# A SELECT LIBRARY

OF

# NICENE AND POST-NICENE FATHERS

OF

# THE CHRISTIAN CHURCH

## Second Series

TRANSLATED INTO ENGLISH WITH PROLEGOMENA AND EXPLANATORY NOTES.

UNDER THE EDITORIAL SUPERVISION OF

PHILIP SCHAFF, D.D., LL.D.,      AND      HENRY WACE, D.D.,

*Professor of Church History in the*          *Principal of King's College,*
*Union Theological Seminary, New York.*                *London.*

*IN CONNECTION WITH A NUMBER OF PATRISTIC SCHOLARS OF EUROPE*
*AND AMERICA.*

## VOLUME XIII

### PART II

### GREGORY THE GREAT

### EPHRAIM SYRUS

### APHRAHAT

## T&T CLARK
### EDINBURGH

## WM. B. EERDMANS PUBLISHING COMPANY
### GRAND RAPIDS, MICHIGAN

**British Library Cataloguing in Publication Data**

Nicene & Post-Nicene Fathers. — 2nd series
1. Fathers of the church
I. Schaff, Philip    II. Mace, Henry
230'.11      BR60.A62


T&T Clark ISBN 0 567 09422 7


Eerdmans ISBN 0-8028-8127-0

*Reprinted, March 1989*

PHOTOLITHOPRINTED BY EERDMANS PRINTING COMPANY
GRAND RAPIDS, MICHIGAN, UNITED STATES OF AMERICA

# SELECTED EPISTLES

OF

# GREGORY THE GREAT

BISHOP OF ROME,

## (BOOKS IX.—XIV.)

TRANSLATED, WITH NOTES AND INDICES,

BY THE LATE

## REV. JAMES BARMBY, D.D.

# GENERAL LITERATURE

OF

# GREGORY'S LIFE AND TIMES

BARMBY (James), D.D., Gregory the Great; part of "The Fathers for English readers." Lond., 1879, 8°.
——— — re-issue. Lond., 1892, 8°.
(QY.), Gregorius I., Pope, in Dictionary of Christian Biography, Vol. II. Lond., 1880.
BIANCHI-GIOVINI (A.), Pontificato di San Gregorio il Grande. Milano, 1844, 8°.
CALLIAS CARYON (A.), Apologie pour S. Gregoire evecque de Rome premier du nom, autrement dit, Gregoire le Grand ... a Sedan, 1603, sm. 8°.
DU MOULIN (P.), the Elder. La vie et religion de deux bons papes Leon premier et Gregoire premier ...
Sedan, 1650, 12°.
EWALD (P.), Die älteste Biographie Gregors I. (p. 17 of Histor. Aufsätze dem Andenken an G. Waitz.)
Hannover, 1886, 8°.
GUETTÉE (F. R.), La Papauté moderne condamnée par le Pape Saint Grégoire le Grand. ... Extraits des ouvrages de St. Grégoire ... Paris., 1861, 8°.
JOANNES, diaconus : S. Gregorii Migni vita. (Patrol. Lat. ed. Migne, tom. 75, col. 59.) Paris., 1849, 8°.
LAU (G. J. T.), Gregor I. der Grosse nach seinem Leben und seiner Lehre geschildert. Leipzig, 1845, 8°.
LEBLANC (H. J.), Utrum B. Gregorius Magnus litteras humaniores et ingenuas artes odio persecutus sit disputationem proponebat ... H. J. L. Parisiis, 1852, 8°.
LUZARCHE (V.) [Editor], Vie du Pape Grégoire le Grande. Légende française [en vers]. Publiée pour la première fois par V.L. Tours, 1857, 8°.
MAGGIO (G.), Prolegomeni alla storia di Gregorio il Grande e de' suoi tempi. Prato, 1879, 8°.
MAIMBOURG (L.), Histoire du Pontificat de S. Grégoire le Grand. Paris, 1686, 4°.
PAULUS, diaconus Aquileiensis dictus Winfridus : S. Gregorii Magni vita auctore Paulo diacono monacho Cassinensi. (Patrol. Lat. ed. Migne, tom. 75, col. 41.) Paris., 1849, 8°.
PFAHLER (G.), of Ellwangen. Gregor der Grosse und seine Zeit. Bd. I. [No more published.]
Frankfurt am Main, 1852, 8°.
PINGAUD (L.), La politique de Saint Grégoire le Grand. Thèse ... Paris. Paris, 1872, 8°.
POZZO (F. dal), Istoria della vita e del pontificato di S. Gregorio Magno Papa ... Con un ragionamento sopra gli studi ecclesiastici. Rome, 1758, 4°.
SAINTE-MARTHE (Denys de), Histoire de S. Grégoire le Grand, ... Tirée principalement de ſes Ouvrages.
a Rouen, 1697, 4°.
SAXTON (Rev. A. J.), Saint Gregory the Great (Penny Biographical series). Lond. [1892], 8°.
SIMROCK (C.) [Editor], Eine schöne merkwürdige Historie des heiligen Bischofs Gregorius auf dem Stein genannt. Berlin [1838 ?), 8°.
SNOW (T. B.), abbot of St. Mary's, Liverpool. St. Gregory the Great. His work and his spirit. (Heroes of the Cross.) Lond., 1892, 8°.
STUTE (J. P.), Gregorius Magnus Papa Lutheranus ; sive Der Lutherische Pabst. Contra Papistas, imprimis Monachos Parienses Ordinis S. Benedicti, S. Marthe, Bellarminum, ... aliosque ex S. Gregorii libris et epistolis vindicatus ... Lipsiae, 1715, 4°.
WELIN (L. G.), Resp.: Legend om Pāſven Gregorius den Store. Praes. J. H. Schröder. Stockholm, 1848, 8°.
WIGGERS (G. F.), De Gregorio Magno ejusque placitis anthropologicis commentatio prior [— posterior].
Rostochii, 1838—40, 4°.
ZYPE (F. vander), Sanctus Gregorius Magnus ... ex ... Dei familia Benedictina oriundus ... Ipris, 1610, 8°.

# REGULA PASTORALIS

## IMPORTANT MSS.

1. Troyes 504. End of the 6th or beginning of the 7th cent. In uncials and majuscules. Formerly in the library of the Collège des Oratoriens de Troyes. (Migne, no. 1.)
2. Corvey no. 93. (Codex Corbeiensis, Migne, no. 2.) [The library at Corvey has now been dispersed.]
3. Chartres 65 (6.) of the 9th cent. (St. Père.)
4-6. St. Gallen 216—217, 219. All of the 9th cent.
7. St. Germain 12260. of the 9th cent.
8. St. Germain 12261. of the 9th cent.
9. Laon 187. of the 9th or 10th cent. (St. Vincent.)
10. Oxford, Bodl. Laud misc. 263. of the 9th or 10th cent.; (probably the 10th).
11. Codex Belvacensis, written about the middle of the 10th cent. (Migne.)
12. Rouen 500 (A. 260.) of the 11th cent. (Cathédrale de Rouen.)
13. Chartres 114 (62.) of the 12th cent. (Chapitre.)
14. Rouen 501 (A. 368.) of the 12th cent. (St. Ouen de Rouen.)
15. Troyes 752. of the 12th cent. (Clairvaux.)
16. Oxford, Bodl. Hatton 20. In English minuscule of the 10th cent., containing the Anglo-Saxon version made by King Alfred. It formerly belonged to Worcester [cathedral].

## EDITIONS.

1. ... lib' Regule pastoral'. [Ulric Zell ? Cologne, 1470?] 4°.
2. ... liber regule pastoral'. [M. Flach : Strasburg, 1475?] 4°.
3. ... liber cure pastoralis. n. pl. 1482, 8°.
4. Pastoralis. Venetiis per Hier. de Paganinis, 1492, 4°.
5. Pastorale. Argentine, 1496, 4°.
6. Pastorale. in vrbe Basilienfi (Mich. Furter) 1496, 4°.
7. Liber cure pastoralis ... Parrhisiis per Vdalricu' gering & Magistru' Berchtoldu' renbolt socioru', 1498, 4°.
8. in Gregorii Magni opera, beneficio Bertholdi Renbolt. In edibus J. Parvi : Parrhisiis, 1518, fol.
9. Do. ed. Franc. Regnault. Rothomagi (Paris), 1521, fol.
10. Pastoralis diui Gregorii ; At fol. cciii. of Opera ... Paris., ex officina Claudii Chevalon, 1523, fol.
11. in opera ... 1533, fol.
12. Do. Basil., 1550.
13. Do. cura Huldrici Coccii. Basil., ap. Froben. 1564, fol.
14. Pastoralia ; at col. 869, tom. I. of Opera ... ed. Ioannes Gillotius Campanus. Paris., 1571, fol.
15. Pastoralis ; at fol. 2, tom. II. of opera, Antverpiae, 1572, fol.
16. [another ed. of no. 14.] Paris., 1586.
17. Liber pastoralis curæ ; at p. 143, tom. III. of opera ... ed. Petrus Tossinianensis episc. Venusinus.
Romæ, ex typis Vaticanis, 1588-93, fol.
18. in Opera, Sixti V. ... jussu emendata ... [by R. Rodulphus, bp. of Venosa.] Paris., 1605, fol.
19. in Opera ... Romæ, 1613, 8°.
20. Do. Dvaci, 1615.
21. Do. emendata ... [by P. Rodulphus]. Antveipiæ, 1615, fol.
22. Do. Paris., 1619.
23. ... Cura Pastoralis ... opera ... Matthiæ Abbatis Admentensis ... in hanc formam recusa. Monaci, 1622, 12°.
24. De cvra pastorali liber verè aureus, accuratè emendatus ... è Vet. MSS. ... ab eximijs aliquot Acad. Oxoniensis theologis ; editus à Ieremia Stephano ... Londini, 1629, 8°.
25. Liber pastoralis curæ ; at p. 169 of ' Septem tubæ orbis Christiani ... , operâ J. M. Horstii ... '
Coloniæ Agrippinæ, 1635, 4°.

26. *in* Opera.                                                                  Paris., 1640.

27. Do.       ed. Petr. Gussanvillaeus.                                          Paris., 1675, fol.

28. Regulæ pastoralis liber; at col. 1—102 of tom. II. of opera ... studio & labore monachorum ord. Sancti Benedicti è congr. S. Mauri ...                                        Par., 1705, fol.

29. ... Regulæ pastoralis liber ... juxta editionem Parisiensium Monachorum Ord. S. Benedicti per B. Campagnolam ... emendatus, variisque lectionibus illustratus .       Veronæ, 1739, 12°.

30. *in* Opera ed. Gallicciolli.                                                Venetiis, 1768—76, 4°.

31. Regulæ pastoralis liber; in tom. 13 of 'Sanctae ... catholicae ecclesiae dogmatum et morum ex selectis veterum patrum operibus veritas demonstrata, &c.' By A. M. Cigheri.       Florentiæ, 1791, 4°.

32. — [another ed.] in vol. I. of Biblio-theca Pastoralis ...                   Oeniponte, 1845, 12°.

33. — Novam editionem curavit E. W. Westhoff.                  Monasterii Westphalorum, 1846, 8°.

34. — [another ed.] col. 13, tom. III. of opera in Migne's Patrologia, tom. 75—9.   Parisiis, 1849, la. 8°.

35. — [another ed.]                                                             Romae, 1849, 12°.

36. — [another ed.] Ex Benedictinorum recensione.   Praemissa est vita S. Gregorii a Paulo Diacono conscripta. [Edited by G. Leonhardi.]                                           Lipsiae, 1873, 8°.

37. — [another ed.] in vol. 20 of 'Sanctorum Patrum opuscula selecta.   Edidit ... H. von Hurter.
                                                                        Oeniponti, 1874—85, 16°.

38. S. Gregorii Magni Regulæ Pastoralis Liber.   S. Gregory on the Pastoral charge ; the Benedictine text, with an English translation by ... H. R. Bramley.                         Oxford, 1874, 8°.

38*. The book of Pastoral rule, and selected epistles, of Gregory the Great, bp. of Rome ; transl., with introduction, notes, and indices, by the Rev. J. Barmby, D.D.   (Pt. I.) (A select library of Nicene and post-Nicene fathers of the Christian Church.   2nd Ser., vol. XII.)       Oxford & New York, 1895, la. 8°.

39. King Alfred's West-Saxon Version of Gregory's Pastoral Care.   With an English translation.   Edited for the Early English Text Society, by H. Sweet.                  Lond., 1871, 2, 8°.

40. Le Livre de S. Gregoire le Grand ... du soin et du devoir des pasteurs. ... Nouvelle traduction [by J. le C. C. de S. ..., i.e. Jean Le Clerc, Curê de Soisy.]                 Paris, 1670, 8°.

41. Die Pastoralschriften des hl. Gregor des Grossen und des hl. Ambrosius von Mailand, übersetzt von. C. Haas.                                                            Tübingen, 1862, 8°.

42. Il libro della Regola Pastorale di S. Gregorio Magno volgarizzamento inedito del secolo xiv., tratto da un Manoscritto della Biblioteca Ambrosiana da A. Ceruti, ...      Milano, 1869, 8°.

[Amongst Rawlinson's MSS. in the Bodleian [MS. Rawl. D. 377, fol. 86] are 2 specimen leaves of an edition, giving the Latin text, with King Alfred's translation, designed by E. Thwaites ;
                                                                        Oxford ? c. 1700, 4°.]

# LITERATURE.

DEWITZ (A.), Untersuchungen über Alfreds des Grossen west-sächsische Übersetzung der "Cura pastoralis" Gregors und ihr Verhaltnis zum Originale.   Inaug.-Diss. ... Breslau.       Bunzlau, 1889, 8°.

FLEISCHHAUER (K. W.), Ueber den Gebrauch des Conjunctivs in Alfred's altenglischer Uebersetzung von Gregor's Cura Pastoralis.   Inaug.-Diss. ... Göttingen.                Göttingen, 1885, 8°.

GIESCHEN (K. L.), Die Charakteristischen Unterschiede der einzelnen Schreiber im Hatton MS. der Cura Pastoralis.   Inaug.-Diss. ... Greifswald.                            Greifswald, 1887, 8°.

GLOSSARIUM zum Werke des heil. Gregorius : Liber regulæ pastoralis, aus einer Handschrift des zehnten Jahrhunderts in der Stiftsbibliothek zu St. Florian, aus geschrieben von F. Kurz.   Aus dem xxxvii. Bde der Jahrbücher der Literatur besonders abgedruckt.                        Wien, 1827, 8°.

WACK (Gustav), Über das Verhältnis von König Aelfreds Übersetzung der Cura Pastoralis ... zum Originale. Inaug.-Diss. ... Greifswald.                                      Greifswald, 1889, 8°.

# REGISTRUM EPISTOLARUM

## IMPORTANT MSS

1. Cologne 92. of the 8th cent.   Held by Ewald to be the best of all the MSS.
2. St. Petersburg 6 F. 1. 7.   (Formerly at Corvey; then at St. Germain-des-Prés.) 8th cent.   The first in the list of MSS. given by Migne.
3. Berlin theol. 322. of the 9th cent.
4. Dusseldorf B. 79. of the 9th cent.
5. Munich 14641. of the 9th cent.
6. Paris 11674. (St. Germain 282.) of the 9th cent.
7. Vienna 934. of the 9th cent.
8. The Escurial d. I. 1. (the Codex Emilianus).   Written in West-Gothic minuscule, and finished in 992.
9. Bamberg 601. of the 10th cent.
10. Cologne 94. of the 10th cent.
11. Paris 2279.   (Formerly in the library of St. Martial de Limoges;) of the 10th cent.
12. St. Gallen 670. of the 10th cent.
13. Trier 171. of the 10th cent.
14. Monte Cassino 71.   Written in a Lombardic hand of the end of the 11th cent.
15. Wolfenbüttel 155. (75.) of the 11th cent.
16. Cologne 95. of the 12th cent.
17. Vatican 619. of the 12th cent.

## EDITIONS.

1. Liber Ep'larum beati Gregorii Pape ...   (Augustae Vindel., G. Zainer, c. 1472) fol.
2. Epiftole ex Regiftro : (cum vita Gregorii praefixa).   Venetiis per Laz. Soardum, 1505, fol.
3. Do.   Parisiis, 1508, 4°.
4. *in* Gregorii Magni opera, beneficio Bertholdi Renbolt.   In edibus J. Parvi : Parrhisiis, 1518, fol.
5. Do.   ed. Franc. Regnault.   Rothomagi (Paris), 1521, fol.
6. ... epiftole ex Regiftro fa'cti Gregorii pape ; At fol. ccclvi. of Opera ...
   Paris., ex officina Claudii Chevalon, 1523, fol.
7. Do.   1533, fol.
8. Registrum Epistolarum.   Lugduni, 1539, 40.
9. Do.   ed. Guillart.   Paris., 1542, fol.
10. *in* Opera ... tom. II.   Basil, 1550.
11. *in* Opera ... cura Huldrici Coccii.   Basil., ap. Froben., 1564, fol.
12. Epiftolæ ex Regiftro ; col. 433—825 of Vol. II. of Opera ... ed. Ioannes Gillotius Campanus.
   Paris., 1571, fol.
13. Registrum Epistolarum.   Venetiis, 1571.
14. Epistolae ex Registro ; fol. 168ᵛ of Vol. II. of Opera,   Antverpiae, 1572, fol.
15. Do.   Venetiis, 1583.
16. [another ed. of No. 12].   Paris., 1586.

17. Registrum Epistolarum ; Vol. **IV.** of Opera ... ed. Petrus Tossinianensis episc. Venusinus.

Romae, ex typis Vaticanis, 1588—93.

18. *in* Opera, Sixti **V.** ... jussu emendata ... [by R. Rodulphus, bp. of Venosa].   Paris., 1605, fol.

19. *in* Opera ...   Romæ, 1613, 8°.

20. Do.   Duaci, 1615.

21. Do. emendata ... [by P. Rodulphus.]   Antverpiæ, 1615, fol.

22. Do.   Paris., 1619.

23. Do.   Paris., 1640.

24. Epistolæ ; col. 1027, Vol. **V.** Conciliorum, studio Ph. Labbei et G. Cossartii.   Paris., 1671, fol.

25. *in* Opera ... ed. Petr. Gussanvillaeus, tom. II. pp. 359—1150.   Paris., 1675, fol.

26. Do. ... studio & labore monachorum ord. Sancti Benedicti è congregatione Sancti Mauri ... tom. II., col. 477—1317.   Par., 1705, fol.

27. *in* Opera ... ed. Gallicciolli, tom. 7—9.   Venetiis, 1768—76, 4°.

28. *in* Opera ... tom. 75—79 bf Migne's Patrologia, tom. III., col. 441.   Parisiis, 1849, la. 8°.

29. Gregorii I. papae Registrvm epistolarvm. Tomi I. pars I. Liber i.—iv. Edidit Pavlvs Ewald. Tomi I. pars II. Libri v.—vii. Tomi II. partes I., II. Libri viii.—xiv. Post Pavli Ewaldi obitvm edidit Lvdovicvs M. Hartmann. (Mon. Germ. Hist.—Epistolarum tomi I., II.)   Berl., 1887—95, 4°.

30. — ; Uebersetzt ... von M. Feyerabend. 6 vols.   Kempten, 1807—9.

[See also no. 38* in list of editions of " Cura Pastoralis."]

The text in Migne's ed. is a reprint of the edition by the monks of St. Maur, of 1705.

By far the best edition of the Epistolae yet attempted is that begun by Ewald, who died after editing pt. I., bks. I.—IV. The work is being continued on the same scale by L. M. Hartmann.

## LITERATURE.

ANTONII DADINI Alteserræ Antecessoris Tolosani, Notæ et observationes in xii. libros epistolarum B. Gregorii papæ...   Tolosæ, 1669, 4°.

BAUMGARTEN (P. M.), Ueber eine Handschrift der Briefe Gregors I. [B. M., King's libr. 6, C. x.] (Neues Archiv d. Gesselsch. f. ä. deutsch. Gesch. xv., 1890, p. 60.)

BEMBUS (Matthæus), Pastor vigilans : sive ars regendi animas ex epistolis D. Gregorii Magni excerpta ...   Colon. 1618, 8°.

EWALD (P.), Studien zur Ausgabe des Registers Gregors I. (Neues Archiv, iii., 1878, pp. 433—625.)

HARTMANN (L. M.), Ueber zwei Gregorbriefe. (Neues Archiv, xvii., 1892, p. 193.)

——— Zur Chronologie der Briefe Gregors I. (——— xv., 1890, p. 411.)

——— Zur Orthographie Papst Gregors I. (——— xv., 1890, p. 529.)

JAFFÉ (Ph.) [Editor]. S. Gregorius I., ed. P. Ewald : pp. 143—219, of vol. I., and p. 738 of vol. II., of Regesta pontificum Romanorum, ed. P. Jaffé.   Lipsiae, 1885, 6, 4°.

JAMES (Thomas), Vindiciæ Gregorianæ, seu restitutus innumeris pæne locis Gregorius ex variis MSS. vt magno labore, ita Singulari fide collatis.   Genevæ, 1625, 4°.

KELLET (F. W.), Pope Gregory the Great and his relations with Gaul. (Cambridge historical essays.)   Lond. 1889, 8°.

LAMPE (Fel.), Qui fuerint Gregorii Magni papae temporibus in imperii Byzantini parte occidentali exarchi et · qualia eorum iura atque officia. Diss. ... Berlin.   Berlin, 1892, la. 8°.

MAASEN (F.), Ueber eine Sammlung von Schreiben Gregors I. u. Verordnungen der Kaiser u. Könige.   Wien, 1877, 8°.

MOMMSEN (Th.), Zu den Gregorienbriefen. (Neues Archiv, xvii., 1892, p. 189.)

PFLUGK-HARTTUNG (J. v.), Papst Gregor d. Gr. (Münchener allgem. Zeitung, 1888. Beilage no. 209—215.)

SAVINI (F.), Se il Castrum Aprutiense delle lettere di s. Gregório Magno fu l'odierna Teramo e se la voce Aprutium servi nel primitivo medio evo a denominare la città di Teramo, ovvero solo il suo territorio. (Archivio storico Italiano Ser. v. tom. X. 1892, p. 3.)

WISBAUM (W.), Die wichtigsten Richtungen und Ziele der Thätigkeit des Papstes Gregors des Grossen. Inaug. Diss. ... Bonn.   Koln (1884), 8°.

WOLFSGRUBER (C.), Die vorpäpstliche Lebensperiode Gregors d. Gr. Nach seinen Briefen Dargestellt. Progr. ... Schotten.   Wien, 1886, 4°.

——— Gregor der Grotze ...   Saulgau, 1890, 8°.

WOLLSCHACK (Th.), Die Verhältnisse Italiens, insbesondere des Langobardenreichs, nach dem Briefwecheb Gregors I. Progr. ... Horn.   Horn, 1888, 4°.

# BOOK IX

## EPISTLE I.

To Januarius, Bishop of Caralis (*Cagliari*).

Gregory to Januarius, &c.

The preacher of Almighty God, Paul the apostle, says, *Rebuke not an elder* (1 Tim. v. 1). But this rule of his is to be observed in cases where the fault of an elder does not draw through his example the hearts of the younger into ruin. But, when an elder sets an example to the young for their ruin, he is to be smitten with severe rebuke. For it is written, *Ye are all a snare to the young* (Isai. xlii. 22). And again the prophet says, *The sinner being an hundred years old is accursed* (Isai. lxv. 20). But so great wickedness has been reported to us of thy old age that, unless we were humanely disposed, we should smite thee with a definitive curse. For it has been told me that on the Lord's day, before celebrating the solemnities of mass, thou wentest forth to plough up the crop of the bearer of these presents, and after ploughing it up didst celebrate the solemnities of mass. Also, after the solemnities of mass thou didst not fear to root up the landmarks of that possession. What punishment ought to follow such deeds all who hear of them know. We had, however, been in doubt as to so great perversity in thee as this; but our son Cyriacus the abbot[1], having been questioned by us, declared that when he was at Caralis he knew it to be the case. And, seeing that we still spare thy gray hairs, bethink thee at length, old man, and restrain thyself from such levity of behaviour, and perversity of deeds. The nearer thou art approaching death, the more careful and fearful oughtest thou to become. And indeed a sentence of punishment had been launched against thee; but, since we know thy simplicity accompanying thy old age, we meanwhile hold our peace. Those, however, by whose advice thou hast done these things we decree to be excommunicated for two months; but so that, if within the space of two months anything should happen to them after the manner of humanity they be not deprived of the blessing of the viaticum. But do thou henceforth be cautious to stand aloof from their counsels, lest, if thou be their disciple in evil whose master thou oughtest to have been in good, we no longer spare either thy simplicity or thy old age.

## EPISTLE II.

To Vitalis, Guardian (*Defensorem*) of Sardinia.

Gregory to Vitalis, &c.

What we have learnt about our brother the bishop Januarius the bearers of these presents, as well as the copies of our letters, will sufficiently inform you; and so let thy Experience judiciously carry into effect the excommunication which we have decreed to be pronounced on his perverse counsellors, that they may learn by falling not to walk unwarily.

Moreover, we have sent back by Redemptus the guardian (*defensorem*), the bearer of these presents, the wheat which had been sent to us under the name of a present. Let thy experience see that neither thou nor he who brought it presume to partake of anything out of it as a bounty[2], but restore the whole of it without abatement to the several persons, or to all of them together, and send me their receipts for the value; for, should I ascertain that anything has been done otherwise than as I direct, I will visit the offence with no slight severity.

## EPISTLE III.

To Januarius, Bishop of Caralis (*Cagliari*).

Gregory to Januarius, &c.

The most distinguished lady Nereida has complained to us that your Fraternity does not blush to exact from her a hundred *solidi* for the burial of her daughter, and would bring upon her the additional vexation of expense over and above her groans of sorrow. Now, if the truth is so, it being a very serious thing and far from a priest's office to require a price for earth that is granted to rottenness, and to wish to make profit out of another's grief, let your Fraternity refrain from this demand, and be no more troublesome to her, especially as she tells us that Hortulanus, to whom she

---

[1] See V. 2, note 1.

[2] *In pretio commodi.* On *commodum*, see I. 44, p. 90, note 4.

asserts she bore this daughter, had formerly been munificent to your Church in no small degree. Now as to this abuse, we ourselves, after we had by God's permission acceded to the dignity of the episcopate, forbade it entirely in our Church, and by no means permitted the evil custom to be taken up anew, remembering that, when Abraham demanded for a price a sepulchre for the burial of his wife's body from the sons of Emor, that is from Ephron the son of Seor, the latter refused to accept a price, lest he should appear to have made profit out of a corpse (*Gen.* xxiii.). If then a man that was a pagan shewed such great consideration, how much more ought we, who are called priests, not to do this thing? Wherefore I admonish you that this abuse, which comes of avarice, be not ventured on any more, even in the case of strangers. But, if at any time you allow any one to be buried in your Church, and the parents, relations, or heirs of such person should of their own accord wish to offer something for lights, we do not forbid it to be accepted. But we altogether forbid anything to be asked for or exacted, this being a very irreligious proceeding, lest (which God forbid) the Church should haply be spoken of as venal, or you should seem to take joy in men's deaths, if you endeavour in any way whatever to seek profit out of their corpses.

With regard to other cases included in the petition of the aforesaid Nereida, we exhort thee, if possible, to settle them by an amicable arrangement, or certainly not to omit sending an instructed person to the court, deputed by us, for which purpose we have sent to your parts Redemptus our guardian (*defensorem*), the bearer of these presents, that he may compel the parties to appear for trial, and carry out with summary execution what may be adjudged.

## EPISTLE IV.

### To Januarius, Bishop of Caralis (*Cagliari*).

Gregory to Januarius, a Bishop of Sardinia.

We knew before the letter of your Fraternity reached us what our enemies had effected in Sardinia. And, having for some time feared that this would be so, we now groan with you on what we foresaw having come to pass. But, if attention had been paid to what we wrote to our most excellent son Gennadius [3], as well as to yourself, telling you that this would be so, the enemy would either not have come into your regions, or, when they came,

they would have incurred the danger which they have caused. Even now, then, let what has happened sharpen your vigilance for the future. For we, too, by no means omit whatever we are able to do for good, the Lord helping us.

Know, moreover, that the abbot [4] whom, now a considerable time ago, we sent to Agilulph, has by the mercy of God arranged a peace with him, so far as was directed in writing by the most excellent Exarch. And so, till such time as the agreements for the confirmation of this peace shall be drawn up, lest perchance our enemies during the present delay should be inclined to come again into those parts, do you cause watches of the walls to be kept up, and careful attention given in all places. And we trust in the power of our Redeemer that the incursions or plots of our adversaries will not injure you anew.

As to your saying in your letter that many persons lay complaints against you before us, this is true ; but among various things nothing has distressed us so much as what our most beloved son, the abbot Cyriacus, has reported to us ; namely, that on the Lord's day before mass you caused a crop of corn to be ploughed up in the field which is in the possession of Donatus, and, as if that were not enough, went, after the sacrifice was finished, in person to the place, and dug up the boundaries [5]. For this reason I exhort thee to consider with anxious attention the office which thou bearest, and to avoid entirely whatever may injure thy reputation or thy soul, and let no one persuade thee to do the like again. For know that thou hast not undertaken the care of earthly things, but the leadership of souls. On this, therefore, thou oughtest to fix thy heart, thy anxiety, thy entire devotion, and to give thy diligent thought to the winning of souls, that when thou shalt render to the Lord at His coming the talents that He has delivered to thee multiplied, thou mayest be counted worthy to receive from Him the fruit of retribution, and to be exalted among His faithful servants in eternal glory. Know, however, that what I now say in the way of reproach or blame comes not from asperity, but from brotherly love, since I desire thee to be found a priest before Almighty God, not in name only, which tends only to punishment, but also in desert, which looks to recompense. For, we being one member in the body of our Redeemer, as I am rent asunder in thy fault, so also am I rejoiced in thy good conduct.

---

[3] Gennadius was Exarch of Africa

[4] Probably the Abbot Probus. See IX. 43, 9
[5] See also IX. 1.

Furthermore, with regard to your desire that we should depute a person from our side (*a nostro latere*), to whom you may communicate in detail the cases that are to be referred to us, write whatever you will to our most beloved son Peter and to Theodore the counsellor (*consiliario*), that, when it has been communicated to us through them, whatever reason may commend may be settled, the Lord revealing the way. Moreover, concerning our brother and fellow-bishop Marinianus[6], cognizance will be taken, when peace with the aforesaid Agilulph shall have been fully confirmed, and whatever the order of reason may dictate will be done.

## EPISTLE V.
### To MARCELLUS, PRO-CONSUL OF DALMATIA[7].

Gregory to Marcellus, &c.

We have received the letter of your Greatness, in which you speak of having incurred our displeasure, and of your wish to be in favour with us through direct satisfaction. And indeed we have heard such things of your Greatness as ought never to have been committed by a faithful man. For all assert that you are the author of all that great mischief in the case of Maximus, and that the spoiling of that Church, and the perdition of so many souls, and the audacity of that unheard-of presumption, had their beginning through you. And indeed, with regard to your seeking to be in favour with us, it is fitting that with your whole heart and soul, and with tears, as becomes you, you should satisfy our Redeemer for such things as these : for, unless satisfaction is made to Him, what certain good can our forgiveness or favour do thee? But while we observe thee to be still implicated in the ruinous conduct of pretenders, or in the advocacy of those who have gone astray, we see not of what sort your satisfaction is either to God or men. For then your Greatness may know that you openly and evidently satisfy God and men, when you bring back both what is devious to rectitude and what is presumptuous to the rule of humility. If this is done, you may know that you will thus be in favour both with God and men.

## EPISTLE VI.
### To JANUARIUS, BISHOP OF CARALIS (*Cagliari*).

Gregory to Januarius, &c.

The Jews who have come hither from your city have complained to us that Peter, who has been brought by the will of God from their superstition to the worship of Christian faith, having taken with him certain disorderly persons, on the day after his baptism, that is on the Lord's day of the very Paschal festival, with grave scandal and without your consent, had taken possession of their synagogue in Caralis, and placed there the image of the mother of our God and Lord, the venerable cross, and the white vestment (*birrum*) with which he had been clothed when he rose from the font. Concerning which thing also the letters of our sons, the glorious *Magister militum* Eupaterius, and the magnificent governor, pious in the Lord, concur in attesting the same. And they add also that this had been foreseen by you, and that the aforesaid Peter had been prohibited from venturing on it. On learning this we altogether commended you, since, as became a truly good priest, you wished nothing to be done whence just blame might arise. But, since by not having at all mixed yourself up in these wrong doings you shew that what was done displeases you, we, considering the bent of your will in this matter, and still more your judgment, hereby exhort you that, having removed thence with fitting reverence the image and the cross, you should restore what has been violently taken away ; seeing that, as legal enactment does not suffer Jews to erect new synagogues, so also it allows them to keep their old ones without disturbance. Lest, then, the above-named Peter, or others who have afforded him assistance or connivance in the wrongfulness of this disorderly proceeding, should reply that they had done it in zeal for the faith, in order that a necessity of being converted might thereby be imposed on the Jews, they should be admonished, and ought to know, that moderation should rather be used towards them ; that so the will not to resist may be elicited from them, and not that they should be brought in against their will : for it is written, *I will sacrifice to thee willingly* (Ps. lviii. 8) ; and, *Of my own will I will confess to him* (Ps. xxvii. 7). Let, then, your Holiness, taking with you your sons who with you disapprove of these things, try to induce good feeling among the inhabitants of your city, since at this time especially, when there is alarm from the enemy, you ought not to have a divided people. But, being anxious with regard to ourselves no less than with regard to you, we think it right to give you to understand that when the present truce is over, the king Agilulph will not make peace with us[8].

---

6 A bishop in Sardinia, see I. 61. What his case was does not appear.
7 See III. 47, note 2.

8 For references to the truce now in course of negotiation

Whence it is necessary for your Fraternity to see to fortifying your city or other places more securely, and to give earnest attention to providing stores of provisions therein, that, when the enemy, with God incensed against him, shall come thither, he may find no harm that he can do, but may retire discomfited. But we also take thought for you as far as we can, and press upon those whose concern it is that they should prepare themselves for resistance, since, as you regard our tribulations as yours, so we in like manner count your afflictions as our own.

## EPISTLE VII.

### To Januarius, Bishop of CARALIS (*Cagliari*).

Gregory to Januarius, &c.

It has been laid down by the plain definition of the law that those who go into a monastery for the purpose of entering on monastic life are no longer at liberty to make wills, but that their property passes into possession of the same monastery 9. This being known to almost all, we have been greatly surprised by the notification of Gavinia, abbess of the monastery of Saints Gavinus and Luxorius, to the effect that Sirica, abbess of her monastery, after receiving the office of government, had made a will leaving certain legacies. And when we enquired of the Solicitude of your Holiness why you endured that property belonging to the monastery should be detained by others, our common son Epiphanius, your archpresbyter, being present before us, replied that the said abbess had up to the day of her death refused to wear the monastic dress, but had continued in the use of such dresses as are used by the presbyteresses [1] of that place. To this the aforesaid Gavinia replied that the practice had come to be almost lawful from custom, alleging that the abbess who had been before the above-written Sirica had used such dresses. When, then, we had begun to feel no small doubt with regard to the character of the dresses, it appeared necessary for us to consider with our legal advisers, as well as with other learned men of this city, what was to be done with regard to law. And they, having considered the matter, answered that, after an abbess had been solemnly ordained by the

bishop, and had presided in the government of a monastery for many years until the end of her life, the character of her dress might attach blame to the bishop for having allowed it so to be, but still could not prejudice the monastery, but that her property of manifest right belongs to the same place from the time of her entering it and being constituted abbess. And so since she [*i.e. the abbess Gavinia*] asserts that a guest-house (*xenodochium*) retains possession unduly of the property unlawfully devised, we hereby exhort you, both the monastery and the guest-house itself being situate in your city, to make provision with all care and diligence, to the end that, if this possession is derived from no previous contract, but from the bequest of the said Sirica, it be restored to the said monastery without dispute or evasion. But, if by any chance it is said to have accrued from another contract, either let your Fraternity, having ascertained the truth between the parties, determine as legal order may seem to demand, or let them by mutual consent choose arbitrators, who may be able to decide between their allegations. And whatever be appointed by them, let it be so observed under your care that no grudge may remain between the venerable places, which ought by all means to be cherished in mutual peace and concord. Wherefore all other things which are detained under the will of the above-named Sirica, seeing that none of them is permitted by legal sanction, must needs be carefully restored to the possession of the monastery through the priestly care of your Fraternity : for it is plainly laid down by the imperial constitutions that what has been done contrary to the laws should not only be inoperative, but also be held as not having been done at all.

## EPISTLE VIII.

### To the Bishops of Sardinia.

Gregory to Vincentius, Innocentius, Marinianus, Libertinus, Agatho, and Victor, Bishops of Sardinia.

We have learnt that it is the custom of your island after the paschal festival, for you to go, or to send your representatives to your Metropolitan, and for him, whether you know the time or not, to give you directions by a written announcement concerning the following Easter. And, as report goes, some of you, neglecting to do this according to custom, pervert the hearts of others also to disobedience. It is added also that some of you, when seeking parts beyond sea in cases that arise touching their churches, venture to travel without the knowledge of their aforesaid metropolitan, or letters from him, such as canonical order prescribes.

---

(A.D. 598-9), with the Lombard King Agilulph, cf. IX. 4, 42, 43, 98.

9 Cf. I. 44, p. 92, note 2.

[1] *Presbyteræ.* So the wives of presbyters who had been married before their ordination were called. So in Canon XIX. of the second council of Tours, "Si inventus fuerit presbyter cum sua presbytera," and Canon XXI. of Council of Auxerre, "Non licet presbytero, post acceptam benedictionem, in uno lecto cum presbytera sua dormire." Or deaconesses may possibly be meant, one designation of whom in Greek was πρεσβύτιδες.

We therefore exhort your Fraternity that, conforming to the custom of your churches, as well with respect to the announcement of Easter, as also if need should compel any of you to travel anywhere for business of your own, you should ask leave of your said metropolitan according to the rule imposed upon you ; except that, if (as we hope will not be the case) you should happen to have a case against your said Metropolitan, then those who are in haste on this account to seek the judgment of the Apostolic See have licence to do so, as you know is allowed in the canons by the institution even of the ancient Fathers.

## EPISTLE IX.

### To Callinicus, Exarch of Italy[2].

Gregory to Callinicus, &c.

In the midst of what you have announced to me of your victories over the Sclaves, know that I have been refreshed with great joy that the bearers of these presents, hastening to be joined to the unity of holy Church from the island of Capritana[3], have been sent by your Excellency to the blessed Peter, Prince of the Apostles. For hereby you will the more prevail over your enemies, if you recall under the yoke of the true Lord those whom you know to be the enemies of God ; and you will prosecute your causes among men with all the more effect as with sincere and devout mind you maintain the causes of God.

Now as to your having desired that a copy should be shewn me of the order[4] that has been sent to you for the defence of the schismatic, your to me most sweet Excellency ought to have considered carefully how that, although that order has been elicited, you are still not therein enjoined to repel those who come to the unity of the Church, but only, at this unsettled time, not to compel those who are unwilling to come. Whence it is necessary for you with all speed to inform our most pious Emperors of these things, to the end that they may be aware how that in their times, through the succour of Almighty God

and your exertions, schismatics are hastening to return of their own accord. What I have decided as to the ordering of things in the island of Caritana, your Excellency will learn through our most reverend brother and fellow-bishop Marinianus[5]. But I would have you know that this has caused me no slight distress ; that your Majordomo, who took charge of the petition of the bishop who was wishing to return, declared that he had lost it, and that afterwards he was got hold of by the adversaries of the Church : which proceeding, in my opinion, was due not to his neglect but to his venality. Wherefore I wonder that your Excellency has not in any way visited his fault in him. And yet I soon blamed myself for wondering at this, for where the lord Justinus gives advice, there heretics cannot be arraigned.

Moreover you tell us that you wish to keep the anniversary of Peter, Prince of the apostles, in the city of Rome. And we pray Almighty God to protect you with His mercy, and grant you a fulfilment of your desires. But I beg that the aforesaid most eloquent man may come with you, or that, if he does not come, he may retire from attendance on you. Or certainly, if your Excellency should be unable to come owing to business that may arise, let him either communicate with the unity of holy Church, or I beg that he may not be a sharer of your counsels. For I hear of him as a good man, were he not in most mischievous error. As to the cause of Maximus, inasmuch as we can no longer stand against the importunity of your Sweetness, you will learn from Castorius, the notary, what we have determined.

## EPISTLE X.

### To Marinianus, Bishop of Ravenna.

Gregory to Marinianus, &c.

The bearers of these presents, the most distinguished men, Vicedominus and Defensor[6], came to us asserting that a certain bishop, by name John, coming from Pannonia, had been constituted in the castle which is called Novæ, to which castle their island, which is called Capritana, had been appended as a diocese[7]. They add that, the bishop having been violently withdrawn and expelled from this same castle, another had been ordained there : concerning whom, however,

---

[2] Callinicus had recently succeeded Romanus at Ravenna as Exarch of Italy. The main purport of this letter to him is to secure his hoped-for co-operation in bringing back the Istrian and Venetian schismatics to Catholic communion. See I. 16, note 3 ; also II. 46, 51. The predecessor of Callinicus, viz. Romanus, had given great dissatisfaction to Gregory by his conduct with regard to the schismatics (see II. 46) ; but better things are expected from the new Exarch. See also below, Ep. XCIII., &c. As to the case of Maximus of Salona, briefly referred to at the end of the letter, see III. 47, note 2.

[3] Capritana was a small island in the Adriatic, not far from the shore of Venetia, containing the episcopal see of Capsula, or Cahorla. More about the desire of the church of this island to return to communion with Rome will be found in the letter which follows to Marinianus, bishop of Ravenna.

[4] Mention of a previous order from the emperors, during the exarchate of Romanus, to Gregory himself, bidding him refrain from compelling the Istrians to return to communion, will be found in II. 46.

[5] See the letter following.

[6] So, with initial capitals as proper names, in the Benedictine Edition. Perhaps rather, " the steward (vicedominus) and the guardian (defensor).

[7] Erat quasi per diocesim conjuncta. The meaning is, that the castellum Novæ on the main land had been made the episcopal see of a diocese of the island of Capritana. though not properly within its limits. Cf. IX. 9, note 3.

they allege that it has been resolved that he ought not to have lived in the aforesaid castle, but in his own island. They say further that, while he abode with them there, he was unwilling to remain in schismatical error, and together with all his people presented a petition to our most excellent son Callinicus the Exarch, desiring to be united, with all those that were with him, to the Catholic Church, as we have already said. But they say that, being persuaded by the schismatics, he afterwards recanted, and that now all the population of the aforesaid island are deprived of the protection of a Bishop, since, while desiring to be united to holy Church, they cannot now receive him who has turned to the error of the schismatics; and they desire to have another ordained for them. But we, inasmuch as it is necessary to investigate all things strictly and thoroughly, have taken the precaution of ordering as follows; namely that thy Fraternity should send to the said Bishop, and admonish him to return to the unity of the Catholic Church and to his own people. If, after admonition, he should scorn to return, the flock of God ought not to be deluded in the error of its pastor; and therefore let thy Holiness in that case ordain a Bishop there, and let him have the said island for his diocese, till such time as the Histrian Bishops shall return to the Catholic Faith; so that each Church may have the rights of its own diocese preserved to it, and that a population destitute of a pastor may not be without the protection and oversight of government. In all these things, however, it becomes thy Fraternity to take vigilant heed that this same people which comes back to the Church be very studiously admonished, to the end that it may be firmly fixed in its return, lest through wavering thoughts it fall back into the pit of error. But take care to request the most excellent Exarch, in his despatches, to notify these same things to the most pious ears of the Emperors, since, although the order which has been conveyed to him appears to have been elicited from them, yet he is not forbidden in that order to allow such as wish it to return to the Church, but only, at the present time, to compel the unwilling. Let, then, our aforesaid son take into his charge the management of this affair, to the end that he may so frame his reports, that whatever he may ordain may not be dubious. We have, however, ourselves also written to our common son Anatolius[8], bidding him notify these things fully to the most pious princes.

I have received repeated and pressing letters from my most excellent son, the lord Exarch Callinicus, in behalf of Maximus[9]. Overcome by his importunity, I see nothing further to be done but to commit the cause of Maximus to thy Fraternity. If, therefore, this same Maximus should come to thy Fraternity, let Honoratus, archdeacon of his Church, appear also; that thy Holiness may ascertain if he was rightly ordained, if he fell into no simoniacal heresy, if there was nothing against him in respect of bodily transgressions, if he did not know himself to be excommunicated when he presumed to celebrate mass; and whatever may seem right to thee in the fear of God do thou determine, that we, under God, may give our assent to thy ordering. But, if our aforesaid son should hold thy Fraternity in suspicion, let our most reverend brother Constantius, bishop of Milan, come also to Ravenna, and sit with thee; and do you decide together on the said cause: and whatever may seem good to both of you, hold it for certain that it will seem good to me. For, as we ought not to be obstinate towards the humble, so we ought to shew ourselves strict towards the proud. Let, then, your Fraternity, as you have learnt in the pages of holy Scripture, decide in this business whatever you may consider just.

## EPISTLE XI.
### To Brunichild, Queen.

Gregory to Brunichild, Queen of the Franks[1].

With what firmness the mind of your Excellency is settled in the fear of Almighty God you shew in a praiseworthy manner, among the other good things that you do, by your love also of His priests; and great joy for your Christianity is caused us, since you study to advance with honours those whom you love and venerate as being truly Christ's servants. For it becomes you, most excellent daughter,

---

[8] At this time Gregory's *apocrisiarius* at Constantinople. Cf. VII. 30.

[9] See III. 47, note 2.
[1] Four Vatican MSS. and Cod. Colbert give a date to this epistle, viz. "mense Octobris, indictione prima," i e. Oct A.D. 597. The Benedictine editors assign it, from certain internal evidence to the following year, and have therefore placed it in this ninth Book of the Epistles. There is this additional reason for placing it later than A.D. 597. Its first purpose is to reply to a request from queen Brunechild that a pallium should be sent to Syagrius, bishop of Augustodunum (*Autun*). Now Autun was in the kingdom of Burgundy, which was reigned over at that time by Brunechild's younger grandson Theoderic II. But it was not till the year 599, according to Gregory of Tours (*Hist. Franc.* xi. 19), that she had been expelled from the kingdom of Austrasia, and taken up her residence with Theoderic. She had previously been guardian of her elder grandson Theodebert II., who reigned over Austrasia, having his capital at Metz, and was more likely to have sought the pall for the bishop Autun after she had become the virtual potentate of the Burgundian kingdom than previously; and indeed she seems to be evidently addressed as ruling the country to which the letter refers. The date assigned to this epistle by the Benedictine editors, viz. Indiction 2 (i.e. from September 598 to September 599), is consistent with these circumstances.

it becomes you to be such as to be able to subject yourself to a lord above you. For in submitting the neck of your mind to the fear of the Almighty Lord you confirm your dominion also over subject nations, and by subjecting yourself to the service of the Creator you bind your subjects the more devotedly to yourself. Wherefore, having received your letters, we signify to you that your Excellency's earnest desire has greatly pleased us, and we have been desirous of sending the pallium to our brother and fellow-bishop Syagrius [2], inasmuch as the disposition of our most serene lord the Emperor is also favourable, and, so far as we have been informed by our deacon, who was the representative of our Church at his Court, he is altogether desirous that this thing should be granted [3], and many good reports have reached us of our aforesaid brother both on your testimony and that of others; and especially we learnt what his life is from John the *Regionarius* [4] on his return to us. And hearing what he did in the case of our brother Augustine, we bless our Redeemer, because we feel that he fulfils in his deeds the meaning of his name of priest.

But there have been many hindrances which have meanwhile prevented us from doing this thing. First indeed, that he who had come to receive this pallium is implicated in the error of the schismatics [5]; further, that you wished it to be understood that it was sent, not on your petition, but from ourselves. But there was this besides; that neither had he who desires to use it requested it to be granted him by a special petition addressed to us: and it was by no means right for us to concede so great a matter without his request; especially as an ancient custom has obtained, that the dignity of the pallium shall not be given except when the merits of a case demand it, and to one who urgently requests it. Still, lest we should seem perchance to wish, under pretext of any excuse, to put off the desire of your Excellency, we have provided for the pallium being sent to our most beloved son Candidus the presbyter, charging him, with befitting precaution, to deliver it in our stead. Hence it is requisite that our above-written brother and fellow-bishop Syagrius must hope for it, when he has of his own motion drawn up a petition with some of his bishops; and this he must give to the aforesaid presbyter, to the end that he may be in a position to obtain properly the use of the same pallium with the favour of God.

In order, then, that the charge you bear may be of fruit to you before the eyes of our Creator, let the solicitude of your Christianity be diligently on the watch, and suffer no one who is under your dominion to attain to holy orders by the giving of money, or the patronage of any persons whatever, or by right of relationship; but let such a one be elected to the episcopate, or to the office of any other sacred order, as his life and manners have shewn to be worthy; lest if, as we do not expect, the dignity of the priesthood should be venal, simoniacal heresy, which was the first to come up in the Church, and has been condemned by the sentence of the Fathers, should arise in your parts, and (which God forbid) should weaken the powers of your kingdom. For it is a serious matter, and a wickedness beyond what can be told, to sell the Holy Spirit, who redeemed all things.

But let this also be your care, that, since, as you know, the excellent preacher entirely forbids a novice to accede to the ruling position of priesthood, you suffer no one to be consecrated bishop from being a layman. For what sort of master will he be who has not been a disciple? Or what kind of leadership can he supply to the Lord's flock who has not been previously subjected to a shepherd's discipline? If, then, any one's life should be such as to shew him worthy of being promoted to this order, he ought first to serve in the ministry of the Church, to the end that by the experience of long practice he may see what to imitate, and learn what to teach; lest perchance the newness of his charge bear not the burden of government, and occasion of ruin arise from the immaturity of his promotion.

Moreover, how your Excellency conducted yourself towards our brother and fellow-bishop Augustine, and how great charity, through the inspiration of God, you bestowed upon him, we have learnt from the relation of divers of the faithful; for which we return thanks, and implore the mercy of Divine Power to keep

---

[2] Bishop of Augustodunum (*Autun*), one of the bishops to whom Augustine had carried commendatory letters from Gregory on his progress to England (VI. 54). The see of Augustodunum was under the metropolitan jurisdiction of Lugdunum (*Lyons*); and Brunechild, for some reason, appears to have desired to have it invested with peculiar dignity. She afterwards founded a church, a nunnery, and a hospital there (see XIII. 6). It is to be observed that the sending of the pallium to a bishop did not in all cases imply metropolitan jurisdiction. It did not in this case. See Epistle CVIII. to Syagrius, in which he is told that the Metropolitan of Lyons was to retain his position unimpaired; only that the bishop of Autun was thenceforth to be next to him in place and dignity.

[3] We observe here the requirement of the Emperor's consent for sending the Pallium to a see not previously thus dignified.

[4] It seems not to be known with any certainty what the title *Regionarius*, thus used absolutely, implies, though no doubt some honourable function. John the Deacon (*Vit. S. Gregor.*) speaks of Gregory's father Gordianus, a layman, as having been a *Regionarius*. As to *Notarii regionarii, Sub-diaconi regionarii, Defensores regionarii*, cf. VIII. 14.

[5] Meaning those who were out of communion with Rome with regard to "The Three Chapters," see I. 16, note 3. There were some in Gaul. as well as in Istria and elsewhere, who long refused assent to the condemnation of the Chapters by the fifth Council. Cf. IV. 2, 3, 4, 38, 39; XVI. 12.

you here under its protection, and cause you to reign, as among men, so also after a course of many years in life eternal.

Furthermore, those whom the error of the schismatics severs from the unity of the Church, strive ye, for your own reward, to recall to the unity of concord. For on no other ground are they enveloped so far in the blindness of their ignorance but that they may escape ecclesiastical discipline, and have licence to live perversely as they please, since they understand neither what they defend nor what they follow. But as for us, we venerate and follow in all respects the synod of Chalcedon, from which they take to themselves the clouds of a pestiferous excuse ; and, if any one should presume to diminish or add anything with regard to the faith thereof, we anathematize him. But they are so impregnated with the taint of error that, giving credence to their own ignorance, they reject the universal Church, and all the four patriarchs, not with reason, but with malicious intent ; so that he who was sent to us by your Excellency, when he was asked by us why he stood separated from the universal Church, acknowledged that he did not know. But neither what he said nor what else he gave ear to had he the power of knowing. As to this also we no less exhort you, that you should restrain the rest of your subjects under the control of discipline from sacrificing to idols, being worshippers of trees, or exhibiting sacrilegious sacrifices of the heads of animals ; seeing that it has come to our ears that many of the Christians both resort to the churches and also (horrible to relate !) do not give up their worshipping of demons. But, since these things are altogether displeasing to our God, and He does not own divided minds, provide ye for their being salubriously restrained from these unlawful practices ; lest (God forbid it !) the sacrament of holy baptism serve not for their rescue, but for their punishment. If therefore you know of any that are violent, if of any that are adulterers, if of any that are thieves, or bent on other wicked deeds, make haste to appease God by their correction, that He may not bring upon you the scourge due to unfaithful races, which, so far as we see, is already lifted up for the punishment of many nations ; lest, if—as we do not believe will be the case—the wrath of Divine vengeance should be kindled by the doings of the wicked, the plague of war should destroy the sinners whom the precepts of God recall not to the way of rectitude. We must, then, needs make haste, with all earnestness and continual prayer, to betake ourselves to the mercy of our Redeemer, wherein there is a place of safety and great security for all.

For whoso steadfastly abides there, him danger crushes not, nor fear alarms.

We have sent the volume, as you desired us by letter, to our aforesaid most beloved son Candidus the presbyter, to be offered to you, being in haste to be sharers in your good purpose. May Almighty God keep you under His protection, and by His outstretched arm defend your kingdom from unbelieving nations, and bring you after long courses of years to eternal joys. Given in the month of October, the first indiction [6].

## EPISTLE XII.
### To John, Bishop of Syracuse.

Gregory to John, &c.

One coming from Sicily has told me that some friends of his, whether Greeks or Latins I know not, as though moved by zeal for the holy Roman Church, murmur about my arrangements [i.e. of divine service], saying, How can he be arranging so as to keep the Constantinopolitan Church in check, when in all respects he follows her usage ? And, when I said to him, What usages of hers do we follow ? he replied ; you have caused Alleluia to be said at mass out of the season of Pentecost [7] ; you have made appointment for the sub-deacons to proceed disrobed [8], and for Kyrie Eleison to be said, and for the Lord's Prayer to be said immediately after the canon. To him I replied, that in none of these things have we followed another Church.

For, as to our custom here of saying the Alleluia, it is said to be derived from the Church of Jerusalem by the tradition of the blessed Jerome in the time of pope Damasus of blessed memory ; and accordingly in this matter we have rather curtailed the former usage which had been handed down to us here from the Greeks.

Further, as to my having caused the sub-deacons to proceed disrobed, this was the ancient usage of the Church. But it pleased one of our pontiffs, I know not which, to order them to proceed in linen tunics. For

---

6 See note 1.

7 I.e. the fifty days between Easter and Whitsuntide. It appears from St. Augustine (see Migne, *Patrolog. note in loc.*) that it was the custom everywhere to sing the Alleluia between Easter and Pentecost, but that its use at other times varied. The point of what Gregory here says seems to be that the Roman custom of saying it at other times had not been derived from the Greeks ; but that, on the contrary, it was said at other times less frequently at Rome than among the Greeks.

8 *Procedere spoliatos* : i.e. to proceed to the altar for celebration without linen tunics on. The verb *procedere* and the noun *processio* are commonly used by Gregory and others in the special sense of 'approaching the altar for mass. It would seem from what is here said that the subdeacons at mass had not been originally distinguished by a vestment, and that some pope before Gregory had first vested them at Rome. He, as further appears, had disrobed the subdeacons ; and his point here is, that his doing so was not an imitation of the Greeks, but a return to ancient usage.

have your Churches in any respect received their tradition from the Greeks? Whence, then, have they at the present day the custom of the subdeacons proceeding in linen tunics, except that they have received it from their mother, the Roman Church?

Further, we neither have said nor now say the Kyrie Eleison, as it is said by the Greeks: for among the Greeks all say it together; but with us it is said by the clerks, and responded to by the people; and as often as it is said, Christe Eleison is said also, which is not said at all among the Greeks. Further, in daily masses we suppress some things that are usually said, and say only Kyrie Eleison, Christe Eleison, so as to devote ourselves a little longer to these words of deprecation. But the Lord's prayer (*orationem Dominicam*) we say immediately after the prayer (*mox post precem*) for this reason, that it was the custom of the apostles to consecrate the host of oblation to (*ad*) that same prayer only. And it seemed to me very unsuitable that we should say over the oblation a prayer which a scholastic had composed, and should not say the very prayer [9] which our Redeemer composed over His body and blood [1]. But also the Lord's Prayer among the Greeks is said by all the people, but with us by the priest alone. Wherein, then, have we followed the usages of the Greeks, in that we have either amended our own old ones or appointed new and profitable ones, in which, however, we are not shewn to be imitating others? Wherefore, let your

---

[9] The word found here is *traditionem*: but, because of the undoubted reference to the Lord's Prayer (*dominica oratio*), and of the verb *composuit*, it is conjectured that the reading ought to be *orationem*.

[1] This whole passage in the original is;—"Orationem vero Dominicam idcirco mox post precem dicimus, quia mos apostolorum fuit ut ad ipsam solummodo orationis oblationis hostiam consecrarent. Et valde mihi inconveniens visum est ut precem quam scholasticus composuerat super oblationem diceremus, et ipsam traditionem (Qy. for *orationem?*) quam Redemptor noster composuit super ejus corpus et sanguinem non diceremus." It is to be observed that, for lack of suitable words in English, the translation does not retain the distinction in the original between *precem* and *orationem*, the former denoting the prayer of consecration in the Canon, exclusive of the Lord's Prayer, the latter the Lord's Prayer itself, which Gregory appended to it. By the *scholasticus*, to whom he assigns the composition of the former, is meant apparently the liturgist, whoever he might be, who had compiled the Canon of the Mass. It would thus seem that, according to the Roman use before the time of Gregory, the Lord's Prayer did not occur at all "over the oblation," or "over the Body and Blood," i.e. (as the expression must be taken to mean) between consecration and distribution, though, of course, it may have been used before or after. Such omission was undoubtedly peculiar. Among other authorities for the general usage, S. Augustine (Ep. CXLIX. *ad Paulin.*) affirms that *nearly* every Church concludes the whole petition (i.e. the prayer of consecration of which he has been speaking) with the Lord's Prayer:—"Quam totam petitionem fere omnis Ecclesia Oratione Dominica concludit." In saying "*fere omnis*," he may possibly have had the Roman Church in view. As to what is said by S. Gregory of the custom of the Apostles, the most obvious meaning of which is, that they used no prayer of consecration but the Lord's Prayer, we have no means of ascertaining whence he derived this tradition, or what the value of it might be. It does not, of course, imply that the words of institution were not said over the elements by the Apostles, but only that they used no other prayer for the purpose of consecration. Ways have been suggested, though not satisfactory, for evading the apparent meaning of the statement.

---

Charity, when an occasion presents itself, proceed to the Church of Catana; or in the Church of Syracuse teach those who you believe or understand may possibly be murmuring with respect to this matter, holding a conference there, as though for a different purpose, and so desist not from instructing them. For as to what they say about the Church of Constantinople, who can doubt that it is subject to the Apostolic See, as both the most pious lord the emperor and our brother the bishop of that city continually acknowledge? Yet, if this or any other Church has anything that is good, I am prepared in what is good to imitate even my inferiors, while prohibiting them from things unlawful. For he is foolish who thinks himself first in such a way as to scorn to learn whatever good things he may see

## EPISTLE XVII.

### To Demetrian and Valerian.

Gregory to Demetrian and Valerian, clerks of Firmum (*Fermo*).

Both the ordinances of the sacred canons and legal authority permit that ecclesiastical property may be lawfully expended for the redemption of captives. And so, since we are informed by you that, nearly eighteen years ago, the most reverend Fabius, late bishop of the Church of Firmum, paid to the enemy eleven pounds of the silver of that Church for your redemption, and that of your father Passivus, now our brother and fellow-bishop, but then a clerk, and also that of your mother, and that you have some fear on this account, lest what was given should at any time be sought to be recovered from you;— we have thought fit by the authority of this precept to remove your suspicion, ordaining that you and your heirs shall henceforth sustain no annoyance for recovery of the debt, and that no process shall be instituted against you by any one; since the rule of equity requires that what has been paid with a pious intent should not be attended with burden or distress to those who have been redeemed.

## EPISTLE XVIII.

### To Romanus, Guardian (*Defensorem*).

Gregory to Romanus, &c.

Our care for the purpose before us prompts us to commit the looking after ecclesiastical interests to active persons. And so, since we have found thee, Romanus, to have been a trusty and diligent guardian, we have thought fit to commit to thy government from this present second indiction the patrimony of the holy Roman Church, which by the mercy of

God we serve, lying in the parts about Syracuse, Catana, Agrigentum, and Mile (*partibus Milensibus*). Hence it is needful that thou go thither immediately, that, in consideration of the divine judgment, and in memory also of our admonition, thou mayest study to acquit thyself so efficiently and faithfully that thou mayest be found to incur no risk for negligence or fraud, which God forbid should be the case. But act thus all the more in order that thou mayest be commended to divine grace for thy faithfulness and industry. Moreover, we have sent orders according to custom to the *familia* of the same patrimony [2], that there may be nothing to hinder thy carrying out what has been enjoined thee.

## EPISTLE XIX.

### To the Husbandmen (*Colonos*) of the Syracusan Patrimony [3].

Gregory to the *Coloni*, &c.

I would have you know that we have arranged for you to be put under the care of our guardian (*defensoris*). And accordingly we order you to obey him without any reluctance in what he may see fit to do, and enjoin on you to be done, for the advantage of the Church. We have given him such power as to enable him to inflict strict punishment on those who may attempt to be disobedient or contumacious. And we have likewise charged him that he delay not with instant attention to recover to ecclesiastical jurisdiction any slaves who are in hiding outside their limits, or any one by whom boundaries have been invaded. For know that he has been warned on his peril, that he presume not ever under any kind of excuse to do any wrong or robbery in regard to what belongs to others.

## EPISTLE XXIII.

### To John, Bishop of Syracuse.

Gregory to John, &c.

Our son the glorious exconsul Leontius has made a serious complaint to us of our brother and fellow-bishop Leo; and his complaint has altogether disturbed us, since a bishop ought not to have acted so precipitately and lightly. This case we have committed, to be thoroughly enquired into, to our Guardian (*defensoris*)

Romanus when he comes to you. Further, the messenger who was sent by him (*i.e. by Leontius*) complains of your Fraternity, that in the defence of the illustrious physician Archelaus the interests of our brother and fellow-bishop, the Metropolitan Domitian, suffer damage [4]. And indeed your Fraternity ought justly to protect your sons, or it may be in this case the interests of holy Church, and to give no occasion for evil-speaking to adversaries. I doubt not, however, even while thus speaking, that you do take heed to this : yet we have enjoined on the same Romanus, when he comes to you, to arrange witn you what is right with regard to this case also

## EPISTLE XXIV.

### To Romanus, Guardian (*Defensorem*).

Gregory to Romanus, &c.

Our son Theodosius, abbot of the Monastery founded by the late Patrician Liberius in Campania, is known to have intimated to us that the late illustrious lady Rustica. about one and twenty years ago, in the will that she made, appointed in the first place Felix, her husband, to be her heir, and delegated to him the foundation of a Monastery in Sicily ; but on this condition,—that if he should not within the space of one year pay all the legacies bequeathed to her freedmen, or establish the aforesaid Monastery as she desired, then the holy Roman Church should have undisputed claim to the portion which she was understood to have in the farm of Cumas, and that it should lend aid for paying the above legacies, and for the construction of the said monastery. Hence, seeing that, as is said, the bequeathed property has not so far been made over in full to this same monastery, and some part of the possession is up to this time detained by her heirs, let thy Experience thoroughly enquire into and examine the case. And in the first place indeed, if under the conditions of the will any heirship comes in wherein our Church may have a plea, we desire thee to investigate and clearly ascertain it, and act for the advantage of the poor, as the order of the business may require ; and then to be instantly solicitous for the due establishment of that cell, and the recovery of the bequeathed property, to the end that the pious desire of the testatrix may be fulfilled in both respects, and the unjust detainers of the property may learn from just loss the guilt of their undue

---

[2] See the following Epistle XIX. For the meaning of *familia* here see note 3 to the same epistle. Gregory sent at the same time letters (which have not been translated) to three influential laymen in Sicily, desiring them to assist and support Romanus in the exercise of his authority. Four other letters (23, 24, 26, 27) are translated, as intimating the kind of duties devolving on Romanus in connexion with his government of the Patrimony.

[3] For the meaning of *Coloni*, see I. 44. The body of them is called the *familia* of the patrimony in the preceding epistle to Romanus (Ep. XVIII.).

---

[4] This Domitian was bishop of Melitina and Metropolitan of Armenia, being a relation of the Emperor's, see III. 67. The physician Archelaus is commended in an epistle not translated (V. 32) to Cyprian, the previous *rector patrimonii* in Sicily, for protection in some question about property.

retention. With all vivacity, then, we desire thee both to enquire into this case and, with the help of the Lord, to bring it to an issue, that the pious devotion of the ordainer may at length take effect. But we desire thee also, as far as justice allows, to succour this monastery in all ways, that lay persons who ought to have rendered the succour of their assistance may not, as is asserted, have power of doing hurt in the name of the founder.

## EPISTLE XXVI.

### To Romanus, Guardian (*Defensorem*).

Gregory to Romanus, &c.

Although the law with reason allows not things that come into possession of the Church to be alienated, yet sometimes the strictness of the rule should be moderated, where regard to mercy invites to it, especially when there is so great a quantity that the giver is not burdened, and the poverty of the receiver is considerably relieved. And so, inasmuch as Stephania, the bearer of these presents, having come hither with her little son Calixenus (whom she asserts that she bare to her late husband Peter, saying also that she has laboured under extreme poverty), demanded of us with supplication and tears that we should cause to be restored to the same Calixenus the possession of a house in the city of Catana, which Ammonia, her late mother-in-law, the grandmother of Calixenus, had offered by title of gift to our Church; asserting that the said Ammonia had not power to alienate it, and that it belonged altogether to the aforesaid Calixenus, her son; which assertion our most beloved son Cyprian, the deacon, who was acquainted with the case, contradicted, saying that the complaint of the aforesaid woman had not justice to go on, and that she could not reasonably claim or seek to recover that house in the name of her son; but, lest we should seem to leave the tears of the above named woman without effect, and to follow the way of rigour rather than embrace the plea of pity, we command thee by this precept to restore the said house to the above-named Calixenus, together with Ammonia's deed of gift with respect to this same house, which is known to be there in Sicily;—since, as we have said, it is better in doubtful cases not to execute strictness, but rather to be inclined to the side of benignity, especially when by the cession of a small matter the Church is not burdened, and succour is mercifully given to a poor orphan.

Given in the month of November, Indiction 2.

## EPISTLE XXVII.

### To Romanus, Guardian (*Defensorem*).

Gregory to Romanus, &c.

It has come to our ears that certain men, having altogether too little discernment, desire us to become implicated in their risks, and wish to be so defended by ecclesiastical persons, that the ecclesiastical persons themselves may be bound by their guilt. Wherefore I admonish thee by this present injunction, and through thee our brother and fellow-bishop, the lord John, or others whom it may concern, that with regard to ecclesiastical patronage of people (whether you should have received letters from me, or none should have been addressed to you), you should bestow it with such moderation that, if any have been implicated in public peculations, they may not appear to be unjustly defended by us, lest we should in any way transfer to ourselves, by venturing on indiscreet defence, the ill repute of evil doers : but so far as becomes the Church, by admonishing and applying the word of intercession, succour whom you can ; so that you may both give them aid, and not stain the repute of holy Church.

## EPISTLE XXXIII.
### To Andrew[5].

Gregory to Andrew.

On hearing that your Glory had been severely afflicted with grief and sickness, I condoled with you exceedingly. But learning presently that the malady had entirely left you, I soon turned my sorrow into joy, and returned great thanks to Almighty God for that He smote that He might heal, afflicted that He might lead to true joys. For hence it is written, *Whom the Lord loveth he chasteneth, and scourgeth every son whom he receiveth* (Heb. xii. 6). Hence the Truth in person says, *My Father is the husbandman, and every branch in me that beareth not fruit, he will take away; but every branch that beareth fruit, he will purge it, that it may bring forth more fruit* (Joh. xv. 1, 2). For the unfruitful branch is taken away, because a sinner is utterly rooted up. But the fruitful branch is said to be purged, because it is cut down by discipline that it may be brought to more abundant grace. For so the grain of the ears of corn, beaten with the threshing instrument, is stript of its awn and chaff. So the olives, pressed in the oil-press, flow forth into the fatness of oil. So the bunches of grapes, pounded with the heels, liquify into wine. Rejoice, therefore, good man, for that in this thy

5 Andreas Scholasticus, so addressed V. 48.

scourge and this thy advancement thou seest that thou art loved by the Eternal Judge.

Furthermore, I beg that my daughter Gloriosa, your wife, be greeted in my name. Now may Almighty God keep you under heavenly protection, and comfort you both now with abundance of gifts and hereafter with the retribution of reward.

## EPISTLE XXXVI.

### To Fortunatus, Bishop of Neapolis (*Naples*).

Gregory to Fortunatus, &c.

Having learnt what zeal inflames your Fraternity in behalf of Christian slaves whom Jews buy from the territories of Gaul, we apprize you that your solicitude has so pleased us that it is also our own deliberate judgment that they should be inhibited from traffic of this kind. But we find from Basilius, the Hebrew, who has come here with other Jews, that such purchase is enjoined on them by divers judges of the republic, and that Christians along with pagans come to be thus procured. Hence it has been necessary for the business to be adjusted with such cautious arrangement that neither they who give such orders should be thwarted, nor those who say they obey them against their will should bear any expense unjustly. Accordingly, let your Fraternity with watchful care provide for this being observed and kept to; that, when they [i.e. the Jewish dealers] return from the aforesaid province, Christian slaves who may happen to be brought by them be either handed over to those who gave the order, or at all events sold to Christian purchasers within forty days. And after the completion of this number of days let none of them in any way whatever remain in the hands of the Jews. But, should any of these slaves perchance fall into such sickness that they cannot be sold within the appointed days, care is to be taken that, when they are restored to their former health, they be by all means disposed of as aforesaid. For it is not fit that any should incur loss for a transaction that is free from blame. But since, as often as anything new is ordained, it is usual so to lay down the rule for the future as not to condemn the past in large costs, if any slaves have remained in their hands from the purchase of the previous year, or have been recently taken away from them by you, let them have liberty to dispose of them while they are with you. So may there be no possibility of their incurring loss for what they did in ignorance before the prohibition, such as it is right they should sustain after being forbidden.

Further, it has been reported to us that the above-named Basilius wishes to concede to his sons, who by the mercy of God are Christians, certain slaves, under the title of a gift, with the view that, under cover of the opportunity thus afforded, they may serve him as their master all but in name; and that, if after this any should perchance have believed that they might fly to the Church for refuge in order to become Christians, they may not be reclaimed to freedom, but to the dominion of those to whom they had before been given. In this matter it befits your Fraternity to keep becoming watch. And, if he should wish to give any slaves to his sons, that all occasion of fraud may be removed, let them by all means become Christians, and let them not remain in his house; but, when circumstances may require that he should have their services, let them be commanded to render him what, even in any case, from his sons, and for God's sake, it is fitting should be supplied to him.

## EPISTLE XLI.

### To Julianus, *Scribo*[6].

Gregory to Julianus, &c.

If in secular offices order and the discipline handed down by our ancestors is observed, who may bear to see ecclesiastical order confounded, to disregard such things when heard of, and postpone their amendment by improperly condoning them? And indeed you do well to love charity and to persuade to concord. But, since we are compelled by consideration of our position, and for God's sake, by no means to leave uninvestigated the things that have come to our knowledge, we shall take care, when Maximus comes, to require a strict account from him of the things that have been said about him. And we trust in the guardianship of our Creator, that we shall not be turned aside by either the favour or the fault of any man from maintenance of the canons and the straight path of equity, but willingly observe what is agreeable to reason. For if (which God forbid) we neglect ecclesiastical solicitude and vigour, indolence destroys discipline, and certainly harm will be done to the souls of the faithful, while they see such examples set them by their pastors. But with regard to your saying in your letter that the good will of the palace and the love of the people are not alienated from him, this circumstance does not recall us from our zeal for justice, nor shall it cause our determination to enquire into the truth to

---

[6] Cf. II. 32, note 7; V. 30, note 8. On the subject of the epistle, see III. 47, note 2.

fail through sin of ours. Every one, then, should strive, magnificent son, to conciliate to himself the love of God. For without divine favour what can I say that human love will do for us hereafter, when even among ourselves it harms us the more?

## EPISTLE XLII.

### To Agilulph, King of the Lombards.

Gregory to Agilulph, &c.

We return thanks to your Excellency, that, hearkening to our petition, you have concluded such a peace as may be of advantage to both parties, as we had confidence in you that you would. On this account we greatly commend your prudence and goodness, since in choosing peace you have shewn that you love God, who is its author. For, if unhappily peace had not been made, what else could have ensued but, with sin and danger on both sides, the shedding of the blood of miserable peasants[7], whose labour profits both? But, that we may feel the advantage to us of this peace, as it has been made by you, we beg you, greeting you with paternal charity, that as often as opportunity offers itself, you would enjoin by letters on your dukes in divers places, and especially those who are constituted in these parts, that they keep this peace inviolate, as has been promised, and not seek for themselves any occasions whence either any contention or any ill-feeling may arise, to the end that we may be able to give thanks still more for your good will. We received the bearers of these presents, as being in very truth your own people, with the affection that was becoming, since it was right both to receive and dismiss with charity men who are wise, and who announced that by the favour of God peace had been concluded.

## EPISTLE XLIII.

### To Theodelinda, Queen of the Lombards.

Gregory to Theodelinda, &c.

How your Excellency has laboured earnestly and kindly, as is your wont, for the conclusion of peace we have learnt from the report of our son, the abbot Probus. Nor indeed was it otherwise to be expected of your Christianity than that you would in all ways shew your assiduity and goodness in the cause of peace. Wherefore we give thanks to Almighty God, who so rules your heart with His loving-kindness that, as He has given you a right faith, so He also grants you to work always what is pleasing in His sight. For you may be assured, most excellent daughter, that for the saving of

so much bloodshed on both sides you have acquired no small reward. On this account, returning thanks for your goodwill, we implore the mercy of our God to repay you with good in body and soul here and in the world to come.

Moreover, greeting you with fatherly affection, we exhort you so to deal with your most excellent consort that he may not reject the alliance of the Christian republic. For, as I believe you know yourself, it is in many ways profitable that he should be inclined to betake himself to its friendship. Do you then, after your manner, always strive for what tends to goodwill and conciliation between the parties, and labour wherever an occasion of reaping a reward presents itself, that you may commend your good deeds the more before the eyes of Almighty God.

## EPISTLE XLIX

### To Anastasius, Bishop of Antioch[8].

Gregory to Anastasius, &c.

I received the letters of thy Fraternity, rightly holding fast the profession of the faith; and I returned great thanks to Almighty God, who, when the shepherds of His flock are changed, still, even after such change, guards the faith which He once delivered to the holy Fathers. Now the excellent preacher says, *Other foundation can no man lay than that is laid, which is Christ Jesus* (1 Cor. iii. 2). Whosoever, then, with love of God and his neighbour, holds firmly the faith that is in Christ, he has laid for himself the same Jesus Christ, the Son of God and man, as a foundation. It is to be hoped therefore that, where Christ is the foundation, the edifice also of good works may follow. The Truth also in person says, *He that entereth not by the door into the sheepfold, but climbeth up some other way, the same is a thief and a robber; but he that entereth in by the door is the shepherd of the sheep* (Joh. x. 1). And a little after He adds, *I am the door.* He, then, enters into the sheep-fold through the door who enters through Christ. And he enters through Christ who thinks and preaches what is true concerning the same Creator and Redeemer of the human race, and holds fast what he preaches; who takes upon him the topmost place of rule for the office of carrying a burden, not for the desire of the glory of transitory dignity. He also watches wisely over the sheep-fold of which he has taken charge, lest either perverse men tear the sheep of God by speaking froward things,

---

7 *Rusticorum.* Cf. I. 44, p. 88, note 1, and *Prolegom.*, p. viii.

8 This was the younger Anastasius, who succeeded the patriarch of the same name to whom previous epistles are addressed.

or malignant spirits ravage them by persuading to vicious delights.

Of a truth we remember how the blessed Jacob, who had served long for his wives, said, *This twenty years have I been with thee ; thy ewes and thy she goats have not been barren. The rams of thy flock have I not eaten, nor shewn unto thee that which had been seized by a beast. I made good every loss ; whatever had been lost by theft, from me didst thou require it. By day and night I was consumed by drought and frost ; sleep fled from mine eyes* (Gen. xxxi. 38). If, then, he who feeds the sheep of Laban labours and watches thus, on what labour, on what watches, should he be intent who feeds the sheep of God ? But in all this let Him instruct us who for our sake became a man, who vouchsafed to become what he had made. May He pour both into my weakness and into thy charity the spirit of His own love, and in all carefulness and watchfulness of circumspection open the eye of our heart.

But for men of a right faith being advanced to sacred orders thanks are to be paid without cease to the same Almighty God, and prayer ever made for the life of our most pious and most Christian lord the Emperor, and for his most tranquil spouse, and their most gentle offspring, in whose times the mouths of heretics are silent ; since, though their hearts seethe with the madness of perverse thought, yet in the time of the Catholic Emperor they presume not to speak out the bad things which they think.

Furthermore, in speaking of your maintenance of the holy councils, your Fraternity declares that you maintain the first holy Ephesine synod. But, seeing that from the account given in an heretical document which has been sent me from the royal city, I have found that, according to it, certain Catholic positions had been censured along with heretical ones, because some suppose that to have been the first Ephesine synod which was got together at some time or other by the heretics in the same city, it is altogether necessary that your Charity should apply to the Churches of Alexandria and Antioch for the acts of this synod, and find how the matter really stands. Or, if you please, we will send you hence what we have here, preserved from of old in our archives. For that synod which was held under pretence of being the first Ephesine asserts that certain positions submitted to it were approved, which are the declared tenets of Cœlestius and Pelagius. And, Cœlestius and Pelagius having been condemned in that synod, how could those positions be approved, the authors of which were condemned 9 ?

Further, since it has come to our ears that in the Churches of the East no one attains to a sacred order except by giving of bribes, if your Fraternity finds it to be so, offer your first oblation to Almighty God by restraining in the Churches subject to you the error of simoniacal heresy. For, to pass over other considerations, what manner of men can they be in sacred orders who are raised to them not by merit, but by bribes ? May Almighty God guard thy Love with heavenly grace, and grant to you to carry with you to eternal joys multiplied fruit and overflowing measure from those who are committed to your charge.

## EPISTLE LV.

### To Fantinus, Guardian (*Defensorem*), of Panormus (*Palermo*).

Gregory to Fantinus, &c.

A little time ago we wrote to Victor, our brother and fellow-bishop, that—inasmuch as certain of the Jews have complained in a petition presented to us that synagogues with their guest-chambers, situated in the city of Panormus, had by him been unreasonably taken possession of—he should keep aloof from their congregation until it could be ascertained whether this thing had been justly done, lest perchance injury should appear to have been alleged by them of their own mere will. And indeed, having regard to his priestly office, we could not easily believe that our aforesaid brother had done anything unsuitably. But, since we find from the report of Salarius, our notary, who was afterwards there, that there had been no reasonable cause for taking possession of those synagogues, and that they had been unadvisedly and rashly consecrated, we therefore enjoin thy Experience, since what has been once consecrated cannot any more be restored to the Jews, that it be thy care to see that our aforesaid brother and fellow-bishop pay the price at which our sons, the glorious Venantius the Patrician, and Urbicus the Abbot, may value the synagogues themselves with the guest-chambers that are under them or annexed to their walls, and the gardens thereto adjoining ; that so what he has caused to be taken possession of may belong to the Church, and they may in no wise be oppressed, or suffer any injustice. Moreover, let books or ornaments that have been abstracted be in like manner sought for. And, if any have been manifestly taken away, we desire them also to be restored without any ambiguity. For, as there ought to be no licence for them, as we have ourselves already written, to do anything in their synagogues beyond what is decreed by law, so neither damage nor any

---

9 Cf. VI. 14.

cost ought to be brought upon them contrary to justice and equity

## EPISTLE LVIII.

### To Martin, *Scholasticus*[1].

Gregory to Martin, &c.

Seeing that questions arising in civil affairs need, as is known to thy Greatness, very full enquiry, let thy wisdom consider with what care and vigilance the causes of bishops should be investigated. But, in the letter which thou hast sent us by the bearer of these presents on the questions with respect to which thou wert sent to us by our brother and fellow-bishop Crementius, thou hast given only a superficial account of them, and hast been entirely silent about their root. But, had their origin and intrinsic character been manifest to us, we should have known what should be decided about them, and would then settle the mind of our aforesaid brother by a plain and suitable reply. This, however, is altogether displeasing to us, that thou givest us to understand that some of the bishops have gone to the court[2] without letters from their primate, and that they hold unlawful assemblies. But since, as we have before said, the origin and nature of the questions are entirely unknown to us, we cannot pronounce anything definitely, lest, as would be very reprehensible, we should seem to pass sentence about things imperfectly known. Hence it was very needful that, for our complete information, thy Greatness should have proceeded hither to reply to our questions during the time of thy lingering in Sicily. Nevertheless, now that thou hast seen our brother and fellow-bishop John, we believe that in him thou hast seen us also. And so, since he has been at pains himself also to write to us about the same questions, we have written in reply to him what seemed to us right. And, since he is a priest of ripe and cautious judgment, if you are willing to treat with him on the questions which he has been commissioned to entertain, we are sure that you will find in

him what is both advantageous and reasonable.

## EPISTLE LIX.

### To John, Bishop of Syracuse[3].

Gregory to John, &c.

I have received your Fraternity's letter, wherein you inform me that the most eloquent Martin has come from the African province and communicated something to you privately. And indeed your Fraternity, as often as you find occasion, ceases not to shew your love towards the blessed apostle Peter. Wherefore we give thanks to Almighty God, that where you are, there we are not found absent. Nevertheless, your Holiness is not yet fully cognizant of the case in hand. For the Byzacene primate[4] had been accused on some charge, and the most pious Emperor wished him to be judged by us according to canonical ordinance. But then, on the receipt of ten pounds of gold, Theodorus the *magister militum* opposed this being done. Yet the most pious Emperor admonished us to commission some one, and do whatever was canonical. But, seeing the contrarieties of men, we have been unwilling to decide this case. Now, moreover, this same primate says something about his own intention. And it is exceedingly doubtful whether he says such things to us sincerely, or in fact because he is being attacked by his fellow-bishops : for, as to his saying that he is subject to the Apostolic See, if any fault is found in bishops, I know not what bishop is not subject to it. But when no fault requires it to be otherwise, all according to the principle of humility are equal. Nevertheless, do you speak with the aforesaid most eloquent Martin as seems good to your Fraternity. For it is for you to consider what should be done ; and we have replied to you briefly on the case, because we ought not to believe indiscriminately men that are even unknown to us. If, however, you, who see him before you in person, are of opinion that anything more definite should be said to him, we commit this to your Charity, being sure of your love in the grace of Almighty God. And what you do regard without doubt as having been done by us.

## EPISTLE LX.

### To Romanus and other Guardians (*defensores*) of the Ecclesiastical Patrimony.

Gregory to Romanus the guardian, Fantinus the guardian, Sabinus the sub-deacon, Sergius

---

[1] On the designation *Scholasticus*, see II. 32, note 2 ; V. 36, note 9. The occasion of this and the following epistle appears to have been as follows. Crementius, who was at that time primate of the province of Bizacia in Africa, had been accused by other African bishops. The Emperor, appealed to by them, had desired Gregory to take cognizance of the case ; but his interference had been objected to in Africa, where, as appears elsewhere, there was still jealousy of the claims of the Roman See. Gregory had commissioned John, Bishop of Syracuse, to investigate the matter, and to him Crementius (who now professed —though Gregory doubted his sincerity—to defer to the Roman bishop) had sent the lawyer Martin to state his case. The latter seems to have been directed to go on to Rome too, but had not done so. Both Martin and John had subsequently written to Gregory on the subject, and to them he now replies. Some three years seem to have afterwards elapsed without anything more being done : see XII. 32, where Gregory urges the bishops of the province to investigate the old charges against their primate in synod : but with what result does not further appear.

[2] *Ad comitatum;* referring to the suffragans of Crementius having complained to the Emperor against their primate.

[3] See preceding epistle, note 1. On this John's election to the See of Syracuse on Gregory's strong recommendation after the death of Maximianus, see V. 17.

[4] Viz. Crementius. See preceding epistle.

the guardian, Boniface the guardian (*a pari-bus*[5]), and the six *patroni*.

Since, even as cautious foresight knows how to block the way against faults, and to avoid what is hurtful, so neglect opens the way to excesses, and is wont to incur what ought to be guarded against, we ought to bestow very careful attention, and see alike to the reputation and to the safeguard of our brethren and priests. Now it has come to our ears that certain of the bishops, under pretext, as it were, of help, associate themselves in one house with women. And so, lest hereby just occasion of detraction should be given to scoffers, or the ancient enemy of the human race should take advantage of an easy matter of deceit, we enjoin thee by the tenor of this mandate that thou study to shew thyself strenuous and solicitous. And, if any of the bishops included within the limits of the patrimony committed to thee are living with women, do thou entirely put a stop to this, and for the future by no means suffer any women to reside with them, except such as the censorship of the sacred canons allows, that is a mother, an aunt, a sister, and others of this sort, concerning whom there can be no ill suspicion. Yet they do better, if they refrain from living together even with such as these. For we read that the blessed Augustine refused to live even with his sister, saying, *Those who are with my sister are not my sisters.*

The caution, then, of a learned man ought to be a great instruction to us. For it is a mark of uncautious presumption for one that is less firm not to fear what a strong man is afraid of. For he wisely overcomes what is unlawful who has learnt not to use even what is allowed him: and indeed we bind none in this matter against their will, but, as physicians are accustomed to do, we prescribe carefulness for health's sake, even though it be for the time distressful. And therefore we impose no necessary obligation; but, if any should choose to imitate a learned and holy man, we leave it to their own will. Let, then, thy Experience act with zeal and solicitude for the observance of what we have ordered to be prohibited. For, if hereafter it should chance to be found otherwise, know that thou wilt incur no slight risk with us. Furthermore, let it be thy care to exhort these same bishops, our brethren, that they admonish those who are subject to them, to wit those who are constituted in sacred orders, to observe in all ways after their example what they themselves observe; this only being added, that these, as canonical authority has decreed, are not to leave wives

whom they ought to govern chastely. Given in the month of March, Indiction 2.

## EPISTLE LXI.

Here begins the epistle of Rechared, King of the Goths, addressed to the blessed Gregory, Bishop of Rome [6].

Rechared to the holy lord and most blessed pope, the bishop Gregory.

At the time when the Lord in His compassion caused us to be dissociated from the impious Arian heresy, and the holy Catholic Church gathered us into her bosom ameliorated in the path of faith, it was then the desire of our mind to seek with delight and with the whole bent of our mind so very reverend a man; thee who art powerful above all other bishops, that he might commend in all ways a thing so worthy and acceptable to God for us men. But, whereas we are engaged in many cares of government, being occupied by divers occasions, three years passed without the desire of our mind being satisfied. And after this we chose, for the purpose of sending them to thee, some abbots of monasteries, who should proceed to thy presence, and offer gifts sent by us to Saint Peter, and bring us word more distinctly of thy holy reverence's health. But, as they hastened on their way, and were almost in sight of the shores of Italy, it befell them that they struck on certain rocks near Marseilles, and were scarcely able to deliver their own souls. And now we have entreated a presbyter whom thy Glory had sent as far as the city of Malaca (*civitatem Malicitanam*) to come into our sight. But he, detained by bodily infirmity, has in no wise been able to reach the soil of our kingdom. But, as we know most certainly that he was sent by thy Holiness, we have sent a golden cup ornamented on the outside with gems for thy Holiness (as I trust thou wilt vouchsafe to do) to offer as worthy of the apostle who shines the first in dignity. For I also beg thy Highness, when an opportunity is found, to seek us out by thy sacred golden letters. For how much I truly love thee I believe is not hidden, the Lord inspiring thee, from the fecundity of thine own breast. It is sometimes the case that those whom tracts of land or sea divide the grace of Christ glues together as if visibly. For to those who do not see thee at all in person fame discloses thy goodness.

---

6 The genuineness of this letter is considered doubtful. It may have been a forgery founded on Epistle CXXII. in this book from Gregory to Reccared. The Latin in the original is in many parts incorrect and ungrammatical; being such indeed Reccared's was not unlikely to be. Other letters relating to the conversion of Reccared are I. 43; IX. 121, 122.

Further, I commend with all veneration to thy Holiness in Christ, Leander, the priest of the church of Hispalis, since through him thy benevolence has been made clearly manifest to us; and when we talk of thy life with this same bishop, we reckon ourselves as your inferiors in regard to your good deeds. I am delighted to hear of thy health, most reverend and most holy man; and I beg of thy Christian prudence that thou wouldest commend frequently in thy prayers to our common Lord us and our people, who are ruled after God under our government, and have been acquired by Christ in your times; that hereby true charity to God-ward may establish in well-being those whom the breadth of the world separates.

## EPISTLE LXII.

### To Romanus, Guardian (*Defensorem*).

Gregory to Romanus, &c.

It has come to our ears that the *tonsuratores*[7] in Sicily, with wicked presumption, take to themselves the name of *defensores*, and that they not only are of no utility for the interests of the Church, but also take occasion hence to commit many irregularities. Consequently we enjoin thy Experience by this present authority to enquire diligently into this. And, if thou findest any, besides those who have letters to empower them in such business[8], usurping henceforth this title, put a stop to this thing by strict correction. If, however, thou shouldest discover any who have proved themselves active and faithful in ecclesiastical affairs, thou must send us a full and particular report of them, that we may judge whether they are worthy of a letter[9].

Furthermore, we desire thee to make a thorough examination of the accounts of Fortunatus; and, when he has satisfied all the debts that appear against him, allow him no longer to have to do with the patrimony, or with any action of our Church, seeing that, as we have heard, he has conducted himself in such a manner that he ought not henceforth to have any communication with our people.

Furthermore, it has been reported to us that one Martianus, who has assumed to himself the name of a *defensor*, has declined to pay obedience to our brother and fellow-bishop John, to whom we had committed the charge of our patrimony. Inquire therefore; and, if it is true, let him be sent into exile,

that his disobedience to him from whose Church he has seized for himself a false title of honour, and who is promoting the interests of the same, may not go unpunished. But, if there are also any others disobedient to the orders of our said brother, thou wilt by all means visit them with strict punishment.

## EPISTLE LXV.

### To Januarius, Bishop of Caralis (*Cagliari*).

Gregory to Januarius, Bishop of Sardinia.

It has come to our ears that some of your clerics, inflated with a spirit of elation (which is a serious thing to be said), neglect obedience to the commands of your Fraternity, and occupying themselves rather in the services and labours of others, desert the business of their own Church in which they are needed. For this reason we greatly wonder why you do not keep up the rule of discipline, and restrain them, when wandering dissolutely at large, with a rein of strict control to the requirements of the office they have undertaken. It is said also that some of these contumacious clerks, in order to obtain support against you, resort to the patronage of our guardian (*defensoris*) Vitalis. Wherefore we have sent a letter to him, telling him not to dare henceforth to support any one of your clerks against you unreasonably; but, if any case of fault should arise which is not a serious one but merits pardon, to approach you rather as an intercessor than as a supporter of the culprit. Be on your guard, then, that no such report shall hereafter reach us of your subjects despising you.

We have learnt also that a certain widow left her substance to the monastery of St. Julian, and that this substance has been plundered by one of your clerks who used to direct the actions of the deceased woman while she lived, and that he now evades making restitution. We therefore exhort thee that, if what is said should prove to be true, you cause him to be constrained by strict proceedings, to the end that he may make haste to restore without diminution the property left to the monastery, and be compelled to give up, even with the loss of his reputation, that which, preserving the purity of his honour, he ought not to have dared to take. But what a cause for shame it is that we should appear as admonishing your Fraternity to restrain your clerk under the vigour of discipline, this I believe that you yourself feel in your own heart.

Also against worshippers of idols, and soothsayers, and diviners, we very earnestly exhort

---

[7] "Tonsuratores dici potuere qui erant præpositi colonis seu possesseribus prædiorum Ecclesiæ Romanæ, qui erant tonsurati in signum subjectionis, more Romanorum." *Alteserra.*
[8] i.e. letters of appointment under the hand of the bishop of Rome. See V. 29, XI. 38, for the form of such letters.
[9] See note above.

your Fraternity to be on the watch with pastoral vigilance, and publicly among the people hold forth against the men who do such things, and recall them by persuasive hortation from the contagion of so great sacrilege, and such temptation of divine judgment, and peril in the present life. If, however, thou shouldest find them unwilling to amend and correct themselves from such doings, we desire thee to lay hold of them with fervent zeal, and, in case of their being slaves, to chastise them with blows and torments, whereby they may be brought to amendment. But, if they are freemen, they should be directed to penitence by suitable and strict confinement; so that they who scorn to listen to salutary words reclaiming them from peril of death may at any rate be brought back by bodily torments to the desired sanity of mind. We have also been informed that, you having committed the care of your patrimony to certain laymen, they, after having been detected in depredations on your peasants and flight in consequence, both refuse to restore the property which, as not being subject to your control, they indecently retain as though it were in their own power, and also scorn to render you an account of their doings. If this be so, it is fitting that the matter be strictly investigated by you, and the case between them and the peasants of your Church be thoroughly examined. And whatever fraud may be discovered in them let them be compelled to make restitution for with the penalty appointed by the laws. But for the future your Fraternity must take care that ecclesiastical property be not committed to secular men not living under your rule, but to approved clerics holding office under you; in whom if any wrong doing should be found, you may be able to correct what has been unlawfully done, as in the case of persons under you, whom the obligation of their condition convenes before you rather than excuses.

## EPISTLE LXVII.

### To Constantius, Bishop of Milan [1].

Gregory to Constantius, &c.

Maximus, the prevaricator of the Church of Salona, after he had failed to obtain anything through the greater powers of the world, has betaken himself to the lesser ones; and by a superfluity of prayers and by attestation to his good works he strives to prevail with us. This being so, I have thought it would be inhuman in me, if he who says that he fears me much

were quite unable to find me in some degree more indulgent. And I have therefore decided that our most reverend brother and fellow-bishop Marinianus should take cognizance of his cause in the city of Ravenna. If, however, by any chance his person is suspected, we desire that your Fraternity also, if it is not too laborious for you, should take the trouble of repairing to the same city, and sit together with our aforesaid brother in the same trial. Whatever, then, may seem good to each of your Holinesses, know that it will seem good to me; and your judgment I accept as my own; and what things you both think should be remitted, be assured that I remit; taking, however, careful heed that we may not appear to be either sinfully remiss or austere to the injury of Holy Church. We have enjoined the execution of this matter on the Chartulary Castorius, that he may fully report to us all that has been done.

## EPISTLE LXVIII.

### To Eusebius of Thessalonica.

Gregory to Eusebius of Thessalonica, Urbicus of Dyrrachium, Andrew of Nicopolis, John of Corinth, John of Prima Justiniana, John of Crete, John of Larissa and Scodra, and many other bishops.

We are constrained by the care of government which we have undertaken to extend vigilantly the solicitude of our office, and to instruct the minds of our brethren by addresses of admonition, that no wrongful presumption may avail to deceive the ignorant, nor any dissimulation to excuse those who know. Be it known then to your Fraternity that John, formerly bishop of the city of Constantinople, against God, against the peace of the Church, to the contempt and injury of all priests, exceeded the bounds of modesty and of his own measure, and unlawfully usurped in synod the proud and pestiferous title of œcumenical, that is to say, universal. When our predecessor Pelagius of blessed memory became aware of this, he annulled by a fully valid censure all the proceedings of that same synod, except what had therein been done in the cause of Gregory, bishop of Antioch, of venerable memory; taking him to task with most severe rebuke, and warning him to abstain from that new and temerarious name of superstition; even so as to forbid his deacon to go in procession [2] with him, unless he should amend so great a wickedness. And we, adhering in all respects to the zeal of his rectitude, observe

---

[1] See III. 47, note 2.

[2] *Procedere*; i.e. proceed to the Holy Table for celebration. Cf. Vii. 34, note 7.

his ordinances, under the protection of God, irrefragably, since it is fitting that he should walk without stumbling along the straight way of his predecessor, whom the tribunal of the eternal Judge awaits for rendering an account of the same place of government. In which matter, lest we should seem to omit anything that pertains to the peace of the Church, we once and again addressed the same most holy John by letter, bidding him relinquish that name of pride, and incline the elation of his heart to the humility which our Master and Lord has taught us. And having found that he paid no regard, we have not desisted, in our desire of concord, from addressing the like admonitions to our most blessed brother and fellow-priest Cyriacus, his successor. But since it is the case, as we see, now that the end of this world is near at hand, that the enemy of the human race has already appeared in his harbingers, so as to have as his precursors, through this title of pride, the very priests who ought to have opposed him by living well and humbly, I exhort and entreat that not one of you ever accept this name, that not one consent to it, that not one write it, that not one admit it wherever it may have been written, or add his subscription to it; but, as becomes ministers of Almighty God, that each keep himself from this kind of poisoned infection, and give no place to the cunning lier-in-wait, since this thing is being done to the injury and rendering asunder of the whole Church, and, as we have said, to the contemning of all of you. For if one, as he supposes, is universal bishop, it remains that you are not bishops.

Furthermore, it has come to our knowledge that your Fraternity has been convened to Constantinople. And although our most pious Emperor allows nothing unlawful to be done there, yet, lest perverse men, taking occasion of your assembly, should seek opportunity of cajoling you in favouring this name of superstition, or should think of holding a synod about some other matter, with the view of introducing it therein by cunning contrivances,—though without the authority and consent of the Apostolic See nothing that might be passed would have any force, nevertheless, before Almighty God I conjure and warn you, that the assent of none of you be obtained by any blandishments, any bribes, any threats whatever; but, having regard to the eternal judgment, acquit ye yourselves salubriously and unanimously in opposition to wrongful aims; and, supported by pastoral constancy and apostolical authority, keep out the robber and the wolf that would rush in, and give no way to him that rages for the tearing of the Church

asunder; nor allow, through any cajolery, a synod to be held on this subject, which indeed would not be a legitimate one, nor to be called a synod. We also at the same time admonish you, that if haply nothing should be done with mention of this preposterous name, but a synod be by any chance assembled on another matter, ye be in all respects cautious, circumspect, watchful, and careful, lest anything should therein be decreed against any place or person prejudicially, or unlawfully, or in opposition to the canons. But, if any question arises to be treated with advantage, let the question in hand take such a form that it may not upset any ancient ordinances. Wherefore we once more admonish you before God and His Saints, that you observe all these things with the utmost attention, and with the entire bent of your minds. For if any one, as we do not believe will be the case, should disregard in any part this present writing, let him know that he is segregated from the peace of the blessed Peter, the Prince of the Apostles. Let, then, your Fraternity so act that when the Shepherd of shepherds comes in judgment, you may not be found guilty with respect to the place of government which you have received.

## EPISTLE LXXVIII.

### To Eulogius, Patriarch of Alexandria.

Gregory to Eulogius, &c.

I have received at the hands of the bearer of these presents the letter of your most sweet Holiness, speaking to me about your cause being terminated speedily. But, as soon as he had come, he learnt how the possession which he sought from our Church was held, and soon satisfied himself about it. The business he had with others he settled without contention.

But concerning the matter which ought by all means to have been written about to me, your Holiness has written nothing, considering me also to be tardy therein. And indeed, for fear of its breaking out into the scandal of division, I have been unwilling to be the author of such division. For I have chosen that whatever may follow should ensue through others. But in time to come, God granting it, you will have proof that in a cause wherein I desire to please God I am not afraid of men. Concerning this I took care to write to you before now, even when you went to Constantinople.

As to the timber, I had prepared pieces of a larger size, as your Blessedness had requested in your letter; but so small a ship has been sent here that it could not carry them, unless they had been cut. But I was unwilling to have them cut, and have reserved for your judgment what should be done about them. If you do not require them, we will adapt them for other uses here. Moreover, I beg of your Holiness to pray for me earnestly, since I am incessantly pressed down by pains of gout, and swords of barbarians, and distressing cares. But, if you bestow on me the help of your prayer, I believe that you will strongly aid me against all adversities.

## EPISTLE LXXIX.

### To Marinianus, Bishop of Ravenna [3].

Gregory to Marinianus, &c.

What is to be done in the case of Maximus you have learnt from the letters which we have before sent to you. But, since we have ascertained from the report of our Chartulary Castorius, the bearer of these presents, what is the wish, or rather the request, of your Fraternity in this matter, therefore if the said Maximus, in the presence of you and our aforesaid Chartulary, shall purge himself on oath from simoniacal heresy, and with respect to other charges shall, before the body of Saint Apollinaris, as we have written, reply only, when interrogated, that he is guiltless, we commit his cause to the judgment of your Fraternity, with regard to his having presumed to celebrate the solemnities of mass while excommunicated, as to what penance such fault shall be purged by. And so, whatever according to God seems good to you, do you settle without fear, and entertain no doubt with regard to us. For whatsoever may be ordained by you concerning this cause we both thankfully accept and willingly allow. Yet we exhort you that you should be careful, and so temper what you provide for being done as both to deal kindly with him, if so it shall seem fit, and by a suitable arrangement to observe, as you ought, the genius of ecclesiastical vigour. We have instructed the above-named bearer, while present with us, how he is to act with you ; and, having learnt all thoroughly from him, do you so acquit yourselves in all respects that in your anxious care we may feel that our presence has been with you.

## EPISTLE LXXX.

### To Castorius, Notary [4].

Gregory to Castorius, &c.

The more thou seest thyself to be trusted by us, and charged with the conduct of cases when need arises, the more oughtest thou to shew thyself energetic and solicitous. Accordingly, if Maximus of Salona, having taken oath, shall affirm that he is not guilty of simoniacal heresy, and, as to other matters, when merely questioned before the body of Saint Apollinaris, shall reply that he is innocent, and shall have done penance, as we have directed, for his disobedience, we desire that, to console him, thy Experience should give him the letter which we have written to him [5], wherein we have signified that we have restored to him both our favour and communion. For, as it befits us to be severe to those who persist in contumacy, so to those who are again humbled and penitent we ought not to deny a place of pardon.

Furthermore, as to our brother Sabinianus, bishop of Jadera [6], and Honoratus [7], archdeacon of Salona, or others who have had recourse to the Apostolical See, Maximus must be very earnestly dealt with, so that he may receive them with becoming charity, and in no way retain in his heart any grudge against them, but live with them with pure goodwill and sincere affection.

## EPISTLE LXXXI.

### To Maximus, Bishop of Salona [8].

Gregory to Maximus, &c.

Although to what was faulty in thy ordination at the first thou hast added serious evil through the fault of disobedience, yet we, tempering with becoming moderation the authority of the Apostolic See, have never been incensed against thee to the extent that the case demanded. But our displeasure which thou hadst excited against thyself continued the longer in that a sense of the responsibility entrusted to us tormented us exceedingly, lest we might seem to be passing over without attention certain unlawful doings of thine that we had heard of. And, if thou considerest well, thou wilt see that thou thyself, by deferring to satisfy us, didst confirm these reports, and thereby didst exasperate us the more against thee. But now that, following wholesome counsel, thou hast submitted thyself humbly to the yoke of obedience, and that thy love, in doing penance [9], has purged itself, as we directed, by fitting satisfaction, understand thou that the favour of brotherly

---

3 See III. 47, note 2.
4 See below, Ep. LXXIX., and III. 47, note 2.

5 See below, Ep. LXXXI.
6 See VII. 15, VIII. 10.
7 See VI. 25, and note there.
8 See above, Ep. LXXX. and III. 47, note 2.
9 According to a narrative found in some few codices of the Registrum Epistolarum, and printed in an appendix by the Benedictine Editors, the penance done by Maximus at Ravenna consisted in his prostrating himself on the pavement of the city for three hours and exclaiming, "Peccavi Deo, et beatissimo papæ Gregorio."

charity is restored to thee, and give thanks that thou art received into our fellowship: for, as it becomes us to be strict with those who persevere in a fault, so does it to be kind in pardoning those who return to a better mind. Now, therefore, that thy Fraternity knows that he has recovered the communion of the Apostolic See, let him send some one to us, according to custom, to receive and convey to him the pallium. For, whilst we do not suffer unlawful things to be perpetrated, we no less refuse not what is customary. Further, though the discharge of the duties of our position might have called upon us to concede this, yet we are greatly constrained thereto by the request of our most sweet and excellent son, the lord Exarch Callinicus, that we would treat thee with moderation. His most dear wish we cannot resist, nor can we cause him sorrow.

## EPISTLE LXXXII.

### To Anatolius, Constantinopolitan Deacon [1].

Gregory to Anatolius, &c.

To good and devoted sons it is worth our labour so to respond as to double, because we are paying a debt, what it would befit us of our own mere motion to bestow upon them. Seeing, then, that the bearer of these presents, our son the magnificent Marcellinus [2], has demeaned himself as he has in the cause of our brother and fellow-bishop Maximus and in that of the Istrians, and is anxious to employ himself for the advantage of our Church, therefore, that he may be able more and more to shew his sincere affection not only in words but also in deeds, we hereby exhort thy Love to co-operate with him when he comes to the royal city with entire zeal and earnestness, and to be at pains so to assist him with all the succour in thy power, that, supported by the aid of Almighty God and thine, he may have the less difficulty to contend with there. Thou wilt also study so to attend to him as to one who is in very truth our own, and so to bestow on him the efficiency of thy charity, that he may both recognise a return made to him for the past, and also be able to entertain a great hope of retribution in the future for his devotion which he promises to exhibit in the service of the Church. But

inasmuch as, so far as we have learnt, the most serene lord the Emperor had commanded our aforesaid magnificent son to hasten to wait upon him immediately, it is fitting for thee to seek an opportunity of intimating that it was no faulty disobedience, but the cause of our brother and fellow-bishop Maximus, that has detained him : which cause, though late, has nevertheless through his exertions been brought to a conclusion. But this we desire thy Love to attend to carefully ; not to allow thyself to be mixed up in any cause whatever where there is oppression of the poor ; lest haply, under pressure to some extent from persons in power, thou shouldest be driven to do what could not be of advantage to thy soul. Dealing, then, with all matters in the fear of God, consider especially the eternal reward.

## EPISTLE XCI.

### To Fortunatus, Bishop of Neapolis (*Naples*).

Gregory to Fortunatus, &c.

Inasmuch as the Father of God's servants whom I had sent to the city of Naples has, by the ordering of God as it hath pleased Him, departed this life, it has seemed good to me to send the bearer of these presents, the monk Barbatianus, for the government of the same monks. For the present we decide that he shall be Prior, so that, if his life should approve itself to thy Fraternity, thou mayest after a little time ordain him as their Father. For he has some good qualities that commend him. But he has this great fault, that he is exceedingly wise in his own conceit. And it is evidently known how many branches of sin may spring from this root. Let thy Holiness, therefore, keep careful watch over him ; and if you shall find him become wary in government and humble in his own mind, then, with the permission of God, advance him to the dignity of Abbot. But, if he makes little progress in humility, defer his ordination, and report to me [3].

## EPISTLE XCIII.

### To Gulfaris, *Magister Militum* [4].

Gregory to Gulfaris, &c.

The bearers of these presents, who come

---

[1] Gregory's *apocrisiarius* at Constantinople.

[2] Supposed to be identical with Marcellus, Proconsul of Dalmatia, who, having originally and for some time afterwards supported Maximus as bishop of Salona against Gregory, had apparently made overtures for reconciliation with the latter. See IX. 5, and on the whole subject III. 47, note 2. He seems to have now fully satisfied Gregory, whose laudation of him in this letter is in marked contrast to the tone of IX. 5, addressed to Marcellus himself previously.

[3] See X. 24.

[4] As to Gregory's renewed efforts, now with better hope after the accession of Callinicus as Exarch of Italy to recover the Istrian schismatics in the matter of "the Three Chapters," see above, IX. 9, 10. Gulfaris, addressed in this epistle, was in military command in Istria, and appears to have exerted himself to further the aims of Gregory, who ever gladly availed himself of the aid of the secular arm. Other letters on the same subject follow.

to us from the Istrian parts, have reported such good things of your Glory as to inflame us ardently to return you thanks. For we learn that, among the cares of the government of those parts which has been committed to you, you are especially anxious to win souls, and that you so take pains to recall the hearts of wanderers to the unity of the Church that, as far as your desire goes, you would have no one there separated from the Apostolic Church; and that so great love of Peter, the Prince of the Apostles, inflames you that you long with all your heart to restore the sheepfold of him to whom the keys were delivered by the Lord the Creator of all. Have, glorious son, from such and so great a work, a confident anticipation of divine retribution, wherein not only our admonition but also the words of the apostle confirm thee, since he who shall have caused a sinner to be converted from the error of his way shall save his soul from death, and cover a multitude of sins (James v.). For, however great be temporal affluence, or at any rate prosperity, it has its end,—the limit of death. But this pursuit of winning souls, which you have taken up, retains the certainty of its hope fixed; to wit, the retribution of eternal life. Wherefore, greeting you with fatherly affection, we exhort your Glory that you the more earnestly give effect to the zeal for the unity of our holy faith which the Author of unity Himself has given you; and that, recalling whomsoever you can from the error of their schism into the bosom of Mother Church, you cherish them with continual admonition. And accomplish this also,—so to protect with the succour of your defence those whom the Lord through you may grant to be restored to His fold that there may be no quarter to which those who are still in error may be able to resort for the accusation of such as return to sound counsels. For, while you uphold the cause of God on earth, He Himself will prosperously direct your actions here with the aid of His protection, and there will remain for you, in the eternal life which you long for, retribution for your so great well-doing.

## EPISTLE XCIV.

To Romanus the Guardian (*Defensorem*).

Gregory to Romanus, &c.

The bearers of these presents, who came hither from the parts of Istria to find their bishop who is now living in the parts of Sicily, have asked us to speed them in their way, and we have arranged for their journey hence. Let, then, thy Experience receive them, and

arrange for their reaching their said bishop as soon as possible; lest, as they allege may be the case, others of the schismatics in those parts should be beforehand to persuade them. For, so far as they indicate, the bishop himself has a desire to come to us in behalf of the unity of the faith. Assistance therefore should be given them, that, with the help of the Lord, they may accomplish the good things they desire. But let thy Experience, in person if he is near at hand, or otherwise by letter, exhort this same bishop to lose no time in hastening, with the Lord's good favour, to the threshold of the Apostles, being assured that he will be received by us with all affection. We also desire thee to pay him the cost of his journey to enable him to come to us. But, if he finds coming here burdensome, and arranges to live in Sicily, and consents, with his security given, to remain in the unity of the Church among the perverters of Scripture, this also do not thou delay to inform us of, that we may arrange, with the help of the Lord, how provision may be made for his expenses there. But lend also thy concurrence and succour for the bearers of these letters to come to their said bishop, so that after leaving us they may experience no less attention.

## EPISTLE XCVIII.

To Theodore, Curator [5] of Ravenna.

Gregory to Theodore, &c.

Although from the report of our *responsalis* we have long heard many things of you to rejoice our heart, yet now our son the abbot Probus, who has returned to us, has reported still further such things of the charity of your Glory as it is becoming should be told of a really good and most Christian son. And, since he has told us of such kind feeling on your part, and such earnestness in arranging the peace as has not appeared even in our own citizens who have previously been in your parts, we beg the mercy of heavenly protection to recompense you for this in body and in soul both here and in the world to come, seeing that you have not ceased to act advantageously for the weal of many.

We inform you therefore that Ariulf [6] has sworn to the observance of the peace, not as his King swore [7], but under the condition that no excess should in any way be committed against himself, and that no one should march

---

5 " Erat forte magistratus municipalis, qui annonæ civitatis curam gerit." *Note to Benedictine Edition.*
6 The Lombard duke of Spoletum, who had besieged Rome, A.D. 592, previously to the invasion of King Agilulph in person Cf. II. 3, 29, 30, 46, and *Prolegom.*, p. xix.
7 For notice of the peace concluded with the Lombard King Agilulph, cf. IX. 4, 42, 43; and *Prolegom.*, p. xx.

against the army of Aroges[8]. This begin altogether unfair and crafty, we take it as if he had not sworn,—since to some extent he will easily find for himself an occasion of exceeding, and will deceive us the more if we are not on our guard against him.

But Warnilfrid, according to whose advice this same Ariulf acts in all respects, has scorned to swear at all. And so it has come to pass that from the peace which we so much desired, we in these parts can have hardly any remedy, since we must still, and for the future, be on our guard against the same enemies that we have been on our guard against so far.

Furthermore, be it known to your Glory that the King's men who have been sent hither press us to subscribe to the compact. But remembering the insults which, to the injury through us of the blessed Peter, Agilulph is said to have addressed to the most illustrious Basilius, though Agilulph himself has entirely denied this, we have still thought it prudent to abstain from subscription, lest we, who are petitioners and mediators between him and our most excellent son the lord Exarch, should find ourselves deceived in any respect, in case of anything being perchance secretly with drawn (*i.e. from the compact*), and he should find an occasion of not assenting to our petition. And so we beg, as we have requested also of our aforesaid most excellent son, that your Glory, with the charity whereby you are united to us, would take measures to the end that, before these men return from Arogis, the king may send them letters post-haste, to be, however, handed on to us, ordering them not to call on us to subscribe. But, if it serves the purpose, we will cause our glorious brother, or one of the bishops, or at any rate an archdeacon, to subscribe.

With regard to Augustus we thank you, and are giving attention to his settling his cause with his adversary in accordance with equity; having been unwilling that the trouble of putting in an appearance with you should be imposed upon him, yet so as not to deny justice to his adversary.

With regard to other matters since it has not been so far in our power to thank you adequately, we will for the future send to you our *responsalis*, through whom, by the mercy of God, we may be the more bound together in the charity wherein we are knit to each other. Moreover, the sorrow of your Glory affects us exceedingly; but since a wise man knows all that can be said in the way of

comfort, we omit comforting you with words; but we attend you with our prayers, beseeching Almighty God to guard the life and health of yourself and all yours under the protection of His loving-kindness, and to console your heart while in a state of affliction.

## EPISTLE CV.
### To Serenus Bishop of Massilia, (*Marseilles*).

Gregory to Serenus, &c.

That we have been so long in sending a letter to your Fraternity attribute not to sluggishness, but to press of business. We now commend to you in all respects the bearer of these presents, our most beloved son Cyriacus, the Father of our Monastery, that no delay may detain him in the city of Massilia, but that he may proceed under God's protection to our brother and fellow-bishop Syagrius [9] with the succour of your Holiness.

Furthermore we notify to you that it has come to our ears that your Fraternity, seeing certain adorers of images, broke and threw down these same images in Churches. And we commend you indeed for your zeal against anything made with hands being an object of adoration; but we signify to you that you ought not to have broken these images. For pictorial representation is made use of in Churches for this reason; that such as are ignorant of letters may at least read by looking at the walls what they cannot read in books. Your Fraternity therefore should have both preserved the images and prohibited the people from adoration of them, to the end that both those who are ignorant of letters might have wherewith to gather a knowledge of the history, and that the people might by no means sin by adoration of a pictorial representation [1].

## EPISTLE CVI.
### To Syagrius, Aetherius, Virgilius, and Desiderius, Bishops [2].

Gregory to Syagrius of Augustodunum (*Autun*), Etherius of Lugdunum (*Lyons*), Virgilius of Aretale (*Arles*), and Desiderius of Vienna (*Vienne*), bishops of Gaul. *A paribus*.

---

[9] It appears from Epistle CIX. below that Cyriacus was being now sent to the bishop of Autun with the special view of getting a synod called by queen Brunechild for restraining the simony and other ecclesiastical irregularities which were prevalent in Gaul. Cf. also above, IX. 11, to Brunechild.
[1] Cf. XI. 13.
[2] This is a circular letter to the metropolitan bishops to prepare them for the general synod which Gregory was anxious should be held in Gaul for checking the simony, and other abuses, continually referred to by him as prevalent there. Cf. in this book, Epistles XI., CVII., CVIII., CIX., CX. On *a paribus*, see I. 25, note 8.

---

[8] Arogis (or *Arigis*) was the Lombard duke of Beneventum. Cf. II. 46.

Our Head, which is Christ, has to this end willed us to be His members, that through the bond of charity and faith He might make us one body in Himself. And to Him it befits us so to adhere in heart, that, since without Him we can be nothing, through Him we may be able to be what we are called. Let nothing divide us from the citadel of our Head, lest, if we refuse to be His members, we be left apart from Him, and wither like branches cast off from the vine. Wherefore, that we may be counted worthy to be the dwelling-place of our Redeemer, let us abide in His love with entire earnestness of mind. For He Himself says, *He that loveth me will keep my word, and my Father will love him, and we will come unto him, and make our abode with him* (Joh. xiv. 23). But, since we cannot keep close to the author of all good, unless we cut away from us covetousness, which is the root of all evil, we therefore by these present writings (which associate us together mutually as in the alternate discourse of a wished for visitation) approach your Fraternity in accordance with apostolic institutes, that, leaning on the rules of the Fathers and the Lord's commands, we may banish from the temple of faith avarice, which is the service of idols, so as to suffer nothing hurtful, and nothing disorderly, to be in the house of the Lord.

I apprize you to wit, that we have long heard it currently reported how that in the regions of Gaul sacred orders are conferred through simoniacal heresy. And we are affected with sorrowful disgust, if money has any place in ecclesiastical offices, and that which is sacred is made secular. Whosoever, then, sets himself to buy this thing by the giving of a price, having regard not to the office but to the title, covets not to be a priest, but only to be called one. What forsooth? What comes of this but that there is no trial of a man's conduct, no carefulness about his moral character, no enquiry into his life, but that he only is counted worthy who has the means to give a price? Hence it ensues, if the matter be weighed in a true balance, that, while one wickedly makes haste to snatch a place of utility with a view to vain glory, he is all the more unworthy from the very fact of his seeking dignity. Moreover, as one who refuses when invited and flies when sought should be brought up to the sacred altar, so one that sues of his own accord and pushes himself forward importunately should without doubt be repelled. For whoever thus strives to climb to higher places, what does he but decrease in increasing, and in rising outwardly sink low inwardly? Where-fore, dearest brethren, in ordaining priests let sincerity prevail, let there be simple consent without venality, let a pure election be preferred, so that advancement to the highest place of the priesthood may be believed to be due, not to the suffrage of sellers, but to the judgment of God. For that it is a grievous crime to wish to procure or to sell the gift of God for a price evangelical authority is witness (Matth. xxi.).

For, when our Lord and Redeemer went into the temple, He overthrew the seats of them that sold doves. What else is it to sell doves but to receive a price for the laying on of hands, and to put to sale the Holy Spirit whom Almighty God gives to men? And that the priesthood of such as do so falls before the eyes of God is plainly signified by the overthrowing of the seats. And yet the perverseness of this iniquity still puts forth its strength. For it drives those to sell whom it deceives into buying. And, while attention is not paid to what is enjoined by the divine voice, *Freely ye have received, freely give* (Matth. x. 8), it is brought to pass that it increases, and becomes doubled in one and the same contagion of sin, to wit of the buyer and of the seller. And, it being well known that this heresy crept into the Church with a pestiferous root before all others, and was condemned in its very origin by apostolic detestation, why is it not guarded against? Why is it not considered that blessing is turned into a curse to him who is promoted to the end that he may become a heretic?

For the most part, then, the adversary of souls, when unable to insinuate into them what is wrong on the face of it, endeavours to supplant them by throwing over it as it were a show of piety, and persuades them, perhaps, that money ought to be received from those who have it, so that there may be wherewith to give to those who have it not, if only he may even so infuse mortal poisons concealed under the appearance of almsgiving. For neither would the hunter deceive the wild beast, nor the fowler the bird, nor the fisherman catch the fish, if the former were to set their snares in open view, or if the latter had not his hook hidden by the bait. By all means, then, the cunning of the enemy is to be feared and guarded against, lest those whom he cannot subvert by open temptation he should succeed in slaying more cruelly by a hidden weapon. For indeed it is not to be accounted almsgiving if that be dispensed to the poor which is got by unlawful dealings, since he who with this intention receives amiss as though with the view of dispensing well is the worse for it rather than the better.

The alms that please the eyes of our Redeemer are not those that are gathered together in unlawful ways and from iniquity, but such as are bestowed out of what has been granted to us and well acquired. Hence this also is certain, that, though monasteries or hospitals or aught else be built with the money given for sacred orders, it profits not for reward; since, when one that is perverse and a buyer of dignity is transferred to a holy place, and constitutes others after the likeness of himself for a consideration given, he destroys more by his evil administration than he who has received money from him for ordination can build up. That we should not, then, try to get anything with sin under pretence of almsgiving we are plainly warned by Holy Scripture, which says, *The sacrifices of the impious are abominable, which are offered of wickedness* (Prov. xxi. 27). For whatever in God's sacrifice is offered of wickedness appeases not, but provokes, the anger of Almighty God. Hence again it is written, *Honour the Lord from thy just labours* (Prov. iii. 9). Whoso, then, takes evilly that he may, as he supposes, give well, it is evident without doubt that he honours not the Lord. Hence also it is said through Solomon, *Whoso offers a sacrifice of the substance of the poor is as though he slew a son in his father's sight* (Ecclus. xxxiv. 24). Now let us consider how great is a father's grief if his son be killed in his sight : and hence we easily understand how much God is grieved when a sacrifice is given Him out of pillage. Exceedingly to be shunned then, most beloved brethren, is the perpetration of the sins of simoniacal heresy under pretence of almsgiving. For it is one thing to do alms on account of sins, but another to commit sins on account of alms.

This also, which has reached our ears, we include as worthy of no dissimilar detestation; that some persons, inflated with desire of dignity, are tonsured on the death of bishops, and from being laymen are suddenly made priests, and shamelessly snatch at the leadership of religious life, not having as yet even learnt to be soldiers. What good do we suppose these will do their subjects, who, before touching the threshold of discipleship, fear not to occupy the place of mastership? In such a case it is needful that, even though any one were of unquestioned merit, he should be exercised in ecclesiastical offices by passing through distinct orders. He should see what he is to imitate, he should be formed into the shape he is to retain, so that afterwards he may not err, when chosen for shewing the way of life to the erring. He should, then, be polished long by religious meditation, that he

may be well-pleasing, and so shine as a candle placed on a candlestick that the adverse force of winds driving against the kindled flame of erudition may not extinguish it, but increase it. For, since it is written, *That one should first be proved, and so minister* (1 Tim. iii. 10), much more ought he first to be proved who is taken as an intercessor for the people, lest bad priests should become the cause of the people's ruin. There can therefore be no excuse, no defence against this, since it is clearly known to all how solicitous about diligent attention to this matter is the holy and excellent teacher, who forbids that a novice should accede to sacred orders (1 Tim. iii.). But, as then one was called a novice who had been newly planted in the conversation of the holy faith, so one is now to be held to be a novice who, having been suddenly planted in the habit of religion, creeps on to canvass for sacred dignities. Orders, then, should be risen to in an orderly way : for he courts a fall who seeks to rise to the topmost heights of a place by steep ascents, disregarding the steps that lead to it. And, seeing that the same apostle teaches his disciple, among other directions with regard to sacred orders, that hands are to be laid hastily on no man (1 Tim. v.), what can be more hasty or what more headlong than to begin at the top, and that a man should commence by being a bishop before he has been a minister? Whosoever, then, desires to obtain priesthood, not for the pomp of elation but for doing good, let him first measure his own strength with the burden he is to undergo, that, if unequal to it, he may abstain, and also approach it with fear, even if he thinks himself sufficient for it.

Further, it will not be beside the mark, if, in addition to the argument from rational beings we draw one from our use of irrational things. For timber suitable for buildings is cut from forests, and yet the weight of the building is not imposed on them while they are yet green, or till a delay of many days has dried their greenness, and rendered them fit for necessary use. And, if by any chance this precaution is neglected, they are soon broken by the mass imposed upon them, and the material provided for support begets ruin.

For hence also medical men, whose care is for the body, do not offer certain remedies to him that needs them while recently concocted, but leave them to be macerated for some time. For, should any one give them immaturely, there is no doubt that the means of health become a cause of danger. Let them learn, therefore, let priests in their office learn, those namely to whom the cure of souls is entrusted, to observe what men of various arts under the teaching of reason attend to, and restrain themselves from ambition, if not of fear, yet at any rate of very shame.

But, lest perchance any one should still wish to defend himself on the pretext of an evil custom, let the discretion of your Fraternity restrain them with the rein of reason, and not allow them to lapse into unlawful doings, since whatever is deserving of punishment ought not to be adduced as an example for imitation, but for correction.

Nor, further, can we suffer you to pass over neglectfully this other matter, which alike requires correction. For of what profit is it to have guarded all besides if through one place pernicious access be afforded to the enemy? Therefore let women be prohibited from living with those who are constituted in any sacred order. With regard to them, lest the old enemy of the human race should exult, it must be laid down by the consent of all that they may have no other women with them but those whom the sacred canons include And, though this interdiction is perhaps bitter for the time to some, there is no doubt that it will afterwards grow sweet from its very benefit to their souls, if the enemy be overcome in that whereby he might have overcome them.

In this part of our solicitude also we must not leave unnoticed what has been ordained by the provision of the Fathers, for the sake of advantage, concerning the holding of councils throughout dioceses. Wherefore, lest there should be any dissension among brethren, or any fomentation of discord between superiors and subordinates, it is necessary that priests should assemble together, so that there may be discussion about cases that arise, and salutary conference about ecclesiastical observances; to the end that, while things past are corrected and things future regulated, the Almighty Lord may be praised on all sides in one accord by brethren. Know ye whose presence will be with you, seeing that it is written, *Where two or three are gathered together in My name, there am I in the midst of them* (Matth. xviii. 20). If, then, He will vouchsafe to be present where there are two or three, how much more will He not be wanting where many priests have come together? And indeed it is not unknown what is appointed by the rules of the Fathers as to the holding of a council twice in the year. But, lest haply any necessity should not allow this rule to be carried out, we decree that still one shall meet, without any excuse allowed, once; so that nothing wrong, nothing unlawful, may be ventured on while a council is being expected. For commonly, though not from love of justice, yet from fear of enquiry, people

abstain from that which it is known may displease the judgment of all. Let us, most beloved brethren, keep this observance to be left to our posterity; and let us meditate on all that is written in the sacred writings for our instruction, and incite all we can to follow it. For it is certain that, if with all our heart we attend to these salutary precepts, we escape all taint of vices, since, while we lean on these whereby we are built up, we shut out, no doubt, all place for deception.

Therefore for the purposes mentioned above, we desire your Fraternity, God willing, to assemble a synod, and in it, through the mediation of our most reverend brother and fellow-bishop Aregius [3], and our most beloved son Cyriacus, let all things that are, as we have before said, opposed to the sacred canons, be strictly condemned under the ban of anathema; that is, that any one should presume to give any consideration for acquiring ecclesiastical orders, or receive any for conferring them; or that any one should all at once from a lay condition dare to enter on a place of rule; or that any other women should live with priests but such as are allowed, as aforesaid, by the sacred canons. Concerning all these things let our most reverend brother the bishop Syagrius, with the whole synod, when our most beloved brother Cyriacus returns to us, take care to send us word of what has been done; in order that, knowing accurately what has been decreed, and with what safeguards and in what manner, we may render thanks without ceasing to Almighty God for your life and manners.

## EPISTLE CVII.

### To Aregius, Bishop of Vapincum [4].

Gregory to Aregius, Bishop in Gaul.

The affliction of your Fraternity, which we have learnt that you have had for the loss of your people, has given us such cause of grief that, since charity makes us two one, we feel our heart to be especially in your tribulations. But in the midst of this we have been much consoled by your having brought your mind to discern how it becomes

---

3 Perhaps an error for Syagrius, bishop of Augustodunum (*Autun*), to whom the use of the pallium had been recently conceded on certain conditions, and to whom the assembling of the synod was committed, though he was not thus authorized to take precedence of his metropolitan, the bishop of Lyons. See Ep. CVIII. and Ep. XI. note 2. Cyriacus, mentioned below, had been sent specially from Rome to forward and regulate the proceedings (see Ep. CIX., note 2), Aregius of Vapincum being also directed to send Gregory a full report of the proceedings (see Ep. CVII.). If the intended synod was held at all, it appears to have failed to put a stop to the abuses complained of. For a year or two later we find Gregory still referring to them, and pressing for a synod to suppress them. See XI. 55, 56, 57, 59, 60, 63.
4 A see in Narbonensis Secunda under the Metropolis of Aquæ (*Aix*); the modern *Gap*

you to bear sorrow patiently, and, in the hope of another life, not to have long continued grief for death. Still, lest some tribulation should still maintain itself in your soul, I exhort you to rest from sorrow, to cease to be sad. For it is unseemly to addict oneself to wearisomeness of affliction for those of whom it is to be believed that they have attained to true life by dying. Those have perhaps just excuse for long continued grief who know not of another life, and have no trust that there is a passing from this world to a better. We, however, who know this, who believe it and teach it, ought not to be too much distressed for them that depart, lest what in others has a show of affection, be to us rather a matter of blame. For it is, as it were, a kind of distrust to be tormented by sadness in opposition to what everyone preaches, as the Apostle says, *But we would not have you to be ignorant, brethren, concerning them that are asleep, that ye sorrow not even as others which have no hope* (1 Thess. iv. 12).

Having, therefore, this reason before us, dearest brother, we should try, as we have said, not to afflict ourselves about the dead, but bestow affection on the living, to whom pity may be of advantage and love bear fruit. Let us henceforth hasten, by reproving, exhorting, persuading, soothing, comforting, to profit all we can. Let our tongue be an encouragement to the good, a goad to the bad ; let it beat down the puffed up, appease the angry, stir up the slow, kindle the idle by exhortation, persuade the shrinkers back, soothe the rough, comfort the despairing ; that, as we are called leaders, we may shew the way of salvation to them that are advancing forward. Let us be vigilant in keeping guard, let us defend all approaches against the snares of the enemy. And, if ever error should have drawn aside a sheep of the flocks committed to us through devious ways, let us strive with all our endeavours to recall it to the Lord's sheepfolds, so that from the name of shepherd which we bear we may reap not punishment, but a reward. Seeing, then, that in all this there is need of the help of divine grace, let us implore the clemency of Almighty God with continual prayers, to the end that for doing these things He may give us the will and grant us the power, and, with the fruit of good work, direct us in that way in which He has declared Himself to be the Shepherd of shepherds ; that so, through Him, without whom we cannot rise to the doing of anything, we may be able to accomplish all.

Furthermore, our common son, Peter the deacon, has given us to understand that your

Fraternity at the time when you were here requested that we would grant to yourself and your archdeacon license to use dalmatics [5]. But, because compelled by the sickness of your people, you departed in such haste that the very grief that weighed upon you did not suffer you to press the matter any longer, as was fit and as the nature of your request required ; and because we had many engagements, and consideration of ecclesiastical propriety did not allow us to concede a new thing inconsiderately and suddenly ; for these reasons the carrying into effect of the thing demanded has been long postponed. Now, however, recalling to mind your Charity's good deservings, by the tenor of this our authority we grant you your request, and have granted to thee or to thy archdeacon to be decorated by the use of dalmatics ; and we have sent the same dalmatics by the hands of our most beloved son, the abbot Cyriacus.

Furthermore, at the synod which we have decreed should be assembled through our brother and fellow-bishop Syagrius against simoniacal heresy, we desire thee to be present ; and we have ordered the pallium which we have sent for our said brother to be accordingly given him, on condition of his promising to remove from holy Church, by a definition of the synod, the unlawful things which we have prohibited. Concerning which synod we desire thy Fraternity to report to us fully by letter all its proceedings, that thou thyself, whose holiness we are well acquainted with, mayest inform us about everything.

## EPISTLE CVIII.

### To Syagrius, Bishop.

Gregory to Syagrius, Bishop of Augustodunum (*Autun*).

Mistress of all good things is charity, which savours of nothing extraneous, nothing rough, nothing confused ; which so exercises and strengthens hearts that nothing is heavy, nothing difficult, but all that is done becomes sweet. Since, then, it is its peculiar quality to foster things that are concordant, to preserve things that are united, to join together things that are dissociated, to set right things that are wrong, and to consolidate all other virtues by the bulwark of its own perfection, whosoever grafts himself into its roots neither falls away from greenness, nor becomes empty of fruits, because effective work loses not the moisture of fecundity. And so I am much

---

[5] For the use of Dalmatics, see Dict. of Christ. Ant. (*Smith and Cheetham,* 1875), under DALMATIC.

delighted with thee, and rejoice with thee in the Lord, most beloved brother, for that I find thee, by the testimony of many, so endowed with this same charity that thou both thyself becomingly exhibitest what befits a prïest, and laudably shewest an example for imitation to others.

Inasmuch, then, as in the work of preaching (which after long thought I have taken care to supply to the nation of the Angli through Augustine, then provost (*præpositum*) of my monastery, and now our brother and fellow-bishop), I have found thee to be, as was right, so solicitous, devoted, and in all ways helpful, as to lay me under a great debt to thee in this matter, therefore moved by the consideration of so great an obligation, I cannot bear to put aside thy Fraternity's petition, lest I should appear towards thee unprofitable. Consequently, according to the tenor of thy request, we have provided under God for thy being dignified by the use of the pallium [6], to be worn within thy church, in the celebration of mass only. Nevertheless we have decided that it should be given thee only on condition of thy first promising to amend by the definition of a synod the things that we have ordered to be corrected; for we certainly deem it fit that, with the gravity of mind in which by the mercy of God we have learnt that thou excellest, a more distinguished adornment of outward apparel should accrue to thee; especially as we think that thou hast asked for it, not with a view to the pomp of needless elation, but with regard to the character and dignity of thy Church. And, lest in this vestment we should seem to be bestowing as it were a bare bounty, we have taken thought at the same time for the granting of this also;—that, while the Metropolitan has in all respects his place and dignity preserved to him, the Church of Augustodunum should be next after the Church of Lugdunum (*Lyons*), and should claim to itself this place and rank by the indulgence of our authority. But as to the other bishops, we decree that they shall take their places according to the date of their ordination, whether for sitting in council, or for subscribing, or in any other matter, and shall claim to themselves the prerogative of their several ranks: for it seems to us consonant to reason that with the use of the pallium we should together with it, as we have said, bestow some privileges.

But, since with augmentation of dignity the sense of responsibility ought also to increase, that the adornments of action may agree with the decoration of vestments, your Fraternity should exercise yourself the more earnestly in all your pursuits. Be vigilant with regard to the doings of those who are under you; let your example be their instruction, and your life their teacher. By the exhortation of your tongue let them learn what to fear, and be taught what to love; that, when thou givest up the talents entrusted to thee with multiplied gain, in the day of retribution thou mayest be counted worthy to hear, *Well done, good and faithful servant: enter thou into the joy of thy lord* (Matth. xxv. 23).

## EPISTLE CIX.

### To Brunichild, Queen of the Franks.

Gregory to Brunichild, &c.

Now that your Excellency's royal solicitude is in all matters of government praiseworthy, you ought, for the increase of your glory, to shew yourself more watchful, and careful not to allow those whom you rule with counsel outwardly to perish inwardly among themselves. So may you, through the fruit of your pious solicitude, after occupying this topmost height of a temporal kingdom, attain under God to kingdoms and joys that are eternal. And this we trust you will be able after the following manner to succeed in; if, among other good deeds, you pay attention to the ordination of priests [7]; whose office, as we have learnt, has come in your parts to be such an object of ambition that priests are ordained all at once from being laymen. This is a very serious matter. For what can they effect, what good can they do the people, who covet being made bishops, not for doing good, but for distinction? These, then, who have not yet learnt what they have to teach—what do they effect, but that the unlawful advancement of a few becomes the ruin of many, and that the observance of ecclesiastical government is brought into confusion, seeing that no regular order is observed? For whoso comes to the control thereof inconsiderately and hurriedly, with what admonition can he edify those who are put under him, his example having taught them, not reason, but error? It is a shame in truth, it is a shame, for one to command others what he knows not how to observe himself.

Nor do we pass over that other thing which in like manner requires amendment, but detest it as utterly execrable and a most serious matter; that in your parts sacred orders are conferred through simoniacal heresy, which was the first to arise against the Church, and was condemned with a rigorous malediction.

---

6 Cf. IX. 11, 109.

7 *Sacerdotibus*, in the usual sense of *bishops*.

Hence, therefore, it is brought about that the dignity of the priesthood comes into contempt, and holy honour under condemnation. And so reverence perishes, discipline is destroyed, since he who ought to have corrected faults committed them ; and by nefarious ambition the honourable priesthood is brought under censure and disparagement. For who will any more venerate what is sold, or not think worthless what is bought ? Hence I am greatly distressed, and condole with that land ; since, while they scorn to have as a divine gift, but compass by bribes, the Holy Spirit which Almighty God deigns to bestow on men through the imposition of hands, I do not think that the priesthood can long subsist there. For where the gifts of heavenly grace are sold, the life is not sought for God's service, but rather money is venerated in opposition to God. Seeing then that so great a wickedness is not only a danger to them, but also in no small degree injurious to your kingdom, greeting your Excellency with fatherly affection we beseech you to make God propitious to you by the correction of this enormity. And, that there may be henceforth no opportunity of committing it, let a synod be held by your order, at which, in the presence of our most beloved son, the abbot Cyriacus [8], it shall be interdicted strictly under pain of anathema that any one should dare to pass suddenly from a lay condition to the degree of the Episcopate, or any one whatever dare to give or receive anything for ecclesiastical orders ; that so our Lord and Redeemer may so deal with the things that are yours as He shall see you to be solicitous with pious devotion in the things that are His. But we have taken special care to delegate the charge and management of this synod, which we have decided should be held, to our brother and fellow-bishop Syagrius, whom we know to be peculiarly your own ; and we beg you to deign both to lend a willing ear to his supplication, and to support him by your aid ; to the end that what may redound to your reward, namely a pious and God-pleasing ordination of priests, the contagion of this evil being removed, may take effect within all the limits of your jurisdiction.

To this our brother, in that he has shewn himself exceedingly devoted with regard to the mission which has been sent, under God, to the nation of the Angli, we have sent a pallium to be used in the solemnities of mass, so that, having given aid in things spiritual, he may find himself advanced by the favour

of the Prince of the apostles in the spiritual order itself.

Furthermore, we have altogether wondered why in your kingdom you allow Jews to possess Christian slaves. For what are all Christians but members of Christ? And we all know that you sincerely honour the Head of these members. But let your Excellency consider how inconsistent it is to honour the Head and to allow the members to be trampled on by his enemies. And so we beg that your Excellency's ordinance may remove the mischief of this iniquity from your kingdom ; so that you may prove yourself the more to be a worthy worshipper of Almighty God, in that you set his faithful ones free from His enemies.

## EPISTLE CX.

### To Theoderic and Theodebert, Kings of the Franks [9].

**Gregory to Theoderic, &c.**

Since the renown of your kingdom has been resplendent of old among all others by the grace of the Christian religion, great pains should be taken that, wherein you stand out more glorious than other nations, you should therein please more perfectly the Almighty Lord who gives health and wealth to kings, and have the faith which you observe in all ways helpful to you. We had wished indeed, most excellent sons, to address to you a discourse of friendly greeting only, so as to shew our fatherly affection in offices of charity. But, seeing that an unlawful proceeding distresses us exceedingly, it befits us so to exhibit one thing as by no means to pass over in silence the other which needs amendment. If you give diligent attention, you will find that we speak entirely for the security of your well-being.

Now it is said that simoniacal heresy (which was the first to creep in by the devil's planting against the Church of God, and was at its very rise smitten and condemned by the weapon of apostolical vengeance) prevails within the limits of your kingdom, though faith together with good life ought to be chosen in priests.

If good life is wanting, faith has no merit, as the blessed James attests, who says, *Faith without works is dead* (Jam. ii. 18). But what can be the works of a priest who is convicted of obtaining the dignity of so great a sacrament by a bribe? Thus it is brought about that even the very persons who are desiring sacred orders take no pains to amend their lives or order their conduct, but busy themselves in amassing wealth wherewith

---

8 Cyriacus, abbot of St. Andrew's monastery at Rome, had been sent, for the purpose indicated, to Syagrius, bishop of Autun. Cf. IX. 105.

9 See VI. 58, note 1.

to buy sacred dignity. Hence also it comes to pass that the innocent and poor recoil from sacred orders, being debarred and looked down upon. And while the innocence of the poor man displeases, there is no doubt that the bribe in the other case commends delinquencies; for, where gold pleases, so does vice. Hence, therefore, not only is a deadly wound inflicted on the souls of the ordainer and of the ordained, but also the Kingdom of your Excellence is weighed down by the fault of your bishops, by whose intercessions it ought rather to have been aided. For, if he is thought worthy of the priesthood who is supported, not by the merits of his doings, but by the abundance of his bribes, it remains that neither gravity nor industry can put in any claim for ecclesiastical dignities, but that the profane love of gold obtains all. And, while vices are remunerated with dignity, he is promoted to the place of the avenger who perhaps ought to have vengeance executed on himself; and hence priests are shewn not to profit others, but rather themselves to perish. For, when the shepherd is wounded, who may apply medicine for healing the sheep? Or how shall he protect the people with the shield of prayer who exposes himself to be stricken by hostile darts? Or what kind of fruit shall he produce out of himself, whose root is infected by sore disease? Greater calamity, then, is to be apprehended in those places where such intercessors are promoted to places of rule, being such as to provoke the more the anger of God against themselves which they ought, through themselves, to have appeased in behalf of the people.

Moreover, we have heard that the farms of the Churches do not pay tribute; and we are consequently lost in great surprise, if unlawful payments be sought from those to whom even lawful ones are remitted [1].

Nor does our solicitude allow us to pass over this evil also; that some, lured by the instigation of vain glory, snatch all at once, from a lay condition of life, at the dignity of priesthood, and (what it shames one to say, though it is too serious a matter to pass over in silence) those who require to be ruled neither blush nor fear to appear as rulers, and those that require to be taught as teachers. Persons assume shamelessly the leadership of souls to whom the whole way to be taken by the leader is unknown, and who know not whither even they themselves are walking. How bad and how venturesome this is, is shewn even by secular order and discipline. For, seeing that a leader of an army is not chosen unless he has been tried in labour and carefulness, let those who desire with immature haste to mount to the height of episcopacy consider, at any rate by the aid of this comparison, of what sort leaders of souls should be; and let them abstain from attempting suddenly untried labours, lest a blind ambition for dignity both be to their own penalty and also sow seeds of pestiferous error to others, they themselves not having learnt what they have to teach. Accordingly, greeting you with fatherly affection, we beg, most excellent sons, that you would be at pains to banish this so detestable an evil from the limits of your kingdom, and that no excuse, no suggestion against your soul, find place with you; since he who neglects to amend what he is able to correct, undoubtedly has the guilt of the doer. Wherefore, that you may be able to offer a great gift to Almighty God, order a synod to be assembled, in which (as we have enjoined our brethren and fellow-bishops), in the presence of our most beloved son the abbot Cyriacus, it may be ordained under the obligation of anathema that no one may ever give and no one ever receive anything for an ecclesiastical order, nor any one of the laity pass all at once to the priesthood; that so our Redeemer, whose priests you suffer not to be ruined among themselves by the enemy, may recompense you for this service both here and in the life to come.

Furthermore, we are altogether astonished that in your kingdom you allow Jews to possess Christian slaves. For what are all Christians but members of Christ? The Head of these members we all know that you honour faithfully: but let your Excellency consider how inconsistent it is to honour the Head and to allow His members to be trodden on by His enemies. And so, we beg that an ordinance of your Excellency may remove the evil of this wrong-doing from your kingdom, that you may thus shew yourselves the more to be worthy worshippers of Almighty God, in that you set free His faithful servants from His enemies.

## EPISTLE CXI.

To Virgilius, Bishop of Arelate (Arles).

Gregory to Virgilius, &c.

Inasmuch as the desire of a pious purpose and the bent of a laudable devotion ought always to be aided by the earnest endeavours

---

[1] The majority of MSS. have here *nunc præbeant* instead of *non tribuant*: but the reading adopted in the text has good support, and seems to give the more intelligible meaning. The drift seems to be, that, while it was the custom in Gaul to relieve Church property even from tribute that might have been exacted lawfully, it was monstrously inconsistent to burden it unlawfully by the exaction of bribes for promotion.

of priests, anxious care should be taken that neither remissness, neglect nor presumption disturb whatever has been ordained for the quiet of monks and of religious conversation. But, as it was right that what reason required should be profitably prescribed, so what has been prescribed ought not to be violated. Now Childebert of glorious memory, King of the Franks, inflamed by love of the Catholic religion, in founding for his own reward a monastery for men within the walls of the city of Arelate, as we find set down in writing, granted certain things there for the sustentation of its inmates. And, lest his purpose should ever be frustrated, and what had been arranged for the quiet of the monks be disturbed, he prayed in his letters that whatever rights he conceded to the said monastery might be confirmed by apostolical authority; adding this also to his petition, that certain privileges might at the same time be accorded to the same monastery, as well in the management of its affairs as in the ordination of its abbot. This he did as knowing such reverence to be paid by the faithful to the Apostolic See that what had been settled by its decree no molestation of unlawful usurpation would thereafter shake. Hence, since the royal purpose as well as the thing desired, urgently demanded effect to be given to it, letters were sent by our predecessor Vigilius, bishop of the Roman See, to your predecessor Aurelius, wherein all things that a desire to embrace that purpose demanded were willingly confirmed by the support of apostolical authority, inasmuch as a thing of this kind, when requested, could not be allowed to encounter difficulty. But, that your Fraternity may know what was decreed at that time, we have seen to the written orders of our aforesaid predecessor being added to this letter. These having been perused, we exhort thee to keep them all inviolate with priestly earnestness, as becomes thee, and to allow nothing undue or unlawful to be imposed on that monastery, or the said orders to be infringed by any usurpation. For, though what has once been sanctioned by the authority of the Apostolic See has no lack of validity, yet we do, over and above, once more corroborate by our authority in all respects all things that were ordained by our predecessor for quiet in this matter. Let your Fraternity, then, so acquit yourself in observing them as both to shut out all occasion of disturbance, and also to persuade others to carry these things out, while you shew yourself careful and devoted, as becomes you, in observing the most pious will of the departed one. .

## EPISTLE CXIV.

### To Virgilius and Syagrius, Bishops.

Gregory to Virgilius, Bishop of Arelate (*Arles*), and Syagrius, Bishop of Augustodunum (*Autun*).

The nature of the office committed to me, dearest brethren, drives me to break out into a cry of grief, and to sharpen your love with the anxiety of charity, for that it is said that you in your parts have been too negligent and remiss, where the rectitude of justice and zeal for chastity ought to have inflamed your earnestness. Now it has come to our ears that a certain Syagria had entered on a religious life, having even changed her dress, and was afterwards united by force to a husband (a thing iniquitous to be told), and that you have been moved by no sorrow to interfere in her defence. If this is so, I groan for it the more heavily for fear lest with the Almighty Lord (which God forbid) you should have the office of hirelings, and not the merit of shepherds, as having left without a struggle a sheep in the mouth of the wolf to be torn. For what will ye say, or what account will ye give of yourselves to the future judge; you whom the lewdness of ravishment has not moved, whom regard to the religious habit has in no wise excited to stand up in defence, whom priestly consideration has not roused to protect the purity of virgin modesty? Even now, then, let your neglect return to your memory; let remembrance of this fault stir you, and consideration of your office impel you to exhortation of the aforesaid woman. And, lest haply in course of time constraint should have passed into willing consent, let your tongue be her cure, and through your exhortations let her give herself diligently to prayer; let not the lamentations of penitence depart from her memory; let her exhibit a penitent heart to our Redeemer; and let her make amends with weeping for the loss of chastity, which in her body it was not allowed her to preserve.

Wherefore, inasmuch as the aforesaid woman desires, as it is said, even now to devote her property to pious uses, we exhort you that she experience the favour and enjoy the support of your Fraternity in this thing, and that it be lawful for her, a competent portion being reserved for her children, to decide as she will about her substance. For without doubt you do good yourselves, if you render aid to those who wish to do good. Consider, therefore, most beloved brethren, from how great love these things which we speak proceed, and take them all in the same spirit of charity that inspires them. For, we being one body in Christ, I burn with you in this which I feel to be to your hurt. And with what earnestness, and what affection I send you this epistle, may the Author of truth disclose to your hearts. And so let not this brotherly admonition distress you, since even a bitter cup is taken gladly, when offered with a view to health. Finally, dearest bethren, let us with united prayers implore the mercy of our God, that He would favourably order our life in His fear, to the end that we may both serve Him here as priests should do, and be able to stand in His sight hereafter secure and without fear.

## EPISTLE CXV.

### To Syagrius, Bishop of Augustodunum (*Autun*).

Gregory to Syagrius, &c.

If in secular affairs every man snould have his right and his proper rank preserved to him, how much more in 'ecclesiastical arrange-ments ought no confusion to be let in; lest discord should find place there, whence the blessings of peace should proceed. And this will in this way be secured, if nothing is yielded to power, but all to equity.

Now it has been reported to us that our most beloved brother Ursicinus, bishop of the city of Taurini [2], after the captivity and plunder which he endured, has suffered serious pre-judice in his parishes [3], which are said to be situated within the boundaries of the Franks, even to the extent of another person being constituted bishop there in contravention of ecclesiastical ordinances, no crime of his demanding it. And, lest this prejudicial pro-ceeding should perchance seem to be a light matter, there has been also some hardship added in the taking from him of the property of his Church which he might have held. Now, if these things are really so, seeing that it is a very cruel thing and opposed to the sacred canons, that the ambition of any should remove from his own altar an innocent priest who does not deserve to be superseded on account of crime, let all regard his cause as their own, and strive against the imposition on others of what they would be unwilling to endure themselves. For if the entrance for an evil thing is not closed before it has been long open, it grows wider by use ; and what is evidently forbidden by reason will be allowed by custom. But, beyond all others, let the solicitude of your Fraternity, in consideration

of our commendation and your own sense of what you owe to God, devote itself earnestly to his defence, and not allow him to be any longer removed against reason from his parishes. But, as well in your own person as by making supplication to the most excel-lent kings [4], whom we believe to cause you no sadness in any respect, do you bring it about that this thing which has been done amiss may be corrected, and that what has been taken away by force may under the patronage of truth be restored ; for, seeing that it is written, *A brother helping a brother shall be exalted* (Prov. xviii. 19), your Charity may know that it will receive by so much the more from Almighty God as His precepts shall have been gladly and constantly executed in helping a brother.

## EPISTLE CXVI.

### To Theoderic and Theodebert, Kings of the Franks.

Gregory to Theoderic, &c.

It is the chief good in kings to cultivate justice, and to preserve to every man his rights, and not to suffer subjects to have done to them what there is power to do, but what is equitable. Our trust that you both love and altogether aim at this invites us to indicate to your Excellency things that call for amend-ment, that so we may be able by our letters both to succour the oppressed and to acquire reward for you.

Now they say that our brother and fellow-bishop Ursicinus, bishop of the city of Taurini (*Turin*), suffers very serious prejudice in his parishes that are within the limits of your kingdom, in such sort that, contrary to eccle-siastical observance, contrary to priestly gravity, and contrary to the definitions of the sacred canons, no crime of his requiring it, another has not feared to be ordained bishop there. And, it being thought not enough unless un-lawfulness were added to unlawfulness, even the property of his church, as is said, has been taken away. If the truth is so, it being exceed-ingly intolerable that one should be oppressed by force whom guilt has not harmed, we beg of you, addressing you in the first place with a greeting of paternal charity, that what out of reverence for the Church and regard to equity your Excellency might of your own accord bestow, you would study to grant all the more kindly on our intercession, and would cause justice to be observed towards him in all

---

[2] *Augusta Taurinarum*, the modern *Turin*.
[3] *In parochiis suis.* Though the term παροικία meant origi-nally what we should now call a bishop's whole diocese, it came after the third century to be applied to parishes within such diocese. Hence here *parochiis* in the plural. Cf. Bingham, Bk. IX., ch. ii., sect. 1 ; Ch. viii., Sect. 1.

[4] *Viz.* Theoderic and Theodebert (see VI. 58, note 1), to whom a letter on the same subject was sent at the same time, viz. Ep. CXVI., which follows. The former would be in this year (A.D. 598-9) about ten, and the latter about thirteen years of age.

respects according to the trust we have in the goodness of your equity ; and that, having ascertained the truth, you would order what has been unlawfully done to be corrected, and the property that has been wrongfully taken from him to be equitably restored to him. Nor should the fact of his church being detained for the present by his enemies be at all to his disadvantage : but this ought to move more and more the disposition of your Christianity to succour him, that, being consoled by the gifts of your bounty, he may not feel the loss arising from the captivity which he has endured. For the good, then, of your soul let this our exhortation find place with you, that to your own reward you may lift up again his dejection with the outstretched hand of justice, to the end that from your observance of equity towards priests you may ever flourish through their prayers before the eyes of God.

## EPISTLE CXVII.

### To Brunichild, Queen of the Franks.

Gregory to Brunichild, &c.

Whereas for the government of a kingdom valour stands in need of justice, and power of equity, nor for this purpose can one suffice without the other, with what great love your care for these things is resplendent is shewn plainly enough by the fact of your governing crowds of nations so laudably. Who then, considering this, can distrust the goodness of your Excellency, or be doubtful of obtaining his request, when he thinks it right to ask for what he knows you would willingly bestow upon your subjects ? The bearer, then, of these presents, Hilarius [5], a servant of your Excellency, supposing that our intervention with your power will aid him, has requested to be supported by letters of commendation from us ; holding it as certain that he will more abundantly obtain such favours as you grant to others if our intercession should speak for him. Accordingly, paying you our address of greeting with the affection of paternal charity, we beg that, as he states that he is labouring under adversities from the iniquity of certain persons, the protection of your Excellence may defend him ; and, lest he should possibly be oppressed against reason, that by your command you would order him to be kept safe ; that so, while no one's opposition shall have place unjustly and of mere will, both we may return thanks for having obtained what rather for your own reward we request, and that the blessed Peter, Prince of the Apostles, whom you will venerate in us with Christian devotion by granting what we ask, may recompense your Excellency.

## EPISTLE CXX.

### To Claudius in Spain [6].

Gregory to Claudius, &c.

The renown of good deeds being fragrant after the manner of ointment, the odour of your glory has extended from the Western parts as far as here. Besprinkled by the sweetness of which breath of air, I declare that I greatly loved one whom I knew not, and within the bosom of my heart seized thee with the hand of love ; nor did I love without already knowing him to be one whose good qualities I had learnt. For of him who is known to me by great intenseness of feeling, but remains unknown by bodily vision, I undoubtedly can say truly that I know his person, though I know not his home. Now herein is a great assertion of your good repute, that your Glory is said to cleave sedulously to the excellent king of the Goths ; since, while good men always displease bad ones, it is certain that you are good, who have pleased one that is good. For this reason, addressing you with the greeting that is due to you, I hope that you are being exercised in these things which you have begun, so that that true sentence of Solomon may be fulfilled in you—*The path of the just is as a shining light, and groweth unto the perfect day* (Prov iv. 18). For, now that the light of truth shines upon us, and the sweetness of the heavenly kingdom discloses itself to our minds, it is indeed already day, but not yet perfect day. But it will then be perfect day, when there shall be no longer anything of the night of sin in our souls. But do you grow unto the perfect day, that, until such time as the heavenly country shall appear, there may be spreading increase of good works here ; to the end that in the retribution hereafter the fruit of reward may be by so much the greater as earnestness in labour has been increasing now. Wherefore we commend to your Glory our most beloved son Cyriacus, the Father of our monastery, that, after he has accomplished what has been enjoined him, there be no hindrance to delay his return. May Almighty God guard you by the protection of His heavenly arm, and grant unto

---

[5] Who this Hilarius was, and what were his grievances, does not appear.

[6] This Claudius appears to have been a person of influence in the court of King Reccared, and no doubt a good Catholic, of whose virtues Gregory may have heard from his friend Leander of Seville. The object of this very complimentary letter to him was to commend to his favour the abbot Cyriacus, who, as appears from preceding epistles, had been sent into Gaul to bring about the assembling of a synod there, and who appears from this epistle to have been sent on into Spain, though for what particular purpose does not appear. Cf. *Proleg.*, p. xi.

you to be glorious both now among men and after long courses of years among the angels.

## EPISTLE CXXI.

### To Leander, Bishop of Hispalis (*Seville*).

Gregory to Leander, Bishop of Spain.

I have the epistle of thy Holiness, written with the pen of charity alone. For what the tongue transferred to the paper had got its tincture from the heart. Good and wise men were present when it was read, and at once their bowels were stirred with emotion. Everyone began to seize thee in his heart with the hand of love, for that in that epistle the sweetness of thy disposition was not to be heard, but seen. All severally were inflamed, and all admired, and the very fire of the hearers shewed what had been the ardour of the speaker. For, unless torches burn themselves, they will not kindle others. We saw, then, with how great charity thy mind was aflame, seeing that it so kindled others also. Your life indeed, which I always remember with great reverence, they did not know; but the loftiness of your heart was manifest to them from the lowliness of your language. As to my life, this your epistle speaks of it as worthy of imitation by all: but may that which is not as it is said to be become so because it is said to be so, lest one should lie who is not wont to lie. In reply to this, however, I speak shortly the words of a certain good woman, *Call me not Noemi, that is, fair; but call me Mara, for I am full of bitterness* (Ruth i. 20). For indeed, good man, I am not to-day the man you knew. For I confess that in advancing outwardly I have fallen much inwardly, and I fear that I am of the number of those of whom it is written, *Thou didst cast them down while they were lifted up* (Ps. lxxii. 18[7]). For he is cast down when he is lifted up who advances in honours, and falls in manners. For I, following the ways of my Head, had determined to be the scorn of men and the outcast of the people, and to run in the lot of him of whom again it is said by the Psalmist, *The ascents in his heart he hath disposed in the valley of tears* (Ps. lxxxiii. 7[8]); that is, that I should ascend inwardly all the more truly as I lay outwardly the more humbly in the valley of tears. But now burdensome honour much depresses me, innumerable cares din me, and, when my mind collects itself for God, they cleave it with their assaults as if with a kind of swords. My heart has no rest. It lies prostrate in the lowest place, depressed by the weight of its cogitation. Either very rarely or not at all does the wing of contemplation raise it aloft. My sluggish soul is torpid, and, with temporal cares barking round it, already almost reduced to stupor, is forced now to deal with earthly things, and now even to dispense things that are carnal; nay sometimes, by force of disgust, is compelled to dispose of some things with accompanying guilt. Why should I say more? Overcome by its own weight, it sweats blood. For, unless sin were reckoned under the name of blood, the Psalmist would not say, *Deliver me from bloodguiltiness* (Ps. l. 16[9]). But, when we add sin to sins, we fulfil this also which is said by another prophet, *Blood hath touched blood* (Hos. iv. 2.) For blood is said to touch blood when sin is joined to sin, so as to multiply the load of iniquity. But in the midst of all this I implore thee by Almighty God to hold me who am fallen into the billows of perturbation with the hand of thy prayer. For I sailed as it were with a prosperous breeze when I led a tranquil life in a monastery: but a storm, rising suddenly with gusty surges, caught me in its commotion, and I lost the prosperity of my voyage; for in loss of rest I suffered shipwreck. Lo, now I am tossed in the waves, and I seek for the plank of thy intercession, that, not being counted worthy to reach port rich with my ship entire, I may at least after losses be brought to shore by the aid of a plank.

Your Holiness writes of being afflicted with the pains of gout, by continual suffering from which I too am grievously worn down. But comfort will be readily at hand, if amid the scourges under which we suffer we recall to mind whatever faults we have committed; and then we shall see that they are not scourges, but gifts, if by pain of the flesh we purge the sins which we did for delight of the flesh.

Furthermore we have sent you, with the blessing of the blessed Peter, Prince of the Apostles, a pallium, to be used only in celebration of Mass. In sending it to you I ought to admonish you much as to how you ought to live: but I suppress speech, since in your manner of life you anticipate my words. May Almighty God keep you under His protection, and bring you to the rewards of the heavenly country with multiplied fruits of souls. As to me, with what amount of business and with what weakness I am weighed down this short letter bears witness, in which I say little to one whom I greatly love.

---

[7] In *English Bible*, lxxiii. 18.
[8] In *English Bible*, lxxiv. 5, 6, differently.

[9] li. 14, in *English Bible*.

## EPISTLE CXXII.

To Rechared, King of the Visigoths [1].

Gregory to Rechared, &c.

I cannot express in words, most excellent son, how much I am delighted with thy work and thy life. For on hearing of the power of a new miracle in our days, to wit that the whole nation of the Goths has through thy Excellency been brought over from the error of Arian heresy to the firmness of a right faith, one is disposed to exclaim with the prophet, *This is the change wrought by the right hand of the Most High* (Ps. lxxvi. 11 [2]). For whose breast, even though stony, would not, on hearing of so great a work, soften in praises of Almighty God and love of thy Excellency? As for me, I declare that it delights me often to tell these things that have been done through you to my sons who resort to me, and often together with them to admire. These things also for the most part stir me up against myself, in that I languish sluggish and unprofitable in listless ease, while kings are labouring in the gathering together of souls for the gains of the heavenly country. What then shall I say to the coming Judge in that tremendous assize, if I shall then come thither empty, where thy Excellency shall bring after thee flocks of faithful ones, whom thou hast now drawn to the grace of a true faith by assiduous and continual preaching? But this, good man, by the gift of God, affords me great comfort, that the holy work which I have not in myself I love in thee. And, when I rejoice with great exultation for thy doings, the results of thy labour become mine through charity. With regard, therefore, to the conversion of the Goths, both for your work and for our exultation, we may well exclaim with the angels, *Glory to God in the highest, and on earth peace to men of goodwill* (Luk. ii. 14). For we, as I think, owe the more thanks to Almighty God for that, although we have done nothing with you, we are nevertheless partakers in your work by rejoicing with you.

Further, how gladly the blessed Peter, Prince of the Apostles, has accepted the gifts of your Excellency your very life witnesses evidently to all. For it is written, *The vows of the righteous are his delight* (Prov. xv. 8). For indeed in the judgment of Almighty God it is not what is given, but by whom it is given, that is regarded.

For hence it is that it is written, *The Lord had respect unto Abel and to his gifts, but unto Cain and to his gifts he had not respect* (Gen. iv. 4, 5). To wit, being about to say that the Lord had respect to the gifts, he was careful to premise that He had respect unto Abel. Thus it is plainly shewn that the offerer was not acceptable by reason of the gifts, but the gifts were so by reason of the offerer. You shew, therefore, how acceptable your offering is, seeing that, being about to give gold, you have first given gifts of souls by the conversion of the nation subject to you.

With regard to your telling us that the abbots who were sent to us to bring your offering to the blessed Apostle Peter had been wearied by the violence of the sea and returned to Spain without accomplishing their voyage [3], your gifts were not kept back, for they reached us afterwards; but the constancy of those who had been sent has been tried, as to whether they knew how with holy desire to overcome dangers in their way, and, though fatigued in body, by no means to be wearied in mind. For adversity which comes in the way of good purposes is a trial of virtue, not a judgment of reprobation. For who can be ignorant how prosperous an event it was that the blessed Apostle Paul came to Italy to preach, and yet in coming suffered shipwreck? But the ship of the heart stood unharmed among the billows of the sea.

Furthermore, I must tell you that I have been led to praise God the more for your work by what I have learnt from the report of my most beloved son Probinus the presbyter; namely that, your Excellency having issued a certain ordinance against the perfidy of the Jews, those to whom it related attempted to bend the rectitude of your mind by offering a sum of money; which your Excellency scorned, and, seeking to satisfy the judgment of Almighty God, preferred innocence to gold. With regard to this what was done by King David recurs to my mind, who, when he longed for water from the cistern of Bethlehem, which was wedged in by the enemy, had been brought him by obedient soldiers, said, *God forbid that I should drink the blood of righteous men* (1 Chron. xi. 19). And, because he

---

[1] Reccared, the Visigoth king of Spain, previously an Arian, had declared himself a Catholic A.D. 587, and had formally adopted Catholicism as the creed of the Spanish Church at the council of Toledo, A.D. 589. See I. 43, note 9. This is the only extant letter addressed to the king himself by Gregory, its date, if rightly placed, being A.D. 598-9, and thus as much as ten years after the council of Toledo. Gregory had been long informed of what had been done at Toledo, as appears in his epistle to Leander (I. 43), written, if correctly placed, A.D. 590-1; and it may appear strange that his letter to the king himself had been so long delayed. He may have waited for a letter to himself from Reccared; and, if Ep. LXI. in this book (see note thereon) be genuine, it would be in reply to it that the letter before us was written. But in Ep. LXI. only three years are said to have elapsed since Reccared's conversion, and gifts spoken of sent at that time to Rome are acknowledged in the Epistle before us. Hence the dates assigned to the Epistles by the Benedictine Editors are open to suspicion.

[2] In *English Bible*, lxxvii. 10, differently.

[3] See IX. 61.

poured it out and would not drink it, it is written, *He offered it a libation to the Lord.* If, then, water was scorned by the armed king, and turned into a sacrifice to God, we may estimate what manner of sacrifice to Almighty God has been offered by the king who for His love has scorned to receive, not water, but gold. Wherefore, most excellent son, I will confidently say that thou hast offered as a libation to the Lord the gold which thou wouldest not have in opposition to Him. These are great things, and redound to the praise of Almighty God.

But in the midst of all these things we must guard with vigilant attention against the snares of the ancient foe, who, the greater gifts he sees among men, with the more subtle snares seeks to take them away. For robbers too do not look out for empty travellers to seize them on their road, but such as carry vessels of gold and silver. For indeed the present life is a road. And every one must needs be the more on his guard against ambushed spirits in proportion as the gifts are greater which he carries. It is the duty, then, of your Excellency, with regard to this so great gift which you have received in the conversion of the nation subject to you, to keep with all your might, first humility of heart, and secondly cleanness of body. For where it is written, *Every one that exalteth himself shall be humbled, and he that humbleth himself shall be exalted* (Luke xiv. 11 ; xviii. 14), it is assuredly evident that he truly loves what is lofty who does not cut off his soul from the root of humility. For often the malignant spirit, in order to destroy the good that previously he had not power to oppose, comes into the mind of the worker after accomplishment of his work, and agitates it with silent thoughts of self-praise, so that the deluded mind admires itself for the great things that it has done. And, being exalted in its own sight through hidden tumour, it is deprived of the grace of Him Who bestowed the gift. For hence it is that it is said through the voice of the prophet to the soul that waxes proud, *Having trust in thy beauty thou playedst the harlot because of thy renown* (Ezek. xvi. 15). For indeed a soul's having trust in its beauty is its presuming within itself on its righteous doings. And it plays the harlot because of its renown, when in what it has done aright it desires not the praise of its Maker to be spread abroad, but seeks the glory of its own reputation. Hence again it is written through the prophet, *In that thou art more beautiful, go down* (Ezek. xxxii. 19). For the soul goes down because of being more beautiful when, owing to the comeliness of virtue whereby it ought to have

been exalted before God, it falls from His grace through elation. What then is to be done in this case but that, when the malignant spirit employs the good things that we have done to exalt the mind, we should ever recall to memory our evil deeds, to the end that we may acknowledge that what we have done sinfully is our own, but that it is of the gift of Almighty God alone when we avoid sins. Cleanness also of body is to be guarded in our strivings after well-doing, since, according to the voice of the apostolic preacher, *The temple of God is holy, which temple ye are* (1 Cor. iii. 17). And again he says, *For this is the will of God, even your sanctification* (1 Thess. iv. 3). As to which sanctification, what he means by it he shews by straightway adding, *That ye should abstain from fornication, that every one of you should know how to possess his vessel in sanctification and honour, not in the lusts of concupiscence.*

The very government also of your kingdom in relation to your subjects ought to be tempered with moderation, lest power steal upon your mind. For a kingdom is ruled well when the glory of reigning does not dominate the disposition. Care also is to be taken that wrath creep not in, lest whatever is lawful to be done be done too hastily. For wrath, even when it prosecutes the faults of delinquents, ought not to go before the mind as a mistress, but attend as a handmaid behind the back of reason, that it may come to the front when bidden. For, if once it begins to have possession of the mind, it accounts as just what it does cruelly. For hence it is written, *The wrath of man worketh not the righteousness of God* (Jam. i. 20). Hence again it is said, *Let every man be swift to hear, but slow to speak, and slow to wrath* (Ib. 19). However I doubt not that under the guidance of God you observe all these things. Still, now that an opportunity of admonition has arisen, I join myself furtively to your good deeds, so that what you do though not admonished you may not do alone, having an admonisher to boot. Now may Almighty God protect you in all your doings by the stretching out of His heavenly arm, and grant you prosperity in the present life, and after a course of many years eternal joys.

We have sent you a small key from the most sacred body of the blessed apostle Peter to convey his blessing, containing iron from his chains, that what had bound his neck for martyrdom may loose yours from all sins. We have given also to the bearer of these presents, to be offered to you, a cross in which there is some of the wood of the Lord's cross, and hairs of the blessed John the Baptist, from which you may ever have the succour of our Saviour through the intercession of His forerunner.

Moreover we have sent to our most reverend brother and fellow-bishop Leander a pallium from the See of the blessed Apostle Peter, which we owe both to ancient custom, and to your character, and to his goodness and gravity [4].

---

A long time ago, when a certain Neapolitan youth came hither, your to me most sweet Excellency had thought fit to charge me to write to the most pious Emperor to the end that he might search in the record office for the treaties that had formerly been concluded with the prince Justinian of pious memory as to the claims of your kingdom, so as to gather from them what he should observe with regard to you. But there were two things seriously in the way of my doing this. One was that the record-office in the time of the aforesaid prince Justinian of pious memory had been so burnt by a fire which had crept in suddenly that hardly any paper of his times remained. The other was that, as no one need be told, thou oughtest to look in thy own archives for the documents that are against thee, and produce these instead of my doing so. Wherefore I exhort your Excellency to arrange matters suitably to your character, and carefully to carry out whatever makes for peace, that the times of your reign may be memorable with great praise through many courses of years. Furthermore, we have sent you another key from the most sacred body of the blessed apostle Peter, which, being laid up with due honour, may multiply with blessing whatever it may find you enjoying.

## EPISTLE CXXIII.
### To Venantius and Italica [5].

Gregory to the lord Venantius, Patrician, and Italica his wife.

I have taken care, with due affection, to enquire of certain persons who have come from Sicily about your Excellency's health. But they have given me a sad report of the frequency of your ailments. Now, when I say this, neither do I find anything to tell you about myself, except that, for my sins, lo it is now eleven months since it has been a very rare case with me if I have been able now and then to rise from my bed. For I am afflicted by so great sufferings from gout, and so great from troubles, that my life is to me most grievous pain. For every day I faint under my sufferings, and sigh .in expectation of the relief of death. Indeed among the clergy and people of this city there has been such an invasion of feverous sicknesses that hardly any freeman, hardly any slave, remains fit for any office or ministry. Moreover, from the neighbouring cities we have news daily of havocs and of mortality. Then, how Africa is being wasted by mortality and sickness I believe that you know more accurately than we do, insomuch as you are nearer to it. But of the East those who come from thence report still more grievous desolations. In the midst of all these things, therefore, since you perceive that there is a general smiting as the end of the world draws near, you ought not to be too much afflicted for your own troubles. But, as becomes wise nobles, bring ye back your whole heart to the care of your souls, and fear the strict judgment all the more as it is so much nearer at hand. Devote yourselves to piety, of which it is written that *It hath promise of the life that now is, and of that which is to come* (1 Tim. iv. 8). But Almighty God is powerful both to preserve the life of your Excellency for a long time here, and to bring you after many courses of years to eternal joys. I beg my most sweet daughters, the lady Barbara and the lady Antonina, to be greeted in my name ; whom I pray that heavenly grace may protect, and grant them to be prospered in all things.

## EPISTLE CXXV.
### To Maximus, Bishop of Salona [6].

Gregory to Maximus, &c.

Having received the letters of our brother and fellow-bishop Marinianus, and Castorius, our *chartularius*, having also returned, we learn that your Fraternity have made most full satisfaction with regard to the matters about which there had been uncertainty ; and we return great thanks to Almighty God that from our inmost heart all rancour of sinister suspicion

---

[4] What follows is preceded by "Item in anagnostico." (The word is thus explained in D'Arnis' *Lexicon Manuale;* "Græcis id omne est quod legitur aut recitatur. Unde Gregorius Magnus pro epistola aut quovis scripto vocem hanc usurpat.") The whole is absent from many MSS., and in one of those preserved in *Bibliotheca Colbertina* it is given, without the heading *Item in anognostico,* as a separate epistle, entitled "Secunda ad Recharedum," and concludes thus : " Furthermore we have received the gifts of your Excellency, which have been sent for the poor of the blessed Apostle Peter, namely three hundred *cocullæ* (*cowls*) ; and, as much as we can, we earnestly pray that you may have as your protector in the tremendous day of judgment Him whose poor you have protected by abundance of clothes. Our not sending at once a man of ours to your Excellency has been owing to the want of a ship : for none can be found that can proceed from these parts to the shores of Spain." The fact of a second key containing filings of St. Peter's chains being referred to as sent to Reccared in this concluding portion of the epistle confirms the probability of its having been part of a subsequent letter. For two such keys were not likely to be sent at the same time.

[5] See I. 34, note 8.

[6] See III. 47, note 2, and IX. 81.

has been eradicated. On this account I have been desirous of dismissing with the utmost speed our common son, your deacon Stephen. But the frequent pains of my sicknesses have compelled me to retain him with me for a few days. As soon, however, as I have begun to be even slightly better, I have provided for sending him forthwith back to you with joy.

Accordingly we send to you, according to custom, the pallium for the sacred solemnities of mass; the meaning of which we desire you in all respects to vindicate. For the dignity of this vestment is humility and justice. Let, then, your Fraternity make haste with all your heart to shew yourself humble in prosperity, and in adversity, if ever it should ensue; upright in justice; friendly to the good, and opposed to the froward; never discount-enancing any one who speaks for the truth; instant in works of mercy according to thy means, and yet beyond thy means desiring to be instant; sympathizing with the weak; rejoicing with men of good will; regarding the woes of others as thine own; exulting for the joys of others as if for thine own; in correcting vices severe, in cherishing virtues, soothing the minds of hearers; in anger, retaining judgment without anger, but in calmness not relinquishing the censorship of your severity. This, dearest brother, is the meaning of the pallium which you will receive, which if you act up to, you will have inwardly what you are seen to have received outwardly.

Furthermore I commend in all respects to your Fraternity our brother and fellow-bishop Sabinianus[7]; and if there be any matters of dispute between you, let them meanwhile be laid aside. Let charity remain fixed between you, that so, in case of contention ever arising about external things, they may be examined without charity deserting the heart. We commend also our common son Honoratus: concerning whom if it is the case, as we have learnt through Castorius our *chartularius,* that through him three previous archdeacons have been compelled to observe the ecclesiastical custom by retiring at the expiration of five years, we desire indeed that he may experience the charity of thy Holiness. For a judgment ought not to be solicited in a case which he himself has judged. If, however, it is not so, then, all swelling of heart being repressed, and all grudge set aside, he ought to be received, and by no means removed from the place which he now occupies. Messianus also, the *cleric* who had taken refuge with us, we have confidently committed to the charge of our common son Stephen the deacon, being assured

that in the case of one whom we ourselves send to your Fraternity, you will not show any grudge, but lend the countenance of your authority. May Almighty God keep you in His protection, and grant us so to act that after the billows of this temporal state we may be able to attain with joy to things eternal.

## EPISTLE CXXVII.
### From S. Columbanus to Pope Gregory [8].

To the holy lord, and father in Christ, the

---

[8] This epistle of the Irish saint Columbanus to Gregory was added to the *Registrum Epistolarum* by the Benedictine editors, having been first published, with other writings of S. Columban, by Patrick Fleming in *Collectanea sacra; Lovan.* A.D. 1667. (See Galland. *Bibliotheca veterum patrum. Sæc. VI. circ.* A.D. 589.) It is assigned by the Benedictines to A.D. 598-9, and hence placed at the end of Book IX. of Gregory's Epistles.

At this time St. Columban was at the monastery founded by him at Luxovium (*Luxueil*) among the Vosges mountains in Burgundy, over which country Theoderic II. was now king. He had already given offence in Gaul, not only by his protest in life and teaching against prevalent laxity, but also by his continuing to observe and uphold the custom of his own Celtic Church with regard to the time for keeping Easter, which differed from what had now been adopted by Rome and prevailed in the West generally. The main purpose of this epistle is to plead with pope Gregory for approval of the Celtic tradition. Subsequently, a synod being held in Gaul for considering the question, he addressed the bishops there assembled in a letter which is also extant, defending, as in this epistle, the Celtic usage, and pleading for being allowed at any rate to follow it himself in peace. (S. Columbani, Ep. II. *in Collectan. sacr.*)

It may be observed in the epistle before us, as also in a subsequent one to pope Boniface IV. with reference to the same subject (*S. Columbani*, Ep. V.; *Collectan. sacr.*), that, though addressing the bishop of Rome in language of the utmost deference, and recognizing his high position, he shews no disposition to submit to his authority; telling him on the contrary that, should he declare himself so as to contradict the supposed teaching of St. Jerome, he would be rejected as heretical by all the Celtic churches. And throughout the letter there runs a vein of sarcasm. There is no extant reply from Gregory to the letter. Probably none was sent. Possibly the letter never reached its destination: for in the subsequent letter, above referred to, to Boniface IV. Columban says, "Once and again Satan hindered the bearers of our letters written formerly to pope Gregory of good memory, which are subjoined below."

The point at issue, and Columban's argument, as it appears in this letter, may be briefly stated thus. Apart from any differences in the cycles for calculating the true day of the Paschal full moon in successive years, there was this difference between the Celtic and Roman usages. While all agreed in keeping Easter on a Sunday, the Celtic use was to keep it on the day of the Paschal full moon itself (i.e. the calculated 14th day of the moon falling on, or next after, the Vernal Equinox), in case of such day falling on a Sunday; whereas the Roman was, in such a case, to defer their Easter celebration till the following Sunday, so as to avoid coincidence with the actual day of the Jewish Passover. Hence, in Bede's account of the controversy on the subject between the British and Scottish (i.e. Irish) Churches on the one hand and the Roman on the other, he speaks of the former keeping their Easter between the 14th and the 20th days of the moon inclusive, but the latter between the 15th and the 21st (Bede, *H.E.* II. 2; III. 25). In Gaul, however, as appears from the letter before us, it was the rule to defer Easter for a week in case of the day of the Paschal full moon (i.e. the 14th) falling on a Saturday, so as to avoid coincidence even with the 15th day of the moon. Hence, agreeing with Bede as to the Celtic usage being to keep Easter between the 14th and 20th days, he speaks not of the 15th and 21st, but of the 16th and the 22nd being the extreme limits according to the Gallic usage. The reason of this difference was, that it had once been the Latin use, as against the Alexandrian, to keep Easter from the 16th to the 22nd days, thus avoiding the 15th; and this rule had been retained in the cycle of Victorius (as to whom see below, note 7), which was still received in Gaul.

The arguments of St. Columban in defence of the Celtic usage may be thus summarized. 1. It had been sanctioned by Anatolius (see below, note 5), whose view had been approved by St. Jerome. 2. To defer Easter to the 22nd, or even the 21st day was incongruous, seeing that the moon then entered her last quarter, rising so late as to give darkness preponderance over light; and the solemnity of light should not be celebrated

---

Roman [*pope*], most fair ornament of the Church, a certain most august flower, as it were, of the whole of withering Europe, distinguished speculator, as enjoying a divine contemplation of purity (?) 9. I, Bargoma 1, poor dove in Christ, send greeting.

Grace to thee and peace from God the Father [*and*] our [*Lord*] Jesus Christ. I am pleased to think, O holy pope, that it will seem to thee nothing extravagant to be interrogated about Easter, according to that canticle, *Ask thy father, and he will shew thee; thine elders and they will tell thee* (Deut. xxxii. 7). For, though on me, who am indeed a trifler (*micrologo*) may be branded that excellent expression of a certain wise man, who is reported to have said, on seeing a certain woman, *contupictam* 2, *I do not admire the art, but I admire the brow*, in that I who am vile write to thee that art illustrious; yet, relying on my confidence in thy evangelical humility, I presume to write to thee, and impose on thee the matter of my grief. For

writing is not in vain, when necessity compels one to write, though it be to one's betters.

What, then, dost thou say concerning Easter on the 21st or 22nd day of the moon, which (with thy peace be it said) is proved by many calculators not to be Easter, but in truth a time of darkness? For it is not unknown, as I believe, to thy Efficiency, how Anatolius 3 (a man of wonderful learning, as says Saint Hieronymus, extracts from whose writings Eusebius, bishop of Cæsarea, inserted in his Ecclesiastical Histoiy, and Saint Hieronymus praised this same work about Easter in his catalogue) disputes with strong disapprobation about this age of the moon. For against the Gallican *Rimarii* 4, who erred, as he says, about Easter, he introduced an awful sentence, saying, *Certainly, if the rising of the moon be delayed till the end of two watches, which indicates midnight, light does not overcome darkness, but darkness light; which thing is certainly not allowable in the Easter Festival. namely, that any part of the darkness should dominate over the light, since the solemnity of the Lord's Resurrection is light, and there is no communion of light with darkness. And, if the moon has not shone forth till the third watch, there is no doubt that the moon has risen on its 21st or 22nd day, in which it is not possible for a true Paschal offering to be made. For those who lay down that it is possible for a true Easter to be celebrated at this age of the moon, not only are unable to affirm this by authority of divine Scripture, but also incur the guilt of sacrilege and contumacy and peril of their souls, while affirming that the true Light, which dominates over all darkness, can be offered while there is any domination of darkness.* Also in the book of holy dogma we read, *Easter, that is, the solemnity of the Lord's Resurrection, cannot be celebrated before the beginning of the vernal equinox is past, to wit, that it may not come before the vernal equinox* 5: which rule assuredly

---

under the domination of darkness. He quotes Anatolius as having insisted on this principle, of which (we may here observe) we find an intimation in Philo with reference to the Jewish Passover:—"That not only by day but also by night the world may be full of all-beauteous light, inasmuch as sun and moon on that day succeed each other with no interval of darkness between." (*De Sept. et Fest.* 1191.) 3. The alleged objection to keeping Easter on the day of the Jewish Passover was unfounded and futile. 4. The Mosaic Law enjoined seven days, beginning with the 14th, as the duration of the Passover festival; and within the same limits should be kept the Easter festival. [This argument, it may be observed, whatever its worth in other respects, appears to be founded on an error. For the Passover. having been killed before sunset on the 14th of Nisan, is believed to have been eaten after sunset, i.e. after the 15th day, reckoned from evening to evening, had begun; and from the latter day inclusive the seven days of unleavened bread were reckoned, thus ending with the 21st, which was a special day of "holy convocation." Cf. below, note 5.]

9 *Theoria utpote divina castulitatis potito.* The word *castulitas* may possibly have been in use among the Irish monks as an endearing diminutive of *castitas* (i.e. chastity or purity), regarded as the object of their affections in the contemplative life. Their writers appear to have been given to the use of such diminutives, not only of the names of people, but of other words also.—"In the following pages (sc. in Adamnan's Life of St. Columba) the reader will observe the liberal employment of diminutives, so characteristic of Irish composition; and he will find them, in many cases, used without any grammatical force, and commutable, in the same chapters, with their primitives." (*Reeve's Adamnan. Appendix to Preface*, Ed., 1857, p. lxi.).

1 Perhaps an error tor Barjona, meaning 'son of a dove,' in allusion to his name, Columba, or Columbanus. He afterwards calls himself "vilis columba." Cf. "Pauperculus præpotenti (mirum dictu! nova res!) rara avis scribere audet Bonifacio patri Palumbus:" "Sed talia suadenti, utpote torpenti actu, ac dicenti potius quam facienti mihi, Jonæ Hebraice, Peristeræ Græce, Columbæ Latine, potius tantum [*al.* tamen] vestræ idiomate linguæ nancto [*al.* nuncupato], (*S. Columbani Ep. V. ad Bonifacium papam IV. Collectan. sacr. Patr. Fleming. Galland. sæc.* VI. c. A D. 598). Cf. "Vir erat vitæ venerabilis et beatæ memoriæ, monasteriorum pater et fundator, cum Joɪa propheta homonymum sortitus nomen; nam licet diverso trium diversarum sono linguarum, unam tamen eandemque rem significat hoc quod Hebraice dicitur Jona, Græcitas vero ΠΕΡΙΣΤΕΡΑ voɔitat, et Latina lingua Columba nuncupatur." (*Adamnan's Life of S. Columba; Secunda Præfatio*.) Du Cange suggests a corruption of Barginna, said to be a low Latin word, equivalent to peregrinus.

2 The meaning of this word is obscure. Patrick Fleming (*Collect. Sacr.*) suggests an error for *compte pictam*; Du Cange for *comptam*, or *acu comptam*, some artificial arrangement of the hair being supposed to be referred to. The intended point of the comparison seems to be, that Gregory will still be admirable, though the writer may set him off unskilfully.

3 Anatolius, an Alexandrian by birth, and bishop of Laodicea, A.D. 269, is referred to by Eusebius (*H.E.* VII. 32), as distinguished for learning, and the writer of a work on the Paschal question, which he quotes. A "Canon Pachalis," purporting to be this work, was published by Bucherius in a Latin version (*Doct. Temp.* Antv. 1634); but its genuineness is doubted. Anatolius was adduced by Colman at the synod of Whitby (Bede, *H.E.* III. 25). as an authority for the 14th and 20th days of the moon being the limits for Easter. But Wilfrid replied that Anatolius had been misunderstood; for that, having in view the Egyptian mode of reckoning days from sunset to sunset, he had meant the day which began after sunset on the 14th day, i.e. really the 15th. And so also with regard to the 20th day. His language, as quoted by Eusebius, supports this explanation of his meaning:—"Given that the day of the Passover is on the fourteenth of the moon *after evening* (μεθ' ἑσπέραν)." See above, end of note 1.

4 "Forte sic dictos, quod obscura et difficilia rimarentur. *Benedictine edit. Migne*.—"Nostri *rimeurs* vocant poetastras, sed an ea sit hic notio non definio." Du Cange.

5 The original here, being probably an incorrect citation, is obscure. It is, "Pascha, ed est solemnitas dominicæ Resurrectionis, ante transgressum vernalis æquinoctii 16 initiam non potest celebrari, ut scilicet æquinoctium non antecedaɪ."

Victorius [6] has gone beyond in his cycle, and hereby has already introduced error into Gaul, or to speak less boldly, has confirmed one of old standing. For indeed how can either of these things stand with reason; either that the Lord's Resurrection should be celebrated before His Passion (the thought of which is absurd), or that the seven days sanctioned by the Lord's command in the Law, during which only it is enjoined that the Lord's Passover could lawfully be eaten (which are to be numbered from the 14th day of the moon to the 20th), should against law and right be exceeded? For a moon in its 21st or 22nd day is out of the dominion of light, as having risen at that time after midnight; and, when darkness overcomes light, it is said to be impious to keep the solemnity of light. Why then dost thou, who art so wise, the brilliant lights indeed of whose sacred genius are diffused, as in ancient times, through the world, —why dost thou keep a dark Easter? I wonder, I confess, that this error of Gaul, *ac si Schynteneum* [7], has not long ago been swept away by thee; unless I should perchance suppose, what I can hardly believe, that, as it is evident that thou hast not corrected it, it has thy approval

In another way, however, may thy Expertness be more honourably excused, if, fearing to subject thyself to the mark of Hermagoric [8] novelty, thou art content with the authority of thy predecessors, and especially of pope Leo.

Do not, I pray thee, in such a question trust to humility only or to gravity, which are often deceived. *Better* by far *is a living dog* in this problem *than a dead lion* (Eccles. ix. 4). For a living saint may correct what had not been corrected by another who came before him. For know thou that by our masters and the Irish ancients, who were philosophers and most wise computists in constructing calculations, Victorius was not received, but held

rather worthy of ridicule or of excuse than as carrying authority. Wherefore to me, as a timid stranger rather than as a sciolist, afford the support of thy judgment, and disdain not to send us speedily the suffrage of thy Placability for assuaging this tempest which surrounds us; since, after so many authors whom I have read, I am not satisfied with that one sentence of those bishops who say only, *We ought not to keep the Passover with the Jews.* For this is what the bishop Victor formerly said; but none of the Easterns accepted his figment [9]. But this the benumbing (*numb ?*) backbone of Dagon; this the dotage of error drinks in [10]. Of what worth, I ask, is this sentence, so frivolous and so rude, and resting, as it does, on no testimonies of sacred Scripture; *We ought not to keep the Passover with the Jews?* What has it to do with the question? Are the reprobate Jews to be supposed to keep the Passover now, seeing that they are without a temple, outside Jerusalem, and Christ, who was formerly prefigured, having been crucified by them? Or, can it be rightly supposed that the 14th day of the moon for the Passover was of their own appointment, and is it not rather to be acknowledged to be of God's, who alone knew clearly with what mysterious meaning the 14th day of the moon was chosen for the passage [*out of Egypt*]. Perhaps to wise men and the like of thee this may be in some degree clearer than to others. As to those who make this objection, although without authority, let them upbraid God for that He did not then beforehand guard against the contumacy of the Jews by enjoining on them in the Law nine days of unleavened bread, if He would not have us keep the Passover with them, so that the beginning of our solemnity should not exceed the end of theirs. For, if Easter is to be celebrated on the 21st

---

6 Pope Leo I. referred the question between the Roman and Alexandrian Churches as to the computation of Easter to his archdeacon (afterwards pope) Hilarius for investigation; and he referred it to Victorius of Aquitaine, who consequently (A.D. 457) drew up a cycle, which was accepted first in the Gallican Churches (*Concil. Aurel.* IV., *an.* 541), and continued to be observed there after it had been superseded in Italy by that of Dionysius Exiguus (A.D. 527). See above, note 1.

7 "*Schynteneum* Græcam vocem σχοινοτενής putat Editor, id est, tanquam si rectum et legitimum esset." Du Cange. This interpretation appears probable from the fact that the Irish writers of the period were given to air their Greek learning by the use of such words.—"He (Adamnan) occasionally employs Greek or Græco-Latin words" (*Reeves's Adamnan*. p. lxi. See also p. 158, note, for other evidence of this Irish tendency). The meaning in the text would thus be, "I wonder that this error should be tolerated by thee as though it were right and legitimate."

8 *Hermagoricæ novitatis*; the epithet being apparently formed from the name of Hermagoras of Temnos, a distinguished Greek rhetorician of the time of Pompey and Cicero. He devoted peculiar attention to what is called the *invention*. Quintilian refers to him and approves his system: Cicero (*De Invent.* i. 6) was opposed to it. The use of a word like this is again characteristic of the Irish writers

9 i.e. pope Victor, in his opposition, towards the end of the second century, to the Asiatic Quarto-decimans, who kept their Pasch on the day of the Paschal full moon, whatever the day of the week might be. Colman at the synod of Whitby had alleged St. John, to whom the Asiatics had traced their tradition, as an authority for the Scottish usage. But Wilfrid truly alleged in reply that the question at issue between the Scots and Romans at that time was a different one, since both parties agreed in keeping Easter on a Sunday only. Still, Columban's argument here is to the point as shewing that the Easterns had not objected to keeping Easter on the actual day of the Jewish Passover. It may be noted here how the authority of Victor, as well as of other popes, is set at naught by S. Columbanus.

10 *Sed hoc soporans spina Dagonis, hoc imbibit bubum erroris.* On these obscure expressions it may be observed that *spina Dagonis* evidently means what was left to the fish-god (ῥάχις in LXX.), after his head and hands had been severed. Gregory, in his comment on 1 Sam. v., interprets it as denoting heathenism prostrate, and at length deprived of even the semblance of rationality, in the presence of the Gospel, which was represented by the ark. Columban may possibly have got the idea from Gregory's own interpretation of the incident, and been pleased to use it against him. *Bubum*, according to Du Cange. is a late Latin word denoting *senium*, or *ianguor*, the noun *bubula* also being used in the sense of *fabula*. The idea seems to be that pope Victor's view was a figment, worthy only to be received (or, as we might now say, swallowed) by senseless heathenism or wandering dotage.

or 22nd day, from the 14th to the 22nd nine days will be reckoned, that is, seven ordered by God, and two added by men. But, if it is allowed for men to add anything of their own accord to divine decree, I ask whether this may not seem opposed to that sentence of Deuteronomy, *Lo* (he saith), *the word which I give unto thee, thou shalt not add unto it nor take from it* (Deut. iv. 2).

But in writing all this more forwardly than humbly, I know that I have involved myself in an Euripus of presumption attended with great difficulty, being perchance unskilled to steer out of it. Nor does it befit our place or rank that anything should be suggested in the way of discussion to thy great authority, and that my Western letters should ridiculously solicit thee, who sittest legitimately on the seat of the apostle and key-bearer Peter, on the subject of Easter. But thou oughtest to consider not so much worthless me in this matter as many masters, both departed and now living, who confirm what I have pointed out, and suppose thyself to be holding a colloquy with them: for know that I open my thick-lipped mouth dutifully, though it may be incoherently and extravagantly. It is for thee, therefore, either to excuse or to condemn Victorius, knowing that, if thou approvest him, it will be a question of faith between thee and the aforesaid Hieronymus, seeing that he approved Anatolius, who is opposed to Victorius; so that whoso follows the one cannot receive the other. Let, then, thy Vigilance take thought that, in approving the faith of one of the two authors aforesaid who are mutually opposed to each other, there be no dissonance, when thou pronouncest thy opinion, between thee and Hieronymus, lest we should be on all sides in a strait, as to whether we should agree with thee or with him. Spare the weak in this matter, lest thou exhibit the scandal of diversity. For I frankly acknowledge to thee that any one who goes against the authority of Saint Hieronymus will be one to be repudiated as a heretic among the churches of the West: for they accommodate their faith in all respects unhesitatingly to him with regard to the Divine Scriptures. But let this suffice with respect to Easter.

But I ask what thy judgment is about those bishops whom thou hast written of as simoniacal, and whom the writer Giltas [1] calls pests. Should communion be had with them? For there are known to be many such in this province, whereby the matter is made more serious. Or as to others, who having been polluted in their diaconate, are afterwards elected to the rank of bishops? For there are some whom we know to have conscientious scruples on these grounds; and in conferring with our littleness about them, they wished to know for certain whether they may minister without peril after such transgressions; that is, either after having bought their rank for money, or after adultery in their diaconate. I mean, however, concealed adultery with their dependents [2], which with our teachers is accounted as no less criminal.

As to a third head of enquiry, say in reply, I pray thee, if it is not troublesome, what should be done in the case of those monks who for a closer sight of God, or inflamed by a longing for a more perfect life, going against their vows, leave the places of their first conversion, and, against the will of their abbots, the fervour of monks compelling them, either go free or fly to deserts. The author Vennianus enquired about these of Giltas, who replied to him most elegantly: yet still to one who is anxious to learn there is ever an increase of greater fear. These things, and much more which epistolary brevity does not admit of, might well have been enquired about more humbly and more clearly in a personal interview, but that weakness of body and the care of my fellow-pilgrims keeps me bound at home, though desirous of going to thee, so as to draw from that spiritual vein of a living well and from the living water of knowledge flowing from heaven and springing up unto eternal life. And, if my body were to follow my mind, Rome would once more be in danger of being itself despised; seeing that—even as we read in the narration of the learned Hieronymus how certain persons once came to Rome from the utmost boundaries of the Heuline coast [3]; and then (wonderful to be told) sought something else outside of Rome— so I too, saving reverence for the ashes of the saints, should seek out longingly, not Rome, but thee: for, though I confess myself not to be wise, but athirst, I should do this same thing if I had time and opportunity.

I have read thy book containing the Pastoral Rule, short in style, lengthy in teaching, full of mysteries; and acknowledge it to be a work sweeter than honey to one that is in

---

[2] *Cum clientelis*: meaning perhaps living with females of their own households as concubines, in distinction from open transgression. The word can hardly denote, as suggested by the Benedictine Editors, wives lawfully married before ordination.
[3] *De ultimis Heulini litoris finibus.*—"Loco *Heulini* esse legendum *Hualini*, vel *Huelini*, constat ex contextu Hieronymiano. Est vox Graeca, a *rad.* ὕαλος, sive ὕελος, *vitrum*, *crystallus.* Sic mare vocatur (*Apocal.* iv.) θάλασσα ὑαλίνη. In Hieronymo hic legimus; *De ultimis Hispaniæ Galliarumque finibus*" (*note in Benedictine Edition*). See above, note 8, as to the fondness of the old Irish writers for the use of Greek words.

need. Wherefore bestow, I pray thee, on me who am athirst for what is thine, the works on Ezekiel, which, as I have heard, thou hast elaborated with wonderful genius. I have read the six books of Hieronymus on that prophet; but he has not expounded the middle part. But, if thou wilt do me the favour, send for me to the city some of thy remaining writings; to wit, the concluding expositions of one book, and (? *namely*) the Song of Songs from that place where it is said, *I will go to the mountain of myrrh and the hill of frankincense*, to the end, treated with short comments, either of others, or thine own: and I beg that thou wouldest expound the whole obscurity of Zachariah, and make manifest its hidden meaning, that Western blindness may give thee thanks for this. I make unreasonable demands, and ask to have great things told me: who can fail to see this? But it is true also that thou hast great things, and knowest well that from a little less, and from much more should be put out to use. Let charity induce thee to write in reply; let not the roughness of my letter hinder thee from expounding, seeing that it is my mode of expression that has been in fault, and I have it in my heart to pay thee due honour. It was for me to provoke, to interrogate, to request: it is for thee not to refuse what thou hast received freely, to put thy talent out to use, to give to him that asks the bread of doctrine, as Christ enjoins. Peace be to thee and thine; pardon my forwardness, blessed pope, in that I have written so boldly; and I pray thee in thy holy prayers to our common Lord to pray for me, a most vile sinner. I think it quite superfluous to commend to thee my people, whom the Saviour judges fit to be received, as walking in His name; and if, as I have heard from thy holy Candidus[4], thou shouldest be disposed to say in reply that things confirmed by ancient usage cannot be changed, error is manifestly ancient; but truth which reproves it is ever more ancient still.

[4] Candidus had been sent by Gregory to Gaul as *rector patrimonii* there. See previous Epistles.

# BOOK X

## EPISTLE X.

### To Romanus, Guardian (*Defensorem*).

Gregory to Romanus, our guardian in Sicily.

It has been reported to us that our most reverend brother the bishop Basilius is occupied in legal suits as though he were one of the last of the people, and unprofitably attends the courts. Now, since this thing both renders the man himself vile and does away with the reverence due to priests, let thy Experience, immediately on receiving this order, so compel him by strict execution of it to return to his duty that, through thy insistency, a delay of five days be not under any excuse allowed him; lest, if thou shouldest in any way permit him to make such delay, thou with him shouldest come to be gravely culpable before us. Given in the month of December, Indiction 3.

## EPISTLE XV.

### To Clementina, Patrician [1].

Gregory to Clementina, &c.

It has reached us by the report of a certain Abbot that your Glory has been told by certain evil-speakers that we have a pique against you. If this is so, whosoever have made up this story have been double towards you under a shew of sincerity, so as to shew themselves off as faithful, and wickedly cause you to doubt us. But I, glorious daughter, knowing thy good qualities of old, and especially the chastity which has been thy companion from youth, have ever regarded thee with great respect and affection. But, lest even now your Glory should suspect that my heart is changed, I declare that there is not in me a scruple of ill-feeling or anger towards you; but be assured that I evince paternal affection for you. One thing, however, that has been told me I ought not to pass over in silence, lest there should begin to be a diminution of charity, if what needs to be said for amendment were suppressed.

For indeed it has been reported to me that, when any one has offended you, you retain soreness unremittingly. Now, if this is true, since the more I love you the more grieved I am, I beg that you would nobly rid yourself of this fault, and not suffer the seed of the enemy to grow to the detriment of your crop of well-doing. Let the words of the Lord's Prayer be brought back to your memory, and let not blame prevail with you over pardon. Let the goodness of your Glory get the better of transgressions, and by salubriously pardoning make the offender devoted to you more than persistent asperity can make him undevoted. Let there be left to him what may make him ashamed, and not kept up what may grieve him. For usually discreet remission has more effect for correction than strictness in executing vengeance; so much so that sometimes the one makes a man more faithful and subdued, while the other makes him obstinate and spiteful. And indeed we do not say this to you in order that you should abate your zeal for righteousness, but lest you should be in the least things such as you ought to be in the greatest. For, if ever the quality of a transgression requires severity, it should be so dealt with that both vengeance may correct the fault and grace not be denied afterwards to those that have been corrected. Seeing, then, that we warn you under the dictates of paternal affection for your soul's good, receive our words with the charity wherewith they are spoken, and take them to yourself for the advantage of your Glory, so that your good qualities may become clearer before men and very pure before Almighty God. But count on us, dearest daughter, confidently in all things, as indeed you may; and, since we always desire to hear of your prosperity, refresh us often by your letters.

## EPISTLE XVIII.

### To Clementina, Patrician [2].

Gregory to Clementina, &c.

Know, glorious daughter, that the presbyter

---

[1] Clementina was one of the ladies of rank whose acquaintance Gregory had made at Constantinople, and with whom he continued to keep up affectionate fatherly intercourse. Cf. I. 11, and the epistle which follows this.

[2] It is a sign of Gregory's habitual courtesy to ladies of rank, as well as of their influential position, that he is moved to send

Amandus has been elected to the episcopate by the people of Surrentum. And, we having written for him to be sent hither, you ought not to be saddened for his absence, seeing that one who is with you in heart should not even be believed to be departing from you. And, since he who once pleased you is acceptable to those who want a bishop, bless Almighty God for this, and with Christian devotion rejoice the more ; and gladly do your best to further his coming to us for the advantage of others speedily, since it is the part of sincere charity to exult when one who is loved is called that he may grow.

## EPISTLE XIX.

### To Anthemius, Subdeacon.

Gregory to Anthemius, Subdeacon of Campania.

After he who had been elected to the episcopate of the city of Surrentum had appeared to us to be unfit, they elected Amandus, presbyter of the oratory of Saint Severinus, which is in the Lucullan camp. Wherefore we enjoin on thy Experience, laying aside excuses, to take care to send the said presbyter to us with all speed, to the end that, if there is nothing to hinder him from coming, the desires of the petitioners may with the help of Christ be fulfilled. As to his life and deeds, seeing that they can be better known where he has long lived, let it be thy care, together with our brother and fellow-bishop, Fortunatus [3], to make diligent enquiry. And if there is nothing in the way of his promotion to the sacred order, he should be sent to us without any delay. But, lest our glorious daughter Clementina should take this amiss, let thy Experience go to her, and do this thing with her consent. If, however, she should be disposed to resist, let thy Experience still send him hither without delay, since we ought so to pacify the minds of our children as still not to obstruct benefit to souls.

## EPISTLE XXIII.

### To Adrian, Notary of Sicily [4].

Gregory to Adrian, &c.

A thing to us altogether detestable and infamous has come to our ears, and we wonder why, if it is true, thou hast not taken notice of it. For Martianus, a monk of the monastery of Saint Vitus, situate on Mount Ætna, has come to us, and presented a petition, complaining among other things that the monks of this monastery live so perversely and wickedly as to dare to have women living with them, which is a thing atrocious to be spoken of. And, seeing that we have written on this matter to our brother and fellow-bishop Leo [5], in order that, having enquired into the truth, he may, if he should find it to be so, be at pains to correct it with the strictest severity, it is necessary for thy Experience also to shew thyself in all respects solicitous for investigation of the truth, and punishment of so great a wickedness ; so that nothing may be found to be done remissly or negligently. Further, for the interests in other respects of the same monastery, lend thy assistance so far as equity may require, to the end that if, as is said, there has been any invasion of it, it may be redressed according to justice, and that for the future nothing prejudicial may in any way arise there contrary to the fear of God and the order of law.

## EPISTLE XXIV.

### To Fortunatus, Bishop of Neapolis (*Naples*).

Gregory to Fortunatus, &c.

When your Fraternity pays too little attention to the monasteries that are under you, you both lay yourself open to reproof, and make us sorry for your laxity. Now it has come to our ears that one Mauricius, who lately became a monk in the monastery of Barbacianus, has fled from the same monastery, taking other monks with him. In this case the hastiness of the aforesaid Barbacianus inculpates him exceedingly in our sight, in that he rashly tonsured a secular person without even previous probation. Did we not write to you that you should prove him first, and then, if he were fit, should make him abbot? Even now, then, look well after him whom you chose. For you are delinquent in his delinquency, if he has begun so to demean himself as to shew himself unfit to have the government of brethren.

Further, let your Fraternity more strictly interdict all monasteries from venturing by any means to tonsure those whom they may have received for monastic profession before

---

her a kind of apology for removing from Constantinople a priest whom she valued, and who may have been her spiritual adviser. See also the epistle which follows, in which the subdeacon in charge of the proceedings is directed to resort to her in person to solicit her consent. Amandus was after his death venerated as a Saint at Surrentum. In the Church of SS. Felix and Baculus there is this epitaph;—" Hic requiescit sacerdos Dei Amandus episcopus sanctæ ecclesiæ Surrentinæ, qui sedit annos xvii. dies xxi. Depositus est die 13, mense Aprilis, indict. 5, imperante D.N. Heraclio R. Aug. anno 7. Orate pro me, sancte Pater." (*Migne, Patrilog., in loc.*)

3 Bishop of Naples.

4 As to the employment of notaries, see *Prolegomena*, p. viii.

5 Bishop of Catana in Sicily, to whom a previous epistle (Ep. XXII., not here translated) on the same subject is addressed. Several years previously he had been summoned to Rome to answer to certain charges against him, but had been honourably acquitted. Cf. I. 72 ; II. 33.

they have completed two years in monastic life. But in this space of time let their life and manners be carefully proved, lest any one of them should either not be content with what he had desired or not keep firm to what he had chosen. For, it being a serious matter that untried men should be associated under obedience to any master, how much more serious is it that any who have not been proved should be attached to the service of God?

Further, if a soldier should wish to become a monk, let no one for any cause whatever presume to receive him [6] without our consent, or before it has been reported to us. If this rule is not diligently observed, know that all the guilt of those that are under thee redounds on thyself, seeing that thou provest thyself by the very facts of the case to be too little anxious about them.

### EPISTLE XXXI.

#### To Libertinus, Ex-prætor.

Gregory to Libertinus, &c.

What straits you are in with regard to the things of this world is not unknown to us. But, since to those who are placed in the utmost tribulation the only comfort is the mercy of the Creator, rest your hope on Him, and turn to Him with your whole heart, Who both justly allows whom He will to be afflicted and will mercifully deliver one who trusts in Him. To Him, then, give thanks, and patiently endure what has been brought upon you. For it is the part of a right mind not only to bless God in prosperity, but also in adversities to join in praising Him. In these things therefore that you are suffering let no murmur against God creep into your heart, since for what purpose our Creator thus works is unknown. For perchance, magnificent son, thou didst offend Him in something when in a state of prosperity, from which He would purge thee by kindly bitterness. And so neither let temporal affliction break thee down nor losses of thy goods distract thee, since if, returning thanks in adversity, thou make God propitious to thee by thy patience, both the things that were lost are multiplied, and in addition to this, eternal joys held out to thee. I beg thee, however, not to take it amiss that we have written through Romanus the guardian to order twenty suits of clothing to be supplied from us to your servants, seeing that things, however small, which are offered from the goods of the blessed Apostle Peter are always to be taken for a great blessing, since he will have power

both to bestow on you greater things, and to hold out to you eternal benefits with Almighty God. The month of June, Indiction 3.

### EPISTLE XXXV.

#### To Eulogius, Patriarch of Alexandria.

Gregory to Eulogius, &c.

In the past year I received the letters of your most sweet Holiness; but on account of the extreme severity of my sickness have been unable to reply to them until now. For lo, it is now almost full two years that I have been confined to my bed, afflicted with such pains of gout that I have hardly been able to rise on feast-days for as much as three hours space to solemnize mass. And I am soon compelled by severe pain to lie down, that I may be able to bear my torment with intervening groans. This pain of mine is sometimes moderate, and sometimes excessive: but neither so moderate as to depart, nor so excessive as to kill me. Hence it comes to pass that, being daily in death, I am daily debarred from death. Nor it is surprising that, grievous sinner as I am, I am long kept confined in the prison of such corruption. Whence I am compelled to exclaim, *Bring my soul out of prison, that I may confess thy name* (Ps. cxli. 8). But, since I am not yet worthy to obtain this by my prayers, I beg that the prayer of your Holiness may afford me the aid of its intercession, and deliver me from the weight of sin and corruption into that liberty, which you know well, of the glory of the children of God.

Your to me most sweet and ever to be honoured Blessedness has informed me in your letter that our common son Anatolius, deacon of the city of Constantinople, had written to you to say that certain monks from the parts about Jerusalem had come to me to make some enquiry concerning the error of the *Agnoitæ* [7], and you say that he begged your Holiness to write to me to express your opinion with respect to this enquiry. But neither have monks come to me from the parts about Jerusalem to make any enquiry, nor do I think that the said our common son

---

[7] The *Agnoetæ* or *Themistiani* arose in connexion with the Monophysite controversy in the sixth century, being led by Themistius, a deacon of Alexandria, who taught the limitation of the human knowledge of Christ, referring especially to Mark xiii. 32, and John xi. 34. The majority of the Monophysites rejected his view, which was condemned also by the orthodox. Eulogius of Alexandria, to whom the letter before us is addressed, wrote a treatise against the Agnoetæ, from which extracts are given by Photius. Sophronius, patriarch of Jerusalem, pronounced the anathema against Themistius. On the same subject, cf. Ep. XXXIX. below. Gregory's arguments in Ep. XXXIX. against the views of the Agnoetæ are interesting to English readers at the present day, when similar views have been lately put forward and discussed.

can have told you in his letters what was not the case ; but I suspect that the interpreter has mistaken the meaning of his letters. For the same deacon, now more than two years ago, wrote to me that monks had come from the aforesaid parts to the city of Constantinople making such enquiries, and he desired to ask me what I thought. To him, long before I received your letters, I made the very same reply against that same heresy as I found afterwards in the epistle of your Holiness : and I returned great thanks to Almighty God that concerning all questions the Fathers of the Romans and of the Greeks, whose followers we are, have spoken with one spirit. For in many parts I found this your epistle to be as though I had been reading the writings of the Latin Fathers against the aforesaid heresy. And consider how much I must love and praise the excellence of my most holy brother, in whose mouth I recognised the venerable Fathers, whom I love so much. Praise therefore be to Him, to Him be glory in the highest, of whose gift the voice of Mark still cries aloud in the See of Peter[8] ; from the effusion of whose spirit, when the priest enters into the Holy of Holies for searching into mysteries, spiritual bells resound in holy Church, as in the tabernacle, from the words of preaching. Right, then, and highly to be praised is your preaching. But we implore the Almighty Lord to keep you long even in this life, that from the organ of God, which you are, the voice of truth may in this world sound more widely. And for me, I pray you, intercede, that the way of this pilgrimage, which has become too rough for me may with speed be finished, to the end that I, who cannot by my own merits, may by yours be able to attain to the promises of the eternal country, and to rejoice with the citizens of heaven.

### EPISTLE XXXVI.

#### To Maximus, Bishop of Salona[9].

Gregory to Maximus, &c.

When our common son the presbyter Veteranus came to the Roman city, he found me so weak from the pains of gout as to be quite unable to answer thy Fraternity's letters myself. And indeed with regard to the nation of the Sclaves[1], from which you are in great danger, I am exceedingly afflicted and disturbed. I am afflicted as suffering already in

your suffering : I am disturbed, because they have already begun to enter Italy by way of Istria. Further, of Julian the *scribo*[2], what shall I say, seeing that I see everywhere how our sins find us out, so as to cause us to be disturbed by the nations from without and by judges from within ? But be not at all saddened by such things, since those who shall live after us will see worse times ; so much so, that they will regard us as having had happy days in comparison with their own. But, so far as thy Fraternity has power, thou oughtest to oppose thyself in behalf of the poor, in behalf of the oppressed. And, even if thou shouldest be unable to do any good, the very devotion of thy heart, which Almighty God has given, is enough for Him. For it is written, *Rescue them that are drawn unto death, and forbear not to deliver them that are ready to be slain* (Prov. xxiv. 11). But if thou shouldest say, My powers are insufficient, He who sees into the heart understands. In all that thou doest, then, desire to have Him Who sees into the heart well-pleased with thee. But whatever there is whereby He may be pleased omit not thou to do. For human terrors and favours are like smoke, which is snatched by a light breeze and vanishes away. Know this most assuredly, that no one can please God and bad men. Let, therefore, thy Fraternity esteem thyself to have pleased Almighty God in such degree as thou knowest thyself to have displeased froward men. Yet let thy defence of the poor itself be moderate and grave, lest, if anything be done too rigidly, men should think you actuated by the pride of youth. But our defence of the poor must needs be found of such sort that both the humble may feel protection and oppressors may not easily find what out of a malevolent disposition they may blame. Attend, then, to what is said to Ezekiel, *Son of man, unbelievers and destroyers are with thee, and thou dost dwell among scorpions* (Ezek. ii. 6). And the blessed Job says, *I have been a brother of dragons, and a companion of owls* (Job xxx. 29). And Paul says to his disciples, *In the midst of a crooked and perverse nation, among whom ye shine as lights in the world* (Philip. ii. 15). We ought, then, to walk all the more cautiously as we know that we are living among the enemies of God. Further, with regard to the Photinianists, let thy Fraternity pay the utmost attention ; and, as thou hast begun, study how to recall them to the bosom of holy Church. But, if any should wish to come to me, and to receive an explanation, let them first make oath that they will not permit their

8 See Lib. VII. 40.
9 For a summary of previous dealings with Maximus of Salona, and his long defiance of the authority of Rome, see III. 47, note 2. It appears from this epistle that all former insubordination, which had called forth such fulminations, was now fully condoned.
1 Cf. IX. 9.

2 As to the designation *Scribo*, see II. 32, note 7 ; V. 30, note 8. As to this Julian, so described, cf. IX. 41.

followers to persist in their error even after an explanation has been received. And then let thy Holiness promise them that they will suffer no wrong from me, but that I will give them an explanation. If they should acknowledge the truth, let them accept it; if they should not acknowledge it, I will dismiss them unharmed. But, if any of them should wish to come to us against you, let thy Fraternity by no means detain them; for, when they come, they shall either accept an explanation, or assuredly they will not see that land any more.

## EPISTLE XXXVII.

### To Innocent, Præfect of Africa.

Gregory to Innocent, &c.

The lucid eloquence of your Eminence, seasoned with the honey of the heart, has so infused its savour into our inmost soul, and ravished us with love of it, that both what you write sounds sweet, and what you do has a pleasant savour; nor this without good cause, since one who is accomplished in good studies is great in the eye of judgment, and not of partiality. Further, as we understand that you have taken upon you the belts [3] of the prefecture, sadness is mingled with our joy. For on the one hand we are rejoiced for the promotion of our most sweet son, but are saddened on the other, because we feel in fact from our own sorrow how heavy a burden it is in times of confusion to be advanced to high positions. Wherefore all pains ought to be taken that troublesome circumstances may become an occasion of reward. For, as you know, corn springs from land that is full of thistles, and the rose is produced from thorns. While, then, you have a time given you meet for sowing, delay not to sow the seed of good works, that in the day of harvest you may carry home the greater armfuls of joy, and from good service in a transitory dignity may come to eternal glory. Knowing, then, of the pains you have taken in the preparation of swift-sailing vessels [4], we relieve your anxiety by wished for news, informing you that, by the mercy of God, we have come to terms about peace with the king of the Lombards until the month of March in the coming fourth Indiction. Whether it will hold or not we know not, since the said king is reported to have died since, though the fact so far is held to be uncertain [5].

We have done what you wrote to ask us to do about Anamundarus, and would that the result might answer to our wish; for, as far as we are concerned, we do not deny the succour of our intercession to the afflicted.

As to your wishing the book on the exposition of holy Job to be sent to you, we altogether rejoice at your earnest desire; since we see that your Eminence earnestly desires what may both prevent you from going entirely outside yourself, and bring your heart back to itself after being distracted by secular cares. But, if you desire to be satiated with delicious food, read the works of the blessed Augustine, your countryman, and seek not our chaff in comparison with his fine wheat.

Furthermore, we have learnt from the testimony of Hilarius our *Chartularius* what patronage and what kindness your Glory has bestowed in the interests of the poor of the blessed Peter, Prince of the apostles, who loves you. On this account, returning you abundant thanks, we implore the mercy of Almighty God, that He would defend you with the protection of His grace, and permit neither bad men to prevail against you without, nor malignant spirits within; but that He would of His mercy so order your doings in His fear that, as He has made you glorious among men, He may also make you so after the course of a long life in the number of His saints.

## EPISTLE XXXIX.

### To Eulogius, Patriarch of Alexandria.

Gregory to Eulogius, &c.

*As cold water to a thirsty soul, so is good news from a far country* (Prov. xxv. 25). But what can be good news to me, so far as concerns the behoof of holy Church, but to hear of the health and safety of your to me most sweet Holiness, who, from your perception of the light of truth, both illuminate the same Church with the word of preaching, and mould it to a better way by the example of your manners? As often, too, as I recall in my heart your oneness of mind with me, and feel that I remain fixed in your heart, I give thanks to Almighty God that charity cannot be divided by distance of place. For, though in body we are far disjoined, yet in soul we are indivisible.

Our common son Anatolius the deacon [6] has notified to me in his letters that in the royal city nothing ecclesiastical has at any time been disturbed from earthly causes. But I believe that he had before announced to me

---

3 *Cingula.* "Speciatim *cingulum* adhibetur in re militari. Est enim militiæ insigne; et metonymice pro ipsa militia ponitur." (Facciolati.)
4 *Dromonibus.* "Est etiam hoc nomine genus navis longæ, transvectionibus aptæ, a celeritate dictæ (δρόμος), a *brigantine*, *cutter, yacht, carvel*: cujus mentio fit in *Cod.* lib. 1, tit. 27, leg. 2, et apud Cassiod. l. 5, Ep. XVII." (Facciolati.)
5 It was not the fact. The Lombard King Agilulph lived till A.D. 616.

6 At this time Gregory's apocrisiarius at Constantinople.

how your Blessedness had spoken in the cause of the Church. And I rejoice to think that, where you chanced to be present, I do not consider that there was any want of me. For I know that you, as a minister of the truth, a follower of Peter, and a preacher of Holy Church, would speak what ought to have been heard through the mouth of a teacher from the Apostle Peter's See [7].

Moreover, before these days, when Abramius of Alexandria came to me, I had written in reply to your Holiness both what I thought of your writings which you issued against the Agnoite heretics [8], and why I had been so late in replying. But the said Abramius, compelled by difficulties of navigation, is reported to have delayed long in the city of Naples ; and so I write again in the same sense in which I had formerly written, since in your teaching against the heretics that are called Agnoitæ there was much for us to admire ; but to displease us there was nothing. And in the same sense I had already written at length to our son Anatolius the deacon. Moreover, your doctrine so agreed in all respects with the Latin Fathers that I find, not to my surprise, that in diverse languages the Spirit has not been diverse.

For, as to what you have said about the fig-tree, Augustine speaks aptly in the same sense ; for, when the evangelist subjoined, *For the time of figs was not yet* (Mark xi. 13), it is plainly shewn that the figs which the Lord had sought were fruit in the synagogue, which had the leaves of the Law, but not the fruit of works. For the Creator of all things could not be ignorant that the fig-tree had no fruit ; which was a thing that all might know, since it was not the time of figs. But concerning what is written, *That the day and hour neither the Son nor the angels know* (Mark xiii. 32), your Holiness has quite rightly perceived that this is most certainly to be referred, not to the said Son with respect to His being the Head, but with respect to His body, which we are. With regard to which matter, the same blessed Augustine in many places adopts this sense (*Quæst. lib.* lxxxiii. *q.* 60 ; *lib.* 1 *de Trinit.*, c. 12 ; *in psalm* vi., *init. ; in ps.* xxxiv. *serm.* 2). He mentions also another thing that may be understood of the same Son, namely that Almighty God sometimes speaks in a human manner, even as He says to Abraham, *Now I know that thou fearest God* (Genes. xxii. 12). It was not that God then came to know that He was feared, but that He then made Abraham know that he feared God. For, as we speak of a glad day, not meaning that the day itself is glad, but that it makes us glad, so

also the Almighty Son says that He does not know the day which He causes not to be known ; not that He Himself does not know it, but that He does not allow it to be known. Whence also the Father alone is said to know it, because the Son Who is consubstantial with Him has His knowledge of what the angels are ignorant of from His divine nature, whereby He is above the angels. Whence also it may be more nicely understood thus ; that the Only-begotten, being incarnate and made for us a perfect man, knew indeed in the nature of His humanity the day and hour of the judgment, but still it was not from the nature of His humanity that He knew it. What then He knew in it He knew not from it, because God, made man, knew the day and hour of the judgment through the power of His Deity : as also at the marriage, when the Virgin Mother said that wine was wanting, He replied, *Woman, what have I to do with thee ? Mine hour is not yet come* (Joh. ii. 4). For it was not that the Lord of the angels was subject to the hour, having, among all things which He had created, made hours and times ; but, because the Virgin Mother, when wine was wanting, wished a miracle to be done by Him, it was at once answered her, *Woman, what have I to do with thee ?* As if to say plainly, That I can do a miracle comes to me of my Father, not of my Mother. For He who of the nature of His Father did miracles had it of His mother that He could die. Whence also, when He was on the cross, in dying He acknowledged His mother, whom He commended to the disciple, saying, *Behold thy mother* (Joh. xix. 27). He says, then, *Woman, what have I to do with thee ? Mine hour is not yet come.*—That is, "In the miracle, which I have not of thy nature, I do not acknowledge thee. When the hour of death shall come, I shall acknowledge thee as my mother, since I have it of thee that I can die." And thus the knowledge, which He had not of the nature of humanity whereby He was with the angels a creature, this He denied that He had with the angels, who are creatures. The day, then, and the hour of the judgment He knows as God and man, but for this reason, that God is man. It is moreover a thing quite manifest, that whoso is not a Nestorian cannot in any wise be an Agnoite. For with what meaning can one that confesses that the very Wisdom of God was incarnate say that there is anything that the Wisdom of God is ignorant of ? It is written, *In the beginning was the Word, and the Word was with God, and the Word was God. All things were made by him* (Joh. i. 1). If all things, then without doubt the day and hour of the judgment. Who then can be so senseless as to presume to say that the Word of the Father made what He is ignorant of? It is written also, *Jesus knowing that the Father had given all things into his hands* (Job xxii. 3). If all things, certainly both the day and the hour of the judgment. Who, then, is so foolish as to say that the Son received into His hands what He knows not?

But, with respect to the passage in which He says to the women about Lazarus, *Where have ye laid him* (Joh. xi. 34), I felt exactly as you felt, that, if they say that the Lord did not know where Lazarus had been buried, and for that reason enquired, they will undoubtedly be compelled to acknowledge that the Lord did not know in what places Adam and Eve had hidden themselves after their sin, when He said in Paradise, *Adam, where art thou* (Gen. iii. 9)? or when He chides Cain, saying, *Where is Abel thy brother* (Gen. iv. 9)? But, if He did not know, why did He forthwith add, *Thy brother's blood crieth unto me from the ground?* However, on this passage Severianus Gabalensis speaks differently, saying that the Lord spoke thus to the women as it were in the way of rebuke, in that He enquired where they had laid the dead Lazarus; as if with plain reference to the sin of Eve He had said, I placed the man in Paradise, whom you have placed in the sepulchre.

But to these things our said common son Anatolius the deacon has replied by putting another question :—What if it should be objected to me that, even as He who is immortal vouchsafed to die that He might deliver us from death, and He who is eternal before all time willed to become subject to time, so the Wisdom of God vouchsafed to take upon Himself our ignorance that He might deliver us from ignorance? But I have not yet given him any reply to this, having been confined until now by grievous sickness. Now, however, through your prayers I have already begun to recover; and, if I should so recover as to be able to dictate, with the help of the Lord I will reply to him. To you it is not for me to say anything on this subject, lest I should seem to teach you what you know, seeing that even medicines lose their power of healing, if applied to sound and strong members.

Furthermore, we apprize you that in this place we suffer from serious difficulty for want of good interpreters. For there are none who can express the sense, while all ever try to translate the words exactly : and so they confuse the whole sense of what has been said. Whence it comes to pass that we are by no means able without severe labour to understand what has been translated.

I have received the blessing of Saint Mark the Evangelist and of your Blessedness. And I have been desirous of sending you some timber; but the ship which came was too small to carry it. And yet even that which the Alexandrians saw when they came is of small size. For I had prepared some that is much larger for you, which has not yet been conveyed to the Roman city : for I waited for it to be conveyed when the Alexandrian ship should arrive; and it has remained in the place where it was felled.

May Almighty God long guard your life for the edification of Holy Church, and inspire you to pray earnestly for me ; that, being pressed down by my own sins, I may be lifted up before Almighty God by your prayers.

## EPISTLE XLII.

### To Eusebius, Archbishop of Thessalonica.

Gregory to Eusebius, &c.

If, most dear brother, we consider attentively how great is the excellence of peace, we shall recognize with what earnestness it should be cultivated by us. For indeed our Lord and Redeemer vouchsafed to leave and give it as a great boon to His disciples, that He might thereby make those who were united to Him in firmness of faith His associates in loving participation with Himself. For it is written, *Blessed are the peacemakers, for they shall be called the children of God* (Matth. v. 9). Whosoever, then, desires to be the father's heir, let him, by keeping peace, not refuse to be his child. For he who gives place to discord surely makes himself to be without lot in so great a gift. Seeing then that by the mercy of God the purity of thy faith has been declared to us, as was meet, with catholic rectitude, we are taken up with great surprise that thou shouldest suffer those whom thou knowest to believe well and to think aright to be needlessly scandalised by the fault of certain persons, so that the reputation of thy Fraternity is clouded by the guilt of others. For how can one avoid suspicion of error who extends sufferance to them that are in error? Or what estimate of himself can he expect, if he provides not for purging by open satisfaction what fervour of faith requires to be purged?

For indeed it is said that Luke thy presbyter and Peter refuse to receive the Chalcedonian synod, and that on this account the hearts of thy orthodox children are perturbed with no slight offence[9]. And, since their zeal is not only to be praised but also to be altogether cherished, we exhort that the care of thy Fraternity hesitate not to investigate the matter with all activity and solicitude. And, if those persons should be found innocent of that pravity, remove offence from the minds of thy children by giving them satisfaction, and among all heresies anathematise especially Severus and Nestorius, so that purification may engender charity among those with whom a sinister suspicion concerning those heretics has, out of love of the faith, produced dissension; and that one feeling of concord may salubriously knit together those whom a pure and single confession of catholic truth unites. Nor let the doubters be thought unworthy of satisfaction, since we are instructed by the Divine voice, *Despise not one of these who are the least* (Matth. xxviii. 18). Whoso, then, desires not that he who instructs us should be despised, let him not reject the words of the instructor; since he also of whom our Redeemer testified that he was a vessel of election unto Himself admonishes us to keep the unity of the Spirit in the bond of peace (Ephes. iv.). Hence whosoever refuses not to be held by this bond of salvation, let him study the things that make for peace, and afford no place for the foe; so that, having been enabled to advance by the fierce dissension of brethren, he may be more stoutly trampled on, when unity is established.

If however, as we do not expect, they should be found to be wounded by the dart of this error, the cure of ecclesiastical exhortation must be applied to them, so that they may either remain among the Lord's sheep if healed, or be cut off from the unity of the ecclesiastical body; to the end that from a slight loss there may be a great gain, and that the removal of a part may make the whole body free. For it is the care also of a provident shepherd not to delay casting out from consort with his sound sheep a sickly one that admits not of cure, lest it should contaminate others with the taint of its sickness, knowing that he cannot preserve the soundness of the rest but by the ejection of this one. Accordingly I once more warn you in brotherly charity to investigate this matter with the utmost vigilance, and to observe what we have written with the utmost care, lest by consort with others you should make the right faith which you hold doubtful. For

he who does not correct things that should be cut off commits them. Wherefore you must take thought with great solicitude and with great provision in all ways, that the persons of those men be not an offence to others, or common opinion injurious to you; that so a shepherd's gains may accrue to your Fraternity from the sheep committed to you all the more as both sincere love and approved care shall have made you solicitous for their custody.

## EPISTLE LXII.
### To the Neapolitans.

Gregory to the clergy and noble citizens of Naples.

It is not a new thing, nor is it reprehensible, that in the election of a bishop the votes of the people should be divided between two parties: but it is a serious matter when in cases of this kind the election goes not by judgment, but by favour only. For before your letter reached us we had learnt from the report of certain persons that the deacon John, who has been elected by the other party, has a little daughter. Hence, if they had had a mind to attend to reason, neither would others have elected him nor would he have consented. For what presumption must his be who dares to approach the episcopate while convicted by the evidence of the little girl, of not having had long control over his own body! Moreover, Peter the deacon, who you say has been elected by you, is, according to what is said, quite without astuteness. And you know that at the present time the person to be constituted in the highest place of government, should be one who knows how to be careful, not only for the salvation of souls, but also with regard to the external advantage and safeguard of his subjects. But know ye further that it has come to our ears concerning him, that he has given money on usury; which thing you ought to enquire into thoroughly, and, if it is so, elect another, and without delay hold yourselves aloof from a person of this kind. For we will on no account lay hands on lovers of usury. If, however, after accurate enquiry made, this should prove to be false (since his person is unknown to us, and we know not whether what has been reported to us of his simplicity be true), he must needs come to us with your decree in his favour, that, having made careful enquiry into his life and manners, we may at the same time become acquainted with his intelligence; and thus, in case of his satisfying this enquiry, we may in him, with the Lord's help, fulfil your desires. Further, let it be your care to look out also for another

---

[9] Those who refused to accept the condemnation of "The Three Chapters" by the fifth council alleged that it contravened the Council of Chalcedon. It may be that the persons referred to here, in their defence of what had been decreed in the fifth council, had seemed to admit that it did contravene the fourth, which they consequently were supposed to reject.

person who may be suitable, so that, if this one should by any chance appear unfit for appointment to this order, there may be some one else to whom you may transfer your choice. For it will be a serious disgrace to your clergy, in case of this man by any chance not being approved, if they should say that they have no one else fit to be elected.

## EPISTLE LXIII.

### To Dominicus, Bishop of Carthage.

Gregory to Dominicus, &c.

We have already learnt what great pestilence has invaded the African parts; and, inasmuch as neither is Italy free from such affliction, doubled are the groans of our sorrows. But amid these evils and other innumerable calamities our heart, dearest brother, would fail from desperate distress, had not the Lord's voice fortified our weakness beforehand. For long ago to the faithful the trumpet of the Gospel lesson sounded, warning them that at the approach of the end of the world wars and many other things, which, as you know, are now feared, would come to pass (Matth. xxiv.; Luke xxi.). We ought not, then, to be too much afflicted in suffering things that we knew of beforehand, as though they had been unknown. Frequently also, in our consideration of another's death, the kind of death may be an alleviation. For what manglings, what cruelties have we seen, where death was the only remedy, and life was a torment! Did not David, when a choice of deaths was offered him, refuse famine or the sword, and choose that his people should fall under the hand of God? Gather ye from this how great favour is granted to such as perish under Divine smiting, since they die by the call that was offered to the holy prophet for a boon. Wherefore let us return thanks to our Creator in all adversities, and, trusting in His mercy, bear all things patiently, since we suffer much less than we deserve. Since, however, we are so scourged temporally that we may not be left without the consolation of life eternal, it is needful (since we are not ignorant, through the announcements of these signs, that the Judge Who is to come is at hand) that we should so much the more, by zeal for good works and the wailing of penitence, make secure our accounts which we shall have to submit to His scrutiny; so that such great smitings may be to us, by the favour of His grace, not the beginning of damnation, but a purgation for our good.

Since, however, the nature of our infirmity is such that we cannot but grieve for those who pass away, let the teaching of your Fraternity be a consolation to the afflicted. Instil into them that the good things which are promised will remain with them; so that, strengthened by a most sure hope, they may learn not to grieve for the loss of temporal things in comparison with the gift to come. Let your tongue, as indeed we believe it does, restrain them more and more from the perpetration of evil deeds; let it announce the rewards of the good, the punishments of the bad, so that those who have little love for good things may at least be greatly afraid of bad things, and keep themselves from the things which must be punished. For to commit things worthy of scourges when placed in the midst of scourges is to be peculiarly proud against the smiter, and provokes the incensed one to fiercer anger. And it is a prime kind of madness for any one to be unwilling to desist justly from his own evil, and to wish God to cease unjustly from His vengeance. But, since in all this there is need of Divine help, let us, beloved brother, with united prayers implore the clemency of Almighty God, that He would both grant unto us thus to acquit ourselves worthily, and mercifully stir the hearts of the people to perform such things; to the end that, while we order our actions wholesomely in His fear, we may be counted worthy both to be delivered from impending evils, and, by the leading of His grace, without which we can do nothing, to come to supernal joys.

The month of August, Indiction 3.

# BOOK XI.

## EPISTLE I.

### To John, Abbot.

Gregory to John, Abbot of Mount Sina [1].

The Epistle of thy Humility testifies to the holiness of thy life; whence we give great thanks to Almighty God, for that we know that there are still some to pray for our sins. For we, under the colour of ecclesiastical government, are tossed in the billows of this world, which frequently overwhelm us. But by the protecting hand of heavenly grace we are raised up again from the deep. Do you, then, who lead a tranquil life in the so great serenity of your rest, and stand as it were safe on the shore, extend the hand of your prayer to us who are on our voyage, or rather who are suffering shipwreck, and with all the supplications in your power help us as we strive to reach the land of the living, so that not only for your own life, but also for our rescue, you may have reward for ever. May the Holy Trinity protect thy Love with the right hand of Its protection, and grant unto thee in Its sight, by praying, by admonishing, by shewing example of good work, to feed the flock committed to thee, that so thou mayest be able to reach the pastures of eternal life with the flock itself which thou feedest. For it is written, *My sheep shall come and shall find pastures* (John x. 27). And these pastures in truth we find, when, freed from the winter of this life, we are satisfied with the greenness of eternal life, as of a new Spring.

We have learnt from the report of our son Simplicius that there is a want of beds and bedding in the *Gerontocomium* [2], which has been constructed by one Isaurus there. Wherefore we have sent 15 cloaks, 30 *rachanæ* [3], and

15 beds. We have also given money for the purchase of mattresses and for their transport, which we beg thy Love not to disdain, but to supply them to the place for which they have been sent. Given on the day of the Kalends of September, Indiction 4.

## EPISTLE XII.

### To Conon, Abbot of Lirinus (*Lerins*).

Gregory to Conon, Abbot of the Monastery of Lirinus [4].

The carefulness of persons in authority is the safeguard of subjects, since one who watches over what is entrusted to him avoids the snares of the enemy. But how skilful thou art in ruling the brethren, and how earnestly watchful in keeping guard over them, we have learnt from the report of our most reverend brother and fellow-bishop Mennas [5]. And as our hearing of the unwary remissness of thy predecessor often saddened us, so the carefulness of thy foresight gladdens us, since there is no doubt that the safeguard of thy earnestness is of profit for reward to thee, and for example to do good to others.

But, since the more our adversary knows himself to be guarded against on all sides, the more he seeks to break in by hidden ways, and strives with cunning art to overthrow his opponent, let the watchfulness of thy Love ever kindle itself to more ardent care; and so, with God's help, fortify all beforehand, that the ravening wolf, running about hither and thither, may have no place for entering among the Lord's sheep. Be it then thine earnest endeavour, the grace of our Redeemer aiding thee, to prohibit and in all ways guard those who are committed to thee from gluttony, from pride, from avarice, from idle speaking, and from all uncleanness; that by so much the greater reward may accrue to thee from the government committed to thee as thy subjects, through thy vigilance, shall be conquerors against the iniquities of the adversary.

---

[1] No doubt the John called *Climacus, Scholasticus*, and *Sinaita*, commemorated as a saint on 30 March. Having entered the monastery of Mount Sinai at the age of 16, he is said to have retired thence to live the life of an anchoret, to have been elected abbot at the age of 75, to have again after a time retired into solitude, and to have died early in the 7th century. While abbot, he wrote a work called *Scala* (κλίμαξ) *Paradisi*, whence his name of *Climacus*. The monastery on Mount Sinai was a place to which pilgrimages were made. Cf. IV. 46.

[2] Properly a hospital for aged persons.

[3] The meaning of the word *rachana, racana*, or *rachina*, is uncertain. It occurs again in XI. 78, where Barbara and Antonina, two young ladies at Constantinople, are thanked for a present of two *racanæ*, which they had alleged to be of their own

workmanship. It is usually supposed to mean some wooller article of dress, worn by monks. Others understand *blankets*.

[4] See VI. 56, note 7. The abbot Stephen, addressed in that letter, was probably the predecessor of Conon.

[5] He was bishop of Telona (*Toulon*). See XI. 58.

Wherefore let the good feel thee sweet. the bad a corrector. And even in correction know thou that this order should be observed, that thou shouldest love persons and visit faults; lest, if thou shouldest perchance be disposed to act otherwise, correction should pass into cruelty, and thou shouldest destroy those whom thou desirest to amend. For thou oughtest so to cut away a sore as not to run the risk of ulcerating what is sound; lest, if thou press in the steel more than the case requires, thou injure him whom thou art in haste to benefit. For let thy very sweetness be wary, not remiss; and let thy correction be loving, not severe. But let the one be so seasoned by the other that both the good may have, in loving, something to beware of, and the bad, in fearing, something to love.

Attend carefully to these things, most beloved son; earnestly observe them; that, when through such management thou shalt have given back safe to God those whom thou hast received from Him, thou mayest be counted worthy in the day of eternal retribution to hear Him say, *Well done, thou good and faithful servant: because thou hast been faithful in a few things, I will set thee over many things: enter into the joy of thy Lord* (Luke xix. 17). Further, we desire that our son Columbus the presbyter, who is commended to thy Charity by his own merits, may advance in thy love from our commendation also.

## EPISTLE XIII.

### To Serenus, Bishop of Massilia (*Marseilles*) [6].

Gregory to Serenus, &c.

The beginning of thy letter so shewed thee to have in thee the good will that befits a priest as to cause us increased joy in thy Fraternity. But its conclusion was so at variance with its commencement that such an epistle might be attributed, not to one, but to different, minds. Nay, from thy very doubts about the epistle which we sent to thee it appears how inconsiderate thou art. For, hadst thou paid diligent attention to the admonition which in brotherly love we gave thee, not only wouldest thou not have doubted, but have perceived what in priestly seriousness it was thy duty to do. For Cyriacus [7], formerly

abbot, who was the bearer of our letter, was not a man of such training and erudition as to dare, as thou supposest, to make up another, nor for thee to entertain this suspicion of falseness against his character. But, while putting aside consideration of our wholesome admonitions, thou hast come to be culpable, not only in thy deeds, but in thy questionings also. For indeed it had been reported to us that, inflamed with inconsiderate zeal, thou hadst broken images of saints, as though under the plea that they ought not to be adored [8]. And indeed in that thou forbadest them to be adored, we altogether praise thee; but we blame thee for having broken them. Say, brother, what priest has ever been heard of as doing what thou hast done? If nothing else, should not even this thought have restrained thee, so as not to despise other brethren, supposing thyself only to be holy and wise? For to adore a picture is one thing, but to learn through the story of a picture what is to be adored is another. For what writing presents to readers, this a picture presents to the unlearned who behold, since in it even the ignorant see what they ought to follow; in it the illiterate read. Hence, and chiefly to the nations [9], a picture is instead of reading. And this ought to have been attended to especially by thee who livest among the nations, lest, while inflamed inconsiderately by a right zeal, thou shouldest breed offence to savage minds. And, seeing that antiquity has not without reason admitted the histories of saints to be painted in venerable places, if thou hadst seasoned zeal with discretion, thou mightest undoubtedly have obtained what thou wert aiming at, and not scattered the collected flock, but rather gathered together a scattered one; that so the deserved renown of a shepherd might have distinguished thee, instead of the blame of being a scatterer lying upon thee. But from having acted inconsiderately on the impulse of thy feelings thou art said to have so offended thy children that the greatest part of them have suspended themselves from thy communion. When, then, wilt thou bring wandering sheep to the Lord's fold, not being able to retain those thou hast? Henceforth we exhort thee that thou study even now to be careful, and restrain thyself from this presumption, and make haste, with fatherly sweetness, with all endeavour, with all earnestness, to recall to thyself the minds of those whom thou findest to be disjoined from thee.

For the dispersed children of the Church

---

[6] Other epistles to Serenus of Marseilles are **VI. 52, IX. 105, XI. 58.** In **IX. 105** he had already been reproved for his inconsiderate zeal in breaking pictures of saints, which is the main subject of the present letter. His reply to the former letter, or which he had affected to suspect the genuineness, seems to have called forth this longer and severer admonition.

[7] Cyriacus, once abbot of Gregory's own monastery of St. Andrew on the Cœlian at Rome, is named in the former epistle to Serenus (**IX. 105**) as its bearer. As to the cause of his being sent at that time into Gaul, see notes to **IX. 105**, and **IX. 109.**

[8] See **IX. 105.**

[9] *Gentibus.* The term *gentes* was used not only to denote Gentiles as usually understood, and pagan races as distinct from Christians, but also nations outside the Roman republic.

must be called together, and it must be shewn then by testimonies of sacred Scripture that it is not lawful for anything made with hands to be adored, since it is written, *Thou shalt adore the Lord thy God, and him only shalt serve* (Luke iv. 8). And then, with regard to the pictorial representations which had been made for the edification of an unlearned people in order that, though ignorant of letters, they might by turning their eyes to the story itself learn what had been done, it must be added that, because thou hadst seen these come to be adored, thou hadst been so moved as to order them to be broken. And it must be said to them, If for this instruction for which images were anciently made you wish to have them in the church, I permit them by all means both to be made and to be had. And explain to them that it was not the sight itself of the story which the picture was hanging to attest that displeased thee, but the adoration which had been improperly paid to the pictures. And with such words appease thou their minds; recall them to agreement with thee. And if any one should wish to make images, by no means prohibit him, but by all means forbid the adoration of images. But let thy Fraternity carefully admonish them that from the sight of the event portrayed they should catch the ardour of compunction, and bow themselves down in adoration of the One Almighty Holy Trinity.

Now we say all this in our love of Holy Church, and of thy Fraternity. Be not then shaken, in consequence of my rebuke, in the zeal of uprightness, but rather be helped in the earnestness of thy pious administration.

Furthermore, it has come to our ears that thy Love gladly receives bad men into its society; so much so as to have as a familiar friend a certain presbyter who, after having fallen, is said to live still in the pollution of his iniquity[1]. This indeed we do not entirely believe, since he that receives such a one does not correct wickedness, but rather appears to give licence to others to perpetrate the like things. But, lest haply by any subornation or dissimulation he should prevail on thee to receive him and keep him still in favour, it becomes thee not only to drive him further from thee, but also in all ways to cut away his excesses with priestly zeal. But as to others who are reported to be bad, study to restrain them from their badness by fatherly exhortation, and to recall them to the way of rectitude. But, if (which God forbid) you seem not to

profit them at all by salutary admonition, these also thou wilt take care to cast off far from thee, lest, from their being received, their evil doings should seem not at all to displease thee, and lest not only they themselves should remain unamended, but others also should be corrupted in consequence of thy reception of them. And consider how execrable it is before men, and how perilous before the eyes of God, if vices should seem to be nurtured through him whose duty it is to punish crimes. Attend therefore to these things diligently, most beloved brother; and study so to act as both wholesomely to correct the bad and to avoid breeding offence in the minds of thy children by associating with evil men.

### EPISTLE XXV.

#### To JANUARIUS, BISHOP OF CARALIS (*Cagliari*[2]).

Gregory to Januarius, &c.

Know ye that your Fraternity's solicitude has pleased us, in that you have evinced, as was right, pastoral vigilance for the guardianship of souls. For indeed it has been reported to us that you have forbidden a monastery to be founded in the house of the late Epiphanius, a reader of your Church, in accordance with his will, for this reason; lest, seeing that this house was adjacent to a monastery of handmaidens of God[3], deception of souls should thence ensue. And we praised you greatly for guarding, as became you, by suitable foresight against the snares of the ancient foe. But, since we have been informed that the religious lady Pompeiana is desirous of taking away the handmaidens of God from this same monastery, and restoring them to their own monasteries whence they had been taken, and establishing there a congregation of monks, it is necessary that if this be accomplished, the disposition of the deceased should in all respects be adhered to. But, if this should not be done, that the will of the testator may not seem to be entirely frustrated, we will that—inasmuch as the monastery of the late abbot Urban, situated outside the city of Caralis, is said to be left so destitute that not even one monk remains there—we will, I say, that John, whom the said Epiphanius appointed to be abbot in the monastery which, as has been said, he had determined should be founded in his house, be ordained abbot (*i.e. of the late Urban's monastery*), provided only that there be no impediment against him.

And let the relics which were to have been deposited in the house of the aforesaid Epi-

---

[1] Cf. Ep. LV. in this book to Virgilius of Arles, the metropolitan of Serenus, in which this laxity on the part of the latter is alluded to.

[2] See I. 62, and *reff*.    [3] See I. 48.

phanius be deposited there, and let whatever the same Epiphanius had contributed for the intended monastery in his own house be in all ways applied to the other ; that so, even though for safeguard, as above written, his will is not carried out with regard to the place, the benefit intended may nevertheless be preserved inviolate. And indeed let your Fraternity, together with the guardian (*defensore*) Vitalis, arrange all this, and endeavour to order it so advantageously that you may have your reward, as for your praiseworthy prohibition, so also for your good settlement of the case. Lastly, though it may be superfluous to commend this monastery to your Fraternity, yet we abundantly exhort you that, as becomes you, with due regard to justice, you hold it as commended to you [4].

## EPISTLE XXVIII.

### To Augustine, Bishop of the Angli [5].

Gregory to Augustine, &c.

*Glory to God in the highest, and on earth peace to men of good will* (Luke ii. 14) ; because a grain of wheat, falling into the earth, has died, that it might not reign in heaven alone ; even He by whose death we live, by whose weakness we are made strong, by whose suffering we are rescued from suffering, through whose love we seek in Britain for brethren whom we knew not, by whose gift we find those whom without knowing them we sought. But who can describe what great joy sprung up here in the hearts of all the faithful, for that the nation of the Angli through the operation of the grace of Almighty God and the labour of thy Fraternity has cast away the darkness of error, and been suffused with the light of holy faith ; that with most sound mind it now tramples on the idols which it formerly crouched before in insane fear ; that it falls down with pure heart before Almighty God ; that it is restrained by the rules of holy preaching from the lapses of wrong doing ; that it bows down in heart to divine precepts, that in understanding it may be exalted ; that it humbles itself even to the earth in prayer, lest in mind and soul it should lie upon the earth. Whose is this work but His who says, *My Father worketh hitherto, and I work*

(John v. 17)? who, to shew that He converts the world, not by men's wisdom, but by His own power, chose unlettered men as His preachers whom He sent into the world? And He does the same even now, having deigned to work mighty works in the nation of the Angli through weak men. But in this heavenly gift, dearest brother, there is ground, along with great joy, for most serious fear. For I know that Almighty God has displayed great miracles through thy Love in the nation which He has willed to be chosen. Wherefore thou must needs rejoice with fear for this same heavenly gift, and tremble in rejoicing :— rejoice, that is, because the souls of the Angli are drawn by outward miracles to inward grace ; but tremble, lest among the signs that are done the infirm mind lift itself up to presumption about itself, and from being exalted in honour outwardly, fall inwardly through vain glory. For we ought to remember how, when the disciples returned with joy from preaching, and said to their heavenly Master, *Lord, in thy name even the devils are subject unto us* (Luke x. 17), they straightway heard, *In this rejoice not ; but rather rejoice because your names are written in heaven* (Ib. v. 20). For they had set their minds on private and temporal gladness, when they rejoiced in the miracles. But they are recalled from private to common, from temporal to eternal gladness, when it is said to them, *In this rejoice ye, because your names are written in heaven.* For not all the elect work miracles ; and yet the names of all of them are kept enrolled in heaven. For to the disciples of the Truth there should not be joy, save for that good which they have in common with all, and in which they have no end to their gladness.

It remains, therefore, dearest brother, that in the midst of the things which through the operation of God thou doest outwardly, thou shouldest ever nicely judge thyself within, and nicely understand both what thou art thyself and how great is the grace in the midst of that same nation for the conversion of which thou hast received even the gift of doing signs. And if at any time thou shouldest remember having offended against our Creator, whether in tongue or in deed, ever recall these things to thy memory, that memory of guilt may keep down the rising glory of the heart. And whatsoever thou mayest receive, or hast received, in the way of doing signs, regard these powers as not granted to thyself, but to those for whose salvation they have been conferred upon thee.

Further, there occurs to my mind, while I think on these things, what took place with

---

[4] For further reference to the subject of this letter, see XIV. 2. It appears there that Epiphanius, mentioned in this letter, had been a son-in-law of Pompeiana. It appears further that this lady afterwards accused both the bishop Januarius and the *defensor* Vitalis of having unjustly withheld her son-in-law's pious bequest, notwithstanding the admonition contained in this letter.

[5] For reasons for supposing this letter to Augustine to have been written earlier than the 4th Indiction (A.D. 600-1), to which it is assigned by the Benedictine Editors, and for a summary of the whole series of letters relating to the English mission, see *Prolegom.*, p. xxv.

one servant of God, even one eminently chosen. Certainly Moses, when he led God's people out of Egypt, as thy Fraternity knows, wrought wonderful miracles. Fasting forty days and nights in Mount Sina, he received the tables of the Law; among lightnings and thunders, while all the people trembled, he was attached to the service of Almighty God, being alone with Him even in familiar colloquy (Exod. xxx., xxxi.); he opened a way through the Red Sea; he had a pillar of a cloud to lead him on his journey; to the people when an hungered he gave manna from heaven; flesh to those who longed for it he supplied in the wilderness by a miracle, even unto overmuch satiety (Exod. xiii., xiv., xvi.). But, when in a time of drought they had come to the rock, he was distrustful, and doubted being able to draw water from the same, which still at the Lord's command he opened without fail in copious streams. But how many and great miracles after these he did during eight and thirty years in the desert who can count or search out (Exod. xvii.; Num. xx.)? As often as a doubtful matter had troubled his mind, he resorted to the tabernacle, and enquired of the Lord in secret, and was forthwith taught concerning it, God speaking to him (Exod. xxxiii. seq.). When the Lord was wrath with the people, he appeased Him by the intervention of his prayer; those who rose in pride and dissented in discord he engulphed in the jaws of the gaping earth; he bore down his enemies with victories, and shewed signs to his own people. But, when the land of promise had at length been reached, he was called into the mountain, and heard of the fault which he had committed eight and thirty years before, as I have said, in that he had doubted about drawing water from the rock. And for this reason he was told that he might not enter the land of promise (Num. xxvii.). Herein it is for us to consider how formidable is the judgment of Almighty God, who did so many signs through that servant of His whose fault He still bare in remembrance for so long a time.

Wherefore, dearest brother, if we find that even he whom we know to have been especially chosen by Almighty God died for a fault after so many signs, with what fear ought we to tremble, who do not yet know whether we are chosen?

But what should I say of the miracles of the reprobate, when thy Fraternity well knows what the Truth says in the Gospel; *Many shall come in that day saying to me, Lord in thy name we have prophesied, and in thy name have cast out devils, and in thy name have done many wonderful works. But I will say unto them, I know not who ye are: depart from me all ye workers of iniquity* (Matth. vii. 22; Luke xiii. 27)? The mind, then, should be much kept down in the midst of signs and miracles, lest haply one seek therein one's own glory, and exult in private joy for one's own exaltation. For through signs gains of souls should be sought, and His glory by whose power these very signs are done. But there is one sign that the Lord has given us for which we may exceedingly rejoice, and acknowledge the glory of election in ourselves, seeing that He says, *In this shall it be known that ye are my disciples, if ye have love one to another* (John xiii. 35). Which sign the prophet demanded, when he said, *Make with me, Lord, a sign for good, that they which hate me may see it, and be confounded* (Ps. lxxxv. 17).

These things I say, because I desire to abase the mind of my hearer in humility. But let thy very humility have its confidence. For I, a sinner, maintain a most certain hope that through the grace of our Almighty Creator and Redeemer, our God and Lord Jesus Christ, thy sins are already remitted, and thou art chosen for this purpose, that those of others may be remitted through thee. Nor will you have sorrow for any guilt in the future, while you strive to cause joy in heaven for the conversion of many. Truly the same our Maker and Redeemer, speaking of the repentance of men, says, *Verily I say unto you there will be joy in heaven over one sinner that repenteth, more than over ninety and nine just persons, which need no repentance* (Luke xv. 7). And if for one penitent there is great joy in heaven, of what kind may we believe the joy to be for so large a people, converted from its error, which, coming to faith, has condemned by penitence the evil things it did. In this joy, then, of heaven and the angels let us repeat the very words of the angels with which we began: let us say therefore, let us all say, *Glory to God in the highest, and on earth peace to men of good will.*

## EPISTLE XXIX.

### To Bertha, Queen of the Angli [6].

Gregory to Bertha, &c.

They who desire, after earthly dominion, to obtain the glory of a heavenly kingdom ought to labour earnestly to bring in gain to their Creator, that they may be able to rise by the steps of their operation to the things they long

---

6 As to the apparent inference from this letter that King Ethelbert of Kent had not been converted when it was written, and as to when it may have been sent to queen Bertha, see *Prolegom.*, p. xxvi., note 2.

for; as we are glad to know you do. For indeed our most beloved son Laurentius the presbyter, and Peter the monk, have brought us word on their return to us how your Glory has exhibited itself towards our most reverend brother and fellow-bishop Augustine, and how great succour and what charity you have bestowed upon him. And we bless Almighty God, who has been mercifully pleased to reserve the conversion of the nation of the Angli for your reward. For, as through Helena of illustrious memory, the mother of the most pious Emperor Constantine, He kindled the hearts of the Romans into Christian faith, so we trust that He works in the nation of the Angli through the zeal of your Glory. And indeed you ought before now, as being truly a Christian, to have inclined the heart of our glorious son, your husband, by the good influence of your prudence, to follow, for the weal of his kingdom and of his own soul, the faith which you profess, to the end that for him, and for the conversion of the whole nation through him, fit retribution might accrue to you in the joys of heaven. For seeing, as we have said, that your Glory is both fortified by a right faith and instructed in letters, this should have been to you neither slow of accomplishment nor difficult. And since, by the will of God, now is a suitable time, so proceed, with the co-operation of divine grace, as to be able to make reparation with increase for what has been neglected. Wherefore strengthen by continual hortation the mind of your glorious husband in love of the Christian faith; let your solicitude infuse into him increase of love for God, and so kindle his heart even for the fullest conversion of the nation subject to him that both he may offer, out of the zeal of your devotion, a great sacrifice to the Almighty Lord, and that the things related of you may both grow and be in all ways proved to be true : for your good deeds are known not only among the Romans, who have prayed earnestly for your life, but also through divers places, and have come even to the ears of the most serene prince at Constantinop'e. Hence, as great joy has been caused us by the consolations of your Christianity, so also may there be joy in heaven for your perfected work. So acquit yourselves devotedly and with all your might in aid of our above-named most reverend brother and fellow-bishop, and of the servants of God whom we have sent to you, in the conversion of your nation that you may both reign happily here with our glorious son your husband, and after long courses of years may also attain the joys of the future life, which know no end. Now we pray Almighty God that He would both kindle the heart of your Glory with the fire of His grace to perform what we have spoken of, and grant you the fruit of an eternal reward for work well-pleasing to Him.

## EPISTLE XXX.

### To Venantius, Ex-Monk, Patrician of Syracuse [7].

Gregory to Venantius, &c.

In addressing to you the greeting which is due I was intending to speak of what I suffer. But I think I need not relate to you what you know. For I am tormented by pains of gout, which, afflicting not dissimilarly both me and you, while they increase upon us exceedingly, have caused our life to decrease. In the midst of them what else should we do but recall our faults to mind, and give thanks to Almighty God? For we who have sinned in many things from the pampering of the flesh are purged by the affliction of the flesh. We are to know also that present pain, if it converts the mind of the afflicted one, is the end of preceding guilt ; but, if it does not convert to the fear of the Lord, is the beginning of pain to follow. We must therefore take care, and in entire conversion of heart watch to the utmost of our power with tears, lest we pass from torment to torments. We are also to consider by how great a dispensation of loving-kindness our Maker deals with us, in that He continually smites us, who are worthy of death, and still slays us not. For He threatens what He will do, and yet does it not, that pains sent in advance may alarm us, and, when we are converted to the fear of the strict Judge, may shield us from His animadversion when life is over. For who may tell, who may count, how many, sunk in their lechery, running headlong also in blasphemies and pride, continuing in robberies and iniquities even to the day of their death, have so lived in this world as never to suffer even a headache, but by a sudden stroke have been delivered to the fires of hell? We, then, have a token that we are not forsaken, in that we are continually scourged, according to the testimony of Scripture, which says, *Whom the Lord loveth He chasteneth, and scourgeth every son whom He receiveth* (Heb. xii. 6). Wherefore under the very stripes of God let us recall to mind both His gifts and the losses of our guilt. Let us consider what good things He has showered upon our ill-doing, and what ill things we have

---

7 See I. 34, note 8. It is significant of Gregory's delicate tact, that he does not in this letter, when his friend was suffering, allude to his past renunciation of monastic life as among the sins to be repented of, or urge him to return to it, though that the subject was still on his mind appears from his letter about the same time to the Bishop of Syracuse (XI. 36).

committed under His goodness. Let us fulfil what the Lord says through the prophet, *Put me in remembrance, that we may plead together* (Isai. xliii. 26). Let us plead now in our thought with God, that we be not hereafter strictly judged by God. For what says Paul? *If we would judge ourselves, we should not be judged of the Lord* (1 Cor. xi. 31). Whosoever, then, would make haste to escape the strictness of the sentence of the judgment to come, let him, through the bitterness of penitence, cut off for himself all the sweetness of the present life. Moreover, whatever gifts of this kind there are, whose gifts are they but our Maker's? But that should not be accounted a gift of God fully to us which separates us through delight in itself from the love of God; lest we should prefer the things given to the Giver, and while receiving good things, though ourselves evil, we should be disjoined from His fear by that whereby we ought to have grown in His fear. Now may the Creator of all things, that is Almighty God, pour into your heart by the inspiration of His Spirit what we speak to you of by letter, and cleanse you from all defilements of sin, and grant you the joy of His comfort here, and hereafter eternal rewards with Himself. I beg that my most sweet daughters, the lady Barbara and the lady Antonina, be greeted in my name.

## EPISTLE XXXII.

### To Marinianus, Bishop of Ravenna.

Gregory to Marinianus, &c.

When the bearer of these presents, Candidus the abbot, came hither to ask for relics (which have also been granted), as much as I rejoiced in thy Fraternity's nursing aid, thy Fraternity's care for me being therein apparent, so much was I distressed that I could not enjoy his presence as I wished to do, seeing that he found me sick, and, when he departed, left me still in a state of weakness. For it is now a long time since I have been able to rise from bed. For at one time the pain of gout torments me, at another a fire, I know not of what kind, spreads itself with pain through my whole body; and it is generally the case that at one and the same time burning pain racks me, and body and mind fail me. Further, what other great distresses of sickness beside what I have mentioned I am affected by, I am unable to recount. This however I may briefly say, that the infection of a noxious humour so drinks me up that it is pain to me to live, and I anxiously look for death, which alone I can hope for to relieve my groans. Accordingly, most holy brother, implore for me the com-

passion of divine loving-kindness, that it would mercifully mitigate towards me the scourges of its smiting, and grant me patience to endure, lest (which God forbid) my heart break out into impatience from excessive weariness, and the guilt which might have been well cured through stripes be increased by murmuring. Given in the month of February, Indiction 4.

## EPISTLE XXXIII.

### To Marinianus, Bishop of Ravenna.

Gregory to Marinianus, &c.

On the arrival here of a certain man of Ravenna, I was smitten by most grievous sorrow for that he told me of thy Fraternity being sick from vomiting of blood. On this account we have caused enquiry to be made carefully and severally of those here whom we know to be well-read physicians, and have sent in writing to your Holiness their several opinions and prescriptions. All, however, prescribe before all else quiet and silence, which I greatly doubt whether thy Fraternity can have in thine own Church. And accordingly it seems good to me that, when the Church there has been provided for—whether with such as may accomplish the solemnities of mass, or with such as may take charge of the episcopate, and may be able to shew hospitality and hold receptions, or such as may superintend the guardianship of monasteries— thy Fraternity should come to me before the summer season, that I may, as far as I can, take special charge of thy sickness, and keep thee from being disturbed, since the physicians say that the summer season is exceedingly dangerous for this kind of sickness. And I greatly fear lest, if thou shouldest have any cares together with the unfavourableness of the season, there might be further risk to thee from this disorder. I too myself am very weak, and it is in all respects advantageous that thou shouldest, with the favour of God, return to thy Church in health; or certainly, if thou art to be called, that thou shouldest be called in the hands of thy friends; and that I, who see myself to be very near death, if Almighty God should be pleased to call me before thee, should pass away in thy hands. But if the circumstances of the present time stand in the way of thy coming, Ago [8] may be treated with, some small present being given him, that he may himself send one of his people with thee as far as Rome. If, then, thou feelest thyself held heavily by this sickness, and

---

[8] i.e. Agilulph, the Lombard king, referred to as Ago also in IV. 11. It was the Lombard occupation of a great part of Italy at that time that was apprehended as kely to impede a journey from Ravenna to Rome.

arrangest to come, thou must come with few attendants, since, while thou stayest with me in the episcopal residence (*episcopium*), thou wilt have daily attendance from this Church.

Furthermore, I neither exhort nor admonish thee, but straitly charge thee, that thou by no means presume to fast, since the physicians say that the practice is very prejudicial to this disorder ; except that, if by chance a great solemnity demands it, I concede it five times in the year.  Thou must also refrain from vigils ; and let the prayers which in the city of Ravenna are wont to be said over the wax-taper, and the expositions of the Gospel which are given by priests about the time of the Paschal solemnity, be delivered by another.  And by no means impose on thyself, beloved, any labour beyond thy powers.  I have said this, that, if thou shouldest feel thyself better, and shouldest put off thy coming, thou mayest know what to observe by my command.

## EPISTLE XXXV.

### To Barbara and Antonina[9].

Gregory to Barbara, &c.

Having received your Glory's letters, which spoke with tears for words, we, most beloved daughters, are affected by no less sorrow than yourselves for your father's sickness.  For we cannot account that sadness as extraneous which is made our own by the law of charity.  But, since in no state of despair ought there to be distrust in the mercy of our Redeemer, raise your spirits for the comforting of your father, place your hope in the hand of Almighty God, and by His protection we trust that He will guard you from all adversity, and cheer your tribulation, and grant you to be favourably disposed of according to your father's desires.  But should He pay the debt of our human lot, even then let not any despair crush you, nor the words of any persons cause you alarm.  For after God, Who is the governor and protector of orphans, we will be so solicitous in behalf of your most sweet Glory, and will so make haste, with the Lord's help, to provide as we can for your advantage, that no rough handling of unjust men may perturb you[1], and that we may repay in all ways the debt we have contracted from the goodness of your parents.  And so may heavenly grace nurture you with its favour and defend you by its protection from all evils, that your safety may become our joy.

## EPISTLE XXXVI.

### To John, Bishop of Syracuse[2].

Gregory to John, &c.

I have received your Fraternity's letters telling me of the sickness of my most sweet son the lord Venantius, and relating how all things are going on about him.  But when I heard at one and the same time that he was desperately and grievously sick, and that unfair men were laying claim to the property of the orphans, the sorrow in my heart could scarce contain itself.  But in this there was comfort, in that tears relieved my groans.  Your Holiness therefore ought not to neglect, what should be your first care, to take thought for his soul, by exhorting him, beseeching him, putting before him God's terrible judgment, and promising His ineffable mercy, so as to induce him to return even at his last moments to his former state of life[3], lest the guilt of so great a fault should stand against him in the eternal judgment.  And then it is your duty to take thought how his daughters, the ladies Barbara and Antonina, may be disposed of, so that no opportunity be afforded to bad men.  For after he had conjured me to take anxious care for them, adding that I should see to the disposal of them, he went on in his letter to mention a thing which, when I consider the matter, I have no doubt might stand in the way.  For he says that I should repeatedly petition the most pious lord Emperor, that he should himself cause provision to be made for the disposal of them.  You observe how different this is from his former wish.  And I fear lest an apt opportunity might hence be given to men in Sicily who are seeking an opportunity for interfering in his affairs.  For, when this is known, what will those men do who have already, as report goes, been attempting to put a seal on his effects[4]?  Would not reason seem to be on their side, and to afford them as it were a just ground for this proceeding ?  If they should say, the girls have been commended to the lord Emperor ; we cannot neglect the matter ; it is at our peril if we do ; we make the property safe till such time as the lord Emperor may order them to be taken to Constantinople ;—tell me, I pray thee, what I could do in such a case, wherein the father's commendation seems to

support a man that has authority. For he con-
jures me to see to their being so disposed of
that they may either be in the Roman city or
not be taken away from Sicily; and he so acts
as to leave no way of either bringing them
hither or retaining them there. But, do you,
as far as you can, oppose these bad men.
Defend their substance for the sake of
Almighty God as if it were your own: and,
if it is still possible, see to all opportunity
for wrong being removed with regard to the
will of the aforesaid lord Venantius. But,
if it is thought fit that they should be commended to the palace, he ought not to impose
such a burden on me as to wish to charge
my soul with the care of the disposal of them;
as to which be it enough that God Almighty
knows how I am taking thought. Hence
I have taken care to write at once to my
most beloved son the deacon Anatolius,
bidding him endeavour to speak with the
glorious patrician lady Rusticiana [5], and telling
him in what manner he should enquire and
inform me about the persons whose names
have been transmitted to me; that so he may
inform us of all things speedily, and what is to
be done, may under the ordering of God be
arranged.

Furthermore, in the letters that have been
sent to us we find that your Fraternity has
been grieved at our not having wished you
to come hither, as though it had been on
account of some displeasure; whereas we
acted with a sole view to utility, knowing
that on account of persons in your locality
your presence there was exceedingly necessary.
But, lest you should hence suppose that we
have any feeling or displeasure towards you
(which God forbid), if you have the will to
come to us, present yourself at a suitable time
at the threshold of the apostles. For, so far
as we are concerned, we so love your Charity
that we desire to see you often.

### EPISTLE XXXVII.

#### To Romanus, Guardian (*Defensorem*).

Gregory to Romanus, Guardian of Sicily [6].

It has come to our knowledge that, if any
one has a suit against any clerics, thou causest
these clerics to be brought before thee for
judgment, setting at nought their bishops.
If this be so, seeing that it is evidently very
unsuitable, we order thee by this our authority
that thou presume not to do it any more.
But, if any one should have a suit against any
cleric, let him go to his bishop, that either

he may take cognizance himself, or at any
rate that judges may be deputed by him; or,
if it should be a case for arbitration, let the
executive authority deputed by him compel
the parties to choose a judge. But, if any
cleric or lay person should have a suit against
a bishop, then thou oughtest to interpose,
so that either thou thyself mayest take cognizance of the matter between them or that
on thy admonition they may choose for themselves judges. For, if each single bishop has
not his own jurisdiction reserved to him, what
else is done but that ecclesiastical order is
confounded through us by whom it ought to
be guarded?

Further, it has been reported to us that,
certain clerics having been sent into penance
for fault requiring it by our most reverend
brother bishop John, thou hast on thy own
authority, without his knowledge removed them
from it. Now, if this is true, know that thou
hast done a thing altogether unseemly, and
calling for no light reproof. Wherefore restore
these clerics without delay to their bishop.
And beware of committing this fault in future:
for, shouldest thou be inattentive, know that
thou wilt incur our anger in no slight degree.

### EPISTLE XXXVIII.

#### To Vitus, Guardian (*Defensorem* [7]).

Gregory to Vitus, &c.

If thou art held bound by no condition or
liability to bodily service, and hast not been
a cleric of any other city, and if there is no
canonical objection to thee, it is our will and
pleasure, with a view to the advantage of the
Church, that thou receive the office of
Guardian of the Church, in order that thou
mayest execute incorruptly and diligently
whatever may be enjoined thee by us for the
benefit of the poor; using this privilege which
after deliberation we have conferred on thee,
so as to do thy diligence faithfully in accomplishing all that may be enjoined thee by us,
as having to render an account of thy doings
before the judgment of our God. This epistle
we have dictated for writing to Paterius,
*secundicerio notario* of our Church [8], and have
subscribed it.

### EPISTLE XL.

#### To Marinianus, Bishop of Ravenna.

Gregory to Marinianus, &c.

Great infirmity constrains us, dearest brother.

---

5 See II. 27, note 2.
6 For the appointment of Romanus, cf. IX. 18.

7 Cf. V. 29.
8 *Primicerius notariarum* occ. III. 22. "*Primicerius*,
Primus cujusque ordinis.—*Secundicerius*, Qui post primicerium
est in schola qualibet." *D'Arnis' Lexicon.*

from which if we were free, we should seem justly blamable. But since, while we are in this fragile body, we cannot subsist but by subservience to its weaknesses, we ought not to blush for what necessity imposes on us. And so, since physicians all say that to those who suffer from eruption of blood fasts are injurious, we exhort thy Fraternity by this present address that, recalling to mind what thou hast been accustomed to endure from sickness, thou by no means impose on thyself the labour of fasting[9]. If, however, by the mercy of God, thou knowest thyself to be so far improved in health as to have sufficient strength, we permit thee to fast once or twice in the week. But of this it befits thee before all things to take care, that thou in no wise subject thyself to any feeling of irritation, lest the sickness, which is believed to be now lighter and as it were suspended, should be experienced afterwards more heavily through exasperation.

## EPISTLE XLIV.

### To Rusticiana, Patrician[20].

Gregory to Rusticiana, &c.

I have received the letters of your Excellency, which altogether relieved me, while I was in a state of most grievous sickness, with regard to your health, your devotion, and your sweetness. One thing however I took amiss, namely that in the same epistles to me what might have been said once was said repeatedly; "Your handmaiden," and "your handmaiden." For, I having been made the servant of all through the burdens of episcopacy, with what reason does she call herself my handmaid whose own I was before I undertook the episcopate? And so I beseech you by Almighty God, that I may never find this word in what you write to me. Further, the gifts which out of a most pure and sincere heart you sent to the blessed Peter, Prince of the apostles, have been received and hung up there[1] in the presence of all the clergy. But my son, the magnificent lord Symmachus, finding me ill from pains of gout and almost despaired of, deferred giving me your letters, and gave them long after the veils had been received: and I found afterwards in your Excellence's letters that they were to have been borne to the Church of the blessed Peter with a litany. And so this was not done, because, as I have already said, we received the veils before the letters. Nevertheless the aforesaid Symmachus did with your

whole household what you wished us to do with the clergy. But, even if the voices of men were wanting, your offering itself has its own voice before Almighty God. In His loving-kindness I trust that the intercession of him whose body you have covered on earth may protect you in heaven from all sins, and in his provision rule your house, and in his watchfulness guard it.

With regard to the affliction of gout which you signify to us has come upon you, I am both distressed and rejoiced exceedingly : rejoiced, because the noxious humour, attacking the lower parts of your body, has entirely left the higher ones ; but distressed, because I fear you suffer excessive pain in so very slender a body. For where there is a deficiency of flesh, what strength can there be to resist pain? For as to myself, you know what I used to be : but now bitterness of soul and continual exasperation, and besides this the affliction of gout so affects me that my body is dried up even as if in burial. Hence it comes to pass that I can rarely now rise from bed. If, then, the pain of gout has reduced the mass of my body to such dryness, what must I think of your body, which was too dry before the pains came on?

As to the alms which you have bestowed on the monastery of the blessed Apostle Andrew, there is no need for me to say anything, since it is written, *Hide thine alms in the bosom of a poor man, and it shall pray for thee* (Ecclus. xxix. 15). If then the good deed itself has its voice in the secret ears of God, whether we cry aloud or keep silence, this very thing which you have well done cries aloud. Moreover I declare that there are so great miracles, there is so great care and custody of the monks in this same monastery of the said apostle that it is as if he himself were specially the abbot of the monastery. For, to speak of a few things out of many which I have learnt from the narration of the abbot and the prior of the monastery, two brethren were one day sent out thence to buy something for the use of the monastery, one a junior who seemed to be distinguished for prudence, the other a senior, sent to be the guardian of the junior. Both went forth, and from the money they received as the price of what they were to purchase, he who had been sent as the guardian of the junior purloined something without the knowledge of the other. Having both of them presently returned to the monastery, and come to the threshold of the oratory, he who had committed the theft fell down seized by a demon, and began to be vexed. And, when the demon had let him go, he was asked by the monks who came round him whether perchance he had purloined anything from what he had received: he denied, and was a second time vexed. Eight times he denied, and eight times was vexed. But after his eighth denial he confessed how much money he had purloined. And repenting he acknowledged, prostrate on the earth, that he had sinned, and, when he had undergone penance, the demon came to him no more.

At another time also, on the anniversary of the same apostle, while the brethren were resting during the mid-day hours, suddenly a certain brother, having become blind with his eyes open, began to tremble, to utter loud cries, testifying by these cries that he could not bear what he was suffering. The brethren ran together to him, saw him blind with his eyes open, trembling, and crying out, abstracted from the scene around him, and having no sense of anything that could be done externally. They lifted him in their hands, and cast him before the altar of Saint Andrew the Apostle, prostrating themselves also in prayer for him. And he at once, coming to himself again, declared what he had suffered; namely that a certain old man appeared to him, and set a black dog at him to tear him, saying, Why wouldest thou flee from this monastery? And, when I could by no means have escaped (said he) from the bites of the dog, certain monks came, and besought that old man for me, who straightway bade the dog depart, and then I came to myself. And he often afterwards confessed, saying, On the day on which I suffered these things I had had a design of flying from this same monastery.

Another monk also secretly desired to depart from the same monastery. And, having considered the matter in his mind, he would have entered the oratory; but he was immediately delivered to a demon and most sorely vexed. But he used to be left by the demon, and if he remained outside the oratory, he would suffer no harm; but, if he attempted to enter it, he was at once delivered to the evil spirit and vexed. And, when this took place frequently, he confessed his fault, namely that he was thinking of going away from the monastery. Then the brethren, assembled in his behalf, bound themselves to continue in prayer for him for three days, and he was so cured that the evil spirit never came to him afterwards. He used to say also that he had seen the same blessed apostle while he was being vexed, and had been reproached by him for wishing to depart from the monastery.

Two other brethren also fled from the same monastery, and gave some intimations previously to the brethren in conversation that they were going down by the Appian way, to make for Jerusalem; but, when they had gone out, they turned aside from the road. And, that there might be no possibility of their being found by any that might follow them, finding some retired crypts near the Flaminian gate, they hid themselves therein. But when they had been looked for in the evening, and not found in the monastery, certain brethren followed them on horseback, going out by the gate of Metronus, to follow them along the Latin or Appian way. But suddenly they conceived the design of looking further for them on the Salarian way: and so, in proceeding outside the city, they turned their course into the Salarian way. But, failing to find them, they decided to return through the Flaminian gate. And, as they were returning, presently when their horses came in front of the crypts in which the men were hidden, they stood still, and, though beaten and urged, refused to move. The monks considered that such a thing could not be without some mystery. They observed the crypts, and saw the entrance to them to be blocked by a piled heap of stones, but, as their horses would not go in any direction, they dismounted. They displaced the stones which were placed at the mouth of the crypts, entered, and found the men in a state of consternation within these dark subterranean hiding-places. They were taken back to the monastery, and were so improved by this miracle that it was of great advantage to them to have fled for a short time from the monastery.

I have told you these things that it may be known to your Excellency whose oratory it is on which you have bestowed your alms. Now may Almighty God keep you under His heavenly protection both in soul and in body and all your house, and grant you to live long for our consolation. I beg that my most beloved son the Lord Strategius[2] with his glorious parents your children may be greeted in my name.

### EPISTLE XLV.

#### To THEOCTISTA, PATRICIAN [3].

Gregory to Theoctista, &c.

We ought to give great thanks to Almighty God, that our most pious and most benignant

---

[2] Strategius (as appears from other letters) was the young grandson of Rusticiana, being the child of Appio and Eusebia. See II. 27, note 2.

[3] Sister of the emperor Mauricius, and governess of the imperial children. See also I. 5, VII. 26. This long letter to her was called forth by her having complained to Gregory of erroneous views in matters of religion being imputed to her at Constantinople, for which she seems to have been maligned in certain quarters. In his reply, with his habitual courtesy, he takes for granted that such imputations were unfounded, though the pains he takes to combat the errors with which she was charged may perhaps suggest the idea of his not being in his heart quite assured of her soundness. The whole letter, both for its tone and for its style of argumentation, is very characteristic of the writer.

Emperors have near them kinsfolk of their race, whose life and conversation is such as to give us all great joy. Hence too we should continually pray for these our lords, that their life, with that of all who belong to them, may by the protection of heavenly grace be preserved through long and tranquil times.

I have to inform you, however, that I have learnt from the report of certain persons how that, owing to the levity of the people, a tumult of detraction has arisen against you. And I hear that your Excellency has consequently been distressed with no slight vexation. If this is so, I wonder much why the words of men on earth should agitate you, who have fixed your heart on heaven. For the blessed Job, when his friends who had come to console him had broken out into rebuke, said, *For behold my witness is in heaven, and he that knows me is on high* (Job xvi. 20). For one who has the witness of his life in heaven ought not to be afraid of the judgments of men on earth. Paul also, a leader of good men, says, *Our glory is this, the testimony of our conscience* (2 Cor. i. 12). And he says again, *Let every man prove his own work, and so shall he have glory in himself, and not in another* (Gal. vi. 4). For, if we are rejoiced by praises and broken down by detractions, we have set our glory not in ourselves, but in the mouth of others. And indeed the foolish virgins took no oil in their vessels, but the wise ones took oil in their vessels with their lamps (Matth. xxv.). Now our lamps are good works; of which it is written, *Let your light shine before men, that they may see your good works, and glorify your Father which is in heaven* (Matth. v. 16). And we then take oil in our vessels with our lamps, when we seek not the splendour of glory for our good deeds from the adulation of our neighbours, but preserve it in the testimony of our conscience. And in regard to all that is said of us outwardly we ought to recur to the secrets of our soul. Although all should revile us, yet he is free whom conscience accuses not, while, even though all should praise, one cannot be free, if conscience accuses him. Whence the Truth says concerning John, *What went ye out into the wilderness to see? A reed shaken with the wind?* (Matth. xi. 7). And this in truth is said in the way of negation, not of assertion, since it is added, *But what went ye out for to see? A man clothed in soft raiment? Behold, they that wear soft clothing are in kings' houses* (Ibid. 8). For although, according to the truth of the Gospel, John was clothed in rough raiment, yet the signification is that they wear soft clothing who are delighted by adulations and praises. And it is denied that John was a reed shaken

with the wind, inasmuch as no breath from any human mouth bent the fortitude of his mind. For we, if we are lifted up by praises, or cast down by revilings, are a reed shaken with the wind. But far be this, far be it from the heart of your Excellency. I know that you read studiously the teacher of the Gentiles, who says, *I, if I yet pleased men, should not be the servant of Christ* (Gal. i. 10).

If, however, any even slight sadness has arisen in your mind from this cause, I believe that Almighty God has kindly allowed this to be the case. For not even to His elect in this life has He promised the joys of delight, but the bitternesses of tribulation; so that, after the manner of medicine, they may be restored through a bitter cup to the sweetness of eternal salvation. For what says He? *The world shall rejoice and ye shall lament* (Joh. xvi. 20). With what hope? With what promise? A little afterwards it is added, *I will see you again, and your heart shall rejoice, and your joy no man shall take from you* (Ibid. 22). Hence again He says to His disciples, *In your patience shall ye possess your souls* (Luke xxi. 19).

Consider, I pray you, where patience would be, if there were nothing to be endured. I suspect that there is no Abel without having a Cain for his brother. For if the good were without the bad, they could not be perfectly good, since they would not be purged: and the very society of the bad is the purgation of the good. There were three sons of Noe in the ark, one of whom was a derider of his father, who, though in himself he was blessed, still received a sentence of condemnation in his son. Abraham had two sons before he took Cethura to wife; and yet his carnal son persecuted the son of promise (Genes. ix.). This the great teacher expounds, saying, *As he who is after the flesh persecuted him that is after the Spirit, even so it is now* (Gal. iv. 29). Isaac had two sons; but one, who was spiritual, fled before the threats of his carnal brother. Jacob had twelve sons, but one, who lived uprightly, was sold by ten into Egypt. In the case of the prophet David, because there was in him what should have been purged, it was brought to pass that he suffered under a son's persecution. The blessed Job says of the society of the reprobate, *I have been a brother to dragons, and a companion to owls* (Job xxx. 29). To Ezekiel the Lord says, *Son of man, unbelievers and destroyers are with thee, and thou dost dwell among scorpions* (Ezek. ii. 6). Among the twelve apostles there was one reprobate, that there might be one by whose persecution the eleven might be tried. The Prince of the apostles speaks thus to his disciples, *He delivered just Lot, oppressed by the injury and conversation of the wicked. For in seeing and hearing he was just, dwelling among those who from day to day vexed the soul of the just one with their unrighteous deeds* (2 Pet. ii. 7, 8). Paul also the apostle writes to his disciples, saying, *In the midst of a crooked and perverse nation, among whom ye shine as luminaries in the world, holding fast the word of life* (Philip. ii. 15).

Seeing then that we know from the witness of Scripture that in this life the good cannot be without the bad, your Excellency ought by no means to be disturbed by the voices of fools, especially as there is then sure confidence in Almighty God, when for well-doing any adversity is given us in this world in order that a full reward may be reserved for us in the eternal retribution. Whence also in the holy Gospel the Truth says, *Blessed shall ye be when men shall say all manner of evil against you falsely for my name's sake* (Matth. v. 11). And for our consolation He deigned to adduce as an example His own reproaches, saying, *If they have called the master of the house Beelzebub, how much more them of his household* (Ibid. x. 25).

But there are many who perhaps praise the life of the good more than they ought ; and, lest any elation should creep in from praise, Almighty God allows bad men to break out into slander and objurgation, in order that, if any sin springs up in the heart from the mouth of them that praise, it may be choked by the mouth of them that revile. Hence it is, then, that the teacher of the Gentiles testifies that he continues in his preaching *through evil report and good report* (2 Cor. vi. 8) ; saying also, *As deceivers and yet true.* If then there were such as laid an evil report on Paul, and called him a deceiver, what Christian now should account it a hard thing in behalf of Christ to hear injurious words? Moreover we know of how great virtue was the precursor of our Redeemer, who in Holy Writ is called not only more than a prophet, but even an angel : and yet, as the history of his death testifies, after his death his body was burnt by his persecutors[4]. But why say we these things of holy men? Let us speak of the Holy of holies Himself, that is of God Who was made man for us, Who before His death heard the injurious charge that He had a devil, and after His death was called a deceiver by His persecutors, when one said, *We know that that deceiver said, After three days I will rise again* (Matth. xxvii. 63). How much, then, must we sinners needs bear from the

tongues and hands of wicked men, we who are to be judged at the coming of the eternal Judge, if He Who will even come as Judge endured so much both before and after His death ?

These things, most sweet and excellent daughter, I have briefly said, lest, as often as thou hearest of foolish men speaking in derogation of thee, thou shouldest be touched by even the least sadness of heart. But, seeing that this very murmuring of foolish men cannot be allayed by quiet reason, I hold it to be sin if the doing of what can be done is neglected. For, when we appease insane minds, and bring them back to a healthy state, we ought by no means to cause them offence. For there are some offences that are to be altogether despised ; but there are some which, when they can be avoided without guilt, are not to be despised, lest there be guilt in keeping them alive. We learn this from the preaching of the sacred Gospel ; since, when the Truth said, *Not that which goeth into the mouth defileth a man ; but that which cometh out of the mouth, this defileth a man* (Matth. xv. 11), and the disciples replied saying, *Knowest thou that the Pharisees were offended after they heard this saying?* (Ibid. 12), straightway He replied, *Every plant which my heavenly Father hath not planted shall be rooted up. Let them alone ; they be blind, and leaders of the blind* (Ibid. 13). And yet, when tribute was demanded, He first gave a reason why tribute should not be paid, and forthwith subjoined, *Notwithstanding, lest we should offend them, go thou to the sea, and cast an hook, and take up the fish that first cometh up ; and when thou hast opened his mouth, thou shalt find a stater. That take, and give unto them for me and for thee* (Matth. xvii. 26). Why is it that of some who were offended it is said, *Let them alone ; they are blind, and leaders of the blind ;* and that to others, lest they should be offended, tribute is paid by the Lord, even though not due? Why is it that He allowed one offence to remain, but forbade another to be caused to others? Why, but that He might teach us on the one hand to despise offences which implicate us in sin, but on the other to mitigate in all ways those which we can appease without sin?

Wherefore your Excellency, God protecting you, may, with great quietness, turn aside the offences of bad men. For the chief of them you should of your own accord call to you privately and give them reasons, and anathematize certain wrong points which they suppose to be held by you. And if too, as it is said may be the case, they suspect such anathema to be insincere, you should confirm it even by an oath, averring that you do not

---

4 Cf. Theodoret, *Eccles. Hist.* lib, ii. c. 6, where this is told : "asseruerunt arcam Joannis Baptistæ, et ossibus combustis dissiparunt cinerem."

hold, and never have held, those points. Nor let it seem beneath you to satisfy them in such a way; nor let there be in your mind any feeling of disdain against them on account of your imperial race. For we are all brethren, created by the power of one Emperor, and redeemed by His blood. And so we ought not in anything to despise our brethren, however poor and abject.

For certainly Peter had received power in the heavenly kingdom, so that whatever he should bind or loose on earth should be bound or loosed in heaven; he walked on the sea, he healed the sick with his shadow, he slew sinners with his word, he raised the dead by his prayer. And because by the admonition of the Spirit he had gone in to Cornelius the Gentile, a question was raised against him by the believers as to why he had gone in among Gentiles and eaten with them, and why he had received them in baptism. And yet this first of the apostles, filled with such gifts of grace, supported by such power of miracles, replied to the complaint of the believers, not by power but by reason, and explained the case to them in order; how he saw a certain vessel, as it had been a sheet, in which were four-footed beasts of the earth, and wild beasts, and creeping things, and fowls of the air, let down from heaven, and heard a voice saying, *Arise, Peter, kill and eat* (Acts xi. 5 seq.); how three men came to him calling him to Cornelius; how the Holy Spirit bade him go with them; how the same Holy Spirit who had been wont to come on those baptized in Judea after baptism, came on the Gentiles before baptism. For if, when he was blamed by the believers, he had paid regard to the authority which he had received in Holy Church, he might have replied that the sheep should not dare to find fault with the shepherd to whom they had been committed. But, had he said anything of his own power in answer to the complaint of the believers, he would not have been truly a teacher of gentleness. He pacified them, therefore, by giving a reason humbly, and even produced witnesses to defend him from blame, saying, *Moreover these six brethren accompanied me* (Acts xi. 12). If, then, the pastor of the Church, the Prince of the Apostles, who singularly did signs and miracles, disdained not, in defending himself from blame, humbly to give a reason, how much more ought we sinners, when we are blamed for anything, to pacify those who blame us by giving a reason humbly!

For to me, as you know, when I was resident at the footsteps of my lords in the royal city, many used to come of those who were accused with respect to the aforesaid points.

But I declare, my conscience bearing me witness, that I never found in them any error, any pravity, or anything of what was said against them. Whence also I took care, despising report, to receive them familiarly, and rather to defend them from their accusers For it used to be said against them that under pretext of religion they dissolved marriages; and that they said that baptism did not entirely take away sins; and that, if any one did penance for three years for his iniquities, he might afterwards live perversely; and that, if they said under compulsion that they anathematized anything for which they were blamed, they were by no means holden by the bond of anathema. Now if there are any who undoubtedly hold and maintain such views, there is no doubt but that they are not Christians. And such both I, and all catholic bishops, and the universal Church, anathematize, because they think what is contrary to the truth, and speak what is contrary. For, if they say that marriages should be dissolved for the sake of religion [5], be it known that, though human law has conceded this, yet divine law has forbidden it. For the Truth in person says, *What God hath joined together let not man put asunder* (Matth. xix. 6). He says also, *It is not lawful for a man to put away his wife saving for the cause of fornication* (Ibid. 9). Who then may contradict this heavenly legislator? We know how it is written, *Two shall be one flesh* (Matth. xix. 5; 1 Cor. vi. 16; Gen. ii. 24). If, then, a man and wife are one flesh, and a man puts away his wife for the sake of religion, or a woman her husband while he remains in this world, even though perchance he turns aside to unlawful deeds, what is this conversion [6], in which one and the same flesh on the one part passes to continence and on the other part remains in pollution? If, however, it should suit both to lead a continent life, who may dare to accuse them, since it is certain that Almighty God, who has granted what is less, has not forbidden what is greater? And indeed we know of many holy persons who have both previously led continent lives with their consorts, and have afterwards passed over to the rules of holy Church. For in two ways holy men are accustomed to abstain even from lawful things. Sometimes that they may increase their merits before Almighty God; but sometimes that they may wipe away the sins of their former life. For when the three children who were brought under obedience to the Babylonian King, asked for pulse for food, being unwilling to make use of the king's

---

5 *Religionis*, in the sense of monastic life.
6 *Conversio*, in the usual sense of embracing monastic life.

meat, it was not because it would have been sin in them to eat what God had created. They were unwilling, then, to take what it was lawful for them to take, that their virtue might increase through continence. But David, who had taken to himself another man's wife, and had been sorely scourged for his fault, desired long afterwards to drink water from the cistern of Bethlehem; which when his bravest soldiers had brought to him, he refused to drink it, and poured it out as a libation to the Lord. For it was lawful for him to drink it, had he been so minded; but, because he remembered having done what was unlawful, he laudably abstained even from what was lawful. And he, who to his guilt previously feared not that the blood of dying soldiers should be shed, afterwards considered that, were he to drink the water, he would have shed the blood of living soldiers, saying, *Shall I drink the blood of these men who have put their lives in jeopardy* (1 Chron. xi. 19)? Accordingly, when good husbands and wives desire either to increase merit or to do away with the faults of previous life, it is lawful for them to bind themselves to continence and to aspire to a better life. But, if the wife does not follow after the continence which the husband aspires to, or the husband refuses that which the wife aspires to, it is not lawful for wedlock to be cut asunder, seeing that it is written, *The wife hath not power of her own body, but the husband; and the husband hath not power of his own body, but the wife* (1 Cor. vii. 4).

But, if there are any who say that sins are only superficially put away in baptism, what can be more against the faith than such preaching, whereby they would fain undo the very sacrament of faith, wherein principally the soul is bound to the mystery of heavenly cleanness, that, being completely absolved from all sins, it may cleave to Him alone of Whom the Prophet says, *But it is good for me to cleave to God* (Ps. lxxii. 28 [7])? For certainly the passage of the Red Sea was a figure of holy baptism, in which the enemies behind died, but others were found in front in the wilderness. And so to all who are bathed in holy baptism all their past sins are remitted, since their sins die behind them even as did the Egyptian enemies. But in the wilderness we find other enemies, since, while we live in this life, before reaching the country of promise, many temptations harass us, and hasten to bar our way as we are wending to the land of the living. Whosoever says, then, that sins are not entirely put away in baptism, let him say that the Egyptians did

not really die in the Red Sea. But, if he acknowledges that the Egyptians really died, he must needs acknowledge that sins die entirely in baptism, since surely the truth avails more in our absolution than the shadow of the truth. In the Gospel the Lord says, *He that is washed needeth not to wash, but is clean every whit* (Joh. xiii. 10). If, therefore, sins are not entirely put away in baptism, how is he that is washed clean every whit? For he cannot be said to be clean every whit, if he has any sin remaining. But no one can resist the voice of the Truth, *He that is washed is clean every whit.* Nothing, then, of the contagion of sin remains to him whom He Himself who redeemed him declares to be clean every whit.

But, if there are any who say that penance is to be done for sin during any three years, and that after the three years one may live in pleasures, these know neither the preaching of the true faith nor the precepts of sacred Scripture. Against these the excellent preacher says, *He that soweth in his flesh shall of the flesh also reap corruption* (Galat. vi. 8). Against these he says again, *They that are in the flesh cannot please God* (Rom. viii. 8); where he subjoins to his disciples, *But ye are not in the flesh, but in the Spirit.*

Now they are in the flesh who live in carnal pleasures. Against them it is said, *Neither shall corruption possess incorruption* (1 Cor. xv. 50). But, if they say that a short season of penitence may suffice against sin, so that one may be allowed to return again to sin, rightly does the sentence of the first pastor hit them, when he says, *It is happened unto them according to the true proverb; The dog is turned to his own vomit again, and the sow that was washed to her wallowing in the mire* (2 Pet. ii. 22). For great is the efficacy of penitence against sin; but only if one persevere in this penitence. For it is written, *He that shall persevere unto the end, the same shall be saved* (Matth. x. 22 : xxiv. 13). Hence again it is written, *He that is baptized from a dead body, and toucheth it again, what availeth his washing?* (Ecclus. xxxiv. 30 [8]). Now a dead body is every perverse work, which draws a man to death, because he lives not in the life of righteousness. He, then, is baptized from a dead body, and again touches it, who deplores the bad works which he remembers having done, but after his tears entangles himself in the same again. Washing, therefore, from such dead body avails not any soul that does again what it has bemoaned, and rises not through the lamentations of penitence to the rectitude of

---

7 In *English Bible*, lxxiii. 28.

8 In *English Bible*, xxxiv. 25.

righteousness. For to do penance truly is not only to bemoan what has been committed, but also to decline from what has been bemoaned.

But, if there are any who say that, if any one shall have anathematised anything under compulsion of necessity, he is not held by the bond of the anathema, these are themselves witnesses that they are no Christians. For they think by vain attempts to loose the binding of holy Church, and hereby neither do they account as real the absolution of holy Church which she offers to the faithful, if they think that her binding is of no avail. Against such as these dispute should be no longer held, since they ought to be altogether scorned and anathematised ; and whence they think to elude the truth, thence let them in reality be bound in their sins.

If, then, there are any who under the Christian name dare either to preach, or to hold silently in their own minds, the points of error which we have spoken of above, these undoubtedly we both have anathematised and do anathematise. Yet, as I have said before, in those who used to come to me in the royal city I observed no error at all as to any one of the aforesaid points, nor do I think there was any. For, if there had been, I should have observed it. However, since there are many of the faithful who are inflamed with unwise zeal, and often, while they attack certain persons as though they were heretics, themselves make heresies, consideration should be had for their infirmity, and, as I have said before, they should be appeased with reason and gentleness. For indeed they are like unto those of whom it is written, *I bear them record, that they have a zeal of God, but not according to knowledge* (Rom. x. 2). Wherefore your Excellency, who live incessantly in reading, in tears, and in alms, should, as I have requested, appease their unwisdom by gentle exhortations and replies, that not only in yourself, but also in them, you may find the glory of eternal retribution. All this my exceeding love has induced me to say to you, since I think that your joy is my gain, and your sadness my loss. May Almighty God guard you with heavenly grace, and, keeping safe the Piety of our lord and the Tranquillity of our most pious lady, prolong your life for the education of the little lords.

## EPISTLE XLVI.

To Isacius, Bishop of Jerusalem [9].

Gregory to Isacius, &c.

In keeping with the truth of history, what means the fact that at the time of the flood the human race outside the ark dies, but within the ark is preserved unto life, but what we see plainly now, namely that all the unfaithful perish under the wave of their sin, while the unity of holy Church, like the compactness of the ark, keeps her faithful ones in faith and in charity ? And this ark in truth is compacted of incorruptible timber, since it is built of strong souls, and such as persevere in good. And, when any single person is converted from a secular life, timber is, as it were, still cut down from the mountains. But when, according to the order of holy Church, one is assigned to have custody of others, it is as though the ark were built of timber sawn and put together for preserving the life of men. And in truth that ark, when the flood was over, rested on a mountain, because when the corruption of this life is over, when the billows of evil works have passed away, holy Church will rest in the heavenly country, as on a high mountain. To the building, therefore, of this ark we rejoice to find, after reading your Fraternity's epistle, that in the compactness of a right faith you lend your aid ; and we render great thanks to Almighty God, who, though the pastors of His flock are changed, keeps the faith which He once delivered to the holy Fathers, even after them unchangeable. Now the excellent preacher says, *Other foundation can no man lay than that is laid, which is Christ Jesus* (1 Cor. iii. 11). Whosoever, then, with love of God and his neighbour, holds firmly the faith which is in Christ, he has laid the same Jesus Christ, Son of God and man, as a foundation for himself from the Father. It is to be hoped, then, that, where Christ is the foundation, the building also of good works may follow. The Truth itself also in person says, *He that entereth not by the door into the sheepfold, but climbeth up some other way, the same is a thief and a robber. But he that entereth in by the door is the shepherd of the sheep* (Joh. x. 1). And a little afterwards He adds, *I am the door*. He, then, enters into the sheepfold by the door who enters by Christ. And he enters by Christ who thinks and preaches what is true concerning the same Creator and Redeemer of the human race, keeps what he preaches, and undertakes the topmost place of government with a view to a burdensome office, not in desire of the glory of transitory dignity. He watches also wisely over the charge of the sheepfold which he has taken in hand, lest either perverse men speaking frowardly tear

---

9 Written in reply to a letter received from the new patriarch of Jerusalem, announcing, as was usual, his election, and containing his confession of faith.

the sheep of God, or malignant spirits waste them by persuading them to vicious delights.

But in all these things may He instruct us Who for our sake was made man. May He Who vouchsafed to become what He made Himself infuse the spirit of His love both into my infirmity and thy charity, and open the eye of our heart in all carefulness and watchful circumspection.

But that men of a right faith are advanced to sacred orders, thanks should be given without cease to the same Almighty God, and prayer should ever be made for the life of our most pious and Christian lord the Emperor, and for his most tranquil spouse, and his most gentle offspring, in whose times the mouths of heretics are silent, since, though their hearts seethe in the madness of perverse opinion, yet in the time of the orthodox Emperor they presume not to speak out the wrong opinions which they hold; so that we plainly see fulfilled what is written, *Gathering the waters of the sea together as in a bottle* (Ps. xxxii. 7)[1]. For the water of the sea is gathered together as in a bottle, because whatever wrong opinions the bitter science of heretics entertains at the present day it keeps within the breast, and presumes not to express them openly. But thy Fraternity, spiritually taught, has set forth in all respects the right faith, and has thoroughly declared the things that should be sought after. Your faith, therefore, is ours. We hold what you say, and say what you hold.

But, inasmuch as it has come to our ears that in the Churches of the East no one attains to sacred orders but by giving of bribes, if your Fraternity finds that this is the case, you should offer as your first oblation to Almighty God the restraining of the error of simoniacal heresy in the Churches subject to you. For, not to speak of other things, what sort of men can they be when in sacred orders who are advanced to them not by merit but by bribes? Now we know with what animadversion the Prince of the apostles attacked this heresy, having pronounced the first sentence of condemnation against Simon, when he said, *Thy money be with thee unto perdition, because thou hast thought that the gift of God may be purchased with money* (Acts viii. 20). Our Lord God Himself also, the Creator and Redeemer of the human race, having made a scourge of small cords, overthrew and cast out of the temple the seats of them that sold doves (Matth. xxi.). For to sell doves in the temple, what else is it but to give for a price in holy Church that im-

position of hands whereby the Holy Spirit is given? But the seats of them that sold doves were overthrown, because the priesthood of such is not accounted as priesthood.

Moreover, I have been informed that in the Church which is called Neas, strifes often arise with your Church in the city of Jerusalem. Wherefore your Holiness ought carefully to consider all things, and to correct some things gently, but bear others that cannot be corrected with equanimity. For we see plainly what is said by holy Church through the voice of the Psalmist, *Sinners have built upon my back* (Ps. cxxviii. 3)[2]. For on the back burdens are borne. Sinners, then, build upon our back, when we bear with sufferance those whom we cannot correct. For the steersman of a ship, when he considers that the wind is against him, surmounts some billows by steering right over them, but some which he foresees cannot be surmounted he prudently avoids by turning his course aside. So, therefore, let your Holiness mitigate some evils by repressing them, and others by bearing them, so as in all respects to conserve the peace of them that dwell together in the holy Church of Jerusalem. For it is written, *Follow peace with all men, and holiness, without which no man shall see God* (Hebr. xii. 14). For in quarrels the very light of the soul, the light of good intent, is blocked. Whence the Psalmist says, *Mine eye is troubled because of anger* (Ps. vi. 8). And what remains in us of well-doing, if we lose peace from the heart, without which we cannot see the Lord? Do you therefore so act as to gather the gain of your reward even from those who through strife might have caused it to perish. May Almighty God guard your Love with heavenly grace, and grant you to carry with you from those who are committed to you manifold fruit and measure running over to eternal joys.

### EPISTLE XLVII.

#### To Anatolius, Deacon at Constantinople.

Gregory to Anatolius, &c.

Thy Love has written to me that our most pious lord orders a successor to be appointed to my most reverend brother John, bishop of Prima Justiniana, on account of the ailment of the head from which he suffers, lest perchance that city, while without the jurisdiction of a bishop, should be ruined by its enemies, which God forbid. And yet the canons nowhere enjoin that a bishop should be superseded on account of sickness. And it is

---

[1] In A.V. xxxiii. 7.

[2] In A.V. cxxix. 3.

altogether unjust that, if bodily ailments come on, the sick person should be deprived of his dignity[3]. Accordingly this thing can by no means be done through us, lest sin should come upon my soul from his deposition. But it is to be suggested that, if he who bears rule is sick, an administrator may be found, to undertake all his charge, and maintain and fill his place, without his being deposed, in the government of the Church and custody of the city; so that neither may Almighty God be offended nor the city be found to be neglected. If, however, the same most reverend John should haply on account of his ailments request to be relieved from the dignity of the episcopate, it should be conceded on his presenting a petition in writing. But otherwise we are altogether unable, with due regard to the fear of Almighty God, to do this thing. But, if he should be unwilling thus to make petition, what pleases the most pious Emperor, whatever he commands to be done, is in his power. As he determines, so let him provide. Only let him not cause us to be mixed up in the deposition of one so situated. Still, what he does, if it is canonical, we will follow. But, if it is not canonical, we will bear it, so far as we can without sin of our own.

## EPISTLE L.

### To Adrian, Notary.

Gregory to Adrian, Notary of Panormus.

Agathosa, the bearer of these presents, complains that her husband has, against her will, been converted[4] in the monastery of the abbot Urbicus. And, since this undoubtedly touches the credit and reputation of the said abbot, we enjoin thy Experience to investigate the matter by diligent enquiry, so as to see whether it may not be the case that the man's conversion was with her consent, or that she herself had promised to change her state. And should it be found to be so, see to his remaining in the monastery, and compel her to change her state, as she had promised. If however neither of these things is the case, and you do not find that the aforesaid woman has committed any crime of fornication on account of

which it is lawful for a man to leave his wife, then, lest his conversion should possibly be an occasion of perdition to the wife left behind in the world, we desire thee, without any excuse allowed, to restore her husband to her, even though he should be already tonsured. For, although mundane law declares that marriage may be dissolved for the sake of conversion against the will of either party, yet divine law does not permit this to be done. For, save for the cause of fornication, a man is on no account allowed to put away his wife, seeing that after the husband and wife have been made one body by the copulation of wedlock, it cannot be in part converted, and in part remain in the world[5].

## EPISTLE LIV.

### To Desiderius, Bishop of Gaul[6].

Gregory to Desiderius, &c.

Many good things having been reported to us with regard to your pursuits, such joy arose in our heart that we could not bear to refuse what your Fraternity had requested to have granted to you. But it afterwards came to our ears, what we cannot mention without shame, that thy Fraternity is in the habit of expounding grammar to certain persons. This thing we took so much amiss, and so strongly disapproved it, that we changed what had been said before into groaning and sadness, since the praises of Christ cannot find room in one mouth with the praises of Jupiter. And consider thyself what a grave and heinous offence it is for bishops to sing what is not becoming even for a religious layman. And, though our most beloved son Candidus the presbyter, having been, when he came to us, strictly examined on this matter, denied it, and endeavoured to excuse you, yet still the thought has not departed from our mind, that in proportion as it is execrable for such a thing to be related of a priest, it ought to be ascertained by strict and veracious evidence whether or not it be so. Whence, if hereafter what has been reported to us should prove evidently to be false, and it should be clear that you do not apply yourself to trifles and secular literature, we shall give thanks to our God, who has not permitted your heart to be stained with the blasphemous praises of the

---

3 Cf. XIII. 5 for a similar assertion of the unlawfulness of superseding a bishop, except at his own request, when incapacitated by illness. See also VII. 19. In this epistle may be observed Gregory's habitual deference to the Emperors, whose subject he ever declared himself to be, even in matters of ecclesiastical import, together with his avoidance of giving his own sanction to anything he regarded as irreligious or uncanonical. Similarly in the case of an imperial prohibition of soldiers becoming monks. See III. 65; VIII. 5; X. 24. Cf. also IV. 47, in the case of Maximus of Salona. We find him, however, in a letter to the empress, in which this case of Maximus is referred to (V. 21), making a respectful protest against imperial interference in matters of ecclesiastical cognizance.
4 *Conversum*, in the usual sense of adopting monastic life.

5 Cf. VI. 48, and XI. 45.
6 Desiderius was bishop of Vienne, cf. VI. 54. This letter, with others that follow (Epp. LV., LVI., LVII., LVIII., LIX., LX., LXI., LXII., LXIV., LXV., LXVI., and possibly also the preceding Epistle, XXIX.) were carried, as appears from its conclusion, by Mellitus and his companions, who, in answer to Augustine's request, were sent by Gregory from Rome to reinforce the mission to Britain (Bede, *H.E.* I. 27, 29). See *Prolegomena*, p. xxvi It is notable as shewing Gregory's views with regard to the study of secular literature.

abominable; and we will treat without misgiving or hesitation concerning the granting of what you request.

We commend to you in all respects the monks whom together with our most beloved son Laurentius the presbyter and Mellitus the abbot we have sent to our most reverend brother and fellow-bishop Augustine, that, through the succour of your Fraternity, no delay may stop their onward progress.

## EPISTLE LV.

### To Virgilius, Bishop of Arelate (*Arles*)[7].

Gregory to Virgilius, &c.

Since by the testimony of Holy Writ avarice is called the service of idols, with what earnestness it ought to be banished from the temple of God is acknowledged; and yet (we say it with groaning) by some priests this is not regarded. For fierce cupidity holds the heart captive, and persuades one that what it commands is lawful, and so proceeds as to slay with the same sword both the giver and the receiver. What safe place, then, can hereafter be of avail against avarice, if the Church of God is opened to it by bad priests? How can he keep the sheepfolds inviolate who invites the wolf to enter? Alas for shame! He pollutes his hands by an unlawful bribe, and thinks to lift up others by his benediction, while himself prostrate under his own iniquity, and captive notwithstanding to his own ambition. Since then this evil of rapacity has never entered the citadel of your mind, and you say that you have your hands unpolluted in the matter of ordinations, give thanks to Almighty God, and acknowledge yourselves to be His debtors in that under His protection you have remained unharmed by the contagion of this disease. But this good in you will profit you less than it might have done if you have not carefully forbidden this thing in others also. As in thyself this evil had displeased thee, thou oughtest to have been zealous against it in thy brother also. For, seeing that the divine precepts admonish us to love our neighbours as ourselves, it is no small fault to disregard them, and not to fear for others what for ourselves we shrink from. Even now, therefore, most beloved brother, give thy mind to repairing what thou hast lost in others through thy negligence in correction, and restrain whomsoever thou canst from this wickedness, and insist on a synod being assembled for rooting out this same heresy, to the end that, with reward to thy

Love, what shall have been condemned, God granting it, by the ordinance of all may be better guarded against by all.

Furthermore, it has come to our ears that our brother and fellow-bishop, Serenus of Massilia (*Marseilles*), receives bad men into his intimate society, so as to have, in fine, as his familiar friend a certain presbyter, who, after lapse, is said to wallow still in his iniquities. This you ought to enquire into closely. And, if it should prove to be so, let it be your care so to correct this matter in our stead that both he who has received such a one may learn not to encourage him by familiarity, but rather to constrain him by punishment, and he who has been received may learn to wash away his sins with tears, and not to pile up iniquity by unclean living.

Let your Fraternity hold as commended to you in all respects the monks whom we have sent to our brother and fellow-bishop Augustine, and take pains so to succour them for proceeding on their way, and so to concur with them, that through your assistance they may be able, under the protection of God, to arrive speedily at their destination.

## EPISTLE LVI.

### To Aetherius, Bishop of Lugdunum (*Lyons.*)

Gregory to Aetherius, Bishop of Gaul.

The language of your epistles, full of venerable gravity, has so engaged our heart's affection that it would please us to be ever mingling mutual discourse, to the end that, if we cannot enjoy your bodily presence, absence may make no difference with us while this intercourse goes on between us. For how great love of ecclesiastical order shines forth in you, and how great is your regard for discipline, and how great your earnestness in the observance of wholesome ordinances, you shew in that you receive our exhortation submissively and altogether willingly, and declare that you will inviolably observe it. Since then you bear a heart prompt for the amendment of others, and condemn with a free voice, as becomes you, an evil of old standing, and seeing that our other brethren and fellow-bishops also are similarly disposed, it is your duty to rise unanimously against the Lord's enemies, and cast avarice out of the house of God by a synodical definition. In the giving of ecclesiastical orders let not fierce hunger for gold find any satisfaction; let not flatteries filch any advantage; let not favour confer anything: let a man's life have the reward of honour, his modesty promote his advancement; that, while this kind of ob-

---

[7] The bishop of Arles had vicariate jurisdiction committed to him under Rome. Cf. V. 53.

servance obtains, both he that seeks to rise by bribes may be judged unworthy, and he to whom his conduct bears good testimony may be worthily honoured.  Let this be your care, most beloved brother, let this anxiety ever keep guard over your thoughts, so that you may prove by action that the zeal which you shew in your letters is the witness of your heart. Wherefore continually and instantly press for the assembling of a synod ; and so earnestly acquit yourself as to act up to the dignity of your title in the administration of your office.

With regard to what you request to have granted to your Church on the ground of ancient custom, we have caused search to be made in our archives, and nothing has been found.  Wherefore send to us the letters which you say you have, that from them we may gather what ought to be granted you.

As to the acts or writings of the blessed Irenæus, we have now long been searching for them, but have not succeeded so far in finding any of them.

Furthermore, let your Fraternity take care to hold as in all respects commended to you the monks whom we despatched to our brother and fellow-bishop Augustine, and for the sake of God display your charity towards them ; and so earnestly concur with them in priestly zeal, and so hasten to help them with your succour for proceeding on their journey, that, while there shall be no cause of delay in your parts to detain them, both they may go on their way more speedily, and you may find a reward for what you have done in their behalf.  Given this 10th day of July, Indiction 4 [8].

## EPISTLE LVII.

### To Aregius, Bishop of Vapincum [9].

Gregory to Aregius, Bishop of Gaul.

There being in brotherly love one heart and one soul, as the mind rejoices in the prosperity of another, so is it afflicted in his adversity, since in both it is bound to be partaker by the law of charity.  And so the greater sorrow had come upon us for your sadness, lest perchance the affliction of a prolonged grief might batter your heart with continual pain, and burden your life with groans.  But, having received the letters of your Charity, we have been consoled with the joy we hoped for, and we give thanks to Almighty God, for that we now know that your equanimity is unimpaired, and that your mind has been restored to comfort.  Nor

indeed was it otherwise to be expected of you than that you would undoubtedly overcome with priestly patience whatever adversity there might be.

Further, we well recollect how the zeal of your Fraternity flamed up of old in uprooting simoniacal heresy.  Wherefore we exhort that you give your earnest attention to this, and that, among other things that we wrote of, it be condemned by the strict definition of a council ; that so, the bent of our desire being fulfilled by the help of your solicitude, you may both offer to Almighty God a most acceptable oblation in the correction of vices, and also shew, for the edification of others, how the care of the pastoral office shines forth in you.  Moreover our experience of your life, which we have known to be much superior to that of many, moves us to presume on great assistance from you in this matter.  And so complete ye your kindness as under God you have begun, that the good which with a right aim has been begun in you may, by the help of God the Creator of all, be brought to completion.

Furthermore, let your Fraternity bestow your accustomed charity on the monks whom we have sent to our most reverend brother and fellow-bishop Augustine ; and so endeavour to succour them for proceeding on their way, as well personally as through others as you can, that, while through your provision they have no difficulties or delays in your parts, both we may feel that our confidence in you was not in vain, and Almighty God may give you the recompense of His grace for the conversion of the souls on whose behalf they have been sent.

## EPISTLE LVIII.

### To divers Bishops of Gaul.

Gregory to Mennas of Telona (*Toulon*), Serenus of Massilia (*Marseilles*), Lupus of Cabillonum (*Châlons-sur-Saône*), Aigulfus of Mettæ (*Metz*), Simplicius of Parisii (*Paris*), Melantius of Rotonius (*Rouen*), and Licinius [1], bishops of the Franks.  *A paribus.*

Though the care of the office you have undertaken reminds your Fraternity how you ought to assist with all your endeavours religious men, and especially those who labour in behalf of souls, yet it is not beside the purpose that an address by letter from us should stimulate your assiduity, since, as a fire becomes larger from a blast of air, so the purposes of a good disposition are advanced by commendation.  Inasmuch, then, as through

---

[8] In two MSS. (*Teller.*) " die decimo Kalendas Julii, indict. 4," i.e. 22 June, A.D. 601.  This may be taken as correct, agreeing with other dated epistles sent through Mellitus and his companions.

[9] Cf. IX. 107, to the same Aregius.

[1] Licinius (afterwards canonized) was bishop of Andegavum (*Angers*).

the co-operating grace of our Redeemer so great a multitude of the nation of the Angli is being converted to the grace of Christian faith that our most reverend common brother and fellow-bishop Augustine asserts that those who are with him cannot suffice for carrying out this work in divers places, we have made provision by sending to him a few monks with our most beloved common sons Laurentius the presbyter and Mellitus the abbot. And so let your Fraternity shew them the charity that becomes you, and so make haste to aid them wherever there may be need, that through your assistance they may have no cause for delay in your parts, and that both they themselves may rejoice with you in being relieved by your consolation, and you, by affording them your succour, may be found partakers in the cause in furtherance of which they have been sent.

## EPISTLE LIX.

### To Theoderic, King of the Franks[2].

Gregory to Theoderic, &c.

The letter of your Excellency, which is the index of your heart, has so shewn, in its flow of lucid language, what great prudence is conspicuous in you, along with royal power, that there can be no doubt of the truth of whatever fame has reported in your praise. And inasmuch as you signify, by what you say in praise of it, that our exhortation has so pleased your royal mind that you wish whatever you know to pertain to the worship of our God, to the veneration of Churches, or to the honour of priests, to be both carefully established and in all ways guarded, we appeal to you with a renewed exhortation, with a view to your greater reward, that you would order a synod to be assembled, and, as we have before written, cause corporal vices in priests and the pravity of simoniacal heresy to be condemned by the definition of all the bishops, and to be cut off within the limits of your kingdom, and allow not any longer money to have more effect than the precepts of the Lord. For, since all avarice is the service of idols, whosoever does not watchfully guard against it, and especially in the bestowal of ecclesiastical honours, is subjected to the perdition of infidelity, even though he may seem to hold the faith which he disregards. As, then, against external enemies, so also against adversaries of souls among yourselves, take ye earnest heed, that on account of this your faithful opposition to God's enemies you may both reign prosperously here under His protection,

and also come hereafter by the leading of His grace to eternal joys.

Furthermore, what benefits your Excellence bestowed on our most reverend brother and fellow-bishop Augustine on his progress to the nation of the Angli we have been told by certain monks who have returned to us from him. Wherefore, returning abundant thanks, we beg that you will deign to afford your support in full measure to these monks also who have been sent to him, and to aid them on their onward journey, so that the more amply you shew your kindness to them, the greater return you may expect from Almighty God, whom they serve.

## EPISTLE LX.

### To Theodebert, King of the Franks[3].

Gregory to Theodebert, &c.

One who receives with willing mind and embraces in the bosom of his heart words of fatherly admonition declares himself without doubt to be one who would be an amender of faults. On which account the absolute promise of your Excellence assures us sufficiently. For we hold in place of a pledge the words of one who is good for payment. Therefore let your Excellency vouchsafe, adhering to the commands of our God, to give zealous attention to the assembling of a synod, that every corporal vice in priests, and simoniacal heresy, which was the first to arise in Churches from iniquitous ambition, may under threat of the censure of your power be removed by the definition of a council, and be cut off by the roots ; lest, if gold is loved in your parts more than God, He who now remains tranquil while His precepts are despised be felt hereafter to be wrathful in vengeance. And indeed, because we say all this for your own behoof, we therefore cease not to press you again and again, that we may be able, even by importunity, to do good to our most excellent and most sweet sons. For it will be in all respects of advantage to your kingdom, if what is done in those parts against God be corrected by the emendation of your Excellency.

Furthermore, what good service your Excellency did to our most reverend brother and fellow-bishop Augustine on his progress to the nation of the Angli we have learnt from the report of certain monks who returned to us from him. Rendering you the greatest thanks for this, we beg you to bestow your benefits abundantly on the monks, the bearers of these

---

presents, whom we have sent to our said brother, to the end that, while under your patronage, they find no difficulties in your parts, but accomplish easily with the help of Christ the journey they have undertaken, you may reap your richer fruit of reward before the eyes of our God.

## EPISTLE LXI.

### To Clotaire, King of the Franks [4].

Gregory to Clotaire, &c.

Among so many cares and anxieties which you sustain for the government of the peoples under your sway, it is to your exceeding praise and great reward that you are helpers of those who labour in the cause of God. And, since you have shewn yourselves by the good things you have already done to be such that we may presume still better things of you, we are moved most gladly to request of you what will be to your own reward. Now certain monks, who had proceeded with our most reverend brother and fellow-bishop Augustine to the nation of the Angli, have returned and told us with what great charity your Excellence refreshed this our brother when he was present with you, and with what supports you aided him on his departure. But, since the works of those who do not recede from the good they have begun are acceptable to our God, we beg of you, greeting you with fatherly affection, to hold as peculiarly commended to you the monks, bearers of these presents, whom we have sent to our aforesaid brother, together with our most beloved sons, the presbyter Laurentius and the abbot Mellitus. And whatever kindness you before shewed to him bestow ye on them also to the richer increase of your praise, to the end that, when through your provision they shall have accomplished without delay the journey they have begun, Almighty God may be the recompenser of your good deeds, and both your guardian in prosperity and your helper in adversity.

Furthermore, it has come to our ears that in your parts sacred orders are conferred with payment of money. And we are exceedingly distressed if the gifts of God are not attained by merit, but pounced upon by bribes. And, because this simoniacal heresy, which was the first to arise in the Church, was condemned by the authority of the apostles, we beg of you for your own reward to cause a synod to be assembled; to the end that, having been put down and eradicated by the definition of all

the priests, it may in future find no power in your parts to endanger souls, nor be allowed henceforth to arise under any pretext whatever, that so our Almighty God may exalt you against your adversaries in proportion as He sees that you have zeal in fulfilling His commands, and as you take thought for the salvation of souls which had been in danger of perishing by the sword of this atrocity.

## EPISTLE LXII.

### To Brunichild, Queen of the Franks [5].

Gregory to Brunichild, &c.

We render thanks to Almighty God, Who, among all the other gifts of His loving-kindness that He has bestowed upon your Excellency, has so filled you with a love of the Christian religion that whatever you know to pertain to the gain of souls, whatever to the propagation of the faith, you cease not to carry into effect with devout mind and pious zeal. As to the great favour and assistance wherewith your Excellence aided our most reverend brother and fellow-bishop Augustine on his progress to the nation of the Angli, fame had already not been silent; and after wards certain monks, returning to us from him, gave us a particular account thereof.

And indeed, let others to whom your benefactions are less known wonder at these evidences of your Christianity; for to us who know them by experience they are not a subject of wonder, but of rejoicing, because through what you bestow upon others you delight yourself. Now of what sort and how great are the miracles which our Redeemer has wrought in the conversion of the above-written nation is already known to your Excellency. On which account you ought to have great joy, since the succours afforded by you claim to themselves the larger share herein, it having been through your aid, after God, that the word of preaching became widely known in those parts. For one who aids the good work of another makes it his own. But, that the fruit of your reward may be richer more and more, we beg of you kindly to afford the support of your patronage to the monks, the bearers of these presents, whom we have sent with our most beloved sons, the presbyter Laurentius and the abbot Mellitus, to our aforesaid most reverend brother and fellow-bishop, because of his telling us that those who are with him are not sufficient; and to vouchsafe to stand by them in all things, to the end that, when by the good auspices of

---

[4] Clotaire II., at this time king of Neustria, his capital being Soissons. There is no letter to him among those which had been carried by Augustine. But it appears from this epistle that the missionaries had passed through his dominions and had been well received.

[5] Brunechild was at this time with her grandson Theoderic in the kingdom of Burgundy, having been expelled from Austrasia, according to Greg. Turon. A.D. 599.

your Excellency they shall have had the better success, and shall have found no delays or difficulties in your parts, you may call down the mercy of our God towards you and your most sweet nephews in proportion as you have demeaned yourselves compassionately for the love of Him in causes of this kind.

[(In *Collect. Pauli Diac.*) Given the tenth day of the Kalends of July, Indiction 4.]

## EPISTLE LXIII.

### To Brunichild, Queen of the Franks.

Gregory to Brunichild, &c.

What good gifts have been conferred on you from above, and with what piety heavenly grace has filled you, this, among all the other proofs of your merits, intimates evidently to all, that you both govern the savage hearts of barbarians with the skill of prudent counsel, and (what is still more to your praise), adorn your royal power with wisdom. And since, as you are above many nations in both these respects, so also you excel them in the purity of your faith, we have great confidence in your amending what is unlawful. For the contents of the letters you have already sent us are witness how your Excellency has embraced our exhortation, and with what devotion you long to fulfil the same. But, since He Who is the giver of good dispositions is wont to be their helper also, we trust that He may direct your causes in His loving-kindness all the more favourably as He sees you to be assiduous in His cause. Do you God's work, and God will do yours. Wherefore order a synod to be assembled, and, among other things, as we have before written, studiously prohibit by the definition of a council the sin of simoniacal heresy in your kingdom. Offer a sacrifice to God by conquering the enemy that is within, that by His help you may conquer the enemies that are without ; and that, according to the zeal you evince against His foes, such you may feel Him to be in aiding you. Believe me, moreover, that, as we have learnt from the experience of many, whatever is gathered together with sin is spent with loss. If, then, you wish to lose nothing unjustly, endeavour to the utmost to have nothing got by injustice. For in earthly matters loss has always its origin in sin. You, therefore, if you wish to stand above adverse nations, if you would speedily, with God's leave, be victorious over them, receive with trembling the commandments of the same Almighty God, that He Himself may fight for you against your adversaries, Who has promised in Holy Writ, saying, *The Lord shall fight for you, and ye shall hold your peace* (Exod. xiv. 14).

[*In Collect. Pauli Diac.: Data die decima Kalend., Indict.* 4. *In Remigiano: Data die x Kalendas Julii, Indict.* 4.]

## EPISTLE LXIV.

### To Augustine, Bishop of the Angli [6].

Here begins the epistle of the blessed Gregory, pope of the city of Rome, in exposition of various matters, which he sent into transmarine Saxony to Augustine, whom he had himself sent in his own stead to preach.

PREFACE.—Through my most beloved son Laurentius, the presbyter, and Peter the monk, I received thy Fraternity's letter, in which thou hast been at pains to question me on many points. But, inasmuch as my aforesaid sons found me afflicted with the pains of gout, and on their urging me to dismiss them speedily were allowed to go, leaving me under the same painful affliction ; I have not been able to reply, as I ought to have done, at greater length on every single point.

### *Augustine's first question.*

I ask, most blessed father, concerning bishops, how they should live with their clergy: And concerning the offerings of the faithful which are received at the altars, both into what portions they should be divided, and how the bishop ought to deal with them in the Church.

### *Answer of Saint Gregory, pope of the city of Rome.*

Holy Scripture, which no doubt thou knowest well, bears witness, and especially the epistles of the blessed Paul to Timothy, in which he studied to instruct him how he ought to behave himself in the house of God. Now it is the custom of the Apostolic See to deliver an injunction to bishops when ordained, that of all emoluments that come in

---

6 This important epistle is given below as published in the Benedictine edition, with notes pointing out its main variations from Bede (*H.E.* i. 27), and with addition of the Preface, first published by Mansi (*Supplem. ad Concil. tom.* vi., p. 385), from a MS. Codex of the eighth century (*Cod. Lucen.*). Bede's copy may be regarded as the most authentic, having been brought to him from Rome by Nothelm, A.D. 715–731 (Bede, *H E. Præf.*). However, he does not give the Preface, which has internal evidence of authenticity. Subsequently to Nothelm's visit to Rome, it would seem that the whole epistle had been mislaid there, not having been kept among the rest of Gregory's letters. For St. Boniface, A.D. 736 (*Epist. XL. ad Nothelm. Episc. Cantuar.*) requests Nothelm to send him a copy of these Questions and Answers from England, saying that no copy of them could at that time be found at Rome. They were, we may conclude, discovered subsequently. Internal evidence, as well as historic probability, supports the superior genuineness of Bede's copy. (Cf. *Councils, &c., relating to Great Britain and Ireland*, Oxf., 1871. Vol. III., p. 32.) The edition of the Epistle (*Cod. Lucen.*) above referred to as, published by Mansi, though containing several variations, agrees in many respects with that of Bede, and especially in the absence of " the request of Augustine " (*obsecratio Augustini*) and " the grant of Gregory " (*Concessio Gregorii*) after the answer to the ninth question. See note there.

four divisions should be made : to wit, one for the bishop and his household on account of hospitality and entertainment ; another for the clergy ; a third for the poor ; and a fourth for the reparation of Churches. But, inasmuch as thy Fraternity, having been trained in the rules of a monastery, ought not to live apart from thy clergy in the Church of the Angli, which by the guidance of God has lately been brought to the faith, it will be right to institute that manner of life which in the beginning of the infant Church was that of our Fathers, among whom none said that aught of the things which he possessed was his own, but they had all things common (Acts iv.).

### Augustine's second question[7].

I wish to be taught whether clerics who cannot contain may marry ; and, if they marry, whether they should return to the world.

### Answer of the blessed pope Gregory.

If, however, there are any clerics, not in sacred orders, who cannot contain themselves, they ought to take to themselves wives, and receive their stipends separately, since we know that it is written of those same Fathers whom we have before mentioned, that distribution was made unto every man according as he had need. Wherefore thought should be taken and provision made for their stipends, and they should be kept under ecclesiastical rule, that they may lead good lives, and give attention to the singing of psalms, and by the help of God preserve their heart and tongue and body from all that is unlawful. But as to those who live in community, what is there more for us to say with regard to assigning portions, or shewing hospitality, or executing mercy, seeing that what remains over and above their needs is to be expended for pious and religious uses, as the Lord and Master of us all says, *Of what is over give alms, and behold all things are clean unto you* (Luke xi. 41)?

### Augustine's third question.

Since there is but one faith, why are the uses of Churches so different, one use of Mass being observed in the Roman Church, and another in the Churches of Gaul ?

### Answer of the blessed pope Gregory.

Thy Fraternity knows the use of the Roman Church, in which thou hast been nurtured. But I approve of thy selecting carefully any-thing thou hast found that may be more pleasing to Almighty God, whether in the Roman Church or that of Gaul, or in any Church whatever, and introducing in the Church of the Angli, which is as yet new in the faith, by a special institution, what thou hast been able to collect from many Churches. For we ought not to love things for places, but places for things. Wherefore choose from each several Church such things as are pious, religious, and right, and, collecting them as it were into a bundle, plant them in the minds of the Angli for their use.

### Augustine's fourth question.

Pray tell me what any one ought to suffer who may have abstracted anything from a church by theft ?

### Answer of the blessed pope Gregory.

In this case thy Fraternity can consider, with regard to the person of the thief, how he may be best corrected. For there are some who commit theft though they have resources, and there are others who transgress in this matter out of want. Hence it is needful that some should be corrected by fines, but some by stripes, and some more severely, but some more lightly. And, when any one is somewhat severely dealt with, he should be dealt with in charity, and not in anger ; since to the man himself who is corrected the punishment is assigned lest he should be given up to the fires of hell. For we ought so to maintain discipline towards believers as good fathers are wont to do towards their sons, whom they both smite with blows for their faults, and yet seek to have as their heirs the very persons on whom they inflict pain, and keep what they possess for the very same whom they seem to assail in anger. This charity, then, should be retained in the mind, so that nothing at all be done beyond the rule of reason.

Thou askest also how they ought to restore what they have abstracted by theft from churches. But far be it from us that the Church should receive back with increase what it seems to lose of its earthly things, and seek gain out of losses. [*al.*, for *de damnis*, de vanis. So Bede.]

### Augustine's fifth question.

I beg to know whether two brothers may marry two sisters, who are far removed from them in descent.

### Answer of the blessed pope Gregory.

This by all means may be done. For nothing at all is found in Holy Writ which seems to be opposed to it.

---

7 In Bede, and *Cod. Luc.*, this question does not appear, what follows as a reply to it being in continuation of the answer to Question I. The form of the beginning of the reply, "Si qui vero sunt clerici," favours its having been so.

### Augustine's sixth question.

As far as what generation believers ought to be joined in marriage with their kin, and whether it is lawful to be joined in marriage with stepmothers and brothers' wives?

### Answer of the blessed pope Gregory.

A certain earthly law in the Roman republic allows the son and daughter, whether of a brother and sister, or of two brothers, or of two sisters, to marry together. But we have learnt by experience that progeny cannot ensue from such marriages. And the sacred law forbids to uncover the nakedness of kindred. Whence it follows that only the third or fourth generations of believers may be lawfully joined together [8]. For the second, which we have spoken of, ought by all means to abstain from each other. But to have intercourse with a stepmother is a grave offence, seeing that is also written in the law, *thou shalt not uncover the nakedness of thy father* (Lev. xviii. 7). Not indeed that a son can uncover his father's nakedness; but, since it is written in the law, *They too shall be one flesh* (Gen. ii. 24), he who has presumed to uncover the nakedness of his stepmother, who has been one flesh with his father, has in truth uncovered his father's nakedness. It is also forbidden to have intercourse with a brother's wife, who, through her former conjunction, has become the flesh of the brother. For which thing also John the Baptist was beheaded, and crowned with holy martyrdom. He was not bidden to deny Christ; and yet for confessing Christ he was slain; because the same our Lord Jesus Christ had said, *I am the truth* (John xiv. 6); and because John was slain for the truth, he shed his blood for Christ.

### Augustine's seventh question [9].

I request to have it declared whether to such as are thus foully joined together separation should be enjoined, and the oblation of sacred communion denied them?

### Answer of the blessed pope Gregory.

But, since there are many in the nation of the Angli who while they were yet in unbelief are said to have been associated in such unholy marriages, they should be admonished, when they come to the faith, to abstain from each other, and be made to understand that this is a grievous sin. Let them fear God's tremendous judgment, lest for carnal delight they incur the pains of eternal torment. Yet they should not on this account be deprived of the communion of the Lord's body and blood, lest we should seem to punish them for what they had bound themselves in through ignorance before the laver of baptism. For at this time holy Church corrects some things with fervour, tolerates some things with gentleness, connives at and bears some things with consideration, so as often to repress what she opposes by bearing and conniving. But all who come to the faith are to be warned not to dare to perpetrate any such thing: and if any should perpetrate it, they must be deprived of the communion of the Lord's body and blood, since, as in those who have done it in ignorance the fault should be to a certain extent tolerated, so it should be severely visited in those who are not afraid to sin in spite of knowledge.

### Augustine's eighth question.

I ask whether, if length of way intervenes, and bishops are not able to assemble easily, a bishop should be ordained without the presence of other bishops.

### Answer of the blessed pope Gregory.

Indeed in the Church of the Angli, wherein thou art so far the only bishop, thou canst not ordain a bishop otherwise than without bishops. For, when bishops shall come from Gaul, they will attend thee as witnesses for the ordination of a bishop [1]. But we desire thy Fraternity so to ordain bishops in England that the bishops themselves be not separated from one another by long distances, to the end that there be no necessary cause why they should not come together in the case of the ordination of any bishop. For the presence of some other pastors also is exceedingly advantageous; and hence they ought to be able to come together as easily as possible. When therefore, God granting it, bishops shall have been ordained in places not far from each other, an ordination of bishops should in no case take place without three or four bishops being assembled. For in spiritual things themselves,

---

[8] This allowance of marriage between second cousins seems to have caused surprise in some quarters. Cf. Epistle of Felix of Messana to Gregory (XIV. 16). The motive of St. Boniface in his letter to Nothelm, referred to above under note 1, in which he asked for a copy of these Questions and Answers, seems to have been a desire to ascertain whether Gregory had really allowed such marriages. He writes, "in qua inter cætera capitula continetur quod in tertia generatione propinquitatis fidelibus liceat matrimonia copulare."

[9] This question is not in Bede, or in *Cod. Lucens.*, what follows being given as a continuation of the preceding answer. It begins with "Quia vero." Cf. note 2.

[1] It is to be observed that Gregory, though aware of the existence of British bishops, as his answer to the following question shews, does not contemplate their taking part in ordinations. He may have been unwilling to invite their co-operation till assured of their orthodoxy and submission to the Roman See. The failure of Augustine's negociations with them has been attributed to his own imperious attitude towards them. But it is at least a question whether his instructions did not justify the position he assumed (see Bede, *H.E.* II. 2.).

that they may be ordered wisely and maturely, we may draw an example even from carnal things. For assuredly, when marriages are celebrated in the world, some married persons are called together, that those who have gone before in the way of marriage may be associated also in the ensuing joy. Why then, in this spiritual ordination too, wherein man is joined to God through a sacred mystery, should not such come together as may both rejoice in the advancement of him who is ordained bishop and pour forth prayers to the Almighty Lord for His protection?

### Augustine's ninth question.

I ask also how we should deal with the bishops of Gaul and of the Britons.

### Answer of the blessed pope Gregory.

Over the bishops of Gaul we give thee no authority, since from the ancient times of my predecessors the bishop of Arelate (*Arles*) has received the pallium, and we ought by no means to deprive him of the authority that he has acquired. If therefore it should happen that thy Fraternity should pass into the provinces of Gaul, thou shouldest act with the same bishop of Arelate in such a way that vices in bishops, if any, may be corrected. And, if he should by chance be lukewarm in the vigour of discipline, he must be stirred up by the zeal of thy Fraternity. To him we have also written letters[2], bidding him aid thee with his whole soul, whenever thy Holiness may be present in Gaul, that you may together repress in the manners of bishops all that is contrary to the command of our Creator. But thou thyself wilt not have power to judge the bishops of Gaul by authority of thine own; but by persuading, alluring, and also exhibiting thine own good works for their imitation, and so moulding the dispositions of the vicious to concern for holiness; seeing that it is written in the law, *One passing through the standing corn of another must not put in a sickle, but rub the ears with his hand and eat* (Deut. xxxii. 25). Thou canst not, then, put in the sickle of judgment into the crop that is seen to be committed to another; but by kindly good offices thou canst strip the corn of the Lord from the chaff of its defects, and by admonishing and persuading, convert it, as it were by chewing, into the body of the Church. But whatever is to be done authoritatively, let it be done with the aforesaid bishop of Arelate, lest there should be any disregard of what the ancient institution of the Fathers has provided. But

of all British bishops we commit the charge to thy Fraternity, that the unlearned may be taught, the weak strengthened by persuasion, the perverse corrected by authority.

### Augustine's request.

I request that the relics of Saint **Sixtus** the martyr may be sent to us[3].

### The grant of Gregory.

We have done what thou hast requested, to the end that the people who formerly said that they venerated in a certain place the body of Saint Sixtus the martyr, which seems to thy Fraternity to be neither the true body nor truly holy, may receive certain benefits from the most holy and approved martyr, and not reverence what is uncertain. Yet it seems to me that, if the body which is believed by the people to be that of some martyr is distinguished among them by no miracles, and if further there are none of the more aged who declare that they had heard the order of his passion from progenitors, the relics which thou hast asked for should be so deposited apart that the place in which the aforesaid body lies, be entirely blocked up, and that the people be not allowed to desert what is certain, and venerate what is uncertain.

### Augustine's tenth question.

Whether a pregnant woman should be baptized, or, when she has brought forth, after what length of time she should be allowed to enter the church. Or, to guard also against her issue being surprised by death, after how many days it may receive the sacrament of holy baptism. Or after what length of time her husband may have carnal intercourse with her. Or, if she is in her sickness after the manner of women, whether she may enter the church, or receive the sacrament of sacred communion. Or whether a man after intercourse with his wife, before he has been washed with water, may enter the church, or even go to the ministry (*ministerium:* in Bede, *mysterium*) of sacred communion. All these things it is right we should have made known to us for the rude nation of the Angli.

### Answer of the blessed pope Gregory.

I doubt not that thy Fraternity has been asked these questions, and I think that I have supplied thee with answers to them. But I believe that thou wishest what thou art able of thyself to say and think to be confirmed by my reply. For why should not a pregnant woman be baptized, fecundity of the flesh

---

[2] Cf. XI. 68.

[3] This question, with the answer to it, is absent from Bede, and *Cod. Lucens.*, and may be regarded as an interpolation.

being no fault before the eyes of Almighty God? For, when our first parents had transgressed in Paradise, they lost by the just judgment of God the immortality which they had received. Therefore, because Almighty God would not utterly extinguish the human race for their fault, He took away immortality from man for his sin, and yet, in the kindness of His pity, reserved to him fruitfulness in offspring. With what reason then can what has been preserved to the human race by the gift of Almighty God be debarred from the grace of holy baptism? For indeed it is very foolish to suppose that a gift of grace can possibly be inconsistent with that mystery wherein all human sin is entirely extinguished.

But as to how many days after her delivery a woman may enter the church, thou hast learnt that by the direction of the Old Testament she ought to keep away xxxiii. days for a male child, but lxvi. for a female. It should be known, however, that this is understood mystically. For, if in the same hour in which she has been delivered she enters the church, she subjects herself to no burden of sin. For it is the pleasure of the flesh, not the pain, that is in fault. But it is in the carnal intercourse that the pleasure lies; for in bringing forth of offspring there is pain and groaning. Whence even to the first mother of all it is said, *In sorrow thou shalt bring forth children* (Gen. iii. 16). If, therefore, we forbid a woman after her delivery to enter the church, we reckon her very penalty to her for a fault. Moreover, it is by no means forbidden that either a woman after delivery or that which she has brought forth should be baptized without delay, if in peril of death; she even in the same hour in which she is delivered, or it in the same hour in which it is born. For, as in the case of those who live and have discretion the grace of the holy mystery should be seen to with great discernment, so to those who are in imminent danger of death it should be offered without any delay, lest, while time is being sought for administering the mystery of redemption, death should shortly intervene, and no way be found of redeeming the time that has been lost.

Further, her husband ought not to cohabit with her till that which is brought forth be weaned. But an evil custom has arisen in the ways of married persons, that women scorn to nurse the children whom they bring forth, and deliver them to other women to be nursed. Which custom appears to have been devised for the sole cause of incontinency, in that, being unwilling to contain themselves, they think scorn to suckle their offspring. Those women therefore who, after an evil custom, deliver their children to others to be nursed ought not to have intercourse with their husbands unless the time of their purification has passed, seeing that, even without the reason of childbirth, they are forbidden to have intercourse with their husbands while held of their accustomed sicknesses; so much so that the sacred law smites with death any man who shall go into a woman having her sickness (Lev. xx. 18). Yet still a woman, while suffering from her accustomed sickness, ought not to be prohibited from entering the church, since the superfluity of nature cannot be imputed to her for guilt, and it is not just that she should be deprived of entrance into the church on account of what she suffers unwillingly. For we know that the woman who suffered from an issue of blood, coming humbly behind the Lord, touched the hem of his garment, and immediately her infirmity departed from her (Luke viii.). If then one who had an issue of blood could laudably touch the Lord's garment, why should it be unlawful for one who suffers from a menstruum of blood to enter in the Lord's Church?

But that woman, thou wilt say, was compelled by infirmity; but these are held of their accustomed sicknesses. Yet consider, dearest brother, how all that we suffer in this mortal flesh is of infirmity of nature, ordained after guilt by the fitting judgment of God. For to hunger and to thirst, to be hot, to be cold, to be weary, is of infirmity of nature. And to seek food against hunger, and drink against thirst, and cool air against heat, and clothing against cold, and rest against weariness, what is it but to search out certain healing appliances against sicknesses? For in females also the menstruous flow of their blood is a sickness. If therefore she presumed well who in her state of feebleness touched the Lord's garment, why should not what is granted to one person in infirmity be granted to all women who through defect of their nature are in infirmity?

Further, she ought not to be prohibited during these same days from receiving the mystery of holy communion. If, however, out of great reverence, she does not presume to receive, she is to be commended; but, if she should receive, she is not to be judged. For it is the part of good dispositions in some way to acknowledge their sins even where there is no sin, since often without sin a thing is done which comes of sin. Whence also, when we hunger, we eat without sin, though it has come of the sin of the first man that we do hunger. For the menstruous habit in women is no sin, seeing that it occurs naturally; yet still that nature itself has been so vitiated as to be seen to be polluted even without the intention of the will is a defect that comes of sin, whereby human nature may perceive what through judgment it has come to be, so that man who voluntarily committed sin may bear the guilt of sin involuntarily. And so females, when they consider themselves as being in their habit of sickness, if they presume not to approach the sacrament of the body and blood of the Lord, are to be commended for their right consideration. But when, out of the habit of a religious life, they are seized with a love of the same mystery, they are not to be restrained, as we have said. For, as in the old Testament outward acts were attended to, so in the New Testament it is not so much what is done outwardly as what is thought inwardly that is regarded with close attention, that it may be punished with searching judgment. For, while the law forbids the eating of many things as being unclean, the Lord nevertheless says in the Gospel, *Not that which goeth into the mouth defileth a man, but the things which come forth from the heart, these are they which defile a man* (Matth. xv. 11). And soon after He added in explanation, *Out of the heart proceed evil thoughts* (Ib. 19). Hence it is abundantly indicated that what is shewn by Almighty God to be polluted in act is that which is engendered of the root of polluted thought. Whence also Paul the Apostle says, *All things are pure to the pure; but unto them that are defiled and unbelieving is nothing pure* (Tit. i. 15). And immediately, to declare the cause of this defilement, he subjoins, *For their mind and conscience is defiled.* If, then, food is not impure to one whose mind is not impure, why should what with a pure mind a woman suffers from nature be reckoned to her for impurity?

Further, a man after sleeping with his own wife ought not to enter the church unless washed with water, nor, even when washed, enter immediately. Now the law enjoined on the ancient people that a man after intercourse with a woman should both be washed with water and not enter the church before sunset. Which may be understood spiritually as meaning that a man has intercourse with a woman when his mind is joined with delight in thought to illicit concupiscence, and that, unless the fire of concupiscence in his mind should cool, he ought not to think himself worthy of the congregation of his brethren, seeing himself to be burdened with by lewdness of wrong desire. For, although in this matter different nations of men have different notions, and some are seen to observe one practice and some another, yet the usage of the Romans

from ancient times has always been for a man after intercourse with his own wife both to seek the purification of the bath and to refrain reverently for a while from entering the church.

Nor do we, in saying these things, account wedlock as sin. But, since even the lawful intercourse of the wedded cannot take place without pleasure of the flesh, entrance into a sacred place should be abstained from, because the pleasure itself can by no means be without sin. For he had not been born of adultery or fornication, but of lawful wedlock, who said, *Behold I was conceived in iniquities, and in sin my mother brought me forth* (Ps. l. 7). For, knowing himself to have been conceived in iniquities, he groaned for having been born in sin, because the tree bears in its branch the vicious humour which it has drawn from its root. Yet in these words he does not call the intercourse of the wedded iniquity in itself, but in truth only the pleasure of the intercourse. For there are many things which are allowed and legitimate, and yet we are to some extent defiled in the doing of them; as often we attack faults with anger, and disturb the tranquillity of our own mind. And, though what is done is right, yet it is not to be approved that the mind is therein disturbed. For instance. he had been angry against the vices of transgressors who said, *Mine eye is disturbed because of anger* (Ps. vi. 8). For, since the mind cannot, unless it be tranquil, lift itself up to the light of contemplation, he grieved that his eye was disturbed in anger, because, though assailing evil doings from above, he still could not help being confused and disturbed from contemplation of the highest things. And therefore his anger against vice is laudable, and yet it troubles him, because he felt that he had incurred some guilt in being disturbed. Lawful copulation of the flesh ought therefore to be for the purpose of offspring, not of pleasure; and intercourse of the flesh should be for the sake of producing children, and not a satisfaction of frailties. If, then, any one makes use of his wife not as seized by the desire of pleasure, but only for the sake of producing children, he certainly, with regard to entering the church or taking the mystery of the body and blood of the Lord, is to be left to his own judgment, since by us he ought not to be prohibited from receiving it who knows no burning though in the midst of fire. But, when not the love of producing offspring but pleasure dominates in the act of .intercourse, married persons have something to mourn over in their intercourse. For holy preaching concedes them this, and yet in the very concession shakes the mind with fear.

For, when the Apostle Paul said, *Who cannot contain let him have his own wife*, he straightway took care to add, *But I speak this by way of indulgence, not by way of command* (1 Cor. vii. 7). For what is just and right is not indulged : what he spoke of as indulged he shewed to be a fault.

Furthermore it is to be attentively considered that the Lord in mount Sinai, when about to speak to the people, first charged the same people to abstain from women. And if there, where the Lord spoke to men through a subject creature, purity of body was required with such careful provision that they who were to hear the words of God might not have intercourse with women, how much more ought those who receive the Body of the Almighty Lord to keep purity of the flesh in themselves, lest they be weighed down by the greatness of the inestimable mystery! Hence also it is said through the priest to David concerning his servants, that if they were pure from women they might eat the shewbread ; which they might not receive at all unless David first declared them to be pure from women. Still a man who after intercourse with his wife has been washed with water may receive even the mystery of sacred communion, since according to the opinion above expressed it was allowable for him to enter the church.

### Augustine's eleventh question.

I ask also whether after an illusion, such is accustomed to occur in dreams, any one may receive the body of the Lord, or, if he be a priest, celebrate the sacred mysteries ?

### Answer of the blessed Pope Gregory.

Such a one the Testament of the old law, as we have already said in the last section, declares indeed to be polluted, and does not allow to enter the church until the evening, or without being washed with water. But one who understands this not only with special reference to that people at that time, but also spiritually, will regard it under the same intellectual conception that we have spoken of before ; namely, that he has, as it were, an illusion in a dream who, being tempted by uncleanness, is defiled in thought by true images. But he is to be washed with water in the sense of washing away the sins of thought with tears. And, unless the fire of temptation has passed away, he should feel himself to be guilty, as it were, until the evening.

But in this same illusion discrimination is very necessary, since it ought to be nicely considered from what cause it occurs to the mind of the sleeper. For sometimes it happens from surfeit, sometimes from superfluity or infirmity of nature, sometimes from cogitation. And indeed when it has come to pass from superfluity or infirmity of nature, it is by no means to be viewed with alarm, since the mind is to be commiserated as having endured it unwittingly rather than as having done it. But when the appetite of gluttony in taking food is carried beyond measure, and consequently the receptacles of the humours are loaded, the mind has therefore some guilt, yet not to the extent of prohibition from receiving the sacred mystery, or celebrating the solemnities of mass, when perchance a festival day demands it, or necessity itself requires the mystery to be exhibited by reason of there being no other priest in the place. For, if others competent to execute the mystery are present, an illusion caused by surfeit ought not to debar from receiving the sacred mystery, though immolation of the sacred mystery ought, as I think, to be humbly abstained from ; provided only that foul imagination has not shaken the soul of the sleeper. For there are some to whom the illusion for the most part so arises that their mind, though in the body which sleeps, is not defiled by foul imaginations. With regard to this, there is one case in which it is shewn that the soul itself is guilty, not being free even from its own judgment ; that is where, while it remembers having seen nothing when the body was asleep, it still remembers having fallen into lewdness when the body was awake. But, if the illusion arises in the soul of the sleeper from foul cogitation while he was awake, the mind's guilt is patent to itself. For a man sees from what root that defilement proceeded, if he has endured unwittingly what he wittingly cogitated. But it is to be considered whether the cogitation ensued from suggestion, or delight, or sinful consent. For there are three ways in which all sin is accomplished ; to wit, by suggestion, by delight, and by consent. Suggestion is through the devil, delight through the flesh, consent through the spirit ; since, in the case of the first sin, the serpent suggested it, Eve, as the flesh, delighted in it, but Adam, as the spirit, consented to it. And great discernment is needed, that the mind may sit as judge of itself to distinguish between suggestion and delight, between delight and consent. For, when the evil spirit suggests sin in the soul, if no delight in sin should follow, no sin is in any wise committed. But, when the flesh has begun to take delight, then sin has its commencement. But, if it sinks to deliberate consent, then sin is known to be completed. In suggestion therefore is the seed of sin, in delight its nutriment, in consent its completion. And it often happens that what the evil spirit sows in the thought the flesh draws into delight, and yet the mind does not consent to this delight. And, while the flesh cannot be delighted without the soul, still the mind, though struggling against the pleasures of the flesh, is in some way bound against its will in carnal delight, so as by force of reason to protest against it and not consent to it, and yet to be bound by the delight, but still to groan exceedingly for being bound. Whence even that chief soldier of the heavenly army groaned, saying, *I see another law in my members fighting against the law of my mind, and bringing me into captivity to the law of sin which is in my members* (Rom. vii. 23). Yet, if he was a captive, he did not fight. But he did fight too, and therefore he was not a captive. And therefore he fought by the law of the mind, which the law which is in the members fought against. If he thus fought, he was not a captive. Behold then, man is, so to speak, both a captive and free : free with regard to the righteousness which he loves ; a captive with regard to the delight which he endures unwillingly.

### EPISTLE LXV.

#### To Augustine, Bishop of the Angli [4].

Gregory to Augustine, &c.

Though it is certain that for those who labour for Almighty God ineffable rewards of an eternal kingdom are reserved, yet we must needs bestow honours upon them, that by reason of remuneration they may apply themselves the more manifoldly in devotion to spiritual work. And, since the new Church of the Angli has been brought to the grace of Almighty God through the bountifulness of the same Lord and thy labours, we grant to thee the use of the pallium therein for the solemnization of mass only, so that thou mayest ordain bishops in twelve several places, to be subject to thy jurisdiction, with the view of a bishop of the city of London being always consecrated in future by his own synod, and receiving the dignity of the pallium from this holy and Apostolical See which by the grace of God I serve. Further, to the city of York we desire thee to send a bishop whom thou mayest judge

fit to be ordained ; so that, if this same city with the neighbouring places should receive the word of God, he also may ordain twelve bishops, so as to enjoy the dignity of a metropolitan : for to him also, if our life is continued, we propose, with the favour of God, to send a pallium ; but yet we desire to subject him to the control of thy Fraternity. But after thy death let him be over the bishops whom he shall have ordained, so as to be in no wise subject to the jurisdiction of the bishop of London. Further, between the bishops of London and York in the future let there be this distinction of dignity, that he be accounted first who has been first ordained. But let them arrange by council in common, and with concordant action, whatever things may have to be done in zeal for Christ ; let them be of one mind in what is right, and accomplish what they are minded to do without disagreement with each other.

But let thy Fraternity have subject to thyself under our God not only those bishops whom thou shalt ordain, and those whom the bishop of York may ordain, but also all the priests of Britain, to the end that they may learn the form of right belief and good living from the tongue and life of thy Holiness, and, executing their office well in their faith and manners, may attain to heavenly kingdoms when it may please the Lord. God keep thee safe, most reverend brother. Given on the tenth day of the Kalends of July, in the 19th year of the empire of our lord Mauricius Tiberius, the 18th year after the consulship of the same lord, Indiction 4.

### EPISTLE LXVI.

#### To Edilbert, King of the Angli.

Gregory to Edilbert, &c.

On this account Almighty God advances good men to the government of peoples, that through them He may bestow the gifts of His loving-kindness on all over whom they are preferred. This we have found to be the case in the nation of the Angli, which your Glory has been put over to the intent that through the good things granted to you, heavenly benefits might be conferred on the nation subject to you And so, glorious son, keep guard with anxious mind over the grace which thou hast received from above. Make haste to extend the Christian faith among the peoples under thy sway, redouble the zeal of thy rectitude in their conversion, put down the worship of idols, overturn the edifices of their temples [5], build up the manners of thy

---

[4] In the scheme, sketched in this letter, for the constitution of the Church in England, which Gregory seems to have contemplated being carried out in Augustine's own day, he shews serious ignorance of the state of things in England at the time, and consequently of possibilities. Among other things he appears to have known little of the ancient British Church, or of the independent position which its bishops would be likely to assume. Still it is interesting to observe that the scheme in its main features—that of two independent Metropolitans, in the North and in the South, each with his suffragan bishops under them— was after all eventually realized, and that the present constitution of the English Church may be traced to this letter ; only that Canterbury never yielded its primitive dignity, as had been proposed, to London.

[5] This direction was modified in a subsequent letter to Mellitus (XI. 76).

subjects in great purity of life by exhorting, by terrifying, by enticing, by correcting, by shewing examples of well-doing; that so you may find Him your recompenser in heaven Whose name and knowledge you shall have spread abroad on earth. For He Himself will make the name of your glory even more glorious to posterity, if you seek and maintain His honour among the nations. For so Constantine, the once most pious Emperor, recalling the Roman republic from perverse worshippings of idols, subjected it with himself to our Almighty Lord God Jesus Christ, and turned himself with his subject peoples with all his heart to Him. Hence it came to pass that that man surpassed in praise the name of ancient princes, and excelled his predecessors as much in renown as in well-doing. And now, therefore, let your Glory make haste to infuse into the kings and peoples subject to you the knowledge of God, Father, Son and Holy Spirit, that you may both surpass the ancient kings of your race in renown and in deserts, and the more you shall have wiped away the sins of others among your subjects, the more secure you may become with regard to your own sins before the terrible scrutiny of Almighty God.

Moreover, you have with you our most reverend brother, Augustine the bishop, learned in monastic rule, replete with knowledge of holy Scripture, endowed by the grace of God with good works. Listen gladly to his admonitions, follow them devoutly, keep them studiously in remembrance: for, if you listen to him in what he speaks in behalf of Almighty God, the same Almighty God will the sooner listen to him when he prays for you. For, if (which God forbid) you disregard his words, when will it be possible for Almighty God to hear him for you, whom you neglect to hear for God? With all your heart, therefore, bind ye yourselves in fervour of faith to him, and aid his endeavours by the power which he gives you from above, that He Whose faith you cause to be received and kept in your kingdom may Himself make you partakers of His own Kingdom.

Furthermore, we would have your Glory know that, as we learn from the words of the Almighty Lord in holy Scripture, the end of the present world is already close at hand, and the reign of the saints is coming, which can have no end. And, now that this end of the world is approaching, many things are at hand which previously have not been; to wit, changes of the air, terrors from heaven, and seasons contrary to the accustomed order of times, wars, famine, pestilences, earthquakes in divers places. Yet these things will not come in our days, but after our days they will all ensue. You therefore, if you observe any of these things occurring in your land, by no means let your mind be troubled, since these signs of the end of the world are sent beforehand for this purpose, that we should be solicitous about our souls, suspectful of the hour of death, and in our good deeds be found prepared for the coming Judge. These things, glorious son, we have now briefly spoken of, that, when the Christian faith shall have been extended in your kingdom, our speech to you may also extend itself to greater length, and that we may be pleased to speak so much the more fully as joy multiplies itself in our heart for the perfected conversion of your nation.

I have sent you some small presents, which to you will not be small, when received by you as of the benediction of the blessed Apostle Peter. And so may Almighty God guard and perfect in you the grace which He has begun, and extend your life here through courses of many years, and after a long life receive you in the congregation of the heavenly country. May heavenly grace keep your Excellency safe, sir son (*domine fili*). Given this 10th day of the Kalends of July, the 19th year of the empire of our most pious lord Mauricius Tiberius Augustus, the 18th year after the consulship of the same our lord, Indiction 4.

## EPISTLE LXVII.
### To Quiricus, Bishop, &c.

Gregory to Quiricus, Bishop, and the other catholic bishops in Hiberia [6].

Since to charity nothing is afar off, let those who are divided in place be joined by letter. The bearer of these presents, coming to the Church of the blessed Peter, Prince of the apostles, asserted that he had received letters for us from your Fraternity, and had lost them, with other things also, in the city of Jerusalem. In them, as he says, you were desirous of enquiring with regard to priests and people who have been bewildered in the error of Nestorian heresy, when they return to the Catholic Church which is the mother of all the elect, whether they should be baptized, or joined to the bowels of the same mother

---

6 Or *Iberia*, corrected from *Hibernia* by the Benedictine Editors, with the support of some few MSS. That the letter was addressed to the bishops of Hibernia (i.e. Ireland) is highly improbable. Not only is it unlikely that the Eastern heresy of Nestorianism would have infected Ireland, but the fact also, mentioned in the beginning of the letter, that the messenger from the bishops addressed had passed through Jerusalem on his way to Rome evidently points to some Eastern locality. For similar reasons it cannot well be supposed that *Iberia* here denotes Spain. It may have been the territory so-called in the neighbourhood of Armenia, between Cholchis on the West, and Albania on the East, now *Gurgistan*.

Church by confession only of the one true faith.

And indeed we have learnt from the ancient institution of the Fathers that whosoever among heretics are baptized in the name of the Trinity, when they return to holy Church, may be recalled to the bosom of mother Church either by unction of chrism, or by imposition of hands, or by profession of the faith only. Hence the West reconciles Arians to the holy Catholic Church by imposition of hands, but the East by the unction of holy chrism. But Monophysites and others are received by a true confession only, because holy baptism, which they have received among heretics, then acquires in them the power of cleansing, when either the former receive the Holy Spirit by imposition of hands, or the latter are united to the bowels of the holy and universal Church by reason of their confession of the true faith. Those heretics, however, who are not baptized in the name of the Trinity, such as the *Bonosiaci* and the *Cataphrygæ*, because the former do not believe in Christ the Lord, and the latter with a perverse understanding believe a certain bad man, Montanus, to be the Holy Spirit, like unto whom are many others;—these, when they come to holy Church, are baptized, because what they received while in their error, not being in the name of the Holy Trinity, was not baptism. Nor can this be called an iteration of baptism, which, as has been said, had not been given in the name of the Trinity. But the Nestorians, since they are baptized in the name of the Holy Trinity—though darkened by the error of their heresy in that, after the manner of Jewish unbelief, they believe not the Incarnation of the Only-begotten—when they come to the Holy Catholic Church, are to be taught, by firm holding and profession of the true faith, to believe in one and the same Son of God and man, our Lord God Jesus Christ, the same existing in Divinity before the ages, and the same made man in the end of the ages, because *The Word was made flesh and dwelt among us* (Joh. i. 14).

But we say that the Word was made flesh, not by losing what He was, but by taking what He was not. For in the mystery of His Incarnation the Only-begotten of the Father increased what was ours, but diminished not what was His. Therefore the Word and the flesh is one Person, as He says Himself, *No man hath ascended up to heaven, but he that came down from heaven, even the Son of man which is in heaven* (Joh. iii. 14). He Who is the Son of God in heaven was the Son of man who spake on earth. Hence John says, *We know that the Son of God is come, and hath given us an understanding* (1 Joh. v. 20). And

as to what understanding He has given us, he straightway added, *That we may know the true God*. Whom in this place does he mean as the true God but the Father Almighty? But, as to what he conceives also of the Almighty Son, he added, *And that we may be in his true Son Jesus Christ*. Lo, he says that the Father is the true God, and that Jesus Christ is His true Son. And what he conceives this true Son to be he shews more plainly; *This is the true God, and eternal life*. If, then, according to the error of Nestorius the Word were one and the man Jesus Christ were another, he who is true man would not be the true God and eternal life. But the Only-begotten Son, the Word before the Ages, was made man. He is, then, the true God and eternal life. Certainly, when the holy Virgin was about to conceive Him, and heard the angel speaking to her, she said, *Behold the handmaid of the Lord; be it unto me according to thy word* (Luke i. 38). And, when she had conceived Him, and went to Elizabeth her kinswoman, at once she heard, *Whence am I worthy that the mother of my Lord should come to me?* Lo, the same Virgin is called both the handmaid and the mother of the Lord. For she is the handmaid of the Lord, because the Word before the Ages, the Only-begotten, is equal to the Father; but the mother, because in her womb from the Holy Spirit and of her flesh He was made man. Nor is she the handmaid of one and the mother of another, because, when the Only-begotten of God, existing before the ages, of her womb was made man, by an inscrutable miracle she became both the handmaid of man by reason of the divinity and the mother of the Word by reason of the flesh. It was not that the flesh was first conceived in the womb of the Virgin, and the divinity afterwards came into the flesh; but that as soon as the Word came into the womb, immediately the Word, retaining the excellence of His own nature, was made flesh. And the Only-begotten Son of God, through the womb of the Virgin, was born a perfect man, that is, in verity of flesh and of rational soul. Whence also He is called Anointed above his fellows, as the Psalmist says, *God, thy God, hath anointed thee with the oil of gladness above thy fellows* (Ps. xliv. 8) [7]. For He is anointed with oil, that is to say with the gift of the Holy Spirit. But He was anointed above His fellows, because all we men first exist as sinners, and afterwards are sanctified through the unction of the Holy Spirit. But He Who, existing as God before the ages, was conceived as man through the

---

[7] xlv. 7.

Holy Spirit in the Virgin's womb at the end of the ages, was there anointed by the same Spirit, even where He was conceived. Nor was He first conceived and afterwards anointed ; but to be conceived by the Holy Spirit of the flesh of the Virgin was itself to be anointed by the Holy Spirit. This truth, then, concerning His nativity let all who are brought back from the perverse error of Nestorius confess before the holy congregation of your Fraternity, anathematising the same Nestorius with all his followers, and all other heresies. The venerable synods also which the universal Church receives let them promise to receive and venerate ; and let your Holiness without any hesitation receive them in your assembly, allowing them to retain their own orders, in order that, while you both carefully sift the secrets of their hearts, and teach them through true knowledge the right things they ought to hold, and in gentleness make no difficulty or contradiction with them with respect to their own orders, you may snatch them from the mouth of the ancient foe ; and that the retribution of eternal glory with Almighty God may increase to you the more as you gather together many who may glory with you in the Lord without end. Now may the Holy Trinity keep you in its protection while you pray for us, and grant you in its love still more manifold gifts.
[In *Colbert.* and *Collect. Paul,* "Given on the tenth day of the Kalends of Jul. Indict. 4."]

## EPISTLE LXVIII.

(To VIRGILIUS, BISHOP OF ARELATE *Arles.*)

Gregory to Virgilius, &c.

What affection should be bestowed on brethren who come to us of their own accord is apparent from the fact that they are usually invited to visit us for the sake of charity. And so, if our common brother the bishop Augustine should chance to come to you, let your Love, as is fit, so affectionately and sweetly receive him as both to refresh him with the boon of your consolation and teach others also how fraternal charity should be cultivated. And, since it often happens that those who are placed at a distance learn first from others of things that require amendment, if he should perchance intimate to your Fraternity any faults in priests or others, do you, in concert with him, enquire into them with all subtle investigation. And do you both shew yourselves so strict and solicitous against things that offend God and provoke Him to wrath that, for the amendment of others, both vengeance may smite the guilty and false report not afflict the innocent. God keep thee safe, most reverend brother. Given the 10th

day of the Kalends of July, the 19th year of the empire of our most pious lord Mauricius Tiberius Augustus, the 18th year after the same our lord's consulship, Indiction 4.

## EPISTLE LXIX.

To BRUNICHILD, QUEEN OF THE FRANKS.

Gregory to Brunichild, &c.

Since it is written, *Righteousness exalteth a nation ; but sin maketh peoples miserable* (Prov. xiv. 34), a kingdom is then believed to be stable when a fault that is known of is quickly amended. Now it has come to our ears by the report of many, what we cannot mention without exceeding affliction of heart, that certain priests in those parts live so immodestly and wickedly that it is a shame for us to hear of it and lamentable to tell it. Lest, then, now that the rumour of this iniquity has extended as far as here, the wrong doing of others should smite either our soul or your kingdom with the dart of its sin, we ought to arise with ardour to avenge these things, lest the wickedness of a few should be the perdition of many. For bad priests are the cause of the ruin of a people. For who may offer himself as an intercessor for a people's sins, if the priest who ought to have prayed for it commits more grievous offences? But, since those whose place it is to prosecute these things are stirred neither by care to enquire into them nor by zeal to punish them, let letters from you be addressed to us, and let us send over, if you order it, a person with the assent of your authority, who together with other priests may search into these things thoroughly, and amend them according to the will of God. For indeed what we speak of is not a thing to be winked at, since one who can amend a fault and neglects to do so without doubt makes himself partaker in it. See therefore to your own soul, see to your grandsons, whom you wish to reign happily, see to the provinces ; and, before our Creator stretches out His hand to smite, take most earnest thought for the correction of this wickedness, lest He afterwards smite by so much the more sharply as He now waits longer and more mercifully. Know moreover that you will offer a great sacrifice of expiation to our God, if you cut off speedily from your territories the infection of so great a sin.

## EPISTLE LXXVI.

To MELLITUS, ABBOT.

Gregory to Mellitus, Abbot in France [8].

Since the departure of our congregation,

---

[8] This letter was sent after the departure of Mellitus with the band of new missionaries from Rome to Britain (see *Pro-*

which is with thee, we have been in a state of great suspense from having heard nothing of the success of your journey. But when Almighty God shall have brought you to our most reverend brother the bishop Augustine, tell him that I have long been considering with myself about the case of the Angli; to wit, that the temples of idols in that nation should not be destroyed, but that the idols themselves that are in them should be. Let blessed water be prepared, and sprinkled in these temples, and altars constructed, and relics deposited, since, if these same temples are well built, it is needful that they should be transferred from the worship of idols to the service of the true God; that, when the people themselves see that these temples are not destroyed, they may put away error from their heart, and, knowing and adoring the true God, may have recourse with the more familiarity to the places they have been accustomed to. And, since they are wont to kill many oxen in sacrifice to demons, they should have also some solemnity of this kind in a changed form, so that on the day of dedication, or on the anniversaries of the holy martyrs whose relics are deposited there, they may make for themselves tents of the branches of trees around these temples that have been changed into churches, and celebrate the solemnity with religious feasts. Nor let them any longer sacrifice animals to the devil, but slay animals to the praise of God for their own eating, and return thanks to the Giver of all for their fulness, so that, while some joys are reserved to them outwardly, they may be able the more easily to incline their minds to inward joys. For it is undoubtedly impossible to cut away everything at once from hard hearts, since one who strives to ascend to the highest place must needs rise by steps or paces, and not by leaps. Thus to the people of Israel in Egypt the Lord did indeed make Himself known; but still He reserved to them in His own worship the use of the sacrifices which they were accustomed to offer to the devil, enjoining them to immolate animals in sacrifice to Himself; to the end that, their hearts being changed, they should omit some things in the sacrifice and retain others, so that, though the animals were the same as what they had been accustomed to offer, nevertheless, as they immolated them to God and not to idols, they should be no longer the same sacrifices. This

then it is necessary for thy Love to say to our aforesaid brother, that he, being now in that country, may consider well how he should arrange all things. God keep thee safe, most beloved son. Given this 15th day of the Kalends of July, the 19th year of the empire of our most pious lord Mauricius Tiberius Augustus, the 18th year after the consulship of the same our lord, Indiction 4.

## EPISTLE LXXVII.
### To Boniface, Guardian (*Defensorem*), in Corsica.

Gregory to Boniface, &c.

Thy experience is not free from blame, in that, knowing Aleria and Adjacium, cities of Corsica, to have been long without bishops, thou hast delayed admonishing their clergy and people to choose for themselves priests. But, since they ought to be no longer without rulers of their own, hasten thou, on receiving this authority, to exhort the clergy and people of these cities severally, that they disagree not among themselves, but that each city with one consent choose for itself a priest to be consecrated. And, when they have made their decree, let such person as shall have been elected come to us. But, if they should be unwilling to come to an unanimous decision, being divided in their choice between two persons, let both in like manner come to us, the decree having been made in the usual way, that, after enquiry made into their lives and characters, the one who may appear to be most fit may be ordained. Seeing, moreover, that many poor persons there are said to be oppressed and to suffer prejudice, let thy Experience give heed to this, and not allow them to be unjustly aggrieved; but so endeavour thyself that neither they who take action be unreasonably hindered nor those against whom action is taken be in danger of sustaining damage unjustly.

Furthermore, it has reached our ears that some of the clergy, thou being on the spot, are held in custody by laymen. If this is so, know that the blame will be imputed to thee, since, if thou wert a man, it would not have been the case. And accordingly thou must needs pay attention in future so that thou permit not the like to be done; but that, if any one should have a cause of complaint against a clerk, he resort to his bishop. And, if perchance the latter should be suspected, a commissioner must be deputed by him—or, if this too should be objected to by the plaintiff, by thy Experience,—who may compel the parties to choose arbitrators by mutual consent. And whatever may be decided by them, let it

be in all ways so carried out, with due observance of law, by thy own or the bishop's
care, that there may be no occasion for them to
weary themselves with disputes.

## EPISTLE LXXVIII.

### To Barbara and Antonina 9.

Gregory to Barbara, &c.

On receiving your epistles, I was in all
manner of ways delighted to hear of your
wellbeing, and I entreat Almighty God that
He would guard you by His protection from
malignant spirits in thought, and from perverse
men, and from all contrariety; and that He
would, with the grace of His fear, settle you
in unions worthy of you, and cause us all to
rejoice in your settlement 1. But do you, most
sweet daughters, rest your hope on His help,
and, being always under the shadow of His
defence, both by praying and by well doing,
escape the plots of bad men. For, whatever
human comforts or adversities there may be,
there are none, unless either His grace protects
or His displeasure troubles you. Rest there-

fore your hope on no one among men, but
bind your whole soul to trust in Almighty God.
While we sleep, then, He will protect you,
of whom it is written, *Behold he that keepeth
Israel shall neither slumber nor sleep* (Ps.
cxx. 4) 2.

As to your saying that you are in haste
to approach the threshhold of the blessed
Peter, Prince of the apostles, I wish exceedingly, and wait with fervent desire, to see you
in his church united to husbands well worthy
of you; that so both you may obtain some
little comfort from me, and I no little joy from
your presence. I have also commended your
causes to my most reverend brother the bishop
John 3, and to Romanus the guardian (*defen-
sori*), that under God they may accomplish
what they have begun.

Your present of two *racanœ* 4, which you
sent me word were your work, I accepted
gladly. But yet know ye that I did not
believe the word you sent me. For you are
seeking praise from the work of others, seeing
that you have perhaps never yet put hand
to spindle. Nor yet does this circumstance
distress me, since I wish you to love the
reading of Holy Scripture, that, so long as
Almighty God shall unite you to husbands,
you may know how you should live and how
you should manage your houses.

---

9 See above, Epp. XXXV., XXXVI., in this book, and I. 34,
note 8, there referred to.
1 If the marriage of the parents, Venantius and Italica, took
place, as conjectured in the note to I. 34, in the eleventh Indiction
(A.D. 592-3), and this letter was written in the fourth (A.D. 600-1),
the daughters would not be more than seven or eight years of age.
Still, even at this early age, their betrothal may have been
contemplated with a view to their settlement in life. But Venantius may have married earlier than 592-3, soon after his return
to a secular life, and so the girls may have been a little older.
Neither, however, if our dates are right, could be more than ten
years old.

2 In *English Bible*, cxxi. 4.
3 Viz. John, bishop of Syracuse. See above, Ep. XXXVI.
4 On the meaning of this word, see XII., note 3.

# BOOK XII

## EPISTLE I.

### To Dominicus, Bishop of Carthage.

Gregory to Dominicus, &c.

How abundant is the charity of your heart you shew by its interpreter—your tongue, while so seasoning the words of your epistles with its sweetness that all you write is pleasant and delightful. Hence it comes that we embrace your Fraternity in the arms of love, though unable to do so in the body. For it is the office of charity to supply to souls that are in concord what distance of place denies. And, since the sickness of our most loving brethren saddens us even as their health refreshes us, we give thanks to Almighty God, who has solaced our sadness by good news. For, having heard that you had contracted a very severe illness, before the receipt of your letter we were in a state of great distress. But since, when we are snatched from peril of death, it is uncertain, dearest brother, for what we are reserved, let us turn the time of respite to the profit of our souls, and, having to render our accounts to the coming Judge, let us fortify our cause before Him with tears and good works, that we may be counted worthy to have security given us with regard to the things that we have done. For in secular causes also a kind judge frequently grants a respite to this end, that one who had not been prepared before may afterwards come to his trial prepared. And what a thing it would be, were we to neglect for the salvation of the soul what we carefully attend to in matters of earthly concern! And so, since, according to the words of the Apostle John, no one is without sin, let us call to mind enticements of thought, incontinence of tongue, deeds of transgression ; and let us, while we may, with great knocking, do away with the stains of our iniquities, that our just and loving Redeemer may not execute vengeance according to our deservings, but according to His mercy be bent to pardon. And, since we do not sufficiently fulfil our office by weeping for our own sins only, let us the more earnestly devote ourselves to the custody of the flock committed to us, and by persuading, by exhorting, by alarming, by preaching, so far as heavenly clemency gives us power, let us hasten to fulfil our office in very deed, that, through the bounty of our Creator, we may look for the longed for reward. But, since we cannot do anything that is good without divine aid, let us implore Almighty God, most beloved brother, with united prayers, that He would direct us, with the flock committed to us, into the way of His commandments by the leading of His grace, and Himself, who by the gift of His mercy has willed us to have the name of shepherds, grant to us to understand and do what is well pleasing to Him. Moreover, we have received with the charity wherewith you sent it the blessing of the blessed martyr Agileus, transmitted to us by your Holiness. In the month of September, Indiction 5.

## EPISTLE VIII.

### To Columbus, Bishop of Numidia[1].

Gregory to Columbus, &c.

How serious, and intolerable even to be heard of, is the complaint of Donadeus, the bearer of these presents, who describes himself as having been a deacon, will be made manifest to your Fraternity by the petition presented by him, which is contained in what is subjoined below. But, since it has come to our ears that he had been deposed for bodily sin, let your Love make full enquiry into this, and, if it is so, let him be consigned to penance, that he may free himself by tears from the bond of the profligacy of which he has been guilty. If, however, he should be proved innocent of any such transgression, all that his petition contains must be enquired into with diligent examination by you, together with the primate of the council, and others our brethren and fellow-bishops. And, if his complaint is supported by the truth, let both such strictness of canonical discipline be brought to bear on his bishop Victor[2], who has not feared to commit so great a wickedness against God and his own priestly profession, that he may understand the wickedness of what he has done ; and let the man himself be restored to his order : for it is indeed preposterous, and con-

---

[1] Cf. II. 48, note 8.
[2] Victor was Primate of Numidia. See IV. 34, note 4.

fessedly against ecclesiastical order, that any one whom his own fault or crime does not depose from the rank of the office which he fills should be deprived invalidly at the will of this or that person.

## EPISTLE XXIV.

### To John, Subdeacon of Ravenna [3].

Gregory to John, &c.

Some monks who came to me from the monastery of the late abbot Claudius have petitioned me that the monk Constantius should be constituted their abbot. But I was exceedingly set against them as touching their petition, because they appeared to me to be altogether of a worldly mind in seeking to have a very worldly man for their abbot. For I have learnt how this same Constantius studies to possess property of his own : and this is the strongest evidence that he has not the heart of a monk. And I have learnt further that he presumed to go alone, without any one of his brethren with him, to a monastery that is situate in the province of Picenum. From this proceeding of his we know that he who walks without a witness lives not aright : and how can he maintain the rule for others who knows not how to maintain it for himself?

Giving him up, therefore, they asked to have a certain cellarer, Maurus by name, to whose life and industry there are many testimonies, the late abbot Claudius also with certain others having spoken in his praise. Let thy Experience therefore make careful enquiry ; and, if his life should be such as fit him for a place of government, cause him to be ordained abbot by our brother and fellow-bishop Marinianus. But, if there is anything decidedly against him, and they cannot find any suitable person in their own congregation, let them choose some one from elsewhere, and let him whom they may choose be made abbot. Further, take care by all means to tell our aforesaid brother and fellow-bishop to put down with the utmost earnestness the possession of property of their own by four or five of the monks of the monastery, which it has been found so far impossible to correct, and to make haste to cleanse this same monastery from such a pest ; since, if private property is held there by monks, it will not be possible for either concord or charity to continue in this same congregation. What, indeed, is a monk's state of life but a despising of the world? How, then, do they despise the world who while placed in a monastery seek gold? Wherefore

let thy Experience so proceed that neither the ordering of the place be deferred, nor any complaint reach us any more on this subject.

Furthermore, forasmuch as my late most dear son Claudius had heard me speak something about the Proverbs, the Song of Songs, the Prophets, and also about the Books of Kings and the Heptateuch, which on account of my infirmity I was unable to commit to writing, and he himself had dictated them for transcription according to his own understanding of their meaning, lest they should be forgotten, and in order that he might bring them to me at a suitable time, so that they might be more correctly dictated (for, when he read to me what he had written, I found the sense of what I had said had been altered very disadvantageously), it is hence necessary that thy Experience, avoiding all excuse or delay, should go to his monastery, and assemble the brethren, and that they should produce fully and truly whatsoever papers on divers Scriptures he had brought thither ; which do thou take, and transmit them to me with all possible speed.

Further, about thy return, having learnt that thou hast incurred serious trouble, we will consider by and by. Further, I have not been pleased to hear what has been told me by certain persons ; namely that our most reverend brother and fellow-bishop Marinianus causes my comments on the blessed Job to be read publicly at vigils ; seeing that this is not a popular work, and engenders hindrance rather than advancement to rude hearers. But tell him to cause the comments on the Psalms to be read at vigils, which mould the minds of secular persons to good manners. For indeed I do not wish, while I am in this flesh, that what I may have said should be readily made known to men. For I took it amiss that Anatolius the deacon of most beloved memory gave to the lord Emperor, at his request and command, the book of Pastoral Rule, which my most holy brother and fellow-bishop Anastasius of Antioch translated into the Greek tongue. And, as I was informed by letter, it pleased him much ; but it much displeased me that those who have what is better should be occupied in what is least.

Further, in the third part of the blessed Job, in the verse wherein it is written, *I know that my Redeemer liveth*, I suspect that my aforesaid brother and fellow-bishop Marinianus has a corrupt copy. For in the copy in our bookcase this passage is given differently from what I find to be in the copies possessed by others ; and consequently I have had this passage corrected, so that our often-named brother may have it as it is in our bookcase. For there are

---

[3] This subdeacon John appears to have been at this time the pope's representative Ravenna, the seat of the exarch of Italy.

four words, the absence of which from the passage may cause the reader no little difficulty. Execute all these things thoroughly and speedily. And, if thou canst do nothing with the most excellent Exarch, shew thyself not to have neglected to do what is in thy power.

What shall I say concerning the place of Albinus, as to which the answer given us is plainly contrary to justice? Thou oughtest, however, to consider the case attentively. Furthermore, a little time ago we had enjoined thy Experience to treat with our most eminent son the præfect to the end that the care of the conduits (*formarum*) should be committed to Augustus the vicecount, in that he is in all respects a diligent and energetic man [4]. And thou hast so far so put off the business as not even to inform us of what thou hast done. And so, even now, hasten thou with all earnestness to treat with the same our most eminent son, that the conduits may be entirely committed to the aforesaid most distinguished man, to the intent that he may to some extent succeed in repairing them. For these conduits are so scorned and neglected that, unless greater attention be given to them, within a short time they will go utterly to ruin. As thou knowest, then, how necessary this business is, and how advantageous to the general community, thou must use thy best endeavours that it may be committed, as we have said, to the aforesaid man for his careful attention. Given in the month of January, Indiction 5.

## EPISTLE XXV.

### To Romanus, Guardian (*Defensorem*) [5].

Gregory to Romanus, &c.

It is well known to thy Experience that Peter, whom we have made a guardian (*defensorem*), is sprung from the estate belonging to our Church which is called Vitelas. And so, since we ought to shew kindness towards him in such a way that nevertheless the Church may suffer no disadvantage, we command thee by this order to charge him strictly not to presume, under any pretext or excuse, to marry his children anywhere but in that estate to which they are bound by law and their condition [6]. In this matter, too, it is necessary for thy Experience to be very care-

ful, and to threaten them, so that on no occasion whatever they may go out of the property to which by their birth they are subjected. For, if any one of them (as we do not believe will be the case) should presume to depart from it, he may be assured that our *assent will never be given to any of them dwelling or being married outside the estate on which they were born, but that also their land should be superscribed [7]. And then know that you will run no slight risk, if through your negligence any of them should attempt to do any of the things which we forbid.

## EPISTLE XXVIII.

### To Columbus, Bishop of Numidia [8].

Gregory to Columbus, &c.

Inasmuch as it has long been known to us how thy Fraternity is distinguished for priestly gravity and ecclesiastical zeal, we have seen sufficient reason for thy taking part in the cognizance of things that require rebuke, lest, if they should be put off through connivance, every one should suppose that what he is able to do is allowed him. Now after what manner our brother Paulinus, bishop of the city of Tegessis is alleged by his clerics and by those who are constituted in sacred orders, to have been excessive towards them in corporal correction, thou needest not to be told, seeing that, before this complaint reached us, the matter, as we have learnt from their statement, had already been made known to thee. And, since superiors ought not to have the right of punishing their subordinates savagely, we have taken care to write to Victor our brother and fellow-bishop, who holds the primacy among you [9], that, together with thy Fraternity, or with others our brethren and fellow bishops whom you may think fit to call in, he may take cognizance of and thoroughly investigate the case between our aforesaid brother priest and his clergy. And let thy Love so give the matter thy close and careful attention, that the things that have been reported to us may not pass without a hearing, lest discord should be fomented in the Church, whence it ought by all means to be banished. And, if indeed the complaint of his clergy against him is well founded, so take cognizance of his fault, which he has scorned of his own accord to correct, with the

---

[4] The reference is to the conduits or aqueducts for supplying water to Rome, which it was the duty of the officer called "præfectus," who appears to have been at this time resident at Ravenna, to keep in order.

[5] Romanus had been appointed guardian (*defensor*) of the patrimony in Sicily. See IX. 18.

[6] This was a case of a native of Sicily, who had been *ascriptus glebæ*, having been appointed a *Defensor Ecclesiæ*. The purpose of the epistle is to guard against his supposing that such appointment exempted his children from the restrictions imposed by their birth.

[7] *Sed et superscribi terram eorum.* The meaning may be that notices should be put on the land to which such defaulters were attached, declaring that such and such persons belonged to it and were bound to remain on it. Cf. V. 41, note 3, on the phrase *titulos imponere.*

[8] See II. 48, note 1.

[9] For the custom in Africa with regard to the primacy, see I. 74, note 9.

force of our ecclesiastical decision that he may both feel for the present what a grave offence he has committed, and may learn for the future that he cannot do more than it is lawful for him to do. Above all things, then, we exhort thee that thou study ardently to exercise the zeal which we know thee to have for the sake of God.

And, inasmuch as our said brother Paulinus is said to confer ecclesiastical orders through simoniacal heresy, which is a thing awful to hear of, let it be thy care, along with the aforesaid primate or others, to enquire thoroughly into this also with all diligence. And, if it should be found to be so (which God forbid), effort must be made and action taken that both he who has not feared to accept and he who has not feared to give a bribe may be smitten by a sentence of canonical punishment, to the end that their correction may avail as a reproof to many. And, before this deadly root acquires strength and slays many more, let it be condemned by the decision of the whole council, so that no one may ever dare to accept or to give anything for any order whatever, nor any be promoted for favour, but all for merit, lest both ecclesiastical order be confounded, and probity of life be held in contempt, if one that is unworthy should receive the reward of merit.

Further we have given orders to Hilarus our *Chartularius* that, if the case should require it, he refuse not to take part in your enquiry.

If, therefore, it should be necessary, inform him by letter that you wish him to come to you, to the end that by treating the matter together with him you may better determine what ought to be ordained. In the month of March, Indiction 5. [N.B. *This date is absent from several Codices.*]

## EPISTLE XXIX.

### To Victor, Bishop [1].

Gregory to Victor, &c.

While on the one hand it is a joy to us to learn that our brethren are solicitous about their children in fatherly charity, on the other we count it no less a matter for sadness when neither regard for other brethren nor consideration of their priestly office avails to restrain them from unlawful doings. How serious, then, and how harsh is the complaint against our brother Paulinus, bishop of the city of Tegessis, made by his clerics and by those who are in sacred orders, I have no doubt is well known to thy Fraternity, since what has reached us from a distance cannot have been

hidden from thee who art near at hand. And, since there is need of great caution lest this bodily injury which they complain of at his hands in excess of his powers should be ventured on with allowance, or should grow worse by being connived at, manifest excesses should ever be so suppressed by canonical control that one proceeding may serve as a reproof of what is past and a rule for the future. Accordingly it becomes thee, together with our most beloved common brother the bishop Columbus, and with other priests whom you may think fit to call on, to sift the case between our above-named brother and his clergy by means of a thorough investigation. And, if the complaint of the petitioners stands with truth, so correct ye this thing by a regular reformation, that he may both be made aware what evil thing he has done and learn for the future not to exceed the limits of his office. And suffer him not, as is said to be the case, to disregard the rank of thy position, lest his contempt be to his risk and to thy blame. For whatever is committed by an inferior, unless it be carefully corrected, reflects on the person who occupies the superior place.

That other matter also, namely that the same our brother Paulinus is said to confer ecclesiastical orders for money, you should fully and very strictly enquire into. And, if it should clearly appear to be so, as we hope will not be the case, let your zeal for God so kindle itself to avenge this wrong that both the avarice of the ordainer may be turned into a penalty, and, the unlawful ordination being void of effect, the person ordained may not enjoy the longed-for object of his ambition. Herein we exhort you and before all things admonish you, that your Fraternity study to be so solicitous that, before the iniquity of simoniacal heresy shall gain strength in your parts from the offence of one, it may be cut off from the root by the pruning-hook of your sentence after a council diligently held. For whosoever does not, in consideration of his office, burn vehemently to correct this atrocity, let him not doubt that he will have his portion with him from whom this peculiar enormity took its beginning. And so, as we have said, you must act vigilantly and earnestly, that your council, which up to this time, under God's keeping, has been preserved from any bad repute of this kind, may not by any possibility be polluted and ruined by the poison of this wickedness.

Furthermore, we have given orders to Hilarus our *Chartularius*, that, if the case should require it, he defer not to join you. Wherefore, should it be necessary, inform him by your letters of the need of his coming

---

[1] At this time primate of Numidia. See preceding epistle.

to you, to the end that you, together with him, may be able, God helping you, to determine all these things in a salutary way.

## EPISTLE XXXII.
### To all the Bishops of the Council of Bizacium [2].

Gregory to all, &c.

As it is laudable and discreet to shew due reverence and honour to superiors, so it belongs to rectitude and the fear of God, if anything in them needs correction, not to put it off by any connivance, lest disease should begin to invade the whole body (which God forbid), sickness not being cured in the head. Now a considerable time ago certain things were reported to us about our brother Crementius, your primate, such as to pierce our heart with no slight sorrow. But through the pressure of divers tribulations, and especially from enemies raging round us, we had not time to enquire into the matter. And, since it is so serious that it ought by no means to be passed over without investigation, we hereby exhort your Fraternity with all carefulness and activity to search out in all ways the substantial truth, in order that either if these things are so, they may be cut off by canonical punishment, or, if they are false, the innocence of our brother may not long lie under the laceration of an infamous report. Wherefore, that there may be no torpor of idleness in the enquiry, we admonish you that neither the interest nor the favour nor the cajoleries of any person what-

---

[2] Cf. IX. 58, note 1, and IX. 59.

---

ever, nor anything else, soften any one of you in your sifting of what has been reported to us, or shake you from the path of truth; but gird ye yourselves in priestly wise to investigate the truth. For, if any one should presume to be sluggish, or to shew himself negligent in this matter, let him know that he will be a partaker in the said crimes before Almighty God, by zeal for whom he is not moved to enquire fully into the causes of atrocious wickedness.

## EPISTLE L.
### To Eulogius, Patriarch of Alexandria.

Gregory to Eulogius, &c.

The bearers of these presents, coming to Sicily, were converted from the error of the Monophysites, and united themselves to the holy universal Church. Having proceeded to the church of the blessed Peter, Prince of the apostles, they requested of me that I should commend them by letter to your Blessedness, to the end that they may not now be allowed to suffer any wrong from the heretics that are near them. And because one of them says that the monastery in which he was had been founded by his kindred, he desires to receive authority from your Holiness that the heretics who are in it may either return to the bosom of holy Church or be expelled from the same monastery. Let it be enough for us to have indicated this to you: for we know of your Blessedness that whatever pertains to zeal for Almighty God you hasten with all fervour to do. But for me I beg you to pray, since amid the swords of the Lombards which I endure I am excessively afflicted by pains of gout.

# BOOK XIII

## EPISTLE I.

### TO THE ROMAN CITIZENS.

Gregory, servant of the servants of God, to his most beloved sons the Roman citizens.

It has come to my ears that certain men of perverse spirit have sown among you some things that are wrong and opposed to the holy faith, so as to forbid any work being done on the Sabbath day. What else can I call these but preachers of Antichrist, who, when he comes, will cause the Sabbath day as well as the Lord's day to be kept free from all work. For, because he pretends to die and rise again, he wishes the Lord's day to be had in reverence; and, because he compels the people to judaize that he may bring back the outward rite of the law, and subject the perfidy of the Jews to himself, he wishes the Sabbath to be observed.

For this which is said by the prophet, *Ye shall bring in no burden through your gates on the Sabbath day* (Jerem. xvii. 24), could be held to as long as it was lawful for the law to be observed according to the letter. But after that the grace of Almighty God, our Lord Jesus Christ has appeared, the commandments of the law which were spoken figuratively cannot be kept according to the letter. For, if any one says that this about the Sabbath is to be kept, he must needs say that carnal sacrifices are to be offered: he must say too that the commandment about the circumcision of the body is still to be retained. But let him hear the Apostle Paul saying in opposition to him, *If ye be circumcised, Christ profiteth you nothing* (Galat. v. 2).

We therefore accept spiritually, and hold spiritually, this which is written about the Sabbath. For the Sabbath means rest. But we have the true Sabbath in our Redeemer Himself, the Lord Jesus Christ. And whoso acknowledges the light of faith in Him, if he draws the sins of concupiscence through his eyes into his soul, he introduces burdens through the gates on the Sabbath day. We

introduce, then, no burden through the gates on the Sabbath day if we draw no weights of sin through the bodily senses to the soul. For we read that the same our Lord and Redeemer did many works on the Sabbath day, so that he reproved the Jews, saying, *Which of you doth not loose his ox or his ass on the Sabbath day, and lead him away to watering* (Luke xiii. 15)? If, then, the very Truth in person commanded that the Sabbath should not be kept according to the letter, whoso keeps the rest of the Sabbath according to the letter of the law, whom else does he contradict but the Truth himself?

Another thing also has been brought to my knowledge; namely that it has been preached to you by perverse men that no one ought to wash on the Lord's day. And indeed if any one craves to wash for luxury and pleasure, neither on any other day do we allow this to be done. But if it is for bodily need, neither on the Lord's day do we forbid it. For it is written, *No man ever hated his own flesh, but nourisheth it and cherisheth it* (Ephes. v. 29). And again it is written, *Make not provision for the flesh to fulfil the lusts thereof* (Rom. xiii. 14). He, then, who forbids provision for the flesh in the lusts thereof certainly allows it in the needs thereof. For, if it is sin to wash the body on the Lord's day, neither ought the face to be washed on that day. But if this is allowed for a part of the body, why is it denied for the whole body when need requires? On the Lord's day, however, there should be a cessation of earthly labour, and attention given in every way to prayers, so that if anything is done negligently during the six days, it may be expiated by supplications on the day of the Lord's resurrection.

These things, most dear sons, being endowed with sure constancy and right faith, observe; despise the words of foolish men, and give not easy belief to all that you hear of having been said by them; but weigh it in the scale of reason, so that, while in firm stability you resist the wind of error, you may be able to attain to the solid joys of the heavenly kingdom.

[In two MSS., one *Colbert.* and *Vatic.* F., " mense Septembri, indict. 6."]

## EPISTLE V.

To Etherius, Bishop of Lugdunum (*Lyons*).

Gregory to Etherius, Bishop.

Although what we say is very distressing to us, and fraternal compassion rather moves us to weep than allows us to lay down anything concerning the things we have heard of, yet solicitude for the government undertaken by us pricks our heart with an urgent spur to see with great care to the good of churches, and to arrange what should be done before their interests might possibly suffer irretrievably. It has come, then, to our ears from the report of certain persons that an affection of the head has so befallen a certain bishop that it is a matter of groaning and weeping to hear of what he is wont to do under alienation of mind. Lest, therefore, while the shepherd is sick, the flock should be exposed to be torn by the teeth of the lyer-in-wait (which God forbid), or the interests of the Church itself should suffer irretrievably, it is necessary for us to treat the case with cautious provision. And so, since during the life of a bishop, whom unavoidable infirmity and not crime withdraws from his office, no reason allows another to be ordained in his place except on his resignation [1], let him, if he is accustomed to have intervals of sanity, himself make petition, declaring that he is no longer equal to this ministry owing to subversion of his intellectual faculties by infirmity, and let him request that another be ordained in his place. Which being done, let another who may be worthy be solemnly consecrated bishop in his place, by the election of all ; yet so that, as long as life shall retain the said bishop in this world, his due expenses be supplied to him by the same Church. If, however, he at no time recovers the faculties of a sound mind, a trustworthy person of approved life must be chosen, who may be fit for the government of the Church, take thought for the benefit of souls, restrain the unquiet under the bond of discipline, take care of ecclesiastical property, and exhibit himself in all respects ripe and efficient. And also, should he survive the bishop who is now sick, he should be consecrated in his place.

But as to ordinations of presbyters or dea-

cons, or of any other order, if cause requires any to be made in that Church, know that this is to be reserved to thy Fraternity, to the end that, it being in thy diocese, thou mayest enquire concerning the life, manners, and conduct of him who is chosen to such office. And if thou shouldest be satisfied, and there is nothing in him liable to the censure of canonical strictness, let him attain to his destined order not otherwise than through ordination by thee. Let thy Fraternity then, so proceed, and so order these things with vigilant provision, that the Church of God may no longer suffer from any neglect, and that thou mayest warn thy fellow-priests, not only by word but also by example, to have a care laudably for venerable places.

## EPISTLE VI.

To Brunichild, Queen of the Franks [2].

Gregory to Brunichild, &c.

Among other excellencies in you this holds the chief place beyond the rest, that in the midst of the waves of this world, which are wont with turbulent vexation to confound the minds of rulers, you so bring back your heart to the love of divine worship and to providing for the quiet of venerable places as if no other care troubled you. Whence, since conduct of this kind on the part of potentates is wont to be a great defence to subjects, we declare the nation of the Franks happy beyond other nations, having been accounted worthy to have a queen thus endowed with all good qualities.

On learning from the information contained in your letters that you have built the Church of Saint Martin in the suburbs of Augustodunum (*Autun*), and a monastery for handmaidens of God, and also a hospital in the same city, we rejoiced greatly, and returned thanks to Almighty God, who stimulates the sincerity of your heart to the doing of these things. In this case, that we may be held to some degree sharers in your good deeds, we have granted privileges according to your wish, to those places for the quiet and protection of those who live in them ; nor have we borne to defer even in the least degree our embracing of your Excellency's desires.

Furthermore, addressing you in the first place with the greeting of paternal charity, we inform you that to our illustrious sons, but

---

[1] On this head, see also XI. 48.

[2] On Brunechild, see VI. 5, note 4. Having after the death of her son Childebert II. acted as guardian of his son Theodebert II., who had received the kingdom of Austrasia with his Capital at Metz, she had been expelled by the Austrasians in the year 599, and been received by her other grandson, Theoderic II., who reigned over Burgundy with his Capital at Orleans. When this letter was sent (A.D. 602) Theoderic would be about fifteen years of age, and, as appears from the letter to himself which follows, under the management of his grandmother.

your servants and legates, Burgoaldus and Varmaricarius, we have granted a private interview in accordance with what you wrote to us; and they have disclosed to us in detail all that they said they had been charged with. It will be our care in time to come to inform your Excellency of whatever is done with regard to these things. For, as for us, whatever is possible, whatever is profitable, and tends to the settlement of peace between you and the republic, we desire, under God, with the utmost devotion, that it should be accomplished.

As to Mennas, our most reverend brother and fellow-bishop, after we had enquired into what had been said about him, and found him in no way culpable, and he having made satisfaction under oath before the most sacred body of the blessed apostle Peter, and so proved himself to be unaffected by what had been objected against his reputation, we have allowed him to return to his post purged and acquitted, since, as it was right, if he were in any respect guilty, that we should punish his fault canonically, so it was not right when he had the support of innocence, that we should detain him longer, or any way distress him.

Moreover, with respect to a certain bishop who, as the aforesaid magnificent men have told us, is prevented by infirmity of the head from administering his office, we have written to our brother and fellow-bishop Etherius [3], that if he should have intervals of freedom from this infirmity, he should make petition, declaring that he is not competent to fill his own place, and requesting that another be ordained to his Church. For during the life of a bishop, whom not his own fault but sickness, withdraws from the administration of his office, the sacred canons by no means allow another to be ordained in his place. But, if he at no time recovers the exercise of a sound mind, a person should be sought adorned with good life and conversation, who may be able both to take charge of souls, and look with salutary control after the causes and interests of the same church; and he should be such as may succeed to the bishop's place in case of his surviving him. But, if there are any to be promoted to a sacred order, or to any clerical ministry, we have ordained that the matter is to be reserved and announced to our aforesaid most reverend brother Etherius, provided it belong to his diocese [4], so that, enquiry having then been made, if the persons are subject to no fault which the sacred canons denounce, he himself may ordain

them. Let, then, the care of your Excellency conjoin itself with our ordering, to the end that the interests of the Church, which you have exceedingly at heart, may not suffer damage, and that increase of reward may accrue to the good deeds of your Excellency.

Having been asked likewise concerning a certain bigamist whether he might be admitted to a sacred order, we have, according to canonical rule, altogether forbidden it. For God forbid that in your times, in which you do so many pious and religious things, you should allow anything to be done contrary to ecclesiastical ordinance.

Moreover the aforesaid magnificent men, our sons, having delivered us a schedule, have requested among other things, what they said had been enjoined on them by your order, that such a person may be sent from us into Gaul as may, on the assembling of a synod, correct under the guidance of Almighty God whatever has been perpetrated against the most sacred canons. Herein we recognize the care of your Glory, how you take thought for the life of the soul and the stability of your kingdom, seeing that, fearing our Redeemer, and observing His precepts in all ways, you act in this case also so that the government of your kingdom may long subsist, and that after long courses of years you also may pass from an earthly to a heavenly kingdom. At a fitting time, if what we have said should be pleasing to God, we will take care to fulfil the venerable desires of your Excellency.

We, then, for the defence of the places about which your Excellency has written to us have been careful to order all things as you wish. But, lest haply our decrees should be suppressed at any time by the governors of those places on the ground that they are found to be interdicted from doing certain things, this same ordinance must be inserted among the public acts, that so it may be kept in your royal archives as well as in ours.

May Almighty God ever keep your Excellency in His fear, and so fulfil your desires and those of our sons the most excellent kings your grandsons, through the intercession of the blessed Peter, Prince of the apostles, to whom you commend them, as to grant you to have stable joy in their continual welfare, as you desire. Given in the month of November, Indiction 6.

## EPISTLE VII.

To THEODERIC, KING OF THE FRANKS [5].

Gregory to Theoderic, &c.

We have received with joy your written address to us indicating your health and safety,

---

3 See preceding epistle.
4 i.e. his metropolitan province, Lyons being a metropolitan See.

and we thereby perceive that you so transcend your age in prudence as to make it evident that it is for the happiness of the nation of the Franks that the government of royal dominion has been committed by the favour of heavenly grace to your Excellency. And this in you among other things is enough to call for praise and admiration, that in such things as you know that our daughter your most excellent grandmother desires for the love of Almighty God, in these you make haste most earnestly to lend your aid, so that thereby you may reign both happily here, and in a future life with the angels[6]. Seeing, then, that this comes, by the gift of God, from great discreetness of judgment, we have so speedily and gladly fulfilled what your Excellency desires as to shew by the celerity of our execution how much your good deeds have pleased us.

Furthermore, greeting you with paternal sweetness, we inform you that all the matters which you enjoined on the illustrious men your servants Burgoaldus and Varmaricarius, our sons, to be transacted with us have been disclosed to us in a private interview. And we praised you greatly, that you both attend wisely, as becomes you, to the present, and also make haste so to provide for security in the future by means of a lasting peace between you and the Republic that, being made one, you may extend the stability of your kingdom salutarily to all time. With regard to this we will announce to you in time to come what it may please God to order. For, as to us, whatever is proved to be advantageous and conducive to peace, we desire and strive that it should be brought to pass. The one thing is that, as our will is with regard to what is expedient, so should be the will of God, without whom we can do nothing. May the Holy Trinity make you to advance always in His fear, and so dispose your heart in moderation well-pleasing to Him as both to grant to your subjects now joy from you, and to you from Himself joy without end hereafter.

## EPISTLE VIII.

### To Senator, Abbot.

Gregory to Senator, presbyter and abbot of a hospital (or guest-house, *xenodochii*).

When the hearts of Catholic Kings, &c.
[See the epistle following (Ep. ix.), with

which this agrees throughout, as does also Epistle X. to Lupo, except for the different designations of the persons addressed and places referred to, and the addition in epistles VIII. and IX., after the words "or absolve her (*him*) as innocent," of the following paragraph.]

By a similar definition, according to the desire of the founders, we decree that none of those who may in future have been ordained as abbot or presbyter to the same guest-house and monastery shall dare by any secret scheming whatever to take the office of the Episcopate, unless he has been first deprived of the office of abbot, and another has been substituted in his place; lest, by consuming the property of the guest-house or monastery in unfair expenditure, he should cause most serious pressure of want to the poor and strangers, or to others who live from its resources. Moreover, we forbid that the bishop have licence, without the consent of the abbot and presbyter, to remove from the same place any monk for promotion to an ecclesiastical order, or for any cause whatever, lest usurpation in this regard should be carried to such an extent that places which have to be built up by the acquisition of men be destroyed by their removal.

## EPISTLE IX.

### To Thalassia, Abbess.

Gregory to Thalassia, &c.
When the hearts of catholic kings are so inflamed with ardent desire, by divine grace preventing them, as of their own accord to demand the things that pontifical admonitions should provoke them to, such things are to be granted with cheerful and joyful mind all the more as the very things which they desire ought to have been demanded of them, had they been unwilling to do them. Accordingly, in accordance with the letters of our most Excellent royal children, Brunichild and her grandson Theoderic, to the monastery of Saint Mary, where there is constituted a congregation of handmaidens of God, founded in the city of Augustodunum by the bishop Siagrius of reverend memory, over which you preside, we indulge, grant and confirm by the decree of our present authority privileges as follows;—Ordaining that no king, no bishop, no one endowed with any dignity whatsoever, or any one else whatsoever, shall have power, under show of any cause or occasion whatsoever, to diminish or take away, or apply to his own uses, or grant as if to other pious uses for excuse of his own avarice, anything of what has been given to the same monastery by the above-written

---

[6] If the accounts given by the Frankish historians be true, Brunechild's influence over her grandson was not in all respects such as to prepare him for life with the angels. She is said to have encouraged him in licentious living for fear of her own power being undermined by the introduction into his court of a lawful queen. (*Greg. Turon., Hist. Franc.* XI. 36; *Fredegar.* XXX., XXXVII.).

king's own children, or of what shall in future be bestowed on it by any others whatever of their own possessions. But all things that have been there offered, or may come to be offered, we will to be possessed by thee, as well as by those who shall succeed thee in thy office and place, from the present time inviolate and without disturbance, provided thou apply them in all ways to the uses of those for whose sustentation and government they have been granted.

We also appoint that on the death of an abbess of the aforesaid monastery no other shall be ordained by means of any kind of craftiness of secret scheming, but such a one as the king of the same province, with the consent of the nuns, shall have chosen in the. fear of God, and provided for the ordination of.

Under this head we also add, in order that we may exclude all place for avarice, that no one of the kings, no one of the priests, or any one else in person or by proxy, shall dare to accept anything in gold, or in any kind of consideration whatever, for the ordination of such abbess, or for any causes whatever pertaining to this monastery, and that the same abbess presume not to give anything on account of her ordination, lest by such occasion what is offered or has been offered to places of piety should be consumed. And, inasmuch as many occasions for the deception of religious women are sought out, as is said, in your parts by bad men, we ordain that an abbess of this same monastery shall in no wise be deprived or deposed unless in case of criminality requiring it. Hence it is necessary that if any complaint of this kind should arise against her, not only the bishop of the city of Augustodunum should examine the case, but that he should call to his assistance six other of his fellow-bishops, and so fully investigate the matter, to the end that, all judging with one accord, a strict canonical decision may either smite her if guilty, or absolve her if innocent.

All these things, therefore, which the paper of this our precept and decree contains we decree to be observed in perpetuity for thee as well as for all who may succeed thee in the same rank and place, and for all whom they may concern. Moreover, if any one, whether king, priest, judge, or secular person, being aware of this our written constitution, should attempt to contravene it, let him be deprived of the dignity of his power and honour, and know that he stands guilty before divine judgment for the iniquity that he has perpetrated. And, unless he either restore what he has wrongfully taken away, or lament what he has done unlawfully with fit penitence, let him be debarred from the most sacred body and blood of our God and Lord, the Redeemer Jesus Christ, and be subject to strict vengeance in the eternal judgment. But the peace of our Lord Jesus Christ be to all who observe what is just to this same place, to the end that they may both receive here the fruit of their welldoing, and find the rewards of eternal peace at the hands of the strict Judge.

## EPISTLE X.

### To Lupo, Abbot.

Gregory to Lupo, Presbyter and Abbot.

When the hearts of catholic kings, &c. [7]

## EPISTLE XII.

### To Paschasius, Bishop of Neapolis (Naples).

Gregory to Paschasius, &c.

Those who with pure intent desire to bring to the true faith aliens from the Christian religion should study kindness, and not asperity; lest such as reason rendered with smoothness might have appealed to should be driven far off by opposition. For whosoever act otherwise, and under cover of such intention would suspend people from their accustomed observance of their own rites, are proved to be intent on their own cause rather than on God's. To wit, the Jews dwelling in Naples have complained to us, asserting that certain persons are endeavouring unreasonably to drive them from certain solemnities of their holidays, so that it may not be lawful for them to observe the solemnities of their festivals, as up to this time since long ago

---

[7] For the rest of this epistle, see preceding Epistle IX., with which, *mutatis mutandis*, it is identical, as was Epistle VIII., save for an additional paragraph, given under Epistle VIII. See what has been said with regard to that Epistle. The genuineness, or at any rate the freedom from interpolation, of all these three Epistles is disputed. The Benedictine Editors of Gregory's works defend their authenticity. See their note (b) to Ep. VIII. (*Patrologiæ Tomus LXVII. Sancti Gregorii Magni tomus tertius*). The purport of all three letters is to confer privileges on, and provide for the future security and regulation of, three recent foundations of Queen Brunechild at Augustodunum (*Autun*); viz. 1. A hospital, or guest-house (*xenodochium*) in Autun, over which a Senator, described as "presbyter and abbot," had been appointed to preside; 2. A monastery for women, of which Tnalassia had been appointed Abbess; 3. The Church of St. Martin in the suburbs, over which Lupo, "presbyter and abbot," presided. These foundations are referred to, though not described, in Epistle VI. to Brunechild herself, where Gregory speaks of having issued decrees for their protection in the future, which he desires should be kept among the royal archives. In those times of continual conflict among the Frank potentates royal founders might naturally wish to protect their foundations from disturbance by means of spiritual fulminations; and the queen's desire in this respect might account for the anathemas in these epistles, which have been said to be characteristic of a later age than that of Gregory. It may be observed further that the appointment of the heads of these religious institutions is, in the letters before us, reserved to "the kings of the province," instead of free election, subject to episcopal approval, being left to the inmates, as was usual in other cases. This might be due, if the letters are genuine, to the request of Brunechild, whom, as a staunch Catholic and a supporter of the Church, Gregory ever shews himself anxious to conciliate. With regard to his politic flattery of her, or of others similarly situated, cf. VI. 5, note 4.

it has been lawful for them and their forefathers to keep and observe them. Now, if this is true, these people appear to be taking trouble to no purpose. For what is the use, when even such long unaccustomed prohibition is of no avail for their faith and conversion? Or why should we lay down rules for the Jews as to how they should observe their ceremonies, if we cannot thereby win them? We should therefore so act that, being rather appealed to by reason and kindness, they may wish to follow us, and not to fly from us; and that proving to them from their own Scriptures what we tell them, we may be able, with God's help, to convert them to the bosom of Mother Church.

Wherefore let thy Fraternity, so far as may be possible, with the help of God, kindle them to conversion, and not allow them any more to be disquieted with respect to their solemnities; but let them have free licence to observe and celebrate all their festivals and holidays, even as hitherto both they and their forefathers for a long time back have kept and held them.

## EPISTLE XVIII.

### To certain Bishops of Sicily.

Gregory to Leo, Secundinus, John, Donus, Lucidus, Trajan, bishops of Sicily.

Even as we are admonished through the speech of the apostles to impart one to another spiritual aids,—so, in matters that by God's ordering we may have to settle in virtue of the government imposed on us for administration of the affairs of the poor, it is fit that priestly succour be not wanting. Accordingly in sending the bearer of these presents, Adrian our *Chartularius* [8], to govern the patrimony of our Church, to wit in the Syracusan district, we have thought it necessary to commend him to your Fraternity, that, wherein custom may demand it, you may afford him your succour, to the end that, while he is supported by you with bodily aid for doing his work, and with the spiritual aid of your prayers for carrying out with facility whatever he may undertake, he may be able, God also working with him, to accomplish prosperously what has been by us enjoined on him. But, as for yourselves, you should so acquit yourselves in good works before the face of Almighty God that there be not found in your doings anything that may be smitten by the judgment of God, or for which you may be accused by any man whatever lying in wait against you. For we have charged our aforesaid *Chartularius* that, if he should come to know of any inordinate doings on the part of our most reverend brethren the bishops, he should first himself take them to task by private and modest admonition; and, that, if such things are not amended, he should inform us of them speedily.

Furthermore, it has been reported to us that in the times of our predecessor of holy memory it was arranged by the deacon Servusdei, who then had charge of the ecclesiastical patrimony, that the priests [9] of your several dioceses, when you go forth to seal infants [1], should not be immoderately burdened. For a certain sum had been fixed, and this, as I hear, with your consent, to be given by the same priests for the services of the clerks (*clericorum*). And this, which was then approved of, is said to be by no means kept to now. Wherefore I admonish your Fraternity to endeavour not to be burdensome to your subjects, and, if they have any grievances, to abate them, seeing also that you ought not to have departed from what had once been determined. For you will be seeing to your own interest both in the future and the present life, if you keep those who have been committed to you free from grievance.

## EPISTLE XXII.

### To Rusticiana, Patrician lady.

Gregory to Rusticiana, &c.

As often as any one comes to us from the royal city, we take care to enquire of your bodily health; but, my sins being the cause, I always hear what I am sorry to hear, since, frail and weak as you already are, it is reported that the pains of gout still grow upon you. But I pray the Almighty Lord that whatever befalls your body may be ordered to the health of your soul, and that temporal scourges may prepare for you eternal rest, and that through the pains which have an end He may grant you joys without end. As for me, I live in such a state of groaning and in the midst of such occupations that it irks me to have arrived at these days which now I spend, and my only consolation is the expectation of death. Wherefore I beg you to pray for me, to the end that I may be soon released from this prison of the flesh, so as

---

[9] *Sacerdotes*, meaning here apparently parish priests, though more commonly, in Gregory's epistles, denoting bishops. The abuse complained of seems to have been that of charging priests of parishes unreasonably for the remuneration of the *clerici* who attended the bishops on their confirmation progresses.
[1] *Ad consignandos infantes;* i.e. for confirmation, cf. IV. 26, note 6.

---

[8] Adrian, who had already been commissioned as *notarius Siciliæ* (X. 23). had now been made *rector patrimonii*, being succeeded as notary by Pantaleo (XIII. 34).

to be no longer tormented by such great pains.

Furthermore, I have to inform you that a certain person has come here, Beator by name, who gives himself out as *comes privatarum*[2], and is doing many things against all, but principally against your Excellency's people, or those of your most noble granddaughters, as though he were making enquiry into matters of public import. And we indeed will not permit him to act wrongfully, but neither can we stand in the way of public interests. Do you therefore treat as you can with the most pious princes, that they may countermand any wrongful proceeding on his part. For neither is the public interest served by any kind of turmoil, nor does he appear to reclaim anything of great amount. I beg that my most sweet son the lord Strategius[3] be greeted in my behalf, whom may Almighty God nourish for Himself and for you, and ever comfort you by His own grace and by the young lord's life. Further, what should I write to you concerning your return hither, knowing as you do how much I desire it? But, when I look to the obligations of the business that detains you, I am in despair; and so I implore the Creator of all that, wherever you are, and wherever you may be, He would protect you by the extension of His right hand, and preserve you from all evil.

### EPISTLE XXVI.

#### To Anthemius, Subdeacon.

Gregory to Anthemius, Subdeacon of Campania.

It has reached our ears that our brother and fellow-bishop Paschasius[4] is so idle and negligent in all ways that he is in no respect recognised as bishop; and that so neither his own Church, nor the monasteries, nor any, whether the sons of the Church[5], or the oppressed poor, are conscious of any earnestness of love on his part towards them; nor does he afford any help in what is just to those who supplicate him, and (what is a still more serious thing to say) he cannot bear on any account to receive the counsels of the

wise and of such as admire what is right, so that he might at any rate learn from another what he cannot attend to of himself; but, passing over the things that pertain to a pastor's charge, he occupies himself with his whole attention unprofitably in the building of ships. Whence, as is reported, it has come to pass that he has already lost four hundred *solidi*, or more. This also is added to his faults, that he is said to go down daily to the sea with one or two clerics in so mean a guise as to be the talk among his own people, and to seem to strangers so vile and despicable that he is judged to have nothing in him of the character or venerableness of a bishop. If this be so, know that it is not without fault of thine, who hast delayed to rebuke and restrain him, as is fit. Seeing, then, that all this not only discredits him, but also evidently brings reproach on the office of the priesthood, we desire thee to summon him for this thing before other priests[6], or some of his noble sons[7], and exhort him that, shaking off the vice of sluggishness, he be not idle, but vigilant in the care of his Church and of the monasteries, exhibit fatherly charity to his sons, stand up for the defence of the poor with discretion in cases that are commended by justice, and receive gladly the counsels of the wise, to the end that both that city may be comforted by his solicitude, and he himself succeed in covering the faults of his idleness. If however, as we do not believe will be the case, after this our exhortation he should venture to be negligent after his accustomed manner, he must by all means be sent to us, that in our presence he may learn what it becomes a priest to do, and how to do it, after the fear of God. Given in the month of March, Indiction 6.

### EPISTLE XXVII.

#### To Anthemius, Subdeacon.

Gregory to Anthemius, Subdeacon of Campania.

As often as we hear things of our brethren and fellow-bishops that shew them to be to blame and cause us sadness, necessity compels us in no slight degree to take thought for their amendment. Seeing, then, that it has been reported to us that the bishops of Campania are so negligent that, unmindful of the dignity and character of their office, neither towards their Churches nor towards their sons do they shew the care of paternal vigilance, nor concern themselves about monasteries, nor bestow their protection on the oppressed and the poor,

---

[2] This designation may mean a kind of private secretary to the Emperor, or one to whom the secret service of the government was committed.

[3] See II. 27, note 2.

[4] Bishop of Naples. A few epistles not included in this translation are addressed to him as such.

[5] *Filii ecclesiæ*, or, according to the authority of MSS., simply *filii*. Cf. III. 56, where the expression occurs. It is understood to denote the lay members of any Church, among whom those of the highest social position were called *nobiles* (see below), and others *plebs*. Mandates for the election of bishops are addressed to *clero, nobilibus, ordini, et plebi* (as in II. 6), or to *clero ordini, et plebi* (as in I. 58), or occasionally *clero et nobilibus* (as in I. 80); *ordo* being understood to denote persons of position, though not ranking as nobles.

[6] i.e. bishops, as commonly meant by *sacerdotos*.

[7] See above, note 5.

we therefore enjoin thee and hereby give thee authority to call them together, and strictly admonish them in virtue of our mandate, that they be not any longer idle, but so evince their priestly zeal and solicitude, and be so vigilant in what it becomes them justly and according unto God to do, that no murmur concerning them may exasperate us any more. If, however, thou shouldest find any one of them to be negligent after this being done, send him to us without allowing any excuse, that by regular exercise of discipline they may be made to feel how serious a matter it is to refuse to be corrected in things that are reprehensible and exceedingly to be condemned.

## EPISTLE XXXI.

### To Phocas, Emperor [8].

Gregory to Phocas Augustus.

Glory to God in the highest who, according as it is written, changes times, and transfers kingdoms, seeing that He has made apparent to all what He vouchsafed to speak by His prophet, *That the most High ruleth in the kingdom of men, and giveth it to whomsoever he will* (Dan. iv. 17). For in the incomprehensible dispensation of Almighty God there are alternate controlments of mortal life ; and sometimes, when the sins of many are to be smitten, one is raised up through whose hardness the necks of subjects may be bowed down under the yoke of tribulation, as in our affliction we have long had proof. But sometimes, when the merciful God has decreed to refresh the mourning hearts of many with His consolation, He advances one to the summit of government, and through the bowels of His mercy infuses the grace of exultation in Him into the minds of all. In which abundance of exultation we believe that we shall speedily be confirmed, who rejoice that the Benignity of your Piety has arrived at imperial supremacy. *Let the heavens rejoice, and let the earth be glad* (Ps. xcv. 11) ; and let the whole people of the republic, hitherto afflicted exceedingly, grow cheerful for your benignant deeds. Let the proud minds of enemies be subdued under the yoke of your domination. Let the crushed and depressed spirits of subjects be revived by your mercy : let the power of heavenly grace make you terrible to your enemies, your piety kind to your subjects. Let the whole republic have rest in your most happy times, the pillage of peace under colour of processes at law being exposed. Let plottings about

wills cease, and benevolences exacted by force. Let secure possession of their own return to all, that they may rejoice in having without fear what they have acquired without fraud. Let every single person's liberty be now at length restored to him under the yoke of empire. For there is this difference between the kings of the nations and the emperors of the republic, that the kings of the nations are lords of slaves, but the emperors of the republic lords of freemen. But we shall better speak of these things by praying than by putting you in mind of them. May Almighty God in every thought and deed keep the heart of your Piety in the hand of His grace ; and whatever things should be done justly, whatever things with clemency, may the Holy Spirit who dwells in your breast direct, that your Clemency may both be exalted in a temporal kingdom, and after courses of many years attain to heavenly kingdoms. Given in the month of June, Indiction 6.

## EPISTLE XXXIV.

### To Pantaleo, Notary

Gregory to Pantaleo, &c.

Thy Experience remembers what and what kind of oath thou tookest over the most sacred body of the blessed apostle Peter. Whence also we committed to thee without fear the charge of enquiry in the patrimony of the Syracusan district. It is, then, incumbent on thee to have thine own good faith and the fear of the same blessed apostle Peter ever before thine eyes, and so to act that neither with men in this present life nor with Almighty God in the last judgment thou mayest be open to blame. Now from the report of Salerius our *chartularius* we have learnt that thou hast found the *modius* in which the husbandmen (*coloni*) [9] of the Church have been compelled to give their corn to be one of twenty-five *sextarii* [1]. This we altogether execrated, and were sorry thou hadst been late in making it a subject of enquiry. We rejoice, therefore, at thy telling us that thou hast broken the said *modius* and made a just one. But, inasmuch as the aforesaid *chartularius* has taken care to mention also what has already been collected under thy Experience by the fraudulent dealings of the farmers (*conductores*) [2] from two territories, therefore, even as with a view to the future, we rejoice that thou hast acted zealously in breaking the unjust *modius*, so also we think of sins in the past ; lest, if what the farmers have fraudulently taken away from the peasants (*rusticis*) [3] accrues to us, we should

---

[8] Phocas succeeded Mauricius as Emperor in November, A.D. 602. With regard to Gregory's adulatory tone towards this sanguinary usurper and his consort Leontia, see *Prolegomena*, p. xxvii.

[9] Cf. I. 44, note 1.   [1] Cf. ib., note 4.   [2] Cf. ib., note 5.
[3] Cf. ib., note 1.

be implicated in their sins. And accordingly we desire thy Experience, with all faithfulness, with all integrity—having regard to the fear of Almighty God, and recalling to mind the strictness of the blessed apostle Peter—to make a list throughout each several estate (*massam*) [4] of poor and indigent husbandmen, and with the money found to have been got by fraud to procure cows, sheep, and swine, and distribute them among the several poor husbandmen. And this we desire thee to do with the advice of the most reverend lord bishop John [5], and Adrian our *chartularius* and *rector* [6]. If, moreover, it should be necessary for the sake of consultation, our son also the lord Julian should be called in, so that no one else may know, but all be kept quite secret. Do you therefore consult among yourselves whether this same assistance should be given to the said poor husbandmen in money or in kind. But, whatever be the common fund, first, as I have said, make a list, and afterwards take pains to distribute to each according to the degree of his poverty. For I, as the teacher of the Gentiles testifies, have all and abound ; nor do I seek money, but reward (Phil. iv.). So act therefore that in the day of judgment thou mayest shew me fruit of thy labour from the service that has been committed to thy Experience. If thou do this purely, faithfully, and strenuously, thou wilt both receive it back here in thy children, and hereafter wilt have plenary retribution in the scrutiny of the Eternal Judge.

## EPISTLE XXXVIII.

### To Phocas, Emperor.

Gregory to Phocas Augustus.

It pleases us to consider, with rejoicings and great thanksgivings, what praises we owe to Almighty God, that the yoke of sadness has been removed, and we are come to times of liberty under the imperial Piety of your Benignity. For that your Serenity has not found a deacon of the Apostolic See resident at the court according to ancient custom, is not owing to my negligence, but to most grave necessity. For, while all the ministers of this our Church shrunk and fled with fear from times of such oppression and hardship, it was not possible to impose on any of them the duty of going to the royal city to remain at the court. But now that they have learnt that your Clemency, by the ordering of God's grace, has attained to the summit of Empire,

those who had before greatly feared to go there hasten even of themselves to your feet, moved thereto by joy. But, seeing that some of them are so weak from old age as to be hardly able to bear the toil, and some are deeply engaged in ecclesiastical cares, and the bearer of these presents, who was the first of all our guardians (*defensores*), has been long well known to me for his diligence, and approved in life, faith, and character, I have judged him fit to be sent to the feet of your Piety [7]. I have accordingly, by God's permission, made him a deacon, and have been at pains to send him to you with all speed, that he may be able, when a convenient time is found, to inform your Clemency of all that is being done in these parts. To him I beg your Serenity to deign to incline your pious ears, that you may find it in your power to have pity on us all the more speedily as you learn the more truly from his account what our affliction is. For in what manner by the daily swords, and by how many invasions, of the Lombards, lo now for the length of five and thirty years, we have been oppressed, by no words of description can we fully express. But we trust in the Almighty Lord, that He will complete for us the good things of His consolation which He has begun, and that, having raised up pious lords in the republic, He will also extinguish cruel enemies. And so may the Holy Trinity guard your life for many years, so that we may the longer rejoice in the good of your Piety, which we have received after long waiting.

## EPISTLE XXXIX.

### To Leontia, Empress.

Gregory to Leontia Augusta.

What tongue may suffice to speak, what mind to think, what great thanks we owe to Almighty God for the serenity of your empire, in that such hard burdens of long duration have been removed from our necks, and the gentle yoke of imperial supremacy has returned, which subjects are glad to bear ? Glory, then, be given to the Creator of all by the hymning choirs of angels, thanksgiving be paid by men on earth, for that the whole republic, which has endured many wounds of sorrow, has now at length found the balm of your consolation. Hence we must needs implore the more earnestly the mercy of Almighty God, that He would keep the heart of your Piety ever in His right hand, and dispose your thoughts by the aid of heavenly grace, to the end that your Tranquillity may be able to rule those who

---

4 Cf. ib., note 5.      5 Bishop of Syracuse. Cf. V. 17.
6 Adrian, previously addressed as *notarius Siciliæ* (X. 23), had been succeeded by Pantaleo and made *rector patrimonii* (XIII. 18).

7 The person thus sent was Boniface (see below, Ep. XL., and XIV. 8), who afterwards became pope.

serve you the more righteously as you know more truly how to serve the Sovereign of all. May He make you His champions in love of the catholic faith, having, of His benign dealing, made you our emperors. May He infuse into your minds zeal together with gentleness, that you may always be able with pious fervour not to leave unavenged whatever is done amiss with regard to God, and in case of any delinquency against yourselves to bear and spare. May He give us in your Piety the clemency of Pulcheria Augusta, who for her zeal for the catholic faith was called in the holy synod the new Helena (*Act.* 1 *synodi Chalcedonensis*). May the Almighty mercy of God grant to you fuller length of days to live with our most pious lord, that the longer your life is extended, the more strongly may the consolation of your subjects be confirmed.

I ought perhaps to have requested that your Tranquillity should hold as especially commended to you the Church of the blessed apostle Peter, which up to this time has laboured under grievous plots against it. But, knowing that you love Almighty God, I ought not to ask what you will exhibit of your own accord out of the benignity of your piety. For the more you fear the Creator of all, the more fully may you love the Church of him to whom it was said, *Thou art Peter, and upon this rock I will build my Church, and the gates of hell shall not prevail against it ;* and to whom it is said, *To thee I will give the keys of the kingdom of heaven ; and whatsoever thou shalt bind on earth shall be bound in heaven ; and whatsoever thou shalt loose on earth shall be loosed in heaven* (Matth. xv. 18). Whence it is not doubtful to us with what strong love you will bind yourself to him through whom you earnestly desire to be loosed from all sins. May he, then, be the guardian of your empire, may he be your protector on earth, may he be an intercessor for you in heaven : that through your relieving your subjects from hard burdens, and causing them to rejoice in your empire, you may, after many years, rejoice in the heavenly kingdom.

## EPISTLE XL.

### To Cyriacus, Patriarch of Constantinople.

Gregory to Cyriacus, &c.

Observing diligently, most dear brother, how great is the virtue of peace from the Lord's voice, which says, *My peace I give unto you* (Joh. xiv. 27), it becomes us so to abide in the love thereof as in no wise to give place to discord. But, since we cannot otherwise live in its root except by retaining in mind and in deed the humility which the very author of peace has taught, we entreat you with befitting charity, that, treading down with the foot of your heart the profane elation which is always hostile to souls, you make haste to remove from the midst of the Church the offence of a perverse and proud title, lest you should possibly be found divided from the society of our peace. But let there be in us one spirit, one mind, one charity, one bond in Christ, who has willed us to be his members. For let your Holiness consider how hard it is, how indecent, how cruel, how alien from the aim of a priest, not to have that peace which you preach to others, and so abstain from offending your brethren out of pride. But study this rather, how you may prostrate with the sword of humility the author of vain and profitless elation, to the end that in such a victory the grace of the Holy Spirit may claim you as a habitation for Himself, so that what is written may be plainly fulfilled in you ; *the temple of God is holy, which temple ye are* (2 Cor. vi. 17.)

We commend to you in all things the bearer of these presents, our most beloved common son, the deacon Boniface, that in whatsoever may be needful he may find, as is becoming, the succour of your Holiness.

## EPISTLE XLI.

### To Eulogius, Patriarch of Alexandria.

Gregory to Eulogius, Bishop of Alexandria.

A conversation having arisen one day between me and my familiar friends about the customs of churches, one who had studied the art of medicine in the great city of Alexandria told us that he had a fellow-student attending the same lectures, a boy of extreme depravity, who, he said, had been suddenly ordained a deacon. And he added that he had procured ordination by bribes and gifts ; for he acknowledged that this custom had prevailed in the holy Alexandrine Church. On hearing this I was amazed, and exceedingly surprised that the tongue of the most holy and blessed man the lord Eulogius, which recalls so many heretics to the catholic faith, has not extirpated simoniacal heresy from the holy Alexandrine Church. And who will there be whose exhortation or correction will be able to amend this, if his great and admirable teaching shall have left it without amendment ?

Wherefore, for the absolution of your soul, for the increase of your reward, that your works may be in all respects perfect before the eyes of the tremendous Judge, you ought to make haste utterly to pull up and eradicate simoniacal heresy, which was the first to arise in the Church, from your most holy See, which is our's [8].

For on this account it comes to pass that the holiness of ecclesiastical orders falls away from very many, because persons are promoted to these orders, not for their life and deeds, but for bribes. But if meritorious character, and not bribes, be sought after, unworthy persons will not come to ordination. And by so much the more will reward begin to accrue to you as any good men who have been promoted to sacred orders shall have devoted themselves to the care of winning souls.

### EPISTLE XLII.

To Eulogius, Patriarch of Alexandria.
Gregory to Eulogius, &c.

We return great thanks to Almighty God, that in the mouth of the heart a sweet savour of charity is experienced, when that which is written is fulfilled, *As cold water to a thirsty soul, so is good news from a far country* (Prov. xxv. 25). For I had previously been greatly disturbed by a letter from Boniface the *Chartularius*, my *responsalis*, who dwells in the royal city, saying that your to me most sweet and pleasant Holiness had suffered from failure of bodily sight. From this letter I was smitten by heavy sorrow. But suddenly, by the prospering grace of our Creator and Redeemer, I received the epistle of your Blessedness, and, learning that the bodily trouble of which I had heard was cured, I rejoiced exceedingly, since gladness of heart succeeded which was as great as the bitterness of the sadness which had come before. For we know that, with the help of Almighty God, your life is the health of many. For sailors sail secure through the waves when an instructed and skilful steersman sits at the helm.

Moreover in my joy for your health I have this additional cause for exultation, that I have learnt how through your mouth the enemies of the Church are decreased in number, and the flocks of the Lord multiplied. For through the ploughshare of your tongue heavenly corn increases daily, and is multiplied in the garners on high; so that in you we rejoice that what is written is fulfilled, *Where there is much increase, there is manifest the strength of the oxen* (Prov. xiv. 4). Whence we gather plainly that the more you bring back fugitives to the service of Almighty God, the more merit you have with Him. And by how much the more merit you receive, the more fully can you obtain what you ask for. I beseech you therefore to pray the more earnestly for me a sinner, since both pain of body, and bitterness of heart, and immense ravages of mortality among the swords of so many barbarians, afflict me exceedingly. In the midst of all these things it is not temporal but eternal consolation that I require, which of myself I am not able to win by prayer, but which I trust that I shall obtain by the intercessions of your Blessedness. Last year I received no letters from your Holiness, and I was much distressed. It is true that your blessing, which you sent without a letter, was both given and received. But, since your tongue delights me more than your gifts, I was less gratified than I might have been by what was given. But I directed our common son, the deacon Epiphanius, to write to Alexander and Isidore, deacons of your most holy Church, to acknowledge the receipt of what had been sent.

I wrote to you, further, that I had got ready large pieces of timber for making masts and rudders, but that the small ship which had come could not carry them; and you have since written nothing in reply. Wherefore, if you need them, write to our common son Boniface, whom we are now sending as our representative (*responsalem*) to the royal city, that he may send me word that they may be prepared, and that they may be found ready when your Blessedness shall send for them.

Furthermore, we have sent you a small cross, in which is inserted a blessing from the chains of your lovers the apostles Saint Peter and Saint Paul; and let this be continually applied to your eyes, seeing that many miracles have been wont to be wrought through this same blessing.

May Almighty God inspire the heart of your Blessedness to be careful to pray for me continually, and may He protect you and all yours with His right hand, and after many courses of years bring you to the heavenly kingdom.

We have received, corresponding with your description of them, the blessings [9] of Saint Mark, sent to us by your most blessed Fraternity, and we return thanks for your kindness, since from these outward things we learn what you are towards us inwardly.

---

[8] See VII 40, for Gregory's view of the three sees of Rome, Antioch, and Alexandria, all representing the see of St. Peter.

[9] *Eulogias*, apparently in the same sense as *benedictiones*, used elsewhere as denoting presents.

# BOOK XIV

## EPISTLE II.

### To Vitalis, Guardian (*Defensorem*) of Sardinia.

Gregory to Vitalis, &c.

From the information given us by thy Experience we find that the hospitals [or guesthouses, *xenodochia*] founded in Sardinia are suffering from grievous neglect. Hence our most reverend brother and fellow-bishop Januarius[1] would have had to be most strongly reprehended, did not his old age and simplicity, and the sickness which thou hast told us of coming on besides, keep us in check.

Seeing, then, that he is so situated that he cannot be fit to order anything, do thou warn the steward of that Church, and Epiphanius the archpresbyter, under our strict authority, that they themselves at their own peril endeavour themselves carefully and profitably to set those same hospitals (*xenodochia*) in order. For, if there should be any neglect there hereafter, let them know that they will not be able in any manner, or to any extent, to excuse themselves before us.

Further, since the proprietors of Sardinia have petitioned us that, seeing that they are afflicted by diverse burdens, thou mightest go to Constantinople for their redress, we grant thee leave to go. And we have also written to our most beloved son Boniface, desiring him to do his best to lend thee his aid in obtaining redress for that province.

Moreover, with regard to the Churches which thou hast informed us are without priests[2], we have written to our aforesaid most reverend brother and fellow-bishop Januarius, that he should supply them; yet so that all be not chosen for the episcopate from his own Church. For it becomes him so to supply other Churches as not to cause want in his own of persons who may be of advantage to it.

As to what thou hast told us of persons having been preferred to the government of certain monasteries who, while they were in a lower monastic order, had fallen into sin, they ought not indeed to have undertaken the office of abbot except after entire reformation of life and after due preceding penance. But since, as thou sayest, they have undertaken the office of abbots, heed must be given to their life, manners, and attention to duty. And, if their conduct should not be found inconsistent with their office, let them persevere in the order in which they are. Otherwise let them be removed, and others ordained who may profit the souls committed to them.

Furthermore, in the case of the monastery of Saint Hermas, which was founded by our brother in the house of the religious lady Pomponiana, inasmuch as it should be treated with tenderness rather than with strictness, let thy Experience endeavour to deal sweetly with the said lady, to the end that neither may she, to her own sin, disregard the will of the founder, nor thou fail to provide salubriously for the advantage of the monastery. Further, as to the girls of whom the aforesaid Pomponiana had formerly changed the religious dress, and converted them in the monastery[3], thou must by no means suffer them to be withdrawn from her, or disquieted; but let them continue, God protecting them, in the state of life in which they are.

With regard to the recovery of the property of Churches, or of monasteries, or any other devoted to pious uses, about which thou hast written, those who are interested must be admonished that it is for them to seek in all ways to recover it with thy support and aid. But, if they should haply prove negligent, or in any case if such as ought to recover it should not be found, then do thou search it all out and so get it back, when discovered, as not to appear to take legal action against any one with a high hand. As to what thou hast told us with respect to the hospitals (*xenodochia*) of Hortulanus and Thomas, we so far have no knowledge. Wherefore let thy Experience look diligently into the order of the Emperor so far given, and arrange all according to its tenour, and make known to us whatever thou hast done.

Concerning what thou hast written about our brother and fellow-bishop Januarius at the time when he celebrates the sacrifice often suffering such distress that he can hardly after long intervals return to the place in the canon

---

[1] See I. 62, note 9.
[2] *Sacerdotes*, here as elsewhere meaning bishops.

[3] "Convertit in monasterio.' *Conversio*, as usually, means here monastic profession.

where he has left off, and as to many doubting whether they should receive the Communion from his consecration, they are to be admonished to be in no alarm at all, but communicate with full faith and security, since a person's sickness neither alters nor defiles the benediction of the sacred mystery. Nevertheless our said brother should by all means be exhorted privately, that, as often as he feels any trouble coming on, he should not proceed to celebration, lest he thus expose himself to contempt, and cause offence to the minds of the weak.

Furthermore, the religious lady Pomponiana [4] has complained to us that the inheritance of her late son-in-law Epiphanius—of which the said Epiphanius had appointed his wife Matrona, daughter of the aforesaid Pomponiana, to be usufructuary for the benefit of the monastery which he had directed to be founded in his house, and for its benefit also in all ways after the extinction of the usufruct—together with other things which are proved to belong to the same Matrona by right of possession, have been unjustly taken away by thy Experience and by our most reverend brother and fellow-bishop Januarius, and that nothing therefore has so far been paid to her daughter, or been of profit to the monastery. Now if the truth is so, and thou art aware of having done anything unbecomingly, without any delay restore what has been taken away; or at any rate, if thou thinkest it to be otherwise, lest the opposite party should seem to be aggrieved prejudicially, by no means defer submitting the case to arbitrators chosen with her concurrence, that it may be declared by a definite decision whether her complaint be true and just.

## EPISTLE IV.

### To Fantinus, Guardian (*Defensorem*) of Panormus.

Gregory to Fantinus, &c.

Such things about our brother and fellow-bishop Exhilaratus, as thou thyself also knowest, have come to our ears as ought by all means to be visited with severe punishment. But, since it has been smoothed over by our most reverend brother and fellow-bishop Leo [5], who has also declared that he was judge in that case, we have thought it fit that he [i.e. Exhilaratus] should be sent back to his Church, considering that what we have inflicted on him by keeping him here so long may be enough for him. Therefore we enjoin thy

Experience to pay attention to his manners and deeds, and to admonish him frequently, to the end that he may shew himself solicitous in extending kind charity to his clerks (*clericis*), and, should need require, in correcting faults. But we desire thee also to admonish his clergy that they exhibit humility towards him, and the obedience which the Lord commands, nor in any respect presume to behave proudly with regard to him. And if any one of them, that is, either bishop or clerk, should disregard thy admonition, do thou, under this authority from us, either correct the sin of disobedience by canonical coercion, as thou seest fit, or make haste to send a report to us, that we may be able to arrange how the rein of discipline may keep from going off their road those whom the goad of evil inclination provokes to transgression.

## EPISTLE VII.

### To Alcyson, Bishop of Corcyra.

Gregory to Alcyson, &c.

Not undeservedly does the ambition of an elated heart require to be quelled, when, disregarding the force of the sacred canons, the excess of rash presumption in coveting unlawfully what belongs to others is shewn to be not only harmful in causing expense, but also opposed to the peace of the Church. Having, then, perused thy Fraternity's epistles, we have learnt what has been done formerly or of late by the bishop of the City of Euria with regard to the camp of Cassiopus [6], which is situated in thy diocese, and we are distressed that those who should have been debtors to thy Church for charity bestowed upon them, should rather become its enemies, no shame restraining them; and at last that, in a way contrary to ecclesiastical arrangement, contrary to priestly moderation, contrary to the ordinances of the sacred canons, they should attempt to withdraw the aforesaid camp from thy jurisdiction and subject it to their own power, so as to become as it were masters where they had before been received as strangers. Concerning which matter, seeing that Andrew, our brother of venerable memory, Metropolitan of Nicopolis, with the support also of an imperial order whereby the cognizance of this case had been enjoined on him, is known to have determined in a sentence promulged by him, as has been made manifest to us, that the aforesaid camp of

---

4 As to this Pomponiana (*al.* Pompeiana), cf. I. 48; XI. 25.
5 Bishop of Catana in Sicily. Cf. IV. 36.

6 *Castrum Cassiopi*, which appears to have been a fortress in the isle of Corcyra, to which refugees from the mainland of Epirus had resorted in time of war. Euria was one of the sees in Epirus Vetus under the jurisdiction of which these refugees had been; and it seems that the bishop of Euria had been complained of by Alcyson, bishop of Corcyra, for asserting jurisdiction over them in their new abode. See also Ep. VIII., which follows, and Ep. XIII.

Cassiopus should remain under the jurisdiction of thy Church as it always has been, we, approving of the form of that sentence, confirm it, as justice approves, by the authority of the Apostolic See, and decree that it remain firm in all respects. For no reason of equity, no canonical order, sanctions that one person should in any way occupy the parish [7] of another. Wherefore, though the guilt of this contentiousness seems to require no slight strictness of treatment, in that they have returned evil for good, nevertheless care should be taken that kindness be not overcome by excess, nor that what is due to strange brethren, when they are suffering constraint too, be denied them, lest charity should be judged to have no operation in the minds of bishops, if those to whom great compassion is due should be left without the remedy of consolation. It is right, then, that the priests and clergy of the city of Euria be not repelled from habitation of the aforesaid camp of Cassiopus, but that they should have leave also to deposit with due reverence the holy and venerable body of the blessed Donatus, which they have brought with them, in one of the churches of the aforesaid place such as they may choose. Yet so that protection be procured for thy Love, in whose diocese this camp is situate, by the issue of a security whereby the bishop of Euria shall promise not to claim for himself any power therein, or any privilege, or any jurisdiction, or any authority in future, as though he were cardinal bishop; but that, peace being restored by the favour of God, they shall return by all means to their own places, taking away with them, if they will, the venerable body of Saint Donatus. So, this promise being kept in mind, neither may they dare on any pretext whatever to claim further to themselves any right of rule there, but acknowledge themselves guests there at all times, nor may the Church of thy Fraternity in any degree incur prejudice to its rights and privileges.

## EPISTLE VIII.

### To Boniface, Deacon.

Gregory to Boniface, Deacon at Constantinople [8].

As often as the discord of those who ought to have been preachers of peace makes us sad, we should study with great solicitude that cause of contention may be removed, and that those who differ among themselves may return to concord. Now what has been done with respect to the camp of Cassiopus, which is situate in the island of Corcyra, and how the bishop of Euria is endeavouring to withdraw it from the jurisdiction of the bishop of Corcyra, and iniquitously to subject it to his own jurisdiction, it would be very tedious to tell [9]. But, that your Love may understand all things fully, we have sent to you the letters of our brother Alcyson, the bishop of Corcyra, and have caused his man to go to you to inform you of everything more particularly by word of mouth. This, however, we briefly mention, that an order having been surreptitiously obtained from the late Emperor Mauricius, which order, having been given in opposition to the laws and sacred canons, had no effect, and the dispute between the parties remaining undecided, he gave another order to our late brother Andrew, then Metropolitan of Nicopolis, to the effect that, as both parties were subject to his jurisdiction, he should take cognizance of the case and terminate it canonically. The said Metropolitan, having taken cognizance of the case and pronounced sentence, of which we send you a copy, decided the aforesaid camp of Cassiopus to be under the power and jurisdiction of the bishop of Corcyra, in whose diocese it always was; and we, approving his sentence, have thought fit to confirm it by the authority of the Apostolic See. And, lest what we decreed should be so strict as to seem to have no admixture of benignity, we took care so to order the matter for the time being (as the text of our sentence which we send to thee shews) that neither should the bishop or clergy of the city of Euria incur the necessity of residence, nor the privileges of the Church of Corcyra be in any way disturbed. But inasmuch as at the very beginning of proceedings an order was surreptitiously got from the most serene lord the Emperor, and (contrary to the judgment of the Metropolitan of Nicopolis, which rested on ecclesiastical propriety and canonical reason) the aforesaid camp of Cassiopus is said to have been handed over to the bishop of Euria (a thing we cannot hear without grief or tell without groans), with still greater wrong to the bishop of Corcyra and his clergy, in such sort as (sad to say) to take away entirely the jurisdiction of the Church of Corcyra, and give as it were to the bishop of Euria the whole principal jurisdiction there; this being so, we have thought right to deliver our sentence to no one, lest we should seem to do anything contrary to the order of our most clement lord the Emperor, or (which God forbid) in contempt of him. Wherefore let thy Love

---

7 *Parochiam*, in the then usual sense of what is now called a *diocese*.
8 See XIII. 38, note 1.

9 Cf. preceeding epistle.

diligently represent the whole matter to his Piety, and steadily insist that the thing is altogether unlawful, altogether bad, altogether unjust, and greatly opposed to the sacred canons. And so may he not allow a sin of this sort to be introduced in his times to the prejudice of the Church. But represent to him what is contained in the judgment of the aforesaid late metropolitan on the business, and in what manner his decision had been confirmed by us, and endeavour so to act that our sentence, with an order from him, may be sent to those parts, to the end that we may be seen to have paid due deference to his Serenity, and to have corrected reasonably what had been presumptuously done amiss. In this affair pains must by all means be taken that, if it can be effected, he may contribute also his own order, enjoining the observance of what has been decided by us. For if this is done, all place for subornation hereafter will be shut out. Make haste, then, so to exercise thy vigilance, with the help of Almighty God, for abating these wrongs, that neither may the will of those who attempt perverse things obtain any advantage now against the ancient settlement of ecclesiastical usage, nor a nefarious proceeding gain ground for example afterwards.

Furthermore, that thou mayest know what wrongs and what oppressions the above-written Alcyson, our brother and fellow-bishop, asserts that he endures from the agents (*actionariis*) of the Church of Thessalonica, we have forwarded to thy Love the letter which he has sent to us. And do thou accordingly cause the *responsalis* of the aforesaid Church to come to thee, and take cognizance of the case in his presence, and write to our brother and fellow-bishop Eusebius, on such heads as reason may suggest to thee, that he may prohibit his men from acting unjustly, and warn them not to oppress inferiors, but rather help them in whatever may be just. This also we desire; that thy Love should write to him who may have been ordained as Metropolitan in the city of Nicopolis, to the end that he may take cognizance of the case with regard to the injuries which our aforesaid brother Alcyson complains of having been inflicted on his Church, and decide what is just, seeing that the matter itself is stated not to have been decided by his predecessors, but reserved.

### EPISTLE XII.

#### To Theodelinda, Queen of the Lombards.

Gregory to Queen Theodelinda.

The letters which you sent us a little time ago from the Genoese parts have made us partakers of your joy on account of our learning that by the favour of Almighty God a son has been given you, and, as is greatly to your Excellency's credit, has been received into the fellowship of the catholic faith [10]. Nor indeed was anything else to be supposed of your Christianity but that you would fortify him whom you have received by the gift of God with the aid of Catholic rectitude, so that our Redeemer might both acknowledge thee as His familiar servant, and also bring up prosperously in His fear a new king for the nation of the Lombards. Wherefore we pray Almighty God both to keep you in the way of His commandments, and to cause our most excellent son, Adulouvald [11], to advance in His love, to the end that, as he is in this world great among men, so also he may be glorious for his good deeds before the eyes of our God.

Now as to what your Excellency has requested in your letter, that we should reply in full to what our most beloved son, the abbot Secundus has written [1], who could think of putting off his petition or your wishes, knowing how profitable they would be to many, did not sickness stand in the way? But so great an infirmity from gout has held us fast as to render us hardly able to rise, not only for dictating, but even for speaking, as also your ambassadors, the bearers of these presents, are aware, who, when they arrived, found us weak, and when they departed, left us in the utmost peril and danger of our life. But, if by the ordering of Almighty God I should recover, I will reply in full to all that he has written. I have, however, sent by the bearers of these presents the Synod that was held in the time of Justinian of pious memory, that my aforesaid most-beloved son may acknowledge on reading it that all that he had heard against the Apostolic See or the Catholic Church was false. For far be it from us to

---

[10] i.e. the child had been baptized a catholic. It would seem from Gregory's way of speaking, and the absence of allusion to the conversion of the father, that king Agilulph had not yet announced his Arianism. Paul Diaconus alleges that he did so eventually through the influence of Theodelinda.

[11] The child who had been baptized (*al*. Adaloaldus, or Adoaldus). He succeeded his father as king of the Lombards, A.D. 616, being still a boy, reigning under his mother's guardianship. According to Paul Diaconus, Gregory's hopes were for a short time fulfilled :—"Under them Churches were restored, and many endowments were bestowed on venerable places ;"—but before long he became insane, and after ten years (A.D. 626) was deposed, Arioald being appointed to succeed him (*Hist. Longob*. iv. 43).

[1] On the subject of the "Three Chapters," as appears from what follows. It is evident that the able and conscientious queen Theodelinda never found herself able to accept the ruling of the See of Rome on this question (cf. IV. 2, note 3); and she seems now to have employed the abbot Secundus to draw up a statement of the arguments on her side, inviting Gregory to reply to them. He did not, however, on this account cease to address her cordially as a good Catholic. He seems to have condoned in her what he so strongly condemned in others as involving them in schism. On the schism arising from the matter of the "Three Chapters," see I. 16, note 3; and *Prolegom*., p. x.

accept the views of any heretic whatever, or to deviate in any respect from the tome of our predecessor Leo, of holy memory; but we receive whatever has been defined by the four holy synods, and condemn whatever has been rejected by them.

Further, to our son the King Adolouvald we have taken thought to send some phylacteries; that is, a cross with wood of the holy cross of the Lord, and a lection of the holy Gospel enclosed in a Persian case. Also to my daughter, his sister, I send three rings, two of them with hyacinths, and one with an *albula*[2], which I request may be given them through you, that our charity towards them may be seasoned by your Excellency.

Furthermore, while paying you our duty of greeting with fatherly charity, we beg you to return thanks in our behalf to our most excellent son the King your consort for the peace that has been made, and to move his mind to peace, as you have been accustomed to do, in all ways for the future; that so, among your many good deeds, you may be able in the sight of God to find reward in an innocent people, which might have perished in offence.

## EPISTLE XIII.

### To Alcyson, Bishop of Corcyra[3].

Gregory to Alcyson, &c.

To brethren who bethink themselves and return to wholesome counsels kindness is not to be denied, lest a fault seem to weigh more in the minds of bishops than charity. We have therefore received, in the presence of thy Love's *responsales*, Peter, reader of the Church of Euria, who came to us with letters from our brother and fellow-bishop John, and, when the letters which he had brought had been read, we took care to ask him if he had anything to say against the allegation of those thy *responsales*. And on his stating that he had been charged with nothing, and had no answer to make, beyond what the epistle of his bishop contained, we decreed without tardiness, under God, what was agreeable to the canons. After a long time, however, the above-written Peter produced a document which he asserted had been given him by his bishop; and so the case underwent delay. But inasmuch as in this document the above-mentioned bishop was found to say that he had hoped to have leave to deposit the holy and venerable body of the blessed Donatus in the church of the blessed John which is

within the camp called that of Cassiopus, saying that he is prepared, on account of its being proved to be in thy diocese, to give thy Love a security that no prejudice to thee should thence arise, we thought it right that his petition should not be left without effect, now that in a time of necessity he desires provision to be made for him in such a way as to secure his acknowledgment in all respects of the jurisdiction of thy Church. Moved therefore by this reason, we exhort thy Fraternity by this present letter, that, without any delay or excuse thou afford opportunity for depositing the venerable body of the above-written Saint in the aforenamed Church of the blessed John; on condition only that he previously protect thee by a security in writing that he will never on any plea whatever claim to himself any jurisdiction or privilege in the aforesaid Church or camp, as though he were the bishop of the place, but guard there inviolably all the right and power of thy Church, the place being in thy diocese. At the same time it becomes thee also, as the same our brother has requested, to reply to him that whenever, peace being restored by the mercy of God, he may be at liberty to return to his own place, it shall be lawful for him to take away with him, without any objection made, the aforesaid venerable body. Herein, lest what is done should seem to be personal, and occasion should possibly be found for stirring up the contention anew, your successors also should be in all respects included in this promise to keep things as they are, to the end that through this preventional security neither may he in future presume to claim anything there in thy diocese against equity and the decrees of the sacred canons, nor the rights of thy Church ever in any manner sustain any prejudice from such concession.

## EPISTLE XVI.

### From Felix Bishop of Messana[4] to St. Gregory.

To the most blessed and honourable lord, the holy father Pope Gregory, Felix lover of your Weal and Holiness.

---

2 Some precious stone, probably of a white colour.
3 See XIV. 7.

4 Messina in Sicily. This Felix cannot be identified with Felix, bishop of the same See, to whom previous letters (viz. I. 66, together with two others, I. 40, and II. 5, which have not been translated) had been addressed. For he had been succeeded in the see by Donus, probably in the 14th Indiction, i.e. A.D. 595-6, (see VI. 9), when Gregory's reply to Augustine's interrogatories, which is the main subject of the epistle before us, had not yet been sent. Augustine does not appear to have even arrived in Britain till A.D. 597. But there seems to be no reason against the supposition that a second Felix had succeeded Donus at Messina before the death of Gregory, the last mention of Donus being in the superscription of Ep. XVIII. in Book XIII., assigned to the 16th Indiction, i.e. A.D. 602-3.

The claims under God of your most blessed Weal and Holiness are manifest. For, though the whole earth was filled with observance of the true faith by the preaching and doctrine of the apostles, yet the orthodox Church of Christ, having been founded by apostolical institution and most firmly established by the faithful fathers, is further built up through the teaching of divine discourses, while instructed by your hortatory admonition. To it did all the most blessed apostles, endowed with an equal participation of dignity and authority[5], convert hosts of peoples; and by salutary precepts and admonitions, piously and holily, brought such as were foreknown in the grace of divine predestination from darkness to light, from error to the true faith, from death to life. Following the merits of these holy apostles, and perfectly acting up to their example, your honoured Paternity adorns with them the Church of God by probity of manners and holiness of deeds; and, strong in sacred faith and Christian manners, enjoins what should be done to please God, and unceasingly follows and fulfils pontifical duties, thus observing the precepts of divine law; since (as says the Apostle) *Not the hearers of the law are just before God, but the doers of the law shall be justified* (Rom. ii. 13).

As we were meditating on these things, news was brought us by certain who came from Rome that you had written to our comrade Augustine (afterwards ordained Bishop for the nation of the Angli, and thither sent by your venerable Holiness), and to the Angli (whom we have long known to have been converted to the faith through you), that persons related in the fourth degree of descent, if married, should not be separated[6]. Now this was not formerly the custom either in those or in these parts, when I was brought up and taught together with you from infancy; nor have I read of it in any decrees of your predecessors, or in the institutes of other Fathers generally or specially, or learnt that it had been allowed hitherto by any of the wise. But I have found from your holy predecessors, and from the rest of the holy Fathers, assembled as well in the Nicene synod as in other holy councils, that this [i.e. *this prohibition of marriage*] should be observed down to the seventh degree of de-

scent; and I know that this is carefully seen to by men who live aright and fear the Lord. While these things were being discussed among us, other things also supervened, concerning which it seems necessary for us to consult your authority. For there came to us both Benedict, bishop of the Syracusan Church, and also others of our brethren, being bishops, weeping, and saying that they were greatly disturbed and afflicted in mind on account of the immoderate proceedings of secular and lay persons, in consequence of which some unjust things were also being said against them.

There are also some churches in our province about the consecration of which doubt is felt; and, because both of their antiquity and of the carelessness of their custodians, it is unknown whether they have been dedicated by bishops or not. As to all these things we beg to be instructed by your Holiness, and by the authority of your holy see; and we ask to be informed by your letters whether what, as we have before said, we have heard that you had written to our aforesaid comrade Augustine and to the nation of the Angli was written specially to them or generally to all; and we desire to be fully informed both on this matter and on the others above written.

For we do not signify to you what we have read, and what we know to be observed by the faithful, by way of finding fault (which be far from us); but we seek to know what we may reasonably and faithfully observe in this matter. And, since no slight murmuring is going on among us on this question, we seek an answer from you, as from the head, as to what we should reply to our brethren and fellow bishops; lest we should remain doubtful in the matter, and lest this murmuring should remain among us both in your times and in times to come, and your reputation, which has always been good and excellent, should be lacerated or disparaged through detractions, or your name (which God forbid) should be evil spoken of in succeeding times. For we, observing under God what is right with humble heart, being bound to you in one bond of charity, and defending your religion in all things as faithful pupils, seek knowledge of what is right from you. For we know that, as the apostles in the first place who were prelates of the holy See, and their successors afterwards, have always done, so you also take care of the universal Church, and especially of bishops, who on account of their contemplation and speculation are called the eyes of the Lord; and that you think continually about our religion and law, as it is written,

---

5 See also below—"the apostles in the first place who were prelates of the Apostolic See." It would seem from these expressions that the Sicilian bishops went on the tradition of St. Paul and St. Peter having been joint founders of the Roman Church: and throughout the epistle, though the supremacy of the See of Rome is acknowledged, it is not spoken of as derived especially from St. Peter.

6 See XI., 64 (*Responsio ad Interrog.* vi.).

*Blessed is he who shall meditate in the law of the Lord day and night* (Ps. i. 2). Which meditation of yours is not only seen by reading, through the outward expression of letters, but, by the grace of Christ abounding in you, is known to be immoveably engrafted in your conscience; while the most holy law of Christ the Lord in no wise departs from your heart; as says the Prophet in the Psalms, *The mouth of the righteous will meditate wisdom, and his tongue will be talking of judgments: the law of God is in his heart* (Ps. xxxvi. 30); written not with ink, but in secret by the Spirit of the living God; not therefore on tables of stone, but on the tables of the heart. Let all gloom of darkness, we pray you, be dispelled by your most wise replies and assistance, that the morning star may shine upon us through you, most holy Father, and a dogmatic definition causing joy to all everywhere, because the glorious Fathers of holy Church are known to have preached proper and most pious dogmas unto secure inheritance of eternal life.

*Subscription.* May the Lord keep you safe and well-pleasing to God for ever, holy father of fathers, while you pray for us.

## EPISTLE XVII.

### To Felix, Bishop of Messana.

To our most reverend brother, the Bishop Felix. Gregory, servant of the servants of God [7].

Our Head, which is Christ, to this end has willed us to be His members, that through His large charity and faithfulness He might make us one body in Himself, to whom it befits us so to cling that, since without Him we can do nothing, through Him we may be enabled to be what we are called. From the citadel of the Head let nothing divide us, lest, if we refuse to be His members, we be deserted of Him, and wither as branches cast off from the vine. That we may be counted worthy, then, to be the habitation of our Redeemer, let us abide with the whole desire of our heart in His love. For he says, *He that loveth me will keep my word, and my Father will love him, and we will make our abode with him* (Joh. xiv. 23). Now thy Love, most dear brother, has demanded of us that we should reply to thy enquiries with the authority of the Apostolic See. And, though we make haste to do this, not at length but succinctly (because of certain pressing cares that have come upon us, through the hindrance of our sins), yet we commit what follows to thy attention for wider enquiry, and investigation of other institutes of holy fathers. For a mind worn and weighed down with burdens and pressing cares cannot effect so much good, or speak of these things so freely, as can one that is joyful and free from depression. We have not therefore given the preference to such cares as wishing to deny to thy Holiness this and such other information as we might find to be needful, but in order that what is here found deficient may be more fully enquired into.

For, following the examples of thy predecessors, thou hast thought it right to consult the Apostolic See, in which thou hast been brought up and educated, on three points; that is on marriages of consanguinity, on vexation of bishops by subordinates, and on doubt with respect to the consecration of churches. Know then that what I wrote to Augustine, bishop of the nation of the Angli (who was, as thou rememberest, thy pupil), about marriages of consanguinity was written specially to him and to the nation of the Angli which had recently come to the faith, lest from alarm at anything too austere they should recede from their good beginning; but it was not written generally to others. Of this the whole Roman city is my witness. Nor did I thus order in those writings with the intention that, after they had been settled in the faith with a firm root, they should not be separated, if found to be below the proper degree of consanguinity, or should be united, if below the proper line of affinity, that is as far as the seventh generation. But for those who are still neophytes it is very often right in the first place to teach them, and by word and example to instruct them, to avoid unlawful things, and then afterwards, reasonably and faithfully, to shut out things that they may have done in matters of this kind. For according to the Apostle who says, *I have fed you with milk, not with meat* (1 Cor. iii. 2), we have allowed these indulgences for them only, and not (as has been said above) for future times, lest the good which had been planted so far with a weak root should be rooted up, but that what had been begun should rather

---

7 The genuineness of this epistle is, to say the least, open to grave suspicion. Jaffé (*Regesta Pont. Lit. Spur.*) rejects it as spurious. Its style in some parts reminds us of Gregory, and it contains passages identical with what he had written elsewhere: but its prolixity, bad composition, and repetitions are unworthy of his pen. It reads like an unskilful imitation of his style. Nor is it difficult to understand why such a letter may have been forged. If, as supposed in our note to Ep. XVI., a letter from Sicily had been addressed to Gregory not long before his death with reference to his answers to Augustine's questions, to which letter he had been unable to reply, it was not unlikely that such a letter as the one before us would afterwards be composed in his name. For anxiety might naturally be felt to vindicate from inconsistency the teaching of the Roman See on the subject of marriages of consanguinity. Such a letter, too, if forged, would be likely to attempt an imitation of Gregory's style, and to bring in (as this does) extracts from his previous writings. It may be observed that the plea set forth of the directions to Augustine having been meant only as temporary concessions is not borne out by the actual language of those directions. See XI. 64.

be made firm, and guarded till it reach perfection. Certainly, if in these things we have done anything otherwise than as we ought to have done, know that it has been done, not of wantonness, but in commiseration. Wherefore, too, I invoke God as my witness, who knows the thoughts of all men, and to whom all things are naked and open. For, if I were to destroy what those who came before me established, I should be justly convicted of being not a builder but an overthrower, as testifies the voice of the Truth, who says, *Every kingdom divided against itself shall not stand* (Luke xi. 17); and every science and law divided against itself shall be destroyed. And so it is needful for us all with one accord to hold to the appointments of our holy Fathers, doing nothing in contention, but, unanimous in every aim of good devotion, to obey, the Lord helping us, the divine and apostolical constitutions.

O how good is charity, which through love exhibits absent things in an image to one's self as though they were present, unites things divided, sets in order things confused, associates things unequal, consummates things imperfect! How rightly the excellent preacher calls it the bond of perfectness, since the other virtues indeed produce perfectness, but yet charity so binds them that they cannot now be unloosed from the mind of him that loves. This being duly considered, in what has been already spoken of I indulged charitably; nor did I give a command, but advice; nor did I deliver a rule to be held to by any who should come after, but shewed of two dangers which might be more easily avoided. If, then, in secular affairs every one should have his own right and his proper rank preserved to him, how much more in ecclesiastical arrangements ought no confusion to be induced, lest discord should find place there whence the blessings of peace ought to proceed. And this will be thus secured, if nothing is yielded to power, but all to equity. On this account our heart rejoices greatly with your greatness, because we find you so earnest in your doings as to have a care for us, and at pains to enquire about such things by questioning us, to the end that such things may acquire for you not only glory with men, but also rewards of recompense with the Almighty Lord.

But with regard to vexation of bishops, about which you wish to consult us, we know that the life of prelates ought to be perturbed by no excesses, since it is very unfit that those who are called thrones of God should be disturbed by any motion from kings or subjects. For, if David who was the most righteous of kings presumed not to lay his hand

on Saul who was evidently already rejected of God, how much more should heed be taken that none lay the hand of detraction or vituperation or indiscreetness or dishonour on the Lord's Anointed, or on the preachers of holy Church, since vexation or detraction of them touches Christ, in whose stead they fill the office of legates in the Church! Hence all the faithful should be exceedingly cautious not either secretly or publicly, by detractions or vituperations rend their bishop, that is, the Lord's Anointed, considering that example of Mary [i.e. *Miriam*], who for speaking against Moses the servant of God because of the Ethiopian woman was punished with the uncleanness of leprosy (Num. xiii.); and that of the Psalmist, *Touch not mine anointed, and do my prophets no harm* (Ps. civ. 15)[8]. And in the divine law we read, *Thou shalt not revile the gods, nor curse the ruler of thy people* (Ex. xxii. 28). Hence great care should be taken by subordinates, whether clerical or lay, that they dare not to blame rashly the lives of their bishops or superiors, if perchance they see them do anything blameable, lest from their position of reproving evil they be sunk into greater depths through the impulse of elation. They are to be admonished also that, when they consider the faults of their superiors, they grow not too bold against them. But let them so consider with themselves the things that are bad that, constrained by divine fear, they refuse not to carry the yoke of reverence, seeing that the things done by bishops and superiors are not to be smitten with the sword of the mouth, even when they may seem to be such as may be properly blamed; since we are aware that it has been laid down by our predecessors and by many other holy bishops that sheep should not readily blame their shepherds, or presume to criminate or accuse them, because, when we sin against our superiors, we go against His ordinance Who gave them to us. Hence Moses, when he had learnt that the people complained against himself and Aaron, said, *For what are we? Not against us is your murmuring but against God* (Ex. xvi. 8). Wherefore subordinates of either order are to be admonished that, when they observe the deeds of their masters, they return to their own heart, and presume not in upbraidings of them, since *The disciple is not above his master, nor the servant above his lord* (Matth. x. 24).

Concerning doubt as to the dedications of churches, about which among other things you have wished to consult us, you ought duly to hold to this which we have received as handed

---

8 Ps. cv. 15.

down to us from those who have gone before us ; namely, that, as often as doubt is entertained as to the baptism or confirmation of any persons, as well as the consecration of churches, and there is no certain account to be given, either from writings or witnesses, as to whether persons have been baptized or confirmed, or whether churches have been consecrated, that such persons should be baptized and confirmed, and that such churches should be canonically dedicated, lest such doubt should become ruin to the faithful ; inasmuch as what does not appear by certain proofs to have been duly done is not in such case done a second time. This, divine grace supporting us, we desire so to hold ; and we enjoin it on you, as you have requested, to hold and teach ; and we wish not wantonly to break through, but faithfully to observe, what has been determined by holy Fathers before us. Wherefore we implore the mercy of our Redeemer to assist you with His grace, and give unto you to carry into effect what He has granted you to will, since in this matter the good gifts of retribution by so much the more accrue to us as the zeal of labour is increased.

But we decree that every one of those who have been faithfully taught, and already stand ineradicably planted with a firm root, shall observe his descent even to the seventh generation. And as long as they know themselves to be related to each other by affinity, let them not presume to approach the association of this union ; nor is it lawful, or shall be lawfully for any Christian to marry a woman of his own kindred whom he has lived with as a wife, or whom he has stained by any unlawful pollution ; since such intercourse is incestuous and abominable to God and to all good men. But we read that it has long been determined by holy Fathers that incestuous persons are not to be reckoned under any title of wedlock. And so we desire not to be blamed by you or any other of the faithful in this matter, seeing that in our indulgence herein to the nation of the Angli we have acted, not as laying down a rule, but as taking thought lest they should leave imperfect the good which they had begun, &c. [9]

---

[9] The rest of this long prolix epistle, not being of any peculiar interest, has not been translated.

SELECTIONS

TRANSLATED INTO ENGLISH

FROM THE

# HYMNS AND HOMILIES

OF

EPHRAIM THE SYRIAN,

AND FROM THE

# DEMONSTRATIONS

OF

APHRAHAT THE PERSIAN SAGE;

EDITED, WITH AN INTRODUCTORY DISSERTATION, BY

# JOHN GWYNN, D.D., D.C.L.

REGIUS PROFESSOR OF DIVINITY IN THE UNIVERSITY OF DUBLIN.

# PREFACE

In the following selection from the voluminous writings of Ephraim, the great light of the Syrian Church of the fourth century, I have endeavored to give adequate specimens of his *Hymns* and of his *Homilies ;* but have not included any part of his *Commentaries* on Holy Scripture. These last contain much that is worthy of study, but would not be found attractive to the general reader ; nor could they be fairly represented by a series of extracts such as the limits of the present volume would admit of.

The Hymns (with small exceptions, presently to be specified), and the Homilies, which I have selected, appear now for the first time in an English version ; and are translated from Syriac texts which have come to light within the last fifty years, in the great collection of manuscripts acquired by the British Museum by the purchase of the library of the monastery of the Theotokos in the Nitrian Desert, in Egypt.

To these I have added eight chosen from the twenty-three *Demonstrations*, or Epistles, of Ephraim's contemporary Aphrahat. These also appear for the first time in English, and are translated from a Syriac text, long lost, and lately recovered from the same famous collection.

Of the Hymns of Ephraim, I have placed the Nisibene series first, including forty-six of the total number (originally seventy-seven ; but a few are lost). The first twenty-one, relating to the history of Nisibis and of its Bishops, I have given in full, because of their special interest and historic value. The translation of these is the work of the Rev. Joseph T. Sarsfield Stopford, B.A. (Dublin), Rector of Castle Combe in the Diocese of Gloucester. It follows the text edited by Dr. Bickell (Leipzig, 1866), from Nitrian MSS.

Of the Hymns *On the Nativity*, which stand next in order, the first thirteen have already appeared in the Oxford "Library of the Fathers" (1847), translated by the Rev. J. B. Morris, M. A., from the text printed in the great Roman edition, *S. Ephræmi Syri Opera Syriaca* (Rome, 1743). These were all of the series known when that edition was published ; but since then six complete hymns, and some fragments of the same have been recovered from Nitrian MSS. I have reprinted Mr. Morris's version of the thirteen, with some modifications, and have subjoined the Nitrian six, rendered from the text published by Professor Lamy, of Louvain, in Tom. II of his edition of Ephraim (Mechlin, 1889). These last, and the series of fifteen Hymns *For the Epiphany* which follow them, have been translated by the Rev. Albert Edward Johnston, B. D. (Dublin), formerly Assistant-Lecturer in Divinity in the University of Dublin, and now Principal of the Church Missionary Society's College, Benares. The remaining series, of seven Hymns *On the Faith*, also called *The Pearl*, is borrowed, like the thirteen *On the Nativity*, from Mr. Morris's version.

I have carefully revised and in parts rewritten all these translations of the *Hymns*, chiefly with a view to bringing into some approach to uniformity the style and method of rendering of a collection which thus includes the work of three independent translators.   While very sensible of the high merit of Mr. Morris's work, and conscious that by retouching and altering it I may incur the blame of presumptuousness, I have thought it expedient to tone down somewhat of the exceeding severity of his faithfulness to his original, and to remove some of the harsh expressions and harsher inversions which make his version, valuable as it is to the student, almost repulsive, and often barely intelligible, to the English reader.   Of his learned Notes, I have retained a few, some of them in a curtailed form, of those which seemed most useful for the illustration of the text.

The three *Homilies* of Ephraim, which follow the *Hymns*, have been translated by Mr. Johnston from Professor Lamy's text (as above, Tom. I., 1889).

The selections from the *Demonstrations* of Aphrahat are the work of the same translator, and follow the text of Dom Parisot's edition, forming Tom. I of the *Patrologia Syriaca* (Paris, 1894).

The versions of the *Homilies* and of the *Demonstrations*, being all the work of one and the same hand, have called for but few and trivial alterations from the editor.   I have, however, revised them throughout ; and am responsible for the general accuracy of the rendering of the originals in these, and in the whole of the selections now presented to the public.

In the *Introductory Dissertation* prefixed to the work, I have drawn largely on the materials supplied by the *Prolegomena* of Dr. Bickell's *Carmina Nisibena*, and of Professor Lamy's *S. Ephræmi Hymni et Sermones*, Tom. I. and Tom. II. ; and by Dr. Forget's Treatise *De Vita Aphraatis*, and the Preface of Dom Parisot to Tom. I. of the *Patrologia Syriaca*.

JOHN GWYNN.

TRINITY COLLEGE, DUBLIN, 31*st* *March*, 1898.

# CONTENTS

---

## INTRODUCTORY DISSERTATION.

# SECOND PART.

### APHRAHAT THE PERSIAN SAGE.

# SELECTIONS FROM EPHRAIM.

### HYMNS.

### HOMILIES.

# SELECTIONS FROM APHRAHAT.

### DEMONSTRATIONS.

# INTRODUCTORY DISSERTATION

## EPHRAIM THE SYRIAN

AND

## APHRAHAT THE PERSIAN SAGE

### PRELIMINARY

THE two Fathers of the Syrian Church, from whose writings the present Volume presents a selection, are from more than one point of view fitly associated as examples of the leaders of Syriac theological thought and literature. They are the earliest Syriac authors of whom any considerable remains survive; and they both represent the religious mind of the Syrian Church, but little affected by influences from without, other than the all-pervading influence of the Jewish and Christian Scriptures.

Syriac Literature is, on the whole, of derivative growth. It consists largely of versions or adaptations from the Greek. The Syriac language, in the hands of those to whom the Syriac Church owes the admirable version of the Scriptures known as the "Peshitto," proved itself capable of reproducing adequately, not only the sublime conceptions of God and of man's relations to God which belong to the cognate Hebrew of the Old Testament, but also—the wider, subtler, and more complex religious ideas for which the writers of the New Testament found their fit vehicle in the Greek. But the Peshitto, great as its value must have been to the religious life of Syriac-speaking Christians, never became to them what Luther's Bible has been to Germany, and the "Authorized" Bible of King James's translators to England—an inspiring force in literature, not merely to elevate and enrich its language, but to quicken it in every branch. Syriac literature was indeed deeply penetrated by the Syriac Bible, but its level was never raised above mediocrity. For the most part it is imitative not original;—nay, it rarely succeeds in assimilating so as to make its own what it has borrowed. The Syriac translator, if he worked on the writings of a Greek divine, would often paraphrase or even interpolate; if of a Greek historian, would subjoin a continuation; but he would seldom venture farther. Those who essayed independent authorship were few. A home-grown Syriac literature began with Ephraim and Aphrahat; but [setting aside a very small number of the writers who followed] it may almost be said to have ended with them. These two, and these alone, in place of being imitators or translators, were translated and imitated by the writers of foreign nations. Aphrahat's literary lot was the singular one, that his work survived in an alien tongue for alien readers. when the original had wellnigh perished out of the memory of his own people.　To Ephraim pertains the high and unique distinction of having originated—or at least given its living impulse to—a new departure in sacred literature ; and that, not for his own country merely, but for Christendom.　From him came, if not the first idea, at all events the first successful example, of making song an essential constituent of public worship, and an exponent of theological teaching ; and from him it spread and prevailed through the Eastern Churches, and affected even those of the West.　To the Hymns, on which chiefly his fame rests, the Syriac ritual in all its forms owes much of its strength and richness ; and to them is largely due the place which Hymnody holds throughout the Church everywhere.　And hence it has come to pass that, in the Church everywhere, he stands as the representative Syrian Father, as the fixed epithet appended to his name attests—" Ephraim *the Syrian*,"— the one Syrian known and reverenced in all Christendom.

Of the two, it has been usual of late to reckon Aphrahat as the elder.　Further on, it will be shown in this Dissertation that the reasons for so reckoning him are inadequate.　For the present it suffices to note that they were contemporaries—both living and writing about the middle of the fourth century, and that priority of treatment cannot with confidence be claimed for either.　On grounds of convenience, therefore, we may properly proceed to deal first with Ephraim, as being indisputably far the first in order of importance, of copiousness, and of celebrity.

# FIRST PART

## EPHRAIM THE SYRIAN.

### I.—Summary of the Authenticated Facts of his Life.

All that is known, on early and trustworthy evidence, of the person and life of Ephraim may be briefly summed up.　He was born within the Roman pale, in the ancient and famous city of Nisibis in Mesopotamia, in, or before, the earliest days of the reign (A.D. 306–337) of Constantine the Great : he was a disciple of St. Jacob, Bishop of that city, who died A.D. 338 : and he lived in it, under Jacob and the three Bishops who successively followed him, through three unsuccessful sieges laid to it by Sapor, King of Persia, down to its final surrender under the terms of the ignominious peace concluded with Sapor by the Emperor Jovian after the defeat and death of his predecessor Julian (A.D. 363).　Nisibis was then abandoned by its Christian inhabitants ; and Ephraim finally settled at Edessa, and took up his abode as a " Solitary " in a cell on the "Mount of Edessa "—a rocky hill close to the city, where many anchorites sought retreat.　Here he rose into repute as a teacher, and a champion against heresy ; and no less as an ascetic and saint.　The fame of St. Basil, metropolitan of Cæsarea in Cappadocia (370–379), drew him from his solitude to visit that great prelate and doctor, and from him he received the diaconate ; but (though some affirm that he was advanced to the priesthood) it is agreed that he never became a Bishop. He died at an advanced age, in his retreat, in the year 373 according to most authorities, but some suppose him to have lived to 378.　He was a most copious writer, and left an immense quantity of writings of which a large part is extant,—Sermons, Commentaries, and Hymns.　These constitute such a body of instruction in the substance of Scripture and the faith of the church, that they have justly earned for him the title of *malpono*, or *teacher*.　And not only have his Hymns done much to shape the ritual of the Syrian Churches, in which large portions of them are embodied, but to his

Sermons this singular honour is paid, that lessons selected from them were appointed, and are still read, in the regular course of public worship.

## II.—MATERIALS FOR HIS BIOGRAPHY.

Fuller details, of more or less authentic character, are forthcoming in many quarters. In Syriac, we have two Lives, a longer and a shorter ; but whether the latter is an abridgment of the former, or is rather the nucleus from which the other has been expanded, is questionable. Of both alike, the date and the authorship are undetermined. The longer of the two is entitled, the *History* [*tash itha*] of the holy Mar Ephraim. It varies not a little in the two copies of it [the Vatican and the Parisian] which have been edited ;[1] and contains many things that are not easily credible, and some things that are irreconcilable with one another, or with established facts. In the main facts, however, this *History* is borne out by the Greek authorities—the narrations of three fifth-century historians, Socrates, Sozomen and Theodoret, the brief notices of Jerome, *De Viris Illustribus* (392), and of Palladius, in his *Lausiac History* (circ. 420) ci., and (what is of most weight) the almost contemporary biographical particulars contained in the *Encomium* pronounced on Ephraim by Gregory of Nyssa. Other Greek Lives are extant ;—one which bears the name of a writer coeval with Gregory, Amphilochius of Iconium, but is certainly by a later hand ; one anonymous, and one ascribed to Simeon the Metaphrast, a writer of the tenth century.[2]

We proceed to give an outline of the contents of the Syriac History, adding to it here and there such further noteworthy details or incidents as have reached us from the other sources indicated. Further on, it will be our business to examine this narrative and ascertain how far its statements are in themselves credible, or attested by other and earlier evidence.

## III.—THE LIFE, AS AMPLIFIED BY MEDIÆVAL BIOGRAPHERS.

1. *His Early Years.*—Ephraim, according to this biography, was a Syrian of Mesopotamia, by birth, and by parentage on both sides. His mother was of Amid (now Diarbekr) a central city of that region ; his father belonged to the older and more famous City of Nisibis, not far from Amid but near the Persian frontier, where he was priest of an idol named Abnil (or Abizal) in the days of Constantine the Great (306-337). This idol was afterwards destroyed by Jovian (who became Emperor in 363 after the extinction of the Flavian dynasty by the death of Julian). In Nisibis, then included within the Roman Empire, Ephraim was born. The date of his birth is not stated, but it cannot have been later than the earliest years of Constantine's reign. Though the son of such a father, he was from his childhood preserved, by Divine grace which " chose him like Jeremiah from his mother's womb," from all taint of idolatrous worship and its attendant impurities, to be, like St. Paul, a "chosen vessel" to spread the light of truth and to quench heresy. The biographer records farther on, but without fixing its time, an intimation of his future work which Ephraim himself relates in his "Testament" as belonging to the days "when his mother carried him on her bosom." He saw in dream or vision a vine springing from his mouth, which grew so high as to fill all that was under the heavens, and produced clusters whereon the fowls of the air

---

[1] The former in the Roman edition, *Opera Syr.*, Tom. III, p. xxiii ; the latter in Lamy's *Hymni et Sermones*, Tom. II.
[2] Of these, the one, which is ascribed to Amphilochius, is perhaps the basis on which the longer Syriac Life was constructed.

fed, and which multiplied the more, the more they were fed on. These clusters (the Testament explains) were his Sermons ; the leaves of the vine, his Hymns.

But his entrance into the Christian fold was not to be without hindrance and suffering. His father, finding the youth one day in converse with some Christians, was filled with anger, chastised him with cruel and almost fatal severity, and repaired to the shrine of his god to seek pardon for his son by sacrifice and prayer. A voice issuing from the idol rejected his intercession, warned him that his son was destined to be the persecutor of his father's gods, and commanded his expulsion from home. The father obeyed : the son received the sentence with joy, and went out from his father's house, carrying nothing with him and not knowing whither he went. His way was divinely directed to the famous and saintly Bishop, Jacob of Nisibis, to whom he told his story and by whom he was affectionately welcomed and admitted into the number of " Hearers," —that is, Catechumens in the first stage of preparatory instruction. From the first he showed himself a diligent disciple, in fasting and prayer, and in daily attendance on the teaching of the Scriptures. He frequented the Bishop's abode, imitated his virtues, attracted his special notice, and acquired a high place in his love as well as in that of all the Church.

A slanderous charge, however, was laid against him in his youthful manhood, which, but for supernatural interposition granted to his prayer, would have ruined his good name. A damsel of noble birth had been seduced by an official (*Paramonarius, i.e.*, sacristan, *or perhaps rather*, steward) of the church, named likewise Ephraim. When pregnancy ensued and her frailty was detected, she at the instance of her paramour charged Ephraim the pious Catechumen as being the author of her shame. Her father laid the matter before the Bishop, who in much grief and consternation summoned his disciple to answer the accusation. The youth received it at first in amazed silence ; but finally made answer, " Yea, I have sinned ; but I entreat thy Holiness to pardon me." Even after this seeming acknowledgment of guilt, however, the Bishop was unconvinced, and prayed earnestly that the truth might be revealed to him : but in vain,—a more signal clearing was in store for the humble and blameless youth. When the child of shame was born, and the father of the frail damsel required him to undertake the charge of it, he repeated his seeming confession of guilt to the Bishop ; he received the infant into his arms : he openly entered the church carrying it ; and he besought the congregation with tears, saying, " Entreat for me, my brethen, that this sin be pardoned to me." After thus bearing for some days the burden of unmerited reproach, he perceived the great scandal caused to the people, and began to reflect that his meek acceptance of calumny was doing harm. On the following Sunday, therefore, after the Eucharist had been administered, he approached the Bishop in church in presence of the people, carrying the infant under his mantle, and obtained his permission to enter the *bema* (not the pulpit, but the raised sanctuary where the altar stood). Before the eyes of the astonished congregation, he produced the babe, held it up in his right hand, facing the altar, and cried aloud, " Child, I call on thee and adjure thee by the living God, who made heaven and earth and all that therein is, that thou confess and tell me truly, who is thy father ? " The infant opened its mouth and said, " Ephraim the paramonarius." Having thus spoken, it died that same hour. The people and the Bishop received this miraculous vindication of the wrongfully accused with amazement and tears ; the father of the sinful mother fell on his knees and cried for forgiveness ; the true partner of her sin fled and was seen in Nisibis no more ; Satan was confounded ; and Ephraim was restored to more than all the favour and affection he enjoyed before.

Not long after, the young disciple received a singular proof of the high esteem in which he was held by his Bishop. When summoned with the other prelates to the great Council of Nicæa (A.D. 325), Jacob took Ephraim with him as his attendant or secretary, and brought him into that holy Synod. It is to be inferred that a youth so chosen must have shown early maturity and zeal for the Faith. His presence on this first great battlefield of the Church's war against heresy must have given a keen stimulus to his polemic activity, and influenced his subsequent life as a student and teacher of theology.

2. *Siege of Nisibis.*—After some years his course of assiduous study, obedience, and devout piety, was rudely broken by the alarm of war. Soon after the death of Constantine (A.D. 337), Sapor, king of Persia was moved to seize the opportunity offered by the removal of the great Emperor and the inexperience of his sons, and to attempt the recovery of the provinces on the Tigris which had been ceded by Narses his predecessor to Diocletian (under the treaty of A.D. 297), so as to push his border westward in advance of the line which had for forty years defined the eastern limits of the Roman Empire. To this end it was essential that he should obtain possession of Nisibis,[1] the strength and situation of that city marking it as a necessary safeguard for the frontier he sought to attain ; and to it accordingly he laid siege in great force. After seventy days' successful resistance, he had recourse to a novel mode of assault by which the city was wellnigh overpowered. The river (Mygdonius[2]) which flowed through it was by his orders embanked and its waters intercepted, and then let loose so as to bear with destructive rush against the city wall. It gave way ; and Sapor prepared to enter and take possession. To his dismay he found his advance vigorously repelled ; he saw the breach filled by a fresh wall, manned and equipped with engines of war. The holy Bishop Jacob and the devout Ephraim, by their unceasing prayers within the church and their exhortations, had stimulated the garrison and the people to accomplish this work with incredible rapidity, and had secured the divine blessing on its timely completion. But a more amazing sight than the newly-built wall awaited Sapor. On the ramparts there appeared a Figure in royal apparel of radiant brightness,—the Emperor Constantius in outward semblance ; though he was known to be far off, in Antioch. Sapor in blind fury assailed this majestic phantom with missiles, but soon desisted when he perceived the futility of his attack. His final discomfiture was brought to pass by Ephraim. Having first sought and obtained the Bishop's sanction, he ascended a tower whence he could view the besieging host, and there he offered prayer to God that He should send on them a plague of gnats and mosquitos, and show by what puny agents Divine Power could effectually work the ruin of its adversaries. The prayer was instantly answered by a cloud of these insects, tiny but irresistible assailants, descending on the Persian host. Maddened by this plague, the horses flung their riders ; the elephants broke loose and trampled down the men ; the camp was thrown into irretrievable confusion ; a storm of wind, rain, and thunder (adds another chronicler) enhanced the panic ; and Sapor was forced to raise the siege and retire with ignominy and heavy loss instead of success.

Soon after, the saintly Bishop Jacob died, in the fulness of his virtues and his fame ; and Ephraim in deep affliction conducted his funeral.

3. *Removal to Edessa.*—Our biographer then, passing over the remaining years of Constantius, goes on to the accession of Julian (A.D. 361). The troubles of the intervening period he assigns to the reign of Constans, whom (though he died before his

---

[1] The strong and ancient city . . . which, since the time of Lucullus had been deservedly esteemed the bulwark of the East. Gibbon, *Decline and Fall*, ch. xviii.

[2] Now called Jaghjagh,—an affluent of the Khabur (Chaboras) which joins the Euphrates at Circesium.

brother Constantius) he supposes to have reigned after him and before Julian.  He records the persecutions suffered by the Christians under the latter, the judgment that overtook him in his defeat and death by the hands of the Persians, the succession of Jovian, and the treaty concluded by him with Sapor, under which Nisibis was surrendered to Persia and emptied of its Christian inhabitants.  Of Ephraim he tells us only that he raised his voice against Julian and his persecutions, and remained in Nisibis until its surrender, and then retired to a place called Beth-Garbaia,[1] where he had been baptized at the age of eighteen and had received his first instruction in the Scriptures and in psalmody.  Persecution having arisen there against the Church, he fled to Amid, where he spent a year ; and thence proceeded to Edessa (now Urfa), which city, as soon as he came in sight of it, he fixed on as his permanent and final abode.  As he was about to enter it, an incident occurred which nearly all the narratives of his life relate with variations, and which the historian Sozomen states to have been recorded in one of the writings of Ephraim himself.  Beside the river Daisan which surrounds the city, he saw some women washing clothes in its waters.  As he stood and watched them, one of them fixed her eyes on him and gazed at him so long as to move his anger. "Woman," he said, "art thou not ashamed?"  She answered, " It is for thee to look on the ground, for from thence thou art ; but for me it is to look at thee, for from thee was I taken."  He marvelled at the reply and acknowledged the woman's wisdom ; and left the spot saying to himself, " If the women of this city are so wise, how much more exceedingly wise must its men be ! "

Other authorities (including Ephraim's contemporary, Gregory of Nyssa, who professes to collect the facts of his *Encomium* exclusively from Ephraim's own written remains) give a somewhat different turn to this story.  According to them, Ephraim approached the city, praying and expecting to meet at his first entrance there some holy and wise man by whose converse he might profit.  The first person whom he encountered at the gate was a harlot.  Shocked and bitterly disappointed, he eyed her, and was passing on ; but when he noticed that she eyed him, in turn, he asked the meaning of her bold gaze.  In this version of the incident, her answer was, " It is meet and fit that I gaze on thee, for from thee, as man, I was taken ; but look not thou on me, but rather on the ground whence thou wast taken."  Ephraim owned that he had learned something of value even from this outcast woman ; and praised God, who from the mouth of such an unlooked-for teacher, had fulfilled his desire for edification.

Another woman of Edessa is related by some of these authorities to have accosted the holy man, expecting that, even if she failed to tempt him to unchastity, she might at least move him to the sin, against which he strove no less sedulously to guard himself, of anger.  He affected to yield to her solicitation ; but when she invited him to fix on a place of assignation, he proposed that it should be in the open and frequented street.  When she objected to such shameless publicity, he replied, " If we are ashamed in sight of men, how much more ought we to be ashamed in the sight of God, who knows all secret things and will bring all to His judgment ! "  By this reply the woman was moved to repentance and amendment, and gave up her sinful life,—and finally (as some add) retired from the world into a convent.

In Edessa, Ephraim at first earned a humble livelihood in the service of a bath-keeper, while giving his free time to the task of making the Scriptures known to the heathen who then formed a large part of the population of the city.  But before long he was led, by the advice of a monk whom he casually met, to join himself to one of

---

[1] Not elsewhere named : perhaps we ought to read Beth-Garme ; for which see *B. O.* II., *De Monophysitis, s. v.*

the Solitaries (or anchorites) who dwelt in the caves of the adjacent "Mount of Edessa" (a rocky range of hills, now Nimrud Dagh). There he passed his time in prayer, fasting, and study of the Scriptures.

But a divine intimation was sent to call him back from his retreat into active life in the city. A vision came to the Solitary under whom Ephraim had placed himself. This man, as he stood at midnight outside his cell after prayer and psalmody, saw an angel descending from heaven and bearing in his hands a great roll written on both sides, and heard him say to them that stood by, "To whom shall I give this volume that is in my hands?" They answered, "To Eugenius [1] the Solitary of the desert of Egypt." Again he asked, "Who is worthy of it?" They answered, "Julian the Solitary." The Angel rejoined, "None among men is this day worthy of it, save Ephraim the Syrian of the Mount of Edessa."

He, to whom this vision came, at first regarded it as a delusion; but he soon found reason to accept it as from God. Visiting Ephraim's solitary cell, he found him engaged in writing a commentary on the Book of Genesis, and was amazed at the exegetical power shown in the work of a writer so untrained. When this was speedily followed by a Commentary on Exodus, the truth of the vision became apparent, and the Solitary hastened to the "School" of Edessa and showed the book to "the doctors and priests, and chief men of the city." They were filled with admiration, and when they learned that Ephraim of Nisibis was the author, and heard of the vision by which his merit was revealed, they went at once to seek him out in his retreat. In his modesty he fled from their approach; but a second divine vision constrained him to return. In the valley where he had sought to hide, an Angel met him and asked, "Ephraim, wherefore fleest thou?" He answered, "Lord, that I may sit in silence, and escape from the tumult of the world." "Look to it," rejoined the Angel, "that the word be not spoken of thee, *Ephraim hath fled from me as an heifer whose shoulder hath drawn back from the yoke'* (Hos. iv. 16, x. 11—quoted loosely). Ephraim pleaded with tears, "Lord, I am weak and unworthy;" but the Angel silenced his excuses with the Saviour's words, *No man lighteth a candle and putteth it under a bushel, but on a candlestick that all may see the light* (St. Matth. v. 5, St. Luke, xi. 33). Accepting the rebuke, Ephraim returned to Edessa, with much prayer for strength from on high, to combat false doctrine. There he was ill received, and taunted as one who had fled in hypocritical affectation of reluctance, and was now returning in vainglorious quest of applause. This reproach he met with the meek reply, "Pardon me, my brethren, for I am a humble man;" at which they cried out the more against him, "Come, see the madman, the fool!" He held his ground notwithstanding, and taught many.

But this work which his adversaries failed to put down, the over-zeal of an admirer brought to a sudden close. One of the recluses of the Mount, having occasion to visit the city, saw him and followed him crying, "This is *the fan in the Lord's hand*, wherewith *He will purge all His floor*, and the tares of heresy: this is the fire whereof our Lord said, *I am come to send fire on the earth*" (St. Matth. iii. 12, St. Luke, xii. 49). Hearing this, certain chief men of the city, heretics, heathens, and Jews, seized him and drew him outside the gates, stoned him and left him wellnigh dead. Next morning he fled back to his cell on the Mount.

4. *Work as a Teacher.*—There, he gave himself to the work of refuting with his pen

---

[1] So the Paris text: the Vatican has "Origen." The person meant is probably the Eugenius who came from Egypt with 70 disciples to Nisibis, to introduce the ascetic life into that region, and lived there from the time of the consecration of St. Jacob till the surrender in 363. His life is related in the inedited MS. Ad'd. 12174 (Lives of Saints), of the British Museum.

the heresies and misbeliefs of his time, which he had thus been hindered by violence from combating in speech. Disciples gathered round him, and a school formed itself under the teacher in his retirement. The names are recorded by our narrator of Zenobius, Simeon, Isaac, Asuna, and Julian. Others add those of Abraham, Abba, and Mara. All these are named with favour in his *Testament* (a document of which we shall treat hereafter) except Isaac; but two others, Paulinus and Aurit (*or* Arnad) are denounced as false to the Faith.

The biographer introduces into his narrative of this stage of Ephraim's life an account of his famous dream of the vine (above referred to), which foreshowed his future fertility as a writer, as related in his *Testament*. It will be given farther on, in his own words.

Remote and isolated as was his abode, the fame of the illustrious Basil, Archbishop of Cæsarea in Cappadocia, reached him there, and moved in him a desire to see and hear so great a divine. He prayed for divine guidance in the matter; and in answer a vision was sent to him. Before the Holy Table there seemed to stand a pillar of fire, whereof the top reached unto heaven, and a voice from heaven was heard to cry, "Such as thou seest this pillar of fire, such is the great Basil."

5. *Journey to Egypt, and Sojourn there.*—Thus encouraged, Ephraim set out on his journey, taking with him an interpreter, for he was unable to speak Greek. In the first instance, however (according to the *History*), he made his way, not to Cappadocia, but to a seaport (not named by the writer—but probably Alexandretta is meant) where he took ship for Egypt. In the voyage the ship encountered perils, first in a storm, and afterwards from a sea-monster, but was delivered from both by his faith, which enabled him with words of power and the sign of the cross to rebuke the winds and waves into calm, and to slay the monster. Arrived in Egypt, he made his way to the city Antino (apparently Antinoë or Antinoopolis),[1] and thence towards the famous desert of Scete, in the Nitrian valley—then, and still, the place of many monasteries. Here he found an unoccupied cave, in which, as a cell, he and his companion took up their abode for eight years. His habits of life in this retreat—and (as it appears) at Edessa —were of the most austere. His food was barley bread, varied only by parched corn, pulse, or herbs; his drink, water; his clothing, squalid rags. His flesh was dried up like a potsherd, over his bones. He is described as being of short stature, bald, and beardless. He never laughed, but was of sad countenance. Other authorities, Gregory especially, dwell much and with admiration on his profuse and perpetual weeping.[2]

In this Egyptian retreat he is related to have proved himself a victorious adversary against the Arians. On his arrival he had sought out and found a monk named Bishoi, to whom, because of his special sanctity, he had been divinely directed before he quitted Edessa; and with him he had sojourned for a week, communing with him by means of a miraculous gift which endowed each with the language of the other. By this gift

---

[1] This city lay quite out of the region of the Nitrian monasteries. Possibly in the original form of this biography, the "Enaton" (*i.e.* the Ninth District) of Alexandria was named as the place of Ephraim's sojourn, and subsequent transcribers changed the word into Antino.

[2] As represented by Gregory, Ephraim was a very Democritus among saints :
"As with all men to breathe is a natural function unceasing in exercise, so with Ephraim was it to weep. There was no day, no night, no hour, no moment however brief, in which his eyes were not wakeful and filled with tears, while he bewailed the faults and follies, now of his own life, now of mankind. By groans he made a channel for the streams of his eyes; or rather, by the outflow of the eyes he looked his groans. . . . There was no interval of time between them, groans succeeding to tears and they again to groans, as in a sort of circle ; so that it was impossible to distinguish which made the beginning and which was the cause of the other. Any one who makes acquaintance with his writings will perceive this characteristic; for he will be found lamenting not only in his treatises on penitence, or morals, or right conduct, but even in his panegyrics, in which it is the habit of most writers to show an aspect of rejoicing. But he was everywhere the same, and abounded perpetually in this gift of compunction."

he was enabled to carry on controversy with Egyptian heretics, many of whom he reclaimed to orthodoxy. Over one of these, an aged monk who had been perverted to heresy by the possession of a demon, he exercised a further miraculous power for his restoration, by casting out the evil spirit and restoring the old man at once to his right mind and to the right faith. This gift of language, and the intercourse of Ephraim with Bishoi, are told only in the Vatican form of the History, which adds that he not only spoke Egyptian, but wrote discourses in that tongue. The other version of it represents him as having learned to speak Egyptian in the ordinary way. It is to be noted that the name of Bishoi (in Greek, Pasoës) is known as that of the founder (in the fourth century) of the monastery of Amba Bishoi, still occupied by a community of monks, in the Nitrian Desert; and that in those sequestered regions the tradition of Ephraim's visit to Bishoi was lingering even within the last century and probably still lingers. To this subject we shall have occasion to recur, further on.[1]

6. *Visit to St. Basil of Cæsarea.*—This long sojourn ended, he resumed his purpose of visiting Basil, and left Egypt for Cæsarea (which our narrator evidently supposes to be a maritime city—probably confusing it with the Cæsarea which was the metropolis of Palestine).[2] He was anxious that his first sight of the great Archbishop should be on the Feast of the Epiphany, and he succeeded in so timing his journey as to arrive the day before that Feast. On enquiry, he learned that Basil would take his part in its celebration in the great church; and thither accordingly on the morrow he and his interpreter repaired. On the same day (adds our historian) was the commemoration of St. Mamas.[3] At first, when he saw the great Prelate in gorgeous vestments attended by his train of richly-robed clergy, the heart of the humble ascetic failed him: this man so surrounded with state and splendor could not be (he thought) the pillar of fire revealed to him in his vision. But when Basil ascended the *bema* to preach, Ephraim, though he could understand little if anything of the orator's eloquence, was speedily brought to another mind. As he listened he saw the Holy Ghost (in the form of a dove, says Gregory, as also the Vatican *History*,—or, according to another account,[4] of a tongue of fire), speaking from his mouth, (Gregory says, hovering by his ear and inspiring his words); and he joined in the applause which each period of the oration drew from the audience,—so vehemently that while others were content to utter the cry of approval (*ahâ*) but once, he reiterated it (*ahâ, ahâ*). Basil noticing this sent his Archdeacon to invite the stranger into the Sanctuary; but the invitation was modestly declined. Another version of the story places this invitation before the sermon, attributing to Basil a spiritual insight which discerned the holy man's presence and identified him. Again the Archdeacon was sent to summon him—this time, by name: "Come, my lord Ephraim, before the *bema;* the Archbishop bids thee." Amazed to find himself thus discovered, Ephraim yielded, and praised God, saying, "Great art Thou in very truth; Basil is the pillar of fire; through his mouth speaks the Holy Ghost." He begged, however, to be excused from coming into the Archbishop's presence publicly, and asked to be allowed instead to salute him privately in the "Treasury," "after the Sacred Oblation." Accordingly, when "the Divine Mysteries" had been completed, the Archbishop's Syncellus repeated the invitation, saying, "Draw near, Apostle of Christ, that we may enjoy thy presence." He complied, and in his mean rags, silent, and with

---

[1] For this monastery, see below, p. 143, note [1]. For the history of Pesoës, see Palladius, *Hist. Lausiaca*, XV.
[2] Cæsarea, the see of Basil, lay far from the sea, in the heart of the inland province of Cappadocia. The Cæsarea of the Acts of the Apostles (Stratonis), the metropolis of Palestine, was a seaport.
[3] The feast of St. Mamas (a Cappadocian martyr) falls in August, not in January. A sermon of St. Basil for that feast is extant (Hom. XXIII.). Probably the author of this *History* knew that sermon, and was thus led to mention the commemoration here, carelessly disregarding the time of year.
[4] To the pseudo-Amphilochius.

downcast looks, stood before the magnificent Prelate.    Basil rose from his seat, received
him with the kiss of brotherhood, then bowed his head, and even prostrated himself
before the humble monk, greeting him as the " Father of the Desert," the foe of unclean
spirits ; and asked the purpose of his journey,—" Art thou come to visit one who is a
sinner?   The Lord reward thy labor."    He then proceeded to give the Holy Eucharist
to both the strangers.    In the interchange of speech (through the interpreter) that ensued,
Basil enquired how it was that one who spoke no Greek had followed his discourse with
such applause.    When he heard, in reply, of the visible manifestation of the Holy Ghost,
he exclaimed, " I would I were Ephraim, to be counted worthy by the Lord of such a
boon ! "   Ephraim then entreated of him a boon ; "I know, O holy man, that whatsoever thou shalt ask of God, He will give it thee : ask Him, therefore, to enable me to
speak Greek."    Basil in reply disclaimed such intercessory power, but proposed that
they should join in prayer for the desired gift, reminding him of the promise, " He will
fulfil the desire of them that fear Him " (Ps. cxlv. 19).    They prayed accordingly for a
long space ; and when they had ceased, Basil enquired, "Why, my Lord Ephraim,
receivest thou not the Order of Priesthood, which befits thee ?"    " Because I am a
sinner," answered Ephraim (through the interpreter).    "I would thy sins were mine ! "
exclaimed Basil.    He then desired Ephraim to bow his head, laid his hand on him and
recited over him the Prayer of Ordination to the Diaconate, inviting him to respond.
Forthwith, to the amazement of all, Ephraim answered in Greek, with the due form,
"Save, and lift me up, O God."    And thenceforth he was able to speak Greek with
ease and correctness.    He persisted, however, in declining the higher Order of the
Priesthood ; but his interpreter was admitted both Deacon and Priest by Basil before
they departed.    Their sojourn lasted about a fortnight.    Other writers, however, call
Ephraim a Priest ; and there is a passage where he himself seems to speak of himself,
as holding the Priesthood (koh'niyô) ;[1] but Palladius, Jerome, Sozomen, and others of
the best-informed writers, confirm our History.    He is in fact frequently styled Ephraim
*the Deacon*, as if to emphasize the fact that one so high in repute never rose above that
lowly rank.

Traces of Ephraim's influence are to be found in two places of Basil's writings.    It
can scarcely be doubted that he points to Ephraim when (*De Spiritu Sancto*, xxix. 74),
in defending the familiar formula "Glory to the Father and to the Son *and* to the Holy
Ghost,"—and again (*Homil.* in *Hexaêm.* ii. 6), in explaining the action of the Spirit on
the waters (Genesis i. 2)—he appeals to the authority of an unnamed man of great
knowledge and judgment, " as closely conversant with the knowledge of all that is
true, as he is far removed from worldly wisdom," a " Mesopotamian," a "Syrian."
From him he says he learned—in the former instance, that "*and* " was to be inserted
before the name of the Holy Ghost as well as before that of the Son ;—and, in the latter,
that the Spirit was not to be conceived as being "*carried* upon" the waters (as the
Septuagint represents) ; but (as the Peshitto more truly represents the Hebrew), as
"*brooding* upon " them, to cherish them into life—as a bird on her nest.    The verb
thus variously rendered is common to the Hebrew with the cognate Syriac ; and the
explanation of it given by Basil is in fact found in Ephraim's extant *Commentary* on the
passage of Genesis :[2] but he understands the "spirit" to be the wind—not (as Basil)
the Holy Ghost.

7. *Return to Edessa.*—Ephraim's return to Edessa was hastened by the tidings that in his
absence no less than nine new heresies had appeared there.    His way thither lay through

---

[1] *Parœnesis* xxvi. 11 (*Opera Syr.*), Tom. III. p. 467.    The word, however, is perhaps not to be taken literally
[2] *Opera Syriaca*, Tom. I., p. 8.

Samosata ; and there he fell in with a chief man of the city, a heretic, who was passing by with a train of attendant youths. As the holy man sat by the wayside to eat bread, these followers mocked him, and one of them wantonly smote him on the cheek. The injury was borne in meek silence ; but it was speedily avenged on the smiter, by a viper which came out from under a stone whereon he sat, and bit him so that he died on the spot. His master and companions hastened after Ephraim, and overtook him as he was begging his food in a village beyond the city which he had just passed through. At their entreaty he turned back with them, and by his prayers restored the dead youth to life. The nobleman and his followers, seeing this miracle, were converted to the orthodox faith.

8. *Controversies.*—Arrived at Edessa, he engaged at once in the conflict against the multiform heresies of the place, old and new—Manichean and Marcionite, as well as Arian. Of all the forms of error he encountered, the one that gave him most grief and trouble was that which had been originated about the year 200 by a Syrian, Bardesan.[6] Of this heresiarch he writes, in one of his *Nisibene Hymns* (the 51st ;[7] not included in the following selection) :

1.  I have chanced upon tares, my breth-
    ren,
    That wear the color of wheat,
    To choke the good seed ;
    Concerning which the husbandmen are
    commanded,
    Take them not away nor root them
    out ;
    And though the husbandmen heeded
    not,
    The seed waxed stronger than they,
    Grew and multiplied and covered and
    choked them.

2.  I have chanced upon a book of Bar-
    daisan,
    And I was troubled for an hour's space ;
    It tainted my pure ears,
    And made them a passage
    For words filled with blasphemy.
    I hastened to purge them

With the goodly and pure reading
Of the Scriptures of truth.

3.  I heard as I read them
    How he blasphemes justice,
    And grace her fellow-worker.
    For if the body be not raised,
    It were foul reproach for grace,
    To have created it unto corruption ;
    And it were slander against justice,
    To send it unto destruction.

4.  This then that I read was grievous
    For soul and for body alike ;
    And between these partners it casts
    The severance of despair.
    The body it cuts off from its resurrec-
    tion,
    And the soul from her comrade,
    And the loss which the serpent threw
    on us
    Bardaisan counts it for gain.

The controversy against the disciples of this man gave to the literary work of Ephra-im an impulse to which his fame is largely due. His polemic in the above instance took, as we see, the form of a hymn ; and his biographer informs us that it was in this controversy he first was led to adopt hymnody as a vehicle for teaching truth and con-futing error. Of his hymns we possess some which can be confidently assigned to an earlier period—the first twenty-one of the Nisibene collection (which are the Nisibene Hymns proper), belonging to the epoch of the third siege (A. D. 350); but those are songs of triumph and thanksgiving, or of personal eulogy and exhortation,—not of con-troversy. The idea of the controversial use of hymnody he borrowed (we are told)

---

[6] In Syriac, Bardaisan (*son of Daisan*), so called from his birthplace beside the river above mentioned.
[7] See Bickell, *Carmina Nisibena*, p. 101.

from his adversaries. It appears that Harmodius, the son of Bardesan, had popularized the false teaching of his father, as embodied in a series of a hundred and fifty hymns (in profane rivalry with the Psalms of David), by setting them to attractive tunes, which caught the ear of the multitude, and inclined them to receive his doctrines. So Ephraim himself tells us (attributing the work, however, to Bardesan solely) in his *Homily* (metrical) LIII., "*Against Heretics*" (not included in our selection). "He fashioned hymns, and joined them with tunes; and composed psalms, and brought in moods. By weights and measures, he portioned language. He blended for the simple poison with sweetness. The sick will not choose the food of wholesomeness. He would look to David, that he might be adorned with his beauty, and commended by his likeness. An hundred and fifty psalms, he likewise composed."[8]

To confute the heresies thus circulated, Ephraim borrowed the tunes employed by Harmodius; and his hymns, set to these tunes, soon carried the day in favor of orthodoxy, partly by the force of their truth, partly by their superior literary power, and partly by the help of a choir formed among the nuns whom he employed to sing them, morning and evening, in the churches. Thus the rival hymnody of heresy was superseded, and the hymns of Ephraim gained the place they have ever since held in the Church, wherever Syriac is the ecclesiastical language,—even though it is no longer the vernacular.

He celebrated this victory in the following strain of triumphant imprecation :—

" Cursed be our trust [if it be] on the Seven;[9] the Æons which Bardaisan confesses !
Anathema [be he] who says, as he said: that from them descend the rain and the dew !
Anathema who affirms, like him : that from them are the showers and the frosts !
Cursed be he who says, as he said : that from them are the snow and the ice !
[Cursed be he who affirms, like him] : that from them are the seeds for the husbandmen !
Anathema who confesses, as he confessed : that from them are the fruits for the labourer !
Anathema who believes, like him : that from them are famine and plenty !
Anathema who confesses, as he taught : that from them are summer and winter !
Anathema be on the man : and on the woman who thus speaks !
Anathema be on the house : wherein it is thus affirmed !
Anathema his doctrine which rests : its trust on the Sevenfold !
Cursed be he who reproaches his Creator : and ascribes dominion to the Seven !
Cursed be he who reads the Scriptures : and becomes a gainsayer of the Scriptures !
Cursed be he who reads the Prophets : and breaks the words of the Prophets !
Cursed be he who reads the Apostles : and abides not by their words ! "

To this is subjoined a verse, the response of Balai (Balæus) a disciple :—

" The Lord exalt thy horn : O Church that art faithful !
For the King, and the King's son : are established in thine ark."

Another demonstration of Ephraim's zeal against heresy, which the compiler of the *History* judiciously omits, is (unhappily for the fame of both) attested, and with evident approval, by Gregory of Nyssa.

---

[8] *Opera Syriaca*, Tom. II., p. 554 , see also Homily I.
[9] The Seven *Æons* (or Beings) of Bardesan's heresy ; see *Opp. Syr.* II., p. 550.

Apollinaris, who was his contemporary, and whose erroneous teaching he held in abhorrence, had committed his heresies to writing in two volumes which he gave into the keeping of a woman, a follower of his sect. Ephraim approached this woman and persuaded her to lend him the books, pretending that he agreed with the doctrine of their author and desired to use them in controversy against its opponents. At her instance he returned them in a short time; but before so doing, he treated them with fish-glue in such fashion that the leaves of each cohered into a solid mass, while to outward appearance they were unharmed. Soon after, he challenged Apollinaris to meet him in a public disputation concerning the articles of faith which the heretic had impugned. The latter sought to decline the controversy, pleading his old age[1] and infirmities; but consented to it,—only on condition, however, that he should be allowed to read from these volumes the statement and defence of his tenets therein written by him. On these terms, the disputants met. Apollinaris was called on to maintain his thesis, and his writings were placed in his hands; but when he went to open the books, it was in vain. No part of either volume would yield to his fingers; he was obliged to desist and to retire, baffled and ashamed; in such dismay as to bring on an illness that nearly proved fatal.

Another incident of this period, related in the *History*, is a miracle (a genuine one this time, if true) wrought by Ephraim on a paralytic. Seeing him as he sat and begged at the door of a church in Edessa, the holy man asked him: "Wilt thou be made whole?" "Yea, my Lord; lay thy hand on me," was the reply. With the words, "In the Name of Christ, arise and walk," he was cured instantly; and departed, glorifying God.

At the end of four years, messengers came to him from Basil, summoning him to come and receive consecration to the Episcopate, for some see unnamed (to which, as Sozomen relates, he had been elected;—*Hist. Eccles.* II. 16). When he learned their errand, he feigned madness, going to and fro in the streets in unseemly fashion, in motley garb, eating bread as he went and letting his spittle run down. Thus he succeeded in evading the undesired elevation: the messengers, shocked at his behaviour, returned without him, and reported that they found him a madman. "O hidden pearl of price" (cried Basil) "whom the world knows not! Ye are the madmen, and he the sane."

The city and the Mount of Edessa suffered in these days from an invasion of the Huns, who plundered, murdered, and ravished, without mercy,—not even sparing the cells and convents. This calamity Ephraim is said to have recorded, in writings which have not reached us.

9. *Persecution by Valens.*—From another peril the Edessenes were saved by their faith and constancy. In the days of their Bishop Barses (361–378), the Arian Emperor Valens (364–378), in the course of his persecution of the orthodox, approached the city and summoned the inhabitants to wait upon him in his camp and hear his pleasure there. They disregarded the command, and gathered into the great Church of St. Thomas,[2] where they and their Bishop continued unceasingly in prayer. The historian

---

[1] The heretic Apollinaris seems to have been a younger man than Ephraim, whom he survived by some years. Possibly his father, the elder Apollinaris, is here intended. But he is not recorded as having taught heresy.

[2] To this church were translated the bones of St. Thomas the Apostle, from his burial place in India, in the time of Eulogius the successor of Barses (378–387),—as we learn from Barhebræus, *Chronicon Eccles.* I. 21 (p. 65 of Abbeloos and Lamy's edition). But the above narrative, as confirmed by Socrates (IV. 18), shows that it had been built and was held in special reverence before that. It is the church at which our *History* places the healing of the paralytic (above). Sozomen's account (VI. 17) in the main agrees; also Theodoret's (IV. 17).

Socrates, a trustworthy and early (fifth century) authority, confirms our *History* here ; and explains that Valens had ordered their Church to be surrendered to the Arians, and was enraged against them for resisting his decree, and against his Prefect Modestus for failing to carry it out. Valens then, finding them contumacious, ordered one of his generals (this same Modestus, according to Sozomen, who also relates the story) to enter the city and put the people to the sword. As Modestus, who was a humane man, sought to persuade them to yield, he met a woman leading her two sons to the Church. He strove to stop her, warning her of the danger she incurred ; but her reply was, "I hear that they who fear God are to be slain, and I am in haste to win the crown with the rest." "But what of these boys?" he asked. "Are they thy sons?" "They are," she answered, "and we pray, both I and they, that we may be made an oblation to the Lord." Amazed at her resolve, he reported the matter to Valens, to convince him that the Edessenes were prepared to die rather than submit. The Emperor was moved to relent ; the people and their Bishop and priests came forth ; he heard their plea, was ashamed of his cruel purpose, pardoned their disobedience, and departed. This well-attested incident is to be assigned to 371, or to the preceding or ensuing year.[3]

This victory of faith was celebrated by Ephraim in the following verses :—

"The doors of her homes Edessa
Left open when she went forth
With the pastor to the grave, to die,
And not depart from her faith.
Let the city and fort and building
And houses be yielded to the king ;
Our goods and our gold let us leave ;
So we part not from our faith !
Edessa is full of chastity,
Full of prudence and understanding.

She is clad in discernment of soul ;
Faith is the girdle of her loins ;
Truth her armour all-prevailing ;
Love her crown, all-exalting.
Christ bless them that dwell in her,
Edessa, whose name is His glory,
And the name of her champion her
    beauty !
City that is lady over her fellows,
City that is the shadow
Of the Jerusalem in heaven ! "

After all was thus restored to peace and orthodoxy, Ephraim withdrew to his retreat on the Mount, which he is not recorded to have again quitted, save on one occasion, to be presently related.

10. *Penitent sent to Ephraim by Basil : Basil's Death.*—The death of Basil (at the end of 378) is said by our author to have caused great grief to Ephraim, and to have been lamented by him in hymns. But (as will be shown below) this is hardly possible, even if the latest date for Ephraim's death be accepted.

Another miraculous incident connected with Ephraim's biography, belongs to the year of Basil's death. A woman of high rank, but of evil life, in Cæsarea, being moved to penitence, wrote on a paper a full confession of her sins, and gave it to Basil, who at her entreaty laid it with prayer before the Lord. Her repentance and his intercession prevailed so far, that the record of all her guilt disappeared from the paper, save of one sin, more heinous than the rest. Disappointed thus of her hope of full pardon, she had recourse again to Basil, supplicating that this sin too might be wiped out. He encouraged her to persevere in prayer, and advised her to repair to the Mount of Edessa, to Ephraim, and through him obtain her desire. To Ephraim accordingly she made her way, and cried to him, saying, "Have pity on me, thou holy one of God." When he heard Basil's advice and her petition, he disavowed all such power to prevail with

---

[3] Baronius, *Annales,* IV. p. 308. The Vatican *Life* reads *Julian* for *Valens* in this narrative, thus introducing inexplicable perplexity into the chronology. Julian died before Ephraim became a resident of Edessa.

God as Basil had ascribed to him, and advised her rather to hasten back and obtain her Archbishop's farther intercession. She returned accordingly to Cæsarea ; but, as it seemed, too late : Basil had died before her arrival, and she met his corpse as it was carried to burial. In despair, she prostrated herself in the dust, proclaimed her story to all that stood by, and upbraided the dead saint, "Woe is me, servant of God ! why didst thou send me far away that I should return too late and meet thee borne to the grave ! The Lord judge betwixt me and thee, who hast sent me to another, when thyself couldst have absolved me !" One of the attendant clergy, desiring to learn what was the sin for which pardon was so hard to win, took from her the paper she held, and opening found it blank. The last and deadliest of her list had vanished like the rest : and "thus, by the prayers of Basil and of Ephraim, and by the woman's faith and perseverance, her sins were all of them blotted out."

After this occurrence, the *History* places the following narrative of Ephraim's last intervention in earthly concerns. It is related likewise by Palladius (Ephraim's younger contemporary) and by Sozomen.

11. *Exertions in Relief of Famine.*—In a season of severe famine, he ascertained that grain was being hoarded in the stores of certain persons who gave nothing to the starving poor. When he rebuked their inhumanity, they excused themselves on the plea that none was to be found of such probity as to guarantee fairness and honesty in the distribution of relief. Ephraim at once offered his services, and was accepted as their agent throughout the famine season, to dispense large sums as the treasurer and steward of their bounty. Among other things, he provided three hundred letters, partly for removing the sick to stations where they were duly tended, partly for carrying the dead for interment. A body of helpers worked with him in administering relief, and their care extended not merely through the city, but to the country and villages adjacent. The year of dearth ended, a year of plenty ensued ; Ephraim retired to his cell,—this time to leave it no more. He died a month after the close of the charitable labours. Of them his biographer, following for once the better instinct which recognizes higher worth in services of love than in ascetic practices or in miraculous pretensions, writes thus :—"God gave him this occasion that therein he might win the crown in the close of his life."

12. *His Testament.*—In his *Testament*, which professes to have been composed in immediate anticipation of his end, he laid on his disciples a solemn charge that his body should be buried humbly, covered with no garment save his tunic (*cothênô*). Gregory of Nyssa adds that a rich friend who, though informed of his prohibition, had provided beforehand for this purpose a costly robe, was punished by the possession of an evil spirit, which tormented him until, on his confession, the dying saint relieved him, casting out the demon by prayer and laying on of hands.

From the extant Syriac of this document [4] (which is metrical), the following have been selected as the most striking verses :

" I Ephraim am at point to die : and I write my testament ;
That I may leave for all men a memorial : of whatsoever is mine,
That though it be [but] for my words : they that know me may remember me.
Woe is me, for my times are ended : and the length of my years is fulfilled ;
The spinning for me is shortened : the thread is nigh unto cutting ;
The oil fails in the lamp : my days are spent, yea, mine hours ;

4 Printed in Overbeck's *Ephræmi S. Opera Selecta*, p. 137 ; also in the (Roman) *Opera Græca*, at end of Tom. II., p. 395.

The hireling has finished his year : and the sojourner has fulfilled his season.
Around me are the summoners : on this side and that are they that lead me away.
I cry aloud, [but] none hears me : and I complain, [but] none delivers.

" Woe to thee, Ephraim, for the judgment : when thou shall stand before the Son's
     judgment-seat,
And around thee they that know thee : on the right hand and the left,
Lo ! there shalt thou be confounded : woe to him who is put to shame there !
Jesu, do Thou judge Ephraim : nor give his judgment to another ;
For whoso has God for his Judge : he finds mercy in judgment ;
For I have heard from the wise : yea, I have heard from men of knowledge,
That whoso sees the face of the King : though he has offended, he shall not die.

\*      \*      \*      \*      \*      \*      \*      \*      \*      \*      \*

" By him who came down on Mount Sinai : and by him who spake on the rock,
By that Mouth which spake the " *Eli* " : [5] and made the bowels of creation tremble,
By him who was sold in Judah : and by him who was scourged in Jerusalem,
By the Might which was smitten on the cheek : and by the Glory which endured
     spitting,
By the threefold Names of fire : and by the one Assent and will,
I have not rebelled against the Church : nor against the might of God.
If in my thought I have magnified the Father : above the Son, let Him have no mercy
     on me !
And if I have accounted the Holy Spirit less : than God, let mine eyes be darkened !
If as I have said, I confessed not : let me go into outer darkness !
And if I speak in hypocrisy : let me burn with the wicked in fire !

\*      \*      \*      \*      \*      \*      \*      \*      \*      \*      \*

" I adjure you my disciples : with adjurations that may not be loosed,
That my words be not set aside : that ye loose not my commandments.
Whoso lays me beneath the altar : he shall not see the Altar of heaven ;
For it is not meet that foul stench : should be laid in the Holy Place ;
Whoso has laid me within the temple : he shall not see the temple of the Kingdom.

\*      \*      \*      \*      \*      \*      \*      \*      \*      \*      \*

" Take nought from me as memorial : [6] my beloved, my brothers, my sons,
For as much as ye have a memorial : that which ye have heard of Jesus.
For if ye take aught from Ephraim : into reproach will Ephraim come ;
For He, my Lord, will say unto me : 'More than in Me they have trusted in thee,
For if they had relied on Me : they had not sought a memorial from thee.'

" Lay me not with the martyrs : for I am a sinner and unworthy,
And because of my unworthiness I fear : to be brought beside their bones ;
For if stubble comes near to fire : it will scorch it, yea, devour it.
It is not that I hate their neigbourhood : because of mine unworthiness. I fear it.

\*      \*      \*      \*      \*      \*      \*      \*      \*      \*      \*

" Whoso carries me on his fingers : may his hands be leprous as Gehazi !

---

[5] St. Matth. xxvii. 46.           [6] *i.e.*, as a relic.

"On your shoulders carry me : and in haste conduct me [to the grave],
And as a mean man bury me : for I have worn out my days in sadness.
Why glorify ye me, O men : who before our Lord am ashamed?
And why give ye me [the name of] 'Blessed' : who am disclosed in my works?
Should one show you my transgressions : ye would all of you spit in my face.
For if the stench of the sinner : could strike one that stood by him,
Ye would all of you flee away : from the loathsome stench of Ephraim.

"Whoso lays with me a pall : may he go forth into outer darkness !
And whoso has laid with me a shroud : may he be cast into Gehenna of fire !
In my coat and cowl shall ye bury me : for ornament beseems not the hateful,
Nor does praise profit the dead : who is laid and cast into the tomb.

\* \* \* \* \* \* \* \* \* \*

"Arise, my brethren of Edessa : my lords and my sons and my fathers !
Bring whatsoever ye have vowed : to lay along with your brother,
Bring and set it before me : whatsoever ye my brethren have vowed.
While I have yet a little memory : let me set on it a price ;
And let there be bought pure vessels : and let there be hired workmen therewith,
And distribution be made among the poor : the needy and them that are in want.

\* \* \* \* \* \* \* \* \* \*

"Blessed is the city wherein ye dwell : Edessa, mother of the wise,
Which from the living mouth of the Son : was blessed by His Disciple.[7]
This blessing shall abide in her : until the Holy One shall be revealed.

"Whoso withholds from me aught that he has vowed : shall die the death of Ananias,
Who sought to deceive the Apostles : and was stretched [dead] before their feet.

"Whoso carries before me a taper : may his fire be kindled beside him !
For to what end avails fire : for him whose fire is from himself?
For when the visible fire is kindled : in it is consumed the secret fire.
Sufficient for me is the pain without : add ye not to me that which is within.

\* \* \* \* \* \* \* \* \* \*

"Lay me not with sweet spices : for this honour avails me not ;
Nor yet incense and perfumes : for the honour benefits me not.
Burn sweet spices in the Holy Place : and me, even me, conduct to the grave with
    prayer.
Give ye incense to God : and over me send up hymns.
Instead of perfumes of spices : in prayer make remembrance of me.
What can goodly odour profit : to the dead who cannot perceive it ?
Bring them in and burn them in the Holy Place : that they which enter in may smell
    the savour.
Wrap thou not the fetid dung : in silk that profits it not.
Cast it down upon the dunghill : for it cannot perceive honour [done to it].

\* \* \* \* \* \* \* \* \* \*

---

[7] The allusion is to the legend that Abgar, King of Edessa, hearing the fame of the Lord Jesus, sent a letter inviting him to his city, and received in reply a letter from Him conveying His blessing, and a promise to send a disciple to teach him and his people. This promise was afterwards fulfilled by the mission of Thaddeus (Addae) to Edessa. (Eusebius, *Hist. Eccles.* I. 13.)

" Lay me not in your sepulchres : for your magnificence profits me not ;
For I have a covenant with God : that I shall be buried with strangers.
I am a stranger, as they were : with them, O my brethren, lay me !
For every bird loves its kind : and man loves him that is like himself.
In the cemetery lay me : where are the broken of heart,
That when the Son of God comes : He may embrace me [8] and raise me among them."

\*     \*     \*     \*     \*     \*     \*     \*     \*     \*

[After blessing by name the five faithful disciples above mentioned (page 126), he leaves an anathema on the two, Paulinus and Urit, who had erred from the faith ; and against]

" Arians and Anomœans : Cathari and those of the Serpent, [9]
Marcionites and Manichœans : Bardesanites and Kukites,
Paulites and Vitalianites : Sabbatarians and Borborites,
With all the other doctrines : of superstitions that are unseemly."

\*     \*     \*     \*     \*     \*     \*     \*     \*     \*

[The dying Saint recalls in the following lines the vision of his childhood, and praises God for its fulfilment.]

" I swear by your lives I lie not : in this thing that I tell.
For when I was a little child : and lay in my mother's bosom,
I saw (I was as in a dream) : a thing which has come to pass in truth.
There grew a vine-shoot on my tongue : and increased and reached unto heaven,
And it yielded fruit without measure : leaves likewise without number.
It spread, it stretched wide, it bore fruit : all creation drew near,
And the more they were that gathered : the more its clusters abounded.
These clusters were the Homilies ; and these leaves the Hymns.
God was the giver of them : glory to Him for His grace !
For He gave to me of His good pleasure : from the storehouse of His treasures."

This farewell strain has no doubt suffered interpolation, but the main part of what is above translated is confirmed as genuine by the references to it of Gregory, who had undoubtedly read it in a Greek version. [1]   As it has reached us, it ends with a narrative, which at most can only claim to be an appendix added by a disciple, of the lamentations uttered at his deathbed by a maiden named Lamprotate, daughter of a man of rank in Edessa, who entreated permission to make a tomb for him and another at his feet for herself.   The narrative concludes with his consent to this petition, his parting commands to her, and her promise of obedience.

His body was followed to the grave by all the people of the city and neighborhood, and by the Bishops, priests, and deacons of the province, with the monks, whether " anchorites, stylites, or cœnobites "—solitary, or living in communities.   It was laid (as he had desired) in the strangers' burial-ground ; but not long after, the citizens removed it thence, and made a grave for him, deacon as he was, among those of their Bishops,—probably in the monastery (now belonging to the Armenians) of St. Sergius

---

[8] The Greek version has " may heal."   The Syriac may be brought to agree with this, by changing *t* into *r* in the verb used.
[9] The sect of Ophites.
[1] The Greek version that has reached us is paraphrastic, and interpolated ; but on the whole represents the original with no great divergence.   See *Opera Græca*, Tom. II., p. 230 ; *Ephraim Syr. Græce*, p. 365 ( Oxford edition).

on the Mount of Edessa, where his tomb is shown to this day, as we learn from the *Reise in Syr. u Mesopot.* of Dr. Sachau (p. 202).

13. *Death and Burial.*—His death occurred in Haziran (June), on the 15th according to our History (Vat.), but other authorities differ, assigning it to the 9th, 18th, or 19th. The shorter Syriac *Life* gives the year as 372,—thus contradicting the *History* which represents him as living in the year of Basil's death (378).

Even in the time of Gregory of Nyssa, an annual commemoration of Ephraim had become customary in the Church, which gave occasion for the *Encomium* above referred to. In the East, it was held on the 28th of January ; but in the Roman Martyrology his name is recorded on the 1st of February.

## IV.—RECAPITULATION OF AUTHENTIC FACTS OF LIFE.

The *Life*, whence the above narrative is mainly derived, though evidently put into its present form by compilers many generations later than the time of Ephraim, is in its leading outlines to be accepted as historically trustworthy, though it has no doubt been largely amplified by the incorporation of exaggerated or fictitious details. Of its essential points, not a few are confirmed by his own writings ; and many more (as has been said above, p. 121), by evidence of hardly later date,—especially by the *Encomium* of Gregory of Nyssa (d. 395), who assures us that he derives his account from Ephraim's written statements and from no other source.[2] This Father, as being brother of Basil with whom Ephraim was so closely associated in his later life, may well have known personally the man of whom he wrote, and was at least in a position to collect and verify with discrimination the facts of his life. Further, the general historical framework of the biography is sufficiently attested as correct by the contemporary secular historians, non-Christian as well as Christian—notably (as will appear farther on), as regards the siege of Nisibis, by one whom Ephraim most abhorred, the Emperor Julian.

It may be briefly affirmed that the external independent evidence covers all the facts included in the summary given above (pp. 120, 121), at the opening of this Section. It extends farther to many incidents related in the *Life*,—such as the attempt of Sapor to take Nisibis by turning the river against its walls, Ephraim's encounter with the woman who met him as he entered Edessa and her retort to his rebuke, his borrowing the music of the heretic in order to popularize the orthodox teaching of his own hymns, the call to the Episcopate and his evasion of it, the constancy of the faith of the Edessenes when threatened by the persecutor Valens, the famine and the work of relief organized by Ephraim in the last year of his life ; also to a few of the details which belong to or verge on the supernatural,—the dream of the vine-shoot which foreshadowed his literary fertility, the vision of the Angel with the book who appeared to his brother-anchorite, and that of the dove, which he himself seemed to see, inspiring the discourses of Basil. In these facts, greater and smaller taken together, we have sufficient data for the derivation of the main outlines of his life and the leading features of his character.

## V.—HISTORICAL CRITICISM OF MEDIÆVAL AMPLIFICATIONS.

But along with the genuine and trustworthy matter, the compiler has embodied much that is unattested and in many cases inherently improbable, and even some things that are demonstrably untrue.

---

[2] There is no ground for supposing that Gregory could read Syriac. It follows therefore that some of Ephraim's writings must have been at a very early date translated into Greek ; and that one of these was the *Testament* which Gregory refers to no less than five times in the *Encomium*.

i. *The Miraculous Details.*—To the category of the improbable—the fiction of hagiology or the growth of myth—belong the miracles so freely ascribed to Ephraim and the miraculous events represented as attending on his career. It is noteworthy that Ephraim himself, though no doubt he believed that he was the recipient of Divine intimations in dream or vision, never lays claim to supernatural powers. Nor does Gregory in the *Encomium* attribute to him any such—except in the case of the rich friend who for his mistaken zeal was given over to an evil spirit ; and on his repentance relieved through Ephraim's intercession.[3] The voice that issued from his father's idol foretelling his future war against idolatry—the answer of the new-born babe that cleared him from calumny—the crowned phantom on the walls of Nisibis that scared the besiegers—the plague of insects that drove them into disastrous flight— the Angel sent to call him back to Edessa when he had fled thence—the storm hushed and the sea-monster slain by his word on the voyage to Egypt—the monk whom he delivered at once from demoniacal possession and from heresy—the sudden gift of tongues which enabled him to speak Coptic with Bishoi and Greek with Basil—the restoration to life of the youth who had died of a viper's bite at Samosata—the paralytic healed at the church door in Edessa—the disappearance of the record of guilt from the scroll on which the penitent of Cæsarea had written her confession—all these belong to the later growth of legend that springs up naturally over the tomb of a saint. Some of them may be safely set aside as purely fictitious ; others are probably due to metaphoric expressions mistaken for literal assertions, or to rhetorical amplification throwing a false coloring of the supernatural over ordinary events. Most of them, moreover, bear evident signs of having been dressed by the compiler into spurious resemblance to the miraculous narrations in the Old and New Testaments, of the Divine dealings with Prophets and Apostles,—Elisha, Jonah, St. Peter, St. Paul, or even of the works of power which attested the mission of our Lord Himself on earth. In reading these, one cannot fail to feel painfully—though the narrator seems quite unconscious of—the irreverence of the travesty. It is noteworthy that some, even of the non-miraculous incidents of the *Life* appear to have been similarly handled. Thus the account of the stoning of Ephraim outside of Edessa seems modelled after that of St. Paul at Lystra, (Acts. xiv. 19, 20) : and the simulated madness by which he evaded the call of the Episcopate is apparently borrowed from the history of David's behavior before Achish and his servants at Gath (1 Sam. xxi. 13-15).

ii. *The Demonstrably Incorrect or Contradictory Statements.*—Farther, even when we have laid aside all that is seemingly exaggerated, invented or mythical in the *Life*, there remains much in it that, when critically examined, proves to need correction or to deserve rejection. We proceed to deal with some questions which arise affecting the historical credibility of its narrative.

1. *Ephraim's Alleged Heathen Parentage.*—The heathen parentage assigned to Ephraim, and consequently the whole narrative of his conversion to Christianity and his consequent troubles, may be without hesitation discredited. They are irreconcilable with his own words[4] (*Adv. Hæreses*, XXVI.), "I was born in the way of truth : though my boyhood understood not the greatness of the benefit, I knew it when trial came." So again more explicitly (if we may trust a *Confession* which is extant only in Greek), "I had been early taught about Christ by my parents ; they who begat me

---

[3] This is related also in the Greek version of the Testament, but is an evident interpolation. It is not in the Syriac.
[4] This has been pointed out by Dr. Payne'Smith (*Dict. of Christian Biography*, Vol. II., p. 137), who cites the passages here adduced, from *Opp. Syr.* II. 499 ; *Opp. Gr.* I. 129.

after the flesh, had trained me in the fear of the Lord. . . . My parents were confessors before the judge : yea, I am the kindred of martyrs."

2. *The First and Third Sieges of Nisibis.*—In the narrative of the siege of Nisibis, and especially of the presence and intercession of St. Jacob the Bishop, there is confusion and grave error. It is certain that in the reign of Constantius (337–361), Nisibis was three times besieged by Sapor.[5] The siege in which St. Jacob was within the city took place in the year 338, and he died the same year. The attempt of Sapor to employ the intercepted waters of the Mygdonius for the destruction of its walls, belongs to a later siege—the third, of the year 350—twelve years after the death of Jacob. These two sieges are expressly recorded in the "*Paschal* (otherwise *Alexandrine Chronicle*)," followed by Theophanes in his *Chronographia* (who also mentions briefly the intervening siege of 346) ; and the account given by the former of these chroniclers (who wrote in the seventh century) rests on the authority of an Epistle written by Valgesh, Bishop of Nisibis in 350, who is eulogized by Ephraim in five of the *Nisibene Hymns* contained in the present volume (XIII.–XVII.). Other contemporary evidence, fuller, and at first hand, to the same effect, is forthcoming from two widely different sources. —As already intimated, the Apostate is here alone with the champion of the Faith.

In his second *Oration*[6] (addressed, probably in the year 358, to Constantius, then Emperor) Julian describes the siege with even more circumstantial detail than our biographer, placing it after the death of Constans, which took place in January 350, and thus confirming the date assigned by the Paschal chronicler and by Theophanes. According to Julian's account, the embankment formed by Sapor, the work of four months,[7] was so constructed as to encompass the whole circuit of Nisibis, so that the river intercepted by it "formed a lake in the middle of which the city stood as an island," with "the battlements of its walls barely appearing above the surrounding waters" ; and on the surface of this encircling lake, he launched armed vessels and floating war-engines. By these the fortifications were ceaselessly battered for several days,—till of a sudden the river (then in flood) burst its barrier, and carried away not only the embankment but a hundred cubits of the city wall. Through the breach thus made, Sapor pushed forward his cavalry to lead the advance upon the city which lay thus seemingly at his mercy. But they proved unable to overcome the difficulties of the intervening ground—torn up and flooded as it was by the torrent, and traversed moreover by an ancient moat—while the Nisibenes in the energy inspired by their deadly peril, showered missiles upon their assailants as they strove to struggle onward. The Persian next sent on his elephants ; but their unwieldly bulk served only to enhance the panic and confusion, and to complete the disaster of his repulse. And when, the next morning, he prepared to renew the assault, he found himself confronted by a new wall, hurriedly raised in the night, to fill the gap in the ramparts, reaching already the height of six feet and manned by fresh and well-armed defenders. Despairing of success against a resistance so obstinate, he raised the siege on which he had in vain expended so much time, labour, treasure, and blood, and retired ignominiously.

It is needless to add that of the miraculous incidents of the siege as related in the *Life*, no trace appears in Julian's account. The only Providence he discerns in the successful defence of Nisibis, is that which he attributes to his imperial kinsman to whom his fulsome oratory is addressed.

---

[5] This was first clearly established by Spanheim (*Observationes in Julianum*, pp. 183 *ff.*, 188 *ff.* ; 1696) in part anticipated by Petave (Petavius) and de Valois (Valesius). He has been followed in this by nearly all historians, including Gibbon (*Decline and Fall*, chap. xviii).

[6] *Juliani Orationes*, ed. Spanheim (1666), *Orat.* II., pp. 62 *ff.* : see also pp. 26 *ff.* (*Orat.* I.).

[7] The *Life* gives but seventy days as the whole duration of the siege—a period quite insufficient for the construction of the embankment.

Of the leading facts, as related by Julian, ample corroboration will be found in the first three of the *Nisibene Hymns* above referred to. In the first, Ephraim makes Nisibis herself tell the tale of her peril : she compares herself to the Ark of the Flood, compassed, not like it by waters merely, but by "mounds and weapons and waves" (I., 3) ; but (*ib.*, 6, 8) the wall had not yet given way, for he still speaks of it as standing, and prays that it may continue to stand. This *Hymn* was therefore written while the siege was still in progress. In the second *Hymn* he celebrates her deliverance and the manner of it,—the very breach of her walls turned into triumph (II. 5, 7) by their reconstruction and the assault of the besiegers with their elephants (*ib.*, 17, 18, 19), repulsed in disgrace, ending in immediate retreat.[8] In the third *Hymn*, he follows on similar lines ; and adds a point, significant in his apprehension, that whereas the wall fell on the Sabbath, it was raised again on the Lord's day, the Day of the Resurrection (III. 6). In all three *Hymns*, it is again and again implied or asserted that this was the third siege of Nisibis (I. 11 ; II. 5, 19 ; III. 11, 12)—and farther (as it seems) the third time that a breach had been effected in her walls (I. 11 ; II. 19). In later *Hymns* also (XI. 14, 15 ; XIII. 17) the embanked river, bursting forth and breaking down the defences of the city, more than once appears. From one of these we learn incidentally that the Mygdonius flowed past, not through, Nisibis (XIII. 18, 19) ;[9] from which fact it follows that the description in the *Life*, of the manner in which the Persian engineers employed the river waters against the walls, is to be set aside in so far as it differs from Julian's account as confirmed by the *Hymns*.

It is remarkable how closely these two accounts, both contemporary with the facts they treat of, agree in all essential points, though coming to us from sources not only independent, but even adverse, *inter se*,—and in forms so little favourable to exactness of statement as thanksgiving Hymns and encomiastic Orations. When from Ephraim's strophes we omit his pious ascriptions of praise to God, and from Julian's periods, the fulsomeness of his panegyric on the Emperor, the residuum of material fact is in either case much the same ; the main outlines of narrative (related or implied) are identical in both writers, each unconsciously attests the truthfulness of the other. Both are farther confirmed in great measure by the account of this siege embodied in the *Pascha Chronicle* above referred to, which (as already stated) rests on information drawn from a written record left by Valgesh who was Bishop of Nisibis at the time, and to whose prayers Ephraim (*Hymn* XIII. 17)[1] attributed the speedy restoration of the breach in the city wall.

In confusing this siege (of 350, in the time of Valgesh), with the previous one (of 338, in the time of Jacob), our biographer, with most subsequent writers down to the eighteenth century, has been misled by following Theodoret's narration in his *Ecclesiastical History* (II. 30).[2] The account of the siege given in the *Life* is in fact a mere

---

[8] Ephraim seems to convey that Sapor, when repulsed, at once withdrew : Julian represents his withdrawal as gradual. The former probably has in view the raising of the siege ; the latter, the retreat from the invaded territory.

[9] Compare Sachau's description, *Reise*, pp. 390, 391.

[1] That Valgesh is the "third" Bishop here meant, appears by comparison with Hymn XVII. 2, where the three are named, Jacob, Babu (not elsewhere mentioned), and Valgesh.

[2] So (*e. g.*) Baronius, *Annales* (*s. q.* 338) ; *Acta Sanctorum*, Febr. (I. p. 51). A few quite recent writers follow these. This error of Theodoret thus ascribing to the first siege the events which belong to the history of the third, is easily accounted for. His narrative of the siege and the breaching of the walls, the apparition, and St. Jacob's prayer answered by the plague of mosquitoes, originally appeared in his earlier work, the *Religious History*—a collection of lives of miracle-working saints of whom St. Jacob stands first—from which (as he himself notes) he has transferred it with little change, to his *Ecclesiastical History*. As the biographer of this, the greatest Bishop of Nisibis, Theodoret would naturally associate with his name all that history or tradition reported of Divine protection extended to the city in her perils—especially in those of her last and most signal siege which ended in her most signal deliverance. He probably knew that a siege of Nisibis had occurred in St. Jacob's time, and would readily overlook the brief interval of twelve years by which the saint's death preceded the later siege.

reproduction, somewhat abridged, and slightly varied, of Theodoret's, from which it derives also its computation of the time occupied by the siege as but twenty days,—a period obviously inadequate for the vast engineering works for which the four months assigned by Julian are certainly not too much,—as well as its description of the method and aim of those works. In Theodoret likewise are found the two supernatural incidents of Sapor's discomfiture, both repeated in the *Life*,—neither of which is affirmed or even hinted at by Ephraim any more than by Julian ; the appearance of the Imperial Phantom on the wall, and the plague of insects sent in answer to Jacob's, or, as the *Life* has it, to Ephraim's prayer. Of these, the former, but not the latter, finds place in the *Paschal Chronicle*, and (in exaggerated form) in Theophanes. Whether, in this instance, the chronicler's statement, which is guardedly expressed,[3] or any nucleus of it, was derived from the *Epistle* of Valgesh,—or whether he borrowed it from Theodoret or some one of Theodoret's sources, or some such authority—is matter of conjecture.[4]

3. *Constantius and Constans.*—The *Life* errs grossly (as already noticed) in making Constans, who died in 350, and never reigned in the East, the successor of his brother Constantius, who survived till 361.

4. *The Alleged Sojourn in Egypt.*—The sojourn of Ephraim for eight years in Egypt, after he had taken up his abode in Egypt, and before his visit to Cappadocia, is impossible. It was in July, 363, that Nisibis was surrendered to Persia by Jovian, which court was the cause, as the *Life* (no doubt rightly) states, of Ephraim's final departure from that city to Beth-Garbaia, thence to Amid, and finally, "at the end of the year," to Edessa. It follows, therefore, that he did not reach Edessa till 364. In Edessa, or in his cell on the adjacent "Mount" according to the *Life*, he lived, worked, wrote commentaries and polemical discourses, taught, and formed a school of disciples, before his alleged journey to Egypt. It is therefore implied that he spent years in or near Edessa before he set out on that journey, which cannot therefore be placed so early as 365. Even if we assign to it the improbably early date of 366, the eight years in Egypt bring us to

One of the *Nisibene Hymns* (XIII. 18, 19, 21) suggests a further explanation how this third siege came to be attached to the legend of St. Jacob. His body was treasured reverently in the city, and to its presence her deliverance was attributed. Thus he was still (in Ephraim's words) "the fountain within her," "the fruit in her bosom," "the body laid within her that became for her a wall without." The traditions of that dead presence in the last siege, and of his living presence in the first, would soon blend together ; and the expressions of pious gratitude for the protection ascribed by the besieged of 350 to the virtue of his remains, would be mistaken as evidence that the man himself was among them to help them by his prayers and exhortations in the struggle by which the fall of their city was so narrowly averted.

[3] In the Chronicle, we read that Sapor saw, in the daytime, "a *man* running to and fro on the walls," in the likeness of the Emperor ; but again, we are told of "the *angel* that appeared." In Theodoret's narratives the apparition wears the royal "purple and diadem," and is described as "divine" (*Hist. Relig.*), and "incorporeal" (*Hist. Eccles.*). In the *Chronography*, "an angel stands on the tower, in shining raiment, holding by the hand the Emperor Constantius" ; a duplication of the vision which seemingly arose from a misunderstanding of the *Chronicle*.

That Constantius was not in Nisibis during this siege, is a point on which all authorities are agreed. Julian, while lavishing on the Emperor unmeasured praises for the repulse of Sapor, attributes it not to his personal presence, but to his foresight in previous preparations made a year before. He is known, however, to have sojourned in the city in May, 345,—see *Cod Theodosianus* (XI. 7, 5) for a law issued thence by him on the 12th of that month (Lex. 5 *de exactionibus*).

[4] The *Nisibene Hymns*, only recovered some fifty years ago from the Nitrian Monastery of the Theotokos, and first printed in 1866, yielding as they do authoritative and contemporary confirmation of the accounts of the siege given by Julian and by Valgesh, come in as decisive evidence to prove that the Chronicler of the seventh century and the Chronographer of the ninth had better fortune or better judgment in their choice of authorities than Theodoret in the fifth. It is, moreover, a signal instance of the true historical instinct that guided Gibbon in his great work, that in relating this history (ch. xviii. ), he followed Julian and the *Chronicle*, and refused to be misled (as our biographer was) by Theodoret—except as regards St. Jacob, whom he supposed to have been still Bishop in 350.

The first to point out this error as to St. Jacob, was Valesius in his note on the passage in Theodoret (*H. E.* II. 30), as above. He remarked that "the *Alexandrine (Paschal) Chronicle* makes Vologeses (Valgesh), not Jacob, Bishop of Nisibis in 350." It was replied (and with justice) that the *Chronicle*, though it records the siege, and cites the *Epistle* of Valgesh, Bishop of the city, does not say that he was Bishop at the time of the siege. Another Chronicle, the Edessene (a relic of the sixth century), first printed by Assemani in 1719 (*Biblioth. Orient.* I., pp. 388 *ff.*) determines 338 as the date of Jacob's death, and 361 as that of Valgesh. Our *Nisibene Hymns* (see above, note [4]) make it plain that Valgesh was bishop in 350, as Valesius rightly (though on insufficient grounds) laid down.

374, or at earliest 373, for his visit to the Cæsarean Cappadocia.   Now there is a prevailing weight of testimony to the effect that Ephraim died in 373, which date, if
accepted, leaves no time for the incidents of his life after his return to Edessa.   This,
however, cannot be urged against our biographer, who (as will be shown) assumes
that he lived till 379.   But the *Life* represents him as resident in or near Edessa during
the persecution which that city suffered from the Emperor Valens, which (as stated
above, p. 132) took place probably in 371 ; certainly not later than 372, at which date
(according to the biographer) he was still in Egypt.   In fact, even without going into particulars, it is evident that between Ephraim's arrival in Edessa in 364 and the persecution
of Valens in 370–2, the eight years' sojourn in Egypt and the visit to Cappadocia would
so fill the interval as to leave no time for the prolonged Edessa residence, before and
after that sojourn, which the *Life*, in common with all other authorities, attributes to
Ephraim, and in virtue of which his name is inseparably associated with the history of
Edessa.

If, with the Vatican recension of the *Life*, we read " Julian " for Valens, as the name
of the persecutor of Edessa, the impossibility becomes yet more absurdly glaring.   For
Julian died in 363, and before that year Ephraim had not migrated from Nisibis to
Edessa.

It is no doubt possible that Ephraim may have visited Egypt,[5] as the *Life* affirms,
before proceeding to Cæsarea : as an anchorite he would naturally be drawn to the
land where the anchorite life had its origin and its greatest development.   Yet it is
hardly probable that, eager as he was to see Basil at Cæsarea, he would, when setting
out on his travels, have directed his course to Egypt first,—a country so distant, and
lying in a direction so different, from Cappadocia.   This improbability would naturally
fail to strike our biographer, who appears to have supposed Basil's Cæsarea (if indeed
he had any definite idea of its situation) to have been the maritime city of that name in
Palestine.   One can hardly avoid suspecting that this whole narrative of the visit to
Egypt—unknown as it is to all authorities save our *Life* (in its twofold recension), and
the shorter form of the same—may have been invented by some compiler or reviser,
writing in, or for, one of the Egyptian monasteries of the Nitrian Desert, and seeking to
gratify the Syrian ascetics who were numerous in that region, by making it the scene of an
episode in the life of the most famous of Syrian ascetics.   It certainly has the air of an
interpolation, coming as it does between the description of Ephraim's longing desire to
see Basil, and the narrative of the fulfilment of that desire by his visit to Cæsarea.
More particularly, as regards the story of the visit of Ephraim to the Nitrian Saint
Pesoës (or Bishoi), it is to be noted that it is mentioned, not in the Parisian recension
of the *Life*, but only in that of the Vatican MS.   It is a significant fact that this MS.,
which is thus our only written authority for the alleged visit, was written (probably)
about the year 1100, in the Nitrian monastery of "Amba Bishoi" (St. Pesoës).[6]   On
the other hand, it is to be added that a tradition of Ephraim's sojourn in Egypt, connecting him with Pesoës, lingered in quite recent times, and may probably still linger,
among the monks, Syrian and Coptic, of the Nitrian region.   Travellers of the seventeenth, and even eighteenth, century, tell of a tamarind tree which was shown to them
within the precincts of the Syrian monastery of the Theotokos in that region, reputed
to have grown from Ephraim's staff which he set in the ground on his arrival there, as

---

[5] The shorter Syriac *Life* agrees in affirming the fact of his visit to Egypt, but says nothing of its duration.   No other authority, earlier or contemporary, hints at it.
[6] Assemani, *Biblioth Orient.*, I., p. 46, note 1.

he was about to enter the cell of Pesoës.[7]   It is probable that this legend of the staff (which reminds one of that of the staff of St. Joseph of Arimathea and the Glastonbury thorn tree) may have grown out of the belief that Ephraim once visited the monastery,—which belief again may have been originated by the pious fiction of the compiler or interpolator of the *Life* in its Vatican form.   It is easy to imagine how gladly a community of Syrian monks in this Egyptian solitude would listen to what professed to be a record of the greatest of Syrian monks, a recluse like themselves, the author of the Sermons to Ascetics which they had read or listened to, and of the many hymns which enriched their offices and quickened their devotions ;—and how ready they would be to welcome as fact the story of his sojourn in their valley, and to imagine that a memorial of it survived among the trees of their garden.

5. *Interval between Visit to Basil and Persecution by Valens.*—The interval of four years or more, which the *Life* seems to place between Ephraim's return from Cæsarea to Edessa, and the persecution of the Edessenes by Valens, is likewise impossible.   For at Cæsarea all agree that Ephraim found Basil Archbishop.   But Basil was consecrated late in 370, and therefore Ephraim's first meeting with him, which was on the Feast of the Epiphany, cannot be placed earlier than January, 371.   But the persecution took place probably in 371, or at latest in 373—thus reducing the possible length of interval to two years at most—probably to a few months.   It may be said, however, that the biographer, though he relates the persecution after mentioning the four years' interval, does not mean to imply that it was subsequent in time to that interval.   But it will be shown farther on (under next head) that the four years' interval is inadmissible, independently of the date of that persecution ; inasmuch as Ephraim survived only three years after his visit to Basil.

6. *Death of Basil before that of Ephraim.*—The story of the lady who was sent by Basil to Ephraim, and by Ephraim back to Basil, only in time to see his corpse,—and of Ephraim's grief for Basil's death, cannot be accepted unless we set aside the consent of the chronologers, who agree that Ephraim died in 373,[8]—whereas Basil survived to 1st January, 379.   It is true that there is extant among the Greek works ascribed to Ephraim, an encomium on Basil,[9] which seems to be genuine.   This, however, is not to be regarded as an eulogium pronounced after Basil's death ; but rather as a panegyric in which the living man is apostrophized.[1]   We may safely conclude that the story, which rests on a basis of erroneous chronology, is itself a fiction.

But the story of Ephraim's helpful intervention and activity in a time of famine, which is undated, having early attestation, may well be accepted as true, and assigned to the winter of 372–3.   The authorities who attest the date of his death as 373, place it in the month of Haziran (June) ;[2] and we may reasonably conjecture that the exer-

---

[7] It is mentioned by Huntington (afterwards Provost of Trinity College, Dublin, and finally Bishop of Raphoe) who visited the place, 1678-9 (see his *Epistolæ*, XXXIX., p. 69) : again by J. S. Assemani in 1715 (see reference in note [6]).   More recent visitors (Lord de la Zouche in 1837, and Archdeacon Tattam in 1839) do not speak of it.

Of the Nitrian monasteries (reputed to have once numbered fifty, or even more), the principal one, that of the Theotokos, whence the libraries of the Vatican and of the British museum have derived their most precious acquisitions of Syriac MSS., belongs to the Syrian Jacobites, whose Church has always been in full communion with that of the Copts.   A second belongs to the Copts ; a third to the Greeks.   The fourth (that of St. Pesoës) does not appear to be specially appropriated, but to be mainly Coptic, though (as appears above) not to the exclusion of Syrians.

[8] See Professor Lamy's edition of Ephraim, II., coll. 94 *ff*, for the authorities on this point,—of which the chief are :—The *Edessene Chronicle* (sixth century) and Jacob of Edessa (seventh century—cited by Elias of Nisibis), both of whom give 373 as the date, as does also the early Chronicle contained in the "*Book of the Caliphs.*"   Jerome (*De Viris. Illustr.* cxv.) merely says that Ephraim died in the reign of Valens,—*i. e.* not later than 378, and therefore before Basil.                              [9] *Opp. Græc.*, II., 289 *ff*.

[1] See Lamy as above, coll. 84 *ff.*

[2] On the 9th, according to *Chron. Edes.* and the shorter *Life ;* the Vatican *Life* says the 15th ; the *Book of the Caliphs* (see Land's *Anecdota*, Tom. I., p. 15 [Syr. text]), and most other authorities, the 18th ; Dionysius, in his *Chronicle*, the 19th (ap. Assemani, *B. O.* II., p. 54).

tions and anxieties of the season of famine had told too heavily on a frame already wasted by years and by excessive austerities, and had thus hastened his end.

### VI.—Rectification of the Vatican Text of the Life.

If the *Life* had reached us in its Vatican form only, it would have been necessary to correct one or two farther errors :

1. *Date of his Baptism Mistaken.*—According to the Vatican *Life*, Ephraim was baptized at the age of 28, after the surrender of Nisibis by Jovian.   The surrender was in 363, and the age assigned to him would therefore make 334 the earliest admissible date for his birth—ten years after the Council of Nicæa, at which the *Life* records that he was present !   The Parisian *Life* corrects this absurdity and shows how the mistake arose.   The statement, in this version of the story, is that after quitting Nisibis, " he retired to Beth-Garbaia, where he *had* received baptism at the age of 18."   By omitting the auxiliary "had" (which in Syriac, as in English, expresses the pluperfect) the Vatican scribe or editor introduces this blunder about the date of the baptism.   It is probable that, without having any distinct knowledge of the date of the departure from Nisibis, he felt that Ephraim must have been more than 18 at this stage of the narrative, and strove to make the age cohere better with the time required for the events related, by changing 18 into 28.

2. *Julian substituted for Valens.*—The substitution of the name of Julian for that of Valens as the persecutor of Edessa, has been already noticed.   That the story (with the incident of the martyr-mother with her two sons) belongs to the time of Valens, is established by the united testimony of Socrates, Sozomen, and Theodoret.   The whole history is clear, and coherent with itself and with chronology, in the Parisian *Life* ; whereas the Vatican version of it, by bringing Ephraim to Edessa in the reign of Julian, makes hopeless confusion.[3]   It is to be noted that the names *Julianus* and *Valens*, so distinct as written in Latin, differ but little when transliterated (without vowel-points) into Syriac.

### VII.—Chronology of the Life of Ephraim.

Thus the fixed points for determining the chronology of Ephraim's life are :

1. The death of his patron, St. Jacob, Bishop of Nisibis, in 338, after the first siege of that city.

2. The third siege, in which he was among the defenders of the city, in 350.

3. The surrender of Nisibis by Jovian, and its abandonment by its Christian inhabitants, 363 ; followed by Ephraim's removal to Edessa.

4. The consecration of Basil to the see of Cæsarea, late in 370, followed by Ephraim's visit to him there.

5. The deliverance of the Edessenes from the persecution of Valens (370–372), celebrated by Ephraim in a hymn.

6. Ephraim's death, 373.

To this list it would be right to prefix the meeting of the Council of Nicæa in 325, if the evidence of Ephraim's presence at it, along with St. Jacob, were sufficient.   But it has no early attestation ; and no writer prior to Theodoret (*Hist. Eccles.* II. 30) associates the name of Jacob with any incident in Ephraim's life.

---

[3] It is to be regretted that neither the Parisian *Life*, nor the *Nisibene* Hymns, was before the writer of the article EPHRAIM in Smith and Wace's *Dictionary of Christian Biography.*   The former would have warned him from being misled by the Vatican *Life* into the error of ascribing to Julian the persecution under Valens ; the latter would have shown him that both versions of the *Life* confuse the first siege of Nisibis with the third.

The date of Ephraim's birth is nowhere directly stated, but it is usually assumed to have been early in the reign of Constantine (306–337), on the authority of the Vatican *Life*, which says, "In the days of the victorious Constantine, true believer, *was born* the holy man Ephraim." But the statement of the Parisian *Life* is less explicit, and is capable of a different meaning :—"*He was* in the days of the victorious Constantine." This merely implies that Ephraim (if the pronoun represent him) lived in the reign of that emperor. But it rather appears that Ephraim's father is meant, inasmuch as he is the subject of the immediately preceding sentence which describes him as a heathen priest ; and the purport of the passage is, that the saint was the son of a man who not merely had been one of an idolatrous priesthood, but continued to be so after Constantine had acknowledged the Christian religion.[4]

The earlier authorities give no express statement on this point ; but a late tenth-century Greek *menologium*, that of the Emperor Basil (Porphyrogenitus), says that he "continued from the reign of Constantine to that of Valens,"[5]—implying as it seems that he was born, as the Vatican *Life* represents, after Constantine's accession in 306.

Considering, however, that the *Life* in both its forms affirms that Ephraim was brought by St. Jacob to the Council of Nicæa in 325—in which it is borne out by Gregory Barhebræus in his *Ecclesiastical Chronicle*[6] (who though a very late writer (1226–1286) had access to early authorities and judgment in using them)—it is hard to reconcile the chronology, for the improbability of the admission of a lad of nineteen, in any capacity, to that venerable assembly, is very great. If we accept it as a fact that he was chosen by Jacob to accompany him, and was permitted to be present among the Fathers at Nicæa, it seems almost necessary to place his birth before Constantine became emperor.[7]

Farther : the *menologium* above cited adds that he died "in *extreme* old age ;" and the tone and tenor of his *testament* go far to confirm the truth of these words. But as he died in 373, he cannot have been more than 67 years old in that year if he was born in 306. No doubt 67 is a ripe age, but hardly sufficient to warrant the strong expression of the *menologium*. Without pressing its language unduly, we may surely take it as implying that he had passed the "threescore years and ten" of the Psalmist at the time of his death—in other words that he was born not later than the first or second year of the fourth century.

Thus by rectifying the text and rendering of the opening sentences of the *Life*, we relieve ourselves of the supposed necessity of placing his birth in or after 306. And his presence in the Council of 325, and his extreme old age in 373, concur in pointing to the beginning of the fourth century—if not to the later years of the third—as the probable time of that event.

However this may be, whether he was born in 306 or earlier, it is certain that by far the greater part of the long life of the "Deacon of Edessa"—all of it save its last

---

[4] The passage is as follows : "Ephraim was a Syrian by birth. His father was of Nisibis, and his mother of Amid. And his father was priest in Nisibis of an idol named Abizal, which afterwards the victorious Emperor Jovian broke. He [or it, *scil.*, the idol] was in the days of the victorious Emperor Constantine, true believer. But his father had this famous son, of whom is our narrative." The meaning may be that the idol was suffered to exist during Constantine's reign and after, till Jovian destroyed it : but it is now natural to understand it, as above, of Ephraim's father. The Vatican editor seems to have misunderstood his original, which the Parisian transcriber has preserved faithfully,—and to have altered it into accordance with his misunderstanding, by recasting the passage and substituting "*was born*" for "*was*."

[5] In Migre's *Patrologia Græca*, CXVII., p. 254.

[6] I., 23 (Abbeloos and Lamy's edition).

[7] Gregory Barhebr. (*Chron. Eccles.*, II., 10) mentions, but doubtfully, a tradition that Ephraim wrote a letter circ. 334 in which he took the part of Papas, the Catholicus, against "the Bishops of the East" who accused him of neglect and misconduct. If this be accepted, it is additional evidence for the early date of Ephraim's birth.

ten or eleven years (363–373) was passed in his native Nisibis ; and that he did not even attain the diaconate till he was considerably over sixty years of age, and within three years of his end.

### VIII.—His Writings : Their Characteristics.

Of the innumerable writings—controversial, expository, hortatory, devotional—which were for Ephraim the fulfilment of his dream in childhood, the fruit of the many years of literary activity that exercised his full heart and busy brain, enough remains to give an adequate idea of his powers and to amaze us by its variety and abundance.   The exaggeration of Sozomen who reckons the number of lines written by him at "three hundred myriads" (three millions) is not to be taken as more than a rough guess at the probable total ; but it is evidence of the impression made on the men of the generations to whom his works were transmitted by his fertility.   That he himself was conscious of this gift appears in the fact that he records the dream and claims for his hymns and sermons that in them is to be found its interpretation.   His faculty of speech, as Gregory informs us in a remarkable passage, though adequate to utter the thoughts of any other mind, was sometimes overborne by the rapid rush and abounding throng of the ideas with which his inspiration filled him, in such measure that he was forced to pray for the intermission of its flow, " Restrain, O Lord, the tide of Thy grace ! " [8]   Copiousness is the characteristic, and its excess is the chief fault, of Ephraim as an author.   The Syriac language has great capacity for condensation ; and the parallelism of balanced clauses which Syriac literature affects, conduces to brevity.   But on the other hand, the Syrian mind has a tendency to amplify ; amplification is the besetting sin of Syriac writers,—of Ephraim not least.   And thus, while each sentence has the severe precision of an epigram, the manifold reiteration of epigrammatic clauses amounts to verbosity : one and the same thought or fact is presented in a long-drawn series of slightly varied aspects, with change of expression or at most of illustration, till the recurrence becomes tedious.   This criticism is meant primarily for his hymns ; but it applies also to too many of his metrical homilies (to be described presently).   In all his writings, metrical or otherwise, this habit of amplification leads him, in handling the narrations of Scripture, to fill out their simple outline with elaborate detail that wrongs their beauty and dignity.   Of such treatment, examples will be found in this volume, in some of the hymns (such as the XIVth and XVth *On the Epiphany*, and in the *Discourse on the Woman who was a Sinner*.

His extant works (some of which are known to us only in a Greek version), and those of his lost works of which the titles are recorded, divide themselves into three classes ; —*Commentaries on Scripture*, Homilies (*mimrē*), and *Hymns* (*madrashē*).

1. *Commentaries.*—His *Commentaries* belonged (if we may trust the *Life*) to his later years, after his migration to Edessa, when he was past middle life.   There he is related to have begun his exposition (still extant) of Genesis, in the preface to which he refers to the homilies and hymns which he had previously produced (*Opp. Syr.* Tom. I., p. 1). He seems to have commented on almost all the canonical books of the Old Testament. His expositions of the Pentateuch, the chief historical books,[9] the Prophets (including Lamentations), and Job, survive, and have been printed (in the Roman edition of 1732–43,

---

[8] This passage is mistranslated in the Latin version of the *Encomium*, by P. F. Linus of Verona (in his *Divina S. Ephraem Opera*, Dillingen, 1562), from whom it has been borrowed by Gerard Voss for his Latin version of Ephraim (Cologne, 1603), and by the editors of Gregory's Works.
[9] Not including Ruth, Ezra, Nehemiah, Esther.   It is not known whether he commented on Ecclesiastes and Canticles, or on the deutero-canonical books (commonly called " Apocrypha ").

supplemented by that of Professor Lamy, of Louvain, Tom. II., 1886) ;[1] but those which he is recorded to have written on the Psalms and Proverbs, the books which may be presumed to have most influenced the religious spirit and literary form of his works, have not been preserved. None of the above, however, have reached us in a complete form, but rather as a series of extracts, apparently abridged, from the *Commentaries* as originally issued by their author. In commenting on the New Testament, he treated of the Gospels, not in their separate form, but in the continuous narrative known as the " Diatessaron " compiled from them by Tatian in the second century. This work, long lost, has been lately recovered in an Armenian version. His *Commentary on the Epistles of St. Paul* has likewise been preserved for us in Armenian. Both have been published by the Mechetarist Fathers of St. Lazaro ; first in Armenian, afterwards in a Latin version.[2] In the present volume it has been judged best to include none of the *Commentaries*, inasmuch as the method and spirit of Ephraim's treatment of Scripture are shown adequately, and in a more interesting form, in his *Homilies* and *Hymns*.

2. *Homilies.*—The *Homilies* are very varied in character. Many are controversial,— directed against the Jews, against heathenism in the person of the Emperor Julian, against the heresies of Manes, of Marcion, of Bardesan, of the Anomœan followers of Arius. Others set forth articles of the Faith—the Creation, the Fall, Redemption by the Passion and Crucifixion of Our Lord, His Descent into Hades, His Resurrection, the Mission of the Holy Spirit, the Rest of Paradise, the Second Coming, the End of the World. Others are expository, treating of narratives from the Old and the New Testaments, such as the life of Joseph, the Repentance of Nineveh, or the story of "the woman who was a sinner" of St. Luke vii.—Others again are hortatory—calling to repentance, warning against sin, threatening future retribution, extolling virginity. Of the *Homilies* two—one doctrinal, *of Our Lord* ; one expository, *of the sinful woman*, are given in this selection. It is to be noted that the *Homilies* are usually metrical in form, being written in regular *stichoi* (lines of uniform length). And some of them—for example, a series of nine for the "Rogation Days,"[3] and another of eight for the "Passion Week" (week before Easter), and the vigil of "New Sunday" (first after Easter)—were and still are regularly read as lessons, as part of the offices of the Church ;[4] a singular mark of reverence—extended, it seems, to the sermons of no other divine.

3. *Hymns.*—But it is in his *Hymns* that Ephraim lives,—for the Syrian Churches, and indirectly for the Christian world, of the East if not of the West.[5] Throughout Syrian Christendom, divided as it has been for ages—in the Malkite, Nestorian, Jacobite, and Maronite communities, from the Mediterranean to the Tigris, and beyond, even to the Malabar remnant of the Syro-Indian Church, all of which retain Syriac as the language of their ritual,—the whole body of public worship is shaped by his hymnody and animated with his spirit. It is literally the fact that the Hymns of Ephraim go with every member of every one of these Churches from the first to the last of his Christian

---

[1] Lamy has supplied the Commentaries on Jonah, Nahum, Habakkuk, Zephaniah, and Haggai, with part of Isaiah and Lamentation—which was wanting from the Roman edition.

[2] Both in the Armenian edition of Ephraim (Vol. II., *Diatessaron* ; Vol. III., St. Paul), Venice, 1836 : also in Latin,—the *Diatessaron*, in 1876 ; *St. Paul.* 1893.

[3] Of these the most complete copy is in MS. B. 5.18, Trinity College, Dublin (formerly the property of Archbishop Ussher), which has been used by Professor Lamy in his edition of three homilies (Tom. III. of his *Ephraim*, 1889).

[4] This remarkable distinction dates from the fourth century ; it is noticed by St. Jerome (*De Viris Ill.*, CXV.), writing within twenty years after Ephraim's death.

[5] St. Hilary of Poitiers (*d.* 368) is reputed (see Isidore of Seville, *De Off. Eccl.*) the earliest writer of Latin Hymns, and some extant Hymns are ascribed to him. But St. Augustine tells us (*Confess.* IX. 7) that at Milan hymns were first used, "*after the manner of the Eastern Church*," in the time when the Empress Justina was persecuting St. Ambrose (386).

life, from the font to the grave.   The *Epiphany Hymns* (included in the present selection) are interwoven into the Baptismal Office ; among the *Funeral Hymns* (which Dr.
Burgess has made accessible to English readers) [6] are to be found dirges proper for the
obsequies of each and all, lay and cleric, young and old, male and female.   Nor is it
to be doubted that it was from these Syriac offices that those of the Greek-speaking
Churches derived this characteristic, common to both, by which both are differentiated
from those of the West,—"hymns occupying in the Eastern Church" (as Dr. Neale
observes) [7] "a space beyond all comparison greater than they do in the Latin," so that
" the body of the Eastern breviary is ecclesiastical poetry."   That the Syrian Church,
and not the Greek, took the initiative in the development of ritual, appears from the facts
that, though there is evidence of the use of Psalms and Canticles from Scripture throughout Christendom from the first, it is only with Ephraim's contemporary, Gregory
Nazianzen, that Greek sacred poetry can be said to have taken shape,—and that his
verses failed to gain a place in public worship.   He wrote in the metres of the heathen
classics ; and it was not until a later day, and from the hands of other writers, working
on other lines, that the hymns appeared which won their way into the Greek ritual,—
hymns written in rhythmic prose, in what seems to be conscious imitation of the
Syriac model. [8]

The imitation, however, is by no means complete ; it is apparent in the general tone
and manner, but does not extend to the form : just as the Greek version of Ephraim's
Hymns, though faithfully reproducing his thoughts and literary method, makes no
attempt to retain his metrical system ; but is a rendering into what in form is prose of
an original which is in verse.   That this should be so is unavoidable, for Syriac metres
are incapable of adaptation to the Greek language.   Syriac literature, in all else imitative, here and here only has found out for itself an independent course.   Elsewhere it
leans on one side to the Hebrew model to which it was drawn by affinity of language
and by the influence of the Old Testament ; on the other to the Greek, as found in the
New Testament and in the writings of the great Divines of the Alexandrian and
Antiochian patriarchates, who were the leaders of religious thought for Eastern Christendom.   In hymnody alone it struck out a line of its own ; it set an example for the
Greek-speaking Churches to follow, so far as was possible for them under the conditions
above indicated.   The Syriac Hymnody is constructed on the Hebrew principle of
parallelism, in which thought answers to thought in clauses of repetitive or antithetical
balance : but, unlike the Hebrew, its clauses are further regulated by strict equivalence
of syllabic measure.   But though in this latter respect it seems to approach to the forms
of Western verse, ancient or modern, yet the resemblance is but superficial : Syriac
verse is not measured by feet—whether determined by syllabic quantity, as in Greek
and Latin, or by accent, as in English and other modern languages.   Thus the metre
of Syriac poetry is substantially the "thought-metre" (as it has been well called) of
Hebrew, reduced to regularity of form by the rule that each of the lines into which the
balanced clauses fall, shall consist of a fixed number of syllables.   There is no sys-
tematic rhyme ; but the nature of the language which by reason of its uniformity of
etymological structure abounds in words of like terminations, often causes correspond-

---

[6] *Metrical Hymns of Ephraim*, 1853.
[7] *Hymns of the Holy Eastern Church*, pp. 34, 35, 49 (1870).   Note the contrast between the wide acceptance
of Ephraim's Hymns, through the East, and the scanty survival of those of his contemporary, in the West.
[8] A few exceptional Greek hymns may be pointed out of earlier date (*e.g.*, that mentioned by St. Basil, *De
Spiritu S.*, XXIX ; but the statement above made is in the main accurate.   Anatolius, Patriarch of Constantinople (440–458) seems to have been the first to devote himself to the composition of hymns of the type above
described.   See Neale (as above).

ences of sound amounting to rhyme, or at least to assonance. The lines are very short; not exceeding twelve syllables, sometimes confined to four. Ephraim, though not the actual inventor, was the first master of this metrical system, the first to develop it into system and variety.[9] His favorite metres are the five-syllabled and the seven-syllabled. In his more elaborate poems, such as the Nisibene series, which are rather Odes than Hymns, the strophes or stanzas into which the lines are arranged are often long and of complicated structure, each strophe consisting of many lines (ranging from four up to fourteen or more) of various lengths according to a fixed scheme rigidly adhered to throughout the poem—sometimes throughout a group of cognate poems. In other poems, especially in Hymns intended for popular or ecclesiastical use, where simplicity of structure is suitable, the lines which compose each strophe, whatever their number, are of uniform length. So easily do the Syriac tongue, and the genius of Syriac litera- ture, lend themselves to this scheme of short, syllabically equal clauses, that (as has been already stated) many even of the Homilies are metrical ; arranged not indeed in strophes, but in continuous succession of brief *stichoi*, all of one and the same length— usually of seven syllables ; a sort of blank verse, but a blank verse with no animating accents, no varying pauses. A Homily so constructed would fatigue the ear of a modern audiencè by its monotony : but inasmuch as some portions of Ephraim's Homilies were used in certain ecclesiastical Offices, probably recited in a sort of chant, it may be that in such use we have the explanation of their quasi-versified structure.

In point of literary value as poems, a high place cannot be claimed for these Hymns. Some of them indeed have much of the devotional fervor, and not a little of the human pathos, of the Psalms of David : others show something of the antithetic point and epigrammatic terseness of the Proverbs of Solomon. Yet the devout aspirations and confessions of the poet are too often forced and artificial in their utterance ; in his fu- neral dirges we seem here and there to detect the false note of the professional mourner in the effort to exhaust all possible topics of grief ; in all his poems he tends to prolong the series of his parallelisms to a wearisome length and with an iteration that, though labo- riously varied, is tedious,—an iteration that has no precedent in the poetry of the Old Testament, save in one or two of the latest Psalms, such as the CXXXVIith with its recurring burden " For His mercy endureth for ever," or the CXIXth with its artificial arrangement (often emulated in Syriac Hymnody) by which each of the twenty-two letters of the alphabet in turn is made to head each one of eight consecutive verses in praise of the Law of the Lord. On the whole, it must be admitted that the greater qualities of poetry, such as abound everywhere in nearly every writer of the Hebrew Scriptures,—of truth in rendering the inmost feelings of man's heart in words of abso- lute simplicity, of aspiration that rises without effort to the highest things of God—to these Ephraim's Hymns have no claim.

For these shortcomings in his poetry, two main causes may be assigned.

One is in the man himself,—or rather, in his mode of life. Naturally, he was prone to feel for and with his fellow-men ; for the sorrows of the bereaved, the cares of the toiling poor whose lot (as he proved in the last and best episode of his history) moved him to sympathy and active succour. He can be simple accordingly when he deals with the homely facts of life. But the main tenor of his course was ascetic ; he looked on this life and the life beyond—on man and to God—with a vision clouded by the gloom

---

[9] Probably the earliest extant Syriac poem is the *Hymn of the Soul* (printed by Dr. Wright in *Apocryphal Acts*, p. 174 ; also by Mr. Bevan in *Texts and Studies*, V. 3). Its metre, though less regular, is substantially the seven-syllabled of Ephraim. Whether Bardesan (or Harmonius) wrote in metres like those of Ephraim has been questioned ; but if it is true that Ephraim's hymns were adapted by him to the tunes of Harmonius, it seems to follow that his metres were those of the hymns to which those tunes belonged.

of unnatural solitude and self-mortification. An assiduous student of Scripture, he had an ear for its threatenings rather than its promises and consolations ; dread and dismay entered into his heart more deeply than hope ; the "Stand in awe and sin not" of the Psalmist was more familiar to his spirit than the "Rejoice in the Lord, ye righteous." The perpetual proneness to tears on which his biographers dwell with admiration, and which he seems to have thought it right to foster, has its reflex in his writings, in the hysterical overflow of his fears, his lamentations and his self-reproach. He had lived as an anchorite till his nature became morbid, and its moral fibre was weakened. But to reach the highest levels in religious literature, whether in prose or in poetry, a man must be sane, his mind healthy and strong,—with a health and strength sustained and exercised by wholesome daily contact with the lives of other men.

The second cause is to be found in the method, above described as his—developed though not actually invented by him, and made his own—which he chose as the vehicle of his thoughts and emotions. The "thought-metre" of the Hebrew poets was regulated (as we have seen) by balance of sense, not of sound—member answering to member, verse by verse, in equivalence or contrast of substance merely, not of verbal form : and in this metre, which has been happily likened to the alternating beat of a bird's wings as it mounts aloft, they had shown it to be possible to attain the highest reach of sublime expression of the utmost that man's spirit can conceive of God and Heaven. The Syriac Hymnists had the unhappy idea of effecting a compromise between their two contrasted models, the Hebrew and the Greek ; and to this end they compelled their verses into conformity by syllabic measure, of sound, as well as of sense. This artificial structure has an effectiveness of its own, and is suited to the popular ear ; but it is incapable of the elevation which the earlier and simpler method attained without effort. As its Semitic parallelism of substance excluded Syriac poetry from the variety in topic and largeness in conception of the Greek, so this grecized regularity of form hampered its efforts to rise to the upper regions where the Hebrew is at home. The wings are free and ample by whose regulated stroke Hebrew poetry is borne, and they carry it to the supreme height : in Syriac poetry the flight is too commonly low and feeble, because its wings are clipped. In the former we are conscious of a uniformity as of the unconstrained waves of the sea, following in a succession of endless change—a uniformity that is majestic : in the latter we detect the uniformity of the water-wheel, that with artificial movement draws up and dispenses the waters of the well in vessels of fixed measure—a uniformity that is mechanical and monotonous.

### IX.—The Selections Included in the Present Collection.

The specimens of Ephraim's compositions offered in these selections are :—

(1) The *Nisibene Hymns*, (2) The *Hymns of the Nativity*, (3) The *Hymns for the Epiphany*, (4) Three *Homilies* (i., *On our Lord;* ii., *On Reproof and Repentance ;* iii., *On the Sinful Woman*).

Of (2) the *Nativity* Hymns, the first thirteen are reprinted from the version by the Rev. J. B. Morris (Oxford, 1847), made from the Roman Edition of the Syriac *Works of Ephraim*. The rest of the series as translated (six [1] in number, making nineteen in all) were unknown when that edition was completed in 1743. These latter, and also (3) the *Epiphany* Hymns (with one exception) [2] have since come to light in the Nitrian collection of the British Museum, and were printed by Professor Lamy in his *St. Ephraim*

---

[1] From the Nitrian MS., 14506.
[2] Hymns 1-14 from MSS., 14506, 14572 ; No. 15 from the Maronite *Breviary*.

(Tom. I., cc. 1–144 ; Tom. II., cc. 427–504), 1882–1889. In the same edition (Tom. I., cc. 145–274 ; 311–338) were first printed (4) the three Homilies.[3] Our translations of these follow Lamy's text, with here and there a slight variation where errors seem to exist. These two series of Hymns belong to the ecclesiastical class : their titles appropriate them to two great Festivals of the Church, and portions of these are embodied in Syriac Rituals still in use. Of the two Homilies, the former was written for the Feast of the Epiphany, like the Hymns which precede it.

The *Nisibene Hymns* (1) are translated from the text as first printed by Dr. Bickell (1866), whose edition, like that of Dr. Lamy, rests upon MSS. of the Nitrian collection.[4] They also were unknown to the Roman editors of the last century, and to the English translator of 1847 ; and they have not till now appeared in English. The series when complete consisted of 77 Hymns. Of these the first division (I.–XXXIV.) treat of the fortunes of the Church in Nisibis, Carrhena [Haran], and an unnamed city (probably Edessa).[5] The remainder (XXXV. to end) deal with the topics of Death and the Resurrection. The present selection comprises 46 of these, namely :—of the *first* division, the first 21, those which relate to Nisibis and which are the *Nisibene Hymns* proper ; of the *second* division, two series—one of 8 hymns (XXXV.–XLII.) in which Death and Satan hold monologue or dialogue,—the other of 17 (LII.–LXVIII.), similar in character, but with Man as a third interlocutor.

### X.—Probable Dates of His Works.

Of the compositions contained in this volume, none yields internal evidence of its date, except the Nisibene Hymns of the first division. Hymns XXXV.–XLII. (not included here), apparently belong to the later (or Edessene) period of Ephraim's life, and to the reign of Valens,—*i.e.*, they are later than the year 363. The 21 Hymns which stand first in our collection may confidently be assigned to the year of the third siege (350) and the thirteen following years. Hymn I. was indubitably composed while the siege was still urgent ; Hymns I. and III. immediately after the deliverance ; Hymns IV.–XII. deal with the fortunes of the city and country in a troubled time of invasion that succeeded ; the rest (XIII.–XXI.) treat of the four successive Bishops of Nisibis under whom Ephraim lived—Jacob, Babu, Valgesh, and Abraham. The last-named is not elsewhere recorded except by Elias of Nisibis, but the death of Valgesh is known to have occurred in 361.[4] The Hymns therefore which celebrate the accession of Abraham to the See (XVII.–XXI.) must be placed in the interval, 361–363, the latter being the year when Ephraim with all the Christian population of the city was driven out by Sapor. Hymns XIII.–XVI., being written while Valgesh was Bishop—for they compare him with his two predecessors—fall into the interval between the year of the siege (350), which they speak of as past,—and the year of the death of Valgesh (361). Bickell assigns IV.–XII. to the months of Sapor's invasion in 359 ; XIII.–XVI. to 358 and 359 ; XVII.–XXI. to 363, in the short space between Julian's death and the surrender of Nisibis.

It is probable that most of his Hymns that are definitely controversial belong, like most of his controversial writings, to the years of his later life, at Edessa. And as we have seen, the earliest of them that can be confidently dated, is not earlier than 350. But it would be hasty to conclude that he had composed no Hymns before that date,

---

[3] From MSS. 14570, 14651, 17266 ; and a fragment from 14654 (printed in Tom. II., pp. xx–xxiii.).
[4] MSS. 14572, 17141 chiefly ; with a few others of secondary value. Five Hymns are lost (viii. and xxii.–xxv.), and part of two others (ix. and xxvi.).
[5] Note the mention of Edessa in Hymn xlii. 1.
[6] *Chron. Edess.*, as above ; *Chronol. of Elias Nisib.*

and that in the Nisibene Hymns of the siege we have the first fruits of the vine of his vision. In 350 he must have been over forty—perhaps over fifty years of age ; and it is highly improbable that a fertility which proved to be so abundant, did not begin to manifest itself at a much earlier age ; or that a literary offspring of such bulk and importance was all produced in the last five and twenty years of a long life. The earlier authorities concerning his life give no definite information on this head ; and the Syriac *Life* is vague in its statements and untrustworthy in its chronology. The account given of Barhebræus, a well-informed but very late writer (thirteenth century), can hardly be accepted as embodying any genuine tradition, but has probability in its favor :—"From the time of the Nicene Council (he writes [1]), Ephraim began to write canticles and hymns against the heresies of his time,"—for few of his hymns are without a polemic spirit, though (as has been said) those that are purely controversial seem to be of a later period. A much later author indeed, Georgius "Bishop of the Arabians" (writing in 714) warns us that there is no evidence to assign any of Ephraim's writings to the twenty years' interval between the Nicene Council and the year 345—"especially (he adds) to the years before 337." [2] This writer, however, is here arguing in support of the claim of Aphrahat to be an independent author, against those who regarded him as a disciple of Ephraim ; and he rests his case on the ground that whereas the *Demonstrations* of Aphrahat are (as we shall see presently) dated from 337 to 345, no composition of Ephraim's can be shown to have been written so early. And it must be admitted that the earliest date (as above noted) that can be fixed with certainty for any of Ephraim's innumerable productions in 350,—thirteen years later than Aphrahat's earlier *Demonstrations*. Against this is to be set the tradition of Ephraim's presence at Nicæa, implying as it does that even in 325 he had made himself a notable person,— and the probability that one who has left such ample proof of the copiousness of his literary gift, must have begun to exercise it before a date at which he would have passed his thirtieth year (supposing his birth to have been in 306), or even have entered middle life (if we place it at the beginning of the century). The two writers were unquestionably contemporary, and as yet no sufficient data have been discovered to determine to which of them seniority belongs.

# SECOND PART.

## APHRAHAT THE PERSIAN SAGE.

1. *Name of Author of Demonstrations long Unknown.*—The author of the *Demonstrations*, eight of which appear (for the first time in an English version) in the present volume, has a singular literary history. By nationality a Persian, in an age when Zoroastrianism was the religion of Persia, he wrote in Syriac as a Christian theologian. His writings, now known to us as the works of Aphrahat, were remembered, cited, translated, and transcribed for at least two centuries after his death ; but his proper name seems to have been for a time forgotten, so that in the MSS. of the fifth and sixth centuries the *Demonstrations* are described as composed by "the Persian Sage," or "Mar Jacob the Persian Sage ; " and a writer of the eighth century, who had made a minute study of these writings and ascertained their date, admits that he has been unable to find out "who or what he was, his rank in the Church, his name or abode." Not only so, but the name Jacob assigned (rightly or wrongly) to him has led to a

---

[1] *Ap.* Assemani, *B. O.* I. 116.
[2] *Ap.* Forget, *De Vita Aphraatis, Introductio*, p. 22 ; see also pp. 121-126 of Forget's *Dissertation* which follows ; also p. 5 of *Introd.*

confusion of identity.  His works have been ascribed for many hundred years—from a date not long after their composition down to quite recent times, to an earlier Jacob, the famous and saintly Bishop of Nisibis in the days of Constantine the Great.  It is not until the tenth century that the true name of "the Persian Sage" emerges to light as Aphrahat, by which he is unhesitatingly designated by several well informed and accurate authorities of that and the three succeeding centuries. and under which he is known to modern scholars.

2.  *Their Subjects, and Arrangement.*—The *Demonstrations* are twenty-two in number, after the number of the letters of the Syriac alphabet, each of them beginning with the letter to which it corresponds in order.  The first ten form a group by themselves, and are somewhat earlier in date than those which follow : they deal with Christian graces, hopes, and duties, as appears from their titles :—"*Concerning Faith, Charity, Fasting, Prayer, Wars, Monks, Penitents, the Resurrection, Humility, Pastors.*"  Of those that compose the later group, three relate to the Jews ("*Concerning Circumcision, the Passover, the Sabbath*") ; followed by one described as "*Hortatory,*" which seems to be a letter of rebuke addressed by Aphrahat, on behalf of a Synod of Bishops, to the clergy and people of Seleucia and Ctesiphon ; after which the Jewish series is resumed in five discourses, "*Concerning Divers Meats, The Call of the Gentiles, Jesus the Messiah, Virginity, the Dispersion of Israel.*"  The three last are of the same general character as the first ten,—"*Concerning Almsgiving, Persecution, Death, and the Latter Times.*"  To this collection is subjoined a twenty-third *Demonstration,* supplementary to the rest, "*Concerning the Grape,*" under which title is signified the blessing transmitted from the beginning through Christ, in allusion to the words of Isaiah, "As the grape [3] is found in the cluster and one saith, Destroy it not" (lxv. 8).  This treatise embodies a chronological disquisition of some importance.

3.  *Dates of Composition.*—Of the dates at which they were written, these discourses supply conclusive evidence.  At the end of section 5 of *Demonstr.* V. (*Concerning Wars*), the author reckons the years from the era of Alexander (B.C. 311) to the time of his writing as 648.  He wrote therefore in A.D. 337—the year of the death of Constantine the Great.  *Demonst.* XIV. is formally dated in its last section, "in the month Shebat, in the year 655 (that is, A. D. 344).  More fully, in closing the alphabetic series (XXII. 25) he informs us that the above dates apply to the two groups—the first ten being written in 337 ; the twelve that follow, in 344.  Finally, the supplementary discourse "Concerning the Grape" was written (as stated, XXIII. 69) in July, 345.  Thus the entire work was completed within nine years,—five years before the middle of the fourth century,—before the composition of the earliest work of Ephraim of which the date can be determined with certainty.

4.  *Extent and Limits of their Circulation.*—These *Demonstrations,* though they fell far short of attaining the unbounded popularity which was the lot of the countless Hymns and Homilies of Ephraim, appear to have won for themselves a recognized place in Syriac literature.  It is true that, in striking contrast with the overwhelming numbers of MSS. containing portions, great or small, of Ephraim's works, which are to be met with in nearly every collection of Syriac written remains, one complete and two incomplete copies are all that have reached us of this series of twenty-three treatises ; and extracts or quotations from them very rarely occur. [4]  Yet it is clear that com-

---

[3] So in Peshitto ; "*unripe grape,*" in LXX. ; "*new wine,*" in A.V. and R.V., with the Hebrew ; but the Latin Vulgate agrees with Peshitto.
[4] In Rosen-Forshall's and Wright's *Catalogues of Syriac MSS., British Museum,* while but few MSS. (Add. 14619, Add. 17182, Orient. 1017. Rich. 7197) contain any portion of Aphrahat, the list of MSS. of Ephraim's works and fragments nearly fills three columns.

positions which were thought worthy at an early date of translation into at least one foreign tongue, must have had some considerable reputation in the country of their origin ; and it may be presumed that these two or three MSS. (of the fifth and sixth centuries), are the survivors of a fairly large number of which the majority have perished.

The Armenian translation is probably the earliest evidence now extant of the circulation (though under a wrong ascription of authorship) of the *Demonstrations*, of which it comprises nineteen. Armenian scholars seem to agree in the belief that it was made in the fifth century, before its original was more than a hundred years in being. An Ethiopic translation of the discourse " On Wars " is extant, but there is no evidence that it formed part of a version extending to all or any of the remaining twenty-two, nor is its date even approximately determinable.

The manuscript evidence hardly reaches so far back as that of the Armenian version. The oldest extant MS. of these discourses (Add. 17182 of the British Museum) contains the first ten, and is dated 474. With it is bound up (under the same number) a second, dated 512, containing the remaining thirteen. A third (Add. 14619) of the sixth century likewise, exhibits the whole series. A fourth (Orient, 1017), more recent by eight centuries, will be mentioned farther on. Of the three early MSS., the first designates the author as " the Persian Sage " merely, as does also the third : the second prefixes his name as " Mar Jacob the Persian Sage."

Among Syriac authors, the first to show an acquaintance with these treatises, at a date prior to that of the earliest of these MSS., is Isaac of Antioch, known as " the Great," whose literary activity belongs to the first half of the fifth century. In his works passages have been pointed out [5] which are evidently borrowed with slight change from the *Demonstrations*,—especially from that *Concerning Fasting*, and (though less distinctly) from that *Concerning Faith*. The imitation, however, is tacit, and Isaac nowhere names the work (or its author) whence he derived the illustrations and even the expressions he uses in treating of these topics.

Before the close of the same century, we find evidence that they were known—by repute, though apparently no farther—to a Latin writer of Western Europe, Gennadius of Marseilles, the continuator of St. Jerome's work *De Viris Illustribus*, who wrote about the year 495. Though mistaken (as will presently be shown) about their parentage, and incorrectly informed as to their number (which he supposes to be twenty-six), Gennadius states their titles with such an approach to accuracy, as to leave no room for doubt that the discourses he describes are those of which we now treat. He shows himself aware that they are in Syriac, but gives no hint that he has ever seen them, or that he is able to read them. [6]

In the seventh century, or (however) early in the eighth, tokens appear of a revival of interest in them. Georgius, " Bishop of the Arabs," [7] a Jacobite prelate, having been applied to by one Joshua an anchorite for information concerning the " *Epistles* " (as he styles them) of " the Persian Sage " and their authorship, wrote (in Syriac) in the year 714 a very full and elaborate reply, in which he cites at length passages from several of them, including those (above referred to) in which the dates of writing are stated with precision,—and he infers from these dates, that the author, of whose name he professes himself to be ignorant, wrote too early to be a disciple of Ephraim. To

---

[5] Forget, *De Vita e Scriptis Aphraatis* (1882), pp. 139–148 ; also (cited by him *S. Isaaci Antiocheni Opp.* (ed. Bickell, 1873).

[6] The titles given by Gennadius do not number 26 ; some titles he omits ; others he divides, treating as two what is really one, in several instances.

[7] See the text in Wright's *Aphraatis*, pp. 29 *ff*. ; in Lagarde's *Analecta Syr.*, pp. 108 *ff*. ; or Forget (as above) pp. 8 *ff*.

this inference we may safely assent, even though we hold that Ephraim wrote and taught earlier in the century than Georgius endeavours to place him. The point to be noted is, that this learned and acute writer, though he had by careful study made himself familiar with the *Demonstrations*, neither knows, nor can guess at, the name of their author, nor can he record any tradition concerning his identity. He can only tell what he has learned from their contents, that they were written from 337 to 345, by one who was a monk, and a cleric, and that they were characterized by certain peculiarities of doctrine.

5. *Ascribed to Jacob of Nisibis.*—Thus it appears that the series of discourses now known as the *Demonstrations of Aphrahat*, were imitated, and transcribed, and translated, into Armenian, and their titles cited by a Latin biographer, and their contents minutely investigated by an able critic, within the four centuries that followed the time of their composition ; while through all that long period the name of Aphrahat had passed out of memory, and the "Persian Sage" simply, or else with the addition of an ambiguous and misleading name, "Jacob, the Persian Sage," was the designation by which their author was usually known. As we have seen, the scribes of two MSS., of the fifth and sixth centuries, and Georgius in the early eighth, confine themselves to the former ; and the scribe of the sixth, thirty-eight years later than the earlier of the other two, uses the latter. Misled by it, the Armenian translator, and Gennadius in his biographical work, fell into the error of identifying the Jacob who wrote the *Demonstrations* with a namesake, the earlier and more conspicuous Jacob of Nisibis, of whom we have had occasion to speak in treating of the life of Ephraim. But of this celebrated personage no writings are recorded, nor was he a Persian,[8] but a native of Nisibis (in his time a city of the Roman Empire), in 338, seven years before the completion of the treatises in question. As Jacob of Nisibis is thus too early to be the author of them, so, on the other hand, Jacob of Sarug, whom Assemani suggested in correcting the mistake of Gennadius,[9] is too late ; for he was not born till more than a century after the date of the last *Demonstration*.

6. *Reappearance of the Name of Aphrahat.*—It is not until some years after the middle of the tenth century, that the "Persian Sage" first appears under his proper name, —of which, though as it appears generally forgotten in the Syriac world of letters, a tradition had survived.—The Nestorian Bar-Bahlul (circ. 963) in his Syro-Arabic *Lexicon*, writes thus :—"Aphrahat [mentioned] in the Book of Paradise, is the Persian Sage, as they record."—So too, in the eleventh century, Elias of Nisibis (Barsinæus, d. 1049), embodies in his *Chronography*, a table, compiled from *Demonstr.* XXIII., of the chronography from the Creation to the "Era of Alexander" (B.C. 311), which he describes as "The years of the House of Adam, according to the opinion of Aphrahat, the Persian Sage."[1]—To the like effect, but with fuller information, the great light of the mediæval Jacobite Church, Gregory Barhebræus (d. 1286), in Part I. of his *Ecclesiastical Chronicle*, in enumerating the orthodox contemporaries of Athanasius, mentions, after Ephraim, "the Persian Sage who wrote the *Book of Demonstrations ;*"[2] and again in

---

[8] The Armenian *Menologium*, subjoined by Antonelli to the Armenian version, as printed by him, makes Jacob to have been sister's son to Gregory the Illuminator, the Apostle of Armenia, to whom that version (impossibly) ascribes the letter prefixed to *Demonstr.* I. But this statement is probably an invention, devised in order to connect Jacob with the Armenian Church.

[9] *Biblioth. Orient.* I., p. 5. A note in MS. Orient. 1017, suggests Jacob of Tagrit,—ignorantly, for he was of the 13th century.

[1] For this extract, see Wright's *Aphraates*, pp. 38, 39.

[2] The MS. of Barhebræus which Wright (*Aphraates*, pp. 2, 3), follows in treating of this notice, seems to identify the "Persian Sage," with one "Buzitis," who is mentioned immediately before ; and he conjectured therefore that "Buzitis" was a scribe's error for *Parhatis* (=Aphraates). But other MSS. insert the copulative particle so as to distinguish "the Persian Sage" from the "Buzitis," whose name precedes.

Part II., supplies his name under a slightly different form, as one who "was of note in the time of Papas the Catholicus," "the Persian Sage by name Pharhad, of whom there are extant a book of admonition [*al.*, admonitions] in Syriac, and twenty-two Epistles according to the letters of the alphabet."[3] Here we have not only the name and description of the personage in question, but a fairly accurate account of his works, under the titles by which the MSS. describe them, "*Epistles* and *Demonstrations ;*—and moreover a sufficient indication of his date, in agreement with that which the *Demonstrations* claim: for one who began to write in 337 must have lived in the closing years of the life of Papas (who died in 334), and in the earlier years of the life of Ephraim. So yet again, a generation later, the learned Nestorian prelate, Ebedjesu, in his *Catalogue* of Syrian ecclesiastical authors,[4] writes, "Aphrahat, the Persian Sage, composed two volumes with Homilies that are according to the alphabet." Here once more the name and designation are given unhesitatingly, and the division of the discourses into two groups is correctly noted ; but the concluding words appear to distinguish these groups from the alphabetic Homilies. Either, therefore, we must take the preposition rendered "*with*" to mean "containing,"—or we must conclude that Ebedjesu's knowledge of the work was at second-hand and incorrect. Finally, in a very late MS.,[5] dated 1364, is found the first or chronological part of *Demonstration* XXIII., headed as follows:—"The Demonstration concerning the Grape, of the Sage Aphrahat, who is Jacob, Bishop of Mar Mathai." Here (though the prefix "Persian" is absent) we have the author's title of "Sage"; and the identification of the "Aphrahat" of the later authorities with the "Jacob" of the earlier is not merely implied but expressly affirmed. Here, moreover, we have what seems to account for the twofold name. As author, he is Aphrahat ; as Bishop, he is Jacob—the latter name having been no doubt assumed on his elevation to the Episcopate.[6] Such changes of name, at consecration, which in later ages of the Syrian Church became customary, were no doubt exceptional in the earlier period of which we are treating. But the fact that Aphrahat was a Persian name, bestowed on him no doubt in childhood—when he was still (as will be shown presently) outside the Christian fold—a name which is supposed to signify "Chief" or "Prefect," and which may have seemed unsuited to the humility of the sacred office—supplies a reason for the substitution in its stead of a name associated with sacred history, both of the Old and of the New Testament. Here finally we have the direct statement of what Georgius had justly inferred from the opening of *Dem.* XIV., that the writer was himself of the clergy, and in this Epistle writes as a cleric to clerics.

We have now brought together all the known authorities who yield information concerning this collection of treatises, and its author. It remains that we should put into a connected form the facts to which they testify, and point out the inferences yielded by their notices, and by the treatises themselves.

7. *His Nationality Persian, and Probably Heathen.*—That the author was of Persian nationality, is a point on which all the witnesses agree, except the fourteenth-century scribe of the MS. *Orient.* 1017, who however is merely silent about it. The name Aphrahat is, as has been already said, Persian—which fact at once confirms the tradition that he belonged to Persia, and helps to account for what seems to be the reluctance[7]

---

[3] Part I., s. 26, c. 83 ; Part II., s. 10, c. 33.
[4] *Ap. B. O.* III. i. (see p. 95).
[5] British Museum, *Orient.* 1017,
[6] The alternative explanation has been suggested that Jacob was the name received by Aphrahat at baptism. This is refuted by Wright's objection, that, if the name Jacob had been given so early, the name Aphrahat would have been entirely disused or forgotten.
[7] Basil (*Homil in Hexaem.* II. 6) shows alike avoidance of the name of the foreigner Ephraim, and designates him as "the Syrian." See above, p. 128.

of early writers to call him by a name that was foreign, unfamiliar, unsuited to his subsequent station in the Church, and superseded by one that had sacred associations. As a Persian, he dates his writings by the years of the reign of the Persian King : the twenty-two were completed (he says) in the thirty-fifth, the twenty-third in the thirty-sixth of the reign of Sapor.[8]—Again : as a Persian of the early fourth century, it is presumable that he was not originally a Christian. And this is apparently confirmed by the internal evidence of his own writings ; for he speaks of himself as one of those "who have cast away idols, and call that a lie which our father bequeathed to us ; " and again, "who ought to worship Jesus, for that He has turned away our froward minds from all superstitions of vain error, and taught us to worship one God our Father and Maker."[9] —But it is clear that he must have lived in a frontier region where Syriac was spoken freely ;[1] or else must have removed into a Syriac-speaking country at an early age ; for the language and style of his writings are completely pure, showing no trace of foreign idiom, or even of the want of ease that betrays a foreigner writing in what is not his mother-tongue. It is clear also that, at whatever age or under whatever circumstances he embraced Christianity, he must have taken the Christian Scriptures and Christian theology into his inmost heart and understanding as every page of his writings attests.

8. *Evidence that he was a Cleric, and a Bishop.*—We have already seen that Georgius in his study of the *Demonstrations* perceived the indications which prove the writer to be of the Clergy. He goes farther, and notes that the sixth (*Concerning Monks*) is evidently written by a monk. He might have added, what is yet more important, that the fourteenth (which he rightly fixes on as evidently written by a cleric) can hardly have been written by one of lower rank than that of Bishop. The translation of the opening sentence of this discourse (which is an Epistle to the Bishops, Clergy and people of the Church of Seleucia and Ctesiphon) is disputed ; for "we being gathered together have taken counsel to write this Epistle to our brethren . . . the Bishops, Priests, and Deacons, and the whole Church" (XIV. 1) may be read so as to make the "Bishops, Priests, etc.," either, the "*we*" who write,—or, the "*brethren*" who are written to.[2] Whichever construction is adopted, the fact remains that Aphrahat here writes on behalf of a body of men assembled in council, who through him admonished their "dear and beloved brethren" whom they designate (farther on) as "the Bishops, Priests and Deacons . . . and all the people of God who are in Seleucia and Ctesiphon." It is not conceivable that any body of men but a synod of Bishops (with their clergy and people present and assenting) would, in that age of the Church, have taken upon itself to meet and consult and address such an epistle of admonition and implied rebuke to that great see, the seat of the "Catholicus of the East,"[3] the prelate who in the oriental hierarchy was inferior in dignity to the Antiochian Patriarch alone, and in authority almost coequal with him. And it may be safely assumed that the writer of the Epistle was one—probably the chief—of the Bishops in whose name it is written. If we accept the late, but internally probable, statement of the Scribe of MS. *Orient.* 1017

---

[8] *Demonstr.* XIV. 50 ; XXII. 25 ; XXIII. 69.
[9] *Ib.* XVI. 7 ; XVII. 8.
[1] Philoxenus of Mabug, likewise a Persian, and a writer of pure Syriac, came from the border-region of Beth-garme (*B. O.* II. p., 10).
[2] Some prefer the latter construction ; but Wright (*Aphr.*, pp, 8, 9), Forget (pp. 82 *ff.*), and Parisot (*Patrologia Syr.* I., Tom. I., p. xix) seem to be right in maintaining the former. Another passage of *Dem.* XIV. (25) is translated by Wright (*Ib.*), Parisot, and Antonelli (*Opp. S. Jacobi Nis.*, p. 423), "The laying on of hands which certain *men receive of us ; *" but by Forget (pp. 100, 101) . . . . "which certain *men of us receive.*" If the former are right, the writer speaks as a Bishop ; but Forget's seems the true rendering.
[3] This ancient title is still borne by the Head of the Nestorian Church : the Jacobites from the sixth century downwards have substituted that of "Maphrian" (*Maphrino-fructificator*), *i. e.* propagator of the Episcopal succession ; which continues in use to the present day.

(above mentioned), that " the Persian Sage " was " Bishop of the monastery of Mar Mathai," we arrive at a complete explanation of the circumstances under which this Epistle was composed.    For the Bishop of Mar Mathai was Metropolitan of Nineveh, and ranked among the Bishops of " the East " only second to the Catholicus ; and his province bordered on that which the Catholicus (as Metropolitan of Seleucia) held in his immediate jurisdiction.    The Bishop of Mar Mathai therefore would properly preside in a Synod of the Eastern Bishops, met to consider the disorders and discussions existing in Seleucia and its suffragan sees.    It thus becomes intelligible how an Epistle of such official character has found a place in a series of discourses of which the rest are written as from man to man merely.    The writer addresses the Bishops, Clergy, and people of Seleucia and Ctesiphon in the name of a Synod over which he was President, a Synod probably of Bishops suffragan to Nineveh, and perhaps of those of some adjacent sees.    Thus the admonition comes officially from " Mar Jacob Bishop of Mar Mathai ; " but the thoughts, and language, and literary form are the production of Aphrahat personally, and he accordingly embodies it as fourteenth in his alphabetic series of twenty-two treatises, in which it is duly distinguished by its initial letter *nun*, the fourteenth of the Semitic alphabet.    It certainly breaks the sequence of subjects, coming after and before treatises relating to Judaism : but for the alphabetic sequence it is essential.—This alphabetic arrangement was overlooked or ignored (as it seems) by the Armenian translator, who has omitted four of the twenty-two and transposed others, placing the fourteenth apart from the rest,—although in *Demonstr*. XXII. (which however is not included in the Armenian version) the author recites all their titles, arranging them in their order, and noting that it is the order of the alphabet.[4]    In the Syriac original the fact is beyond question that *Demonstr*. XIV. is an integral part of the series ; and we may rely with confidence on the internal evidence it yields of the high ecclesiastical rank of the writer[5]—evidence confirmed by, and in its turn confirming, the statement of the fourteenth-century scribe who makes him Bishop of the second see of the East.[6]

Reverting to the subject of the Persian nationality of Aphrahat, we note that this monastery of Mar Mathai was on the eastern, that is, the Persian, side of the Tigris, not far from what once was Nineveh and is now Mosul, on the precipitous mountain Elpheph (now *Maklob*) where it still stands, though ruinous, and is known by the name of *Sheikh Matta*, and is occupied by the *Metram* (or Metropolitan) and a few monks.

9. *His Writings little Concerned with Current Controversies.*—To the remoteness of his

---

[4] The Roman editor (Antonelli) of the Armenian text (1756) was misled by the displacement of *Demonstr*. XIV., and its omission from the list of Gennadius, as well as by its synodical character, to reject it as spurious. Had he known *Demonstr*. XXII., or had he been aware of the alphabetical arrangement of the series, he would have been guarded against this error.    The Synod however in whose name *Demonstr*. XIV. is written cannot have been (as Wright supposed) that of 334 ; for it was written in 344.

[5] See also *Demonstr*. X. (below) ; especially s. b., where he exhorts " pastors " (evidently Bishops) as one set over them, in other words, their Metropolitan.

[6] An examination of this MS. leads to the conclusion that its scribe was probably well informed in this matter.    Its principal contents are, the " Book of Rays " of Gregory Barhebræus and three of his minor works. Between the first named and that which follows is inserted the extract from *Demonstr*. XXIII., above specified (p. 156), headed as we have seen with the author's names and additions,—" Aphrahat, the Sage, who is Jacob Bishop of Mar Mathai."    Now Gregory himself, as Maphrian, was Bishop of Mar Mathai, and died and was buried in that monastery in 1286.    It may be conjectured that this MS., written in 1364 (not 80 years after his death), may have obtained this passage of Aphrahat, and the heading which assigns his see, from some collection made by Gregory, among whose writings it here finds place.    If so, the statement that he was Bishop of Mar Mathai rests on the authority of Gregory, who would no doubt have within his reach authentic lists of the names of his predecessors in that see.

For the monastery of Mar Mathai, see Rich, *Koordistan*, Vol. II., ch. xv., pp. 73 *ff.* ; Badger, *Nestorians*, Vol. I., ch. ix,, pp. 95 *ff*.    The former visited it in 1820 ; the latter in 1843 and 1850 ; and his account is illustrated with an engraving of the monastery, and a plan of the Church.    He found the *Metran* residing there, with two monks ; and five villages, with some 350 families, formed his diocese.    In 1880 Sachau visited Mosul, and records (*Reise*, ch. iv., p. 352) that a Bishop still resided in this monastery.

see, and probably of the place of his obvious origin and abode, from the centres of religious thought and controversy, is probably due the notable absence from these discourses
of all reference to the great theological questions that had employed, and in his time were
engrossing, the leading minds of Christendom.    He began to write within ten years after
the Nicene Council and the Arian controversy, and the  disputations that grew out of it
were still ripe, and continued to abound long after.    The writings of Ephraim show how
vehemently in Aphrahat's lifetime, or possibly a few years later, the theologians of Nisibis
and of Edessa deemed  themselves bound to  strive for the Faith against Arians, Ano-
mæans, Apollinarians,—and not less against the surviving or revived heresy of home-
grown production—that of Bardesan.[7]    But in Seleucia and Ctesiphon it is not heresy,
but strife, self-seeking, and neglect of duty, that are censured by the Synod through the
letter which we know as *Demonstr*. XIV., and the errors which the Bishop of Mar
Mathai combats  for the benefit of those whom  he addresses are the errors of the Jews
who refused and  resisted the  creed and  the customs of the  Church.    There is in one
place (*Demonstr*. III. 9) a passing reference to the heresiarchs of  the second and third
centuries, Valentinus, Manes, and Marcion ; but it merely amounts to a brief statement
in which the  false teaching of  each is summed up in a sentence, each  followed by the
question, Can one who holds such doctrine find acceptance before God by his fasting ?
No later heresy is even mentioned.

These facts not only confirm the tradition which places him at Nineveh, but they go
far to account for the obscurity in which his name and his writings lay so long.    In an
age of excited controversy, these quiet hortatory discourses, marked by no striking eloquence of style or subtlety of reasoning, dealing with no burning question of the time,
nor with any disputes more recent than those of the two previous centuries, or those
between Jew and Christian, would hardly attain to more than a local circulation ; and
when they penetrated to Edessa or other such centres of Syriac theological life, would
awaken but a languid interest.    That they did so penetrate is certain ; for of the existing MSS. whence we derive their text, one (the oldest) was  written in Edessa in 474,
and Isaac of Antioch, who knew and imitated them, before that time, was a disciple of
Zenobius of Edessa.    But the paucity of such MSS., and still more  the oblivion which
so long covered the  name of Aphrahat, prove, either, that the work failed to  attain
popularity—or, that it provoked some prejudice which led to its  practical suppression.
It would be difficult, however, to point out anything in it to which  exception could be
so seriously taken as to be a bar to its acceptance.    None of the errors which so keen
a critic as Georgius detected in its theology—even if we admit the justice of his censure
—is such as to shock the orthodoxy of the fourth or fifth century.

10. *Possibly Suspected of a Nestorian Tinge.*—Yet it is possible that theological prepos-
session may indirectly have brought about the disfavour or at least disuse into which
the *Demonstrations* fell.    In Edessa there was an institution  known as the "School of
the Persians," to which as it seems disciples from Persia resorted for theological instruction.    From Ibas, Bishop of Edessa (435–457), who was  infected with Nestorianism,
the Nestorian taint passed to Maris, a Persian (and through him to Persia generally),
and likewise to Maro, a teacher in the school.    After the death of Ibas, the Persian
and others who had followed him were expelled from Edessa, by Nonnus his orthodox
opponent and successor ; and the school was finally closed by the next Bishop, Cyrus,
in the reign of Zeno[8] (who died 491).    These facts may well be supposed to have raised
a prejudice against all writings coming from a Persian source ; and the works of "the

---

[7] See Ephraim's words, cited above, pp. 129, 136.
[8] Simeon of Beth-Arsam, *ap.*, Assem, *B. O.* I. 346, is our authority for this narrative.

Persian Sage," absolutely free,though they are from any thought or phrase which could
be construed as favouring or tending in the direction that led to the errors of Nestorius,
may have come undeservedly under the ban issued against the School of the Persians
and all that was connected with it, by the orthodox zeal of Cyrus.   It is probable that
his writings were read in that school, and that he himself may have studied them in
early life.   Prescribed in Edessa, the centre of Syriac theology, these discourses would
be effectually checked in their circulation in all churches of Syriac-speaking Christendom that were anti-Nestorian.[9]

   11. *Their Popularity in the Armenian Church.*—How the book made good and held
its footing in the Armenian Church is perhaps more difficult to explain.   It is not indeed
the only instance in which an author, of whom no works are extant in their original
tongue, has survived and been widely known in a translation.   A notable example is
that of Irenæus, of whose great work on *Heresies,* so well known in its early Latin
dress, but a few fragments have reached us, through citations, in Greek.   There is no
obvious ecclesiastical channel through which the knowledge of the writings of Aphrahat
can be supposed to have reached Armenia, unless by way of Edessa, before they fell
(as above suggested) into discredit in that city.   But it is to be borne in mind that from
and after the close of the fourth century "greater (*i.e.* Eastern) Armenia was ruled as
a dependency of Persia, by Persian Kings."[1]   Of these the earlier at least were Christians,
and their policy led them to promote the Syriac language and literature, as against the
Greek, among their people ; until, under the Catholicus Isaac (d. 441), the Armenian
tongue was reduced to writing (in the characters then invested by Mesrob), and a
beginning made of an Armenian sacred literature by the translation of the Scriptures
into Armenian from the Syriac.   Versions of the works of Syriac divines would naturally
follow before long.   That among these *Ephraim's Commentaries* were conspicuous we
have already mentioned (p. 147) : that those of a Syriac Divine of Persian ·nationality
should be passed over is unlikely—a Divine too of such repute as to have won the
honourable title of "the Persian Sage," and who as occupant of a great Persian see was
also known as Jacob of Mar Mathai, metropolitan of Nineveh.   How readily his assumed name would lead to his being confused with his far more widely known namesake of Nisibis, we have already pointed out ; and it is obvious that the name, once
attributed and accepted, would lend fictitious vogue to the book.

   12. *First Printed in an Armenian Version.*—The mistake of the Armenian translator
became, in later times, the means of first making the work—though not the name—of
Aphrahat known to European scholars.   The Armenian version, containing nineteen of
the *Demonstrations* (XX. being omitted), was printed at Rome in 1756, edited, with a

---

   [9] Note that the authorities who know the author as Aphrahat are of "the East" (in the ecclesiastical sense
—namely, the regions beyond the Tigris).   Bar-Bahlul and Ebedjesu are Eastern, as being Nestorians.   Of
the Jacobites, Elias Barsinneus was of Mosul originally, and Gregory Barhebræus as Maphrian had his see in
Mosul and the whole East under his rule.   The scribe of the MS. *Orient.* 1017 wrote indeed in the Jacobite convent of Kartamin, but he was merely the copyist of a MS. of the works of Barhebræus, obtained no doubt
from Mosul.   On the other hand, of the three scribes of the earlier MSS., who knew him only as "the
Persian Sage," or as "Mar Jacob," one was of Edessa, and all were presumably Jacobites of the same
regions ; as likewise Georgius (also connected with Edessa), and his correspondent (Joshua, of Anab).   Isaac
of Nineveh was Eastern, and Nestorian ; but as he nowhere mentions the author of the works with which
he was evidently acquainted, he does not come here into consideration.   Nor does Ennadius ; inasmuch as
we have no means of discovering how he came to hear of their existence, or to attribute them to Jacob of
Nisibis : we can only conjecture that his informant may have been an Armenian.
   As to Barhebræus, the significant fact is farther to be noted that in Part I., where he treats of the Patriarchs and the western provinces, presumably drawing from Western documents, he only speaks of "the
Persian Sage :" and the name Aphrahat first appears in Part II., where the writer records, as Maphrian,
no doubt, from the tradition of his own church at Mosul, the names of the notable persons of the time of
his predecessor, Papas the Catholicus of the East.
   [1] See Gibbon, *Decline and Fall,* ch. xxxii. (p. 392, Vol. III. of Prof. Bury's edition ; also his *Appendix* 25,
p. 504).

Latin version, by Antonelli. Its text is derived from a transcript made in 1719, after an ancient copy in the Armenian Monastery at Venice, by order of the Abbot Peter Mechitar, and presented by him to Pope Clement XI. for the Vatican Library. In this edition, entitled *S. Patris Jacobi Episcopi Nisibeni Sermones*, the discourses are not merely ascribed to Jacob of Nisibis, but the theory is advanced by the editor, that the Armenian text is the original. It is hardly necessary to point out that the alphabetic arrangement of the twenty-two discourses—which is not and could not be reproduced in Armenian,[2] a language with an alphabet of thirty-eight letters—is alone sufficient to expose the impossibility of this idea.

13. *Recovery of the Post-Syriac Original.*—The Syriac text, so long forgotten, was first discovered among the MSS. of the great Nitrian collection in the British Museum, by Dr. Cureton, whose name is so honourably known as a great Syriac scholar, and editor of Syriac documents. He did not live, however, to accomplish his desire of publishing it, but bequeathed that task to his still more eminent successor, in the leadership of Syriac studies in England, the late Dr. William Wright, then assistant keeper of MSS. in the British Museum, and afterwards Professor of Arabic in the University of Cambridge. To him is due the admirable *editio princeps* of the Syriac text of all the twenty-three *Demonstrations* (from the MSS. 14617 and 17182), issued in London, 1869. He did not, however, carry out his intention of adding to this work a second volume, containing an English translation of the whole.

Since then, another edition of the series of twenty-two has been published in Paris (Firmin-Didot, 1894), as the first volume of a *Patrologia Syriaca*, under the general editorship of Dr. R. Graffin, lecturer in Syriac in the Theological Faculty of the Catholic Institute of Paris. This excellent work includes a Latin Version, and is preceded by a learned and copious Introduction, in which all questions relating to Aphrahat and his writings are fully treated,—both of which are the work of Dom Parisot, Benedictine Priest and Monk.

14. *Was Aphrahat Prior to Ephraim?*—In thus placing Aphrahat first as their projected series of Syriac Divines, the learned editors follow the opinion which, ever since Wright published his edition, has been adopted by Syriac scholars—that Aphrahat is prior in time to Ephraim. This is undoubtedly true (as pointed out above) in the only limited sense, that the *Demonstrations* are earlier by some years (the first ten by thirteen years, the remainder by five or six) than the earliest of Ephraim's writings which can be dated with certainty (namely, the first Nisibene Hymn, which belongs to 350). It is then assumed that Ephraim was born in the reign of Constantine, therefore not earlier than 306, and that Aphrahat was a man of advanced age when he wrote (of which there is no proof whatever), and must therefore have been born before the end of the third century—perhaps as early as 280. It has been shown above (p. 145) that even if we admit the authority of the Syriac *Life* of Ephraim, we must regard the supposed statement of his birth in Constantine's time as a mistranslation or rather perversion of the text. Thus the argument for placing Ephraim's birth so late as 306 disappears, while for placing Aphrahat's birth no argument has been advanced, but merely conjecture ; and the result is, that the two may, so far as evidence goes, be regarded as contemporary. It is true that Barhebræus, in his *Ecclesiastical History*, reckons Aphrahat as belonging to the time of Papas, who died 335 ; but it is to be noted that in the very same context he mentions that letters were extant purporting to be addressed by Jacob of Nisibis and Ephraim to the same Papas,—and though he admits that some discredited the genuine-

---

[2] In the Armenian alphabet the number of letters is 38.

ness of these letters, he gives no hint that Ephraim was too young to have written them. In fact he could not do so, for in the earlier part of this *History* he had already named Ephraim as present at the Nicene Council in 325, and had placed his name before that of Aphrahat in including both among the contemporaries of the Great Athanasius.[3]

15. *His Use of Holy Scripture.*—Concerning the canon and text of the Books of the Bible as used by Aphrahat,—a subject hardly within the scope of this Introduction—a few words must suffice.

In citing the Old Testament, he shows himself acquainted with nearly all the Books of the Jewish Canon, and with some, but not all, of the deutero-canonical books commonly called Apocrypha—with Tobit, Ecclesiasticus (and perhaps Wisdom), and Maccabees, but not Judith, Susanna, Bel and the Dragon, or Baruch. He follows the Peshitto rather than the Greek, but not seldom departs from both; and he shows a knowledge of the Chaldee Paraphrase.

His New Testament Canon is apparently that of the Peshitto;—that is to say, he shows no signs of acquaintance with the four shorter Catholic Epistles, and in the one citation which seems to be from the Apocalypse, it has been shown to be probable that he is really referring to the Targum of Onkelos on Deut. xxxiii. 6.[4] But he omits all reference also to the longer Catholic Epistles, except 1 John. He also passes over (of St. Paul's Epistles) 2 Thessalonians, Titus, and Philemon. But as regards the last, its shortness accounts for the omission; and as to the former two, he can hardly have been unacquainted with them, inasmuch as he knew 1 Thessalonians and 1 and 2 Timothy. He designates the writer of Hebrews as "the Apostle," probably meaning to ascribe it to St. Paul.

In citing the Gospels, he seems sometimes to follow the *Diatessaron*, which, as we have said, was in the hands of his contemporary Ephraim, and which is known to have circulated largely in the East until far on in the following century. Sometimes, however, his references seem to be to the separate Gospels as commonly read. It cannot be claimed for the Peshitto that he always or even usually follows its text; nor yet does he uniformly agree with the Curetonian, or with the probably earlier form of the Syriac Gospel recently discovered by Mr. Lewis. With each of these last, however, his text has many points of coincidence. In the rest of the New Testament, we can only say that he must have had before him a text which diverged not seldom from the Peshitto.[5]

16. *Literary and Theological Value of his Writings.*—From the *Demonstrations*, eight have been selected for the present volume, viz.: I. *Of Faith* (with *Letter of an Inquirer* prefixed); V. *Of Wars;* VI. *Of Monks;* VIII. *Of the Resurrection of the Dead;* X. *Of Pastors;* XVII. *Of Christ the Son of God;* XXI. *Of Persecution;* XXII. *Of Death and the Latter Times.* Of these, one only (XVII.) is controversial,—directed against the Jews: it is painfully inadequate in the treatment of its great theme,—so inadequate as to suggest the surmise that doubts may have arisen about the orthodoxy of the writer, such as to discredit his works, and to account for the neglect in which they lay (as we have seen) for centuries. But in all his writings his mastery of the Scriptures, of the Old Testament especially, is conspicuous; and in many of them, especially in those of a hortatory character, there is much force of earnest persuasiveness, rising at times into eloquence.

---

[3] Cp. *Eccles. Hist.* II. 10, cc. 31, 33, with I. 26, cc. 83, 85.
[4] See *Demonstr.* VIII. 19 (also VII. 25), and cp. Apoc. II. 11. (Parisot, Introduction, p. xliii.)
[5] It is important to note that he quotes in full three (16, 17, 18) of the disputed "Last Twelve Verses" of St. Mark's Gospel. (*Demonst.* I. 17.)

# EPHRAIM

---

## HYMNS.

### A. The Nisibene Hymns.

### B. The Hymns *On the Nativity*.

### C. The Hymns *For the Epiphany*.

### D. The Hymns *On the Faith* (THE PEARL).

---

## HOMILIES.

# THE NISIBENE HYMNS

(Translated by Rev. J. T. Sarsfield Stopford, B.A.).

# NISIBENE HYMNS

## I.

1. O GOD of mercies Who didst refresh Noah, he too refreshed Thy mercies. He offered sacrifice and stayed the flood; he presented gifts and received the promise. With prayer and incense he propitiated Thee: with an oath and with the bow Thou wast gracious to him; so that if the flood should essay to hurt the earth, the bow should stretch itself over against it, to banish it away and hearten the earth. As Thou hast sworn peace so do Thou maintain it, and let Thy bow strive against Thy wrath!

*R.* Stretch forth Thy bow against the flood, for lo! it has lifted up its waves against our walls!

2. In revelation, Lord! it has been proclaimed, that that lowly blood which Noah sprinkled, wholly restrained Thy wrath for all generations; how much mightier then shall be the blood of Thy Only Begotten, that the sprinkling of it should restrain our flood! For lo! it was *but* as mysteries of Him that those lowly sacrifices gained virtue, which Noah offered, and stayed *by them* Thy wrath. Be propitiated by the gift upon my altar, and stay from me the deadly flood. So shall both Thy signs bring deliverance, to me Thy cross and to Noah Thy bow! Thy cross shall cleave the sea of waters; Thy bow shall stay the flood of rain.

3. Lo! all the billows trouble me; and Thou hast given *more* favour to the ark: for waves alone encompassed it, mounds and weapons and waves encircle me. It was unto Thee a storehouse of treasures, but I have been a storehouse of debts: it in Thy love subdued the waves; I in Thy wrath, am left desolate among the weapons; the flood bore it, the river threatens me. O Helmsman of that ark, be my pilot on the dry land! To it Thou gavest rest in the haven of a mountain; to me give Thou rest also in the haven of my walls!

4. The Just One has chastened me abundantly, but it He loved even among the waves. For Noah overcame the waves of lust, which had drowned in his generation the sons of Seth. Because his flesh revolted against the daughters of Cain, his chariot rode on the surface of the waves. Because women defiled him not, he coupled the beasts, whereof in the ark he joined together, all pairs in the yoke of wedlock. The olive which with its oil gladdens the face, with its leaf gladdened their countenances: for me the river whereof to drink is wont to make joyful, lo! O Lord, by its flood it makes me mournful.

5. The foulness of my guilt Thy righteousness has seen, and Thy pure eyes abhor me. Thou hast gathered the waters by the hand of the unclean, that Thou mightest make for me purification of my guilt; not that in them Thou mightest baptize and purify me, but that in them Thou mightest chasten me with fear. For the waves will stir up to prayer, which shall wash away my guilt. The sight of them which is full of repentance, has been to me a baptism. The sea, O Lord, which should have drowned me, in it let Thy mercies drown my guilt. In the Red Sea Thou didst drown bodies; in this *sea* drown Thou my guilt instead of bodies!

6. An ark in Thy mercy Thou didst prepare, that Thou mightest preserve in it all the remnants. That Thou shouldest not desolate the earth in Thy wrath, Thy compassion made an earth of wood. Thou didst empty them one into the other; Thou didst

167

render them back one unto the other. *But* my lands have thrice been filled and emptied again ; and now against me the waves rebel, to overwhelm the remnant that has escaped in me. In the ark Thou didst save a remnant ; save in me, O Lord, yea in me a leaven. The ark upon the mountain brought forth ; let me in my lands bring forth my imprisoned ones !

7. O Lord, gladden Thou in me the imprisoned ones of my fortresses, Thou Who didst gladden those prisoners with the olive leaf ! Thou sentest healing by means of the dove to the sick ones that were drowning in every wave ; it entered in and drove out all their pains. For the joy of it swallowed up their sorrow, and mourning vanished away in its consolation. And as the chief of a host gives heartening to the fugitives, so *the dove* disseminated courage among the forsaken. Their eyes tasted the sight of peace, and their mouth hasted to open in Thy praise. As the olive leaf in the waves, save Thou me, that Thou mayest gladden in me the prisoners of my fortresses !

8. The flood assails, and dashes against our walls : may the all-sustaining might uphold them ! It falls not as the building of the sand, for I have not built my doctrine upon the sand : a rock shall be for me the foundation, for on Thy rock have I built my faith ; the secret foundation of my trust, shall support my walls. For the walls of Jericho fell, because on the sand she had built her trust. Moses built a wall in the sea, for on a rock his understanding built *it.* The foundation of Noah *was* on a rock ; the dwelling place of wood it bore up in the sea.

9. Compare the souls which *are* in me, with the living things that *were* in the ark ; and instead of Noah who mourned in it, lo ! Thy altar mourning and humbled. Instead of the wedded wives that *were* in it, lo ! my virgins that are unmarried. Instead of Ham who went forth *from it* and uncovered his father's nakedness, lo ! workers of righteousness, who have nourished and clothed apostles. In my pains, O my Lord, I rave

in my speech ; blame me not if my words provoke Thee ! Thou puttest to silence the prosperous when they murmured : have mercy on me as on them that were silenced aforetime !

10. Before Thy wrath Thou madest a house of refuge, and all the nations rebelled against it. Noah was refreshed in rest, that his dwelling-place should give rest according to his name. Thou didst close the doors to save the righteous one ; Thou didst open the floods to destroy the unclean. Noah stood between the terrible waves that *were* without, and the destroying mouths that *were* within : the waves tossed him and the mouths dismayed him. Thou madest peace for him with them that were within ; Thou broughtest down before him them that were without : Thou didst speedily change his troubles, for light to Thee, O Lord, are hard things.

11. Hear and weigh the comparison of me with Noah, and though my suffering be light beside his, let Thy mercy make our deliverance alike ; for lo ! my children stand like him, between the wrathful and the destroyer. Give peace, O Lord, among them that are within, and humble before me them that are without ; and give me twofold victory ! And whereas the slayer has made his rage threefold, may He of the three days show me threefold mercy ! Let not the Evil One overcome Thy lovingkindness : seeing he has assailed me twice and thrice overcome Thou him ! Let my victory fly abroad through the world, that it may earn Thee praise in the world ! O Thou who didst rise on the third day, give us not over to death in *our* third peril !

## II.

1. This day are opened, our mouths to give thanks. They who opened the breaches, have opened my sons' mouths. Thank the Merciful, who has delivered the men of our *city*, nor thought at that time of exacting the debts that were due by us. When they rose up they that took us cap-

tive, the worlds in our deliverance, tasted of Thy graciousness.

*R.* From all that have mouths, glory be to Thy grace !

2. He has saved us without wall, and taught us that He is our wall : He has saved us without king and made us know that is our king : He has saved us, in each and all, and showed us that He is All : He has saved us in His grace and again reveals, that freely He has mercy and quickens. From every boaster, He takes away his boasting, and gives it to His own grace.

3. The sound of all mouths, is too little for Thy praise : for lo ! in the hour when our light was smoking, and was at the point to be quenched (seeing that all is easy to Thee) of a sudden it awoke and shone ! Who has seen these two marvels, that for him whose hope was cut off, hope has sprung up and increased ; the hour of mourning has been turned into good tidings ?

4. This is a festival day, whereon hang the feasts : for if wrath had taken us captive, lo ! our feasts too had ceased. Whereas our peace has conquered and triumphed, lo ! our festivals resound. This blessed day supports all : upon it depends the city, on the city depends the people, on the people depends peace, on peace depends all.

5. Out of these breaches, Thou hast multiplied triumphs. Praise unto the Triune God goes up from the three breaches ; for that He descended and repaired them, in His mercy which restrains wrath. He smote *the enemy* who understood not that He was teaching us. He taught those within, for in His justice He made the breaches ; He taught those without, for in His goodness He repaired them.

6. Speak and give glory, my delivered ones on this day ; old men and boys, young men and maidens, children and innocents, and thou, O Church, mother of the city ! For the old men have been rescued from captivity, the youths from torture, the sucklings from being dashed in pieces, the women from dishonour, and the Church from mockery.

7. He came to us with hardness ; we were afraid for a moment : He came in gentleness, and we rejoiced for an hour. He turned and left us for a little, we wandered without end ; like a beast of prey which is trained by blandishments and by fear, but if so be that men turn *from it*, rebels and strays and becomes savage in the midst of peace.

8. He punished us and we feared not ; He rescued us, and we were not shamed : He straitened us and our vows were multiplied ; He enlarged *us* and our crimes were multiplied. When He constrained there was a covenant, when He gave breathing-space there was straying. Though He knew us He lowered Himself to establish us. In the evening we exalted Him ; in the morning we rejected Him. When necessity left us, faithfulness left us.

9. He afflicted us by the breaches, that He might punish our crimes : He raised the mounds that thereby, He might humble our boasting. He made a breach for the seas that thereby, He might wash away our pollution. He shut us in that we might gather together in His Temple. He shut us in and we were quenched ; He set us free and we went astray. We are like unto wool, which passes into every colour.

10. We know that when the blessed sons of Nineveh repented, it was not because of mounds they repented, nor yet by means of waters, nor was it by reason of a breach, nor yet by reason of bows; it was not at the sound of the bowstring they feared and repented. They harkened to a feeble voice ; they caused their little ones to fast ; they made their youths chaste, they made their kings humble.

11. Thou smotest us and we justified Thee, for it befel not by chance ; Thou deliveredst us and we gave thanks, for it was not that we were worthy. Thou hadst mercy on us not because Thou erredst, in hoping that we should repent. It was manifest to Thee that when Thou hadst mercy on us we strayed. Thou knewest that we had sinned ; Thou knewest that we are sinners : with our

iniquity that has been and is, Thou wast acquainted when Thou hadst mercy on us.

12. Weigh our repentance, that it may outbalance our crimes! But not in even balance, ascends either weight; for our crimes are heavy and manifold, and our repentance is light. He had commanded that we should be sold for our debt: His mercy became our advocate; principal and increase, we repaid with the farthing, which our repentance proffered.

13. Ten thousand talents for that little *payment,* our debt He forgave us. He was bound to exact it, that He might appease His justice: He was constrained again to forgive, that He might make His grace to rejoice. Our tears for the twinkling of an eye we gave Him; He satisfied His justice, in exacting and taking a little; He made His grace to rejoice, *when* for a little He forgave much.

14. Ten thousand *are the* crimes that He has pardoned; ten thousand tongues, are unable to suffice, in presence of His goodness. He has pardoned us and we have not pardoned; we have requited to Him contrariwise; the guilt committed we write up afresh. "Pardon, O Lord," we cry; "Requite, O Lord," we pray: "pardon" verily when we have done wrong; "requite" verily when wrong is done us.

15. Yea not as those without, have we laboured for our lives. They have raised their mounds, but we not even our voices: they have broken through the wall, but we —not even the chains, the frail chains on our heart within have we broken. *God* has rejected the diligent, for the sake of the slothful; He has rejected the labour done without, though He was rejected from within.

16. He has set free them that talked, and smitten the silent; the wall was beaten, and the people were instructed: He spared them that can suffer, He smote that which knows no suffering. For instead of souls that feel, He smote the stones that feel not, that He might chasten us. In His love He spared our bodies, and hasted to smite our wall.

17. Who has ever seen, that a breach became as a mirror? Two parties looked thereinto; it served for those without and those within. They saw therein as with eyes, the Power that breaks down and builds up: they saw Him who made the breach and again repaired *it.* Those without saw His might; they departed and tarried not till evening: those within saw His help; they gave thanks yet sufficed not.

18. Let the day of thy deliverance, arouse thee from sloth! When the wall was broken through, when the elephants pressed in, when the javelins showered, when men did valiantly, then was there a sight for the heavenly ones. Iniquity fought there; mercy triumphed there; lovingkindness prevailed below; the watchers shouted on high.

19. And thine enemy wearied himself, *striving* to smite by his wiles, the wall that encompassed thee, a bulwark to thine inhabitants. He wearied himself and availed not; and in order that he might not hope, that if He broke through He should also enter and take us captive, he broke it through and not once only; and was put to shame, nor was that enough, even unto three times, that he might be shamed thrice in the three.

20. Let my happiness by *God's* grace, be also multiplied in thy midst! Whereas in thee my crimes have been many, many be in thee my fruits! Whereas in thee I have sinned in my youth, in thee let there be mercy for my old age! By the mouth of thy sons pray for thy son, for I have sinned beyond my ability, and have repented below my ability; I have scattered above measure, and have gathered below measure.

## III.

1. Fix thou our hearing, that it be not loosed and wander! For it is a-wandering if one enquire, who He is and what He is like. For how can we avail, to paint in us the likeness, of that Being which is like to the mind? Naught is there in it that is limited, in all of it He sees and hears; all of

it as it were speaks ; all of it is in all senses.

*R., Praise to the One Being, that is to us unsearchable!*

2. His aspect cannot be discerned, that it should be portrayed by our understanding : He hears without ears ; He speaks without mouth ; He works without hands, and He sees without eyes. Because our soul ceases not nor desists, in presence of Him Who is such ; in His graciousness He put on the fashion of humankind and gathered us into His likeness.

3. Let us learn in what way that Being is spiritual and appeared as corporeal ; and how it also is tranquil and appears as wrathful. These things were for our profit ; that Being in our likeness was made like to us, that we may be made like Him. One there is that is like Him, the Son Who proceeded from Him, Who is stamped with His likeness.

4. O Nisibis, hear these things, for, for thy sake these things were written and spoken. Both to thyself and to others, thou hast been in the world a cause of strife and of disputations. Mouths over thee, O thou that wast shut up, even over thee mouths sang ; when thou didst triumph and wast enlarged, in thee mouths were opened, for lamentation and for thanksgiving.

5. The prayer of thy inhabitants, sufficed for thy deliverance ; it was not that they were righteous, but that they were penitent : according as they were disgraced, so did they haste *to submit* to the rod. In transgressions and in triumphs they had like part. They whose crimes were great, so be their fruit great ; they who triumphed in their sackcloth, have triumphed also in their crowns.

6. The day of thy deliverance, is king of all days. The Sabbath overthrew thy walls, it overthrew the ungrateful ; the day of the Resurrection of the Son, raised *again* thy ruins ; the day of Resurrection raised thee according to its name, it glorified its title. The Sabbath relaxed its watch ; for the making of the breaches, it took blame to itself.

7. In Samaria hunger prevailed, but in thee fulness prevailed. In Samaria there broke in and came on her, abundance of a sudden ; but in thee there roared and came in on thee a sea of a sudden. In her was eaten a child, and it saved her alive ; in thee was eaten the body, living and all life-giving ; of a sudden He delivered them, the Eaten *delivered* the eaters.

8. We know that the Blessed wills not the afflictions, that have been in all ages; though He has wrought them, it is our offences that are the cause of our troubles. No man can complain against our Creator ; it is for Him to complain against us, who have sinned and constrained Him, to be wrathful though He wills it not, and to smite though He desires it not.

9. The Earth, the vine, and the olive, are in need of chastisement. When the olive is bruised, then its fruit smells sweet ; when the vine is pruned, then its grapes are goodly ; when the soil is ploughed its yield is goodly. When water is confined in channels, desert places drink of it ; brass, silver and gold, when they are burnished shine.

10. If *then* it be that man, by chastening makes all things goodly ; and if he who despises and rejects *chastening*, is hated and all rebels against him ; *then* by that which he chastens, let him learn Him that chastens him ; since whoso chastens *does so* that he may profit *thereby*. For whoso chastens his servants, *does so* that he may possess them ; the good God chastens *His* servants that they may possess themselves.

11. Let thy afflictions be, books to admonish thee, for the thrice-besieged, suffice to become for thee, books to meditate therein, every hour on their histories. Because thou despisedst the two Testaments, wherein thou mightest read thy life, therefore He wrote for thee, three hard books wherein thou shouldst read thy chastisements.

12. Let us avert by that which has been, the thing that is yet to be ; let us be taught by that which has come, to escape that which is coming ; let us remember that which is past, to avoid that which is future.

Because we had forgotten the first stroke, the second fell on us; because we forgot the second, the third bore heavy on us. Who will yet again forget!

### IV.

1. My God, without ceasing, I will tread the threshold of Thy house; I who have rejected all grace, I will ask with boldness, that I may receive with confidence.    *R., Our hope, be thou our Wall!*

2. For if, O Lord, the earth, enriches manifold, a single grain of wheat, how then shall my prayers, be enriched by Thy grace!

3. Because of the voices of my children, their sighs and their groans, open to me the door of Thy mercy! Make glad for their voices, the mourning of their sackcloth!

4. O firstborn that wast a weaned *child*, and wast familiar with the children, the accurst sons of Nazareth, hearken to my lambs that have seen the wolves, for lo! they cry.

5. For a flock, O my Lord, in the field, if so be it has seen the wolves, flees to the shepherd, and takes refuge under his staff, and he drives away them that would devour it.

6. Thy flock has seen the wolves, and lo! it cries loudly. Behold how terrified it is! Let thy Cross be a staff, to drive out them that would swallow it up!

7. Accept the cry of my little ones, that are altogether pure. It was He, the Infant of days, that could appease, O Lord, the Ancient of days.

8. The day when the Babe came down, in the midst of the stall, the Watchers descended and proclaimed, peace—may that *peace* be, in all my streets for all my offspring.

9. Seventy and two old men, the elders of that people, sufficed not for its breaches. The Babe it was, the Son of Mary, that gave peace on every side.

10. Have mercy, O Lord, on my children! In my children call to mind Thy childhood, Thou Who wast a child! Let them that are like Thy childhood, be saved by Thy grace!

11. Mingled in the midst of the flock, are the cry of the innocents, and the voice of the sheep, that call on the Shepherd of all, to deliver them from all.

\*　　\*　　\*　　\*　　\*

13. There is a joy that is affliction, misery is hidden in it; there is a misery that is profit, it is a fountain of joys, in that new world.

14. The happiness that my persecutor has gained, woes are hidden in it; therefore I rejoice. The wretchedness that I have gained from him, happiness is concealed for me in it.

15. Who will not give praise, to Him that has begotten us, and can beget again, from the midst of evil rumours, the voices of glad tidings!

16. Thou Healer of all, hast visited me in my sicknesses! Payment for Thy medicines, I cannot give Thee, for they are priceless.

17. Thy mercies in richness, surpass Thy medicines: they cannot be bought, they are given freely, it is for tears they are bartered.

18. How, O my Master, can a desolate city, whose king is far off, and her enemy nigh, stand firm without *aid* of mercy?

19. A harbour and refuge, art Thou at all times. When the seas covered me, Thy mercy descended and drew me out. Again let Thy help lay hold on me!

20. Apply to my afflictions, the medicine of Thy salvation, and the passion of Thy help! Thy sign can become, a medicine to heal all.

21. I am greatly oppressed, and I hasten to complain, against him that troubles me. Let Thy mercy, my Lord, take the bitterness from the cup, that my sins have mixed.

22. I look on all sides, and weep that I am desolate. Very many though be my chiefs and my deliverers, one is He that has delivered me.

23. My young men have fled, O Lord, and gone forth, and are like chickens, which an eagle pursues; lo! they hide in a secret place: may Thy peace bring them back!

24. The sound of my grape-gatherers, lo! my ears miss it, for their voices fail. Let it

resound with the glad tidings, O Blessed One of Thy salvation !

25. A voice of terror, I have heard on my towers ; as my defenders cry, while they guard my walls. Still Thou it with the voice of peace !

26. The noise of my husbandmen, shall speak peace without my walls : the shouting of my dwellers shall speak peace within my walls, that I may give peace without and within.

27. Make an end, O Lord, of the mourning, of this Thy pure altar, and of Thy chaste priest, who stands clothed in mourning, covered over with sackcloth !

28. The Church and her ministers shall give praise for Thy salvation ; the city and its dwellers. Be the voice of peace, O Lord, the reward of their voices !

## V.

1. Cause to be heard in Thy grace, the tidings of Thy salvation: for an hearing has been made, a path of passage; our minds have been downtrodden, by messages of terror.  *R., Praises to Thy victory ! Glory to Thy Dominion !*

2. Comfort Thou with profits, *though* small and scanty, those that have had harvest, of hurt by their labour : at a time of profit, they have gained *but* loss.

3. It is manifest that He has stood, portioning wrath upon earth: loss and profit in anger He divided. There are whom He has cast down of a sudden, and there are whom He has puffed up of a sudden.

4. To teach *us* that He can, chastise in all ways; when He saw the persecutors, were terrible before mine eyes, He laid me out before my children, and they my beloved chastised me.

5. Lo ! He taught me to fear, Himself and not man: for when there was none to smite us, His wrath gave command of a sudden, and every man stretched himself out, and chastised himself.

6. In like manner that Babylonian, who struck down all kings when he was confi-

dent and hoped that there was none to smite him, God caused that by his own hands. he should strike himself down.

7. His majesty and his mind, of a sudden became mad together: he rent and cast off his garments ; he went forth and wandered in the desert ; he drove himself out first, and then his servants drove him out.

8. He showed to all kings, whom he had led captive and brought down, that not by his own power, could he have overcome : the power that struck him down, was that which punished them.

9. I have stood and borne, O my Lord ; the blows of my deliverers. Thou art able in Thy grace, to make me profit by the smiters: Thou art able in Thy justice to punish me by *my* helpers.

10. The day when the host was bold, to come up against Samaria; their plenty and their pleasure, their treasures and their possessions, they cast away and forsook and fled. He crowned her by her persecutors.

11. My beloved ones crowned me, and my deliverers healed me. Through the guilt of my dwellers, my helpers chastised me, give me drink from Thy vines, of the cup of consolation !

12. The corn and the vine, preserve, O my Lord, by Thy grace! Be the husbandman cheered, by the vine of the grape-gatherer ; be the vinedresser glad, in the corn of the husbandman !

13. They are joined each to each, the corn and the grape. In the field the reapers, wine can make cheerful, in the vineyard the dressers, bread strengthens in turn.

14. These two things have power, to comfort my troubles : the Trinity has power, to comfort more exceedingly; whom I will praise because of a sudden, I was delivered through grace.

15. But the man whose life, is preserved through grace, if he goes away to murmur, at the loss of his goods, he is thankless for the grace, of Him who had pity on him.

16. Of His own will He destroys, one

thing instead of another. He destroys possession, and spares the possessor : He destroys our plants, instead of our lives.

17 Let us fear to murmur, lest His own wrath be roused, and He spare the possessions, and smite the possessor; that we may learn in the end, His mercy in the beginning.

18. Let us learn against whom, it is meet for us to murmur. Learn thou to murmur, not against the Chastener, but against thine own will, that made thee sin and thou wast punished.

19. Let us put away murmuring, and turn unto prayer : for it the possessor dies, his possessions also cease for him; but while he survives, he seeks to recover his losses.

20. Let consolations be multiplied, in mercy to my dwellers : let the remainder and residue, console us in the midst of wrath; and cause Thou us to forget in the residue, the mourning of our devastation !

21. Heal and increase O my Lord, the fruits Thy wrath has left ! They seem to me like sick ones, that have escaped in pestilence. Make me to forget in these weak ones, the suffering of the many !

22. While I speak, O my Lord, I call to mind that this too is the month, when the blossom pined, and dropped off in blight, may it return to soundness, to be a consolation !

23. For these escaped the pestilence, that carried off their brethren. The vines though voiceless, wept when before them, a multitude was cut down and felled, of trees that they loved.

24. The company of plants, lo ! the earth misses ! The roots for the husbandmen, weep and cause them to weep. Their beauty had spread and gave shade, and it was torn away in one hour.

25. The axe came nigh and struck ; and struck the husbandman; the blow was on the trees, and it caused the husbandman to suffer; every axe that smote, he bore the pain of it.

## VI.

1. I will run in my affections, to Him who heals freely. He who healed my sorrows, the first and the second, He who cured the third, He will heal the fourth. R., Heal me, Thou Son the First Born !

2. My sons, O my Lord, drank and were drunken, of the tidings which wrath had mixed ; and they rushed on my adornments, and spoiled and cast away my ornaments ; they rent and spared not, my garments and my crowns.

3. They uncovered me and I was made bare. Because I was shamed a little, by means of that stripping, the first and the second, because I was shamed a third time, lo ! they have stripped me a fourth time.

4. For they have seized and taken away my garments, my ornaments and my gardens. On the sackcloth that girds my altar, look Thou, O my Lord, and have pity on me ! Let the sackcloth be to me, O my Lord, the breastplate of salvation !

5. Lo ! it is not by the hand of the chaste, that Thou hast chastised me, O my Master ! For lo ! his shame is before him, and behind him his disgrace ; for as to his marriage, adultery is better than it.

6. Lo ! his daughter is his wife, and his sister his consort; and his mother whence he came forth, he turns again and takes her to wife ! The heavens are astonished that thus, he provokes Thee, and lo ! he prospers.

7. And though, O my Lord, my crimes are many, are my offences so heavy, that Thou shouldst make over a chaste woman, mother of chaste daughters, to foul Assyria, mother of defiled daughters ?

8. Restrain him that he come not, and wag at me his head, and stamp on me his heel, and rejoice that the voice of his fame, thus troubles the world; and be uplifted yet a little !

9. My sons, O my Lord, have seen my nakedness, yea have uncovered me and wept. Uncover Thou me before my children, who are pained by my pain, and let

not those mock at me, the accursed that *have* no pity!

10. My lands had brought forth fruits and pleasant things; good things in the vineyard, abundance in the fields. But as I rested secure, of a sudden wrath overtook *me*.

11. The husbandmen *were* plundered, the spoilers heaped *the grain;* what thou had borrowed and sown these destroyed. With one's debt his hunger, haply will also remain unsatisfied, for his bread *is* snatched from him.

12. The husbandman, O my Lord, *is* plundered, for he lent to the earth; she has received the deposit, and given it to a stranger; she has borrowed it of the husbandman; and paid it to the spoiler.

13. Be jealous over me who am Thine, and to Thee, O my Lord: am I betrothed! The Apostle who betrothed me to Thee, told me that Thou art jealous. For *as a* wall to chaste *wives* is the jealousy of their husbands.

14. Samson stirred up seas, because he was mightily jealous over his wife, though she was greatly defiled, and was divided against him. Keep Thy Church, for no other, has she beside Thee!

15. Whoso is not jealous, over his spouse despises her. Jealousy it is that can make known, the love that is within. Thou art called jealous, that thou mayest show me Thy love.

16. The nature of woman is this; it is weak and rash: it is jealousy keeps it, under fear every hour. Thou hast been named among the jealous, that Thou mightest make known Thy solicitude.

17. Every man has been master, of something that *was* not his own; every man has gone forth gathering, something that he scattered not. The day of confusion, I have prepared for myself by my crimes.

18. How shall they bear the suffering, the labourers and tillers? In the face of the vinedresser, they have cut down the vines and driven away the flocks of the husbandman; his sowing they have reaped and carried off.

19. They had yoked cattle sown and harrowed, they had ploughed, planted, nurtured. They stood afar and wept; and they went away bereft of all. The labour *was* for the toilers, the increase for the spoilers.

20. The rulers, O my Lord, maintained not, order in the midst of *Thy* wrath. If they had willed *it* they might have kept order, but our iniquity suffered it not. Though wrath had greatly abated, wrath compelled *them* to spoil.

21. To whom on any side, shall I look for comfort, for my plantations that are laid low, and my possessions that are laid waste? Let the message of the voice of peace, drive away my sadness from me!

22. Give me not over; lest it be thought that Thou, hast given me a writing of divorce, and sent me away and driven me out! Let them not call me, O my Lord, the forsaken and the disgraced!

23. I have not anything, to call to mind before Thine eyes, for I am wholly despised. Call Thou to mind for me, O my God, this only that none other, have I set before me beside Thee!

24. Who would not weep for me, with voice and wailing? for before the days of full *moon* I was chaste and crowned; and after the days of full moon, I was uncovered and made bare.

25. My chaste daughters of the chambers, wander in the fields; for the wrath that makes all drunken, has caused my honourable women to be despised. Let Thy mercy which gives peace to all, restore these beloved ones to honour!

26. My elder *daughters* and my younger, lo! they cry before Thee; the damsels with their voices, they that are aged with their tears; my virgins with their fasts, my chaste ones with their sackcloth!

27. Mine eyes to all the streets, I lift up and lo! they are deserted. There are left of a hundred ten, and a thousand of ten thousand. Give Thou peace and fill my streets, with the tumult of my dwellers!

28. Bring back them that are without, and make them glad that are within! Mighty is Thy grace, that Thou extendest it within and without. Let the wings of Thy grace gather my chickens together!

29. Let the prayer of my just men, save my fugitives! The unbelievers have plundered me, and the believers have sustained me. In them that believe put Thou to shame them that believe not!

30. There came together on one day, two festivals as one : the Feast of Thine Ascension, and the Feast of Thy Champions ; the feast that wove Thy Crown, and the memorial of the crowning of Thy servants.

31. Have thou mercy because there were doubled for us, *these* feasts on one day ; and there were doubled for us instead of them, *even* the two feasts in one, suffering from the voice of *ill* tidings, and mourning from desolation!

32. Give peace to my festivals! for both my feasts have ceased ; and instead of rejoicing, *of* my remnants in festivals, tremblings and desolations meet me in every place.

33. Bring home mine that are far off, make glad mine that are nigh ; and in the midst of our land shall be preached, good tidings of joy ; and I shall render in return for peace, praise from every mouth!

## VII.

1. Wrath came to rebuke, the greedy who in the midst of peace, bargained, defrauded and plundered. In calamity the greedy have waxed rich : lo! what was theirs they have scattered, what was not theirs they have gathered. *R., Give peace, O Son, to our land!*

2. Twenty years my troubles, have been like branches, O my Saviour! which are kept back throughout winter, but when it is time to shoot forth, my troubles shoot forth : with our fruit our heart ripens.

3. Nisan is the time of buds : in it the *ill*

tidings budded. When our delights crowded on us, then crowded on us our ills. At the time of winnowing of wheat, came the winnowing of cities.

4. For the three brethren in Babylon fled not from the fire that men kindled, because they were steadfast : from lust they fled, because they were perfect.

5. The fire of them that have triumphed, is able to turn the black kids into white : the fire of vain men is able to make the lambs into spotted leopards.

6. How great will be my cries, to be cried at any alarm! How great my indignation to ripen at every ill tidings! How great my harvests, to perish every month!

7. For the crimes of my sons He has chastened me, in their struggling for my deliverance. The people who deliver me, bring chastisement upon me. Restrain ye your sins, and lo! my chastisements are restrained!

8. In ill tidings they are afflicted ; in time of wrath they are tortured ; in time of peace they are distressed ; for when every man breathes freely, and *all* are unthankful for grace, they render *thanks* on behalf of every man.

9. Their sackcloth *is* humble for my sake ; their ashes *are* sprinkled in my affliction ; their prayer *is* for my victory ; their fast for my deliverance. Lo! the debt is on my ascetics, the guilt with my nobles.

10. Great is in every age, the folly of the wise ; the scribes and elders envied and killed the teacher, who taught all people the Law of Moses.

11. Wisdom in this age *is* a possession that brings loss : he who has a little folly, very small *is* his guilt ; but he who has a little prudence, his iniquity passes measure.

12. They build with their words, and overthrow in their deeds ; for the teachers were many and foolish, but the mouth of the judge is both of these things, the judge and the accuser.

[Hymn VIII. is wanting, as also the earlier part of IX.]

## IX.

. . . My afflictions are as Job's. Thy justice delivered him ; let Thy grace have mercy on me !

2. In these two things is profit ; that neither should the just, be weary in supplication, nor should the rebellious, multiply transgression.

3. With the sons Thou labourest, to chastise and help *them ;* and that the fathers should not be grieved, by the sound of the scourge, they left me in peace.

4. Look, O my Lord, on my woods without, how they have been cut down ! behold, O my Lord, my breasts within, that they are *too* weak, for me to bear my beloved ones !

5. With swords they have cut off, my wings that are without ; again the fire kindles, in my bosom within, the incense of burnt offering.

6. The sun-worshippers have killed, my sons in the plain : and they that offer to Baal, have sacrificed my bulls in the city, my sheep with my babes.

7. In my fields is lamentation ; in my halls wailing ; in my vineyards terror ; in my streets confusion. Who can suffice for me ?

8. The Evil One who dealt treacherously, and disturbed me with his words, stirred up trouble within, so that my inward part, is wholly as my outward part.

9. With what face, O my Lord, shall I call on Thee to send, a camp of holy ones, to guard my bosom, which is full of uncleanness ?

10. With Thy new leaven, Thou hast chastened creation. Make Thou the old leaven, which ensnares and humbles, to be like the new leaven !

11. By the manifest striving, of Thy power let us conquer ; lest error should crown, those that strive for Thee, cleaving *to them* with blandishment !

12. If we look into our time, it is like our deceit ; [1]—for in the years of truthfulness, we practised divinations,—and secretly used enchantments.

13. If I look into the time, it provokes and into light,—brings secret things, that our deceit may be shamed,—which wore the raiment of Truth.

14. Verily it is truth, that overcomes all ; [2]—and the sea with its bitterness, cannot trouble it,—for it is pure in its nature.

15. In wisdom Thou hast made it, O my Lord, that it has laid bare our lust.—That the foolish should come to nought, and should not be encouraged,—*Truth* has withheld the crown.

16. On the tottering walls, whereon Thou hast given me victory,—the unthankful repay Thee, with sacrifice and libation, which provoke Thee openly.

17. If it were at that time, sacrifices had been offered ;—there had been room even, for delusion to suppose,—that in these I was delivered.

18. Through the multitude of deliverances, Thou hast rebuked two things :—the delusion of graven images, and the teaching of magicians ;—for in Thee, O my Lord, have I been delivered !

---

[1] An attempt is here made to represent by means of dashes the metrical versification of the Syriac hymns. See above, pp. 147 sq.
[2] 1 Esdr.

## X.

1. My children have been slain ; and my daughters *that are* without me,—their walls are overthrown, their children scattered,—and their holy places trodden down. *R.*, *Blessed is Thy chastisement !*

2. The fowlers have taken, my doves out of my strongholds,—which quitted their nests, and fled to the caves ;—in the net have they taken them.

3. After the manner of wax, that melts before the fire,—thus melted and dissolved, the bodies, of my sons before the heat—and the drought of my strongholds.

4. And instead of streams, of milk that used to flow,—for my sons and my little ones, milk fails the sucklings, and water the weaned children.

5. The suckling falls, from its mother and gasps,—because it cannot suck, nor can she give suck :—they breathe out their spirit and die.

6. How is it possible, that Thy grace can refrain—the welling of its stream, when it is not possible to restrain—the abundance of its flow ?

7. And why has Thy grace, shut up its mercies,—and withheld its streams, from the people that cry,—for one to moisten their tongue ?

8. And there was a pit, between them and their brethren ;—like the rich man who cried, and there was none to answer,—to moisten his tongue.

9. And as into the midst of fire, the wretched ones were cast ;—and heat in the midst of thirst, the fire was blowing,—and kindling upon them.

10. Their carcases were melted, and dissolved by the heat ;—they that had thirsted gave in turn the earth to drink,—of the reek of their bodies.

11. And the fort that with thirst, had killed, its dwellers,—it drank in its turn of the flux from the corpses,—that were melted by thirst.

12. Who has seen a people—that were burning with thirst,—while there surrounded them a wall of water and they could not—moisten their tongue !

13. Surely with the judgment of Sodom, were my beloved judged,—and my children smitten, with the torment of Sodom ;—though that was but *for* one day.

14. The torment of fire, though it be *for* one hour, O my Lord,—in lingering thirst, is a lingering death, and a subtle punishment.

15. After my sorrows, O my Lord, and my bitter sufferings,—this is the best comfort, wherewith Thou hast comforted me,—that Thou hast multiplied my afflictions.

16. The medicine that I hoped, it is sorrow decreed ;—the binding up that I looked for, it is bitter calamity,—that it seeks to work for me.

17. And whereas I hoped to escape, from the midst of the storm ;—worse for me is the storm in it, even in the harbour,—than that in the sea.

18. Whereas I thought in my folly, that I should anchor and escape—from the midst of the Gulf ; my sins have cast me back—again into the midst of it.

19. Look, O my Lord, on my limbs, how the swords are thick in me,—and have left *their* mark on my arms ; and the scars of the spears,—are planted in my sides !

20. Tears in mine eyes, and in my ears *ill* rumours,—wailing in my mouth, and mourning in my heart !—Add no more, O my Lord, to me !

## XI.

1. Thy chastening is, *as* a mother of our infancy :—her rebuke is merciful, in that Thou hast restrained,—the children from folly, and they have been made wise !    *R.,* *Glory* be *to thy justice !*

2. Let us search out Thy justice ; for who is sufficient—to measure its help ? since by it the wanton—are oftentimes made chaste.—

3. Oftentimes Thy hand, O my Lord, has made the sick whole,—for it is the healer in secret of their diseases,—and the fount of their life.

4. Exceeding gently, the finger of Thy justice,—in love and compassion, touches the wounds—of him that is to be healed.

5. Exceeding mild and merciful, is her cutting to him that is wise :—her sharp remedy, in its mighty love,—consumes the corrupt *part.*

6. Exceeding welcome her wrath, to him that is discerning ;—but her remedies are hated, of the fool who has delight—in the trouble of his limbs.

7. Exceeding eager is she, to bind the cut she has made ;—when she has smitten she pities, that from between these two—she may breed healing.

8. Exceeding welcome her wrath, and her anger pleasant,—and sweet her bitterness, sweetening bitter things—that they may be made pleasant.

9. A cause of negligence is Thy indulgence to the careless ;—a cause of profit, is Thy rod among the slothful—so that they become *as* traffickers.

10. The cause of our affliction, it is Thy justice ;—the cause of our carelessness, it is Thy graciousness,—for our understanding has turned foolish.

11. Pharaoh hardened himself, because of Thy graciousness ;—for when the plagues were stayed, his cruelties waxed strong,—and he lied to his promises.

12. Justice requited him, because he lied greatly against her,—even *Grace* her free-born sister ; yea she restrained him again—that he should not again provoke.

13. Rebuke, O my Lord, my guide, for it has been false as Egypt !—my prayers testify, that I am not as she,—for Thy door have I not forsaken.

14. Let Thy cross, O my Lord, which stands, in my breaches that are open,—repair again the *breaches* that are hidden ; for instead of those without,—those within have cleft me asunder !

15. A sea has broken through, and cast down, the watch tower wherein I had triumphed.—Iniquity has dared to set up, a temple wherein I am shamed : its drink-offering chokes me.

16. My prayers on my walls, my persecutors have heard :—the sun and his worshippers, are ashamed of their magicians,—for I have triumphed by Thy cross.

17. *All* creatures cried out, when they saw the struggle,—while Truth with falsehood, on my battered walls, fought and was crowned conqueror.

18. The force of Truth, chastised falsehood :—in its chastisement it felt *Truth,* and through its *own* sins, it earned her victory.

19. I have great alarm ; for since my deliverance,—the honourable and mighty, who were devoted to my altar, have built in me high places.

20. My seven senses, O my Lord, even though they had been as fountains of tears, yet my tears were *too* little—to lament our ruin.

21. The streets that *were* in sackcloth, and ashes cried out,—disturbed by the play, akin to that which *was,*—in the wilderness before the calf.

22. Poison seeks and wears, the beauty of lilies ;—and though their buds may conceal, and hidden disguise it,—it blossoms in their bitter flowers.

## XII.

1. I will call in my affliction, on the Power that subdues all;—that is able to subdue, the Captor in his wrath,—as it overcame Legion.     *R., Glory to His grace!*

2. The Evil One has repaid me my brethren, debts that he borrowed not of me :—
the good *God* likewise has repaid me, mercies that I lent Him not.—Come and marvel
ye at these two things!

3. The good *God* has divided and given, my misdeeds to His grace,—my offences
to His justice ; His mercy has blotted out my misdeeds—His judgment has requited
my offences.

4. Sin was exceeding wroth, and abode in alarm,—when she saw how grace, put
restraint on freedom, that she might overcome transgressions.

5. Glow Thou, O my Lord, and send down Thy love, break out and pour forth Thy
wrath !—Thy wrath to destroy, Thy love to rescue—the captives from the captor !

6. The days wherein the Evil One, decreed to cast me forth,—as with a sling into
perdition, in them the good God has bound up and kept—my soul in the bundle of
life.

7. The men of speech who keep not silence, from praising continually,—who
have kept me in the midst of waves, and supported me that I fell not, let them give
praise in my stead, O my Lord !

8. For who has at any time sufficed, in presence of the grace,—of the mercies
which surrounded him, that I should suffice to praise—the mercies that encompass
me ?


## XIII.

### Concerning Mar Jacob and his Companions.

1. Three illustrious priests, after the manner of the two great lights,—have carried
on and handed down one to another, the See and the Hand and the Flock.—To us
whose mourning was great for the two, this last *is* wholly a consolation.     *R., Glory
to Thee Who didst choose them !*

2. He Who created two great lights, chose for Himself *these* three Lights,—and set
them in the three dark seasons of siege that have been.—When *that* pair of Lights
was quenched, the other shone wholly forth.

3. These three priests were treasures, who held in their faithfulness,—the key of the
Trinity ; three doors they opened for us ;—each one of them with his key, unlocked
and opened his door.

4. In the first was opened the door, for the chastisement that befel us ;—in the
next was opened the door, for the King's power that came down on us,—in the last
was opened the door, for the good tidings that came up for us.

5. In the first was opened the door, for battle between two hosts ;—in the next
were opened doors, for the kings from either wind ;—in the last was opened the door,
for ambassadors from either side.

6. In the first was opened the door, for battle because of misdeeds ;—in the next
was opened the door,—for the kings because of strife ;—in the last was opened the
door, for ambassadors because of mercies.

7. Lo ! in these three successions, as in a mystery and a figure,—wrath is likened
to the sun : it began under the first ;—it waxed strong under the next ; it sank and
was quenched under the last.

8. Three figures the Sun also, shows forth in the three quarters :—its rising *is* keen and bright; its meridian strong and overpowering ;—and like a torch that is burnt out, its setting *is* mild and pleasant.

9. Small yet bright *is* its rising, when it comes to waken sleepers ;—hot and over-powering its meridian, when it comes to ripen the fruits ;—tender and pleasant its set-ting, when it reaches its consummation.

10. Who is this daughter born of vows, enviable above all women,—whose succes-sions thus proceed, and her ranks are thus manifold,—and her degrees thus ascend, and her teachers thus excel.

11. Do these similitudes belong, only to the daughter of Abraham,—or to thee too, O daughter, born of vows, whose adorning is according as thy beauty ?—for as thine occasion, *so was* thy help, and as thy help *so was* its minister.

12. According to the measure of her need, there came to her the supply of her need.—Her fathers were as *was* her birth ; her teachers were as *was* her understanding ;—her training as *was* her growth ; her raiment as *was* her stature.

13. Grace weighed out *to her* and gave all these things as in the scales ;—she laid them in *her* balance, that therefrom there might be profit ;—she drew them into suc-cession, that therefrom might be perfection.

14. In the days of him that *was* first, peace abounded and peace vanished ;—in the days of him that was next, kings came down and kings went back ;—but in the days of the last, hosts assailed and hosts retreated.—

15. By the first order came in, it came in with him and went out with him ;—by the next the diadem that gladdened our churches, came nigh and withdrew far away ;—but by the last there dawned on us, grace that was not thankfully received.

16. Against the wrath that was first, the labour of the first contended ;—against the heat that was at noon, the shade of the second stood up ;—against peace that was thankless, the last multiplied warnings.

17. For the first invader of the land *was* the first and illustrious priest ;—for the sec-ond invader of the land, was the second and merciful priest :—but the prayers of him that was last, repaired our breaches secretly.

18. Nisibis is set [3] upon waters, waters secret and open :—living streams *are* within her ; a noble river without her. The river without deceived her ; the fountain within has saved her.

19. The first priest was her vinedresser ; he made her branches to grow even unto heaven.—Lo ! being dead and buried within her, he has become fruit in the midst of her bosom :—when therefore the pruners came, the fruit that *was* in her midst preserved her.

20. The time of her pruning came ; it entered and took from her her vinedresser,—that there should not be one to pray for her. She made haste in her subtlety ;—He laid in her bosom her vinedresser, that she should be delivered through her vine-dresser.

21. Be ye wise like Nisibis, O ye daughters of Nisibis,—for that she laid the body within her, and it became a wall without her.—Place ye within you the living body, that it be a wall for your lives !

---

[3] The verb is *n'sab*,—a play on the name of the city.

## XIV.

1. Under the three pastors,—there were manifold shepherds ;—the one mother that *was* in the city,—had daughters in all regions.—Since Wrath has destroyed her dwellings,—Peace shall build up her churches.      *R. Blessed be He who chose out those three !*

2. The kindly labour of the first,—bound up the land in her affliction :—the bread and wine of the next,—healed the city when she was broken :—the sweet speech of the last,—sweetened our bitterness in affliction.

3. The first tilled the land with his labour,—he rooted out of her the briars and thorns :—the next fenced her round about,—he made a hedge for her of them that were saved :—the last opened the garner of his Lord,—and sowed in her the words of her Lord.

4. The first priest by means of a fast,—closed up the doors of *men's* mouths :—the second priest for the captives,—opened the mouths of the purse :—but the last pierced through the ears,—and fastened in them the ornament of life.

5. Aaron stripped off from the ears,—the earrings and made a calf.—That lifeless calf in secret,—pierced and slaughtered the camp :—those who had fashioned his horns, —he ripped them up with his horns.

6. But our priest *who was* the third,—pierced through the ears of the heart :—and fastened *there* the earrings he had fashioned,—of the nails that were fixed in the cross, —whereon his Lord was crucified,—and gave life to His fellow-men.

7. A son unto death the fire brought forth ;—Death feeds upon all bodies :—the son of Death who surpassed Death,—upon the souls of men he fed.—The calf forsook his provender,—for *men's* minds were the food for him.

8. To the first Tree that which killed,—to it grace brought forth a son,—O Cross offspring of the Tree,—that didst fight against thy sire !—The Tree was the fount of death ;—the Cross was the fount of life.

9. The son that was born to Death,—all mouths were opened to curse him.—He devoured bodies and souls,—and multiplied the disgrace of his father.—But the Cross caused to pass away the rebuke,—of its father that first Tree.

10. The two sons were even as were—the *two* mothers that bare them.—The calf which the fire brought forth,—the fire consumed in the midst of the people :—the Cross the offspring of grace,—divided good gifts to *all* creation.

11. O my tongue hold thy peace and be silent of the histories of the Cross that press *to be told !*—for my mind of a sudden has conceived,—and lo ! pangs of travail smite it :—it has conceived these among the last,—and they strive to become the firstborn.

12. The babes struggled in the womb ;—the elder made haste to come forth :—the younger desiring the birthright,—laid his hand upon his heel ;—that which he obtained not by birth,—he obtained by the mess of pottage.

13. After the like sort these later histories,—lo ! they make light of the former *ones*, —that *themselves* may come forth and take the birthright.—Let us bring forth the history of our fathers,—for lo ! the histories of the Cross—*are* the firstborn of *all* creatures.

14. For if that which has no beginning—is the first of all created things,—its histories also are the firstborn,—for they are elder than *all* creatures.—Let the histories of Thee, O my Lord, yield place,—that we may tell of Thy ministers !

15. The first in degree of doctrine,—His eloquence was like as *was* his degree ;—the next who was second in degree,—his interpretation mounted to the height of his degree ;—the last who was third in degree,—his eloquence was great as he *was*.

16. The first in his simple words,—gave milk unto his infants ;—the next in his plain sayings,—gave victual to his children ;—the third in his perfect sayings,—gave meat to his *that were* of perfect age.

17. She too the daughter of instruction,—mounted from degree to degree,—along with her teachers and fathers.—A young child she was with the first ; a simple *maid* was she with the next ;—she came to perfect age in the third.

18. The first *dealing* with her as a child,—loved her and taught her to fear ;—the next as with a damsel, rebuked her and make her glad ;—the third as with one fully instructed,—was to her a solace of pleasantness.

19. Even the Most High with the daughter of Jacob,—*gave* blandishment and the rod to her childhood ;—and in her frowardness and full age,—gave part in the sword and the Law ; —and according to her discipline and instruction,—He came to her in mildness and pleasantness.

20. The first that begat the flock,—his bosom bare her infancy ;—the next of gladsome countenance,—cheered with song and made glad her childhood ;—the last grave of countenance,—lo ! he guards *her* chastity in her youth.

21. The first priest who begat *her*,—gave milk to her infancy ;—the next priest interpreted,—and gave victual to her childhood ;—the third priest nourished *her*, and gave meat to her perfect age.

22. The wealthy father who *was* first,—laid up treasures for her childhood ;—the next for her maturity—multiplied provision for her journey ;—the third the goodly olive tree,—multiplied oil in her vessels.

23. When she comes before Him who is rich,—she will show the treasure of the first ;—when she comes before the Saviour, she will show the saved ones of the next ;—when she goes forth to meet the Bridegroom,—she will show the oil of her lamps.

24. Before Him who rewards the weary toilworn,—she will offer the labour of the first ;—before Him who loves *cheerful* givers,—she will show the almsgiving of the next ;—before Him who judges doctrines,—she will offer the discourse of the last.

25. And I the sinner who have striven to be—the disciple of these three,—when they shall see Him of the Third Day,—that he has closed the door of His chamber,—may these three pray *Him* for me, that He keep the door *open* a little while for me !

26. May the sinner press into and enter—rejoicing and fearing to behold !—May the three masters call in—the one disciple in *their* grace !—May he gather up under the table—the crumbs that are full of life !

## XV.

1. If the head had not been right,—haply the members had murmured :—for when because of a perverse head—the course of the members is put astray,—they are wont to lay the blame on the head.  *R. Blessed be He who chose thee the pride of our people !*

2. If now on one that is all goodly,—on it we lay our hatred ;—how much *more* if we were hateful !—Yea even God though He is kind,—bitter men complain against Him.

3. Be like the head O ye members !—Get repose in his purity—and pleasantness in his tranquillity ;—in his sanctity renown,—and in his wisdom learning !

4. Get discernment in his mildness,—and chastity in his gravity,—and bounty in his poverty !—As he is fully and altogether fair,—let us be altogether fair with him !

5. See ye how meted and weighed—are his words and his actions !—Take heed how even his steps—keep the measure of peace !—With all his might he holds the bridle of all himself.

6. He was master over his youth ;—he bound it in the yoke of chastity :—his members were not enticed *by lust ;*—for they were kept under the rod :—his will he had in subjection.

7. For he was ready beforehand for his degree,—as he was ready beforehand in his conversation,—as he laid his foundations securely.—He became Head in his youth,—when they made him preacher to the people.

8. Excellent was he among preachers,—learned was he among scholars,—and understanding was he among the wise :—chaste was he among his brethren,—and grave among his familiar friends.

9. In two abodes was he—a solitary recluse from *his early* days ;—for he was holy within his body,—and solitary within his dwelling ;—openly and secretly was he chaste.

10. But although we my brethren—have put astray those measures,—and we have lost that savour,—and have become teachers to ourselves,—unto the perfection that called us.

11. Yet that measure of Truth—preserves itself in its vessel :—*Truth* chose it because she saw it chose her ;—she has preserved in it her fragrance and savour,—from the beginning to the end.

12. The Head both chaste and grave,—that was not wrathful nor hard,—nor transgressed even as we *did*,—set and kept his own measures,—and cast a bridle on his thoughts.

13. He gave example in his person,—that as he kept the measure of his time,—*so* was it meet that we should know our time.—We have become strangers to our time,—for we have been witless in the time of discernment.

14. In the beginning the blast of the wind—in its might chastens the fruit·;—then in the meantime the might of the sun :—but when its mightiness is passed,—its end gathers his sweetness.

15. But we—they that were first chastened us ;—and also they that came next rebuked us ;—and they that were last added sweetness to us :—then when the time of tasting *us* arrives,—great was our savourlessness.

16. For we came to maturity,—that we might wean the children from wantonness,—and lead them to gravity :—*but* our old age stood in need—that we should be rebuked as youths.

17. Accordingly he in kindness endured, nor did he make use of force,—that he might increase honour to our old age :—and even if it knew not its degree,—let him be magnified who knew its time !

18. And if one say that for the multitude,—force and the rod should govern it ;—even *as* for the thief fear,—and for the spoiler threatening,—and for fools open shaming.

19. Yet if with the head as first,—the members had hasted *to move* as second,—they would have drawn that which was third,—and the whole body from the end—would have followed after them.

20. They that *were* second despised those that *were* first,—and that *were* third those that *were* second :—the degrees were set at naught one by another.—While these within despised one another,—they were trodden down likewise by those without.

## XVI.

1. Herein *is* a mirror to be blamed,—if its clearness is darkened—because there are spots on its substance ;—for the foulness that is on it becomes—a covering before them that look on it.    *R. Blessed be He Who polished our mirror !*

2. For that comeliness is not adorned in it,—and blemishes are not brought to view in it,—it is altogether a damage to comely things ;—seeing that their comeliness gain not—adornments as *their* profit.

3. Blemishes are not rooted out by it,—likewise adornments are not multiplied by it.—A blemish that remains is as a loss ;—that there is no adornment is a defect :—loss is met together with defect.

4. If our mirror *be* darkness,—it is altogether joy to the hateful ;—because their blemishes *are* not reproved :—but if polished and shining,—it is our freedom that is adorned.

5. Twofold is the loss in defect,—for the hateful and for the goodly ;—in that the goodly gain no crown,—and likewise the hateful get no adorning :—the mirror divides the loss.

6. Never does the mirror drive—by compulsion him that looks therein :—so likewise grace which followed—upon the righteousness of the Law,—does not possess the compulsion of the Law.

7. Righteousness was unto childhood,—its adorner of compulsion ;—for when mankind was in childhood,—she adorned it by compulsion,—while she robbed it not of its freedom.

8. Righteousness used blandishment,—and the rod *to deal* with childhood ;—when she smote it she roused it ; her rod restrained frowardness, her blandishment softened the minds.

\*　　　\*　　　\*　　　\*　　　\*　　　\*　　　\*

9. [If one turn from the Gospel,] wherewith we are adorned to-day, my brethren,—to another gospel he is a child :—in a time of greatness of understanding,—he is become without understanding.

10. For in the degree of full age,—he has gone down to childhood ;—and he loves the law of bondmen,—which when he is confident smites him,—and when he rejoices buffets him.

11. Whatsoever ornament *is* compulsion,—is not true but is borrowed.—This is a great thing in God's eyes,—that a man should be adorned by himself :—therefore took He away compulsion.

12. For even as of *His* prudence—in its *own* time He employed compulsion,—so *likewise* of His prudence,—He took it away at a time—when gentleness was desired in its stead.

13. For as it is befitting to Youth,—that it should be made to haste under the rod ;—*so is* it very hateful that under the rod—Wisdom should be brought to serve,—that compulsion should be lord over her.

14. Behold therefore how likewise—God has ordered my successions—in the pastors I have had,—and in the teachers He has given me,—and in the fathers He has reckoned unto me !

15. For weighed out according to their times—*were* the helps of their qualities ;—namely in him in whom it was needful, fear ; and in whom it was profitable, heartening ; and in whom it was becoming, meekness.

16. By measure He made my steps advance :—to my childhood He assigned terror ; likewise to my youth, fear ;—to my *age of* wisdom and prudence,—He assigned and gave meekness.

17. In the frowardness of the degree of childhood,—*my* instructor was a fear to me : —his rod restrained me from wantonness,—and from mischief the terror of him,—and from indulgence the fear of him.

18. Another father He gave to my youth :—what there was in me of childishness, —that was there in him of hardness ; what there was in me of maturity,—that was in him *as* meekness.

19. When I rose from the degrees—of childhood and of youth,—there passed away the terror *that was* first,—there passed away the fear *that was* second ;—He gave me a kind pastor.

20. Lo ! for my full age his food ;—and for my wisdom his interpretations ;—and for my peace his meekness ;—and for my repose his kindness ;—and for my chastity his gravity !

21. Blessed is He who as in a balance—weighed out and gave me fathers :—for according to my times *were* my helps ;—and according to my sicknesses my medicines ; —and according to my comelinesses my adornments !

22. We then *are* they that have disturbed—the succession and fair order ;—for in a time of mildness—lo ! we crave for hardness,—that Thou should rebuke us as though *we were* children !

## XVII.

### Concerning Abraham, Bishop of Nisibis.

1. Suffer, O Lord, that even my lowliness, should cast into Thy treasury its farthing, even as the merchant of our flock, who made increase of his talent of Thy doctrine, and has departed and entered Thy haven. I will speak of the shepherd, under him who has become head of the flock ; who was disciple of the Three, and has become our fourth master. *R., Blessed be He Who has made him our comfort !*

2. In one love will I cause them to shine, and as a crown will I weave them, the splendid blossoms, and the fragrant flowers of the teacher and of his disciple, who remained after him as Elisha ; for the horn of his election and he was consecrated and became head, and he was exalted and became master. *R., Blessed be He Who made him chief !*

3. And they in heaven rejoiced for the flock, that by the pastor whom they fed, they feed it ; the abode of the shepherds under him rejoiced, because they saw the succession of their degrees. He took and set him as a mind in the midst of the great body of the church, and his members came round him to buy of him life, doctrine, new bread. *R., Blessed be He Who made him their treasury !*

4. He chose him from the multitude of shepherds, because he had given trial of his stedfastness ; the time tested him in the midst of the flock, and length of days proved him as a crucible ; for that he gave proof in his person, He made him a wall for many. Let thy fasting be armour to our country, thy prayer a shield to our city, let thy censer purchase reconcilement. *R., Blessed be He Who has hallowed thy sacrifices !*

5. The Pastor who has been parted from his flock, fed them on spiritual pastures, and by his exalted staff, he defended them from secret wolves. Fill thou up the room of thy master, which thirsts for the sound of his melody ; set up thyself as a pillar, in the city of the trembling people ; support her with thy prayers. *R., Blessed be He Who has made thee our pillar !*

6. He has committed the Hand to his disciple, the Throne to one that is worthy of it, the Key to one that is proved faithful, the Flock to one that has excelled. To thy hand belongs the laying-on, to thy offering propitiation, and to thy tongue consolation. May peace adorn thy Dominion; be the watchmen within and the congregations without. *R., Blessed be He Who has chosen thee for rejoicings!*

7. May thy doctrine abound, in deeds more than words! In saying few words, till Thou our land with labour, that by much tillage the scanty seed may become rich, the increase of the old seed, may come among us thirtyfold, and thy new seed sixtyfold. *R., Blessed be He Who multiplies an hundredfold!*

8. The wrath that was against thee ceases, because peace flows over thee altogether; the jealousy against thee is quenched, for thy love hourly flames forth: thou hast broken the string of envy, that it should smite none in secret; slander that confounds, to it thy ear turns not, for open truth is pleasing to thee. *R., Blessed be He Who adorned thy members!*

9. Thou shalt give counsel in the midst of thy people, like Jethro among the Hebrews; thou shalt altogether go with him, who for thy profit counsels thee, thou shalt altogether flee from him, who otherwise counsels thee: Rehoboam shall be a sign to thee; thou shalt choose counsels of profit, thou shalt refuse counsels of envy. *R., Blessed be He Who has counselled comfort!*

10. The gift that has been given thee, from on high it flew and came down: thou shalt call it by a name of man, thou shalt not bear it in another power, lest haply to its place there should come, Satan in his guile, supposing, that the sons of men have given it to thee, so that this freeborn gift should serve in bondage to man. *R., Blessed be He Who has handed down his gift!*

11. Thy master is painted in thy person; lo! his likeness is on thee altogether; parted from us one with us is he. In thee we shall see those three, the excellent ones who are parted from us. Thou shalt be unto us a wall as Jacob, and full of tenderness as Babu, and a treasury of speech as Valgesh. *R., Blessed be He Who in one has painted them!*

12. I, too, the offscouring of the flock, have not withholden aught that was meet: I have painted the similitude of these two, in the colours of these two; that the sheep may see their adornment, and the flock their beauties. And I who have become a lamb endowed with speech, unto Thee, O God of Abraham, in the posture of Abram will give Thee praise. *R., Blessed be He Who has made me His harp!*

## XVIII.

1. O thou who art made priest after thy master, the illustrious after the excellent, the chaste after the grave, the watchful after the abstinent, thy master from thee has not departed; in the living we see the deceased: for lo! in thee is his likeness painted; and impressed upon thee are his footprints, and all of him shines from all of thee. *R., Blessed be He Who in His stead has given us thee!*

2. The fruit wherein its tree is painted, bears witness concerning the root. Hitherto there has not failed us, the savour of his sweetness. His words thou showest forth in bodily act, for thou hast fulfilled them in deed. In thy conversation is painted his doctrine, in thy conduct his exposition, in thy fulfilment his interpretation. *R., Blessed be He Who has made thy lustre to excel!*

3. The last pastor who was exalted, and became head unto the members, the younger who obtained the birthright, not for price like Jacob, not in jealousy like Aaron, whose brethren the Levites envied him, *but* by love obtained he it like Moses, though he was older than Aaron. In thee thy brethren rejoiced as in him. *R., Blessed be He Who chose thee in unanimity!*

4. There is no envy or jealousy, among the members of the body; for in love they

give ear unto him, with tenderness they are visited by him. A watch tower is the head unto the members, for on every side he looks forth. Exalted is he yet meek in his graciousness, even to the feet he humbleth himself, that he may turn away harm from them. *R., Blessed be He Who instilled thy love into us !*

5. A small thing verily had this been, if by an old man apostasy were overcome. Old age in its prudence submitted ; youth in its season conquered ; for a youthful combatant endured, the hateful conflict waged, by force that was full of apostacy, which like smoke waxed and passed : with its beginning was its end. *R., Blessed be He Who blew upon it that it vanished !*

6. The voice of the cornet on a sudden, amazed and called Thee to battle. Thou wentest up like a new David, by Thee was subdued a second Goliath. Thou wast not untried in combat, for a secret warfare day by day, *Thou art waging against the Evil One.* Exercise in secret is wont to attain the crown openly. *R., Blessed be He Who chose Thee for our glory !*

7. In face of trial Job trained his body and his mind, and in temptation he was victorious. And Joseph conquered in the chamber ; Ananias and his company in the furnace, and in the midst of the den Daniel. Satan did foolishly, when in tempting, he confirmed their victory openly. *R., Blessed be He Who has multiplied shame on him !*

8. And the husbandman who apostatized and was urgent, to sow thorns with his left hand ; zealous against him was the righteous husbandman, stopped and cut off his left hand. He filled His own right hand and sowed in the heart the words of life ; and lo ! our understanding is tilled, by His prophets and His apostles. By Thee may our souls be tilled ! *R., Blessed be He Who chose Thee for our husbandman !*

9. And if so be Thy words are too little, till Thou our land with deeds, that amid much tillage, stock and root may be strengthened. Better is a goodly deed, than the hearing of ten thousand words. Thy

seed shall yield an hundredfold, and the after crop sixtyfold, yea that which grows of itself thirtyfold. *R., Blessed be He Who multiplied Thy increase !*

10. That light should be darkened it is not meet, that salt should lose its savour it is not right ; defilement for the head is not seemly, nor yet foulness for the mirror. Nor if medicines have lost their savour. sicknesses also are not cured ; and if so be the torch is quenched, the stumbling also are many. Thy light shall chase away our darkness. *R., Blessed be He Who hath made Thee our lamp !*

11. Appoint for thee scribes and judges, exactors also and dispensers, overseers also and officers : to each assign his work, lest haply by care should be rusted, or by anxiety should be distracted, the mind and the tongue, wherewith thou offerest supplication, for the expiation of all the people. *R., Blessed be He Who makes illustrious Thy ministry !*

12. That he should purge his mind, and cleanse also his tongue ; that he should purify his hands, and make his whole body to shine ; this is too little for the priest and his title, who offers the Living Body. Let him cleanse all himself at all hours ; for he stands as mediator, between God and mankind. *R., Blessed be He Who has cleansed His ministers !*

## XIX.

1. Thou who answerest to the name of Abraham, in that Thou art made father of many ; but because to Thee none is spouse, as Sarah was to Abraham,—lo ! Thy flock is Thy spouse ; bring up her sons in Thy truth ; spiritual children may they be to Thee, and the sons be sons of promise, that they may become heirs in Eden. *R., Blessed be He Who foreshowed Thee in Abraham !*

2. Fair fruit of chastity, in whom the priesthood was well pleased, youngest among Thy brethren as was the son of Jesse ; the horn overflowed and anointed Thee, the hand alighted and chose Thee, the Church

desired and loved Thee; the pure altar *is* for Thy ministry, the great throne for Thy honour, and all as one for Thy crown. *R., Blessed be He Who multiplied Thy crowning!*

3. Lo! thy flock, O blessed one, arise and visit it, O diligent one! Jacob ranged the flocks in order; range Thou the sheep that have speech, and enlighten the virgin-youths in purity, and the virgin-maids in chastity; raise up priests in honour, rulers in meekness, and a people in righteousness. *R., Blessed be He Who filled Thee with understanding!*

4. Guard thou the sheep that are whole, and visit them that are sick, and bind up them that are broken, and seek out them that are lost; feed them in the pastures of the Scriptures, and give them drink ot the spring of doctrine: let the truth be a wall unto thee, let the cross be a staff unto thee, and truthfulness be peace unto thee. *R., Blessed be He Who multiplied Thy virtues!*

5. Let there be with Thee in Thy flock, the power that was with David; for if he plucked a straying lamb, from the mouth of the lion, how meet is it for Thee, O exalted one, to be zealous to snatch from the Evil One the souls that are precious above all, for by nothing can they be bought, save by the blood of Christ! *R., Blessed be He Who was sold and bought all!*

6. Unto Moses Joshua ministered, and for the reward of his ministry, from him received the right hand. Because to an illustrious old man thou hast ministered, he too gave thee the right hand. Moses committed unto Joshua, a flock of which half were wolves; but to thee is delivered a flock, whereof a fourth yea a third is sanctified. *R., Blessed be He who adorned thy flock!*

7. Let the love of Moses abide in thee, for his love was a discerning love, his zeal a discreet zeal. When Korah and Dathan sundered themselves, he sundered the earth from beneath them; by sundering he made the sundering to cease. In Eldad and Medad he made known, that his good will was altogether this that all the people should pro-phesy. *R., Blessed be He who in His good will was reconciled!*

8. The poor estate of Elijah, Elisha loved above wealth; a poor man gave to a poor man, a gift that was great above all. Because thou hast loved the poverty, of thy master who in secret was rich, the fountain of his words shall flow from thee, that thou mayst become a harp for the Spirit, and mayst sing to thyself inwardly His good will. *R., Blessed be He who made thee His treasurer!*

9. There is none that envies thy election, for meek is thy headship; there is none angered by the rebuke, for thy word sows peace; there is none terrified by thy voice, for pleasant in thy visitation; there is none that groans against thy yoke, for it labors instead of our neck, and lightens the burden of our souls. *R., Blessed be He who chose thee for our rest*

10. Contend not with the mighty, despair not of the outcast; soften and teach the rich, exhort and win the poor; with the harsh join the forbearing, and the long suffering with the wrathful; catch them that are evil by them that are good, and them that spoil by them that give, and the defiled by means of the sanctified. *R., Blessed be He who made thee our hunter!*

11. Take to thee ten thousand medicaments, and arise and go forth among the sick; to the diseased offer medicine, and to him that is sound a preservative; not one medicine only shalt thou offer, for the sickness lest haply it be not meet: offer many remedies, that the sickness may find healing; likewise thou shalt learn experience. *R., Blessed be He who laboured to heal our wounds!*

12. May the land be according to thy desire; may the vineyard be according to thy husbandry; may the flock be in the midst of thy dwelling, and the sheep sound under thy staff! Mayest thou be a great Head, and we the jewels of thy crown! May we be beautiful in thee and thou be beautiful in us! for they are goodly each in the other, people and priest when they are

at one.    *R., Blessed be He who has sowed among us unity!*

13. Hearken to the Apostle when he saith, to that virgin whom he had espoused ; I am jealous over you with jealousy, with a jealousy verily of God, not of the flesh but of the spirit.   Be jealous therewith thou also in pureness, that He may know what she is and whose she is.   In thee may she cherish, and in thee may she love, Jesus the Bridegroom in truth.    *R., Blessed is he whose zeal is holy!*

14. As are her masters, so are her manners : for with the teacher that lags a laggard is she, and with him that is noble, excellent is she.   The Church is like unto a mirror, for according to the face that gazes into it, thus does it put on the likeness thereof.   For as is the king so also his host, and as is the priest so also his flock ; according as these are it is stamped on them. *R., Blessed be He Who stamped her in His likeness !*

15. Without a testament they departed, those three illustrious priests ; who in Testaments used to meditate, those two Testaments of God.   Great gain have they bequeathed to us, even this example of poverty. They who possessed nothing the blessed ones, made us their possessions ; the Church was their treasure.    *R., Blessed is he who possessed in them his possessions !*

16. The priest Jacob the noble, with him she was ennobled as he was : because he joined his love to his jealousy, with fear and love he was clothed.   With Babes a lover of bounty, for money she redeemed the captives.   With Valgesh a scribe of the law, her heart she opened to the Scriptures. With thee then may her profit be manifold ! *R., Blessed be He Who has magnified her merchantmen !*

## XX.

1. O virgin-youth that art become bridegroom, move to a little jealousy thy mind, towards  her who is the wife of thy youth : cut off the attachments which she had, in her girlhood with many others ; rebuke her and call together her affections, that she may know what she is and whose she is.   In thee may she desire yea love, Christ the Bridegroom of truth.    *R., Blessed be He Who betrothes her to His Only Begotten!*

2. Be jealous O husbandman against the tares, which have sprung up and entangled themselves among the wheat.   Easy is it to root up the thicket, rather than the despised          : if a slight breeze bears it, it attacks the sowing and conquers it. That which three husbandmen have sown, may it return in threefold measure ! thirty-fold  and  sixty  and  an  hundred !    *R., Blessed be He Who makes rich thine increase !*

3. A new shepherd for him it is right, that he should oversee the flock in new wise, and should know what is the number of it, and should see what are its needs.   A flock it is that was purchased with the blood, of that chief of the shepherds.   Call thou and cause to pass each sheep by its name, for it is a flock whereof the name is written, and its reckoning in the Book of life.    *R., Blessed be He Who will require the number thereof !*

4. Lo the spouse of thy Lord is with thee ! keep her from all harm, and from  men that deal corruptly, and call the congregations by their own names.   The name of her spouse is set on her ; let her not go a-whoring for another name, for she was not baptized in the name of man ; with Names wherein she was baptized let her make confession, of the Father and the Son and the Holy Spirit.    *R., Blessed be He by Whose Name she is called!*

5. The Apostle her betrother was jealous over her, that she should not be corrupted by names, yet not by names that were false, but not even by names that were true ; not by Cephas yea not by his *name.*   They who were true betrothers, set the Name of her betrothed upon her ; the false *betrothers* like whoremongers, set their own names on the flock.    *R., Glory be to Thy Name, our Creator !*

6. The stamp on living creatures, O my brethren, no man destroys openly; and a

name that is signed to a letter, no man adds to or alters: whoso effaces the stamp is a thief ; and whoso alters the name is a falsifier. The name of Christ has been altered; names of falsehood lo! have been set, upon the congregations that have been corrupted. *R., Blessed be He Who has called His flock by His Name !*

7. Look at the Prophets and Apostles, how like they are each to the other! By the Prophets the Name of God, was set on the flock of God; and by the Apostles the Name of Christ, was set on the Church of Christ. The false *betrothers also* are like one another, for by their names are called, the congregations who commit whoredom with them. *R., Blessed be He in Whose Name we were sanctified !*

## XXI.

1. John who was a torch, laid bare and rebuked the wanton ones: they made haste and quenched the torch, that they might let loose the desire of their lust. Be thou a lamp in brightness, and make the works of darkness cease, that whensoever thy doctrine shines, no man may dare at its rising, to give ear to the lusts of darkness. *R., Blessed be He Who made thee our lamp !*

2. A great blessing was hidden in it, even in the reproof of Elijah. Elisha ministered unto him and sought, a twofold reward of his ministration. Twofold glory it gave to him, for in double measure was he clad with his virtues. Thou who hast loved the reproof of Valgesh thy master rich *in gifts*, mayest thou inherit the treasure of his wisdom ! *R., Blessed be He Who makes thy Doctrine rich !*

3. May greediness be overcome by thy fasting even as by the fasting of Daniel ! May lust be confounded before thy body, like as it was confounded before Joseph ! May lust of money be overcome by thee! like as it was overcome before Simeon, Mayest thou bind on earth even as he, and loose on high after his likeness; for thy faith *is* even as his ! *R., Blessed is He Who committed to thee His ministry !*

4. Thy chastity be as Elisha's, and thy celibacy Elijah's, the covenant with thine eyes as Job's, thy tender mercies as David's; without envy as Jonathan, thy firmness *as* Jeremiah's, thy gentleness the Apostles' ! Thine be the ancient things of the prophets, thine the new things of the Apostles, *R., Blessed be He Who filled thee with their treasures !*

5. Be a crown to the priesthood, and in thee be the ministry made to shine ! Be a brother to the elders, likewise an overseer to the deacons; be a master to youth, a staff and a hand to old age ; be a wall to the consecrated virgins. In thy conversation may the covenant prevail, and the Church in thy comeliness be adorned. *R., Blessed be He Who chose thee to be priest !*

6. In thy poverty be brought to nought, the hateful custom of the house of Gehazi ; in thy sanctity be abolished, the abominable custom of the house of Eli; in thy unity be done away, the treacherous greeting of the lips of Iscariot the deceiver ! Pour forth all our thought, and form it anew from the beginning ! *R., Blessed be He Who in thy crucible refines us !*

7. In thy conversation let Mammon be put to shame, who has been lord over our freedom ! Let the disease be done away from us, which is customary with us and pleasant to us ; abolish the causes that have maintained, customs that are full of harm ! Evil things have possessed us through custom: let good things possess us through custom ! Be thou, O Lord, the cause of help to us. *R., Blessed be He Who chose Thee in order to our life!*

8. Let evil customs be cut off: let not the Church possess wealth ; that she be sufficed let her possess souls, and if thus she be sufficed *let it* be in marvellous measure ! And let not her deceased be buried in the cutting off of hope heathenishly, with vestments and wailing and lamentation ; for the living is clothed in raiment, but the deceased his all is a coffin. *R., Blessed be He Who to our dust turns us again !*

9. A cause of evil is the lust, also the

greediness of the house of Eli, and the thievishness of the house of Gehazi, and the reviling of Nabal. These hateful well-springs close thou up, lest there be a great outpouring, and there come from it defilement, and even thou be reached by its overflow. The Lord restrain their outpourings! *R., Blessed be He Who dried up their overflowings!*

10. For the old man commit speech to him; for the young enjoin silence on him; for the stranger who comes in unto thee, learns of thee from thy discipline, namely who speaks first, and who second and third: and if every man keeps his mouth, and every man knows his degree, they will call thee happy. *R., Our Lord perform thy desire!*

11. Let the voice of thy truth be single and thy assumed voices without number; the image of truthfulness on thy heart, and on thy face all aspects, sadness, gladness, and feebleness. To him that errs show that thou art wrathful, to him that is chaste show that thou art glad. Be single towards the Godhead, and to mankind be manifold. *R., Blessed be He Who with all men is all things!*

12. If thou hearest an evil report, from truthful men that deceive not, pour forth tears that thou mayst quench the fire that burns in others; let them that are wise pray with thee, and appoint thou a fast for them that have knowledge, and let thy dwelling be in mourning, for him who is lost in sin, that he may turn back in repentance. *R., Blessed be He Who found the sheep that was lost!*

13. To every man give not thy ear, lest liars overwhelm thee; to every man lend not thy foot, lest vile ones misguide thee; to every man give not thy soul, lest the insolent trample thee. Keep thy hand from the false man, lest he gather thorns into thy hand. Be far off and near at hand. *R., Blessed be He Who is near though far!*

14. Lo the fame of the new king, resounds and comes into the world! To the spoiled he is a comfort, and to the spoilers a terror.

On the covetous vomiting has come, that they may render up all that they have swallowed. Let them be put to fear from before thee also, that between a priest and a righteous king, the former customs may be done away. *R., Blessed be He Who was angry, and turns and has mercy!*

15. There is that finds opportunity and ventures, and there is that forces and compels his will. One thinks that judgment is reserved, and another that it is not to be at all. There is that steals and quenches his thirst, and there is that steals and thirsts to steal. The rich steal and the poor; but the hungry steal by measure, and the full steal without measure. *R., Blessed be He Who has searched out all wills!*

16. But now has He given opportunity, and every man has shown his will, of what kind it is and to what it is like, and what he has chosen for himself rather than what. He has removed temptation from every man, lest even he who is not hateful should deny him. He has given us opportunity that we may understand, that better think this power *is* chastisement which profits much. *R., Blessed is He Who for our profit rebukes us!*

17. For He wills not by compulsion, to cast his yoke on our neck; He gave us opportunity and we waxed proud, that so when we rebelled and were punished, we might love His light yoke, might choose His pleasant staff. Our rest is very wearisome to us, for in His compulsion is restfulness, and in His yoke is lightening. *R., Blessed be He Whose labour is pleasantness!*

18. The whole world like a body, had fallen into a heavy sickness; for in the fever of heathenism, it burned and pined and fell. The right hand of tender mercy touched it, and dealt with its soul in pity; and cut off speedily its heathenism, for that was the cause of its sickness, and it was purged and sweated and restored. *R., Glory be to the Hand that has healed it!*

19. The land shall have peace in thy days, for it has seen thee that thou art full of peace. In thee shall the churches be

built, and shall be clothed with their ornaments, and their books shall be opened in
them, and their tables shall be spread, and
their ministers shall be adorned ; from them
shall go up thanksgiving, *as* first fruits to the
Lord of peace. *R., Blessed is He Who
revives our Churches !*

20. Let thy prayer go up to heaven, with
it let reconciliation go up ! May the Lord
of Heaven rain down His blessings upon
our [      ], and His consolations upon our
afflictions, and His gathering upon our dispersion : may He waken His jealousy with
His love ; may His righteousness avenge
our disgrace, may His grace blot out our
iniquity ! *R., Blessed is He Who blesses
His flock !*

21. The *first* priest and first king, even as
if depicted each in the other, were balanced
as if in scales. So too Valgesh and so too
the son of that king, for they were gentle
and calm. May these latter be like each to
other ; the priests be shining lights, the king
be glowing lights, likewise illustrious judges !
*R., Blessed be He Who has enlightened our
souls !*

22. From the king's office laws, and from
the priest's office propitiations. That both
should be mild is hateful ; that both should
be strong is grievous. Let one be strong
and one be tender ; in prudence and in discretion, let fear with mercy be mingled.
Let our priesthood be tender, likewise our
king strong. *R., Blessed be He Who has
mingled our helps !*

23. Let the priests pray for the kings,
that they may be a wall to mankind ! From
beside the kings be victory ; and from beside the priests faith ! May victory save
*our* bodies, and faith *our* souls ! May kings
put an end to war ; priests put an end
to strife ! May disputing and quarrelling
cease ! *R., Blessed be the Son of Him
Who gives peace to all ! Praise to Thee for
Thy gift !*

[XXII.–XXV. (wanting) ; XXVI. (only a
fragment remains) ; XXVII.–XXXIV. (relate
to Edessa and Carrhæ).]

VOL. XIII.—13

## XXXV.

### Concerning our Lord, and Concerning Death and Satan.

1. The Voice made proclamation : and
they gathered and came ; the hosts of the
Evil One, together with his ministers. The
army of the tares was gathered altogether,
for they saw that Jesus had triumphed, to
the grief of all them on the left hand, for
there was none of them but had been tormented. They began one by one to relate
all whatsoever they had endured. Sin and
Hell were terrified : Death trembled and
the dead rebelled ; and Satan because sinners rebelled against him. *R., To Thee be
glory because the Evil One saw Thee and was
troubled !*

2. Sin cried aloud ; she gave counsel to
her sons, to the demons and the devils, and
unto them she said, Legion the head of
your ranks is not, the sea has swallowed
him and his company ; and likewise ye my
sons if ye despise, this Jesus will destroy
you. Ye who in a snare took Solomon, it
is therefore a reproach to you, that ye
should be overcome by his disciples, takers
of fish and ignorant men ; for lo ! they have
taken the draught of men, which had been
taken by us.

3. This is great, above all evils (saith the
Evil One, concerning our Saviour) ; for this
suffices Him not that He has spoiled us,
but likewise on us He has begun retribution for Jonah son of Amittai. On Legion
therefore He was avenging him when He
seized and cast him into the sea. Jonah
emerged, after three days and came up ;
but Legion yea not after a long season, for
the depth of the sea closed upon him at the
command.

4. I tempted Him, after his past, with
pleasant bread, but He desired it not. To
my grief I strove to learn a psalm, that by
His psalm I might take Him as a prey : I
paused and learned it a second time, but
He made my second *trial* to be vain. I
brought Him up to a mountain and showed
Him all possessions ; I gave *them* to Him

and He was not moved. Better was it for me in the days of Adam, who gave me no great trouble in teaching him.

5. The Evil One ceased, from his activity and said, A cause of idleness to me, is this Jesus; for lo! the publicans and harlots take refuge in Him. What work shall I seek for myself? I who was master to all men, to whom shall I be a disciple? Sin again said, It must be, that I forsake, therefore, and change from that which I am; for this Son of Mary who is come, as a new creation, has created mankind.

6. Gluttonous Death, lamented and said, I have learned fasting, which I used not to know; lo! Jesus gathers multitudes, but as to me, in His feast a fast is proclaimed for me. One man has closed my mouth, mine who have closed the mouths of many. Hell said I will restrain my greed; hunger, therefore, is *mine :* this Man triumphs as at the marriage, when He changed the water into wine, *so* He changes the vesture of the dead into life.

7. And moreover, God made a flood, and washed the earth, and purged her crimes; fire and brimstone again He sent on her, that He might make white her stains. By fire He gave me the Sodomites, and by flood the Giants. He closed the mouth of the hosts of Sennacherib, and opened the mouth of Hell. These things and such as these, I loved. *But now*, in place of deadly visitations of justice, He has wrought in His Son, the quickening of the dead by grace.

8. Prophets and righteous men, said the Evil One, unto his companions, have been seen by me; and though their strength was exceeding mighty, there was in them a savour of that which is mine; for the stuff whereof the sons of man are made, is near akin to our heaven. This man has clothed Himself with the body of Adam, and is troubling us, for our leaven has no power on Him. He is man, therefore, and God; for His manhood in His Godhead is intermingled.

9. Adam was seen by me, that fountain from whence flowed all races of *men ;* his children has been sought out by me, and proved one by one. Yet have I not seen from the beginning a man, of whom one part was of God, and the other half, man. Moses, who shone in his splendour, I tempted again, and in his tongue I made him to err; but this man, yea, not in His mind, for pure exceedingly is the fountain of His thoughts.

10. The lust of the body, is in all bodies; for even while they sleep, it wakes in them. Him, who in his waking hours keeps himself pure, by means of a dream, I disturb. The dregs of the body are stirred in him, by a shaking movement in secret inwardly. The sleeping and the waking besides, I trouble alike. This is He Who alone keeps Himself pure, Whom not even in a dream can I disturb, Who even in His sleep is pure and holy.

11. But separate was even His childhood, from that of the children who have been seen by me; for I have not seen in Him *any* part of that which is of me. I was afraid of His childhood; therefore, I stirred up Herod, that among the infants He might be slain. Because of this also that He escaped, I was greatly afraid, for our mystery how did He find out! He received the offerings of the Wise Men; He scorned us and departed and escaped from our sword.

12. Children have been seen by me, sons of righteous men; yea, also youths, sons of chaste women; and I have moved them from the womb, one by one, and I have seen in them our leaven. For they were wrathful men and revilers, yea, also furious and gluttonous; fruits were they that by instruction were to be ripened and sweetened. But this man from His *first* planting, was a good fruit that possessed sweetness, wherewith sinners were made sweet.

13. Even while He was an infant, He was a teacher of the sons of men, by the splendour that was upon Him. Even the priest as he carried Him was amazed at Him. In the prudence of old men was He clad. Joseph stood aloof from Him: His mother

gloried in His presence. He was a help in His childhood, to every one that saw Him; He was a profit to them that knew Him, from the day when He entered into the world, He was a helper of mankind by His excellencies.

14. From whence has it sprung up before me, this fruit of Mary, the grape whereof the wine is not according to nature? For lo! I stand between doubts. To turn away and leave Him, I am afraid, lest by His teaching, they should be sweetened, they, who have acquired by bitterness. But again to tread on Him and crush Him, is a terror to me, lest haply He turn and become, new wine unto sinners, and when they are drunken therewith, lo! they forget their idols.

15. Lo! I am afraid of both things, as well His death, as also His life. Then unto the Evil One His ministers made answer and counselled Him. Though both these things be grievous, somewhat lighter to us is the trouble, that we should choose His death rather than his life. Let Death tell us whether any one from among the righteous, has ever from the first been aroused again. The sons of the Giants and the renowned ones, there is none that has issued forth from her, even Hell, the Devourer.

16. The blowing of the wind, a man may feel after; but the Son of Mary, who shall search him out? for when He wept, by His tears He robbed me; and again when I bid Him cast Himself, from the holy Temple, I thought, that it was through fear He cast Himself not: yet when they threw Him from the hill-top, He flew through the air. On the well again when He was weary He sat. His variableness I understand not, for on the dry land alike and on the water He walks.

17. I have seen Him that He hungered, as a Son of man; yet this was done away by the bread which He multiplied. From the beginning I proved Him and I came *to Him;* He questioned *me* as though He knew *me* not; but this, too, was done away, when He showed that He knew *our* secrets.

Again He chose Iscariot, as though He knew him not; then He turned and showed that He knew him, though he was binding and loosing. I was mistaken in Him, for He was baptized and emerged and overwhelmed me.

18. But one token there is which I have seen in Him that heartens me exceedingly above all. For while He was praying I saw Him and was glad, because He changed colour and was afraid: His sweat was as drops of blood, because He felt that His day was come. This is pleasant to me, exceedingly above all, if it be not that deceiving He has deeived me therein. But if beguiling He has beguiled me, this is both for me and for you alike, my ministers.

19. Then shouted the host of devils and said, Hateful is the sign that we see in thee, for never from the beginning has it thus happened to thee. In prompt counsels thou wast excellent: the Son of Mary captures *our* cities, while thou art prolonging thy discourse. Arise, go forth, let us fight with Him, for this were to us a reproach, that we being many should be overcome by one. And if thou art in pain or fear, give us counsel for the battle and stay thou *behind.*

20. This Jesus out of His own words it is, that I shall teach *Him,* and war with Him; for He said that he, even Satan, is divided, himself against himself, and that he cannot stand. Though He desires to fight with us, He has given us arms which are against Himself, gage and divide for me His disciples, for if ye divide them, with these you will conquer them, even with Eve and the serpent, the weak *powers,* whereby I conquered the first Adam.

21. Death unto the Evil One, made answer and said to him, Wherefore tarriest thou not according to thy wont? for lo! it is those that are despised and least, that thou ensnarest after thy custom: Jesus Who is great above all, wherewith hast thou sought to ensnare Him? The experience of His weapons moves thee to fear, which He hurled against thee when he was tempted of thee. Thou and I with thy followers,

the host of us is too little for the battle with Him, the Son of Mary.

22. I counsel, then, if this our strife permits us to do anything : go thou into that disciple, let thyself loose, that head may speak with heads ; and let loose all thy host, let it go and stir up the Pharisees. And *beware*, lest thou speak contentiously as thou art wont. If thou be a god, descend from hence, with fondness kiss them and betray Him ; and, lo ! we will bring on Him the envy and the sword of the Levites.

## XXXVI.

1. Our Lord subdued His might and constrained it, that His living death might give life to Adam. His hands He gave to the piercing of the nails, instead of the hand that plucked the fruit : He was smitten on the cheek in the judgment hall, instead of the mouth that ate *it* in Eden. And because his foot bore Adam *thence*, His feet were pierced. Our Lord was stripped, that He might make *us* modest : with the gall and vinegar He made sweet the bitterness of the serpent, which he had poured forth into mankind. *R. Blessed is He Who gave me the victory and quickened the dead to His glory !*

2. (DEATH.)—If Thou be God show Thy power ; and if Thou be man, feel our power. And if it be Adam that Thou seekest, get Thee hence ! because of his transgressions he is shut up here ; Cherubim and Seraphim await not, in his stead to pay his debt. There is none among them mortal, so as to give his life in his stead. Who can open the mouth of hell, and plunge and bring him up from her, who has swallowed him and keeps a hold on him, and that forever !

3. I am He who has conquered all the wise men ; and lo ! in the corners they are heaped for me in hell. Come, enter, son of Joseph, and see terrible things ; the limbs of the giants, the mighty corpse of Samson, and the skeleton of the stubborn Goliath ; Og, moreover, the son of the giants, who made for himself a bed of iron and lay thereon, from whence I hurled him and cast him down ; that cedar I laid low to the gate of hell.

4. I by myself alone have conquered multitudes, and one may single-handed seek to conquer me. Prophets and priests and men of renown have I carried off ; I have conquered kings in their armies, and mighty men in their hunts, and righteous men in their excellencies. Streams of corpses are hurled by me into hell, and though they pour into her she is athirst. Though one be near or though he be far off, the end brings him to the gate of hell.

5. Silver I despised at the hand of the rich, and their offerings corrupted me not. The lords of slaves never once persuaded me, to take a slave instead of his lord, and a poor man instead of a rich man, or an old man instead of a child. As for wise that are able to charm wild beasts, their charms enter not into my ears. Hater of persuasion all men call me ; and I the thing that is commanded me that I do.

6. Who is this, or whose son is He, or what His lineage who has conquered me ? The book of families is by me ; lo ! I went in and read and studied the names from Adam till now, and not one of the dead do I forget. Family by family, lo ! they are written, upon my limbs. Because of Thee, O Jesus, I went in and made a reckoning, that I might show Thee that there is none that escapeth my hands.

7. Yet were there two men (that I lie not) whose names have escaped me in Hell. For Enoch and Elijah came not to me. In all the world I have sought them ; yea thither where Jonah descended, I descended and sought and they were not. And though I suppose that into Paradise, they have entered and escaped, a mighty Cherub guards it. The ladder Jacob saw, what if haply by it they have entered into Heaven !

8. Who is there that has measured the sand of the sea, and has spilt only two grains ? This harvest wherein every day there labour, diseases as harvesters, I alone carry the handfuls and gather them up ; other gatherers in making haste, drop

handfuls. Vintagers overlook clusters ; *but* two grapes have escaped me, in that great vintage which I alone have plucked.

9. I am He that has taken (said Death), on sea and on dry land, all prey in chase. Eagles of the air come to me ; yea and dragons of the deep : creeping things and fowl and cattle ; old men, youths and children. These will convince Thee, O Son of Mary, that this my power rules over all. Thy Cross how shall it conquer me, who by a tree lo ! I have prevailed and conquered from old time ?

10. But I was desirous to speak yet farther, for I am not wanting in words ; yea words are not to be sought by me, for lo ! deeds call on me close at hand. Not as you do I make promise, to the simple of secret things, that forsooth there is to be a resurrection at some time or other. If then Thou art very powerful, give a present pledge, that Thy distant promise also may be believed.

11. Death ended his speech of derision : and the voice of our Lord sounded into Hell, and He cried aloud and burst the graves one by one. Tremblings took hold on Death ; Hell that never of old had been lighted up, into it there flashed splendours, from the Watchers who entered in and brought out the dead to meet Him, who was dead and gives life to all. The dead came forth, and the living were ashamed, they who thought that they had conquered the Life Giver of all.

12. But who gave me the day of Moses, (said Death) who made a feast for me ? For that lamb that *was slain* in Egypt gave me, from every house the first fruit : heaps and heaps of the first born, at the gate of Hell he piled me them. But this Lamb of the festival, has robbed Hell ; of the dead He has taken title and carried them off from me. That lamb filled the graves for me ; but this has emptied the graves that were full.

13. The death of Jesus to me is a torment ; I prefer for myself His life rather than His death. This is the Dead whose death (lo !) is hateful to me ; in the death of all men *else* I rejoice, but His Death, even His, I detest ; that He may come back to life I hope. While He was living He brought to life and restored three that were dead ; but now by His death, at the gate of Hell they have trampled on me, the dead who have come to life, whom I was going to shut in.

14. I will haste and will close the gates of Hell, before this Dead, Whose death has spoiled me. Whoso hears will wonder at my humiliation, that by a dead man who is without I am overcome. All the dead seek to go forth, but this one presses to enter in. A medicine of life has entered into Hell, and has restored life to its dead. Who then has brought in and hidden from me, that living fire wherein have reposed, the cold and dark recesses of Hell ?

15. Death has seen the Watchers in Hell ; the immortal instead of the mortal ; and he said Confusion has entered our abode, for in these two things is torment *to me :* That the dead have come forth out of Hell, and the Watchers that die not have entered therein. Lo ! one at the pillow in this tomb, has entered and sat down by it, and a second his companion at His feet. I will entreat of Him and will persuade Him, with His pledge to ascend and go to His Kingdom.

16. Be not wroth against me, gracious Jesus, for the words that my pride has spoken before Thee ! Who is there that when seeing Thy Cross, shall have doubted that Thou art man ? Who is there that shall have seen Thy Power, and shall not believe that Thou art also God ? Lo ! thus by these two things I have learnt to confess that Thou art man and likewise art God ! For as much as the dead in Hell repent not, go up among the living, O Lord, and preach repentance.

17. O Jesus King, receive my supplication, and with my supplication take to Thyself a pledge, even Adam the great pledge accept for Thyself, him in whom are buried all the dead ; even as when I received him, in him were hidden all the living. The first pledge I have given Thee, the body of Adam ; go Thou up therefore and reign over all ; and when I shall hear Thy trumpet, I with mine

own hand will lead forth the dead at Thy Coming.

18. Our King living has gone forth and gone up, out of Hell, as Conqueror. Woe He has doubled to them that are of the left hand; to *evil* spirits and demons *He is* sorrow, to Satan and to Death *He is* pain, to Sin and Hell mourning. Joy to them that are of the right hand, has come to-day. On this great day, therefore, great glory let us give to Him, who died and *is* alive that, unto all He may, give life and resurrection!

## XXXVII.

1. Death was weeping for her, even for Sheol, when he saw her treasury that it was emptied. And he said, Who, then, has plundered thy riches? Gehazi stole and was discovered; I am stealing every day, *but* theft has not been laid to my charge. I am sent to Kings, in their sicknesses, their guards are set around them, guards are also at their gate. The soul of kings I snatch and I go forth. *R., Blessed is He Who has broken the sting of Death by His Cross!*

2. All women grieve that are barren; Sheol rejoices because of her barrenness; she is desolate if so be that she brings forth. The all-compelling Power constrained it, even the bosom *that was* barren and cold, and it rendered back though wont to deny its debts. Rebekah, when the two babes afflicted her, asked for death. How great then the pain of Sheol, when there smote her strange pangs; the dead were roused and brake forth and came out from her bowels.

3. Is this then perchance that saying, which was heard by me from Isaiah? (but I despised it) when he arose and said, "Who hath heard such a thing as this? that the earth should travail in one day, and bring forth a nation in one hour." Is it this that has come to pass? or else, is it reserved for us hereafter? And if it be this it is a vain shadow that I thought I am a king; I knew not it was but a deposit I was keeping.

4. Two utterances that were different, have I heard from him, even this Isaiah. For he said that a virgin should conceive and bring forth; and he said again that the earth should bring forth. But lo! the Virgin has brought Him forth, and Sheol the barren has brought Him forth; two wombs that contrary to nature, have been changed by Him; the Virgin and Sheol both of them. The Virgin in her bringing forth He made glad; but Sheol He grieved and made sad in His Resurrection.

5. I saw in the valley that Ezekiel, who quickened the dead when he was questioned; and I saw the bones that were in heaps and they moved. There was a tumult of bones in Sheol, bone seeking for his fellow, and joint for her mate. There was there none that questioned, or that was questioned, whether those bones lived. Unquestioned, the voice of Jesus, the Master of all creatures quickened them.

6. Sheol was made sorrowful when she saw them, even the sorrowful dead made to rejoice. She wept for Lazarus when he went forth, "Go in peace *thou* dead that livest, bewailed by two houses of mourning." Within and without were lamentations for him; for his sisters wept for him when he came into the grave unto me, and I wept for him as he went forth. In his death there was weeping among the living; likewise in Sheol is great mourning at his resurrection.

7. Now it is that I have tasted the taste of his sorrow, even of him who weeps over his beloved. The dead that are thus beloved of Sheol, how dear *were* they to their fathers! The limbs which I severed and carried away, lo! they are shorn away and carried off from me. If I thus suffer for the departure of him, the youth who was restored to life, blessed is He Who had compassion on the widow; in her only son He gave peace to her dwelling that had been made desolate.

8. Lo! this suffering which I cause men to suffer in their beloved ones, in the end on me it gathers itself altogether. For when the dead shall have left Sheol, for every

man there will be resurrection, and for me alone torment. And who is he then that shall bear for me all these things, that I shall see Sheol left alone, because this voice which has rent the graves, makes her desolate and sends forth the dead that were in her midst?

9. If a man reads in the Prophets, he hears there of righteous wars. But if a man meditate in the story of Jesus, he learns of grace and tender mercy. And if a man think of Jesus, that He is a strange God it is a reproach against me. No other strange key into the gate of Sheol could ever be fitted. One is the key of the Creator, that which has opened it, yea, is to open it at His Coming.

10. Who is he that is able to join the bones, save that Power which created them? What is it that shall reunite the shreds of the body, save the hand of the Maker? What is it that shall restore the forms, save the finger of the Creator? He, who created and turned and destroyed, is He that is able also to renew and raise up. Another God is unable to enter in and restore creatures not his own.

11. But were he another Power, I should be very joyful that He is coming to me. Into the bosom of Sheol He would descend and learn that One alone is God. Mortals that have erred and preached that there are Gods many, lo! they are bound for me in Sheol, and their Gods have never grieved because of them. One God do I know, and His Prophets and His Apostles do I acknowledge.

## XXXVIII.

1. My throne was set for me in Sheol: and one arose that was dead, and hurled me from it. Every man feared me alone, and I feared no man. Terror and trouble *were* among the living, rest and peace among the dead. In a man that was slain lo! there has entered into Sheol He that takes her captive. I used to take all men captive: the Son of Captivity Whom I took captive has taken me captive. He Whom I took captive has led her away and is gone to Paradise. *R., Blessed is He Who has quickened the dead of Sheol by His Cross!*

2. All men complain much against me; and I against one only have complained. Who is there among men so just as I? Has corruption touched my integrity? I held all men in affection, and whoso hates me knows *it;* I know not all my days what a bribe is. The person of a king have I not accepted. By me is preached equality, for bondman and his lord in Sheol I make equal.

3. Before God it is that I minister, with Whom is no acceptance of persons. What other is there that endures as I do, I that am cursed when I do good? Perversely are requited to me the benefits I have rendered. Though my deeds are goodly, my name is not goodly. Yet my mind rests in its integrity: in God it is that I comfort myself; for though He is good He is denied every day and endures *it.*

4. The old I remove from all sufferings, likewise the young from all sins. Secret contention I quell in Sheol; in our land there is no iniquity: it is Sheol and Heaven alone, that are removed from all sins; this earth that lies between, in her iniquity dwells. He therefore that is prudent will either go up into Heaven, or, if that be *too* hard, will go down to Sheol which is easy.

5. To one man because of one that is dead, every man hastes to comfort *him.* But for me though many of my dead have come to life, there is none that comes in and comforts me. Satan came in, against Whom, had been proclaimed seven woes even against him; though mightily the Son of Mary had trodden on him, *yet* uplifted is his spirit; for he is the serpent that strives though bruised. Better is it for me to fall and worship, before this Jesus Who has conquered me by His Cross.

6. When He enters at the gate of Sheol, in place of John who preached before His coming, then will I cry "Lo! He that quickens the dead is come; Thy servant am I from henceforth, Jesu! Because of The Body I

reviled Thee, for it covered Thy Godhead. Be not angry, O Son of the King, against Thy treasury; at Thy command I have opened and closed. Though my wings *be* very swift it is at thy nod I haste to every quarter.

7. All that have been raised were not first born; for our Lord is the First-born of Sheol. How can *any that is* dead go before Him, that power whereby he was raised? There are last that are first, and younger that have become first-born. For though Manasseh was first-born, how could it be that Ephraim should take the birthright? And if the second born was set before him, how much rather shall the Lord and Creator prevent *all* in His Resurrection!

8. Lo! John as a herald declares that he is later, though he was elder-born; for he said, "Behold a man cometh after me, and yet He was before me." For how could he be before Him, that Power in Whom he preached? For everything that comes to pass because of *another* thing, is after *that other* even though it *seem to* be before. For the cause which called it *into being*, is elder *than it* and before *it* in all things.

9. The cause of Adam was elder than *all* creatures, which were made for him, for to him even to Adam He had respect continually, the Creator even while he was creating. Thus though Adam as yet was not, he was elder than *all* creatures. How much more then, my Lord, must this Thy manhood be elder, which in Thy Godhead is, from eternity with Him that begat Thee! To Thee *be* praise and through Thee to Thy Father from us all!

10. To Thee *be* praise for Thou art the first, in Thy Godhead and in Thy manhood! For even though Elijah was first to go up, he was not able to prevent Him, for whose sake he was taken up. For his type depended on Thy verity: and even though the types apparently are before Thy fulfilment, it is before them secretly. Creatures were before Adam; he was before them because for his sake they were made.

11. O my Lord, work for me this resurrection, not of Thy compulsion but of Thy love.

For Thy compulsion gives life to sinners also: Iscariot would rather again choose for himself the death of Sheol, than the life of Gehenna. Work for me then the resurrection that is of Thy mercy; and even though Thy justice permits not, let there be occasion for Thy grace. This only let it remember for me, that in it I have sought refuge.

### XXXIX.

1. There have come to me ransomers from among the saints, but none has plundered me like the Son of Mary. For lo! Elijah brought a dead man to life; and even though he himself escaped from my hands, yet had I consolation after him, for the dead man whom he quickened, I carried off from him. By Elisha son of Shaphat, I was beaten *as* with rods, for he brought two dead men to life. By one staff I in turn bore away both the prophet and the dead men whom he had raised. *R., Blessed is He Who cleft the tombs of Sheol by His voice!*

2. I feared him even Gehazi when I saw, him lay the staff upon the youth. The thief took the staff away and returned; Elisha came and bowed himself; laid himself low as the child and raised himself up, and walked hither and thither. I marvelled at the new mysteries which I saw there, which restored but one youth to life. It was well with me *then* when those were *but* mysteries, and not now when the dead have rebelled and conquered me.

3. Moses when I saw the mighty splendour upon his face, I feared him: yet not according to what I feared befel it me. Nisan in Sheol he caused to spring for me; for a pasture, a pasture of corpses, of six hundred thousand fell.—This lowly and despised one whom I contemned, has healed the sick and the diseased: to others He has multiplied bread, but our bread *even* ours from our mouths He snatches.

4. A mighty feast there was in Sheol, when I swallowed up Korah and his company. A great delight Satan made for me, when he made strife among the Levites. A

fount of milk and honey, made he flow for me in a dry place, when the congregation of transgressors went down to Sheol.—Lo! the righteous have lived and come forth: Moses sent down the living thither, but Jesus has revived and brought up the dead.

5. It was well with me then, in the day of the zealous, those in whose swords I had delight. Phinehas the zealous pierced and gave me, on the head of his spear *for* my delight, Zimri and Cozbi both together; on the head of his lance he presented *them* to me. To whom then were there ever two fatted oxen, offered on the head of a spear?—But instead of Cozbi, daughter of princes, the daughter of Jairus has Jesus rescued from my hands.

6. The censer of Aaron caused me to fear, for he stood between the dead and the living and conquered me. The Cross causes me to fear more exceedingly, which has rent open the graves of Sheol. The Crucified Whom on it I slew, now by Him am I slain. Not very great is his reproach, who is overcome by a warrior in arms. Worse to me *is* my reproach than my torment, in that by a crucified man my strength has been overcome.

7. The lance of Phinehas again has caused me to fear, for by the slaughter he wrought with it he hindered the pestilence. The lance guarded the tree of life, it made me glad and made me sad; it hindered Adam from life, and it hindered death from the people. But the lance that pierced Jesus, by it I have suffered; He is pierced and I groan. There came out from Him water and blood; Adam washed and lived and returned to Paradise.

8. The Sadducees were *as* a mouth for me, and disputed with Him after my mind, that there is no rising of the dead at all. Jesus answered them in a saying, which I alone understood; He spake aloud the hateful word and saddened me, "I am the God of him even of Abraham, and God is not *the* God of the dead." It was well with me then these were *but* words, and He had not *yet* showed me the life of the dead indeed.

9. Jesus son of Nun, slew thirty kings, and filled the graves and pits for me; he laid waste Jericho and filled Sheol. But this Jesus who is come, has wasted the graves of *their* dead, and has filled the cities of the upper world. Wherefore thus when lo! they are like in their names, are they unlike in their doings? *That* gave me the body of Achor, but *this* snatched from me the body of Lazarus.

10. Moses trod down that Egyptian, with his meekness he mingled justice. Whence has this new law sprung for me, "If one smite thee on thy cheek, turn to him thy other cheek, and see that thou hate him not?' Instead of the strong man of zeal who trod down and slew, a new man of mercy has risen for us. Samuel hewed Agag in pieces, but Jesus healed the paralytic.

11. Tender mercy which had as it were waxed less, lo! in this time has waxed great. And moreover it was *then* detested, lest *through* it one should transgress the commandment; for without mercy Saul and Ahab, were slain because they desired, to have mercy on the evil ones, and they were not slain who were deserving of punishment. In my time Jesus has changed this, by giving life to all men and having compassion on His slayers.

12. I remember Samson that lion's whelp, who brake and gave me the pillars of Philistia; also that mighty man of valor Abner son of Ner, took for me that fleet wild roe, Asahel son of Zeruiah, and smote him and cast him on the ground. Benaiah in the holy temple slew Jacob, justly as it is written.—Because justice has restrained her sword, henceforth penitents shall rejoice in grace.

13. David measured the Edomites, by line and line and destroyed them. How merciful then art Thou, O Son of David! David's justice was twofold, when he put to death two lines, and saved *one* full line alive.—Lo! the Son of David teaches us, "Forgive thy brother even unto seventy times seven." There justice was measured; but here clemency is without measure.

14. Of zeal and strength David was possessed; the lion and the bear he slew together. He left that mighty lion and hasted, to meet the strong giant. With a stone he quenched his light, and his soul left him and he perished. But Jesus cried to the young man that was dead "Young man!" Even the dead to Him are sleepers. That young man He brought to life and rescued from me. The despised swine He drowned for me in the sea.

15. The Levites slew because of the calf, their fathers and their brethren. Jephthah by his own hands was ready to slay his daughter. The King of Moab on the wall, was sacrificing his first-born son: In presence of his sword I rejoice.—By Jesus the sword was blunted; yea the fever was rebuked, the sister of Sheol: the mother-in-law of Simeon was healed, but the fame of her healing smote Sheol with pain.

16. This Jesus though he be the Son of the Just One, all that He preaches is grace. But to me this His grace is torment. Envy is the cause of pleasure to us, for Envy at the beginning mixed for me the first shedding of blood. Why is it guilty in the sight of the Son of Mary Who is come commanding, "Thou shalt not be angry against thy brother?" He has taken away the sword from between brethren; while in the sword of Cain I had pleasure from the beginning.

17. An honeycomb in the midst of the skeleton, Samson found—was it then a mystery? This Jesus has multiplied for us mysteries. Amid billows of mysteries have I fallen, which show me in parable the life of the dead, in all mysteries and in all types. "Out of the eater came forth meat" was Samson's parable. But to me it has befallen contrariwise; for the eater has come forth to me out of the meat, for out of Adam lo! *has come* the Son of Adam Who has destroyed me.

18. Just men likewise have robbed me manifold, when by them was preached the rising of the dead: but they mingled with my sorrows great consolation. By the prayer of Asa and Hezekiah, I was fed upon the dead, yea I feasted upon corpses. Elijah slew the prophets of Baal and gave them to me, who on the bread of Jezebel had waxed fat. The righteous has constrained me to devour, but Jesus has compelled me to disgorge all that I had eaten.

19. I was afraid because of the sprinkled blood, which Moses sprinkled on every door; for though the blood of the slain, it was that which saved the living. Blood from of old I feared not, save that blood that was on the doors, and this moreover that was on the Tree. The blood of the slain is a delight, and is as sweet perfume: but the blood of Jesus is to me a terror; for whenever I come and smell His blood, the savour of life that lurks therein terrifies me.

20. Priests and pontiffs, anointed men and kings, who foreshow types of the rising of the dead, have never triumphed through their crosses. Crowns and diadems were *set on them;* and when I engaged in struggles with them, I was smitten *sometimes* and *sometimes* also I smote. But this carpenter's son with his crown of thorns, has humbled and cast down my pride, in His shame and His dying: Sheol has seen Him, yea, and fled from before Him.

21. When the sea saw Moses and fled, it feared because of his rod, and likewise because of his glory. His splendour and his rod and his power, the rock also saw which was cleft. But Sheol when her graves were rent, what saw she in Him even in Jesus? —Instead of splendour He put on the paleness of the dead and made her tremble. And if His paleness when slain slew her, how shall she be able to endure, when He comes to raise the dead, in His Glory!

XL.

1. The Evil One perceived his great humiliation, and boasted himself in the presence of his servants: he spoke great words to persuade them and said: "The knowledge which I possess, little of it is by nature; and much of it, yea all of it, is by learning. I to myself have been master, and have exer-

cised my understanding. Without a teacher I have learnt all ; I have armed myself with every weapon, and have won by it the crown which I desired among mankind." *R., Blessed is He that has come and undone the snares of sin !*

2. Among the Pharisees I clothed myself in hatred, that I might contend with Him, even the Son of Mary. Wrath like a bow rained shafts ; boldness railed upon Him ; fury rebelled against Him ; ingratitude slandered Him ; envy and jealousy in *their* wrath, strove with Him ; and blasphemy took up stones. The Healer came in and stood among the sick, and I stirred up the diseased in contention against Him.

3. Because He fell not under reproach, it was in questions that I took refuge. Many times did I stir up occasions, but I saw that my falsehood was rebuked, and my impudence was made known, and my vain babbling was despised. To the windings of contention I betook myself. Everywhere that I disputed with Him, all my labor was as chaff, and the word of truth scattered it on every side.

4. I saw that there is a warrior and a mighty lord, in cunning within man : [and the snake that *is* without makes it fear.] His lusts within him is coiled continually ; his jealousy hisses like a serpent. Deadly desires he begets, and of a fever he is in dread. Command as a drug, is able to quell derision, which smites unto destruction. It is love that avails to break the sting secret and bitter of the tongue.

5. Who is more foolish than men, who rather than for himself cares for his dwelling ! The garments that *are* in his chest he examines daily, and a worm is lurking in his members. The rents that are in his clothes he mends, but a rent is made in his soul. His house is lighted up but his heart is dark. He shuts up his senses but opens his windows. He closes his door and guards his money ; his mouth is open and the treasure of his thought *is* stolen.

6. The fool makes more of his beasts than of himself, for he cares for his possessions rather than for his soul. Good seed he sows in his ground ; in his heart he sows tares. His understanding is thrown open and cast down ; but at the fences of his vineyard he labours. He chooses and plants vine-plants ; while his mind is a vine of the vines of Sodom. He keeps off the wild ass from his sowing ; but the wild boar of the wood devours his thoughts.

7. I am a furnace to the sons of men, and in me are tried their counsels. Therefore is it lawful to me to weave deceit. I teach the Chaldean art : by reason of the true things that befall, the false things are believed. In the midst of Egypt I closed *men's* eyes ; I showed insects, *men* thought they were though they were not. By closing *men's* eyes I teach the signs of the Zodiac, though they are not in the heavens.

8. By reason of my swiftness I fly and see, and I show beforehand to the soothsayer ; they who err concerning me count me a prophet. But sometimes I make bold ; and I ask that for an hour, secret things be revealed to me, that true men may be proved by me even as Job, likewise deceivers as Saul. For the one I revealed his sorcery ; and for the other I purged his truth and he was praised.

## XLI.

1. The Evil One said, " I fear Him, even Jesus, lest He destroy my arts. For lo ! I am thousands of years old, and never have I had repose. I have seen nothing established, that I have turned from and left. There has come One making the unchaste pure : there is sorrow since He has destroyed all that I had built. Many have been my labours and my teachings, that I might cover all creation with all evils. *R., Blessed is He Who came and laid bare the wiles of the Crafty One !*

2. I matched my speed with the swift, and I outstripped them : I waged war ; the tumult of multitudes was armour to me. In the tumult of the people I rejoiced, because it gave me ready room, for grievous is the

onslaught of multitudes. By the strength of multitudes I raised a great mountain, a tower I stretched unto heaven. If they waged war with the Height, how *much more* shall they conquer Him whose warfare is on earth?

3. As time serves and as help offers, I wage war, but cautiously. The people used to hear that God is one; they made for themselves a multitude of gods. And when they saw the Son of God, they made haste to the One God, that as though confessing God they might deny Him, and as though in zeal might flee from Him; so that they in all times perverse shall be found to be without God.

4. Lo! I am ancient of many years, and no infant have I ever rejected. The burden of children have I ofttimes borne, so that from the beginning I might make them acquire habits that are not goodly, that their faults might grow up with them. But there are foolish fathers, who do not crush the seed that I have sown in their sons; and there are *some* who like good husbandmen, root up faults from the mind of their children.

5. As with a chain I have bound men with sloth, and they sat in idleness. I have drawn away their senses from all good things; their eyes from reading, their mouths from singing praise, their understanding from doctrine. For hurtful and vain fables how eager *are they;* for empty talk *how* ready! If the word of life fell among them, they either thrust it from them, or rose and went forth from its presence.

6. How many Satans are there among men! and me even me alone every man curses. For lo! the anger of men—it is a devil that grinds him every day. Demons are like wayfarers, who depart if they are compelled: but against anger though all righteous men adjure, it is not rooted out from its place. Instead of pernicious envy, every one hates a weak and wretched demon.

7. The enchanter is put to shame with the wizard, who every day tames serpents. The viper that is within him is out of his power; for the lust that is within him he tames not. Secret sin like an asp, when it breathes on him he is scorched. Even when he takes the viper through his cunning, delusion smites him secretly. He lulls the snake by his incantations: he wakens against himself mighty wrath by his incantations.

8. I set *my* stings and I sat and waited: who is long-enduring *as I* with all? Beside the patient-spirited I sat, and step by step I bewitched him, so that he came unto despair. Him who was ashamed of his transgressions, habits subdued him: little by little I mastered him, till he became under the yoke, till he came in to it and was used to it and did not even wish to go forth.

9. I perceived and saw that the long-enduring is he that can subdue all. At the time when I conquered Adam, he was *but* one. I left him till he had begotten *children*, and I sought for myself another task, for idleness is not to my taste. I counted the sands of the sea, that thereby I might make my spirit patient, and might ·prove my memory whether it would suffice, for the sons of men when they were multiplied. Before they were multiplied, I proved them in many things.

10. The servants of the Evil One disputed with him, and they refuted his words with their rejoinder. "But lo! Elisha brought the dead to life, and conquered death in the upper chamber, and brought to life the widow's son. Lo! now is he in bondage in Sheol." But because the reasoning of the Evil One was very powerful, with their own words he refuted their words. "How has Elisha been overcome? Lo! in Sheol he brought the dead to life by his bones."

11. "If Elisha, who was *of* small *power,* was great in might in the midst of Sheol, and if so be he brought one dead to life therein, how many dead then will be raised therein, by the death of Jesus the mighty! Hence even from this consider ye, how much greater therefore is Jesus, than we, my comrades. For lo! by His craftiness He de-

ceived you, and ye sufficed not to determine, His greatness when ye compared Him to the prophets.

12. "Your consolations are *of* small power," said the Evil One to them of his company. "For He Who brought Lazarus to life though dead, how can Death suffice against Him? And if Death conquers Him, it is that He wills to be subdued unto him; and if so be He wills to be subdued, fear ye greatly, for He dies not in vain. He has wrought in us great terror, lest when dying He may enter in to raise Adam to life."

13. Death looked forth from within his den, and marvelled when he saw our Lord crucified, and he said "O raiser of the dead to life where *art* thou! Thou shalt be to me *for* meat, instead of the sweet Lazarus, whose savour lo! it is still in my mouth. Jairus' daughter shall come and see this Thy cross. The widow's son gazes on Thee. A tree caught Adam for me: blessed be the Cross which has caught for me the Son of David!"

14. Death opened his mouth and said, "Hast Thou not heard, O Son of Mary, how Moses was great and excellent above all? became a God and wrought *the works* of God? slew the first-born and saved the first-born? turned aside the pestilence from the living? To the mount I went up with Moses, and He Whose glory be blessed gave him to me from hand to hand. For however great the son of Adam becomes, dust he is and to his dust returns, because he is of the ground."

15. Satan came with his servants, that he might see our Lord cast into Sheol, and might rejoice with Death his Counsellor; and he saw Him sorrowful and mourning, because of the dead who at the voice of the Firstborn, lived and came forth thence even from Sheol. The Evil One arose to console Death his kinsman. "Thou hast not destroyed as much as thou wast able. Even as Jesus is in thy midst, to thy hand shall come they that have lived and that live.

16. "Open for us to see Him, yea and mock Him: let us answer and say, 'Where is Thy power? For lo! three days have passed for Him, and let us say to Him, O Thou of three days, Who didst raise Lazarus, when he had lain four days, raise Thine own self.'" Death opened the gates of Sheol, and there shone from it the splendour of the face of our Lord; and like the men of Sodom they were smitten; they groped and sought the gate of Sheol, which they had lost.

## XLII.

1. The Evil One wailed "Where now, is there a place for me to flee to from the righteous? I stirred up Death to slay the Apostles, that I might be safe from their blows. By their deaths now more exceedingly am I cruelly beaten. The Apostle whom I slew in India is before me in Edessa: he is here wholly and also there. I went there, there was he: here and there I have found him and been grieved." *R., Blessed is the might that dwells in the hallowed bones!*

2. The bones that merchantmen carried, or was it then that they carried him? For lo! they made gain each of the other. But for me what did they profit me? yea they profited each by each, while to me from both of them there was damage. O that one would show me that bag of Iscariot, for by it I acquired strength! The bag of Thomas has slain me, for the secret strength that dwells in it tortures me.

3. Moses the chosen carried the bones, in faith as for gain. And if he a great prophet believed, that there is benefit in bones, the merchant did well to believe, and did well to call himself merchant. That merchant made gain, and waxed great and reigned. His storehouse has made me very poor: his storehouse has been opened in Edessa, and has enriched the great city with benefit.

4. At this storehouse of treasure I was amazed, for small was its treasure at first; and though no man took from it, poor was the spring of its wealth. But when multitudes have come round it, and plundered it and carried off its riches, according as it is plundered, so much the more does its wealth

increase. For a pent-up spring, if one seeks it out, when deeply pierced it flows forth mightily and abounds.

5. It is evident that Elisha was a fountain in a thirsting people : and because they that thirsted sought him not out, his outflow was not great. But when Naaman sought him out, he abounded and poured forth healing. The fountain into the midst of a fountain, he took him and plunged him ; for in the river he cleansed the leper. Jesus the Sea of benefits, into Siloam sent the blind man whose eyes were opened.

6. Gehazi, with the staff that brought to life the dead, was unable to raise the child. And how could the famous prophet have been brought up by the sorceress ? We were they that mocked Saul, for instead of one demon whom he questioned, two demons came up and mocked him. From the bones of Elisha learn also of *the bones of* Samuel ; for though *Elisha's* bones brought to life the dead, the sorcerers could not bring up the dead, the living and sacred bones.

7. And though I asked this petition, He who gives all gave it not to me. For though the demons were troubled, by the bones of some priest, or magician or wizard, of Chaldean or soothsayer, yet I was aware that this was but mockery. In two ways I cause *men* to err : either I make the Apostles to lie, or I make my Apostles like the Apostles.

8. The party of the demons lo ! it is spoiled ; the party of the devils endures stripes : though there be none that lifts the rod openly, the demons cry out with pain ; though there be none that fetters and binds, the spirits hang bound. This silent judgment, which is calm and still, and works not even by questioning, the one power that is all sufficing, lo ! it dwells in the bones of this second Elisha.

9. He gave judgment unto His Twelve, that they might judge the twelve Tribes. And if so be that they are to judge the sons of the great Abraham, this is then no great matter, that they shall judge demons now. And unless they make the crucifers fulfil the judgment that is to be, by our judgment shall they be proved. For worse than we did they cry out, in presence of the Apostles the judges of the tribes.

10. For a wolf was Saul the Apostle, and on the blood of the sheep I reared him ; and he waxed strong and became a singular wolf. But nigh to Damascus suddenly, the wolf was changed into a sheep. He said that the Apostles, are to judge Angels ; for by the Angels he signified the priest as it is written. If so be then they are thus powerful, woe to the demons from the strokes of their bones !

## LII.

### Concerning Satan and Death.

1. I heard Death and Satan, as they disputed, which was the more powerful, among men. *R., To Thee be glory, Son of the Shepherd of All, Who deliveredst His flock from the secret wolves that devoured it,* the Evil One and Death !—2. Death showed his power, that he conquers all ; Satan showed his guile, that he makes all to sin.— 3. *Death,* To thee, O Evil One, none hearkens save he that wills : to me he that wills and he that wills not, even to me they come.—4. *Satan,* Thine, O Death, is but the force of tyranny : mine are snares and nets of subtlety.—5. *D.,* Hear, O Evil One, that who so is subtle breaks off thy yoke : but none is there that is able to escape my yoke.—6. *S.,* Thou, Death, on him that is sick provest thy might : but I over them that are whole, am exceeding powerful.— 7. *D.,* The Evil One prevails not over all those that revile him : but for me he that has cursed me and he that curses me, come into my hands.—8. *S.,* Thou, Death, from God, hast gotten thy might : I alone by none am I helped, when I lead *men* to sin.—9. *D.,* Thou, O Evil One, like a weakling : while like a king I exercise my dominion.—10. *S.,* Thou art a fool, O Death, not to know how great am I : who suffice to capture free will, the sovereign power.—11. *D.,* Thou, O Evil One, like a thief, lo ! thou goest round : I like a lion break in pieces and

fear not.—12. *S.*, To thee, O Death, none does service or worship : to me kings do service of sacrifice as to God.—13. *D.*, On Death there are many that call, as on a kind Power : on thee, O Evil One, none has called or calls.—14. *S.*, Markest thou not this, O Death, how many there are : who in sundry fashions call on me and make oblation?—15. *D.*, Hated is thy name, O Satan, nor canst thou clear it : thy name every one curses, hide thy reproach.—16. *S.*, Thine ear, O Death, has waxed dull, that thou hearest not : how against thee all men groan, conceal thyself.—17. *D.*, My face is shown to the world, for I am guileless : not like thee who without guile canst not abide. —18. *S.*, Thou hast not in aught surpassed me for it is true : that thou art hateful as I to the sons of men.—19. *D.*, Of me all men are afraid as of a lord : but as for thee they hate thee as the Evil One.—20. *S.*, For thee, O Death, they hate thy name, and also thy work : my name they hate but my delights they greatly love.—21. *D.*, To bitterness of teeth is turned, this thy sweetness : penitence of soul cleaves ever unto thy lusts.— 22. *S.*, Sheol is hated because in her is no repentance : a pit that swallows and closes on all movements.—23. *D.*, Sheol is a gulf wherein whoso falls shall rise again : sin is hated because it cuts off the hope of man.—24. *S.*, Though I mislike penitents, I give place *for repentance :* thou cuttest off hope from the sinner who dies in his sin. —25. *D.*, It was of thee that at first his hope was cut off : for he whom thou hast not caused to sin dies happily.—26. Blessed *is* He who raised against each other those cursed servants : that we might see them as they have seen us and mocked at us.—27. This that we have seen of them is a pledge, my brethren : of what we shall see of them hereafter when we rise again.

## LIII.

1. Come, let us hear how they contend for victory : the guilty ones who never have conquered, nor will conquer.—2. Death said

unto the Evil One, In the end the victory is mine : for Death is master of the close, as a conqueror.—3. *Satan,* This were to be Death indeed, wert thou able : to bring to death a living man, by means of lusts.—4. *D.*, Lo ! I who behold the dead, both good and bad : the righteous who despise thee, O Evil One, me they despise not.—5. *S.*, This dying of the body, is sleep for a time : think not, O Death, that thou art Death, who art as a shadow.—6. *D.*, Thee, O Evil One, the just have conquered, yea will conquer : but these that have conquered thee, lo ! I conquer.—7. *S.*, Even this that thou bringest to death the just, is not of thyself : because of Adam whom I conquered, they drink this cup.—8. *D.*, Lo ! Sheol is full of the men of Sodom, and the Assyrians : and the giants who *were* in the flood, who is like me?—9. *S.*, These, O Death, all of them, by me were slain : I am he that caused them to sin, so that they perished.—10. *D.*, Joseph who conquered thee I conquered, O Satan : in the chamber he conquered thee but I conquered, and cast him into the tomb. —11. *S.*, Moses who conquered thee, O Death, by sprinkling of blood : he conquered thee in Egypt, but at the rock, who conquered him?—12. *D.*, Elijah who feared thee not, O Satan : fled before Jezebel's face, because he feared me.—13. *S.*, Aaron who withstood thee, O Death, with smoke of incense : to him I gave earrings of gold : and he fashioned a calf.—14. *D.*, Thou wentest down to contend with Job, and he conquered thee and came up : but I, after he had conquered thee, then conquered him.—15. *S.*, David who by his sackcloth stayed that pestilence : him on the house-top I conquered, who had conquered Goliath.—16. *D.*, Jehu who destroyed the house of Baal, the temple of the Evil One : was unable to destroy Sheol, the stronghold of my realm. 17. *S.*, Solomon who snatched from thy mouth, a child by *his* judgment : him in his old age I made a builder of idol-altars.—18. *D.*, Samuel who in *respect of* gold scorned thee, O Satan : him I conquered, the conqueror, who conquered bribes.—19. *S.*,

Samson who in *respect of* the lion's whelp, scorned thee, O Death : through Delilah, frail vessel, I yoked him to the mill.—20. *D.*, Josiah from his childhood despised thee, Evil One : but me not even in his old age, could he withstand.—21. *S.*, Hezekiah withstood thee, Death, when he overcame the bound *of life :* I misled him and he neglected the miracle, and showed his treasures.—22. *D.*, John who conquered thee, Evil One, and absolved and baptized : I extinguished that torch, which had disclosed thee.—23. *S.*, Simon overcame thee, when he brought to life that blessed woman : in a woman he overcame thee and by a woman I overcame him and made him deny.—24. *S.*, Apostles and prophets with one voice, curse thee, O Death : "Where is the victory of Death, and the sting of Sheol?"—25. Thy Lord in Sheol thou hast shut up, O cursed servant : God hates thee and also man, hold then thy peace.—26. *S.*, It was the will of Him who gives life to all, that shut him in Sheol : it was thou that called Him to this, when thou madest Adam sin.—27. O comrade of Nabal who in the wilderness reproached his lord : abhorred be thy mouth which said to Him, "Fall down and worship me!"

## LIV.

1. Hear, O Freedom, the dispute of two servants : how they are convicted by each other, that they are powerless.—2. *R.*, *To Thee be glory by Whose humiliation Adam was exalted : and by Whose death he was raised, and regained Eden!*—3. If then the Evil One overcome thee, great is the shame : Death his comrade has convicted him, as being weak.—4. And if again Death subdue thee, lo! what reproach : for the Evil One his comrade derides him, as but a shadow.—5. Their dispute is for thee a mirror, wherein thou mayest see : that they both are but as chaff, before thy breath.—6. Yea and Prophets and Apostles, in their promises : assure thee that they like flowers, shall fade at the rising.—7. *S.*, Thou, Death, art he

whom they hate, the quick and dead : for every combination thou dissolvest, and destroyest.—8. *D.*, It is not open death that kills, O Satan : thy death which is secret kills the sons of men.—9. *S.*, My name is not hateful as thine, for the angel : showed himself in Satan's likeness to Balaam on the way.—10. *D.*, How fit is this thy name, O Satan : who hast erred and made unwary Adam err, from the way!—11. *S.*, Wander not like one ignorant, and lose thy cause : dispute, O Death, if thou are competent, for replying.—12. *D.*, I know that thou art wily, O Satan : so that thou out of sand canst twist a snare.—13. *S.*, Thy disputing, Death, is ended : for he who is worsted : when his words fail and are ended, begins to rail.—14. *D.*, Among all I am conqueror, and by thee am I worsted? Let Adam persuade thee whom I have overcome, O Satan!—15. *S.*, I am he who bound Adam, and cast him before thee : the mighty man whom my wiles had bound, thou didst come and subdue.—16. *D.*, I am he who have been crowned anew, with a diadem in the world : for Adam, chief of the mighty, I hold captive in Sheol.—17. *S.*, I killed him by secret death, even Adam when he sinned : thou, Death, hast slain one that was dead, killed by me.—18. *D.*, In thy desire to conquer, Evil One, thou hast made thyself hated : for thou art Death as well as Satan, and this *seems* a little thing to thee.—19. *S.*, Thou hast then been silenced, Death, as a weakling : for neither in words nor in deeds, hast thou strength to stand.—20. *D.*, It is for thy evil thou conquerest, O Evil One, if thou discernest : thy crown is wholly of shame, if thou perceivest.—21. I shall be defeated and thou shalt be cursed, O Satan : it is well for me to be ignorant, and not mischievous. —22. Blessed be the Just One who divided them, though they were quite of one mind : Blessed be the Good One who made us of one mind, when we were divided.—23. I will overcome the Evil One through Thy forgiveness, O All-Merciful : and I shall overcome death through Thy Resurrection, O All-Life-giver!

## LV.

1. Lo! the Evil One reproached Death, and was in turn reproached : from each and to each and against each, *were* their taunts.—2. *R., To Thee be glory, Son of the Lord of All, Who diedst for all : for He was raised to give life to all, in the day of His Coming!*—3. *S.,* Jonah who conquered thee, and returned back from Sheol, became my advocate *in asking*, why sinners were spared?—4. *D.,* Slander not, O Evil One, the son of Amittai : he showed a face of anger, that they might praise thee more.—5. *S.,* Quite powerless is all thy persuasion, O tyrant Death : for there pleases me nothing, of all thou hast said.—6. *D.,* For when was the word of truth pleasing to thee? A gulf is between thee and truthfulness, O lying one.—7. I am righteous all my days, with nought to repent : I am he that rescues from thee the sons of men.—8. *S.,* Proclaim thy repentance, Death, thou art well come : lo! Saul also among the prophets, great cause of scorn.—9. If thou, Death, be justified, then for myself : I cut not off hope, likewise, of repentance.—10. *D.,* No idol with my Lord have I made, O hater of thy Lord! lo! thou by dead idols, slayest the living.—11. *S.,* That thou, Death, art half of me, I know, and I half of thee : if half of me repents, it repents, but I marvel.—12. *D.,* Thy partner am I in share, but not in sin : mine are the slain and thine the slayers, whom thou madest sin.—13. *S.,* My craftiness weeps for itself, when I dispute with thee : my wiles mourn over me, when I meet thee.—14. *D.,* Workers of witchcraft and soothsayers, with all *their* offences : the fire that thou kindledst in the world, in Sheol I have quenched.—15. *S.,* Thou penitent who strainest out gnats, and swallowest the just : the chaste shall rend thee, who cry, from within thy belly.—16. *D.,* It is the treasure-house *where* I keep all the righteous : their resurrection threatens *ill* to thee, who didst persecute them.—17. *S.,* The greedy one who carries all creatures, in his bowels : lo! he casts up to me that I am robbed, of my possessions.—18. *D.,* Before the stroke lament not, for it has not *yet* reached *thee :* the day will come when thou shalt cry out, and I shall hear and rejoice.—19. The fire will come that shall strip off thee thy very skin : as by the potsherd thou didst strip the skin of Job.—20. *D.,* The savour of sloth begins, as if to hover on me ; it is then a dream that I ceased, for a short space.—21. It was not that words failed me, and therefore I was silent : it is for the time I grieve, that has passed idly.—22. The hurt *done* by thy speech is very great : would I had not heard it! For my whole mind is intent upon my work.—23. This humankind that is lost, was undone by wandering thought : slothfulness, with negligence, brought it under yoke.—24. The madness of desire bid for wealth, and bought it : contention with boastfulness, were the sureties.—25. With persistence for strength, I wage my war : and if I neglect but a little, my sway is naught.—26. By continual dropping, I clean the rocks : for continual dropping can dissolve even a mountain.—27. Habit even over nature, becomes master : it trains and leads even lions, as beasts of burden.—28. Habit, repose, and increase, with persistence ; by these is freedom conquered, though stubborn above all.—29. If its will be firmly set, it breaks the fetters ; but if lax, a fragile net, can capture it.—30. If so be that Freedom shouts, we are scattered : but if she be silent we gather together, to mock at her.—31. Let us cease from much speaking, lest it lead to much sloth: with one mind let us assail the wall, and lo! it is broken down.—32. *S.,* Go thou and see to diseases, and I to snares : for to me sins and to thee pestilences, are great solace.—33. And even though I have paused, I have not paused from my cares : for my will at no time rests, but is ready.

## LVI.

1. With Freedom is thy struggle, O Evil One : it can cast on thee a muzzle, if it so please.—2. *R.,* To Thee be glory in whose

victory we have gained strength : and in whose resurrection we defy even Death itself !—3. Lo ! again these two exposed each other, how weak both are : Death reminded the Evil One of thy mightiness (*O Freedom*).—4. Thy fire is in thy nest, O Death, and thou perceivest not : the fate of the departed, to thee is overthrow.—5. Lo ! Death and the Evil One proclaim thy mightiness (*O Freedom*) : yea, the Evil One calls to mind thy faith.—6. If then these that were against thee are on thy side : this is a great thing that thy persecutors have become thy heralds.—7. *D.*, I confess, O Evil One, that as usury : I lay up the King's treasures, till His Coming.—8. *S.*, I, O Death, rather deny that this belongs to God : this treasure of subtlety, which I have stored.—9. *D.*, Thy coinage is fraudulent, then, O Satan : that into the treasuries of God, is not received.—10. *S.*, A new coinage do I coin, in kingly wise : lo ! my merchantmen bring loss, into the world.—11. God created everything out of nothing : and I created great sin out of nothing—12. *D.*, Closed and bound be thy mouth, Evil One, who art thus bold : to set thyself, lo ! in comparison with the Creator.—13. *S.*, To me, O Death, it is lawful to dare and speak : thy tongue, even thine, is a slave, and under fear.—14. *D.*, A gulf is henceforth between us, O Satan : for madly against thy Lord, lo ! thou assailest.—15. *S.*, Wherefore doubtest thou, O Death, of our concord? Be to us comrade and member : and lo ! we reign.—16. Come, draw we our pair of swords, against mankind : I secretly, thou openly, and lo ! we end them.—17. Sin and Sheol they too gave counsel to those two : saying "If ye be divided, ye are undone."—18. See the waters how if dispersed, they run low : but if gathered they gain strength, and thus ye likewise.—19. If divided ye perish, as the feeble : but yoked together ye reign, as the mighty.—20. Love melts down many, as in a furnace : and makes one powerful mass, that overcomes all.—21. In it are wisdom and cunning, and force and power : it is greater far than an image of sixty cubits.—22. Be reconciled,

let us assemble and go, against that party : which if it be at one can never be defeated. —23. These things the troublers discoursed, and gathered and came : Thy day, Lord, will gather them, into Gehenna.—24. Through Thy mercy, Lord, will I worship Thee, when I have risen : at Thy trumpet I will praise Thy Son, when I am purged.

## LVII.

1. Listen, my brethren, to Death, mocking the Evil One : that caused the head of our race to sin, and its mother.—2. *R.*, *To Thee be glory that by Thy humiliation, Satan is subdued : and that Thy abasement has exalted Adam, who was abased.*—3. *D.*, Thy great nakedness shall be seen, by the sons of Adam ; as thou mockedst his nakedness, when thou madest him sin.—4. Eve will cease from that serpent, and rail at thee : for thou, O Dragon, wast he that beguiled her simpleness.—5. Abel will see him, even, Cain, who has come to thee : the disciple of his wrath will blame his cursed master.—6. *S.*, Noah who conquered the flood, as it were death : by the mouth of Ham I laughed at, when wine overcame him.—7. *D.*, Noah was not harmed, but thy garment, wherewith thou clothedst him : even cursings, he put on, and became a slave.—8. *S.*, Lot who overcame anger which is, thy likeness, Death : to his daughters I gave such counsels, as were pleasing to me.—9. *D.*, And Lot's wife who was thy vessel hearkened, to thy counsel : may half of thee be dried up, as thy whole vessel was dried up !—10. Gehenna be overturned, upon thy head : as thy malice overturned Sodom, its dwellers !—11. Floods of fire be stirred against thee, in the resurrection : who against Moses and Elijah, didst stir the people !—12. Let the just mock thee at the last, and Joseph rejoice ! whose brethren mocked him, set on by thee !—13. Let vapour of smoke come in, and choke thy senses : as the waters of the sea choked, the senses of the wicked !—14. Let chaste women also mock thee, by whose counsel : the daughters of Midian

mocked, the foolish people !—15. Flame be kindled on thy head, for Samson's sake : for by a woman thou shavedst his locks, that lion of strength !—16. *S.*, Saul whom I conquered by envy, by witchcraft conquered thee : for he asked for and brought up Samuel, out of his grave.—17. *D.*, Slander not the living dead, for he came not up : thou wast he that came up in the phantom : for thou wast worthy.—18. Let the commandment hang thee over the flame, thou Evil One ! for by thee they hanged Absalom, upon a tree.—19. In the fire mayst thou see thyself humbled, among vile women ! for Solomon by thee was degraded, among profane women.—20. Justice be measured to thee, as thou didst inflame her ! even Jezebel who devoured the prophets, thou kindledst her.—21. In fire mayst thou justly burn, who madest them drunken ! the two whom Elijah burnt up, when they went up and assailed *him.*—22. On thee also be coals heaped ! may he see and rejoice : that Naboth in whom thou heapedst, a pile of stones !—23. Be thou clad in scorn in the day of judgment, before all beholders ! who clothedst Gehasi in a leprosy, by means of thy theft.—24. With lightning for a dart be thou pierced, O Satan ! who in the heart of Josiah, didst fix *thy* darts.—25. Sink thou in the dregs of Gehenna, O Satan ! who didst sink Jeremiah in the mire of the pit.—26. Daniel escaped from the pit, whither thou didst cast him : may he have comfort in seeing thee, in the furnace for ever !—27. Be thy wickedness returned on thy head, Hater of man : as his wickedness was returned on the head, of Haman thy fellow !—28. May the King's Bride mock thee, as did Esther : when thou beseechest her in the judgment-day, to plead for thee !—29. Fire released the righteous ones, whom thou hadst bound : a mighty bond be to thee, the flame of fire ! —30. Be thou torn in sunder, and may the seven brothers, see thy defeat : the sons of Shemuni who by thy wolves, were torn in sunder !—31. May fire triumph over thy pate, as thou didst mock : the two heads of Nazarites, sons of the barren !—32. May fire make mock of thy head, for mother and daughter : triumphed over John's head, when thou didst madden them !—33. Flame triumphed over thy head, O Evil One : for on the charges thou didst triumph, over John's head !

## LVIII.

1. Lo ! Death was prompt beforehand, to mock Satan : him who was doomed to become a mockery at the last.—2. *R.*, *Glory to Thee Who by Thy crucifixion, didst conquer the Evil One : and by Thy resurrection gain victory, likewise over Death !—*3. And for our Lord's sake Death spake curses on him : who was the cause of His shame, and crucifixion.—4. *D.*, The fiery pit be thy grave, O Satan : who blasphemedst the Voice from the grave, that rent the graves ! —5. My Lord I know, and the Son of my Lord, O thou Satan ! thou hast denied thy Lord, and crucified the Son of thy Lord.— 6. This is the name that fits thee, "Slayer of thy Lord" : when He appears Whom thou slewest, He shall slay thee.—7. At thee shall every one shake the head, for by thee the chiefs : shook their heads at Him, the Lord of life.—8. A bruised reed under the feet, of the just shalt thou be : for through thee they put a reed in His hand, Who upholds all.—9. With a crown of thorns was He crowned, to signify : that He took the diadem of the kingdom, of the house of David.—10. With a crown of thorns was He crowned, the King of kings : but He took the diadem of the kings, of those that shamed Him.—11. In the robes of mockery that they gave him, in those He mocked *them :* for He took the raiment of glory, of priests and kings.—12. To vinegar is thy memory akin, O thou Satan : who didst offer vinegar for the thirst, of the Fount of Life.—13. The hand shall every man lift against thee who strengthenedst the hand that smote Him by Whose hand, all creatures stand.—14. He was smitten by the hand and He cut off the hand, of Caiaphas : the hand of the priesthood is cut off, in the cutting off of the unction.—15. On

the pillar again they stretched Him, as for
scourging: Him Whose pillar went before,
to *guide* their tribes.—16. The pillar on the
pillar, He was scourged: He removed Himself from out of Zion, and its fall came.—
17. When they put two beams together, to
form the Cross: He broke them, even
the two staves, the guardians of them.—
18. Ezekiel put together the sticks, the two
in one: in the two beams of the Cross,
their staves have ceased.—19. The two
sticks, as it were wings, bore the people:
lo! his two staves were broken, even as
his wings.—20. The bosom and wings of
the Cross, He opened in mercy: its pinions
bowed and bore the nations, to go to Eden.
—21. It is akin to the Tree of Life, and unto
the son of its stock: it leads its beloved
that on its boughs, they may feed on its
fruits.—22. Go howl and weep, Evil One,
for me and for you: for not one of us shall
enter the "Garden of Life."—23. *S.*, Now
that thou hast confessed O Death, come let
me tell thee: that all this discourse of thine,
to me is idle talk.—24. I will go and watch
the snares, which I have set: thou too,
Death, fly and look after, all that are sick.
—25. Our Lord has brought both to nought,
on either hand: the Evil One shall be
brought to nought here, and Death hereafter there.

### LIX.

1. Lo! Death for us on Satan, inflicts
vengeance: come let us hear his shame and
rejoice, for he rejoiced in our shame.—2.
*R., To Thee be glory from Thy flock, from
Thee: are subdued both Death and Satan,
under Thy Feet!*—3. D., Evil ones shall
be hung upright, but thou, head down-
ward: for, reversely, thou crucifiedst,
Simon on the tree.—4. *S.*, Touching all else
I am silent, Death, for my time wanes:
Simon himself conjured me, "Crucify me
thus."—5. Were it the just that cursed me, I
had not grieved: the curse of Death unto me,
is worse than hell.—6. D., The shame of
our Lord I have not spoken of, it is too
great for my mouth: that I should weigh

and compare His Passion, with Thy torment.
—7. Twelve *judgment* thrones shall He set,
for His Twelve: for by the twelve tribes
thou, even thou, shall be condemned.—8. A
halter unbought shalt thou hang thee, O
thou Satan: as that Thy disciple hung him,
a halter for a price.—9. Haply yon hell in
mercy, shall be emptied: and thou shalt
dwell there alone, with Thy ministers.—10.
Manifold are Thy curses, and how shall I
count *them?* Lo! the sum of all thy curses,
*is* on thy members.—11. The evil in the fire
shall stab thee, who madest them evil: they
shall upbraid thee "wherefore, broughtest
thou us hither?"—12. Sinners shall rail
against thee, and haply their threats: shall
be worse to thee than the torment, of yonder
hell.—13. These shall be unto thee there, all
of them Satans: as thou hast been to them
here, the one Satan.—14. The Watchers
shall seize and hurl thee down, calling to
mind: how through thee men hurled their
Lord, from the height to the depth.—15. All
men will run to stone thee, not forgetting
that through thee the maddened people ran,
to stone their Maker.—16. On thee, Evil One,
from all mouths *shall be*, the spitting of
wrath: for through thee they spat on Him
Whose spittle, gave sight to the blind.—17.
On thee, Evil One, from all tongues, shall be
all curses: for through thee men blasphemed
Him, Who opened dumb mouths.—18.
Blessed *is* He Who avenged our wrong,
though in silence: and stirred up Death
against the Evil One, to fall upon him!—
19. Sound we Hosannas, my brethren, as *did*
Gideon:[1] who when he sounded, the oppressors, fell on one another!

### LX.

1. O what amazement befel the Evil One,
of a sudden, my brethren: when the sinful
woman was corrected, and gained wisdom!
—2. *R., Glory to the One Who alone, conquered the Evil One: and to Him yea Him be
also confession, Who vanquished Death!*—3.

---

[1] Judg. vii. 18–22.

The Evil One marvelled "Where *is* her laughter? where her perfumes? where her dancing and outward ornament, and inward wickedness?"—4. Instead of that light laughter, she is given up to tears: She has cut off her hair to wipe the dust, off the feet of Jesus. —5. Naught lasts in her of any doctrine, nor abides in her: from our instruction she has escaped and cast away, all that I taught her.—6. She has denied us and our acquaintance, and even as though: she had never seen me she has blotted my image, out of her mind.—7. The living leaven of Jesus flew to her, Jesus was silent: but she made bold to press and enter, though none called her.—8. She forgot our love of *many* years, and in the twinkling of an eye: from between me and her she removed *it, and* set Death *there.*—9. For instead of laughter weeping delights her, and instead of paint: a shower of tears, and instead of ornament, a sad countenance.—10. Zaccheus I made chief of extortioners, and her I made: chief of wantons; my two wings, Jesus has broken.—11. If so be Zaccheus becomes *his* disciple, and if so be she: becomes *his* hearer, henceforth they fetter, my craftiness. —12. Carved images henceforth are a mockery and the carvers: a derision, and the worshippers a laughing-stock.—13. I shut *men's* eyes that they might not perceive, that they are carved images: Jesus opens their eyes to see that they are the works *of men's hands.*—14. If Jesus has chosen for Himself preachers, then our preaching: whereof the whole world is full, is put to silence.—15. For lo! the Chaldeans with the soothsayers, and lo! the wizards: with the diviners they are smitten and the priests, with all evil ones!— 16. Ye priests are ended and have given up the Ghost from henceforth, depart ye diviners! become husbandmen, the Chaldeans likewise, shall close their books.—17. If the Hebrews have become His disciples, who by all miracles: were not subdued, who of the nations, shall not obey him?—18. If he begins to set straight the reverse, He brings to naught our speech: henceforth He will not hesitate against us, He who rebukes all men.—19. In that I was worshipped in all temples, our disgrace is greater: than our honour *was*, for all men spit, upon our altars. —20. Flesh of sacrifice becomes abhorred, into fragments: idols are *broken*, and carven images burn, under their pots.—21. All our work becomes a laughing-stock, and a ruin: all that we have built, and a mockery, all that we have taught.—22. The secret mysteries that I taught them, laboriously: are about to be spread abroad, on the housetops. —23. Of the Egyptians I was more proud, than of any nation: for they used to worship even, the onions and garlic.—24. Lo! I fear lest even here, where delusion was *so* great: truth shall prevail that there exceedingly, Jesus may reign.—25. And if when He was an infant, and fled and went down, Egypt marvelled: yea lulled him—this strangler of babes, loved their Babe.—26. Was it a pledge He went down to give her, as a betrother: giving assurance that when of full age, He will also take her *to wife?*— 27. Pharaoh cannot set his foot *firm*, for this is no stammerer: that he should deceive Him, and no bondman, that he should lie unto Him.—28. Moses smote and the Egyptians rebelled, and he chastised the people: and the Hebrews rebelled—Jesus is smitten, and gives life to all.—29. This is hard *to understand* that not by force; lays He His yoke: on the rebellious: He was rebuked, and He instructs others.—30. The spittle of His mouth, wiped off and took away, the shame of Adam: by the smiting of His cheeks, He rooted out our wrathfulness, from His disciples.—31. By the nails which he received, He made me to suffer. I rejoiced when I crucified Him: and I knew not that He was crucifying me, in His crucifixion.

## LXI.

1. In wisdom let us hearken to Death, O my beloved: how he accuses us for our weeping, and for our mourning.—2. *R., To thee be praise Who cameth down, to follow Adam: and foundest Adam and also in him, the children of Adam.*—3. And rightly per-

haps he says, "Ye slay : without mercy and lo ! ye weep, as though merciful."—4. Ye have made me as a cruel one, O ye murderers : for ye slay one another, without my help ! —5. While Death was *but* desiring to come, the sword came before him : let us see then against whom cries out, the blood of the slain.—6. Against you cry out the strangled, who were suffocated : for it shames me of the rope, of their strangulations.—7. They take away from me even my rest, for without me : how could the strangled and the slain, enter Sheol ?—8. Lo ! your infants are cast out, as those in Egypt : your sons have ye sacrificed to demons, O demoniacs ! —9. While Death was *but* desiring to taste, of your corpses : Cain refreshed me beforehand, with blood of man.—10. While I was but desiring to wait patiently, till Adam should die : before I had power ye gave me power, over your bodies.—11. Cain with his sword overthrew, the gate of Sheol : for it was closed and before the time, he first opened it.—12. He by treading made the way of Sheol, without my help : for in the way ye have trodden out for me, lo ! I walk *therein.*—13. Nine hundred years I sat and waited, for Adam to die : but Cain not even a day, endured his brother. —14. Robbers upon the highways, are worse than I : I am slumbering while they, are watching to slay.—15. Lo ! your slaughtered in the graves, and your murdered in your ways ; and your strangled upon your stakes !—16. "If I rebelled against my lord, yea and slew him : who was he that slew these here," said Jehu.—17. And if I Death have taken, your departed : the strangled, the slain, and the slaughtered, who was it slew them ?—18. Ye are Satan to each other, and the Evil One is abhorred : ye are pestilence to each other, and Death is blamed !—19. Your *own* will to you is Satan, yea and a murderer : but of Death and of Satan, all men complain.—20. Poison of Death ye give also to drink, each to other : lo ! how many Deaths have ye, beside me.—21. Wiles, stratagems, yea and snares, sword and poison : how many

Deaths from you and in you, lo ! are there born.—22. The judge in the judgment-hall, is a second Death : he slays for secret reward, but I for naught.—23. I have seen bribery and marvelled at it, that ran and outran me : how many slain does bribery, slay, and none perceives !—24. I am ashamed that *so* unskilfully, I conduct myself : if I take even one corpse, all men perceive *it.*—25. In the houses weeping and in the streets, also wailing : and even unto the gates of Sheol, they groan over me.—26. Groan over yourselves that ye are thus hateful, and ye hate me : Sheol henceforth shall groan over you, O murderers !—27. With torture, scourging and fire, yea with stoning : ye put to death the sons of men, and ye are proud !—28. I am more modest than you and merciful, also reverent : for with reverence I bear away, your departed. —29. On the bed I deal gently, with him that is sick : and quietly I lay him to sleep, for *but* a while.

### LXII.

1. Lo ! Death, the King of silence, complains, my brethren : that we have filled his abode with the wailing, of Hope cut off.— 2. *R. To Him be great praise Who comest down, to us here below : and suffered and rose again and in His Body, raises our bodies!* —3. While we weep like madmen, at the gates of Sheol : hearken what Death says, reproaching us.—4. It shames me, says Death, that ye, have overcome me : the half of Sheol suffices not, to contain your slain.—5. For alien corpses together, lie heaped in Sheol : there are two divisions there, the dead, the slain.—6. Whereas I should complain that ye have wronged me, lo ! ye are weeping : ye have burst the gate of Sheol, and done me hurt.—7. For ye are like unto an infant, which while yet weeping : laughs again as ye also, over your dead.—8. For there is no discretion in your mourning, and no understanding : in your laughter—for to me ye seem like, to a weaned babe.—9. One hour weeping and wailing, and after a little : both jesting and

wantonness, as of children.—10. For ye are unable to become, perfect men : that weep not yea and laugh not, as the discreet.—11. Touching your books we are grieved, that they have toiled over them : who should read them unto you, *even* the divine Scriptures.—12. The readers are crying aloud, for ye are deaf : this *their* crying proves concerning you, that ye are *as* stocks.—13. For since the reader and the interpreter, are crying aloud : your ears therefore are heavy, or else your hearts.—14. For if there were *with you* an ear, *open* to persuasion : it were meet to hear little, and to do much.—15. But because *its* hearing is closed, whoso knocks at it : the voice returns back to him, who sent it forth.—16. There is no crying with me of mine, I am not deaf : none that reads or interprets *for me*, I am not dull.—17. The breath that *is* from Him commands me, *sons* the God of truth : and with the command there follows, also the fulfilment.—18. With me is no holding back, no turnings aside : I wot no arrow even, could outstrip me.—19. But your voices are scorned by me, when ye are weeping : over the graves of your departed, in the cutting off of hope.—20. Were it possible or permitted, when ye are weeping : I would go forth and tell *you*, to your faces.—21. "I am endeavouring to give, an account of the death : and your voices disturb me, that I err in my count."—22. Ye nations, let not your understanding, become childish : like that nation whose intelligence, was never great.—23. In which prudence bestows not itself, as in a fool : for its thoughts are darkness, without discernment.—24. For your infants and your sons, in the resurrection : they shall be foremost to come forth, as the first fruits.—25. Then after them *shall come* the just, as victorious : last shall come forth the sinner, as put to shame.—26. For although in the twinkling of an eye, they be quickened : yet is it in order that their ranks, come forth from Sheol.—27. Prophets come forth and Apostles, and *holy* Fathers : following them in due array, according to command.—28. Lo ! that which now is sown, in random

mixture : is yielded back in great order, as garden-herbs.—29. For though one in the sowing, should mix all seeds : that which is earlier than its fellow, prevents its fellow.—30. And not as their going down was confused, so disordered shall be : their coming up from the earth, for its order is fixed.—31. Lo ! I have been against myself, in what I have said : for secret things which ye comprehended not, from me ye have learned.—32. Instead of the tears that profit not, which are at the tomb : pour them forth in *your* prayer, in the midst of the Church.—33. For to the dead there is profit in these, and likewise to the living : weep not with a weeping that afflicts, both dead and living !

## LXIII.

1. Who shall weigh the recompense of Abraham ? whom I marvelled at when he bound, his only son.—2. R., *To thee be glory, Voice that bringest to life the dead in Sheol: and they have come up as preachers, of His Son Who quickens all!*—3. At that time I came forth in haste, to see the marvel : how that his knife was drawn out, against his beloved.—4. I gathered my manifold memories, from all quarters : and I collected my spirit to marvel, at that illustrious one.—5. How therefore can ye read, that great story ? ye have despised the reading of it, in your very ears.—6. The sword of Jephthah rebukes, him that laments : his daughter was to him a mirror of life from the dead.—7. She gave herself for her father, so commend ye : your life to the Father of all, in the hope of *your* end.—8. In the womb then did ye not make trial, of a mystery of Sheol ? yet in Sheol ye had more rest, than in the womb.—9. It is stubborn in you to stand up against, my mighty will : for lo ! to succour them I take away, your departed.—10. By the king of Moab who slew, his son with his hands : he is put to shame who laments, for the departed one.—11. He was a profane man, lo ! according, to what you read : but ye are doctors and teachers, as ye suppose.—12. He endured, but ye are furious, in

your mourning : against the will of the Lord of all, while ye are weeping.—13. I fear however to let pass, the story of Job : through this feeble mouth of mine, for I am unworthy.—14. So in like manner I turn aside, from *mention* of their bones : though I praise Him who granted, that they should come to me.—15. Dishonour not your members, by your sins : for in Sheol the bones are despised, of evildoers.— 16. Whenever I see the body of one of the evil : I trample on it and curse, even his memory.—17. But wherever I see a bone, of one of the just ; I set it apart and honour it, and do it worship.—18. Ye feeble ones understand not, all my ordinances : with you orders are confused, for ye are blind.— 19. It is Moses alone that I know, to have honoured like me : the bones of that Joseph whom I magnify.—20. But Moses did such honour, to one pure body : but I to the body and the bones, of all the righteous. —21. Brightly shine the bones of Prophets, and of Apostles : a lamp to me in darkness, are all the righteous.—22. I worship Him Who lightens for me, the darkness of Sheol : the splendour of Moses who was so great, was *as* the sun to me.

## LXIV.

1. O feeble ones, why weep ye, over your dead : who in death are at rest from sorrows and sins ?—2. *R., Glory to Him Who endured all, for the sake of all men : yea tasted death for the sake of all, to bring all to life*—3. I reveal unto you, that even Satan, though much content : at your weeping, yet laughs much, at your mourning.—4. In mockery he winks at me and nods to me, as a jester : "Come let us laugh at sinners, for lo ! they are mad."—5. Truly they have given up remembrance of that fire, which I have hidden for them : and lo ! the fools are drunken with weeping, for their departed.—6. Instead of weeping as though, without provision : I had plundered and sent forth their dead, lo ! they are mad.— 7. The souls of the evil are to be afflicted,

till the judgment day : and these weep over the graves, like to madmen.—8. They care not for their own sins, that haply to-morrow : they must go in shame of face, to join their dead.—9. And thus shall all be put to shame alike, family by family : in Sheol the wretches shall repent without avail.—10. Leave the drunken and the madman, until that day : wherein *each* shall shake off his wine wherewith he was maddened.—11. I will go to gather them, like children : that they may play the wanton and the madman, until they perish.—12. Lo ! I have revealed to you the mystery, the secret of my comrade : go forth therefore, depart, amend, in repentance.—13. Leave me, I too will depart, I will see to my affairs : that with open face I may give my account to my Lord.—14. I know that the wind as it blew, has borne away my words : for ye are the same whom I, ofttimes have proved.—15. I remember Jeremiah how he, compared boldness : to the Indian who changes not *his skin*, though it is of freedom.—16. For this too belongs to it, even to freedom : that it binds itself by the will, as though by nature.—17. For so powerful is the will, in them that are free : that it may be likened to nature, through its workings.[1]

## LXV.

1. *Man*, O Death, despise thou it not, that image of Adam : which like a seed is committed to earth, till the Resurrection.— 2. *R. To thee be glory Who didst descend and plunge, after Adam : and draw him out from the depths of Sheol, and bring him into Eden !* —3. *Death*, I marvel at this seed, and at your words : for lo ! after five thousand years, it springs not yet.—4. *M.,* Its present state passes away, as winter *does :* and as a handful of *corn* it comes in the resurrection, to the garner of life.—5. *D.,* That there is vintage-time, lo ! I know, but I have not seen : the dead at any time sown, or yet reaped.—6. *M.,* There is coming a reaping,

---

[2] *I.e.* though boldness is matter of free will, it becomes a second nature.

O Death, that will leave thee bare: and the Watchers shall go forth as reapers, and make thee desolate.—7. *D.*, When did I become husbandman, instead of vine-dresser? who has turned Sheol the wine-press, into a tilled field?—8. *M.*, Does not the seed then teach thee, which decays and dies: and *is* cut off from hope, yet from the rain, recovers hope?—9. *D.*, A dream have ye seen ye feeble ones, of life from the dead: for in waking time the resurrection, ye do not see.—10. *M.*, Thy drowsiness hinders thee, that thou seest not: the multitudes of mysteries which cry aloud, of the resurrection.—11. *D.*, I know that seeds come to life, but I have not seen: bones that grew in Sheol, and sprang and came up.—12. *M.*, All thy discourse is like thyself, for lo! Ezekiel: has taught thee how in the valley, the dead come to life.—13. *D.*, Trees have I seen how in summer, they put on their garments: but bones in their nakedness, are cast into Sheol.—14. *M.*, Moses broke by his splendour, thy heart, O Death: the son of Adam has regained and put on, the glory of Adam.—15. *D.*, Our law in Sheol is this, to keep silence: for you are words and for me deeds, O feeble ones.—16. *M.*, How are the aged passed over if thou be vinedresser? He Who hindered thee from *taking* their lives, the same quickens all. 17.—The babe in the womb confutes thee, which is *as* buried there: to me it proclaims life from the dead, but to thee despoiling.—18. The despised flower despises thee, for it is shut up and passed over: yet though lost it is not lost, but blossoms again.—19. The chick cries out from the egg, wherein it is buried: and the graves are rent by a Voice, and the body arises. 20. For a body too is the chick, that is in the egg: lo! its body to our body proclaims, the life from the dead.—21. With the locust thy plea is overthrown, and ended, O Death: for in coming forth from the dust it teaches, the life from the dead.—22. *D.*, I had been content if already, the resurrection had been: for the day of resurrection had disturbed me less, than your judgments.—

23. Merciful is the Son of the Highest, yea good and just: and will not harshly avenge on me, the death of Adam.—24. Have ye then no understanding, to perceive this: that your father laid on you, this retribution?

## LXVI.

1. Hold your peace, O mortals (said Death), a little while: and be like me who am so silent, in the midst of Sheol.—2. *R.*, *To Thee be glory, Watcher, that didst come down, after them that slept: and utter the voice from the Tree, and waken them!*—3. Ye are grieving, yea, weeping, for him that has gone: as though he came to grind for me, the mill in Sheol.—4. Great is the peace I give, unto the wearied: I wax not weary as you, nor weary them.—5. I hear all manner of curses, from thankless men: the sons of Adam are like Adam, who was thankless to his Lord.—6. Contrary one to the other are your voices, and your doings: with *your* voices ye weep and in your doings, ye fight daily.—7. I heard weeping and I thought to myself, that none labours: I saw toiling and I thought to myself, that no man dies.—8. The struggles of man made me think, that he is not mortal: his great weeping made me think, that to-morrow he is not.—9. Hear and let me be your counsellor, if ye be willing: for these two, these burdens, are very bitter.—10. Cease a little while from this toil, and from *this* weeping: toil ye and weep as mortals, who to-morrow vanish.—11. Ye are frantic with weeping, for your departed: and ye struggle in toiling, for your possessions.—12. It is well with the infants that die, and blessed are they: for they are freed from the misery, whereunto ye are cast.—13. Suffer me to go to Sheol, and there to say: "Happy are ye silent dead, how tranquil are ye!"—14. Hear the conclusion of our own words, If there be a resurrection: weep not ye, neither labour as though strangers.—15. Ye struggle as one who was to live, here forever: and ye weep as one who never, should rise again.—16. Hear my words, if there be with you

place for hearing: and prepare you provision that when I call ye may answer.— 17. For I hearken even I, to Him that calls me: and will restore your bodies, with your treasures.—18. Let there be peace between us, until that day: and when ye come forth I will cry and say, "Depart in peace!"— 19. Come ye, you and I even now, shall give glory: to Him that brings to death and to life, that He may give aid.—20. Praise from us all be to thee, O Lord, the living Sacrifice! Who by the sacrifice of Thy Body hast given life to quick and dead.— 21. Praise to Him Who clothed Himself in our body, and died and rose again: He died in us and we live in Him, blessed be He Who sent Him!

## LXVII.

1. Come ye, let us hear how Death convicts the People: that harsher than Death was their sword, against the just.—2. *R.,* *To Thee be glory, Who by Thy sacrifice, hast* *redeemed our disgrace: and Whose death* *was instead of all deaths, that Thou mightst* *raise all!*—3. It was not Death indeed that crucified Jesus, but *it was* the People: how hateful then the People, that are yet more hateful than I!—4. Into the pit they cast Jeremiah, the miry *pit:* but I in Sheol allotted, honour to his bones.—5. Naboth they bruised *to death* with stones, as though *he were* a dog: how good am I who have never stoned, even a dog!—6. The Hebrew women in famine, ate their children: Sheol *is* good who delivers and gives them up, without difficulty.—7. To the widow I gave her son, by the hand of Elijah: to the Shunamite her beloved, by the hand of Elisha.—8. The Hebrew women in greed, ate their children: Sheol gave up the dead and learned, to fast soberly.—9. Sheol was not indeed Sheol, but *its* semblance: Jezebel was the true Sheol, who devoured the just.—10. The sons of the prophets and the prophets, she slew and cast down: to heaven Elijah escaped, from her fury.— 11. How many deaths instead of one Death,

were among the People! and how many Sheols instead of one, were there also!— 12. Samaria and Jezrael her daughters, in Israel: and Zion and Jerusalem her sister, in Judea.—13. Prophets and just men in Judea, and in Israel: in these two abysses, they were drowned.—14. Why then is Sheol hated, and she alone: though there be many that are hateful, rather than she?— 15. The dead of the men of Judah, to me are right hateful: yea, abhorred by me are their bones, in the midst of Sheol.—16. Would that then I had a way to cast them out: *to cast* their bones thence from Sheol, for they cause her to rot.—17. I wonder at the Holy Spirit, that He thus dwelt: in the midst of a People whose savour stank, as their conversation.—18. Onions and garlic *are* the heralds of their doings: as *is* the food so is the understanding, of this defiled people. —19. Through the supplication of all that bow, and worship Thy Father: have mercy on Thy worshipper, who is thankless for Thy love.—20. From Hebrews and Aramæans, and also from the Watchers: to Thee *be* praise and through Thee to Thy Father, be also glory!—21. For that I have a mouth to Death, who is without mouth: may the Son Who is all mouths, hold back my offence from His Father!

## LXVIII.

1. *Man.* O, Death, be not thou boastful, over the just: the sons of thy Lord who at His command, come *to dwell with thee.*—2. *R.,* *To thee be glory that by Thy command,* *Death has reigned: and by Thy Resurrection has been humbled to low estate!*—3. *Death.* Herein am I exceeding great, according to thy saying: that though I be bondman I trample on them that are free.—4 *M.,* Adam was chosen and ruler, and under his yoke: thou, Death, and the Evil One, thy fellow, became bondmen.—5. *D.,* This is our pride that lo! the slaves have become lords: Death, and Satan, his fellow, have trampled on Adam.—6. *M.,* Lo! the humbling of thee and thy fellow, accurst servants! how Enoch trampled on you both,

and rose aloft and reigned.—7. *D.*, If so be Enoch made me grieve, yet have I comfort : for on Noah's dust in Sheol, lo ! I trample.— 8. *M.*, Tremble, O Death, before man, for though a servant, the yoke of his dominion reigns on all creatures.—9. *D.*, I rejoice then that they are no mean *foes* that I have overcome : for according to the greatness of the vanquished, he is great that overcomes.—10. *M.*, Well does thy voice sing triumph, O Death, over the just : for Enoch and Elijah have broken thy pair of wings.—11. *D.*, I know *how* to weigh my sorrows with my comforts : in place of two, lo ! many are come and coming.—12. *M.*, All that are come and coming to thee dwell as sojourners, and depart from thy abode as Lazarus.—13. *D.*, This thy saying hurts me not, rather it heals me : for Lazarus who rebelled against me, I again subdued.—14. *M.*, Make answer, O Death, and argue what constrained him, to be raised unless it were a mystery, showing forth his resurrection.—15. *D.*, Ye are famous in arguing as idle ones, while I labour in my task to discern and perform.— 16. *M.*, Thou wast well prepared for argument, what has checked thee? The truth of our resurrection has constrained thee by its reputations.—17. *D.*, Ye have made me hated by you, though I be not hateful : I am he that gives rest to your aged, and your afflicted.—18. Ye have made me as one that troubles, O ye mortals : Adam brought death upon you, and I bear the blame.—19. Gently will I expose you, for I am a slave, and ye are they that by your sins have made me king.—20. The will of Adam roused me for I was at rest : I was dead and ye quickened me, that ye might die by me.—21. I accuse the lying ones, who slew and denied it : for Adam slew himself and charges me. —22. The beginning of strife was the accursed serpent which has rightly been crippled : which crept, entered, and set enmity between me and you.—23. Satan is passed by and it is against me that ye are roused : go, strive with the Evil One who made you transgress.—24. He is my comrade and I deny *it* not, but though he be much hated, what need that I be blamed for him. I deny him henceforth.—25. Hearken to my words, O mortals, and I will console you : I have afflicted you and I confess the life from the dead.—26. For there begins to steal into my ears a voice of preparation : of the trumpet that holds itself ready to sound. —27. Hear my words and put much oil into your lamps : for hindrance from my part there is none for you.—28. *Yet*, Know ye that even although I have said these things, dear is the sound of your voice in the solitude of Sheol.—29. For man has been weighed by me, and great is his peace : for snakes and fishes and birds come to meet him.—30. But it is a marvel that to the Watchers, too, his converse is dear : yea, the Evil One in Gehenna, desires his presence.—31. Ye shall have life from the dead, O ye mortals, and I who am bereft shall be bereft in the midst of Sheol.—32. Let praise ascend from all to Thee Who quickenest all, and from every quarter gatherest the dust of Adam !

# NINETEEN HYMNS

## ON THE NATIVITY OF CHRIST IN THE FLESH.

(Translated, I.-XIII. by Rev. J. B. Morris, M.A., [Oxford *Library of the Fathers*]; XIV.-XIX. by Rev. A. Edward Johnston, B.D.).

# HYMNS ON THE NATIVITY

## HYMN I.

THIS is the day that gladdened them, the Prophets, Kings, and Priests, for in it were their words fulfilled, and thus were the whole of them indeed performed! For the Virgin this day brought forth Immanuel in Bethlehem. The voice that of old Isaiah spake,[1] to-day became reality. He was born there who in writing should tell the Gentiles' number! The Psalm that David once sang, by its fulfilment came to-day![2] The word that Micah once spake,[3] to-day was come indeed to pass! For there came from Ephrata a Shepherd, and His staff swayed over souls. Lo! from Jacob shone the Star,[4] and from Israel rose the Head.[5] The prophecy that Balaam spake had its interpreting to-day! Down also came the hidden Light, and from the Body rose His beauty! The light that spake in Zachary, to-day shined in Bethlehem!

Risen is the Light of the kingdom, in Ephrata the city of the King. The blessing wherewith Jacob blessed, to its fulfilment came to-day! That tree likewise, [the tree] of life, brings hope to mortal men! Solomon's hidden proverb[6] had to-day its explanation! To-day was born the Child, and His name was called Wonder![7] For a wonder it is that God as a Babe should show Himself. By the word Worm did the Spirit foreshow Him in parable,[8] because His generation was without marriage. The type that the Holy Ghost figured to-day its meaning was [explained.] He came up as a root before Him, as a root of parched ground.[9] Aught that covertly was said, openly to-day was done! The King that in Judah was hidden, Thamar stole Him from his thigh; to-day arose His conquering beauty, which in hidden estate she loved. Ruth at Boaz' side lay down, because the Medicine of Life hidden in him she perceived. To-day was fulfilled her vow, since from her seed arose the Quickener of all. Travail Adam on the woman brought, that from him had come forth. She to-day her travail ransomed, who to her a Saviour bare! To Eve our mother a man gave birth, who himself had had no birth. How much more should Eve's daughter be believed to have borne a Child without a man! The virgin earth, she bare that Adam that was head over the earth! The Virgin bare to-day the Adam that was Head over the Heavens. The staff of Aaron, it budded, and the dry wood yielded fruit! Its mystery is cleared up to-day, for the virgin womb a Child hath borne![10]

Shamed is that people which holds the prophets as true; for unless our Saviour has come, their words have been falsified! Blessed be the True One Who came from the Father of the Truth and fulfilled the true seers' words, which were accomplished in

---

[1] Is. x. 19.    [2] Ps. lxxxvii. 6.    [3] Mic. v. 2.    [4] Num. xxiv. 17.    [5] Hos. i. 11.
[6] Prov. iii. 18.    [7] Isa. ix. 6.    [8] Ps. xxii. 6.    [9] Is. liii. 2.

[1] Notice here, how St. Ephraim (in common with others) speaks of the *celebration* of the day as if it was the day itself, partly in exhibiting his intense realization through faith of the mystery and the re-presentation of it, to use the word in its ancient sense ; partly as evincing, perhaps, a belief in the unabidingness of our conceptions of time—a belief resulting, it may be, from the mystical union with God in Christ which the saints enjoy. For to God time is as nothing, and those who through grace are one with Him, begin to view things as He views them.

their truth. From thy treasure-house put forth, Lord, from the coffers of Thy Scriptures, names of righteous men of old, who looked to see Thy coming ! Seth who was in Abel's stead shadowed out the Son as slain, by Whose death was dulled the envy Cain had brought into the world! Noah saw the sons of God, saints that sudden waxed wanton, and the Holy Son he looked for, by whom lewd men were turned to holiness. The brothers twain, that covered Noah,[2] saw the only Son of God who should come to hide the nakedness of Adam, who was drunk with pride. Shem and Japhet, being gracious, looked for the gracious Son, Who should come and set free Canaan from the servitude of sin.

Melchizedek expected Him ; as His vicegerent, looked that he might see the Priesthood's Lord whose hyssop[3] purifies the world. Lot beheld the Sodomites how they perverted nature : for nature's Lord he looked who gave a holiness not natural. Him Aaron looked for, for he saw that if his rod ate serpents up,[4] His cross would eat the Serpent up that had eaten Adam and Eve. Moses saw the uplifted serpent that had cured the bites of asps, and he looked to see Him who would heal the ancient Serpent's wound. Moses saw that he himself alone retained the brightness from God, and he looked for Him who came and multiplied gods by His teaching :[5]

Caleb the spy bore the cluster on the staff, and came and longed to see the Cluster, Whose wine should comfort the world. Him did Jesus son of Nun long for, that he might conceive the force of his own surname : for if by His name he waxed so mighty,[6] how much more would He by His Birth? This Jesus that gathered and carried, and brought with him of the fruit, was longing for the Tree of Life to taste the Fruit that quickens all. For Him Rahab too was looking ; for when the scarlet thread in type redeemed her from wrath, in type she tasted of the Truth. For Him Elijah longed, and when Him on earth he saw not, he, through faith most throughly cleansed, mounted up in heaven to see Him. Moses saw Him and Elijah ; the meek man from the depth ascended, the zealous from on high descended, and in the midst beheld the Son. They figured the mystery of His Advent: Moses was a type of the dead, and Elijah a type of the living, that fly to meet Him at His coming.[7] For the dead that have tasted death, them He makes to be first : and the rest that are not buried, are last caught up to meet Him.

Who is there that can count me up the just that looked for the Son, whose number cannot be determined by the mouth of us weak creatures ? Pray ye for me, O beloved, that another time with strength endued, I in another legend may so set forth their foretaste, as I am able. Who is adequate to the praising of the Son of the Truth that has risen to us ? For it was for Him the righteous longed, that in their generation they might see Him. Adam looked for Him, for He is the Cherub's Lord, and could minister an entrance and a residence hard by the branches of the Tree of life. Abel longed after Him, that in his days He might come; that instead of that lamb that he offered, the Lamb of God he might behold. For Him Eve also looked ; for woman's nakedness was sore, and He capable to clothe them ; not with leaves, but with that same glory that they had exchanged away. The tower that the many builded, in mystery looked for One, who coming down would build on earth a tower that lifts up to Heaven. Yea the ark of living creatures looked in a type for our Lord ; for He should build the Holy Church, wherein souls find a refuge. In Peleg's days earth was divided into tongues,

---

[2] Gen. ix 23.   [3] Lev. xiv. 52.   [4] Exod. vii. 12.
[5] St. E. refers here to St. John x. 34, where the Word Himself teaches us that it was by His coming to them that Saints of old were called Gods.
[6] Heb. iv. 8.   [7] 1 Thess. iv. 17.

threescore and ten.[8] For Him Who by the tongues, to His Apostles divided earth. Earth which the flood had swallowed up, in silence cried to her Lord. He came down and opened Baptism, and men were drawn by it to Heaven. Seth and Enos, Cainan too, were surnamed sons of God; for the Son of God they looked, that they by grace might be His brethren. But little short of a thousand years did Methuselah live: He looked for the Son Who makes heirs of life that never ends! Grace itself in hidden mystery was beseeching on their behalf that their Lord might come in their age and fill up their shortcomings. For the Holy Spirit in them, in their stead, besought with meditation:[9] He stirred them up, and in Him did they look on that Redeemer, after whom they longed.[1]

The soul of just men perceive in the Son a Medicine of life; and so it felt desires that He might come in its own days, and then would it taste His sweetness. Enoch was longing for Him, and since on earth the Son he saw not, he was justified by great faith, and mounted up in Heaven to see Him. Who is there that will spurn at grace, when the Gift that they of old gained not by much labour, freely comes to men now? For Him Lamech also looked who might come and lovingly give Him quiet from his labour and the toiling of his hands, and from the earth the Just One had cursed.[2] Lamech then beheld his son, Noah,—him, in whom were figured types relating to the Son. In the stead of the Lord afar off, the type at hand afforded quiet. Yea Noah also longed to see Him, the taste of whose assisting graces he had tasted. For if the type of Him preserved living things, Himself how sure to bestow life upon souls! Noah longed for Him, by trial knowing Him, for through Him had the ark been established. For if the type of Him thus saved life, assuredly much more would He in person. Abraham perceived in Spirit that the Son's Birth was far of; instead of Him in person he rejoiced to see even His day.[3] To see Him Isaac longed, as having tasted the taste of His redemption;[4] for if the sign of Him so gave life, much more would He by the reality.

Joyous[5] were to-day the Watchers,[6] that the Wakeful came to wake us! Who would pass this night in slumber, in which all the world was watching? Since Adam brought into the world the sleep of death by sins, the Wakeful came down that He might awake us from the deep sleep of sin. Watch not we as usurers, who thinking on money put to interest, watch at night so oft, to reckon up their capital, and interest. Wakeful and cautious is the thief, who in the earth hath buried and concealed his sleep. His wakefulness all [comes to] this, that he may cause much wakefulness to them that be asleep. Wakeful likewise is the glutton, who hath eaten much and is restless; his watching is to him his torment, because he was impatient of stint. Wakeful likewise is the merchant; of a night he works his fingers telling over what pounds are coming, and if his wealth doubles or trebles. Wakeful likewise is the rich man, whose sleep his riches chase away: his dogs sleep; he guards his treasures from the thieves. Wakeful also is the careful, by his care his sleep is swallowed: though his end stands by his pillow, yet he wakes with cares for years to come. Satan teaches, O my brethren, one watching instead of another; to good deeds to be sleepy, and to ill awake and watchful. Even Judas Iscariot, for the whole night through was wakeful; and he sold the righteous Blood, that purchased the whole world. The son of the dark one put on darkness, having stripped the Light from off him: and Him who created silver, for silver the thief sold. Yea, Pharisees, the dark one's sons, all the night through kept awake: the

---

[8] This in round numbers is the received account of the number of languages at the dispersion.
[9] Rom. viii. 26.     [1] I Pet. i. II.     [2] Gen. v. 29.     [3] John viii. 56.     [4] Heb. xi. 19.
[5] Dan. iv. 13.     [6] I. e., the Angels; as usually in St. E.'s writings.

dark ones watched that they might veil the Light which is unlimited. Ye then watch as [heaven's] lights in this night of starry light. For though so dark be its colour yet in virtue it is clear.

For whoever is like this clear One, wakeful and prayerful in darkness, him in this darkness visible a light unseen surrounds! The bad man that in daylight stands, yet as a son of darkness deals; though with light clad outwardly, inly is with darkness girt. Be we not deceived, beloved, by the fact that we are watching! For whoso does not rightly watch, his watch is an unrighteous watch. Whoso watches not cheerfully, his watching is but a sleeping: whoso also watches not innocently, even his waking is his foe. This is the waking of the envious one! a solid mass, compact with harm. That watch is but a trafficking, with scorn and mockery compact. The wrathful man if he wakes, fretful with wrath his wake will be, and his watching proves to him full of rage and of cursings. If the babbler be waking, then his mouth becomes a passage which for sins is ready but for prayers shows hindrance.

The wise man, if so be he that watches, one of two things chooseth him; either takes sweet, moderate, sleep, or a holy vigil keeps.[7] That night is fair, wherein He Who is Fair [8] rose to come and make us fair. Let not aught that may disturb it enter into our watch! Fair be kept the ear's approach,[9] chaste the seeing of the eye! hallowed the musing of the heart! the speaking of the mouth be cleared. Mary hid in us to-day leaven that came from Abraham. Let us then so pity beggars as did Abraham the needy. To-day the rennet fell on us from the gentle David's house. Let a man show mercy to his persecutors, as did Jesse's son to Saul.[1] The prophets' sweet salt [2] is to-day sprinkled among the Gentiles. Let us gain a new savour [3] by that whereby the ancient people lost their savour. Let us speak the speech of wisdom; speak we not of things outside it, lest we ourselves be outside it!

In this night of reconcilement let no man be wroth or gloomy! in this night that stills all, none that threatens or disturbs! This night belongs to the sweet One; bitter or harsh be in it none! In this night that is the meek One's, high or haughty be in it none! In this day of pardoning let us not exact trespasses! In this day of gladnesses let us not spread sadnesses! In this day so sweet, let us not be harsh! In this day of peaceful rest, let us not be wrathful in it! In this day when God came to sinners, let not the righteous be in his mind uplifted over sinner! In this day in which there came the Lord of all unto the servants, let masters too condescend to their servants lovingly! In this day in which the Rich became poor for our sakes, let the rich man make the poor man share with him at his table. On this day to us came forth the Gift, although we asked it not! Let us therefore bestow alms on them that cry and beg of us. This is the day that opened for us a gate on high to our prayers. Let us open also gates to supplicants that have transgressed, and of us have asked [forgiveness.] To-day the Lord of nature was against His nature changed; let it not to us be irksome to turn our evil wills. Fixed in nature is the body; great or less it cannot become: but the will has such dominion, it can grow to any measure. To-day Godhead sealed itself upon Manhood, that so with the Godhead's stamp Manhood might be adorned.

---

[7] Ps. xlv. 5.

[8] Cant. i. 15.

[9] St. E. here alludes to the early days of David; he brought cheeses to his brethren; these were made by separating the curd from the whey with rennet, a small quantity of which will curdle much milk, as a little leaven leavens the whole lump.

[1] 1 Sam. xxvi., xxvi.

[2] 2 Kings ii. 20.

[3] Matt. v. 13.

## HYMN II.

BLESSED be that Child, Who gladdened Bethlehem to-day! Blessed be the Babe Who made manhood young again to-day! Blessed be the Fruit, Who lowered Himself to our famished state! Blessed be the Good One, Who suddenly enriched our necessitousness and supplied our needs! Blessed He Whose tender mercies made Him condescend to visit our infirmities!

Praise to the Fountain that was sent [4] for our propitiation. Praise be to Him Who made void the Sabbath by fulfilling it! Praise too to Him Who rebuked the leprosy and it remained not, Whom the fever saw and fled! Praise to the Merciful, Who bore our toil! Glory to Thy coming, which quickened the sons of men!

Glory to Him, Who came to us by His first-born! Glory to the Silence,[5] that spake by His Voice. Glory to the One on high, Who was seen by His Day-spring! Glory to the Spiritual, Who was pleased to have a Body, that in it His virtue might be felt, and He might by that Body show mercy on His household's bodies!

Glory to that Hidden One, Whose Son was made manifest! Glory to that Living One, Whose Son was made to die! Glory to that Great One, Whose Son descended and was small! Glory to the Power Who did straiten His greatness by a form, His unseen nature by a shape! With eye and mind we have beheld Him, yea with both of them.

Glory to that Hidden One, Who even with the mind cannot be felt at all by them that pry into Him; but by His graciousness was felt by the hand of man! The Nature that could not be touched, by His hands was bound and tied, by His feet was pierced and lifted up. Himself of His own will He embodied for them that took Him.

Blessed be He Whom free will crucified, because He let it: blessed be He Whom the wood also did bear, because He allowed it. Blessed be He Whom the grave bound, that had [thereby] a limit set it. Blessed be He Whose own will brought Him to the Womb and Birth, to arms and to increase [in stature]. Blessed He whose changes purchased life for human nature.[6]

Blessed He Who sealed our soul, and adorned it and espoused it to Himself. Blessed He Who made our Body a tabernacle for His unseen Nature. Blessed He Who by our tongue interpreted His secret things. Let us praise that Voice whose glory is hymned with our lute, and His virtue with our harp. The Gentiles have assembled and have come to hear His strains.

Glory to the Son of the Good One, Whom the sons of the evil one rejected! Glory to the Son of the Just One, Whom the sons of wickedness crucified! Glory to Him Who loosed us, and was bound for us all! Glory to Him Who gave the pledge, and redeemed it too! Glory to the Beautiful, Who conformed us to His image! Glory to that Fair One, Who looked not to our foulnesses!

Glory to Him Who sowed His Light in the darkness,[7] and was reproached in His hidden state, and covered His secret things. He also stripped and took off from us the clothing of our filthiness.[8] Glory be to Him on high, Who mixed His salt[9] in our minds, His leaven in our souls. His Body became Bread, to quicken our deadness.

---

[4] There is perhaps an allusion here to the pool of Siloam, which comes from the root employed in the original.
[5] This name is given by St. E. to the Father, to suggest to the mind that there was a period when the Father had not begun to work by His Word.
[6] St. E. seems to mean, that whereas the alterations man undergoes in his body tend ultimately to decay the same when undergone by our Lord tended to life.
[7] Ps. xcvii. ii.       [8] Zech. iii. 3.       [9] Mark ix. 49.

Praise to the Rich, Who paid for us all, that which He borrowed not;[1] and wrote [His bill], and also became our debtor! By His yoke He brake from us the chains of him that led us captive. Glory to the Judge Who was judged, and made His Twelve to sit in judgment on the tribes, and by ignorant men condemned the scribes of that nation!

Glory to Him Who could never be measured by us! Our heart is too small for Him, yea our mind is too feeble. He makes foolish our littleness by the riches of His Wisdom. Glory to Him, Who lowered Himself, and asked;[2] that He might hear and learn that which He knew; that He might by His questions reveal the treasure of His helpful graces!

Let us adore Him Who enlightened with His doctrine our mind, and in our hearing sought a pathway for His words. Praise we Him Who grafted into our tree His fruit. Thanks to Him Who sent His Heir, that by Him He might draw us to Himself, yea make us heirs with Him! Thanks to that Good One, the cause of all goods!

Blessed He Who did not chide, because that He was good! Blessed He Who did not spurn, because that He was just also! Blessed He Who was silent, and rebuked; that He might quicken us with both! Severe His silence and reproachful. Mild His severity even When He was accusing; for He rebuked the traitor, and kissed the thief.

Glory to the hidden Husbandman of our intellects! His seed fell on to our ground, and made our mind rich. His increase came an hundredfold into the treasury of our souls! Let us adore Him Who sat down and took rest; and walked in the way, so that the Way was in the way, and the Door also for them that go in,[3] by which they go in to the kingdom.

Blessed the Shepherd Who became a Lamb for our reconcilement! Blessed the Branch Who became the Cup of our Redemption! Blessed also be the Cluster, Fount of medicine of life! Blessed also be the Tiller, Who became Wheat, that He might be sown; and a Sheaf,[4] that He might be cut! [Blessed be] the Architect Who became a Tower for our place of safety![5] Blessed He Who so tempered the feelings of our mind,[6] that we with our harp should sing that which the winged creatures' mouth knows not with its strains to sing! Glory to Him, Who beheld how we had pleased to be like to brutes in our rage and our greediness; and came down and was one of us, that we might become heavenly!

Glory be to Him, Who never felt the need of our praising Him; yet felt the need as being kind to us, and thirsted[7] as loving us, and asks us to give to Him, and longs to give to us. His fruit was mingled with us men, that in Him we might come nigh to Him, Who condescended to us. By the Fruit of His stem He grafted us into His Tree.

Let us praise Him, Who prevailed and quickened us by His stripes! Praise we Him, Who took away the curse by His thorns! Praise we Him Who put death to death by His dying! Praise we Him, Who held His peace and justified us! Praise we Him, Who rebuked death that had overcome us! Blessed He, Whose helpful graces cleansed out the left side![8]

Praise we Him Who watched and put to sleep him that led us captive. Praise we Him Who went to sleep, and chased our deep sleep away. Glory be to God Who cured weak manhood! Glory be to Him Who was baptized, and drowned our iniquity

[1] Ps. lxix. 4. Comp. Luke xvi. 6.        [2] Luke ii. 46.        [3] John x. 9, xiv. 6.
[4] Alluding to the wave-offering, Levit. xxiii. 11, which was ordinarily interpreted of Christ.
[5] Ps. lxi. 3.        [6] Prov. xviii. 10.        [7] Mat. xxv. 40.
[8] Allusion is here made perhaps to Eccles. x. 2, "a wise man's heart is at his right hand, but a fool's heart is at his left."

in the deep, and choked him [9] that choked us! Let us glorify with all our mouths the Lord of all creatures!

Blessed be the Physician Who came down and amputated without pain, and healed wounds with a medicine that was not harsh. His Son became a Medicine, that showed sinners mercy. Blessed be He Who dwelt in the womb, and wrought therein a perfect Temple, that He might dwell in it, a Throne that He might be in it, a Garment that He might be arrayed in it, and a Weapon that He might conquer in it.

Blessed be He Whom our mouth cannot adequately praise, because His Gift is too great for skill of orators [to tell]; neither can the faculties adequately praise His goodness. For praise Him as we may, it is too little.

And since it is useless to be silent and to constrain ourselves, may our feebleness excuse such praise as we can sing.

How gracious He, Who demands not more than our strength can give! How would Thy servant be condemned in capital and interest, did he not give such as he could, and did he refuse that which He owed! Ocean of glory Who needest not to have Thy glory sung, take in Thy goodness this drop of praise; since by Thy Gift Thou hast supplied my tongue a sense for glorifying Thee.

## HYMN III.

Blessed be that first day of thine, Lord, wherewith this day of Thy Feast is stamped! Thy day is like Thee, in that it shows mercy unto men, in that it is handed down and comes with all generations.

This is the day that ends with the aged, and returns that it may begin with the young! a day that by its love refreshes itself, that it may refresh by its might us decayed creatures. Thy day when it had visited us and passed and gone away, in its mercy returned and visited us again : for it knows that human nature needs it, in all things like unto Thee as seeking us.

The world is in want of its fountain; and for it, Lord, as for Thee, all therein are athirst. This is the day that rules over the seasons! the dominion of Thy day is like Thine, which stretches over generations that have come, and are to come! Thy day is like unto Thee, because when it is one, it buds and multiplies itself, that it may be like Thee!

In this Thy day, Lord, which is near unto us, we see Thy Birth that is far off! Like to Thee be Thy day to us, Lord; let it be a mediator and a warranter of peace.

Thy day reconciled Heaven and earth, because therein the Highest came down to the lowest.

Thy day was able to reconcile the Just One, who was wroth at our sins; Thy day forgave thousands of sins, for in it bowels of mercy shone forth upon the guilty!

Great, Lord, is Thy day; let it not be small upon us, let it show mercy according as it used to do, upon us transgressors!

And if every day, Lord, Thy forgiveness wells forth, how exceeding great should it be upon this day! All the days from the Treasure of Thy bright day gain blessings.

All the feasts from the stores of this feast have their fairness and their ornaments.

Thy bowels of mercy upon Thy day make Thou to abound unto us, O Lord! Make us to distinguish Thy day from all days! for great is the treasure-house of the day of Thy Birth; let it be the ransomer of debtors! Great is this day above all days, for in

---

[9] Luke viii. 33.

it came forth mercy to sinners. A store of medicines is this Thy great day, because on it shone forth the Medicine of Life to the wounded! A treasure of helpful graces is this day, for that on it Light gleamed forth upon our blindness! Yea, it also brought a sheaf unto us; and it came, that from it might flow plenty upon our hunger. This day is that forerunning Cluster, in which the cup of salvation was concealed! This day is the first-born feast, which, being born the first, overcomes all feasts. In the winter which strips the fruit of the branches off from the barren vine, Fruit sprang up[1] unto us; in the cold that bares all the trees, a shoot was green for us of the house of Jesse. In December[2] when the seed is hidden in the earth, there sprouted forth from the Womb the Ear of Life. In March[3] when the seed was sprouting in the air, a Sheaf[4] sowed itself in the earth. The harvest thereof, Death devoured it in Hell; which the Medicine of life that is hidden therein did yet burst open! In March when the lambs bleat in the wilderness, into the Womb the Paschal Lamb entered! Out of the stream whence the fishers came up,[5] He was baptized and came up Who incloses all things in his net; out of the stream the fish whereof Simon took, out of it the Fisher of men came up, and took him. With the Cross which catches all robbers, He caught up unto life that robber![6] The Living by His death emptied Hell, He unloosed it and let fly away from it entire multitudes! The publicans and harlots, the impure snares, the snares of the deceitful fowler the Holy One seized! The sinful woman, who was a snare for men, He made a mirror for penitent women! The fig that cast its fruit, that refused fruit,[7] offered Zacchæus as fruit; the fruit of its own nature it gave not, but it yielded one reasonable fruit! The Lord spread His thirst over the well, and caught her that was thirsty with the water that He asked of her. He caught one soul at the well, and again caught with her the whole city:[8] twelve fishers the Holy One caught, and again caught with them the whole world. As for Iscariot, that escaped from His nets, the strangling halter fell upon his neck! His all-quickening net catches the living,[9] and he that escapes from it escapes from the living.

And who is able, Lord, to tell me up the several succours that are hid in Thee? How shall the parched mouth be able to drink from the Fountain of the Godhead! Answer to-day the voice of our petition; let our prayer which is in words take effect in deeds. Heal us, O my Master; every time that we see Thy Feast, may it cause rumours that we have heard to pass away. Our mind wanders amid these voices. O Voice of the Father, still [other] voices; the world is noisy, in Thee let it gain itself quiet; for by Thee the sea was stilled from its storms. The devils rejoiced when they heard the voice of blasphemy: let the Watchers rejoice in us as they are wont.[1] From amongst Thy fold there is the voice of sorrowfulness; O Thou that makest all rejoice,[2] let Thy flock rejoice! as for our murmur, O my Master, in it reject us not: our mouth murmurs since it is sinful. Let Thy day, O Lord, give us all manner of joy, with the flowers[3] of peace, let us keep Thy passover. In the day of Thy Ascension we are lifted up:[4] with the new Bread shall be the memorial thereof. O Lord, increase our peace, that we may keep the three feasts of the Godhead. Great is Thy day, Lord, let us not be despised. All men honour the day of Thy birth. Thou righteous One, keep Thou the glory of Thy birth; for even Herod honoured the day of His birth! The dances of the impure one pleased the tyrant; to Thee, Lord, let the voice of chaste women be sweet! Thee, Lord, let the voice of chaste women please, whose bodies Thou guardest holily. The day of Herod

---

[1] Isa 5. 2.    [2] (Conum.)    [3] (Nisan.)    [4] Lev. xxiii. 10.    [5] Ezek. xlvii. 10, etc.    [6] Luke xxiii. 43.
[7] St. E. seems to blend here the account of the withering of the fig-tree and that of Zacchæus climbing into the *wild fig-tree*, as the Peshitto renders it.
[8] John iv. 42.    [9] Mat. xiii. 47.    [1] Mat. xviii. 10.    [2] Luke xv. 7.
[3] Flowers used at Easter in the Churches are here alluded to.    [4] John xx. 17.

was like him : Thy day too is like Thee ! The day of the troubled one was troubled with sin ; and fair as Thou art is Thy fair day ! The feast of the tyrant killed the preacher ; in Thy feast every man preaches glory. On the day of the murderer, the Voice [5] was put to silence ; but on Thy day are the voices of the feast. The foul one in his feast put out the Light, that darkness might cover the adulterers. The season of the Holy One trims lamps, that darkness may flee with the hidden things thereof. The day of that fox [6] stank like himself ; but holy is the feast of the True Lamb. [7] The day of the transgressor passed [8] away like himself ; Thy day like Thyself abideth for ever. The day of the tyrant raged like himself, because with his chain it put to silence the righteous Voice. The feast of the Meek One is tranquil like Himself, because His sun shines upon His persecutors. The tyrant was conscious that He was not a king, therefore to the King of kings he gave place. The whole day, Lord, suffices me not to balance Thy praise with his blame. May Thy Gracious day cause my sin to pass away, seeing that it is with the day of the impure one, that I have weighed Thy day ! For great is Thy day beyond comparison ! nor can it be compared with our days. The day of man is as of the earthy : the day of God is as of God ! Thy day, Lord, is greater than those of the prophets, [9] and I have taken and set it beside that of the murderer ! Thou knowest, O Lord, as knowing all things, how to hear the comparison that my tongue hath made. Let Thy day grant our requests for life, since his day granted the request for death. The needy king swore on his feast that half his king-dom should be the reward of the dance ! Let Thy feast then, O Thou that enrichest all, shed down in mercy a crumb of fine wheat flour ! From the dry land gushed the Fountain, which sufficed to satisfy the thirst of the Gentiles ! From the Virgin's womb as from a strong rock sprouted up the seed, whence was much fruit ! Barns without number did Joseph fill ; [1] and they were emptied and failed in the years of the famine. One true Sheaf gave bread ; the bread of Heaven, whereof there is no stint. The bread which the First-born brake in the wilderness, [2] failed and passed away though very good. He returned again and broke the New Bread [3] which ages and generations shall not waste away ! The seven loaves also that He brake failed, [4] and the five loaves too that He multiplied were consumed ; [5] the Bread that He brake exceeded the world's needs, for the more it was divided, the more it multiplied exceedingly. With much wine also He filled the waterpots ; they drew it out, yet it failed though it was abundant : of the Cup that He gave though the draught was small, very great was its strength, so that there is no stint thereto. A Cup is He [6] that contains all strong wines, and also a Mystery in the midst of which He Himself is ! The one Bread that He brake has no bound, and the one Cup that He mingled has no stint ! [7] The Wheat that was sown, [8] on the third day came up and filled the Garner of Life. [9] The spiritual Bread, as the Giver of it, quickens the spiritual spiritually, and he that receives it carnally, receives it rashly to no profit. This Bread of grace let the spirit receive dis-cerningly, as the medicine of Life. If the dead sacrifices in the name of devils were offered, [1] yea eaten, not without a mystery ; at the holy thing of the offering, how much more does it behove us that this mystery be circumspectly administered by us. He that eateth of the sacrifice in the name of devils, becomes devilish without all contra-

---

5 This was a common name of old for St. John Baptist, with allusion to St. John i. 23.
6 Luke xiii. 32.
7 It may be well to observe once for all, that true is often use, as in John xv. 1, for "real," in opposition to "typical," as in Scripture, so in the Fathers.
8 The same Syriac verb means to *pass*, and to *transgress*.
9 It might seem from this that there were some days kept in their honour in the East.

| | | | | |
|---|---|---|---|---|
| 1 Gen. xli. 49. | 2 John vi. 1, etc. | 3 p. 227. | 4 Mat. xv. 36. | 5 Mat. xiv. 17. |
| 6 Ps. xvi. 5 | 7 Prov. ix. 5. | 8 John xii. 24. | 9 Mat. xiii. 30. | 1 1 Cor. x. 20. |

diction. He that eateth the Heavenly Bread, becomes Heavenly without doubt! Wine teaches us, in that it makes him that is familiar therewith like itself: for it hates much him that is fond of it, and is intoxicating and maddening, and a mocker [2] to him! Light teaches us, in that it makes like unto itself the eye the daughter of the sun : the eye by the light saw the nakedness, and ran and chastely hid the chaste man. [3] As for that nakedness it was wine that made it, which even to the chaste skills not to show mercy !

With the weapon of the deceiver the First-born clad Himself, that with the weapon that killed, He might restore to life again ! With the tree wherewith he slew us, He delivered us. With the wine which maddened us, with it we were made chaste ! With the rib that was drawn out of Adam, the wicked one drew out the heart of Adam. There rose from the Rib [4] a hidden power, which cut off Satan as Dagon : for in that Ark a book was hidden that cried and proclaimed concerning the Conqueror ! There was then a mystery revealed, in that Dagon was brought low in his own place of refuge ! [5] The accomplishment came after the type, in that the wicked one was brought low in the place in which he trusted ! Blessed be He Who came and in Him were accomplished the mysteries of the left hand, and the right hand. [6] Fulfilled was the mystery that was in the Lamb, and fulfilled was the type that was in Dagon. Blessed is He Who by the True Lamb redeemed us, and destroyed our destroyer as He did Dagon ! In December when the nights are long, rose unto us the Day, of Whom there is no bound ! In winter when all the world is gloomy, forth came the Fair One Who cheered all in the world ! In winter that makes the earth barren, virginity learned to bring forth. In December, that causes the travails of the earth to cease, in it were the travails of virginity. The early lamb no one ever used to see before the shepherds : and as for the true Lamb, in the season of His birth, the tidings of Him too hasted unto the shepherds. That old wolf saw the sucking Lamb, and he trembled before Him, though He had concealed himself ; for because the wolf had put on sheep's clothing, the Shepherd of all became a Lamb in the flocks, in order that when the greedy one had been bold against the Meek, the Mighty One might rend that Eater. [7] The Holy One dwelt bodily in the womb ; and He dwelt spiritually in the mind. Mary that conceived Him abhorred the marriage bed ; let not that soul commit whoredom in the which He dwelleth. Because Mary perceived Him, she left her betrothed : He dwelleth in chaste virgins, if they perceive Him. [8] The deaf perceive not the mighty thunder, neither does the heady man the sound of the commandment. For the deaf is bewildered in the time of the thunderclap, the heady man is bewildered also at the voice of instruction ; if fearful thunder terrifies the deaf, then would fearful wrath stir the unclean ! That the deaf hears not is no blame to him ; but whoso tramples [on the commandments] it is headiness. From time to time there is thunder : but the voice of the law thunders every day. Let us not close our ears when their openings, as being opened and not closed against it, accuse us ; and the door of hearing is open by nature, that it might reproach us for our headiness against our will. The door of the voice and the door of the mouth our will can open or close. Let us see what the Good One has given us ; and let us hear the mighty Voice, and let not the doors of our ears be closed.

Glory to that Voice Which became Body, and to the Word of the High One Which became Flesh ! Hear Him also, O ears, and see Him, O eyes, and feel Him, O hands, and eat Him, O mouth ! Ye members and senses give praise unto Him, that came and quickened the whole body ! Mary bare the silent Babe, while in Him were hidden all

---

[2] Prov. xx. 1.                [3] Gen. ix. 23.              [4] Gen. iii. 15.              [5] 1 Sam. v. 4.
[6] Mat. xxv. 33.               [7] Judg. xiv. 6.            [8] Mat. v. 28.

tongues! Joseph bare Him, and in Him was hidden a nature more ancient than aught that is old! The High One became as a little child, and in Him was hidden a treasure of wisdom sufficing for all! Though Most High, yet He sucked the milk of Mary, and of His goodness all creatures suck! He is the Breast of Life, and the Breath of Life; the dead suck from His life and revive. Without the breath of the air no man lives, without the Might of the Son no man subsists. On His living breath that quickeneth all, depend the spirits that are above and that are beneath. When He sucked the milk of Mary, He was suckling all with Life. While He was lying on His Mother's bosom, in His bosom were all creatures lying. He was silent as a Babe, and yet He was making His creatures execute all His commands. For without the First-born no man can approach unto the Essence, to which He is equal. The thirty years He was in the earth, Who was ordering all creatures, Who was receiving all the offerings of praise from those above and those below. He was wholly in the depths and wholly in the highest! He was wholly with all things and wholly with each. While His body was forming within the womb, His power was fashioning all members! While the Conception of the Son was fashioning in the womb, He Himself was fashioning babes in the womb. Yet not as His body was weak in the womb, was His power weak in the womb! So too not as His body was feeble by the Cross, was His might also feeble by the Cross. For when on the Cross He quickened the dead, His Body quickened them, yea, rather His Will; just as when He was dwelling wholly in the womb, His hidden Will was visiting all! For see how, when He was wholly hanging upon the Cross, His Power was yet making all creatures move! For He darkened the sun and made the earth quake; He rent the graves and brought forth the dead! See how when He was wholly on the Cross, yet again He was wholly everywhere! Thus was He entirely in the womb, while He was again wholly in everything! While on the Cross He quickened the dead, so while a Babe He was fashioning babes. While He was slain, He opened the graves; while He was in the womb, He opened wombs. Come hearken, my brethren, concerning the Son of the Secret One that was revealed in His Body, while His Power was concealed! For the Power of the Son is a free Power; the womb did not bind it up, as it did the Body! For while His Power was dwelling in the womb, He was fashioning infants in the womb! His Power compassed her, that compassed Him. For if He drew in His Power, all things would fall; His Power upholds all things; while He was within the womb, He left not His hold of all. He in His own Person shaped an Image in the womb, and was shaping in all wombs all countenances. Whilst He was increasing in stature among the poor, from an abundant treasury He was nourishing all! While she that anointed Him was anointing Him, with His dew and His rain He was anointing all! The Magi brought myrrh and gold, while in Him was hidden a treasure of riches. The myrrh and spices which He had prepared and created, did the Magi bring Him of His own. It was by Power from Him that Mary was able to bear in Her bosom Him that bears up all things! It was from the great storehouse of all creatures, Mary gave Him all which she did give Him! She gave Him milk from Himself that prepared it, she gave Him food from Himself that made it! He gave milk unto Mary as God: again He sucked it from her, as the Son of Man. Her hands bare Him in that He had emptied. His strength; and her arm embraced Him, in that He had made Himself small. The measure of His Majesty who has measured? He caused His measures to shrink into a Raiment. She wove for Him and clothed Him because He had put off His glory. She measured Him and wove for Him, since He had made Himself little.

⁹ Ps. cxxxix. 16.　¹ Mat. xxvii. 52.　² p. 11. n. d.　³ Jer. xxxi. 22.

The sea when it bore Him was still and calmed, and how came the lap of Joseph to bear Him ?  The womb of hell conceived Him and was burst open, and how did the womb of Mary contain Him ?  The stone that was over the grave He broke open by His might, and how could Mary's arm contain Him ?  Thou camest to a low estate, that Thou mightest raise all to life !  Glory be unto Thee from all that are quickened by Thee !  Who is able to speak of the Son of the Hidden One who came down and clothed Himself with a Body in the womb ?  He came forth and sucked milk as a child, and among little children the Son of the Lord of all crept about.  They saw Him as a little Child in the street, while there was dwelling in Him the Love of all.  Visibly children surrounded Him in the street ; secretly Angels surrounded Him in fear.  Cheerful was He with the little ones as a child ; awful was He with the Angels as a Commander : He was awful to John for him to loose His shoe's latchet : He was gentle to sinners that kissed His feet !  The Angels as Angels saw Him ; according to the measure of his knowledge each man beheld Him : according to the measure of each man's discernment, thus he perceived Him that is greater than all.  The Father and Himself alone are a full measure of knowledge so as know Him as He is !  For every creature whether above or below obtains each his measure of knowledge ; He the Lord of all gives all to us.  He that enriches all, requires usury of all.  He gives to all things as wanting nothing, and yet requires usury of all as if needy.  He gave us herds and flocks as Creator, and yet asked sacrifices as though in need.  He made the water wine as Maker : and yet he drank of it as a poor man.  Of His own He mingled [wine] in the marriage feast, His wine He mingled and gave to drink when He was a guest.  In His love He multiplied [the days of] the aged Simeon ; that he, a mortal, might present Him who quickeneth all.  By power from Him did Simeon carry Him ; he that presented Him, was by Him presented [to God].  He gave imposition of hands to Moses in the Mount,[4] and received it in the midst of the river from John.  In the power of His gifts John was enabled to baptize, though earthy, the heavenly.  By power from Him the earth supported Him : it was nigh to being dissolved, and His might strengthened it.  Martha gave Him to eat : viands which He had created she placed before Him.  Of His own all that give have made their vows : of His own treasures they placed upon His table.

## HYMN IV.

THIS is the month which brings all manner of joy ; it is the freedom of the bondsmen, the pride of the free, the crown of the gates, the soothing of the body, that also in its love put purple upon us as upon kings.

This is the month that brings all manner of victories ; it frees the spirit ; it subdues the body ; it brings forth life among mortals ;  it caused, in its love, Godhead, to dwell in Manhood.

In this day the Lord exchanged glory for shame, as being humble ; because Adam changed the truth for unrighteousness as being a rebel : the Good One had mercy on him, justified and set right them that had turned aside.

Let every man chase away his weariness, since that Majesty was not wearied with being in the womb nine months for us, and in being thirty years in Sodom among the madmen.[5]

Because the Good One saw that the race of man was poor and humbled, He made feasts as a treasure-house, and opened them to the slothful, that the feast might stir up the slothful one to rise and be rich.

---

[4] Exod. xxxiii 22.    [5] Is. i. 10.  Rev. xi. 8.

Lo ! the First-born has opened unto us His feast as a treasure-house. This one day in the whole year alone opens that treasure-house : come, let us make gain, let us grow rich from it, ere they shut it up.

Blessed be the watchful, that have taken by force [6] from it the spoil of Life. It is a great disgrace, when a man sees his neighbor take and carry out treasure, and himself sits in the treasure-house slumbering, so as to come forth empty.

In this feast, let each one of us crown the gates of his heart. The Holy Spirit longs for the gates thereof, that He may enter in and dwell there, and sanctify it, and He goes round about to all the gates to see where He may enter.

In this feast, the gates are glad before the gates, [7] and the Holy One rejoices in the holy temple, and the voice resounds in the mouth of children, and Christ rejoices in His own feast as a mighty man.

At the Birth of the Son the king was enrolling all men for the tribute-money, that they might be debtors to Him : the King came forth to us Who blotted out our bills, [8] and wrote another bill in His own Name that He might be our debtor. The sun gave longer light, and foreshadowed the mystery by the degrees which it had gone up. [9] It was twelve days since it had gone up, and to-day is the thirteenth day : a type exact of the Son's birth [1] and of His Twelve.

Moses shut up a lamb in the month Nisan on the tenth day ; a type this of the Son that came into the womb and shut Himself up therein on the tenth day. [2] He came forth from the womb in this month in which the sun gives longer light.

The darkness was overcome, that it might proclaim that Satan was overcome ; and the sun gave longer light, that it might triumph, because the First-born was victorious. Along with the darkness the dark one was overcome, and with the greater light our Light conquered !

Joseph caressed the Son as a Babe ; he ministered to Him as God. He rejoiced in Him as in the Good One, and he was awe-struck at Him as the Just One, greatly bewildered.

"Who hath given me the Son of the Most High to be a Son to me ? I was jealous of Thy Mother, and I thought to put her away, and I knew not that in her womb was hidden a mighty treasure, that should suddenly enrich my poor estate. David the king sprang of my race, and wore the crown : and I have come to a very low estate, who instead of a king am a carpenter. Yet a crown hath come to me, for in my bosom is the Lord of crowns ! "

With rival words Mary burned, yea she lulled Him, [saying,] Who hath given me, the barren, that I should conceive and bring forth this One, that is manifold; a little One, that is great ; for that He is wholly with me, and wholly everywhere?

The day that Gabriel came in unto my low estate, he made me free instead of a handmaid, of a sudden : for I was the handmaid of Thy Divine Nature, and am also the Mother of Thy human Nature, O Lord and Son !

Of a sudden the handmaid became the King's daughter in Thee, Thou Son of the King. Lo, the meanest in the house of David, by reason of Thee, Thou Son of David, lo, a daughter of earth hath attained unto Heaven by the Heavenly One !

How am I astonied that there is laid before me a Child, older than all things !

---

[6] Mat. xi. 12.
[7] I. e., the gates of the heart, before the gates of the Church.
[8] Col. ii. 14.
[9] The increase of light at the time of the Nativity is meant.
[1] Exod. xii. 3.
[2] Of Nisan. So St. E. writes on Exod. xii. 3. "The Lamb is a type of our Lord, who on the tenth of Nisan entered into the womb ; for from the tenth day of the seventh month when Zachary received the message of John's birth, even to the tenth day of the first month when Mary received the message from the Angel, are six months."

His eye is gazing unceasingly upon Heaven.  As for the stammering of His mouth, to my seeming it betokens, that with God its silence speaks.

Who ever saw a Child the whole of Whom beholdeth every place?  His look is like one that orders all creatures that are above and that are below !  His visage is like that Commander that commandeth all.

How shall I open the fountain of milk to Thee, O Fountain ?  Or how shall I give nourishment to Thee that nourishest all from Thy Table?  How shall I bring to swaddling clothes One wrapped round with rays of glory ?

My mouth knows not how I shall call Thee, O Thou Child of the Living One : for to venture to call Thee as the Child of Joseph, I tremble, since Thou art not his seed : and I am fearful of denying the name of him to whom they have betrothed me.

While Thou art the Son of One, then should I be calling Thee the Son of many.  For ten thousand names would not suffice Thee, since Thou art the Son of God and also the Son of man, yea, David's Son and Mary's Lord.

Who hath made the Lord of mouths to be without a mouth?  For my pure conception of Thee wicked men have slandered me.  Be, O Thou Holy One, a Speaker for Thy Mother.  Show a miracle that they may be persuaded, from Whom it is that I conceived Thee !

For Thy sake too I am hated, Thou Lover of all.  Lo ! I am persecuted who have conceived and brought forth One House of refuge for men.  Adam will rejoice, for Thou art the Key of Paradise.

Lo, the sea raged against Thy mother as against Jonah.  Lo, Herod, that raging wave, sought to drown the Lord of the seas.  Whither I shall flee Thou shalt teach me, O Lord of Thy Mother.

With Thee I will flee, that I may gain in Thee Life in every place.  The prison with Thee is no prison, for in Thee man goes up unto Heaven : the grave with Thee is no grave, for Thou art the Resurrection ! [3]

A star of light which was not nature, shone forth suddenly ; less than the sun and greater than the sun, less than it in its visible light, but greater than it in its hidden might, by reason of its mystery.

The Morning Star cast its bright beams among the darknesses, and led them as blind men, and they came and received a great light : they gave offerings and received life, and they worshipped and returned.

In the height and the depth two preachers were there to the Son : the bright star shouted above ; John also preached below, two preachers, an earthly and a heavenly.

That above showed His Nature to be from the Majesty, and that below too showed his Nature to be from mankind.  O great marvel, that His Godhead and His Manhood each was preached by them.

Whoso thought Him earthly, the bright star convinced him that He was heavenly ; and whoso thought Him spiritual, John convinced him that He was also corporeal.

In the Holy temple Simeon carried Him, and lulled Him, [saying,] "Thou art come, O Merciful One, showing mercy on my old age, making my bones to go into the grave in peace.  In Thee shall I be raised from the grave into Paradise !"

Anna embraced Him, and put her mouth to His lips, and the Spirit dwelt upon her own lips.  As when Isaiah's mouth was silent, the coal [4] which approached his lips opened his mouth ; so Anna burned with the Spirit of His mouth, yea, she lulled Him, [saying,] "Son of the Kingdom, Son of the lowliness, that hearest and art still, that

---

[3] John xi. 25.　　　　　　　　　　　　　　　　　　　[4] Isai 6.

seest and art hidden, that knowest and art unknown, God, Son of Man, glory be unto Thy Name."

The barren also heard, ran, and came with their provisions : the Magi came with their treasures, the barren came with their provisions. Provisions and riches were suddenly heaped up in the house of the poor.

The barren woman cried out, as at that which she looked not for, Who hath granted me this sight of thy Babe, O Blessed One, by whom the heaven and earth are filled ! Blessed be thy Fruit, which made the barren vine to bear a cluster.

Zacharias came and opened his venerable mouth and cried, "Where is the King, for whose sake I have begotten the Voice that is to preach before His face ? Hail, Son of the King, to whom also our Priesthood shall be given up !"

John approached with his parents and worshipped the Son, and He shed glory upon his countenance ; and he was not moved as when in the womb ! Mighty miracle, that here he was worshipping, there he leaped.

Herod also, that base fox, that stalked about like a lion, as a fox crouched down, and howled, when he heard the roaring of the Lion, who came to sit in the kingdom according to the Scriptures. The fox heard that the Lion was a whelp, and as a suckling ; and he sharpened His teeth, that while He was yet a child the fox might lie in wait and devour the Lion ere He had grown up, and the breath of His mouth should destroy him.

The whole creation became mouths to Him, and cried concerning Him. The Magi cried by their offerings ! the barren cried with their children, the star of light cried in that air, lo ! the Son of the King !

The Heavens were opened, the waters were calmed, the Dove glorified Him, the voice of the Father, louder than thunder, was instant and said, This is my beloved Son. The Angels proclaim Him, the children shout to Him with their Hosannas.

These voices above and below proclaim Him and cry aloud. The slumber of Sion was not dispersed by the voice of the thunders, but she was offended, stood up, and slew Him because He aroused her.

## HYMN V.

At the birth of the Son, there was a great shouting in Bethlehem ; for the Angels came down, and gave praise there. Their voices were a great thunder : at that voice of praise the silent ones came, and gave praise to the Son.

Blessed be that Babe in whom Eve and Adam were restored to youth ! The shepherds also came laden with the best gifts of their flock : sweet milk, clean flesh, befitting praise ! They put a difference, and gave Joseph the flesh, Mary the milk, and the Son the praise ! They brought and presented a suckling lamb to the Paschal Lamb, a first-born to the First-born, a sacrifice to the Sacrifice, a lamb of time to the Lamb of Truth. Fair sight [to see] the lamb offered to The Lamb !

The lamb bleated as it was offered before the First-born. It praised the Lamb, that had come to set free the flocks and the oxen from sacrifices :[5] yea that Paschal Lamb, Who handed down and brought in the Passover of the Son.

The shepherds came near and worshipped Him with their staves. They saluted Him with peace, prophesying the while, "Peace, O Prince of the Shepherds." The rod of Moses[6] praised Thy Rod, O Shepherd of all ; for Thee Moses praises, although his lambs have become wolves, and his flocks as it were dragons, and his sheep fanged beasts. In the fearful wilderness his flocks became furious, and attacked him.

---

[5] Ps. l. 9 ; Is. lxvi. 3.  [6] Exod. iv. 4, etc.

Thee then the Shepherds praise, because Thou hast reconciled the wolves and the lambs within the fold ; O Babe, that art older than Noah and younger than Noah, that reconciled all within the ark amid the billows !

David Thy father for a lamb's sake slaughtered a lion. Thou, O Son of David, hast killed the unseen wolf that murdered Adam, the simple lamb who fed and bleated in Paradise.

At that voice of praise, brides were moved to hallow themselves, and virgins to be chaste, and even young girls became grave : they advanced and came in multitudes, and worshipped the Son.

Aged women of the city of David came to the daughter of David ; they gave thanks and said, " Blessed be our country, whose streets are lightened with the rays of Jesse !   To-day is the throne of David established by Thee, O Son of David."

The old men cried, " Blessed be that Son Who restored Adam to youth, Who was vexed to see that he was old and worn out, and that the serpent who had killed him, had changed his skin and had gotten himself away.   Blessed be the Babe in Whom Adam and Eve were restored to youth."

The chaste women said, O Blessed Fruit, bless the fruit of our wombs ; to Thee may they be given as first-born.   They waxed fervent and prophesied concerning their children, who, when they were killed for Him, were cut off, as it were first-fruits.

The barren also fondled Him, and carried Him ; they rejoiced and said, Blessed Fruit born without marriage, bless the wombs of us that are married ; have mercy on our barrenness, Thou wonderful Child of Virginity !

## HYMN VI.

Blessed be the Messenger that was laden, and came ; a great peace ! The Bowels of the Father brought Him down to us ; He did not bring up our debts to Him, but made a satisfaction to that Majesty with His own goods.

Praised be the Wise One, who reconciled and joined the Divine with the Human Nature.   One from above and one from below, He confined the Natures as medicines, and being the Image of God, became man.

That Jealous One when He saw that Adam was dust, and that the cursed serpent had devoured him, shed soundness into that which was tasteless, and made him [as] salt, wherewith the accursed serpent should be blinded.

Blessed be the Merciful One, who saw the weapon by Paradise, that closed the way to the Tree of Life ; and came and took a Body which could suffer, that with the Door, that was in His side, He might open the way into Paradise.

Blessed be that Merciful One, who lent not Himself to harshness, but without constraint conquered by wisdom ; that He might give an ensample unto men, that by virtue and wisdom they might conquer discerningly.

Blessed is Thy flock, since Thou art the gate thereof, and Thou art the staff thereof. Thou art the Shepherd thereof, Thou art the Drink thereof, Thou art the salt thereof, yea, the Visitor thereof.   Hail to the Only-Begotten, that bare abundantly all manner of consolations !

The husbandmen came and did obeisance before the Husbandman of Life.   They prophesied to Him as they rejoiced, [saying,] "Blessed be the Husbandman, by Whom the ground of the heart is tilled, Who gathereth His wheat into the garner of Life."

The husbandmen came and gave glory to the Vineyard that sprang of the root and stem of Jesse, the Virgin Cluster of the glorious Vine. "May we be vessels for Thy new Wine that renews all things."

"In Thee may the Vineyard of my Well-beloved that yielded wild grapes[7] find peace ! Graft its vines from Thy stocks ; let it be laden entirely from Thy blessings with a fruit which may reconcile the Lord of the Vineyard, Who threatens it."

Because of Joseph the workmen came to the Son of Joseph saying, "Blessed be Thy Nativity, Thou Head of Workmen, the impress whereof the ark bore, after which was fashioned the Tabernacle of the congregation that was for a time only ! "[8]

"Our craft praises Thee, Who art our glory. Make Thou the yoke which is light, yea easy, for them that bear it ; make the measure, in which there can be no falseness, which is full of Truth ; yea, devise and make measures[9] by righteousness ; that he that is vile may be accused thereby, and he that is perfect, may be acquitted thereby. Weigh therewith both mercy and truth, O just One, as a judge."

"Bridegrooms with their brides rejoiced. 'Blessed be the Babe, whose Mother was Bride of the Holy One ! Blessed the marriage feast, whereat Thou wast present, in which when wine was suddenly wanting, in Thee it abounded again ! '"

The children cried out, "Blessed He that hath become unto us a Brother, and Companion in the midst of the streets. Blessed be the day which by the Branches[1] gives glory to the Tree of life, that made His Majesty be brought low, to our childish age ! "

Women heard that a Virgin should conceive and bring forth a Son : honourable women hoped that thou wouldest rise from them ; yea noble ladies that Thou mightest spring up from them ! Blessed be Thy Majesty, that humbled Itself, and rose from the poor !

Yea the young girls that carried Him prophesied, saying, "Whether I be hated or fair, or of low estate, I am without spot for Thee. I have taken Thee in charge for the bed of Childbirth."

Sarah had lulled Isaac, who as a slave[2] bare the Image of the King his Master on his shoulders, even the sign of His Cross ; yea, on his hands were bandages and sufferings, a type of the nails.

Rachel cried to her husband, and said, Give me sons.[3] Blessed be Mary, in whose womb, though she asked not, Thou didst dwell holily, O Gift, that poured itself upon them that received it.

Hannah with bitter tears asked a child ;[4] Sarah and Rebecca with vows and words, Elizabeth also with her prayer, after having vexed themselves for a long time, yet so obtained comfort.

Blessed be Mary, who without vows and without prayer, in her Virginity conceived and brought forth the Lord of all the sons of her companions, who have been or shall be chaste and righteous, priests and kings.

Who else lulled a son in her bosom as Mary did? who ever dared to call her son, Son of the Maker, Son of the Creator, Son of the Most High?

---

[7] *S.* husks.

[8] So too St. E. himself upon Exodus xxxvii. "And Bezaleel made an ark of undecaying wood, a type of the Body of Immanuel, which is incorruptible, and not soiled by sin. By the gold within and without he indicates the Divine Nature of the Word, which was united unto all the functions (*S.* vessels) of the Soul and the Body in a manner no discourse can reach, seeing he anointed our manhood with His Godhead." These words appear to make it plain, that St. E. means the same *ark* above as in this passage ; he, however, uses a different word, and one which others contend is only applied to Noah's ark.

[9] St. Mark, vi. 3, intimates that our Lord was a carpenter Himself, while on earth.

[1] He alludes to Palm Sunday, on which the children carried them.

[2] Gen. xxii. 6.         [3] Gen. xxx. 1.         [4] 1 Sam. i. 7.

Who ever dared to speak to her son as in prayer? O Trust of Thy Mother as God, her Beloved and her Son as Man, in fear and love it is meet for thy Mother to stand before Thee!

## HYMN VII.

The Son of the Maker is like unto His Father as Maker! He made Himself a pure body, He clothed Himself with it, and came forth and clothed our weakness with glory, which in His mercy He brought from the Father.

From Melchizedek, the High Priest, a hyssop came to Thee, a throne and crown from the house of David, a race and family from Abraham.

Be thou unto me a Haven, for Thine own sake, O great Sea. Lo! the Psalms of David Thy Father, and the words also of the Prophets, came forth unto me, as it were ships.

David Thy father, in the hundred and tenth Psalm, twined together two numbers as it were crowns to Thee, and came [to Thee], O Conqueror! With these shalt Thou be crowned, and unto the throne shalt Thou ascend and sit.

A great crown is the number that is twined in the hundred, wherein is crowned Thy Godhead! A little crown is that of the number ten, which crowns the Head of Thy Manhood, O Victorious One!

For Thy sake women sought after men. Tamar desired him that was widowed, and Ruth loved a man that was old, yea, that Rahab, that led men captive, was captivated by Thee.

Tamar went forth, and in the darkness [5] stole the Light, and in uncleanness stole the Holy One, and by uncovering her nakedness she went in and stole Thee, O glorious One, that bringest the pure out of the impure.

Satan saw her and trembled, and hasted to trouble her. He brought the judgment to her mind, and she feared not; stoning and the sword, and she trembled not. He that teacheth adultery hindered adultery, because he was a hinderer of Thee.

For holy was the adultery of Tamar, for Thy sake. Thee it was she thirsted after, O pure Fountain. Judah defrauded her of drinking Thee. The thirsty womb stole a dew-draught of Thee from the spring thereof.

She was a widow for Thy sake. Thee did she long for, she hasted and was also an harlot for Thy sake. Thee did she vehemently desire, and was sanctified in that it was Thee she loved.

May Tamar rejoice that her Lord hath come and hath made her name known for the son of her adultery! Surely the name she gave him [6] was calling unto Thee to come to her.

For Thee honorable women shamed themselves, Thou that givest chastity to all! Thee she stole away in the midst of the ways, who pavest the way into the kingdom! Because it was life that she stole, the sword was not able to put her to death.

Ruth lay down by a man in the threshingfloor for Thy sake; her love made her bold for Thy sake, O Thou that teachest all penitents boldness. Her ears refused [to listen to] any voices for the sake of Thy voice.

The live coal that glowed went up into the bed, of Boaz, lay down there, saw the High Priest, in whose loins was hidden a fire for his incense! [7] She hasted and was a heifer to Boaz, that should bring forth Thee, the fatted Calf.

---

[5] Gen. xxxviii.  [6] Gen. xxxviii. 29.
[7] The introduction of Ruth after Tamar was doubtless suggested by Ruth iv. 12. Mat. i. 3, etc. St. E. seems to mean, " Ruth saw by faith Christ the High Priest, in whose loins was to be that Fire of Righteousness which alone could make the incense (*i.e.* the child which rose up from Ruth, who is called a coal) to be acceptable."

She went gleaning for her love of Thee ; she gathered straw. Thou didst quickly pay her the reward of her lowliness ; and instead of ears of corn, the Root of Kings, and instead of straws, the Sheaf of Life, didst Thou make to spring from her.

## HYMN VIII.

That Thy Resurrection might be believed among the gainsayers, they sealed Thee up within the sepulchre, and set guards ; for it was for Thee that they sealed the sepulchre and set guards, O Son of the Living One !

When they had buried Thee, if they had neglected Thee and left Thee, and gone, there would have been room to lie [and say] that they did steal, O Quickener of all ! When they craftily sealed Thy sepulchre, they made Thy Glory greater.

A type of Thee therefore was Daniel, and also Lazarus ; one in the den, which the Gentiles sealed up, and one in the sepulchre, that the People opened. Lo ! their signs and their seals reproved them.

Their mouth had been open, if they had left Thy sepulchre open. But they went away because they had shut Thy sepulchre and sealed it, and closed up their own mouths. Yea they closed it, and when they had senselessly covered Thy sepulchre, all the slanderers covered their own heads.

But in Thy Resurrection Thou persuadest them concerning Thy Birth ; since the womb was sealed, and the sepulchre closed up ; being alike pure in the womb, and living in the sepulchre.[8] The womb and the sepulchre being sealed were witnesses unto Thee.

The belly and hell cried aloud of Thy Birth and Thy Resurrection : The belly conceived Thee, which was sealed ; hell brought Thee forth which was closed up. Not after nature did either the belly conceive Thee, or hell give Thee up !

Sealed was the sepulchre whereto they had entrusted Thee, that it might keep the dead [safe]. Virgin was the womb which no man knew. Virgin womb and sealed sepulchre, like trumphets, proclaimed Him in the ears of a deaf people.

The sealed belly and the closed rock were amongst the accusers. For they slandered the Conception as being of the seed of man, and the Resurrection as being of the robbery of man ; the seal and the signet convicted them, and pleaded that Thou wert of Heaven.

The people stood between Thy Birth and Thy Resurrection. They slandered Thy Birth, Thy Death condemned them : they set aside Thy Resurrection, Thy Birth refuted them ; they were two wrestlers that stopped the mouth that slandered.

For Elijah they went and searched the mountains :[9] as they sought him on earth, they the more confirmed that he was taken up. Their searching bare witness that he was taken up, in that it found him not.

If then prophets that had had forewarning of Elijah's ascension, doubted as it were of his going up, how much more would impure men speak slander of the Son ? By their own guards He convinced them that He was risen again.

To Thy Mother, Lord, no man knew what name to give. Should he call her Virgin, her Child stood [there] ; and married no man knew her to be ! If then none comprehended Thy Mother, who shall suffice for Thee ?

For she was, alone, Thy Mother ; along with all, Thy Sister. She was Thy mother, she was Thy Sister. She along with chaste women[1] was Thy betrothed. With everything didst Thou adorn Her, Thou ornament of Thy Mother.

---

For she was Thy Bride by nature ere Thou hadst come; she conceived Thee not by nature after Thou wast come, O Holy One, and was a Virgin when she had brought Thee forth holily.

Mary gained in Thee, O Lord, the honours of all married women. She conceived [Thee] within her without marriage. There was milk in her breasts, not after the way of nature. Thou madest the thirsty land suddenly a fountain of milk.

If she carried Thee, Thy mighty look made her burden light; if she gave Thee to eat, it was because Thou wert hungry; if she gave Thee to drink [it was], because Thou wert thirsty; willingly if she embraced Thee, Thou, the coal of mercies, didst keep her bosom safe.

A wonder is Thy Mother. The Lord entered her, and became a servant: the Word entered her, and became silent within her; thunder entered her, and His voice was still: the Shepherd of all entered her; He became a Lamb in her, and came forth bleating.

The Belly of Thy Mother changed the order of things, O Thou that orderest all! The rich went in, He came out poor: the High One went in, He came out lowly. Brightness went into her and clothed Himself, and came forth a despised form.

The Mighty went in, and clad Himself with fear from the Belly. He that giveth food to all went in, and gat hunger. He that giveth all to drink went in, and gat thirst. Naked and bare came forth from her the Clother of all.

The daughters of the Hebrews that cried in the Lamentations of Jeremiah, instead of lamentations of their Scriptures, used lulling-songs from their own books: a hidden Power within their words was prophesying.

Eve lifted up her eyes from Sheol and rejoiced in that day, because the Son of her daughter as a medicine of life came down to raise up the mother of His mother. Blessed Babe, that bruised the head of the Serpent that smote her!

She saw the type of Thee from the youth of Isaac the fair. For Thee Sarah, as seeing that types of thee rested on his childhood, called him, saying, O child of my vows, in whom is hidden the Lord of vows.

Samson the Nazarite shadowed forth a type of Thy working. He tore the lion, the image of death, whom Thou didst destroy, and caused to go forth from his bitterness the sweetness of life for men.

Hannah also embraced Samuel; for Thy righteousness was hidden in him who hewed in pieces Agag as [a type] of the wicked one. He wept over Saul, because Thy goodness also was shadowed forth in him.[2]

How meek art Thou! How mighty art Thou, O Child![3] Thy judgment is mighty Thy love is sweet! Who can stand against Thee? Thy Father is in Heaven, Thy Mother is on earth; who shall declare Thee?[4]

If a man should seek after Thy Nature, it is hidden in Heaven in the mighty Bosom of the Godhead; and if a man seek after Thy visible Body, it is laid down before their eyes in the lowly bosom of Mary.

The mind wanders between Thy generations, O Thou Rich One! Thick folds are upon Thy Godhead. Who can sound Thy depths, Thou great Sea that made itself little?

We come to see Thee as God, and, lo! Thou art a man: we come to see Thee as man, and there shineth forth the Light of Thy Godhead!

Who would believe that Thou art the Heir of David's Throne? A manger hast Thou inherited out of [all] his beds, a cave has come down to Thee out of all his palaces. Instead of his chariots a common ass's colt, perchance, comes down to Thee.

---

How fearless art Thou, O Babe, that dost let all have thee [to carry] : upon every one that meets with Thee dost Thou smile : to every one that sees Thee, art Thou gladsome ! Thy love is as one that hungers after men.

Thou makest no distinction between Thy fathers and strangers, nor Thy Mother and maidservants, nor her that suckled Thee and the unclean. Was it Thy forwardness or Thy love, O Thou that lovest all ?

What moves Thee that Thou didst let all that saw Thee have Thee, both rich and poor ? Thou helpedst them that called Thee not. Whence came it that Thou hungeredst so for men ?

How great was Thy love, that if one rebuked Thee, Thou wast not wroth ! if a man threatened Thee, Thou wast not terrified ! if one hissed at Thee, Thou didst not feel vexed ! Thou art above the laws of the avengers of injuries.

Moses was meek, and [yet] his zeal was harsh, for he struggled and slew. Elisha also, who restored a child to life, tore a multitude of children in pieces by bears. Who art Thou, O Child, whose love is greater than that of the Prophets ?

The son of Hagar who was wild, kicked at Isaac.[5] He bore it and was silent, and his mother was jealous. Art Thou the mystery of him, or is not he the type of Thee ? art thou like Isaac, or is it not he that is like Thee ?

## HYMN IX.

Come rest, and be still in the bosom of Thy Mother, Son of the Glorious. Forwardness fits not the sons of kings. O Son of David, Thou art glorious, and [yet] the Son of Mary, who dost hide Thy beauty in the inner chamber.

To whom art Thou like, glad Babe, fair little One, Whose Mother is a Virgin, Whose Father is hidden, Whom even the Seraphim are not able to look upon ? Tell us whom Thou art like, O Son of the Gracious !

When the wrathful came to see Thee, Thou madest them gladsome : they exchanged smiles one with another : the angry were made gentle in Thee, O sweet One. Blessed art Thou, little One, for that in Thee even the bitter are made sweet.

Who ever saw a Babe that was gladsome when in arms to those that came near him, lo ! reached Himself unto them that were far off ? Fair sight [to see] a Child, that takes thought for every man that they may see him !

He that hath care came and saw Thee, and his care fled away. He that had anxiety ; at Thee forgat his anxiety ; the hungry by Thee forgat his victuals ; and he that had an errand, by Thee was errant and forgot his journey !

O still Thyself, and let men go to their works ! Thou art a son of the poor, learn from Thyself that all the poor had to leave their work to come. Thou who lovest men, hast bound men together by Thy gladsomeness.

David, that stately king, took branches,[6] and in the feast amongst the children as he danced, he gave praise. Is it not the love of David Thy father that is warm in Thee ?

That daughter of Saul ! her father's devil spake in her : she called the stately [king] a vile fellow, because he gave an ensample to the elders of her people of taking up branches with the children in the day of praise to Thee.

Who would not fear to lay it to Thee that Thou art forward ? For lo, the daughter of Saul who mocked the child, cut off her womb from childbearing ; because her mouth derided, the reward of its mouth was barrenness.[7]

---

[5] Gen. xvi. 12, and xxi. 9.      [6] Scripture does not mention this.      [7] 2 Sam. vi. 23.

Let mouths tremble at blasphemy, lest they be shut up! Refrain, O daughter of Sion, thy mouth from Him, for He is the Son of David, Who is gladsome before thee. Be not unto Him as the daughter of Saul, whose race is extinct.

Because Elijah restrained the desire of the body, he withheld rain from the adulterous; because he kept under his body, he withheld dew from the whoremongers, who let their fountains be loosely poured out.

Because the hidden fire of the lust of the body ruled not in him, to him the fire from on high was obedient. And since he subdued on the earth the lust of the flesh, he went up thither where holiness dwells and is at peace.

Elisha also who deadened his own body, quickened the dead. The resurrection of the dead was in the usual course by a sanctification not in the usual course; He raised the child, because he purified his soul like a weaned child.

Moses, who divided and separated himself from his wife, divided the sea before the harlot. Zipporah though daughter of a heathen priest kept sanctity : with a calf the daughter of Abraham [8] went a whoring.

## HYMN X.

In Thee will I begin to speak, Thou Head that didst begin all created things. [9] I, even I will open my mouth, but it is Thou that fillest my mouth. [1] I am the earth to Thee, and Thou art the husbandman. Sow Thy voice in me, [2] Thou that sowedst Thyself in the womb of thy Mother.

"All the chaste daughters of the Hebrews, [3] and the virgins' daughters of the chief men, are astonished at me! For Thee doth the daughter of the poor meet with envy, for Thee, the daughter of the weak with jealousy. Who hath given Thee to me?

"O Son of the Rich One, Who abhorred the bosom of the rich women, who led Thee to the poor? for Joseph was needy and I also in want, yet Thy merchants have come, and brought gold, to the house of the poor."

She saw the Magi : her songs increased at their offerings ; "Lo! Thy worshippers have surrounded me, yea thy offerings have encircled me. Blessed be the Babe who made His Mother a harp for His words :

"And as the harp waiteth for its master, my mouth waiteth for Thee. May the tongue of Thy Mother bring what pleases Thee ; and since I have learnt a new Conception by Thee, let my mouth learn in Thee, O new born Son, a new song of praise.

"And if hindrances are no hindrances to Thee, since difficulties are easy to Thee, as a womb without marriage conceived Thee, and a belly without seed brought Thee forth, it is easy for a little mouth to multiply Thy great glory.

"Lo! I am oppressed and despised, and yet cheerful : mine ears are filled with reproof and scorn ; and it is a small thing to me to bear, for ten thousand troubles can a single comfort of Thine chase away.

"And since I am not despised by Thee, O Son, my countenance is bright ; and I am slandered for having conceived, and yet have brought forth the Truth who justifies me. For if Tamar was justified by Judah, how much more shall I be justified by Thee!"

David Thy father sung in a psalm of Thee before Thou hadst come, that to Thee should be given the gold of Sheba. [4] This psalm that he sung of Thee, lo! it, whilst Thou art yet a child, in reality heaps before thee myrrh and gold.

---

[8] *I.e.* the Jewish Church.　　　　[9] Rev. iii. 14.　　　　[1] Ps. lxxxi. 10.
[2] Heb. vi. 7.　　　　[3] The Virgin Mother here speaks.　　　　[4] Ps. lxxii. 15.

And the hundred and fifty Psalms that he wrote, in Thee were seasoned, because all the sayings of prophecy stood in need of Thy sweetness, for without Thy salt all manner of wisdom were tasteless. [5]

## HYMN XI.

### (THE VIRGIN MOTHER TO HER CHILD.)

I SHALL not be jealous, my Son, that Thou art with me, and also with all men. Be Thou God to him that confesses Thee, and be thou Lord to him that serves Thee, and be Brother to him that loves Thee, that Thou mayest gain all !

When Thou didst dwell in me, Thou didst also dwell out of me, and when I brought Thee forth openly, Thy hidden might was not removed from me. Thou art within me, and Thou art without me, O Thou that makest Thy Mother amazed.

For [when] I see that outward form of Thine before mine eyes, the hidden Form is shadowed forth "in my mind," O holy One. In Thy visible form I see Adam, and in Thy hidden form I see Thy Father, who is joined with Thee.

Hast Thou then shown me alone Thy Beauty in two Forms? Let Bread shadow forth Thee, and also the mind; dwell also in Bread and in the eaters thereof. In secret, and openly too, may Thy Church see Thee, as well as Thy Mother.

He that hates Thy Bread is like unto him that hates Thy Body. He that is far off that desires Thy Bread, and he that is near that loves Thy Image, are alike. In the Bread and in the Body, the first and also the last have seen Thee.

Yet Thy visible Bread is far more precious than Thy Body ; for Thy Body even unbelievers have seen, but they have not seen Thy living Bread. They that were far off rejoiced ! their portion utterly scorns that of those that are near.

Lo ! Thy Image is shadowed forth in the blood of the grapes [6] on the Bread ; and it is shadowed forth on the heart with the finger of love, with the colors of faith. Blessed be He that by the Image of His Truth caused the graven images to pass away.

Thou art not [so] the Son of Man that I should sing unto Thee a common lullaby ; for Thy Conception is new, and Thy Birth marvellous. Without the Spirit who shall sing to Thee? A new muttering of prophecy is hot within me.

How shall I call Thee a stranger to us, Who art from us? Should I call Thee Son ? Should I call Thee Brother ? [7] Husband should I call Thee? Lord should I call Thee, O Child that didst give Thy Mother a second birth from the waters?

For I am Thy sister, of the house of David the father of us Both. Again, I am Thy Mother because of Thy Conception, and Thy Bride am I because of Thy sanctification, Thy handmaid and Thy daughter, from the Blood and Water wherewith Thou hast purchased me and baptised me.

The Son of the Most High came and dwelt in me, and I became His Mother ; and as by a second birth I brought Him forth, so did He bring me forth by the second birth, because He put His Mother's garments on, she clothed her body with His glory.

Tamar, who was of the house of David, Amnon put to shame ; and virginity fell and perished from them both. My pearl is not lost : in Thy treasury it is stored, because Thou hast put it on.

The scent of her brother-in-law stank from Tamar, whose perfume she had stolen.

---

[5] Job. vi. 6.
[6] The Roman Editor points out that this alludes to a rite in the Syrian Liturgy, in which the officiating Priest is instructed to dip one portion of the consecrated bread into the cup and sprinkle the rest with it.
[7] Mat. xii. 50.

As for Joseph's Bride, not even his breath exhaled from her garments, since she conceived Cinnamon.[8] A wall of fire was Thy Conception unto me, O holy Son.

The little flower was faint, because the smell of the Lily[9] of Glory was great. The Treasure-house of spices stood in no need of flower or its smells! Flesh stood aloof because it perceived in the womb a Conception from the Spirit.

The woman ministers before the man, because he is her head. Joseph rose to minister before his Lord, Who was in Mary. The priest ministered before Thy ark by reason of Thy holiness.

Moses carried the tables of stone which the Lord wrote, and Joseph bare about the pure Tablet in whom the Son of the Creator was dwelling. The tables had ceased, because the world was filled with Thy doctrine.

## HYMN XII.

THE Babe that I carry carries me, saith Mary, and He has lowered His wings, and taken and placed me between His pinions, and mounted into the air; and a promise has been given me that height and depth shall be my Son's.

I have seen Gabriel that called him Lord, and the high priest the aged servant, that carried Him and bare Him. I have seen the Magi when they bowed down, and Herod when he was troubled because the King had come.

Satan also who strangled the little ones that Moses might perish,[1] murdered the little ones that the Living One might die. To Egypt He fled, Who came to Judea that He might labour and wander there: he sought to catch the man that would catch himself.

In her virginity Eve put on the leaves of shame: Thy Mother put on in her Virginity the garment of Glory that suffices for all. She gave the little vest of the Body to Him that covers all.

Blessed is she in whose heart and mind Thou wast! A King's palace she was by Thee, O Son of the King, and a Holy of Holies by Thee, O High Priest! She had not the trouble nor vexation of a family, or a husband!

Eve, again, was a nest and a den for the accursed serpent, that entered in and dwelt in her. His evil counsel became bread to her that she might become dust. Thou art our Bread, and Thou art also [of] our race and our garment of glory.

He that has sanctity, if he be in danger, lo! here is his Guardian! He that has iniquity, lo! here is his Pardoner! He that has a devil, here is the Pursuer thereof! They that have pains, lo! here is the Binder up of their breaches.

He that has a child, let him come and become a brother to my Well-beloved![2] He that has a daughter or a young woman of his race, let her come and become the bride of my Glorious One! He that has a servant, let him set him free, that he may come and serve his Lord.

The son of free men that bears Thy yoke, my Son, shall have one reward; and the slave that bears the burden of the yoke of two masters, of Him above and of Him below, there are two blessings for him, and two rewards of the two burdens.[3]

The free woman, my Son, is Thy handmaid: also if she who is in bondage serve Thee, in Thee she is free: in Thee she shall be comforted, because she is freed; hidden apples in her bosom are stored up,[4] if she love Thee!

---

[8] Cant. iv. 14.     [9] Cant. ii. 1.     [1] Ex. i. 16.     [2] Mat. xii. 15.
[3] This passage is to be observed as one of the many in which the Fathers encourage masters to set slaves free, although they pretty uniformly held (as St. E. here seems to do also) that slaves. if they had the choice, should use slavery rather.     [4] Cant. ii. 3.

O chaste woman, long ye for my Well-beloved, that He may dwell in you ; and ye also that are impure that He may sanctify you ! ye Churches also, that the Son of the Creator Who came to renew all creatures, may adorn you !

He received the foolish who worshipped and served all the stars ; He renewed the earth which was worn out through Adam, who sinned and waxed old. The new formation was the creature of its Renewer, and the all-sufficient One repaired the bodies along with their wills.

Come ye blind, and without money receive lights ! Come ye lame, and receive your feet ! ye deaf and dumb, receive your voice ! come thou also whose hand is cut off ; the maimed also shall receive his hands.

It is the Son of the Creator Whose treasure-houses are filled with all manner of helps. Let him that is without eyeballs come to Him that makes clay and changes it, that makes flesh, that enlightens eyes.

By the small portion of clay He shows that it was with His hand that Adam was formed : the soul of the dead also bears Him witness, that by Him it was that the breath of man was breathed in ; by the last witnesses He was accredited to be the Son of Him Who is the First.

Gather ye together and come, O ye lepers, and receive purification without labour. For He will not wash you as Elisha, who baptized seven times in the river : neither will He trouble you as the priests did with their sprinklings. Foreigners and also strangers have betaken themselves to the Great Physician.

The rank of strangers hath no place with the King's Son ; the Lord makes not Himself strange to His servants, [or conceal] that He is Lord of all. For if the Just makes the body leprous, and Thou purifiest it ; then, the Former of the body hateth the body ; but Thou lovest it.

And if it be not Thy forming, being Just, Thou wouldest not have healed it ; [5] and if it were not Thy creature, when in health, Thou wouldest not have afflicted it. The punishments that Thou has cast upon it, and the pains which Thou hast healed, proclaim that Thou art the Creator's Son.

## HYMN XIII.

### (Compare Hymn II. *For the Epiphany.*)

1. In the days of the King whom they called by the name of Semha,[6] our Lord sprang up among the Hebrews : and Semha and Denha [7] ruled, and came, King upon earth, and Son in Heaven ; blessed be His rule !

2. In the days of the king who enrolled men in the book of the dead, our Redeemer came down and enrolled men in the book of the living. He enrolled, and they also : on high He enrolled us, on earth they enrolled Him. Glory to His Name !

3. In the days of the king whose name was Semha, the type and the Reality met together, the king and the King, Semha and Denha. His Cross upon His shoulders, was the sign of His Kingdom. Blessed be He Who bare it.

4. Thirty years He went in poverty upon the earth ! The sounds of praise in all their measures let us twine, my brethren, to the years of the Lord, as thirty crowns to the thirty years. Blessed be His Birth !

5. In the first year, that is chieftain over the treasures and Dispenser of·abundant

---

[5] Deut. xxxii. 39.      [6] *I.e.*, August.      [7] *I.e.*, Dayspring.

blessings, let the Cherubim who bare up the Son in glory,[8] praise Him with us! He left His glory, and toiled and found the sheep that was lost. To Him be thanksgiving!

6. In the second year, let the Seraphim praise Him yet more with us. They that had proclaimed the Son Holy,[9] by and by saw Him when He was reviled among the gainsayers; He bore the contempt and taught praise. To Him be Glory!

7. In the third year, let Michael and his followers, that ministered to the Son in the highest, praise Him with us. They saw Him on the earth when He was ministering, washing feet, cleansing souls. Blessed be His lowliness!

8. In the fourth year, let the whole earth praise Him with us. It is but small for the Son, and it marvelled because it saw that it entertained Him in its bed that is so very mean. He filled the bed, and filled the Heaven. To Him be Majesty!

9. In the fifth year, the Sun shone unto the earth. With its breath let it praise our Sun Who brought His breadth down low, and humbled His mightiness, that the subtle eye of the unseen soul might be able to look upon Him. Blessed be His brightness!

10. In the sixth year again, let the whole air praise Him with us, in whose wide space it is that all things are made glorious, which saw its mighty Lord that had become a little Child in a little bosom. Blessed be His dignity!

11. In the seventh year, the clouds and winds rejoiced with us and sprinkled the dews over the flowers, for they saw the Son who enslaved His brightness and received disgrace and foul spitting. Blessed be His Redemption!

12. In the year also that is eighth, let the fields give praise, that suckle their fruits from His fountains. They worshipped because they saw the Son in arms and the pure One sucking pure milk. Blessed be His good pleasure!

13. In the ninth year, let the earth glorify the might of her Creator, Who laid seed in her in the beginning that she might bring forth all her produce; for it saw Mary, a thirsty land, who yielded the fruit of a Child that was a wonder, yea, a marvel. [Then] it praised Him more exceedingly, for that He was a great Sea of all good things. To Him be exaltation!

14. In the tenth year, let the mount Sinai glorify Him, it which trembled before its Lord. It saw that they took up stones against its Lord; He received stones, Who should build His Church upon a Stone.[1] Blessed be His building!

15. In the eleventh year, let the great sea praise the fists of the Son that measured it,[2] and it was astonished and saw that He came down, was baptized in a small water, and cleansed the creatures. Blessed be His noble act!

16. In the twelfth year, let the holy Temple praise Him, that saw the Child when He sat amongst the old men: the priests were silent when the Lamb of the Feast bleated in His feast. Blessed be His propitiation!

17. In the thirteenth year, let the crowns praise with us the King who conquered, that died and was crowned with a crown of thorns, and bound upon Adam a great crown at His right hand. Blessed be His Apostleship!

18. In the fourteenth year, let the passover in Egypt praise the Passover that came and passed over all, and instead of Pharaoh sunk Legion,[3] instead of horses choked the devil. Blessed be His vengeance!

19. In the fifteenth year, let the lamb of the gluttons praise Him: since our Lord was so far from slaughtering it as Moses did, that He even redeemed mankind with His own Blood. He that feeds all, died for all. Blessed be His Father!

20. In the sixteenth year, let the wheat praise by its type that Husbandman,[4] Who

---

8 Ps. xcix. 1.  
2 Is. xl. 12.  
9 Is. vi. 2; Mat. xxvi. 53; 1 Tim. iii. 16.  
3 Mark v. 9; Luke viii. 30.  
1 Cephas—Petros—*stone.*  
4 John xii. 24.

sowed His Body in the barren earth, since it covers all, spreads itself out and yields new Bread. Blessed be the Pure One!

21. In the seventeenth year, let the Vine praise the Lord that garnished it. He planted a vineyard, souls were as vineplants. He gave peace to the vineyard, but destroyed the vineyard that brought forth wild grapes. Blessed be its Uprooter!

22. In the eighteenth year, let the Vine which the wild boar out of the wood had eaten, praise the True Vine which trimmed Himself, and kept His fruit, and brought the fruits to the Lord of the Vineyard.[5] Blessed be His Vintage!

23. In the nineteenth year, let our leaven praise the true leaven which worked itself in among those that were in error, and drove them all together, and made them one mind by one Doctrine. Blessed be thy doctrine!

24. In the twentieth year, let salt praise Thy living Body, wherewith are salted the bodies and the souls of all the faithful, and faith is the salt of men wherewith they are preserved.[6] Blessed be Thy preserving!

25. In the twenty-first year, let the waters of the desert praise Thee. They are sweet to them afar off, they are bitter to them[7] that are near, who did not minister to Him. The [chosen] people and the nations were bitter in the desert, and He destroyed them. They were sweetened by the Cross which redeemed them. Blessed be Thy pleasantness!

26. In the twenty-second year, let arms and the sword praise Thee : they sufficed not to kill our adversary. It was Thou that killed him, even Thou who didst fix the ear on, which Simon's sword cut off. Blessed be Thy healing!

27. In the twenty-third year, let the ass praise Him, that gave its foal for Him to ride on, that loosed the bonds, that opened the mouth of the dumb, that opened also the mouth of the wild asses[8] when the race of Hagar gave a shout of praise.[9] Blessed be the praise of Thee!

28. In the twenty-fourth year, let the Treasury praise the Son. The treasures marvelled at the Lord of treasures, when in the house of the poor He was increasing, Who made Himself poor that He might enrich all.[1] Blessed be Thy rule!

29. In the twenty-fifth year, let Isaac praise the Son, for by His goodness he was rescued upon the Mount from the knife, and in his stead there was the victim, the type of the Lamb for the slaughter.[2] The mortal escaped, and He that quickens all died.[3] Blessed be His offering!

30. In the twenty-sixth year, let Moses praise Him with us, for that he was afraid and fled from his murderers. Let him praise the Lord that bore the spear and that received the nails in His hands, in His feet. He entered into hell and spoiled it,[4] and came forth. Blessed be Thy Resurrection!

31. In the year which is the twenty-seventh, let the eloquent speakers praise the Son, for they found no cloke to save our cause. He was silent in the judgment-hall, and He carried our cause. Honour be to Him!

32. And in this year let all judges praise Him, who, as being just men, killed the ungodly ; let them praise the Son who died for the wicked, as being good. Though Son of the Just One, He gave them all manner of good things in abundance. Blessed be His bowels of mercy!

33. In the eight and twentieth year, let all mighty men of valour praise the Son, because they delivered not from him who took us captive. He only is to be praised, who being slain showed us life.[5] Blessed be His delivery!

---

[5] John xviii. 9.  [6] Mark ix. 49.  [7] Exod. xv. 25.  [8] Gen. xvi. 12.  [9] Acts ii. 11.
[1] 2 Cor. viii. 9.  [2] Heb. xi. 19.  [3] Is. liii.  [4] Is. xlix. 24.  [5] Rev. v. 9.

34. In the twenty-ninth year, let Job praise Him with us, who bore sufferings for himself, and our Lord bore for us the spitting and the spear, and the crown of thorns, and scourges, contempt and reproach, yea mocking.   Blessed be His mercy !

35. In the year that is thirteenth, let the dead praise Him with us, because they are quickened, and the living, because they have turned to repentance,[6] because height and depth were set at one by Him.   Blessed be He and His Father !

## HYMN XIV.

(Resp. —*Blessed be he who became beyond measure low, that he might make us beyond measure great*)

1. Of the Birth of the Firstborn, let us tell on His Feast-day.[7]—He gives on His day, secret comforts.—If the unclean *King* at his feast, in memory of his day,—gave the gift of wrath, the head in a charger,—how much more shall the Blessed, give blessings to him—who sings praise at His Feast !

2. Let us not count our vigil like vigils of every day.—His feast, its reward, exceeds an hundredfold.—For this feast makes war, on sleep by its vigil ;—speaking it makes war, on silence by its voice ;—clad with all blessings, it is chief of feasts,—and of every joy.

3. To-day the angels, and the archangels,—descended to sing—a new song on earth. —In this mystery they descend, and rejoice with the vigil-keepers.—At the time when they gave praise, blasphemy abounded.—Blessed be the Birth by which, lo ! the world resounds—with anthems of praise.

4. For this is the night that joined, the Watchers on high with the vigil-keepers.— The Watcher came to make watchers in the midst of creation.—Lo ! the vigil-keepers are made comrades with the Watchers :—the singers of praise are made, companions of the Seraphs.—Blessed be he who becomes, the harp of Thy praise !—and Thy grace becomes his reward.

5. The Birth then of the Firstborn, I will sing *and tell* how—the Godhead in the womb wove itself a vesture.—He put it on and came forth in birth, in death again put it off ;—once he put it off, twice He put it on.—On the left He wore it, then took it off thence,—and laid it at the right.

6. He dwelt in a narrow bosom, the Might that rules all.—While He was dwelling there, He held the reins of the whole :—to His Father He made offering, that He might fulfil His Will :—Heaven was filled by Him, and every creature.—The Sun entered the womb, and in the height and the depth—his splendour abode.

7. He dwelt in the wide bosoms, of all the creatures ;—too narrow to hold, the greatness of the Firstborn.—How then sufficed for it, that bosom of Mary ?—Marvellous if it sufficed, bewilderment if it sufficed not.—Of all bosoms that held Him, one bosom sufficed for Him,—His, the Supreme Who begat Him.

8. The bosom that held Him, if it held Him Wholly,—equals the wondrous bosom, of the Supreme Who begat Him.—But who dare say the bosom, that is narrow weak and lowly,—is equal to His, Who is the Supreme Being ?—He dwelt there of His mercy, though so great is His Nature :—it is without bound.

9. Reconciling Peace, sent to the nations !—gladdening Brightness, that camest to the sad !—Mighty Leaven in silence, overcoming all !—Patient One that hast taken, man after man in Thy net !—Happy he who has welcomed, thy joy in his heart,—and forgot his groans in Thee !

---

[6] Mal. iv. 6.                                                                [7] See p. 177 n.

10. They sounded forth peace, the Watchers to the vigil-keepers.—Among the vigil-keepers the good tidings, were announced by the Watchers.—Who would sleep on that night, which has waked all creatures?—For they bear good tidings of peace, where warfare had been.—Blessed is he who has pleased, the *Divine* Majesty by his silence,—when speaking moved His wrath!

11. Watchers mixed with watchers, they rejoiced that the world came to life.—The Evil One was shamed who was king, and had woven a crown of lies;—and set up his throne, as God in the world.—The Babe laid in the manger, cast him from his dominion.—The Sun rendered worship, doing Him homage by his Magi;—in his worshippers he worshipped Him.

12. God saw that mankind, worship things created:—He put on a created body, that in our custom He might capture us.—Lo! in this *our* form, He that formed us healed us;—and in this created shape, our Creator gave us life.—He drew us not by force: blessed be He Who came in ours,—and joined us in His!

13. Who would not marvel, at Mary, David's daughter,—bearing an infant, and her virginity kept!—She lays Him on her breast, and lulls Him with song and He rejoices.—The Angels raise hymns, the Seraphs cry "Holy,"—the Magi offer, acceptable gifts,—to the Son Who is born.

14. O great above measure, immeasurably made low,—praised beyond praises, debased to humiliation!—the tender mercies laid on Thee, bowed Thee down to all this;—let Thy grace bow me down, though evil to give praise!—Happy he who becomes, a fountain of voices,—all praising Thee in all!

15. He was servant on earth; He is Lord in Heaven.—Heir of height and depth, He became a stranger:—Whom men judged in guile, He is judge in truth:—He Whose face they spat on, breathes His Spirit on theirs:—He Who held the frail reed, is become the staff of the world,—which grows old and leans on Him.

16. He Who rose to wait on His servants, now sits to be worshipped.—Whom the scribes despised, before Him Seraphs cry "Holy."—This praise Adam desired, to steal privily.—The serpent which made him fall, saw to what height he was raised:—he crushed it because it deceived him; the feet of Eve trod it down,—which had sent venom into her ears.

17. The wife proved barren, and withheld her fruit;—but the bosom of Mary, holily conceived.—To wonder at fields, and to admire plants—she needed not who received, and rendered what she borrowed not.—Nature confessed its defeat; the womb was aware of it,—and restored what *Nature* gave not.

18. Mary was defeated, in the judgment by Elizabeth.—She that was barren pleaded, that the Will which prevailed—to close the open door, has opened the closed.—He has made childless the married womb; He has made fruitful the virgin womb.—Because the People were accurst faithless, He made her that was married,—held from bearing before the face of the maiden.

19. He Who could give moisture, to breasts barren and dead,—caused them to fail in youth, made them to flow in age;—forced and changed nature, in its season and out of its season.—The Lord of natures changed, the Virgin's nature.—Because the People were barren, He made her that was aged,—a mouth on behalf of the damsel.

20. And as He began at birth, He went on and fulfilled in death.—His Birth received worship; His Death paid the debt.—As He came to His Birth, the Magi worshipped Him;—again He came to His Passion, and the thief sought refuge in Him—Between His Birth and Death, midway He set the world:—in birth and Death he gave it life.

21. Thousand thousands stand, and ten thousand thousands haste.—The thousands

and ten thousands, cannot search out the One :—for all of them stand, in silence to serve.—He has no heir of His Throne, save the Son Who is of Him.—In the midst of silence *is* the enquiry into Him, when the watchers come to search Him out,—they attain to silence and are stayed.

22. The Firstborn entered the womb, and the pure Virgin was not harmed.—He stirred and came forth in *her* travail, and the fair Mother was troubled by Him.—Glorious and unseen in entering, humble and manifest in issuing ;—for He was God in entering, and He was man in issuing.—A marvel and bewilderment to hear : fire entered the womb ; put on a body and came forth !

23. Gabriel chief of Angels, called Him " My Lord " :—he called Him " My Lord," to teach that He was his Lord, not his fellow.—Gabriel had with him, Michael as fellow : —the Son is Lord of the servants ; exalted *is* His Nature as His Name.—*No* servant can search Him out ; for the greater the servant,—He is great above His servant.

24. When they stand before Thee, the watchers with songs of praise,—they know not in what part, they shall discern Thee.—They have sought Thee above in the height ; they have seen Thee below in the depth :—they have searched for Thee in the midst of heaven ; they have seen Thee in the midst of the abyss :—they have discerned Thee beside Him that is worshipped ; they have found Thee in the midst of the creatures : —they have come down to Thee and sung Glory to Thee.

25. Thou art all wonderful, in all parts where we seek Thee.—Near art Thou,—and far, and who may attain to Thee?—No seeking avails, that its stretch should reach unto Thee.—Whereon it stretches to reach Thee, it is checked and stops,—it falls short of Thy mountain ; Faith reaches thither,—and Love with prayer.

26. The Magi also sought Him, and in the manger when they found Him,—instead of scrutiny worship, they offered Him in silence ;—for empty strivings, oblations gave they Him.—Seek thou too the Firstborn, and if thou find Him in the height,—instead of troubled questionings, open thy treasures before Him,—and offer Him thy works.

## XV.

RESP.—*Blessed is He above all in His Birth !* (bis).

1. Celebrate, O nations, this feast, first fruits of all feasts ;—recount the sufferings that were, and the wounds and pains,—that we may know what plagues, He healed, the Son Who was sent.    *R., Blessed be He Who sufficed to heal our pains !*

2. Celebrate, O saved nations, Him Who saves all in His Birth.—Even my feeble tongue, has become a harp through *His* mercy.—The excellency of the Firstborn, in His Festival let us sing.    *R., Blessed is He Who has made us meet for His Feast!*

3. How then can any one, admire a physician,—until he hear and learn, what were the pains he healed ?—And when our plagues are proclaimed, then is our Healer magnified.    *R., Blessed be He Who is exalted in our pains !*

4. Created things were worshipped : because the worshipper was foolish,—he used to worship all things ; but One they worshipped not.—He came down therefore in mercy and broke, the yoke that enslaved all.    *R., Blessed is He Who loosed our pains !*

5. The mercies of the Highest were revealed ; He came down and set free His creature.—In this blessed month, wherein are made releases of *slaves*,—the Lord underwent bondage, to call the bond to freedom.    *R., Blessed is He Who brought freedom !*

6. The Lord of the months chose Him, two months for His doings.—His Conception was in Nisan, and His Birth in Conun.—In Nisan He sanctified them that were con-

ceived ; and them that were born He set free in Conun.  *R., Blessed be He Who makes glad His months !*

7. The Sun revealed in silence, his worshippers to his Lord :—it was grievous to him, a servant, to be worshipped instead of his Lord.—Lo ! creation is glad, that the Creator is worshipped.  *R., Blessed is the Child that is worshipped.*

8. The months wore three *crowns*, and crowned Him in His triumphs.—Blessed *is* the Sun for His Birth, and for His Resurrection desired,—and for His Ascension blessed ; the months have borne Him crowns.  *R., Blessed be He Who has triumphed in His months !*

9. Unveil and make glad thy face, O Creature, in our feast.—Let the Church sing with voice ; Heaven and earth in silence !—Sing and praise the Child, who has brought release for all !  *R., Blessed be He Who has annulled the bonds !*

10. When fools did reverence to the Sun, in reverence to him they disgraced him.— But now when all know he is a servant, in his course his Lord is worshipped ;—all servants rejoice, that as servants they are reckoned.  *R., Blessed be He Who ordered* their *natures !*

11. We have done perverse things, who have become servants of servants.—Lo ! our freedom compelled him, a servant, to become lord to us :—the Sun, the servant for all, we have made Lord for all.  *R., Blessed is He Who to Himself has turned us !*

12. And the Moon too which was worshipped, has been set free by His Birth.—For 'tis strange that by her light, which enlightens the eyes,—by it the eyes were darkened, that they gazed on her as a God.  *R., Blessed be the beam that has enlightened us !*

13. Fire commended Thy Birth, which drew away worship from it.—The magi used to worship it : they who have worshipped before Thee.—They left it and worshipped its Lord ; they exchanged fire for the Fire.  *R., Blessed is He Who has bathed us in His light !*

14. In place of the senseless fire that eats up its own body of itself,—the magi adored the Fire Who gave His Body to be eaten.—The live coal drew near and sanctified, the lips that were unclean.  *R., Blessed is He Who has mixed His Fire in us !*

15. Delusion blinded men, to worship created things :—fellow servants were worshipped, and the God of all was wronged.—He Who is to be worshipped came down *to* His birth, and gathered to himself worship.  *R., Blessed is He Who by all is worshipped !*

16. The All-knowing saw, that *men* worship things that were made :—He put on a body that was made, that in our custom He might take us captive,—and by a body that was made, drew us to the Creator.  *R., Blessed be He Who drew us with guile !*

17. The Evil One knew how to harm us ; and by lights he blinded us,—by possessions he hurt us, through gold he made us poor,—by the graver's graven images, he made us a heart of stone.  *R., Blessed is He Who came and softened it !*

18. They graved and set up stones, whereon men should stumble.—They set them not on the highway, for the blind to stumble on :—they called them Gods, that on them *with* open *eyes* men might stumble.  *R., Blessed is He Who exposed the idols which they feared !*

19. Sin had spread its wings, and covered all things,—that none could discern, of himself or from above, the truth.—Truth came down into the womb, came forth and rolled away error.  *R., Blessed is He Who dispelled Sin by His Birth !*

20. For Mercy endured not, to see the way hindered.—When He came down for conception, He opened the way *and made it* easy :—when He came forth in birth, He trod it and marked its miles.  *R., Blessed is the peace of Thy Way !*

21. He chose the Prophets; they cleared the way for the people :—He sent the Apostles; they smoothed paths for the nations.—The snares of the Evil One were shamed, when feeble men cleared them away.    *R., Blessed is He Who made our paths plain !*

22. The graven images blinded, their gravers in secret :—they graved eyes on stone, and darkened the eyes of the soul.—Praise to Thy Birth that opened, the sight that was blinded.    *R., Blessed be He Who has restored sight !*

23. Let women praise Her, the pure Mary,—that *as* in Eve their mother,—great was their reproach,—lo ! in Mary their sister,—greatly magnified was their honour.    *R., Blessed is He Who sprang from women !*

24. Let the nations praise Thy Birth, that they have gained eyes to see,—how their wine has made them reel; and they have seen their own humiliation ?—They come to know themselves, and worship Him who has rescued them.    *R., Blessed is He Who has taught repentance !*

25. Its worship mankind—had spread everywhere :—Him Who is *to be* worshipped it sought not, that worship should be paid Him.—But He endured not—worshippers that err.    *R., Blessed is He Who came down and is worshipped !*

26. The gold of the idols worshipped Thee, that Thou didst treat it as alms; which availed not apart, for the uses of life.—It hasted to Thy purse, as it had hasted to the manger.    *R., Blessed be He Whom Creation has loved !*

27. The frankincense worshipped Thy Birth, which had served demons.—It sorrowed *then* in its vapour : it exulted when it saw its Lord.—Instead of *being* the incense of delusion, it was an oblation before God !    *R., Blessed is Thy Birth which is worshipped !*

28. The myrrh worshipped Thee for itself, and for its kindred ointments.—The hands that bore its ointment, had anointed abominable graven images.—To Thee the perfume was sweet, from the anointing wherewith Mary anointed Thee.    *R., Blessed is Thy savour which is sweet to us !*

29. The gold that had been worshipped worshipped thee, when the magi offered it. —That which had been worshipped in molten images, gave worship to Thee.—With its worshippers it worshipped Thee, it confessed that Thou art He that is to be worshipped.    *R., Blessed is He Who claimed worship for Himself !*

30. The Evil One fled and his hosts, he that used to exult in the world.—In the high places they sacrificed heifers to him, in the gardens they slew bulls for him.—He swallowed up all creation, he filled his belly with prey.    *R., Blessed be He Who came and made him disgorge !*

31. Of him the Lord said, that he had fallen from Heaven.—The Abhorred One had exalted himself; from his uplifting he has fallen.    The foot of Mary has trod him down, who bruised Eve with his heel.    *R., Blessed be He Who by His Birth laid him low !*

32. Chaldeans went about, in all places and led astray :—the preachers of delusion, were shamed through the world,—they were shamed and overcome,—by the preachers of truth.    *R., Blessed be the Babe Whom they preached !*

33. Sin had spread out, her nets for the draught.—Praise *be* to Thy Birth that captured, the nets of delusion.—The soul took flight on high, which had been taken in the deep.    *R., Blessed is He Who prepared for us wings !*

34. His Will was able, even by force to rescue us. —*But* since it was not force that made us guilty, *it was* not by force He purged us.—The Evil One by enticement enslaved us : Thy Birth enticed to give us life.    *R., Blessed be He Who planned and gave us life !*

35. The creatures complained that they were worshipped; in silence they sought release.—The All-Releaser heard, and because He endured it not He came down,—put on *the form of* a servant in the womb, came forth, set free Creation.  *R., Blessed be He Who made his Creation his gain!*

36. Mercy was kindled on high, at the voice of Creation that cried out :—Gabriel was sent; he came and gave tidings of Thy Conception.—When Thou camest to the Birth, Watchers gave tidings of thy coming forth.  *R., Blessed be by Thy Worship above all!*

37. For greater is the joy of the Birth than the Conception.—Yea it was one angel, that brought us tidings of Thy Conception :—*but* in the joy of Thy Birth, a multitude of Watchers brought tidings.  *R., Blessed be Thy tidings in Thy day!*

38. Glory to Thee I too in Thy day, will offer, O Thou that art worshipped !—Take of the fruit that is mine ; and give me mercy which is Thine !—For if the evil that is in me gives gifts, how much more shalt Thou give Who art good !  *R., Blessed is Thy wealth in Thy servant!*

39. The two things Thou soughtest, in Thy Birth have been done for us.—Our visible body Thou hast put on ; Thy invisible might we have put on :—our body has become Thy clothing ; Thy Spirit has become our robe.  *R., Blessed be He Who has been adorned and has adorned us!*

40. Height and depth were amazed, that Thy Birth subdued the rebels.—For that we gave Thee hostages, Thou gavest us the Paraclete :—when the hostages went up from us, the Captain of the host came down to us.  *R., Blessed be He Who took away and sent down!*

41. Come ye mouths of all and pour forth, and be in the likeness of waters, and wells of voices !  May the Holy Spirit come,—and sing glory through us all, to the Father Who has redeemed us through His Son !  *R., Blessed is He above all in His Birth!*

## XVI.

(Resp.—*Glory to all of Thee from all of us!* (bis.)

1. Who then that is mortal man, can declare concerning the All-Life giver,—Who quitted the height of His Majesty, and abased Himself to humility ?—*Thou* Who exaltest all in Thy Birth, exalt my weak mind,—to declare of Thy Birth ; not that I should search out Thy Majesty,—but that I should proclaim Thy grace.  *R., Blessed be He Who conceals and reveals in His discourses!*

2. It is a great marvel that the Son, dwelt wholly in a body ;—abode therein wholly and it sufficed for Him ; dwelt therein though not bounded *thereby*.—His Will was wholly therein ; His bounds reached wholly to His Father.—Who is sufficient to tell, how though He dwelt wholly in a body.—He likewise dwelt wholly in all ?  *R., Blessed is He Who though without bounds was bounded!*

3. Thy Majesty is concealed from us ; Thy Grace is revealed before us.—I will be silent, O Lord of Thy Majesty ; and I will tell of Thy grace.—Thy grace clove to Thee, and bowed Thee down to our vileness :—Thy grace made Thee a babe ; Thy grace made Thee man :—it straitened, it enlarged, Thy Majesty.  *R., Blessed be the might that became little and became great!*

4. Glory to Him Who became lowly, though lofty He was by His nature !—He became in His love the firstborn of Mary, Firstborn though He be of Godhead.—He became in name the offspring of Joseph, offspring though He be of the Most High.—

He became by His own Will man, God though He be by His Nature.— Glorified *be* Thy Will and Thy Nature!    *R., Blessed be Thy Glory which put on our image!*

5. Yea, O Lord, Thy Birth, has become mother of *all* creatures ; for it travailed anew and gave birth, to mankind which gave birth to Thee. Thou wast born of it bodily ; it was born of Thee spiritually.—All that Thou camest *for* to birth, *was* that man might be born in Thy likeness.—Thy Birth became the author of birth to all.   *R., Blessed be He Who became a youth and to all gave youth!*

6. When man's hope had broken down, hope was increased by Thy Birth.—Good tidings of hope they bore, the Heavenly Ones to men.—Satan who cut off our hope, his own hope by his own hands had cut off.—when he saw that hope was increased : Thy Birth became to the hopeless,—a fountain teaming with hope.   *R., Blessed be He Who bore the tidings of hope!*

7. The day of Thy Birth is like Thee, for it is desired and loved as Thou.—We who saw not Thy Birth, and its flame as in its own time,—in this Thy day we see Thee, even as Thou wast a babe ;—beloved by all men, lo ! in Thee the Churches rejoice ;— Thy day adorns and is adorned.   *R., Blessed be Thy day which was ordained for us!*

8. Thy day has given us a gift, to which the Father has none other like ;—It was not Seraphim He sent us, nor yet did Cherubim come down among us ;—there came not Watchers *or* Ministers, but the Firstborn to Whom they minister.—Who can suffice to give thanks, that the Majesty which is beyond measure—is laid in the lowly manger !   *R., Blessed be He Who gave us what He had won!*

9. That generation Thy Birth made glad, and our generation Thy day makes glad : twofold *was* the happiness of that generation, for they saw Thy Birth and also Thy day : —less *is* the happiness of them that come after, for the day of Thy Birth they see only. —Yet because they that then were, doubted, greater is the happiness of them that come after,—who though they have not seen Thee have believed in Thee.   *R., Blessed be Thy happiness that is added to us!*

10. The Magi exalted from afar ; the Scribes murmured near at hand ;—the prophet showed his message, and Herod his wrath ;—the scribes showed their doctrine, the Magi showed their offerings. It is a marvel that to Him, the Babe, they of His own house hasted with their swords, and they that were strangers with their offerings.   *R., Blessèd be Thy Birth which has stirred up all!*

11. The bosom of Mary amazes me, that it sufficed for Thee, Lord, and embraced Thee.—All creation were too small, to conceal Thy Majesty ;—Heaven and earth too narrow, to be in the likeness of wings,[1] to cover Thy Godhead.—Too small for Thee was the bosom of earth ; great enough for Thee was the bosom of Mary.—He dwelt in the bosom and healed in her bosom.   *R.,*

12. He was wrapped meanly in swaddling clothes, and offerings were offered Him. —He put on garments in youth, and from them there came forth helps : He put on the waters of baptism, and from them there shone forth beams :—He put on linen cloths in death, and in them were shown forth triumphs ; with His humiliations. His exaltations.   *R., Blessed be He Who joined His Glory to His Passion!*

13. All these *are* the changes of raiment, which Mercy put off and put on,—when He strove to put on Adam, the glory which he had put off.—He was wrapped in swaddling-clothes as *Adam* with leaves ; and clad in garments instead of skins.—He was baptized for *Adam's* sin, and buried for *Adam's* death :—He rose and raised *Adam* into Glory.   *R., Blessed be He Who came down and clothed him and went up!*

---

[1] The word used for " bosom " in this stanza, also means " wing."

14. Though Thy Birth had sufficed, for Adam's sons as for Adam ;—O Mighty One Who didst become a babe, in Thy Birth anew hast Thou begotten me !—O pure One Who wast baptized, let Thy Washing wash away our filth—O Living One who wast buried, may we gain life in Thy death !—I will praise all of Thee in Him that fills all. *R., Glory to all of Thee from all of us !*

## XVII.

(RESP., *Praise to Thee from every mouth on this Day of Thy Birth !*)

1. Infants were slain because of Thy Birth, Thou Giver of life to all—But because He Who was slain was a King, our Lord the Lord of Kingdoms,—the tyrant in subtlety, gave for Him slain hostages,—clad in the mysteries of His slaying : the ranks of heaven received,—the hostages that they of earth offered. *R., Blessed be the King who magnified Him !*

2. All the Kings of the house of David, transmitted and hauled on each to each,— the throne and crown of the Son of David, as guardian of a deposit.—In one they reached their bound and limit, when He came, the Lord of all things,—and took away from them all things, and cut off the transmission of all things. . . . *R., Blessed be He Who is clad in that which is His !*

3. The doves moaned in Bethlehem, that the serpent destroyed their offspring.— The eagle betook himself to Egypt, to go down and receive the promises.—Egypt rejoiced in Him that there came, abundance for payment of debts,—which had failed the sons of Joseph. Among the sons of Joseph He laboured and paid—the debts of the sons of Joseph. *R., Blessed is He Who called Him out of Egypt !*

4. The Scribes read daily, that the Star arises out of Jacob.—For the People *were* the Voice and the reading, for the nations the rising *of the Star* and the interpretation :— for them were the Books and for us the facts ; for them boughs and for us fruits.—The Scribes read in things written ; the Magi saw in things done, the outshining of that which was read. *R., Blessed be He Who added to us their books !*

5. Who is able to tell, of the withdrawal and the appearings,—of the shining star that went, before the bearers of the offerings ?—It appeared and proclaimed the crown ; it was hid and concealed *His* Body.—It was for the Son in twofold wise, herald and guardian ;—it guarded His Body, it proclaimed His Crown. *R., Blessed is He Who has given wisdom to them that proclaim Him !*

6. The tyrant gazed on the Magi, as they asked "Where is the son of the King ?"— While his heart was gloomy, he sought for himself a cheerful countenance.—With the sheep he sent wolves, that should kill the Lamb of God.—The Lamb went down to Egypt, that thence He might judge them,—whence He had saved them. *R., Blessed be He Who yet again subdued them.*

7. The Magi declared to the tyrant, "When thy servants joined us,—the bright star withdrew itself, yea the paths hid themselves."—The blessed ones knew not, that the king had sent bitter *foes,*—murderers as *if* worshippers, to destroy the sweet fruit,— whereof the bitter eat and are made sweet. *R., To Thee be glory, Medicine of life !*

8. When there the Magi received, commandment to go and seek Him.—it is written of them that they saw, that bright star and rejoiced.—*Thus* it is known that it had been withdrawn ; therefore rejoiced they at its aspect.—It was hid and hindered the murderers, it arose and called the worshippers ;—it overthrew a part and it called a part. *R., Blessed be He Who has triumphed in both parts !*

9. The abhorred one who slew the children, how did he overlook the Child ?—Justice

hindered him that he thought, the Magi would return to him.—While he stayed waiting to seize, the Worshipped and His worshippers,—everything escaped his hands, the offerings and the worshippers took flight,—from the tyrant to the Son of the King. *R., Glory to Him who knows all counsels !*

10. The blameless Magi as they slept, meditated on their beds :—sleep became a mirror, and a dream rose *on it* as light.—The murderer they saw and trembled, as his guile and his sword flashed forth.—He taught the men guile, he sharpened the sword to sharpness :—the Watcher taught the sleepers.     *R., Blessed is He who gives prudence to the simple !*

11. The simple who believe have known, two Comings of Christ :—but the foolish scribes have not even perceived one Coming.—Yet the nations have life in the first, and shall rise again there in the second.—The People whose mind is blinded, the first Coming has dispersed ;—the second shall blot out their memory.     *R., Blessed be the King Who is come and is to come !*

12. When the Saviour arose as the blind, the Sun showed forth his beams,—and they were clothed in darkness : the Brightness sent forth his light,—and He brought the sons of the stars, to make manifest the sons of darkness.—For lo ! among you is the star, but on your eyes the veil.     *R., To Thee be glory, newborn Sun !*

13. Prophets declared concerning His Birth, but they made not plain the time thereof. —He sent the Magi, and they came and showed of its time.—Yet the Magi who made known the time, made not plain who the Child *should be.*—A star of splendid light, in its course showed who the Child *was,*—*how* splendid was *His* lineage.     *R., Blessed be He Who by them all was pointed out !*

14. They scorned the trumpet of Isaiah, which sounded forth His pure Conception,— they silenced the lute of the Psalms, which sang of His Priesthood ;—the harp of the Spirit they hushed, which sang again of His Kingdom ;—under deep silence they closed up, the great Birth that joined the cry—of them above with them below. *R., Blessed be He Who appeared in the midst of silence !*

15. His voice was the secret key that opened the mouths of the Magi.—Whereas preachers were silent in Judah, they made their voice sound through creation ;—and the Gospel which those had scorned, these who came from far took and departed.—The scorners began to hear their *own* orders from strangers, who cried out *the name of* the Son of David.     *R., Blessed be He Who by our voice has put them to silence !*

16. Whereas the People scorned offerings, and brought them not to Him the Son of the King,—He sent His herald to the nations, and caused them to come with their offerings :—yet not all of them caused He to come, for it could not suffice for them,— the narrow bosom of Bethlehem ; but the bosom of Holy Church,—enlarged itself and contained her children.     *R., Blessed be He Who has made the barren fruitful !*

17. The slayers of Bethlehem mowed down the tender flowers that among them— should perish the tender seedling, wherein was hidden the Bread of life.—But the ear of corn that has life had escaped, that it should come to the sheaves in harvest :—the grape that escaped when young, gave itself to the treading,—that its wine might give life to souls.     *R., Glory to Thee, Treasury of life !*

18. The murderers went into a paradise, full of tender fruits :—they shook off the flowers from the bough, blossoms and buds they destroyed,—unblemished oblations he offered, the persecutor unwittingly.—To him woe, but to them blessing ! Bethlehem was first to give, virgin fruits to the Holy One.     *R., Blessed is He Who receives the first fruits !*

19. The Scribes were silenced in envy, the Pharisees in jealousy.—Men of stone

cried out and gave praise, who had a heart of stone.—They applauded in presence of the Stone, the rejected that has become the Head.—Stones were made flesh by that Stone, and obtained mouths to speak; stones cried out through that Stone.   *R., Blessed be Thy Birth that has caused stones to cry out!*

20. The Star that is written in Scripture, the nations beheld from afar,—that the People might be shamed which is near; O People instructed and puffed up! which by the nations hast been in turn instructed, how and where they saw,—that vision whereof Balaam spake; a stranger he who spread abroad concerning it,—strangers they who saw it.   *R., Blessed is He Who has provoked to jealousy them of His own house!*

21. Let my supplication draw nigh to Thy Door, yea my poverty to Thy Treasury!—Give to me my Lord without measure, as God unto man!—And though Thou increase gifts as Son of the Blessed, and though Thou add to them as Son of the King;—though I be thankless as *are all* creatures of dust, as Adam *so is* the son of Adam,—and as the Blessed *so* too *is* the Son of the Blessed.   *R., Praise be to Thee Who art like unto Thy Father!*

## XVIII.

R̲e̲s̲p̲.—*Praise be to Him Who sent Him!* (bis)

1. *Blessed art* thou, O Church, for lo! in thee is the sound,—of the great feast the festival of the King!—Sion is deserted, her gates are sore athirst,—and forsaken of festivals.—Blessed thy gates that are open yet not filled,—and thy halls that are enlarged yet suffice not!—In the midst of thee lo! is the sound, of the nations that cry out, and have put to silence the People.

2. *Blessed art* thou, O Church, that in thy festivals,—the Watchers rejoice amid thy festivity!—for one night the Watchers gave praise,—on the earth which withheld and refused praise.—*Blessed* thy voices that have been sown and reaped,—and in Heaven stored up in garners!—Thy mouth is a censer, and thy voices as perfumes, breathing vapour in thy festivals.

3. *Blessed art* thou, O Church, that all oblations,—are brought unto thee in this feast.—The Magi once among traitors, offered them to the Truth.—*Blessed* thy abode that He bowed Himself and dwelt therein, Son of the King Who is worshipped with gifts!—Gold from the West, and spices from the East,—are offered in Thy Festivals.

4. *Blessed art* thou, O Church, that there is not with thee,—a tyrant King slayer of babes! for he killed in Bethlehem the little ones at random,—that he might put to death the Child that gives life to all.—*Blessed* thy children that are envied and worshipped,—by Kings, for those are promised for Thy worship,—the crowns of the East:—he who trod down thy dear ones, shall be trodden down by thy beloved.

5. *Blessed art* thou, O Church, for lo! over thee,—Isaiah too exults in his prophecy,—"Lo a Virgin shall conceive and bear,—a Son" Whose name is great mystery!—O interpretation revealed in the Church!—two names that were joined and became one;—"Emmanuel,"—God be with thee ever, Who joined thee with His members!

6. *Blessed art* thou, O Church, in Micah who cried out,—"A Shepherd shall come forth from Ephrata":—for He came to Bethlehem to take—from thence the rod of Jesse and to rule the nations.—*Blessed* thy lambs that are sealed with His seal,—and thy sheep that are kept by His sword!—Thou art, O Church,—the abiding Bethlehem,—for in thee is the Bread of Life![1]

7. *Blessed art* thou, O Church, for lo! in thee rejoices,—Daniel also the man beloved,

---

[1] Bethlehem = House of Bread.

—who foretold that the glorious Messiah shall be killed,—and the city of holiness be laid desolate at His killing !—Woe to the People that was rejected and is not converted ! —*Blessed* the nations that were called and turned not away !—The bidden guests refused,—and others in their stead enjoyed their banquet.

8. *Blessed art* thou, O Church, for on thy, lute, lo ! King David sings psalms in thee ! In the Spirit he sings of Him " Thou *art* My Son and I—this day have begotten Thee " in the glories of holiness.—*Blessed* thy ears that have been purged to hear !—On His day watch thou as His Body and call on Him ;—be taught by Sion,—which saddened His Feast ; make Him glad Who has gladdened thee.

9. *Blessed art* thou, O Church, that all festivals—have taken flight from Sion and sheltered with thee !—In the midst of thee the wearied Prophets have found rest,— from the labour and the reproach *they bore* in Judah.—*Blessed* the books unrolled in thy temples,—and the festivals celebrated in thy shrines !—Sion *is* forsaken,—and lo ! today the nations shout in thy festivals.

10. *Blessed art* thou, O Church, in ten blessings,—which our Lord has given *as* a mystery complete :—for on ten all the numbers hang, therefore art thou perfect by ten blessings.—Blessed thy crowns that are twined—with all blessings mixed in every crown !—O blessed one,—with every blessing crowned, on me too send thy blessing !

11. *Blessed art* thou, Ephrata, mother of Kings, that from thee sprang the Lord of diadems !—Micah gave thee tidings that He is from everlasting, and the span of His times is not comprehended.—Blessed thine eyes which first of all discerned Him !—thee He deemed worthy to see Him when He appeared,—Chief of benediction,—and Beginning of gladness, thou didst receive first of all.

12. Blessed *art* thou, Bethlehem, that the towns envy thee,—and the fortified cities ! —As they *envy* thee, *so* the women envy Mary,—and the virgins daughters of princes. —Blessed the maiden in whom He deigned to abide,—and the city wherein He deigned to sojourn ;—a poor maiden,—and a small city, He chose Him to humble Himself.

13. Blessed *art* thou, Bethlehem, that in thee was the beginning,—for Him the Son Who from everlasting is in the Father !—It is hard to comprehend, that before Time He is,—Who in thee made Himself subject to Time.—Blessed thine ears, for in thee first was heard the cry—of the Lamb of God who exulted in thee !—Narrow though thy manger,—He spread Himself on all sides, and was worshipped of every creature.

14. Blessed *art* thou too, Mary, that thy name—is great and exalted because of thy child !—Thou canst tell then how and how long—and where He dwelt in thee, the great One in small room.—Blessed thy mouth that praised and enquired not,—and thy tongue that glorified and questioned not !—For His Mother was uncertain concerning Him,—even while she carried Him *in the womb ;* who then shall suffice *to comprehend* Him ?

15. O Woman, thou whom no man knew,—how can we behold the Son thou hast borne?—For no eyes suffice to stand—before the transfigurations of the glory, that is on Him.—For tongues of fire abide in Him—Who sent tongues by His Ascension.—Be every tongue warned,—that our questioning is *as* stubble, and *as* fire our scrutiny.

16. Blessed *is* he the priest who in the sanctuary,—offers to the Father the Son of the Father,—the fruit that is plucked from our tree, though it be wholly of the *Divine* Majesty !—Blessed the hands that are hallowed and offer Him !—and the lips that are spent in kissing Him !—The Spirit in the Temple—longed for His embrace ; and at His Crucifixion rent *the veil* and went forth.

17. The Archangel gave thee greeting,—as the earnest of holiness—Earth became to him new Heavens,—when the Watcher came down and sang glory on it.—The sons

of the Highest encompassed thy habitation—because of the Son of the King that dwelt in thee.—Thy abode below,—to the Heaven above was made like by the host of Watchers.

## XIX.

*(Resp.—Blessed be thy Birth that gladdens all creatures !)*

1. The first year wherein, our Saviour was born,—is source of blessing, and ground of life ;—for by it are borne,—manifold triumphs, the sum of all help :—as the first day of "the beginning,"—the great pillar of all creatures,—bears the building of Creation ; —so the year of the Firstborn *bears* help for man.

2. In the second year, of our Saviour's Birth,—the Magi exult, the Pharisees mourn : —treasures are opened,—kings are hastening, and infants are slain.—For in it are offered in Bethlehem,—oblations precious and terrible ;—for while love made offering of gold,—hatred offered infants by the sword.

3. The day of the All-Lightening, exults in His birth ;—a pillar of radiance, which drives away, by its beams—the works of darkness. After the type of that day, wherein light was created,—and sundered the darkness that spread—over the fair beauty of Creation ;—the radiance of our Saviour's birth—came in to sunder the darkness that *was* on the heart.

4. The first day the source and the beginning,—orders the roots, to make all things grow.—Our Saviour's day—is praised far above it, a tree planted in the world.—For His Death *is* as the root in the earth ; His Resurrection as the head in heaven ; on all sides His words *reach* as boughs ; likewise His Body as fruit for the eaters.

5. Let the second day, sing praise to the Birth—of the second Son, and His voice which first—commanded the firmament and it was made,—divided the waters that *were* above, and gathered the seas that *were* under.—He Who divided waters from waters, divided Himself from the Watchers and came down to man.—For the waters which at His command were gathered.—He cleft the fountain of life and gave drink.

6. Let the third day weave with divers hymns—the crown of psalms and with one voice present it—for His Birth who gave growth—of buds and flowers, on the third day.—But now He the All-giver of growth,—has come down and become the All-holy Flower ; from the thirsting earth has sprang forth and gone up,—that he may decorate and crown the conquerors.

7. Let the fourth day praise, first among the four,—His Birth Who created as the fourth day—the two lightgivers,—which fools worship, and are sightless and blind.—The Lord of Lightgivers has come down,—and from the womb has shone on us as the Sun. —His splendours have opened the eyes of the blind :—His rays have given light to the wandering.

8. Let the fifth day laud Him Who created—on the fifth day creeping things and Dragons—of whose kind is the serpent.—He deceived with guile our mother, a maid void of counsel.—The deceiver who had mocked the maid,—by the Dove was exposed as false,—which from a virgin bosom sprang, and came forth—the Wise that trod down the crafty.

9. Let the sixth day laud Him who created—on Vesper-day Adam, whom Satan envied ; as a feigned friend—cheered him in offering poison in his food.—The medicine of life reached them both,—put on a body and came near to both.—The mortal tasted Him and lived through Him ;—the devourer who ate Him was left void.

10. Let the seventh day hallow the Holy One,—Who halloweth the Sabbath, and gave rest to all that live.—The Blessed One Who wearied not—has care for mankind,

and has care for the beasts.—When Freedom fell under the yoke,—He came to the Birth and became bond to make it free:—He was smitten on the face by servants in the judgment hall ;—He broke the yoke that *was* on the free, as Lord.

11. Let the eighth day, which circumcised the Hebrews,—praise Him Who commanded his namesake Joshua—to circumcise with a flint—the people circumcised in body, while the heart was profane within.—Lo ! as the eighth day, as a Babe,—to circumcision He came Who circumcises all.—Though the sign of Abraham *is* on His Flesh, —the blind daughter of Sion had defiled it.

12. Let the tenth day sing, praises in its turn.—For *God* the *first* letter of Jesus (goodly name ! ), is ten in numbering.—He Who *is* as a lamb, turns back the numbers.— For when the number goes up to ten, it is turned back to begin again from one.  O great mystery of that which is in Jesus, Whose might turns all creation back again !

13. The All-Purifier Firstborn in the day of His purifying,—purified the purification of the firstborn and was offered [1] *in the Temple :*—the Lord of offering needed offerings, —to make offering of birds.—In His Birth were fulfilled the types,—in His purification and circumcision the allegories.—He came and paid over debts in His coming down ;— in His Resurrection He went up and sent down treasures.

---

[1] Sc., in the Presentation, St. Luke ii. 22.

# FIFTEEN HYMNS

## FOR THE FEAST OF THE EPIPHANY.

———

(Translated by Rev. A. Edward Johnston, B.A.)

# HYMNS
# FOR THE FEAST OF THE EPIPHANY.

### I.

*RESP.*—*To Thee be praise from Thy flock in the day of Thy Epiphany!*

1. The heavens He has renewed, for that fools worshipped all the luminaries :—He has renewed the earth, for that in Adam it was wasted.[1]—That which He fashioned has become new by His spittle :—and the All-Sufficing has restored bodies with souls.

2. Gather yourselves again ye—sheep and without labour receive cleansing !—for one needs not as Elisha—to bathe seven times in the river, nor again to be wearied as the priests are wearied with sprinklings.

3. Seven times Elisha purified himself in a mystery of the seven spirits ;—and the hyssop and blood are a mighty symbol.—There is no room for division ;—*He is* not divided from the Lord of all Who is Son of the Lord of all.

4. Moses sweetened in Marah the waters that were bitter,—because the People complained and murmured :—*Thus* he gave a sign of baptism,—wherein the Lord of life makes sweet them that were bitter.

5. The cloud overshadowed and kept off the burning heat from the camp ;—it showed a symbol of the Holy Spirit, which overshadows you in baptism—tempering the flaming fire *that it harm not* your bodies.

6. Through the sea the People then passed, and showed a symbol—of the baptism wherein ye were washed. The People passed through that and believed not :—the Gentiles were baptized in this and believed and received the Holy Ghost.

7. The Word sent the Voice to proclaim before His Coming,—to prepare for Him the way by which He came,—and to betroth the Bride till He should come,—that she might be ready when He should come and take her from the water.

8. The voice of prophecy stirred the son of the barren woman,—and he went forth wandering in the desert and crying,—"Lo! the Son of the Kingdom comes !—prepare ye the way that He may enter and abide in your dwellings !"

9. John cried, "Who comes after me, He is before me :—I am the Voice but not the Word ;—I am the torch but not the Light ;—the Star that rises before the Sun of Righteousness."

10. In the wilderness this John had cried and had said,—"Repent ye sinners of your evils,—and offer the fruits of repentance ;—for lo! He comes that winnows the wheat from the tares."

11. The Lightgiver has prevailed and marked a mystery, by the degrees he ascended :—Lo! there are twelve days since he ascended,—and to-day this is the thirteenth :—a perfect mystery of Him, the Son, and His twelve!

---

[1] See p. 177.

12. Darkness was overcome to make it manifest that Satan was overcome ;—and the Light prevailed that he should proclaim—that the Firstborn triumphs : darkness was overcome—with the Dark Spirit, and our Light prevailed with the Lightgiver.

13. In the Height and the Depth the Son had two heralds.—The star of light proclaimed Him from above ;—John likewise preached Him from beneath :—two heralds, the earthly and the heavenly.

14. The star of light, contrary to nature, shone forth of a sudden ;—less than the sun yet greater than the sun.—Less was it than he in manifest light ;—and greater than he in secret might because of its mystery.

15. The star of light shed its rays among them that were in darkness,—and guided them as though they were blind ;—so that they came and met the great Light :—they gave offerings and received life and adored and departed.

16. The *herald* from above showed His Nature to be from the Most High ;—likewise he *that was* from beneath showed His Body to be from humankind, mighty marvel !—that His Godhead and His Manhood by them were proclaimed !

17. Thus whoso reckons Him as of earth, the star of light—will convince him that He is of Heaven : and whoso reckons Him as of spirit,—this John will convince him that He is also bodily.

18. John drew near with his parents and worshipped the Sun,—and brightness rested on His Face.—He was not moved as when in the womb.—Mighty marvel ! that here he worships and there he leaped !

19. The whole creation became for Him as one mouth and cried out concerning Him.—The Magi cry out in their gifts ;—the barren cry out with their children ;—the star of light, lo ! it cries out in the air, " Behold the Son of the King ! "

20. The heavens are opened, the waters break forth, the dove is in glory !—The voice of the Father is stronger than thunder,—as it utters the word, " This *is* My Beloved " ;—the Watchers brought the tidings, the children acclaimed *Him* in their Hosannas.

## II.

(Nearly identical with Hymn XIII. *On the Nativity*.)

(RESP.—*To Thee be praise Who in this feast makest all to exult !*)

1. In the time of the King whom they called by the name Semha [1]—our Lord was manifested among the Hebrews.—Thus Semha and Denha [2] reigned together,—the King on earth and the Son on high—blessed *be* His power !

2. In the days of the King who wrote down men in the taxing,—our Saviour came down and wrote down men in the Book of Life ; He wrote and was written ;—on high He wrote us, on earth He was written ; glory to His Name !

3. His Birth was in the days of the King whose name was Semha.—Symbol and truth met one another ;—King and King, Semha and Denha.—That kingdom bore His Cross ; blessed *be* He Who took it up !

4. Thirty years abode He on earth in poverty.—Voices of praise in all measures,—let us weave my brethren for our Lord's years ;—thirty crowns for thirty years ; Blessed be His number !

5. In the first year, mistress of treasure and filled with blessings,—let the Cherubin give thanks with us, they who bear—the Son in glory Who gave up His glorious state,—and toiled and found the sheep that was lost ;—to Him *be* thanksgiving !

---

[1] Equivalent to *Augustus*.                                    [2] *i. e.*, *Dayspring*.

6. In the second year let the Seraphin multiply thanksgiving with us ;—they who cried " Holy " to the Son, and turned and saw Him—among unbelievers put to shame. —He endured scorn and taught *us* glory ; to Him be glory given !

7. In the third year let Michael and his hosts give thanks with us ;—they who were wont to serve the Son on high,—*and* saw Him on earth doing service.—He washed *men's* feet and cleansed *men's* souls ; blessed *be* His meekness !

8. In the fourth year let all the heavens give thanks with us ! *Too* narrow for the Son it shall burst to see—how He lay on the couch of despised Zaccheus.—He filled the couch and had filled the heavens ;—to Him *be* thanksgiving !

9. In the fifth year let the Sun that burns the earth with its heat—give thanks to our Sun that He straitened His largeness,—and tempered His force that *the eye* might endure to see Him ;—the inward eye of a pure soul ; blessed *be* His radiance !

10. In the sixth year again let all the air give thanks with us,—in the vastness whereof all things exult.—It saw its great Lord that He became—a little babe in a lowly bosom ; blessed *be* His honour !

11. In the seventh year let the clouds and winds sound *the trumpet* with us,—they whose dew sprinkles the faces of the flowers,—yet saw they the Son that He subdued His brightness,—and endured scorn and shameful spitting ;—blessed *be* His salvation !

12. Yet again in the eighth year let Creation give glory,—from whose fountain the fruits draw nurture.—She adored when she saw the Son at the breast,—pure *babe* nurtured by pure milk ; blessed *be* His good pleasure !

13. In the ninth year let the earth give glory, which when her lap is watered then brings forth the root.—She saw Mary an unwatered soil—whose fruit that she yielded is a mighty sea ; to Him *be* exultation ! *R., To Thee be glory, Son of the Lord of all, Who givest life to all !*

14. In the tenth year let Mount Sinai give glory, which melted—before its Lord ! It saw against its Lord—stones taken up : but He took stones—to build the Church upon the Rock ; blessed *be* His building !

15. In the eleventh year let the great sea give thanks—to the hand of the Son Who measured it ! And it wondered to see how He came down and was washed—in humble waters, He that cleanses Creation ; blessed *be* His triumph !

16. In the twelfth year let the holy Temple give thanks—which beheld the Child as He sat—among the elders : the doctors were silenced—as the Lamb of the feast bleated in the feast ; blessed *be* His atonement !

17. In the thirteenth year let diadems with us give thanks—to the King Who triumphed and was crowned—with a crown of thorns : He wove for man—a mighty diadem at His right hand ; blessed *be* He That sent Him !

18. In the fourteenth year let the Passover of Egypt give thanks—to the Passover that came and made passover for all,—and instead of Pharaoh overwhelmed Legion,—and instead of horsemen drowned demons ; blessed *be* His retribution !

19. In the fifteenth year let the lamb of the flock give thanks,—that our Lord slew it not as *did* Moses,—but redeemed by His Blood mankind.—He the Shepherd of all died for all ; blessed *be* He That begat Him !

20. In the sixteenth year let the seed-corn in mystery give thanks—to that Husbandman Who gave His Body for seed—in a barren soil that corrupts all things.—It proved fertile and yielded new bread ; blessed *be He that is* pure !

21. In the seventeenth year let the Vine give thanks to our Lord,—the Vineyard of truth, *wherein* souls were—as the scions. He gave peace to this vineyard, but laid waste that vineyard which bare wild grapes ; blessed *be* the Uprooter !

22. In the eighteenth year let our leaven give thanks—to the leaven of truth that penetrates and draws—all minds and makes them *to become*—one mind in one doctrine ; blessed *be* His doctrine !

23. In the nineteenth year let the Salt give thanks for Thy Body.—O blessed Babe it is the soul—that is the salt of the Body, and Faith—the salt of the soul whereby it is preserved ; blessed *be* Thy preservation !    *R., Glory to Thy Epiphany, O God and Man !*

24. In the twentieth year let temporal wealth with us give thanks,—which men *that are* perfect have cast off and abandoned—because of the " Woe " ; and have gone and loved—poverty because of its beatitude ; blessed *be* He Who desired it !

25. In the one-and-twentieth year let the waters give thanks that were sweetened— in a mystery of the Son.   In the honey of Samson—the nations tasted bitterness therein that destroyed them :—they had life in the Cross that redeemed them ; blessed be its pleasantness !

26. In the two-and-twentieth year let arms and the sword give thanks,—for they could not slay our Adversary.—Thou art He Who slew him as Thou art He Who restored—the ear that Simon's sword cut off ; blessed *be* Thy healing !

27. In the three-and-twentieth year let the ass likewise give thanks,—that gave the colt whereon He should ride ;—He opens likewise the mouth of wild asses,—the off-spring gave *Him* praise ; blessed *be* the praise of Thee !

28. In the four-and-twentieth year let wealth give thanks to the Son !—Treasures were amazed at the Lord of treasures,—how He grew up among the poor.—He made Himself poor that He might make all rich ; blessed *be* His participation !

29. In the five-and-twentieth year let Isaac give thanks to the Son—Who in the mount saved him from the knife,—and became in his stead the lamb to be slain.—The mortal escaped, and He died Who gives life to all ; blessed *be* His offering !

30. In the six-and-twentieth year let Moses with us give thanks,—who feared and fled from the slayers ;—let him give thanks to the Son, for He it was Who on His feet —entered Sheol and spoiled it and came forth ; blessed *be* His Resurrection !

[31. In the seven-and-twentieth year let the eloquent Orators—give thanks to the Son, for they could not find—means whereby we should prevail in our judgment :—He was silent in judgment and made our judgment prevail ; to Him *be* applause !]

32. In the seven and twentieth year let all Judges give thanks,—who as being just have put to death illdoers ;—let them give thanks to the Son Who instead of the evil —died as being good, though He was Son of the Just One ; blessed *be* His mercies !

33. In the eight-and-twentieth year let them give thanks to the Son,—all the mighty men who saved us not—from the captors.   One is to be worshipped,—Who was slain and laid hold and saved us ; blessed *be* His deliverance !

34. In the nine-and-twentieth year let Job with us give thanks,—who bare sufferings in his own behalf :—but our Lord bare on our behalf—the spitting and the stripes, the thorns and the nails ; blessed is His compassion !

35. In the year that is the thirtieth let them give thanks with us ;—the dead that have lived through His dying,—the living that were converted in His Crucifixion,— and the height and the depth that have been reconciled in Him !   Blessed *be* He and His Father !

### III.

(Resp.—*Christ with chrism, lo! He is sealing the newborn lambs in His flock!*)

1. Christ and chrism are conjoined; the secret with the visible is mingled: the chrism anoints visibly,—Christ seals secretly, the lambs newborn and spiritual, the prize of His twofold victory; for He engendered it of the chrism, and He gave it birth of the water.

2. How exalted are your Orders! For she that was a sinner anointed, as a handmaid, the feet of her Lord. *But* for you, as though *His* minister, Christ by the hand of His servants, seals and anoints your bodies. It befits Him the Lord of the flock, that in His own person He seal His sheep.

3. Since then she, that sinner, stood in need of forgiveness, the anointing was for her an offering, and by it her love reconciled her Lord. But you who are the flock, among the profane and unbelievers, the Truth by the chrism is your seal, to separate you from the strayed.

4. From the peoples he separated the People, by the former seal of circumcision; but by the seal of anointing, the peoples He separates from the People. When the peoples were in error, the People He separated from the peoples; now when the People has erred from Him, He separates the peoples from thence.

5. Of the dust of the pure soil, Naaman bore away and returned to his place; that he by this holy dust, might be separated and known from the unclean. The chrism of Christ separates, the sons of the mystery from strangers: and by it they that are within are separated, and known from them that are without.

6. The oil which Elijah multiplied, might be tasted with the mouth; for the cruse was that of the widow, it was not that of the chrism. The oil of our Lord that *is* in the cruse, it is not food for the mouth: the sinner *that was* a wolf without, it makes him a lamb in the flock.

7. The chrism of the meek and lowly One, changes the stubborn *to be* like its Lord. The Gentiles were wolves and feared, the severe rod of Moses. Lo! the chrism seals *them* and makes, a flock of sheep out of the wolves! And the wolves that had fled from the rod, lo! they have taken refuge in the Cross!

8. The leaf of olive arrived, brought as a figure of the anointing; the sons of the Ark rejoiced to greet it, for it bore good tidings of deliverance. Thus also ye rejoiced to greet it, even this holy anointing. The bodies of sinners were glad in it, for it brought good tidings of deliverance.

9. The oil again that Jacob poured, upon the stone when he sealed it, that it should be between him and God, and that he might offer there his tithes; lo! in it is a symbol of your bodies, *how* by chrism they are sealed *as* holy, and become temples for God, where He shall be served by your sacrifices.

10. When Moses had sealed and anointed, the sons of Aaron the Levite, the fire consumed their bodies; the fire spared their vestments. But ye my brethren blessed are ye, for the fire of grace has come down, has consumed utterly your offences, and cleansed and hallowed your bodies!

11. As for the anointing of Aaron my brethren, it was the vile blood of beasts, *that* it sprinkled in the horns of the altar. The anointing of truth is this; wherein the living and all-lifegiving Blood, is sprinkled inwardly in your bodies. is mingled in your understandings, is infused through your inmost chambers.

12. The anointed priests used to offer, the slain bodies of beasts; Ye, O anointed

and excelling, your offerings *are* your *own* bodies. The anointed Levites offered, the inward parts *taken*, from beasts : ye have excelled the Levites, for your hearts ye have Consecrated.

13. The anointing of the People was—a foreshadowing of Christ; their rod a mystery of the Cross; their lamb a type of the Only begotten; their tabernacle a mystery of your Churches; their circumcision a sign of your sealing. Under the shadow of your goodly thing, sat the People of old.

14. Thus the truth is likened, to a great shadowing tree: it cast its shade on the People; it struck its root among the peoples. The People abode under its shadows, whose shadows were its mysteries; but the Gentiles lodged on its bough, and plucked and ate of its fruits.

15. *As for* the anointing of Saul to be king; the sweeter was its savour, so much fouler was the savour of his heart. The Spirit struck him and fled. Your anointing which ye have is greater; for your minds are censers, in your temples the Spirit exults, a chamber forever shall ye be unto Him.

16. *As for* the anointing of David my brethren; the Spirit came down and made sweet savour, in the heart of the man wherein He delighted; the savour of his heart *was* as the savour of his action. The Spirit dwelt in him and made song in him. Your anointing which ye have is greater, for Father and Son and Holy Ghost, have moved and come down to dwell in you.

17. When the leper of old was cleansed, the priest used to seal him with oil, and to lead him to the waterspring. The type has passed and the truth is come; lo! with chrism have ye been sealed, in baptism ye are perfected, in the flock ye are intermixed, from the Body ye are nourished.

18. What leper when he has been cleansed, turns again and desires his leprosy? Ye have put off transgressions—forsake it! None puts on the leprosy he had put off. It has fallen and sunk—let it not be drawn out! It is wasted and worn—let it not be renewed! Let not corruption come out upon you, whom the chrism of Christ has anointed!

19. The vessel moulded of clay, gains beauty from the water, receives strength from the fire; *but* if it slips it is ruined, it cannot be afresh renewed. Ye are vessels of grace; be ye ware of it, even of justice, for it grants not two renewals.

20. How like are ye in comparison, with the Prophet whom the fish yielded up! The Devourer has given you back for he was constrained, by the Power Which constrained the fish. Jonah was for you *as* a mirror, since not again did the fish swallow him, let not again the Devourer swallow you: being yielded up be ye like Jonah!

21. Goodly ointment on the head of our Lord did Mary pour; its savour was fragrant through all the house. Likewise the savour of your anointing, has been fragrant and perfumed the heavens, to the Watchers on high; doing pleasure to Satan its savour *is* overpowering; to God its odour *is* sweet.

22. The crowds in the desert were like unto sheep that have no shepherd. The Merciful became their shepherd, and multiplied to them the pasture of bread. Yea, blessed *are* ye that are perfect, that are sealed *as* lambs of Christ, that of His Body and Blood are made worthy; the Pastor Himself is become pasture for you!

23. Out of water He made the wine, He gave *it* for drink to the youths in the feast. For you who are keeping the fast, better is the unction than drink. In His wine the betrothed are wedded, by His oil the wedded are sanctified. By His wine *is* union; by His oil sanctification.

24. The sheep of Christ leaped for joy, to receive the seal of life, that ensign of

kings which has ever put sin to flight. The Wicked by Thy ensign is routed, iniquities by Thy sign are scattered. Come, ye sheep, receive your seal, which puts to flight them that devour you !

25. Come, ye lambs, receive your seal, for it is truth that is your seal! This is the seal that separates, them of the household from strangers. The steel circumcised alike, the gainsayers and the sons of Hagar. If circumcision *be* the sign of the sheep, lo! by it the goats are signed.

26. But ye, *who are* the new flock, have put off the doings of wolves, and *as* lambs are made like to the Lamb. One by changing has changed all ; the Lamb to the wolves gave Himself to be slain ; *the wolves* rushed and devoured Him and became lambs ; for the Shepherd was changed into a Lamb ; likewise the wolf forgot his nature.

27. Look on me also in Thy mercy! be not branded on me the seal, of the goats the sons of the left hand! let not Thy sheep become a goat! For though to justify myself I sufficed not, yet to be a sinner I willed not. Turn *thine eyes*, O my Lord, from what I have done, and seek not only what I have willed.

28. From them that write and them that preach, from them that hear and them that are sealed, let glory go up to Christ, and through Him to His Father *be* exaltation! He Who gives words to them that speak, and gives voice to them that preach, has given understanding to them that hear, and consecrates chrism for him that is sealed.

## IV.

(RESP.—*Blessed be He that blots out in water misdeeds that are without measure !*)

1. Descend my sealed brethren, put ye on our Lord,—and be rejoined to His lineage, for He is son of a great lineage,—as He has said in His Word.

2. From on high is His Nature, and from beneath His Vesture.—Each that puts off his vesture, commingled is that vesture, with His Vesture forever.

3. Ye too in the water, receive from him the vesture,—that wastes not or is lost for it is the vesture that vests—them that are vested in it forever.

4. But the blessed Priest, is daysman between two :—the covenant shall be made before Him, He is daysman of his Lord,—and surety on our part.

5. The Godhead in the water, lo! has mingled His leaven ;—for the creatures of dust, that leaven raises up,—and the Godhead joins them.

6. For it is the leaven of the Lord, that can glide into the bondman,—and raise him to freedom ; it has joined the bondman to the lineage,—of Him the Lord of all.

7. For the bondman who has put on Him, Who makes all free in the waters,—though bondman he be on earth, is son of the free on high,—for freedom he has put on.

8. The freeman who has put on, that Angel in the waters,—is as the fellow of servants, that he may be made like to the Lord,—Who became bondman unto bondmen.

9. He Who enriches all came down, and put on poverty,—that He might divide to the poor, the stores that were hidden,—out of the treasure-house of the water.

10. The lowly one again that has put on, the Giver of all greatness, in the water,—even though he be base in the sight of fools, yet is great in the sight of the Watchers,—for that he is clad in greatness.

11. For like as He Who is great, Who became lowly in His love,—by the unbelievers was persecuted, and by the Watchers was worshipped,—was made lowly and makes the lowly great.

12. *Thus* let him be lowly who is great, that in him the lowly may be great :—Let

us be like to Him Who is greater than all, Who became less than all :—He was made lowly, and makes all *men* great.

13. The meek man who has put on Him Who is great, in the water,—though humble *be* his countenance, very great is his discernment,—for He Who is exalted above all dwells in him.

14. For who could be found to despise the bush of thorn,—the despised and humble, wherein the Majesty in fire,—made its dwelling within?

15. Who again could be found, to despise Moses,—the meek and slow of speech,—when that excelling glory—dwelt upon his meekness?

16. They that despised him despised his Lord; the wicked that despised him—the earth swallowed up in anger; the Levites who scorned Him,—the fire devoured in fury.

17. Of Him Christ commanded, "Thou shalt not call him Raca," who is baptized and has put Him on; for whoso despises the despised, despises with him the Mighty.

18. In Eden and in the world, are parables of our Lord ;—and what tongue can gather, the similitudes of His mysteries?—for He is figured all of Him in all things.

19. In the Scriptures He is written of; on Nature He is impressed ;—His crown is figured in kings, in prophets His truth, His atonement in priests.

20. In the rod was He of Moses, and in the hyssops of Aaron,—and in the crown of David : to the prophets *pertains* His similitude, to the Apostles His Gospel.

21. Revelations beheld Thee, proverbs looked for Thee,—mysteries expected Thee, similitudes saluted Thee, parables showed types of Thee.

22. The Covenant of Moses looked forward to the Gospel :—all things of old time, flew on and alighted thereon, in the new Covenant.

23. Lo! the prophets have poured out on Him, their glorious mysteries ;—the priests and kings have poured out upon Him, their wonderful types :—they all have poured *them* out on all of Him.

24. Christ overcame and surpassed, by His teachings the mysteries,—by His interpretations the parables ; as the sea into its midst—receives all streams.

25. For Christ is the sea, and He can receive—the fountains and brooks, the rivers and streams, that flow from the midst of the Scriptures.

## V.

(RESP.—*Blessed be He that ordained baptism, for the atonement of the sons of Adam !*)

1. Descend, my brethren, put on from the waters of baptism the Holy Spirit ;—be joined with the spirits that minister to the Godhead !

2. For lo! He is the fire that secretly, seals also His flock,—by the Three spiritual Names, wherein the Evil One is put to flight.

3. John when he cried and said "This is the Lamb of God,"—thereby showed concerning the Gentiles that they are Abraham's children.

4. This is he that testified of our Saviour, that with fire and the Spirit He should baptize.—Lo ! the fire and the Spirit, my brethren, in the baptism of truth.

5. For greater is Baptism than Jordan that little river ;—for that in streams of water and oil, the misdeeds of all men are washed out.

6. Elisha by seven times *washing*, cleansed Naaman's leprosy :—in Baptism are cleansed the secret misdeeds in the soul.

7. Moses baptized the People in the midst of the sea, yet availed not—to wash their heart within, that was full of the defilements of misdeeds.

8. Lo! the priest in the likeness of Moses purges the defilements of the soul ;—and with oil of anointing, lo! he seals new lambs for the Kingdom.

9. Samuel anointed David to be king among the People :—but lo! the priest anoints you to be heirs in the Kingdom.

10. For with the armour that David put on, after the anointing he fought—and laid low the giant who sought to subdue Israel.

11. Lo! again in the chrism of Christ, and in the armour that is from the water —the haughtiness of the Evil One is humbled, who sought to subdue the Gentiles.

12. By the water that flowed from the rock, the thirst of the People was quenched. Lo! in the fountain of Christ, the thirst of the peoples is quenched.

13. The rod of Moses opened the rock, and the streams flowed forth ; and they were refreshed by its draught, who had grown faint with thirst.

14. Lo! from the side of Christ flowed the stream that bestowed life.—The Gentiles drank that were weary, and in it forgot their pains.

15. With Thy dew besprinkle my vileness, and my crimes in Thy blood shall be atoned!—And I shall be, O my Lord, at Thy right hand, and with Thy Saints I shall be joined!

## VI.

(RESP.—*Blessed be He Who was baptized that He might baptize you, that ye should be absolved from your offences.*)

1. The Spirit came down from on high,—and hallowed the waters by His brooding.—In the baptism of John,—*He* passed by the rest and abode on One :—but now He has descended and abode,—on all that are born of the water.

2. Out of all that John baptized,—on One it was that the Spirit dwelt :—but now He has flown and come down,—that He may dwell on the many ;—and as each after each comes up,—He loves him and abides on him.

3. A marvel *it* is that surpasses all !—To the water He went down and was baptized.—The seas declared it blessed,—that river wherein Thou wast baptized :—even the waters that were in heaven envied,—because they were not worthy to be Thy bath.

4. A marvel *it* is, O my Lord, now also,—that while the fountains are full of water, —it is the water of baptism,—that alone is able to atone.—Mighty is the water in the seas,—yet is it too weak for atonement.

5. Thy might, O my Lord, if it abides,—within the humble it exalts him ;—like as royalty if it abide—within the desert gives it peace.—Water by Thy might has triumphed—over sin, for Life has encompassed it.

6. The sheep exulted when they saw—the hand draw nigh to baptize them.— Receive, O ye sheep, your sealing ; enter and be mingled in the flock !—for more than over all the flock,—over you rejoice the Watchers to-day.

7. The Angels and the Watchers rejoice—over that which is born of the Spirit and of water :—they rejoice that *by* fire and *by* the Spirit,—the corporeal have become spiritual.—The Seraphins who sing " Holy " rejoice,—that they who are made holy have been increased.

8. For lo! the Angels rejoice—over one sinner if he repent :—how much more do they now rejoice—that in all churches and congregations,—lo! Baptism is bringing forth—the heavenly from the earthly !

9. The baptized when they come up are sanctified ;—the sealed when they go down are pardoned.—They who come up have put on glory ;—they who go down

have cast off sin.—Adam put off his glory in a moment;—ye have been clothed with glory in a moment.

10. A house that is of dust when it has fallen,—by means of water can be renewed :—the body of Adam that was of dust,—which had fallen by water has been renewed.—Lo ! the priests as builders—afresh renew your bodies.

11. A great marvel is this of the wool,—that it can take every dye,—as the mind *takes* every discourse.—By the name of its dye it is called ;—as ye who were—baptized *when* " Hearers,"—have gained the name of " Recipients."

12. The common waters he sanctified—*even* Elisha through the Name that is secret.—In them washed the leper openly,—and was cleansed by the Power that is secret :—the leprosy was done away in the water, as transgressions in Baptism.

13. To-day, lo ! your offences are blotted out,—and your names are written down.—The priest blots out in the water ;—and Christ writes down in Heaven.—By the blotting out and the writing down—lo ! doubled is your rejoicing.

14. Lo ! mercy has dawned to-day ;—and from bound to bound it stretches :—the sun has sunk and mercy has dawned.—Justice has drawn in her wrath ; Grace has spread forth her love,—lo ! she pardons and quickens freely.

15. The sheep that beforetime were in *the fold*—lo ! they hasten forth to greet—the new lambs that have been added *to it.*—*They are* white *and* are clad in white ;—within and without white *are* your bodies as your vestments.

16. From every mouth " Blessed *are* ye,"—on every side " Blessed *are* ye."—Sin from you is driven out,—and the Holy Spirit on you is dwelling.—The Evil One is become sad of countenance ;—the Good *God* makes glad your countenance.

17. The gift that ye have received freely,—cease not from watching over it :—this pearl if it shall be lost—cannot again be sought out,—for it is like to virginity—which if it be lost is not to be found.

18. May ye from all defilement—be kept by the power of your white robes !—and he whose freedom has defiled itself—may it be able to wash itself clean by his weeping !—For me who am servant of the community—may the supplication of the community win pardon !

19. To the author who has toiled in words,—be reconciliation in rest !—to the teacher who has toiled with voice,—be forgiveness through grace !—to the priest who has toiled in baptizing,—let there come the crown of righteousness !

20. From every mouth with one consent,—of those beneath and those above,—Watchers, Cherubin, and Seraphin,—the baptized, the sealed, and the hearers,—let each of us cry aloud and say,—" Glory to the Lord of our feasts ! "

## VII.

(Resp.—*Blessed is He Who atoned your sins, that ye might receive His Body worthily !*)

1. The flock of Jacob came down—and stood round the well of water.—In the water they put on the similitude of the wood that was covered *by it.*—Mysteries *these* and types of the Cross,—wherein the parables are interpreted.

2. There are shown in *these* rods similitudes,—and in the sheep, parables.—The Cross in the rods is figured, and in the sheep the souls *of men.*—His wood was a mystery of our Wood ;—likewise his sheep a mystery of our flock.

3. The sheep of Christ rejoice,—and stand round the laver of baptism ;—in the water they put on the likeness—of the living and goodly Cross—whereon gaze all things created,—and all of it is stamped on them all.

4. At the well Rebecca received—in her ears and hands the jewels.—The Spouse of Christ has put on—precious things that are from the water :—on her hand the living Body,—and in her ears the promises.

5. Moses drew *water* and watered the sheep—of Jethro the priest [1] of sin.—But our Shepherd has baptized His sheep—Who is the high priest of truth.—At the well the flocks were dumb,—but here the sheep have speech.

6. The People passed through the water and were baptized :—the People came up on dry land and became *as* heathen.—The Commandment was savourless in their ears ;—the manna corrupted in their vessels.—Eat ye the living Body,—the medicine of life that gives life to all !

7. To the sons of Lot Moses said,—"Give us water for money,—let us only pass by through your border."—They refused the way, and the temporal water.—Lo ! the living water freely [2] *given*,—and the path that leads to Eden !

8. From the water Gideon chose for himself—the men who were victorious in the battle.—Ye have gone down to the victorious waters :—come ye up and triumph in the fight !—receive from the water atonement,—and from the fight the crowning !

9. Ye baptized, receive your lamps,—like the lamps of the house of Gideon ;—conquer the darkness by your lamps,—and the silence by your hosannas !—Gideon likewise in the battle—triumphed by the shout and the flame.

10. David the King longed after—the water of the well, and they brought it him ;—but he drank it not, for he saw that with blood of men it was bought.—In the midst of the water ye have revelled—that was bought with the blood of God.

11. Out of Edom the prophet saw—God *coming* as one that *presses the grapes*.—He made ready the winepress of wrath,—He trod down the peoples and delivered the People.—He has turned and ordained Baptism ;—the peoples live, the People is come to nought.

12. In the river Jeremiah buried—the linen girdle that was marred ;—and [the People] waxed old and decayed.— . . . —The peoples that were decayed and marred,—by the waters have been clad in newness.

13. In Siloam,[3] the blessed stream—the priests anointed Solomon.—His youth was had in honour ;—his old age was despised.—Through the pure waters ye have been clad—in the purity of Heaven.

14. The fleece that was dry from the dew,—Jerusalem was figured in it :—the bason that was filled with water,—Baptism was figured in it.—That was dry after the manner of its type ;—this was full after the manner of its symbol.

15. The wearied body in water—washes and is refreshed from its toil.—Lo ! the laver in which are hidden—refreshing and life and delights.—In it wearied Adam had rest—who brought labour into the creation.

16. The fountain of sweat in the body—is set *to protect* against fever :—the fountain of Baptism—is set *to protect* against the Flame.—This is the water that avails—for the quenching of Gehenna.

17. He who journeys through the desert,—as armour takes to himself water—against all-conquering thirst.—Go ye down to the fountain of Christ,—receive life in your members,—as armour against death.

18. Again, the diver brings up—out of the sea the pearl.—Be baptized and bring up from the water—purity that therein is hidden,—the pearl that is set as a jewel—in the crown of the Godhead.

---

[2] Rev. xxi. 6, xxii. 17.     [3] So in Peshitto, 1 Kin. i. 38 ; but *Gihon* in the Hebrew.

19. Sweet water in his vessel—the seaman lays up as a store ;—in the midst of the sea he lays up and keeps it, the sweet in the midst of the bitter.—So amidst the floods of sin,—keep ye the water of Baptism.

20. The woman of Samaria said to our Lord,—"Lo ! verily the well is deep." —Baptism *though it be* high,—in its mercy has stooped down with us :—for the atonement is from above—that has come down unto sinners.

21. " He that drinks the water that I shall give him,—verily never again shall he thirst."—For this holy Baptism,—for it be ye athirst, my beloved ;—never again shall ye be athirst,—so that ye should come to another baptism.

22. In the baptism of Siloam—the blind man washed, and his eyeballs—were opened and enlightened by the water ;—he cast off the darkness that *was* on them.—The hidden darkness ye have cast off ;—from the water ye have been clad in light.

23. His hands Pilate washed—that he might not be of them that slew.—Ye have bathed your bodies,—your hands together with your mouths.—Go in and be of them that eat,—for this medicine of life gives life to all.

24. " Come after Me and verily I will make you—fishers of men."—For instead of a draught of that which perishes,—they fished for the draught that *is* forever.—They who had taken fishes for death,—baptized and gave life to them that were to die.

25. An hundred and fifty fishes were taken—by Simon's net from the water ;—but there were taken by his preaching,—out of the bosom of Baptism,—ten thousands and thousands of men,—a draught of the sons of the Kingdom.

26. Lo ! our priest as a fisher—over the scanty water is standing ;—he has taken thence a great draught—of every shape and of every kind ;—he has drawn up the draught to bring *it* near—to the King of kings, most high.

27. Simon took the fishes and drew them up,—and they were brought near before our Lord :—Our priest has taken from out of the water,—by the Hand which he received from Simon,—virgins and chaste men who are brought near—in the festival of the Lord of feasts.

28. In Thy mercy I adjure Thee pardon me,—for in mercy Thou too hast sworn,— Rabboni, " In the death of him that dieth,—I have no pleasure, but in his life."—Thou hast sworn and I have adjured :—O Thou Who hast sworn, pardon him who has adjured !

## VIII.

(Resp.—*Happy are ye whose bodies have been made to shine !*)

1. God in His mercy stooped and came down,—to mingle His compassion with the water,—and to blend the nature of His majesty—with the wretched bodies of men.— He made occasion by the water—to come down and to dwell in us :—like to the occasion of mercy—when He came down and dwelt in the womb :—O the mercies of God—Who seeks for Himself all occasions to dwell in us !

2. To the cave in Horeb He stooped and came down,—and on Moses He caused His majesty to dwell ;—He imparted His glorious splendour to mortals.—There was therein a figure of Baptism :—He Who came down and dwelt in it,—tempers within the water—the might of His majesty,—that He may dwell in the feeble.—On Moses dwelt the Breath,—and on you the Perfecting of Christ.

3. That might then none could endure ;—not Moses chief of deliverers,—nor Elijah chief of zealots ;—and the Seraphin too vail their faces,—for it is the might that subdues all.—His mercy mingled gentleness—in the water and by the oil ;—that mankind in

its weakness—might be able to stand before Him—when covered by the water and the oil.

4. The captive priests again in the well—hid and concealed the fire of the sanctuary,[1]—a mystery of that glorified fire—which the Highpriest mingles in Baptism.—The priests took up of the mire,—and on the altar they sprinkled it;—for its fire, the *fire* of that well,—with the mire had been mingled;—a mystery of our bodies which in the water—with the fire of the Holy Spirit have been mingled.

5. The famous Three in Babylon—in the furnace of fire were baptized, and came forth;—they went in and bathed in the flood of flame, they were buffeted by the blazing billows.—There was sprinkled on them there—the dew that *fell* from heaven;—it loosed from off them there—the bonds of the earthly *king*.—Lo! the famous Three went in and found a fourth in the furnace.

6. That visible fire that triumphed outwardly,—pointed to the fire of the Holy Ghost,—which is mingled, lo! and hidden in the water.—In the flame Baptism is figured,—in that blaze *of the furnace.*—Come, enter, be baptized, my brethren,—for lo! it looses the bonds;—for in it there dwells and is hidden—the Daysman of God,—Who in the furnace was the fourth.

7. Two words again our Lord spake—which in one voice agree in unison:—He said, "I am come to send fire,"—and again, "I have a baptism to be baptized with."—By the fire *of Baptism* is quenched the fire,—that which the Evil One had kindled:—and the water *of Baptism* has overcome—those waters of contention—by which he had made trial—of Joseph who conquered and was crowned.

8. Lo! the pure fire of our Redeemer—which he kindled in mankind of His mercy!—Through His fire He quenched that fire—which had been kindled in the defiled and sinful.—This is the fire wherein the thorns—are burnt up and the tares.—But happy are your bodies—that have been baptized in the fire—which has consumed your thickets,—and by it your seeds have sprung up to heaven!

9. Jeremiah in the womb He sanctified and taught.—But if the lowly bosom of wedlock—was sanctified in conceiving and bringing him forth,—how much more shall Baptism sanctify—its conception and its bringing forth—of them that are pure and spiritual!—For there, within the womb—is the conception of all men;—but here, out of the water,—is the birth whereof the spiritual are worthy.

10. For Jeremiah though sanctified in the womb,—they took up nails and cast him into the pit.—Holy was the prophet in his befoulment,—for clean was his heart though he was in the mire.—Be ye afraid, my brethren—for lo! to-day is washed away—your secret befoulment,—and the abomination of your sins.—Turn not again to uncleanness,—for there is *but* one cleansing of your bodies!

11. The presumptuous who is baptized and again sins,—is as the serpent that casts *its slough* and again puts it on, that is renewed and made young, and turns again——putting on anew *its skin* of old;—for the serpent does not—cast off its nature.—Cast ye off the tempter—the corrupter of souls,—even the old man;—let it not make old—the newness ye have put on!

12. Elisha cast the wood into the water, and made the heavy float and the light sink:—their natures were exchanged in the water.—There a new thing came to pass not according to nature.—How much easier then, O Lord,—is this for Thy grace;—that in the water should sink—transgression which is heavy,—but that the soul which is light—should be drawn forth and raised up on high!

13. Joshua, son of Nun, on Jericho—laid a curse on its walls and a doom on its

---

[1] 1 Maccab. i. 19.

fountains.—They whom Joshua cursed to their destruction,—again in the mystery of Jesus have been blessed.—There was cast into them salt,—and they were healed and sweetened:—a mystery of this salt,—the sweet *salt* that came from Mary,—that was mingled in the water,—whereby was healed the noisomeness of our plagues.

14. Lo! quiet waters *are* before you,—holy and tranquil and pleasant ;—for they are not the waters of contention—that cast Joseph into the dungeon ;—nor yet are they the waters,—those *waters* of strife,—beside which the people strove,—and gainsaid in the wilderness.—*There* are waters whereby—there is reconciliation made with Heaven.

15. Hagar saw the spring of water,—and from it she gave drink to *her* forward *son*, him who became *as* a wild ass in the wilderness.—Instead of that fountain of water *is* Baptism.—In it are baptized the sons of Hagar,—and are become gentle and peaceful. Who has seen rams[1] *like these*,—that are yoked, lo! and labour—along with tame bullocks,—and the seed *of* their *tillage* is reaped an hundredfold!

16. In the beginning the Spirit that brooded—moved on the waters ; they conceived and gave birth—to serpents and fishes and birds.—The Holy Spirit has brooded in Baptism,—and in mystery has given birth to eagles,—Virgins and Prelates ;—and in mystery has given birth to fishes,—celibates and intercessors ; and in mystery of serpents,—lo! the subtle have become simple as doves!

17. Lo! the sword of our Lord in the waters !—that which divides sons and fathers : —for it is the living sword that makes—division, lo! of the living from the dying.— Lo! they are baptized and they become—Virgins and saints,—who have gone down, been baptized, and put on—the One Only begotten.—Lo! many have come boldly to Him!

18. For whoso have been baptized and put on Him—the Only begotten the Lord of the many,—has filled thereby the place of many,—for to him Christ has become a great treasure :—for He became in the wilderness—a table of good meats,—and He became at the marriage feast—a fountain of choice wines.—He has become *such* to all in all things,—by helps and healings and promises.

19. Elisha was the equal of the Watchers—in his doings, glorious and holy.—The camp of the Watchers was round about him ;—thus let Baptism be unto you,—a camp of guardians,—for by means of it there dwells in the heart—the hope of them that are below—and the Lord of them that are above.—Sanctify for Him your bodies,—for where He abides, corruption comes not near.

20. They are no more, the waters of that sea—which by its billows preserved the People,—and by its billows laid low the peoples.—Of contrary effect are the waters in Baptism.—In them, lo! the people have life ;—in them, lo! the People perishes :—for all that are not baptized,—in the waters that give life to all,—they are dead invisibly.

21. They are no more, the waters of that sea—which were tempestuous, and boiled against Jonah,—and plunged into the depths the Son of Amittai.—Though he fled he was bound in the prison-house ;—*God* cast him in and bound him—in dungeon within dungeon ;—for he bound him in the sea,—and He bound him in the fish.—For him Grace stood surety,—and she opened the prison and brought forth the preacher.

22. The Prophets have called the Most High a fire,—"a devouring fire," and " who can dwell with it?"[2]—The People were not able to dwell in it ;—its might crushed the peoples and they were confounded.—In it, with the unction ye have been anointed ;— ye have put Him on in the water ;—in the bread ye have eaten Him ;—in the wine ye have drunk Him ;—in the voice ye have heard Him ;—and in the eye of the mind ye have seen Him !

---

[1] 'Arbo = ram ; 'Arboyo = Arab.                                    [2] Isai. xxx. 27.

## IX.

(RESP., *Blessed is He Who came down, and sanctified water for the remission of the sins of the children of Adam !*)

1. O John, who sawest the Spirit,—that abode on the head of the Son,—to show how the Head of the Highest—went down and was baptized—and came up to be Head on earth !—Children of the Spirit ye have thus become,—and Christ has become for you the Head :—ye also have become His members.

2. Consider and see how exalted ye are ;—how instead of the river Jordan—ye have glorious Baptism, wherein is peace ;—spreading her wings to shade your bodies.—In the wilderness John baptized :—in Her pure flood of Baptism,—purely are ye baptized therein.

3. Infants think when they see its glory,—that by its pomp its might is enhanced. —But it is the same, and within itself—is not divided.—But the might which never waxes less or greater—in us is little or again great ;—and he in whom is great understanding,—great in him is Baptism.

4. A man's knowledge, if it be exalted,—exalted also is his degree above his brethren ; —and he whose faith is great,—*so* also is his promise ;—and as *is* his wisdom, so also his crowning.—As is the light, which though *it be* all goodly—and equal all of it with itself,—*yet* goodlier is one eye than another.

5. Jesus mingled His might in the water :—put ye Him on my brethren as discerning *men !*—For there are that in the water merely—perceive that they are washed.— With our body be our soul washed !—The manifest water let the body perceive,—and the soul the secret might ;—that both to the manifest and to the secret ye may be made like !

6. How beautiful is Baptism—in the eye of the heart ; come, let us gaze on it !— Like as by a seal ye have been moulded ;—receive ye its image,—that nought may be lacking to us of our image !—For the sheep that are white of heart—gaze on the glory that is in the water :—in your souls reflect ye it !

7. Water is by nature as a mirror,—for one who in it examines *himself.*—Stir up thy soul, thou that discernest,—and be like unto it !—For it in its midst reflects thy image ;—from it, on it, find an example ;—gaze in it on Baptism,—and put on the beauty that is hidden therein !

8. What profits it him that hears—a voice and knows not its significance ?—Whoso hears a voice and is devoid—of the understanding thereof,—his ear is filled but his soul is empty.—Lo ! since the gift is abundant,—with discernment receive ye it.

9. Baptism that *is* with understanding—is the conjunction of two lights,—and rich are the fountains of its rays.— . . . . . . —And the darkness that is on the mind departs,—and the soul beholds Him in beauty,—the hidden Christ of glory,—and grieves when *the glory* fails.

10. Baptism without understanding—is a treasure full yet empty ;—since he that receives it is poor in it,—for he understands not—how great are its riches into which he enters and dwells.—For great is the gift within it,—though the mean man perceives not—that he is exalted even as it.

11. Open wide your minds and see, my brethren,—the secret column in the air,— whose base is fixed from the midst of the water—unto the door of the Highest Place,— like the ladder that Jacob saw.—Lo ! by it came down the light unto Baptism,—and *by it* the soul goes up to Heaven,—that in one love we may be mingled.

12. Our Lord when he was baptized by John—sent forth twelve fountains ;—and they issued forth and cleansed by their streams—the defilement of the peoples.—His worshippers are made white like His garments,—the garments in Tabor and the body in the water.—Instead of the garments the peoples are made white,—and have become for Him a clothing of glory.

13. From your garments learn, my brethren,—how your members should be kept.—For if the garment, which ever so many times—may be made clean,—is duly kept for the sake of its comeliness,—the body which has *but* one baptism,—manifold more exceeding is *the care of* its keeping,—for manifold are its dangers.

14. Again the sun in a house that is strait,—is straitened therein though he be great :—but in a house that is goodly and large,—when he rises thereon—far and wide in it he spreads his rays ;—and though the sun is one and the same in his nature,—in *divers* houses he undergoes changes :—Even so our Lord in *divers* men.

## X.

(RESP.—*Glory to Him Who came and restored it!*)

1. Adam sinned and earned all sorrows ;—likewise the world after His example, all guilt.—And instead of considering how it should be restored,—*considered* how its fall should be pleasant for it.—Glory to Him Who came and restored it !

2. This cause summoned Him that is pure,—that He should come and be baptized, even He with the defiled,—Heaven for His glory was rent asunder.—That the purifier of all might be baptized with all,—He came down and sanctified the water for our baptism.

3. For that cause for which He entered into the womb,—for the same cause He went down into the river.—For that cause for which He entered into the grave,—for the same cause He makes *us* enter into His chamber.—He perfected mankind for every cause.

4. His Conception is the store of our blessings ;—His Birth is the treasury of our joys ;—His Baptism is the cause of our pardon ;—His Death is the cause of our life.—Death He alone has overcome in His Resurrection.

5. At His Birth a star of light shone in the air ;—when He was baptized light flashed from the water ;—at His Death the sun was darkened in the firmament ;—at His Passion the luminaries set along with Him ;—at His Epiphany the luminaries arose with Him.

6. Revealed was His Glory because of His Majesty ;—revealed was His Passion because of His Manhood ;—revealed was His Love because of His Graciousness ;—revealed was His Judgment because of His Justice.—He has poured forth His attributes, on them that were His.

7. That whoso has looked on His Glory and despised Him,—may look again on His Glory and worship Him ;—and whoso has scorned to taste of His Graciousness,—may fear lest he be made to feel His justice ;—He has poured forth His helps on His worshippers.

8. Lo ! the East in the morning was made light !—lo ! the South at noonday was made dark !—The West again in turn at eventide was made light.—The three quarters represent the one Birth ;—His Death and His Life they declare.

9. His Birth flowed on and was joined to His Baptism ;—and His Baptism again flowed on even to His Death ;—His Death led and reached to His Resurrection,—a fourfold bridge unto His Kingdom ; and lo ! His sheep pass over in His footsteps.

10. And like as, save by the door of birth,—none can enter into creation ;—so, save

by the door of resurrection,—none can enter into the Kingdom,—and whoso has cut off his bridge, has brought to nought his hope.

11. He put on His armour and conquered and was crowned;—He left His armour on earth and ascended,—that if any man desires the crown,—he may resort to the armour and win by it—the crown of victory which he yearns after.

12. He fulfilled righteousness on earth, and ascended.—But if He, the All-cleanser, was baptized,—What man is there that shall not be baptized?—for grace has come to baptism—to wash away the foulness of our wound.

13. The compulsion of God is an all-prevailing force;—[but that is not pleasing to Him which is of compulsion,]¹—as that which *is* of discerning will.—Therefore in our fruits He calls us—who live not *as* under compulsion, by persuasion.

14. Good is He, for lo! He labours in these two things;—He wills not to constrain our freedom—nor again does He suffer us to abuse it.—For had he constrained it, He had taken away its power;—and had He let it go, He had deprived it of help.

15. He knows that if He constrains He deprives us;—He knows that if He casts off He destroys us;—He knows that if He teaches He wins us.—He has not constrained and He has not cast off, as the Evil One *does*:—He has taught, chastened, and won us, as being the good *God*.

16. He knows that His treasuries abound:—the keys of His treasuries He has put into our hands.—He has made the Cross our treasurer—to open for us the gates of Paradise,—as Adam opened the gate of Gehenna.


## XI.

(RESP.—*Let the bodies rejoice which the Evil One had made naked, that in the water they have put on their glory!*)

1. Give thanks, O daughter, that thy crownings have been doubled;—for lo! thy temples and thy sons rejoice.—The dedication of thy temples is in the ministration;—The dedication of thy sons *is* in the anointing.—Blessed art thou that at once . . . . . . — . . . . . . the tabernacle for them that dwell in thee,—and the Spirit has abode upon thy sons!

2. Our Lord opened up Baptism—in the midst of Jordan the blessed river.—The height and the depth rejoiced in Him;—He brings forth the first fruits of His peace from the water,—for they are first fruits, the fruits of Baptism.—The good *God* in His compassion will bring to pass—that His peace shall be first fruits on earth.

3. Moses stretched out the temporal Tabernacle;—the priests bathed themselves in water,—and went in and ministered; and were stricken and punished,—because their heart within was not cleansed.—Blessed art thou that in the Passover of the great Passion,—the priests by the savour of their oblations,—lo! are cleansing souls in thee!

4. Great was the mystery that the Prophet saw,—the torrent that was mighty.—Into its depths he gazed and beheld—thy beauty instead of himself; thee it was he saw,—for thy faith passes not away,—thou whose flood unseen shall overwhelm—the subtleties of idolatry.

5. Though John was great among them that are born of women,—yet he that is little is greater than he,—in this that his baptized were again baptized,—in the baptism

---

¹ The rendering of this line is very conjectural.

that was of the Apostles.—Blessed *art* thou that thy priest is greater than he—in this alone that forever—abides his baptism.

6. The baptism that was of Siloam—did not bring mercy to the man that was laid *there*—who for thirty and eight years awaited it,—for he was a respecter of the persons of the Levites.—Blessed *art* thou that thy healing *is* in thee for all men,—and thy priests are devoted and ready—for all that *are* in need of thy help.

7. The Prophet healed the waters that were unwholesome,—and cured the disease of the land that was barren,—so that its death was done away and its region resounded, for its offspring increased and its bosom was filled.—Greater is Thy grace, *Lord*, than Elisha's !—Multiply my lambs and my flocks—at the great stream of my fountain ! [1]

8. Great is the marvel that is within thy abode ;—the flocks together with the Shepherds,—those at the stream of the waters,—two unseen with one manifest who baptizes.—Blessed *is* he who is baptized in their fountains !—for three arms have upheld him,—and three Names have preserved him !

## XII.

(RESP.—*Blessed is He Who went down and was baptized in Jordan, and turned back the People from error !*)

1. In Baptism Adam found *again*—that glory that *was* among the trees *of Eden.*— He went down, and received it out of the water ;—he put it on, and went up and was adorned therein.—Blessed be He that has mercy on all !

2. Man fell in the midst of Paradise,—and in baptism compassion restored him :— he lost his comeliness through *Satan's* envy,—and found it *again* by *God's* grace.— Blessed be He that has mercy on all !

3. The wedded pair were adorned in Eden ;—but the serpent stole their crowns :— yet mercy crushed down the accursed one,—and made the wedded pair goodly in their raiment.—Blessed be He that has mercy on all !

4. They clothed themselves with leaves of necessity ;—but the Merciful had pity on their beauty,—and instead of leaves of trees,—He clothed them with glory in the water.—Blessed be He that has mercy on all !

5. Baptism is the well-spring of life,—which the Son of God opened by His Life ;— and from His Side it has brought forth streams.—Come, all that thirst, come, rejoice !— Blessed be He that has mercy on all !

6. The Father has sealed *Baptism*, to exalt it ;—and the Son has espoused it to glorify it ;—and the Spirit with threefold seal—has stamped it, and it has shone in holiness.—Blessed be He that has mercy on all !

7. The Trinity that is unsearchable—has laid up treasures in baptism.—Descend, ye poor, to its fountain !—and be enriched from it, ye needy !—Blessed be He that has mercy on all !

---

[1] Ezek. xlvii. 1, sq.

## XIII.

### HYMN OF THE BAPTIZED.

(RESP.—*Brethren, sing praises, to the Son of the Lord of all ; Who has bound for you crowns, such as kings long for !*)

1. Your garments glisten, my brethren, as snow ;—and fair is your shining in the likeness of Angels !

2. In the likeness of Angels, ye have come up, beloved,—from Jordan's river, in the armour of the Holy Ghost.

3. The bridal chamber that fails not, my brethren, ye have received :—and the glory of Adam's house to-day ye have put on.

4. The judgment that *came* of the fruit, was Adam's condemnation :—but for you victory, has arisen this day.

5. Your vesture is shining, and goodly your crowns :—which the Firstborn has bound for you, by the priest's hand this day.

6. Woe in Paradise, did Adam receive :—but you have received, glory this day.

7. The armour of victory, ye put on, my beloved :—in the hour when the priest, invoked the Holy Ghost.

8. The Angels rejoice, men here below exult :—in your feast, my brethren, wherein is no foulness.

9. The good things of Heaven, my brethren, ye have received :—beware of the Evil One, lest he despoil you.

10. The day when He dawned, the Heavenly King :—opens for you His door, and bids you enter Eden.

11. Crowns that fade not away, are set on your heads :—hymns of praise hourly, let your mouths sing.

12. Adam by means of the fruit, *God* cast forth in sorrow :—but you He makes glad, in the bride-chamber of joy.

13. Who would not rejoice, in your bridechamber, my brethren ?—for the Father with His Son, and the Spirit rejoice in you.

14. Unto you shall the Father, be a wall of strength :—and the Son a Redeemer, and the Spirit a guard.

15. Martyrs by their blood, glorify their crowns :—but you our Redeemer, by His Blood glorifies.

16. Watchers and Angels, joy over the repentant :—they shall joy over you my brethren, that unto them ye are made like.

17. The fruit which Adam, tasted not in Paradise :—this day in your.mouths, has been placed with joy.

18. Our Redeemer figured, His Body by the tree :—whereof Adam tasted not, because he had sinned.

19. The Evil One made war, and subdued Adam's house :—through your baptism, my brethren, lo ! he is subdued this day.

20. Great is the victory, but to-day you have won :—if so be ye neglect not, you shall not perish, my brethren.

21. Glory to them that are robed, glory to Adam's house !—in the birth that *is* from the water, let them rejoice and be blessed !

22. Praise to Him Who has robed, His Churches in glory !—glory to Him Who has magnified, the race of Adam's house.

## XIV.

### HYMN CONCERNING OUR LORD AND JOHN.

(RESP.—*Glory to Thee*, my Lord, for Thee—*with joy Heaven and earth worship!*)

1. My thought bore me to Jordan,—and I saw a marvel when there was revealed—the glorious Bridegroom who to the Bride—shall bring freedom and holiness.

2. I saw John filled with wonder,—and the multitudes standing about him,—and the glorious Bridegroom bowed down—to the Son of the barren that he might baptize Him.

3. At the Word and the Voice my thought marvelled :—for lo ! John was the Voice ;—our Lord was manifested as the Word, that what was hidden should become revealed.

4. The Bride was espoused but knew not—who was the Bridegroom on whom she gazed :—the guests were assembled, the desert was filled,—and our Lord was hidden among them.

5. Then the Bridegroom revealed Himself ;—and to John at the voice He drew near :—and the Forerunner was moved and said of Him—"This is the Bridegroom Whom I proclaimed."

6. He came to baptism Who baptizes all,—and He showed Himself at Jordan.—John saw Him and drew back,—deprecating, and thus he spake :—

7. "How, my Lord, willest Thou to be baptized,—Thou Who in Thy baptism atonest all?—Baptism looks unto Thee ;—shed Thou on it holiness and perfection?"

8. Our Lord said "I will *it so ;*—draw near, baptize Me that My Will may be done.—Resist My Will thou canst not :—I shall be baptized of thee, for thus I will *it.*"

9. "I entreat, my Lord, that I be not compelled,—for this is hard that Thou hast said to me,—'I have need that thou shouldst baptize Me ; '—for it is Thou that with Thy hyssop purifiest all."

10. "I have asked it, and it pleases Me that thus it should be ;—and thou, John, why gainsayest thou?—Suffer righteousness to be fulfilled,—and come, baptize Me ; why standest Thou?"

11. "How can one openly grasp—in his hands the fire that burns?—O *Thou that art* fire have mercy on me,—and bid me not come near Thee, for it is hard for me !"

12. "I have revealed to Thee My Will ; what questionest thou?—Draw near, baptize Me, and thou shalt not be burned.—The bridechamber is ready ; keep Me not back—from the wedding-feast that has been made ready."

13. "The Watchers fear and dare not—gaze on Thee lest they be blinded ;—and I, how, O my Lord, shall I baptize Thee?—I am too weak to draw near ; blame me not !"

14. "Thou fearest ; therefore gainsay not—against My Will in what I desire :—and Baptism has respect unto Me.—Accomplish the work to which thou hast been called !"

15. "Lo ! I proclaimed Thee at Jordan—in the ears of the people that believed not ; and if they shall see Thee baptized of me,—they will doubt that Thou art the Lord."

16. "Lo ! I am *to be* baptized in their sight,—and the Father Who sent Me bears witness of Me—that I am His Son and in Me He is well pleased,—to reconcile Adam who was under *His* wrath."

17. "It becomes, me. O my Lord, to know my nature—that I am moulded out of the ground,—and Thou the moulder Who formest all things :—I, then, why should I baptize Thee in water?"

18. "It becomes thee to know wherefore I am come,—and for what cause I have desired that thou shouldst baptize Me.—It is the middle of the way wherein I have walked ;—withhold thou not Baptism."

19. "Small is the river whereto Thou art come,—that Thou shouldst lodge therein and it should cleanse Thee.—The heavens suffice not for Thy mightiness ;—how much less shall Baptism contain Thee ! "

20. "The womb is smaller than Jordan ;—yet was I willing to lodge in the Virgin :—and as I was born from woman,—so too am I *to be* baptized in Jordan."

21. "Lo ! the hosts are standing !—the ranks of Watchers, lo ! they worship !—And if I draw near, my Lord, to baptize Thee,—I tremble for myself with quaking."

22. "The hosts and multitudes call thee happy,—all of them, for that thou baptizest Me.—For this I have chosen thee from the womb :—fear thou not, for I have willed *it*.

23. "I have prepared the way as I was sent :—I have betrothed the Bride as I was commanded.—May Thy Epiphany be spread over the world—now that Thou art come, and let me not baptize Thee ! "

24. "This is My preparation, for so have I willed;—I will go down and be baptized in Jordan,—and make bright the armour for them that are baptized,—that they may be white in Me and I not be conquered."

25. "Son of the Father, why should I baptize Thee ?—for lo ! Thou art in Thy Father and Thy Father in Thee.—Holiness unto the priests Thou givest;—water that is common wherefore askest Thou ? "

26. "The children of Adam look unto Me,—that I should work for them the new birth.—A way in the waters I will search out for them,—and if I be not baptized *this* cannot be."

27. "Pontiffs of Thee are consecrated,—priests by Thy hyssop are purified;—the anointed and the kings Thou makest.—Baptism, how shall it profit *Thee* ? "

28. "The Bride thou betrothedst to Me awaits Me,—that I should go down, be baptized, and sanctify her.—Friend of the Bridegroom withhold Me not—from the washing that awaits Me."

29. "I am not able, for I am weak,—Thy blaze in my hands to grasp.—Lo ! Thy legions are as flame ;—bid one of the Watchers baptize Thee ! "

30. "Not from the Watchers was My Body assumed,—that I should summon a Watcher to baptize Me.—The body of Adam, lo ! I have put on,—and thou, son of Adam, art to baptize Me."

31. "The waters saw Thee, and greatly feared ;—the waters saw Thee, and lo ! they tremble !—The river foams in its terror ;—and I *that am* weak, how shall I baptize Thee ? "

32. "The waters in My Baptism are sanctified,—and fire and the Spirit from Me shall they receive ;—and if I be not baptized they are not made perfect—to be fruitful of children that shall not die."

33. "Fire, if to Thy fire it draw near,—shall be burnt up of it as stubble.—The mountains of Sinai endured Thee not,—and I *that am* weak, wherein shall I baptize Thee ? "

34. "I am the flaming fire ;—yet for man's sake I became a babe—in the virgin womb of the maiden.—And now I am to be baptized in Jordan."

35. "It is very meet that Thou shouldst baptize me,—for Thou hast holiness to purify all.—In Thee it is that the defiled are made holy ; but Thou *that art* holy, why art Thou to be baptized ? "

36. "It is very right that thou shouldst baptize Me,—as I bid, and shouldst not gainsay.—Lo! I baptized thee within the womb ;—baptize thou me in Jordan !"

37. "I am a bondman and I am weak.—Thou that freest all have mercy on me!—Thy latchets to unloose I am not able ;—Thy exalted head who will make me worthy *to touch ?*"

38. "Bondmen in My Baptism are set free;—handwritings in My washing are blotted out ;—manumissions in the water are sealed ;—and if I be not baptized all these come to nought."

39. "A mantle of fire the air wears,—and waits for Thee, above Jordan ;—and if Thou consentest to it and willest to be baptized,—Thou shalt baptize Thyself and fulfil all."

40. "This is meet, that thou shouldst baptize Me,—that none may err and say concerning Me,—'Had He not been alien from the Father's house,—why feared the Levite to baptize Him ?'"

41. "The prayer, then, when Thou art baptized,—how shall I complete over Jordan?—When the Father and the Spirit are seen over Thee,—Whom shall I call on, as priest?"

42. "The prayer in silence is to be completed :—come, thy hand alone lay thou on Me.—and the Father shall utter in the priest's stead—that which is meet concerning His Son."

43. "They that are bidden, lo! all of them stand ;—the Bridegroom's guests, lo! they bear witness—that day by day I said among them,—'I am the Voice and not the Word.'"

44. "Voice of him that cries in the wilderness,—fulfil thou the work for which thou camest,—that the desert whereunto thou wentest out may resound—with the mighty peace thou preachedst therein."

45. "The shout of the Watchers has come to my ears ;—lo! I hear from the Father's house—the hosts that sound forth the cry,—'In Thy Epiphany, O Bridegroom, the worlds have life.'"

46. "The time hastes on, and the marriage guests—look to Me to see what is doing.—Come, baptize Me, that they may give praise—to the Voice of the Father when it is heard !"

47. "I hearken, my Lord, according to Thy Word :—come to Baptism as Thy love constrains Thee !—The dust worships that whereunto he has attained,—that on Him Who fashioned him he should lay his hand."

48. The *heavenly* ranks were silent as they stood,—and the Bridegroom went down into Jordan ;—the Holy One was baptized and straightway went up,—and His Light shone forth on the world.

49. The doors of the highest were opened above,—and the voice of the Father was heard,—"This is my Beloved in Whom I am well pleased."—All ye peoples, come and worship Him.

50. They that saw were amazed as they stood, at the Spirit Who came down and bare witness to Him.—Praise to Thy Epiphany that gladdens all,—Thou in Whose revelation the worlds are lightened !

## XV.

1. In the Birth of the Son light dawned,—and darkness fled from the world,—and the earth was enlightened ; then let it give glory—to the brightness of the Father Who has enlightened it !

2. He dawned from the womb of the Virgin,—and the shadows passed away when He was seen,—and the darkness of error was strangled by Him,—and the ends of the earth were enlightened that they should give glory.

3. Among the peoples there was great tumult,—and in the darkness the light dawned, —and the nations rejoiced to give glory—to Him in Whose Birth they all were enlightened.

4. His light shone out over the east ;—Persia was enlightened by the star :—*His* Epiphany gave good tidings to her and invited her,—" He is come for the sacrifice that brings joy to all."

5. The star of light hasted and came and dawned—through the darkness, and summoned them—that the peoples should come and exult—in the great Light that has come down to earth.

6. One envoy from among the stars—the firmament sent to proclaim to them,—to the sons of Persia, that they might make ready—to meet the King and to worship Him.

7. Great Assyria when she perceived *it*—called to the Magi and said to them,— " Take gifts and go, honour Him—the great King Who in Judea has dawned."

8. The princes of Persia, exulting,—carried gifts from their region ;—and they brought to the Son of the Virgin—gold and myrrh and frankincense.

9. They entered and found Him as a child—as He dwelt in the house of the lowly woman ;—and they drew near and worshipped with gladness,—and brought near before Him their treasures.

10. Mary said, " For whom are these ?—and for what purpose ? and what *is* the cause —that has called you to come from your country—to the Child with your treasures ? "

11. They said, " Thy Son is a King,—and He binds crowns and is King of all ;— and great *is* His power over the world,—and to His Kingdom shall all be obedient."

12. "At what time did this come to pass,—that a lowly woman should bring forth a King ?   I who am in need and in want,—how then could a king come forth from me ? "

13. "In thee alone has this come to pass—that a mighty King from thee should appear ;—thee in whom poverty shall be magnified,—and to thy Son shall crowns be made subject."

14. " Treasures of Kings I have not ;—riches have never fallen to my lot.—My house *is* lowly and my dwelling needy ;—why then proclaim ye that my Son is King ? "

15. " Great treasure is in thy Son,—and wealth that suffices to make all rich ;—for the treasures of kings are impoverished,—but He fails not nor can be measured."

16. " Whether haply some other be for you—the King that is born, enquire ye concerning Him.—This is the son of a lowly woman,—of *one* who is not meet to look on a King."

17. " Can it be that light should ever miss—the way whereon it has been sent ?— It was not darkness that summoned and led us ;—in light we walked, and thy Son is King."

18. " Lo ! ye see a babe without speech,—and the house of His mother empty and needy,—and of that which pertains to a king nought is in it :—how then in it is a king to be seen ? "

19. " Lo ! we see that without speech and at rest—*is* the King, and lowly as thou

hast said :—but again we see that the stars—in the highest He bids haste to proclaim Him."

20. "It were meet, O men, that ye should enquire—who is the King, and then adore .him ;—lest haply *your* way has been mistaken,—and another is the King that is born."

21. "It were meet, O maiden, that thou shouldst receive *it*,—that we have learned that thy Son is King,—from the *star of* light that errs not,—and plain is the way, and he has led us."

22. "The Child is a little one, and lo ! he has not—the diadem of a king and of a throne ;—and what have ye seen that ye should pay honour to Him,—as to a king, with your treasures ?"

23. "A little one, because He willed *it* for quietness' sake,—and meek now until He be revealed.—A time shall be for Him when all diadems—shall bow down and worship Him."

24. "Armies he has none ;—nor has my Son legions and troops :—in the poverty of His mother He dwells ;—why then King is He called by you ?"

25. "The armies of thy Son are above ;—they ride on high, and they flame,—and one of them it was that came and summoned us,—and all our country was dismayed."

26. "The Child is a babe, and how is it possible—He should be King, unknown to the world ?—And they that are mighty and of renown,—how can a babe be their ruler ?"

27. "Thy babe is aged, O Virgin,—and Ancient of Days and exalted above all ;—and Adam beside Him is very babe,—and in Him *all* created things are made new."

28. "It is very seemly that ye should expound—all the mystery and explain *it ;*—who *it* is that reveals to you the mystery of my Son,—that He is a King in your region."

29. "It is likewise seemly for thee to accept this,—that unless the truth had led us we had not wandered hither from the ends of the earth,—nor come for the sake of thy Son."

30. "All the mystery as it was wrought—among you there in your country,—reveal ye to me now as friends.—Who was He that called you to come to me ?"

31. "A mighty Star appeared to us—that was glorious exceedingly above the stars,—and our land by its fire was kindled ;—that this King had appeared it bore tidings to us."

32. "Do not, I beseech you, speak of—these things in our land lest they rage,—*and* the kings of the earth join together—against the Child in their envy."

33. "Be not thou dismayed, O Virgin !—Thy Son shall bring to nought all diadems, and set them underneath his heel ;—and they shall not subdue Him Whom they envy."

34. "Because of Herod I am afraid,—that unclean wolf, lest he assail me,—and draw his sword and with it cut off—the sweet cluster before it be ripe."

35. "Because of Herod fear thou not ;—for in the hands of thy Son is his throne placed :—and as soon as He shall reign it shall be laid low,—and his diadem shall fall on the earth beneath."

36. "A torrent of blood is Jerusalem,—wherein the excellent ones are slain ;—and if she perceives Him she will assail Him.—In mystery speak ye, and noise *it* not abroad."

37. "All torrents, and likewise swords,—by the hands of thy Son shall be appeased ;—and the sword of Jerusalem shall be blunted,—and shall not desire at all to kill."

38. "The scribes of the priests of Jerusalem—pour forth blood and heed not.—

They will arouse murderous strife—against me and against the Child; O Magi, be silent!"

39. "The scribes and the priests will be unable—to hurt thy son in their envy;—for by Him their priesthood shall be dissolved,—and their festivals brought to nought."

40. "A Watcher revealed to me, when I received—conception of the Babe, that my Son is a King;—that His diadem is from on high and is not dissolved,—he declared to me even as ye *do*."

41. "The Watcher, therefore, of whom thou hast spoken—is he who came as a star,—and was shown to us and brought us good tidings—that He is great and glorious above the stars."

42. "That Angel declared to me—in his good tidings, when he appeared to me,—that to His Kingdom no end shall be,—and the mystery is kept and shall not be revealed."

43. "The Star also declared again to us—that thy Son is He that shall keep the diadem.—His aspect was something changed,—and he was the Angel and made *it* not known to us."

44. "Before me when the Watcher showed himself,—he called Him his Lord before He was conceived;—and as the Son of the Highest announced Him to me:—but where His Father is he made not known to me."

45. "Before us he proclaimed in the form of a star—that the Lord of the Highest is He Who is born;—and over the stars of light thy Son *is* ruler,—and unless He commands they rise not."

46. "In your presence, lo! there are revealed—other mysteries, that ye may learn the truth;—how in virginity I bare my Son,—and He is Son of God; go ye, proclaim Him!"

47. "In our presence the Star taught *us*—that His Birth is exalted above the world; and above all beings is thy Son,—and is Son of God according to thy saying."

48. "The *world* on high and the *world* below bear witness to Him,—all the Watchers and the stars,—that He is Son of God and Lord.—Bear ye His fame to your lands!"

49. "All the world on high, in one star,—has stirred up Persia and she has learnt the truth,—that thy Son is Son of God,—and to Him shall all peoples be subject."

50. "Peace bear ye to your lands:—peace be multiplied in your borders!—As apostles of truth may ye be believed—in all the way that ye shall pass through."

51. "The peace of thy Son, it shall bear us—in tranquillity to our land, as it has led us *hither;*—and when His power shall have grasped the worlds,—may He visit our land and bless it!

52. "May Persia rejoice in your glad tidings!—may Assyria exult in your coming!—And when my Son's Kingdom shall arise,—may He plant His standard in your country!"

53. Let the Church sing with rejoicing,—"Glory in the Birth of the Highest,—by Whom the world above and the world below are illumined!"—Blessed *be* He in Whose Birth all are made glad!

# THE PEARL

## SEVEN HYMNS ON THE FAITH

(Translated by Rev. J. B. Morris, M.A. [Oxford *Library of the Fathers*].)

# THE PEARL,
# SEVEN HYMNS ON THE FAITH

## HYMN I.

1. On a certain day a pearl did I take up, my brethren; I saw in it mysteries pertaining to the Kingdom; semblances and types of the Majesty; it became a fountain, and I drank out of it mysteries of the Son.

I put it, my brethren, upon the palm of my hand, that I might examine it: I went to look at it on one side, and it proved faces on all sides. I found out that the Son was incomprehensible, since He is wholly Light.

In its brightness I beheld the Bright One Who cannot be clouded, and in its pureness a great mystery, even the Body of our Lord which is well-refined: in its undividedness I saw the Truth which is undivided.

It was so that I saw there its pure conception,—the Church, and the Son within her. The cloud was the likeness of her that bare Him, and her type the heaven, since there shone forth from her His gracious Shining.

I saw therein His trophies, and His victories, and His crowns. I saw His helpful and overflowing graces, and His hidden things with His revealed things.

2. It was greater to me than the ark, for I was astonied thereat: I saw therein folds without shadow to them because it was a daughter of light, types vocal without tongues, utterances of mysteries without lips, a silent harp that without voice gave out melodies.

The trumpet falters and the thunder mutters; be not thou daring then; leave things hidden, take things revealed. Thou hast seen in the clear sky a second shower; the clefts of thine ears, as from the clouds, they are filled with interpretations.

And as that manna which alone filled the people, in the place of pleasant meats, with its pleasantnesses, so does this pearl fill me in the place of books, and the reading thereof, and the explanations thereof.

And when I asked if there were yet other mysteries, it had no mouth for me that I might hear from, neither any ears wherewith it might hear me. O thou thing without senses, whence I have gained new senses!

3. It answered me and said, "The daughter of the sea am I, the illimitable sea! And from that sea whence I came up it is that there is a mighty treasury of mysteries in my bosom! Search thou out the sea, but search not out the Lord of the sea!

"I have seen the divers who came down after me, when astonied, so that from the midst of the sea they returned to the dry ground; for a few moments they sustained it not. Who would linger and be searching on into the depths of the Godhead?

"The waves of the Son are full of blessings, and with mischiefs too. Have ye not seen, then, the waves of the sea, which if a ship should struggle with them would break her to pieces, and if she yield herself to them, and rebel not against them, then she is preserved? In the sea all the Egyptians were choked, though they scrutinised it not, and, without prying, the Hebrews too were overcome upon the dry land, and how shall ye be kept alive? And the men of Sodom were licked up by the fire, and how shall ye prevail?

"At these uproars the fish in the sea were moved,[1] and Leviathan also. Have ye then a heart of stone that ye read these things and run into these errors? O great fear that justice also should be so long silent!"[2]

4. "Searching is mingled with thanksgiving, and whether of the two will prevail? The incense of praise riseth along with the fume of disputation from the tongue, and unto which shall we hearken? Prayer and prying [come] from one mouth,[3] and which shall we listen to?

"For three days was Jonah a neighbour [of mine] in the sea: the living things that were in the sea were affrighted, [saying,] 'Who shall flee from God? Jonah fled, and ye are obstinate at your scrutiny of Him!'"

## HYMN II.

1. Whereunto art thou like? Let thy stillness speak to one that hears; with silent mouth speak with us: for whoso hears the stammerings of thy silence, to him thy type utters its silent cry concerning our Redeemer.

Thy mother is a virgin of the sea; though he took her not [to wife]: she fell into his bosom, though he knew her not; she conceived thee near him, though he did not know her. Do thou, that art a type, reproach the Jewish women that have thee hung upon them. Thou art the only progeny of all forms which art like to the Word on High, Whom singly the Most High begot. The engraven forms seem to be the type of created things above. This visible offspring of the invisible womb is a type of great things.[4] Thy goodly conception was without seed, and without wedlock was thy pure generation, and without brethren was thy single birth.

Our Lord had brethren and yet not brethren, since He was an Only-Begotten. O solitary one, thou type exact of the Only-Begotten! There is a type of thine in the crown of kings, [wherein] thou hast brothers and sisters.

Goodly gems are thy brethren, with beryls and unions as thy companions: may gold be as it were thy kinsman, may there be unto the King of kings a crown from thy well-beloved ones! When thou camest up from the sea, that living tomb, thou didst cry out, Let me have a goodly assemblage of brethren, relatives, and kinsmen. As the wheat is in the stalk, so thou art in the crown with princes: and it is a just restoration to thee, as if of a pledge,[5] that from that depth thou shouldest be exalted to a goodly eminence. Wheat the stalk bears in the field; thee the head of the king upon his chariot carries about.

O daughter of the water, who hast left sea, wherein thou wert born, and art gone up to the dry land, wherein thou art beloved: for men have loved and seized and adorned themselves with thee, like as they did that Offspring Whom the Gentiles loved and crowned themselves withal.

It is by the mystery of truth that Leviathan is trodden down of mortals: the divers put him off, and put on Christ. In the sacrament of oil did the Apostles[6] steal Thee away, and came up. They snatched their souls from his mouth, bitter as it was.

---

[1] Hos. iv. 3; Zeph. i. 3.      [2] Eccles. viii. 11.      [3] James iii. 10.
[4] Pearls, he means, have their beauty by nature and so are like Christ; other stones must be graven and so are like created natures.
[5] Job. xli. 4; Ps. lxxi. 14.      [6] See Note on Hymn V. 4 (below)

Thy Nature is like a silent lamb in its sweetness, of which if a man is to lay hold, he lifts it in a crucial form by its ears, as it was on Golgotha. He cast out abundantly all His gleams upon them that looked upon Him.

2. Shadowed forth in thy beauty is the beauty of the Son, Who clothed Himself with suffering when the nails passed through Him. The awl passed in thee since they handled thee roughly, as they did His hands; and because He suffered He reigned, as by thy sufferings thy beauty increased.

And if they showed no pity upon thee, neither did they love thee: still suffer as thou mightest, thou hast come to reign! Simon Peter[1] showed pity on the Rock; whoso hath smitten it, is himself thereby overcome; it is by reason of Its suffering that Its beauty hath adorned the height and the depth.

## HYMN III.

1. Thou dost not hide thyself in thy bareness, O pearl! With the love of thee is the merchant ravished also, for he strips off his garments; not to cover thee, [seeing] thy clothing is thy light, thy garment is thy brightness, O thou that art bared!

Thou art like Eve who was clothed with nakedness. Cursed be he that deceived her and stripped her and left her. The serpent cannot strip off thy glory. In the mysteries whose type thou art, women are clothed with Light in Eden.[2]

2. Very glistening are the pearls of Ethiopia, as it is written, Who gave thee to Ethiopia [the land] of black men.[3] He that gave light to the Gentiles, both to the Ethiopians and unto the Indians did His bright beams reach.

The eunuch of Ethiopia upon his chariot[4] saw Philip: the Lamb of Light met the dark man from out of the water. While he was reading, the Ethiopian was baptised and shone with joy, and journeyed on!

He made disciples and taught, and out of black men he made men white.[5] And the dark Ethiopic women[6] became pearls for the Son; He offered them up to the Father, as a glistening crown from the Ethiopians.

3. The Queen of Sheba[7] was a sheep[8] that had come into the place of wolves; the lamp of truth did Solomon give her, who also married[9] her when he fell away. She was enlightened and went away, but they were dark as their manner was.

The bright spark which went down home with that blessed [Queen], held on its shining amid the darkness, till the new Day-spring came. The bright spark met with this shining, and illumined the place.

4. There are in the sea divers fishes of many cubits, and with all their greatness they are very small; but by thy littleness the crown is made great, like as the Son, by whose littleness Adam was made great.

For the head is thy crown intended: for the eye thy beauty, for the ear thy goodliness. Come up from the sea, thou neighbour to the dry land, and come and sojourn by the [seat of] hearing. Let the ear love the word of life as it loveth thee!

In the ear is the word, and without it is the pearl. Let it as being warned by thee,

---

1 Cephas; *i.e.*, Rock.
2 *I.e.* with the mysteries typified in the pearl, women are clothed with light at Baptism.
3 Job. xxviii. 19 (Pesh.).      4 Acts viii. 27.      5 Jer. xiii. 23; Is. i. 18.
6 Ps. lxviii. 31.      7 1 Kings x. 1.
8 Why St. E. contemplates the queen as a sheep appears from his remarks on the place. The following are a part of them: " It was not the fame of Solomon only, but also the Name of the Lord, which called to this queen, who sought to know the God of Solomon, who set out upon a dangerous long journey, and brought presents fit for a king. . . . Our Lord also extolled this queen in the Gospel, and praised her zealousness, when He rebuked the sluggishness of the Jews."
9 This was a tradition of the Jews, a tradition based in part on Canticles i. 5.

by thee get wisdom, and be warned by the word of truth. Be thou its mirror: the beauty of the Word in thine own beauty shall it see: in thee it shall learn how precious is the Word on High! The ear is the leaf: the flesh is the tree, and thou in the midst of it are a fruit of light, and to the womb that brings forth Light, thou art a type that points.

Thee He used as a parable of that kingdom, O pearl! as He did the virgins that entered into it, five in number, clothed with the light of their lamps! To thee are those bright ones like, thou that art clad in light!

5. Who would give a pearl to the daughter of the poor? For when it hangs on her, it becomes her not. Gain without price that faith, all of which becomes all the limbs of men. But for no gold would a lady exchange her pearl.

It were a great disgrace if thou shouldst throw thy pearl away into the mire for nought!

In the pearl of time let us behold that of eternity; for it is in the purse, or in the seal, or in the treasury. Within the gate there are other gates with their locks and keys. Thy pearl hath the High One sealed up as taking account of all.

## HYMN IV.

1. The thief gained the faith which gained him,[1] and brought him up and placed him in paradise. He saw in the Cross a tree of life; that was the fruit, he was the eater in Adam's stead.

The fool, who goes astray, grazes the faith, as it were an eye,[2] by all manner of questions. The probing of the finger blinds the eye, and much more doth that prying blind the faith.

For even the diver pries not into his pearl. In it do all merchants rejoice without prying into whence it came; even the king who is crowned therewith does not explore it.

2. Because Balaam was foolish, a foolish beast in the ass spoke with him, because he despised God Who spoke with him. Thee too let the pearl reprove in the ass's stead.

The people that had a heart of stone, by a Stone He set at nought,[3] for lo, a stone hears words. Witness its work that has reproved them; and you, ye deaf ones, let the pearl reprove to-day.

With the swallow[4] and the crow did He put men to shame; with the ox, yea with the ass,[5] did He put them to shame; let the pearl reprove now, O ye birds and things on earth and things below.

3. Not as the moon does thy light fill or wane; the Sun whose light is greater than all, lo! of Him it is that a type is shadowed out in thy little compass. O type of the Son, one spark of Whom is greater than the sun!—

The pearl itself is full, for its light is full; neither is there any cunning worker who can steal from it; for its wall is its own beauty, yea, its guard also! It lacks not, since it is entirely perfect.

And if a man would break thee to take a part from thee, thou art like the faith which with the heretics perishes, seeing they have broken it in pieces and spoiled it: for is it any better than this to have the faith scrutinised?

The faith is an entire nature that may not be corrupted. The spoiler gets himself

[1] Luke xxii. 42.   [2] Zech. ii. 8.   [3] Matt. xxi. 42.   [4] Jer. viii. 7.   [5] Is. i. 3.

mischief by it : the heretic brings ruin on himself thereby.   He that chases the light from his pupils blinds himself.

Fire and air are divided when sundered.   Light alone, of all creatures, as its Creator, is not divided ; it is not barren, for that it also begets without losing thereby.

4. And if a man thinks that thou art framed [by art] he errs greatly ; thy nature proclaims that thou, as all stones, art not the framing of art ; and so thou art a type of the Generation which no making framed.

Thy stone flees from a comparison with the Stone [which is] the Son.   For thy own generation is from the midst of the deep, that of the Son of thy Creator is from the highest height ; He is not like thee, in that He is like His Father.

And as they tell, two wombs bare thee also.   Thou camest down from on high a fluid nature ; thou camest up from the sea a solid body.   By means of thy second birth thou didst show thy loveliness to the children of men.

Hands fixed thee, when thou wast embodied, into thy receptacles ; for thou art in the crown as upon a cross, and in a coronet as in a victory ; thou art upon the ears, as if to fill up what was lacking ; thou extendest over all.


## HYMN V.

1. O gift that camest up without price [1] with the diver !   Thou laidest hold upon this visible light, that without price rises for the children of men : a parable of the hidden One that without price gives the hidden Dayspring !

And the painter too paints a likeness of thee with colours.   Yet by thee is faith painted in types and emblems for colours, and in the place of the image by thee and thy colours is thy Creator painted.

O thou frankincense without smell, who breathest types from out of thee ! thou art not to be eaten, yet thou givest a sweet smell unto them that hear thee ! thou art not to be drunk, yet by thy story, a fountain of types art thou made unto the ears !

2. It is thou which art great in thy littleness, O pearl !   Small is thy measure and little thy compass with thy weight ; but great is thy glory : to that crown alone in which thou art placed, there is none like.

And who hath not perceived of thy littleness, how great it is ; if one despises thee and throws thee away, he would blame himself for his clownishness, for when he saw thee in a king's crown he would be attracted to thee.

3. Men stripped their clothes off and dived and drew thee out, pearl !   It was not kings that put thee before men, but those naked ones who were a type of the poor and the fishers and the Galileans.

For clothed bodies were not able to come to thee ; they came that were stript as children ; they plunged their bodies and came down to thee ; and thou didst much desire them, and thou didst aid them who thus loved thee.

Glad tidings did they give for thee : their tongues before their bosoms did the poor [fishers] open, and produced and showed the new riches among the merchants : upon the wrists of men they put thee as a medicine of life.

4. The naked ones in a type saw thy rising again by the sea-shore ; and by the side of the lake they, the Apostles [2] of a truth, saw the rising again of the Son of thy Creator. By thee and by thy Lord the sea and the lake were beautified.

---

[1] Is lv. 1.                    [2] The same word in Syriac means *naked* and *Apostle*.

The diver came up from the sea and put on his clothing; and from the lake too Simon Peter came up swimming and put on his coat;[1] clad as with coats, with the love of both of you, were these two.

5. And since I have wandered in thee, pearl, I will gather up my mind, and by having contemplated thee, would become like thee, in that thou art all gathered up into thyself; and as thou in all times art one, one let me become by thee!

Pearls have I gathered together that I might make a crown for the Son in the place of stains which are in my members. Receive my offering, not that Thou art shortcoming; it is because of mine own shortcoming that I have offered it to Thee. Whiten my stains!

This crown is all spiritual pearls, which instead of gold are set in love, and instead of ouches in faith; and instead of hands, let praise offer it up to the Highest!

## HYMN VI.

1. Would that the memory of the fathers would exhale from the tombs; who were very simple as being wise, and reverend as believing. They without cavilling searched for, and came to the right path.

He gave the law; the mountains melted away; fools broke through it. By unclean ravens He fed Elijah at the desert stream; and moreover gave from the skeleton honey unto Samson. They judged not, nor inquired why it was unclean, why clean.

2. And when He made void the sabbaths, the feeble Gentiles were clothed with health. Samson took the daughter of the aliens, and there was no disputing among the righteous; the prophet also took a harlot, and the just held their peace.

He blamed the righteous,[2] and He held up and lifted up [to view] their delinquencies: He pitied sinners,[3] and restored them without cost: and made low the mountains of their sins:[4] He proved that God is not to be arraigned by men, and as Lord of Truth, that His servants were His shadow; and whatsoever way His will looked, they directed also their own wills; and because Light was in Him,[5] their shadows were enlightened.

3. How strangely perplexed are all the heretics by simple things! For when He plainly foreshadowed this New Testament by that of the Prophets, those pitiable men rose, as though from sleep, and shouted out and made a disturbance. And the Way, wherein the righteous held straight on, and by their truths had gone forth therein, that [Way] have these broken[6] up, because they were besotted: this they left and went out of; because they pried, an evil searching, [yea,] an evil babbling led them astray.

They saw the ray: they made it darkness, that they might grope therein: they saw the jewel, even the faith: while they pried into it, it fell and was lost. Of the pearl they made a stone, that they might stumble upon it.

4. O Gift, which fools have made a poison! The People were for separating Thy beauteous root from Thy fountain, though they separated it not: [false] teachings estranged Thy beauty also from the stock thereof.

By Thee did they get themselves estranged, who wished to estrange Thee. By Thee the tribes were cut off and scattered abroad from out of Sion, and also the [false] teachings of the seceders.

Bring Thyself within the compass of our littleness, O Thou Gift of ours. For if love cannot find Thee out on all sides, it cannot be still and at rest. Make Thyself small, Thou Who art too great for all, Who comest unto all!

---

[1] John xxi. 7.　　　[2] Hos. i 2.　　　[3] Matt. ix. 13.　　　[4] Luke xviii. 9.　　　[5] Cant. ii. 17.
[6] Or, pierced—perhaps a word of intentionally uncertain meaning, so as to suit with "the way" in either sense of it.

5. By this would those who wrangle against our Pearl be reproved ; because instead of love, strife has come in and dared to essay to unveil thy beauty.    It was not graven, since it is a progeny which cannot be interpreted.

Thou didst show thy beauty among the abjects to show whereto thou art like, thou Pearl that art all faces.    The beholders were astonied and perplexed at thee.    The separatists separated thee in two, and were separated in two by thee, thou that art of one substance throughout.

They saw not thy beauty, because there was not in them the eye of truth.    For the veil of prophecy, full as it was of the mysteries ; to them was a covering of thy glistering faces : they thought that thou wast other [than thou art], O thou mirror of ours ! and therefore these blind schismatics defiled thy fair beauty.

6. Since they have extolled thee too much, or have lowered thee too much, bring them to the even level.    Come down, descend a little from that height of infidelity and heathendom ; and come up from the depth of Judaism, though thou art in the Heaven.

Let our Lord be set between God and men ![1]    Let the Prophets be as it were His heralds !    Let the Just One, as being His Father, rejoice ! that Word it is which conquered both Jews and Heathens !

7. Come, Thou Gift of Holy Church, stay, rest in the midst of Her !    The circumcised have troubled Thee, in that they are vain babblers, and so have the [false] doctrines in that they are contentious.    Blessed be He that gave Thee a goodly company which bears Thee about !

In the covenant of Moses is Thy brightness shadowed forth : in the new covenant Thou dartest it forth : from those first Thy light shineth even unto those last.    Blessed be He that gave us Thy gleam as well as Thy bright rays.

## HYMN VII.

1. As in a race saw I the disputers, the children of strife, [trying] to taste fire, to see the air, to handle the light : they were troubled at the gleaming, and struggled to make divisions.

The Son, Who is too subtle for the mind, did they seek to feel : and the Holy Ghost Who cannot be explored, they thought to explore with their questionings.    The Father, Who never at any time was searched out, have they explained and disputed of.

The sound form of our faith is from Abraham, and our repentance is from Nineveh and the house of Rahab,[2] and ours are the expectations of the Prophets,[3] ours of the Apostles.

2. And envy is from Satan : the evil usage of the evil calf is from the Egyptians.[4] The hateful sight of the hateful image of four faces is from the Hittites.[5]    Accursed disputation, that hidden moth, is from the Greeks.

The bitter [enemy] read and saw orthodox teachings, and subverted them ; he saw hateful things, and sowed them ; and he saw hope, and he turned it upside down and cut it off.    The disputation that he planted, lo ! it has yielded a fruit bitter to the tooth.

3. Satan saw that the Truth strangled him, and united himself to the tares, and

---

[1] 1 Tim. ii. 5.
[2] On Josh. ii. 9, *For I know that God hath delivered unto you the land*, etc., St. E. makes Rahab say, " This forty years is this land yours ; and now it is that we might repent, that we have continued in it up to this day."
[3] Gen. xv. 6.
[4] The calf might be at once intended for a symbol of God, and also a copy from the worship of Apis.
[5] Elsewhere ( *Opp. Syr.* II. 384) St. E. calls the Teraphim of Micah (Judges xviii. 2, 14) " the idol *with four faces.*"

secreted his frauds, and spread his snares for the faith, and cast upon the priests the darts of the love of pre-eminence.

They made contests for the throne, to see which should first obtain it. There was that meditated in secret and kept it close : there was that openly combated for it : and there was that with a bribe crept up to it : and there was that with fraud dealt wisely to obtain it.

The paths differed, the scope was one, and they were alike. Him that was young, and could not even think of it, because it was not time for him ; and him that was hoary and shaped out dreams for time beyond ; all of them by his craftiness did the wicked one persuade and subdue. Old men, youths, and even striplings, aim at rank !

4. His former books did Satan put aside, and put on others : the People who was grown old had the moth and the worm devoured and eaten and left and deserted : the moth came into the new garment of the new peoples :

He saw the crucifiers who were rejected and cast forth as strangers : he made of those of the household, pryers ; and of worshippers, they became disputants. From that garment the moth gendered and wound it up and deposited it.

The worm gendered in the storehouse of wheat, and sat and looked on : and lo ! the pure wheat was mildewed, and devoured were the garments of glory ! He made a mockery of us, and we of ourselves, since we were besotted !

He showed tares, and the bramble shot up in the pure vineyard ! He infected the flock, and the leprosy broke out, and the sheep became hired servants of his ! He began in the People, and came unto the Gentiles, that he might finish.

5. Instead of the reed which the former people made the Son hold, others have dared with their reed[1] to write in their tracts that He is only a Son of man. Reed for reed does the wicked one exchange against our Redeemer, and instead of the coat of many colours,[2] wherewith they clothed Him, titles has he dyed craftily. With diversity of names he clothed Him ; either that of a creature or of a thing made, when He was the Maker.

And as he plaited for Him by silent men speechless thorns that cry out, thorns from the mind has he plaited [now] by the voice, as hymns ; and concealed the spikes amid melodies that they might not be perceived.[3]

6. When Satan saw that he was detected in his former [frauds]; that the spitting was discovered, and vinegar, and thorns, nails and wood, garments and reed and spear, which smote him, and were hated and openly known ; he changed his frauds.

Instead of the blow with the hand, by which our Lord was overcome, he brought in distractions ; and instead of the spitting, cavilling entered in ; and instead of garments, secret divisions ; and instead of the reed, came in strife to smite us on the face.

Haughtiness called for rage its sister, and there answered and came envy, and wrath, and pride, and fraud. They have taken counsel against our Redeemer as on that day when they took counsels at His Passion.

And instead of the cross, a hidden wood hath strife become ; and instead of the nails, questionings have come in ; and instead of hell, apostasy : the pattern of both Satan would renew again.

Instead of the sponge which was cankered with vinegar and wormwood, he gave

[1] Reeds are used all over the East to write with.
[2] St. E. assumes that the type of Joseph was fulfilled in Christ to the letter.
[3] This alludes probably to Bardesanes, the existence of whose rhythmical compositions induced St. E to try and counteract them by orthodox ones of the same kind.

prying, the whole of which is cankered with death.    The gall which they gave Him did our Lord put away from Him ; the subtle questioning, which the rebellious one hath given, to fools is sweet.

7. And at that time there were judges against them,[1] lo, the judges are, as it were, against us, and instead of a handwriting are their commands.    Priests that consecrate crowns, set snares for kings.

Instead of the priesthood praying for royalty that wars may cease from among men, they teach wars of overthrow, which set kings to combat with those round about.

O Lord, make the priests and kings peaceful ; that in one Church priests may pray for their kings, and kings spare those round about them ; and may the peace which is within Thee become ours, Lord, Thou that art within and without all things ![2]

---

[1] Luke xxiii. 14, 15.                    [2] *I.e.* Omnipresent in space, but not limited by space.

# THREE HOMILIES

(Translated by Rev. A. Edward Johnston, B.D.)

# THREE HOMILIES

## ON OUR LORD.

1. Grace has drawn nigh to mouths, once blasphemous, and has made them harps ; sounding praise.

Therefore let all mouths render praise to Him Who has removed from them blasphemous speech. Glory to Thee Who didst depart from one dwelling to take up thy abode in another ! that He might come and make us a dwelling-place for His Sender, the only-begotten departed from [being] with Deity and took up His abode in the Virgin ; that by a common manner of birth, though only-begotten, He might become the brother of many. And He departed from Sheol and took up His abode in the Kingdom ; that He might seek out a path from Sheol which oppresses all, to the Kingdom which requites all. For our Lord gave His resurrection as a pledge to mortals, that He would remove them from Sheol, which receives the departed without distinction, to the Kingdom which admits the invited with distinction ; so that, from [the plan] which makes equal the bodies of all men within it, we may come to [the plan] which distinguishes the works of all men within it. This is He Who descended to Sheol and ascended, that from [the place] which corrupts its sojourners, He might bring us to the place which nourishes with its blessings its dwellers ; even those dwellers who, with the possessions, the fruits, and the flowers, of this world, that pass away, have crowned and adorned for themselves there, tabernacles that pass not away. That Firstborn Who was begotten according to His nature, was born in another birth that was external to His nature ; that we might know that after our natural birth we must have another birth which is outside

our nature. For He, since He was spiritual, until He came to the corporeal birth, could not be corporeal ; in like manner also the corporeal, unless they are born in another birth, cannot be spiritual. But the Son Whose generation is unsearchable, was born in another generation that may be searched out ; that by the one we might learn that His Majesty is without limit, and by the other might be taught that His grace is without measure. For great is His Majesty without measure, Whose first generation cannot be imagined in any of our thoughts. And His grace is abundant without limit, Whose second birth is proclaimed by all mouths.

2. This is He Who was begotten from the Godhead according to His nature, and from manhood not after His nature, and from baptism not after His custom ; that we might be begotten from manhood according to our nature, and from Godhead not after our nature, and by the Spirit not after our custom. He then was begotten from the Godhead, He that came to a second birth ; in order to bring us to the birth that is discoursed of, even His generation from the Father :—not that it should be searched out, but that it should be believed ;—and His birth from the woman, not that it should be despised, but that it should be exalted. Now His death on the cross witnesses to His birth from the woman. For He that died was also born. And the Annunciation of Gabriel declares His generation by the Father, namely [the power of the Highest shall overshadow thee].[1] If then it was the power of the Highest, it is plain that it was not the seed of mortal man. So then His

---

[1] Luke i. 35.

conception in the womb is bound up with His death on the cross ; and His first generation is bound up with the declaration of the Angel ; in order that whoso denies His birth may be confuted by His crucifixion, and whoso supposes that His beginning was from Mary, may be admonished that His Godhead is before all ; so that whoever has concluded His beginning to be corporeal, [may be proved to err hereby that His issuing forth from the Father is narrated]. The Father begat Him, and through Him created the creatures. Flesh bare Him and through Him slew lusts. Baptism brought him forth, that through Him it might wash away stains. Sheol brought Him forth, that through Him its treasures might be emptied out. He came to us from beside His Father by the way of them that are born : and by the way of them that die, He went forth to go to His Father ; so that by His coming through birth, His advent might be seen ; and by His returning through resurrection, His departure might be confirmed.

3. But our Lord was trampled on by Death ; and in His turn trod out a way over Death. This is He Who made Himself subject to and endured death of His own will, that He might cast down death against his will. For our Lord bare His cross and went forth according to the will of Death : but He cried upon the cross[1] and brought forth the dead from within Sheol against the will of Death. For in that very thing by which Death had slain Him [*i.e.*, the body], in that as armour He bore off the victory over Death. But the Godhead concealed itself in the manhood and fought against Death. Death slew and was slain. Death slew the natural life ; and the supernatural life slew Him. And because Death was not able to devour Him without the body, nor Sheol to swallow Him up without the flesh, He came unto the Virgin, that from thence He might obtain that which should bear Him to Sheol ; as from beside the ass they

brought for Him the colt whereon He entered Jerusalem, and proclaimed concerning her overthrow and the destruction of her children. With the body then that [was] from the Virgin, He entered Sheol and plundered its storehouses and emptied its treasures. He came then to Eve the Mother of all living. This is the vine whose fence Death laid open by her own hands, and caused her to taste of his fruits. So Eve the Mother of all living became the wellspring of death to all living. But Mary budded forth, a new shoot from Eve the ancient vine ; and new life dwelt in her, that when Death should come confidently after his custom to feed upon mortal fruits, the life that is slayer of death might be stored up [therein] against him ; that when Death should have swallowed [the fruits] without fear, he might vomit them forth and with them many. For [He Who is] the Medicine of life flew down from heaven, and was mingled in the body, the mortal fruit. And when Death came to feed after his custom, the Life in His turn swallowed up Death. This is the food that hungered to eat its eater. So then, by one fruit which Death swallowed hungrily, he vomited up many lives which he had swallowed greedily. The hunger then which hurried him against one, emptied out his greed which had hurried him against many. Thus Death was diligent to swallow one, but was in haste to set many free. For while One was dying on the cross, many that were buried from within Sheol were coming forth at His cry.[2] This is the fruit that cleft asunder Death who had swallowed it, and brought out from within it the Life in quest of which it was sent. For Sheol hid away all that she had devoured. But through One that was not devoured, all that she had devoured were restored from within her. He, whose stomach is disordered, vomits forth both that which is sweet to him and that which is not sweet. So the stomach of Death was disordered, and as he was vomiting forth

---

[1] St. Matt. xxvii. 50–52.

[2] St. Matt. xxvii. 50–53.

the medicine of life which had sickened it, he vomited forth along with it also those lives that had been swallowed by him with pleasure.

4. This is the Son of the carpenter, Who skilfully made His cross a bridge over Sheol that swallows up all, and brought over mankind into the dwelling of life. And because it was through the tree that mankind had fallen into Sheol, so upon the tree they passed over into the dwelling of life. Through the tree then wherein bitterness was tasted, through it also sweetness was tasted; that we might learn of Him that amongst the creatures nothing resists Him. Glory be to Thee, Who didst lay Thy cross as a bridge over death, that souls might pass over upon it from the dwelling of the dead to the dwelling of life!

5. The Gentiles praise Thee that Thy Word has become a mirror before them, that in it they might see death, secretly swallowing up their lives. But graven images were being adorned by their artificers; and by their adornments were disfiguring their adorners. But Thou didst draw them to Thy cross; and while the beauties of the body were disfigured upon it, the beauties of the mind shone forth upon it. Then, as for the Gentiles who used to go after gods which were no gods, He Who was God went after them, and by His words, as by a bridle, turned them from many gods to the One. This is that Mighty One, Whose preaching became a bridle in the jaws of the Gentiles, and led them away from idols to Him that sent Him. But the dead idols, with their closed mouths, used to feed on the life of their worshippers. On this account Thou didst mingle in their flesh that blood of Thine, by which death was enfeebled and laid low; that the mouths of their devourers might be driven away from their lives. Also because Israel slew Thee and was defiled by Thy blood, that idolatry, that had been engrafted upon him was driven away from him on account of Thy blood. For he was weaned from that heathenism through Thy blood; because

that from it, he had never before been weaned.

6. But Israel crucified our Lord, on the plea that verily He was seducing us from the One God. But they themselves used constantly to wander away from the One God through their many idols. While then they imagine they crucify Him Who seduces them from the One God, they are found to be led away by Him from all idols to the One God; to the end that because they did not voluntarily learn of Him that He is God, they might by compulsion learn of Him that He is God; when the good which had accrued to them through Him should accuse them concerning the evil which their hands had done. Thus even though the tongue of the oppressors denied, yet the help with which they were helped convicted them. For grace loaded them beyond their power, so that they should be ashamed, while laden with Thy blessings, to deny Thy person. And also Thou didst have mercy on those, whose lives had been made food for dead idols. For the one calf which they made in the desert,[1] pastured on their lives as on grass in the desert. For that idolatry which they had stolen and brought out in their hearts from Egypt, when it was made manifest, slew openly those in whom it was dwelling secretly. For it was like fire concealed in wood, which when it is gendered from within it, burns it. For Moses ground to powder the calf and caused them to drink it in the water of ordeal;[2] that by drinking of the calf all those who were living for its worship might die. For the sons of Levi ran upon them, those who ran to [help] Moses and girded on their swords.[3] For the sons of Levi did not know whom they should slay, because those that worshipped were mingled with those that worshipped not. But He, for Whom it was easy to distinguish, distinguished those who were defiled from those who were not defiled; so that the innocent might give thanks that their innocence had not passed [unseen

---

[1] Exod. xxxii. 4.  [2] Exod. xxxii. 20
[3] Exod. xxxii. 26, 27, 28.

by] the Just One ; and the guilty might be convicted that their offence had not escaped [the eye of] the Judge. But the sons of Levi were the open avengers. Accordingly Moses set a mark upon the offenders, that it might be easy for the avengers to avenge. For the draught of the calf entered those in whom the love of the calf was dwelling, and displayed in them a manifest sign, that the drawn sword might rush upon them. The congregation therefore which had committed fornication in [the worship of] the calf, he caused to drink of the water of ordeal, that the mark of adulteresses might appear in it. From hence was derived that law about women,[1] that they should drink the water of ordeal, that by the mark that came on adulteresses, the congregation might be reminded of its fornication that was in the worship of the calf, and be on its guard with fear against another [fornication] ; and remember the former [fornication] with penitence of soul ; and that when they were judging their women, if they played the harlot against them, they might condemn themselves, who were playing the harlot against their God.

7. To Thee be glory who by Thy cross hast taken away the heathenism in which both circumcised and uncircumcised were caused to stumble ! To Thee be praise, the medicine of life, Who hast converted all that are baptised, to Him Who is life of all, and Lord of all ! The lost that are found bless Thee ; for by the finding of the lost, Thou hast given joy to the angels that are found and were not lost. The uncircumcised praise Thee, for in Thy peace the enmity that was between is swallowed up, for Thou didst receive in Thy flesh the outward sign of circumcision, through which the uncircumcised that were Thine, used to be accounted as not Thine. For Thou didst make as Thy sign the circumcision of the heart ; by which the circumcised were made known, that they were not Thine. For Thou didst come to Thine own[2] and Thine own received Thee not ; and by this they were made known that they were not Thine. But they to whom Thou didst not come, through Thy mercy cry out after Thee, that Thou wouldst satisfy them with the crumbs which fall from the children's table.

8. God was sent from the Godhead, to come and convict the graven images that they were no gods. And when He took away from them the name of God which decked them out, then appeared the blemishes of their persons. And their blemishes were these ;—They have eyes and see not, and ears and hear not.[3] Thy preaching persuaded their many worshippers to change their many gods for the One. For in that Thou didst take away the name of godhead from the idols, worship also along with the name was withdrawn ; that, namely, which is bound up with the name ; for worship also attends on the Name of God. Because, then, worship also was rendered to the Name, by all the Gentiles, at the last the worshipful Name shall be gathered in entirely to its Lord. Therefore at the last worship, also shall be gathered in completely to its Lord, that it may be fulfilled that *all things shall be subjected to Him.* Then, He in His turn *shall be subjected to Him Who subjected all things to Him.*[4] So that that Name, rising from degree to degree, shall be bound up with its root. For when all creatures shall be bound by their love to the Son through Whom they were created, and the Son shall be bound by the love of that Father by Whom He was begotten, all creatures shall give thanks at the last to the Son, through Whom they received all blessings ; and in Him and with Him they shall give thanks also to His Father, from Whose treasure He distributes all riches to us.

9. Glory be to Thee Who didst clothe Thyself in the body of mortal Adam, and didst make it a fountain of life for all mortals. Thou art He that livest, for Thy slayers were as husbandmen to Thy life, for that they sowed it as wheat in the depth [of the

---

[1] Num. v. 17-27.　　　[2] John i. ii.　　　[3] Ps. cxv. 5, 6.　　　[4] 1 Cor. xv. 27, 28.

earth], that it may rise and raise up many with it. Come, let us make our love the great censer of the community, and offer on it as incense our hymns and our prayers to Him Who made His cross a censer for the Godhead, and offered from it on behalf of us all. He that was above stooped down to those who were beneath, to distribute His treasures to them. Accordingly, though the needy drew near to His manhood, yet they used to receive the gift from His Godhead. Therefore He made the body which He put on, the treasurer of His riches, that He, O Lord, might bring them out of Thy storehouse, and distribute them to the needy, the sons of His kindred.

10. Glory be to Him Who received from us that He might give to us ; that through that which is ours we might more abundantly receive of that which is His ! Yea, through that Mediator, mankind was able to receive life from its helper, as through a Mediator it had received in the beginning death from its slayer. Thou art He Who didst make for Thyself the body as a servant, that through it Thou mightest give to them that desire Thee, all that they desire. Moreover in Thee were made visible the hidden wishes of them that slew [Thee] and buried [Thee] ; through this, that Thou clothedst Thyself in a body. For taking occasion by that body of Thine, Thy slayers slew Thee, and were slain by Thee ; and taking occasion by Thy body, Thy buriers buried Thee, and were raised up with Thee. That Power Which may not be handled came down and clothed itself in members that may be touched ; that the needy may draw near to Him, that in touching His manhood they may discern His Godhead. For that dumb man [whom the Lord healed] with the fingers of the body, discerned that He had approached his ears and touched his tongue ;[1] nay, with his fingers that may be touched, he touched Godhead, that may not be touched ; when it was loosing the string of his tongue, and opening the clogged doors of his ears. For the Architect of the body and Artificer of the flesh came to him, and with His gentle voice pierced without pain his thickened ears. And his mouth which was closed up, that it could not give birth to a word, gave birth to praise to Him Who made its barrenness fruitful in the birth of words. He, then, Who gave to Adam that he should speak at once without teaching, Himself gave to the dumb that they should speak easily, tongues that are learned with difficulty.

11. Lo, again, another question is made clear :—We enquire in what tongues our Lord gave the power of speaking to the dumb, who from all tongues came unto Him ? And although this be easy to know, yet our soul impels us to that knowledge which is greater than this. That [knowledge] then is, to know that through the Son the first man was made. For in this fact, that through Him speech was given to the dumb, the sons of Adam, we may learn that through Him speech was given to Adam their first father. And here also defective nature was supplied by our Lord. He, then, Who was able to supply the defect of nature,—it is manifest that through Him is established the supplying of nature. But there is no greater defect than this, when a man is born without speech. For since it is in this, in speech, that we excel all the creatures, the defect of it is greater than all [other] defects. He, then, through Whom all this defect was supplied,—it is manifest that through Him all fulness is established. But because through Him the members receive all fulness in the womb secretly, through Him their defect was supplied openly ; that we might learn that through Him in the beginning the whole frame was constituted. He spat then on His fingers and placed them in the ears of that deaf man ; and He mixed clay of His spittle, and spread it upon the eyes of the blind man ;[2] that we might learn that as there was defect in the eyeballs of that man who was blind from his mother's womb, so there was defect in

---

[1] Mark vii. 32–37.

[2] St. John ix. 6.

the ears of this [man]. So then, by leaven from the body of Him Who completes, the defect of our formation is supplied. For it was not meet that our Lord should have cut off anything from His body to supply the deficiency of other bodies; but with that which could be taken away from Him, He supplied the deficiency of them that lacked; just as in that which can be eaten, mortals eat Him. He supplied then the deficiency, and gave life to mortality, that we may know that from the body in which fulness dwelt, the deficiency of them that lacked was supplied; and from the body in which life dwelt,[1] life was given to mortals.

12. Now the Prophets performed all [other] signs; but on no occasion supplied the deficiency of members. But the deficiency of the body was reserved, that it should be supplied through our Lord; that souls might perceive that it is through Him that every deficiency must be supplied. It is meet, then, that the prudent should perceive that He Who supplies the deficiencies of the creatures, is Master of the formative power of the Creator. But when He was upon earth, our Lord gave to the deaf [and dumb], [the power] of hearing and of speaking tongues which they had not learned; that after He had ascended, [men] might understand that He gave to His disciples [the power] of speaking in every tongue.

13. Now the crucifiers supposed when our Lord was dead that His signs had died with Him. But His signs manifestly continued to live through His disciples; that the murderers might know that the Lord of the signs was living. Beforehand His murderers made trouble, crying out that His disciples had stolen His corpse. But, afterwards, His signs performed through His disciples, filled them with trouble. For His disciples, who were supposed to have stolen the dead corpse, were found to be raising to life the dead corpses of others. But the ungodly were terrified and said;—"His disciples have stolen His body;" that they

might be held in contempt when it should be discovered. But the disciples, who [they said] stole the dead body from the living guards, were found to be assailing Death in the name of Him Who was stolen; that [Death] might not steal the life of the living. So then, before He was crucified, He gave the deaf the power of hearing, that after He was crucified, all ears should hear and believe in His resurrection. For beforehand He confirmed our hearing by [the word] of the dumb whose mouth was opened, that it should not doubt concerning the preaching of the Word. Our Redeemer was in every way equipped, that in every way He might rescue us from our captor. For our Lord did not merely clothe Himself in a body, but also arrayed Himself in members and in garments; that through His members and His garments, they that were afflicted with plagues might be encouraged to approach the treasury of healing, that they who were encouraged by His mercy might approach His body and they who were dismayed by His terror might approach His vesture. For with one woman her fear suffered her merely to approach the hem of His raiment;[2] but with another, her love impelled her even to approach His flesh.[3] Now by her who received healing by His garments, those were put to shame who did not receive healing from His words; and by her who kissed His feet, he was rebuked who did not desire to kiss His lips.

14. Now our Lord bestowed great gifts through small means; that He might teach us of what they are deprived who have scorned great things. For if from the hem of His garment, healing like this was secretly stolen, could He not assuredly heal when His word distinctly granted healing? And if defiled lips were sanctified by kissing His feet, how much more should not pure lips be sanctified by kissing His mouth? For the sinful woman by her kisses received the grace of His sacred feet, which had come with toil to bring her remission of her sins.

---

Col. ii. 9.                    [2] St. Matt. ix. 20.          [3] St. Luke vii. 37, 38.

She was refreshing the feet of her Healer with oil freely, for freely had He brought her the treasure of healing for her sickness. For it was not for the sake of his stomach that He Who satisfies the hungry was a guest ; but for the sake of the sinful woman's repentance He Who justifies sinners made Himself a guest.

15. For it was not for the dainties of the Pharisees that our Lord hungered, but for the tears of the sinful woman He was an hungered. For when He was satisfied and refreshed by the tears for which He hungered, He turned and rebuked him who had bidden Him to the food that passes away, that He might show that it was not for the sake of food for the body that He had become a guest, but for the sake of help to the soul. For it was not for the sake of pleasure that our Lord mingled with gluttonous men and winebibbers, as the Pharisee supposed ; but that in their food as mortals He might mingle for them His teaching as the medicine of life. For even as it was in the matter of eating that the Evil One gave his deadly counsel to Adam and his helpmeet, so in the matter of eating the Good Lord gave His life-giving counsel to the sons of Adam. For He was the fisherman Who came down to fish for the lives of the lost. He saw the publicans and harlots rushing into prodigality and drunkenness ; and He hastened to spread His nets amongst their places of assembly, that He might capture them from food that fattens bodies, to fasting that fattens souls.

16. Now the Pharisee made great preparations for our Lord in His banquet ; and the sinful woman did but little things for Him there. Yet he by his great dainties displayed the smallness of his love to our Lord ; but she by her tears displayed the greatness of her love to our Lord. Thus he that had invited Him to the great banquet was rebuked because of the smallness of his love ; but she by her few tears atoned for the many follies of her offences. Simon the Pharisee received our Lord as a prophet ;

because of the signs, and not because of faith. For he was a son of Israel, who when signs drew near, himself also drew near to the Lord of the signs ; and when the signs ceased, he also stood naked without faith. This man also when he saw our Lord with signs, esteemed Him as a prophet ; but when our Lord ceased from signs, the doubting mind of the sons of his people entered him. *This man if He had been a prophet, He would have known that this woman is a sinner.* But our Lord for Whom in every place all things are easy, here also did not cease from His signs. For He saw that because He had ceased a little from signs, the blind mind of the Pharisee had turned away from Him. For he had said in error, *This man, had He been a prophet, He would have known.* In this reflection therefore the Pharisee doubted concerning our Lord, whether He were a prophet or no ; but by this very reflection he learned that He is Lord of the prophets ; so that from the source from which error entered him, from that source our Lord might bring help to Him.

17. Our Lord then told him the parable of the two debtors ; and made him judge ; that by his tongue He might catch him in whose heart the truth was not. *One owed five hundred dinars.* Here then our Lord showed to the Pharisee the multitude of the offences of the sinful woman. He then who imagined concerning our Lord that He did not know that she was a sinner, in the result heard from Him how great was the debt of her sins. The Pharisee, then, who imagined that our Lord did not know who she was, and what was the reputation of the sinful woman, was found himself not to know who our Lord was, and what was His reputation. Thus he was reproved in his error, who did not even perceive his error. For the knowledge that he was assuredly erring eluded him in his error. But he received a reminder from Him Who came to remind them that err. The Pharisee had seen great signs done by our Lord, as Israel by Moses ; but because there was not faith in him, that those

prodigies which he saw might be conjoined with that faith, a little cause hindered and annulled them. *Had this man been a prophet, he would have known that this woman is a sinner.* For he let slip the wonders that he had seen, and blindness readily entered into him. For he was of the sons of Israel, whom terrible signs accompanied up to the sea, that they might fear ; and blessed miracles surrounded in the waste desert, that they might be reconciled ; but through lack of faith, for a slight cause, they rejected them [saying] ; *As for this Moses who brought us up, we know not what has become of him.*[1] For they ceased to regard the mighty works that had been surrounding them. They perceived that Moses was not near them ; so that for this cause that had come near, they drew [near] to the heathenism of Egypt. For Moses was for a little removed from before them, that the calf that was before them might appear, that they might worship it openly also ; for they had been secretly worshipping it in their hearts.

18. But when their heathenism from being inward became open, then Moses also from being hidden openly appeared; that he might openly punish those whose heathenism had revelled beneath the holy cloud which had overshadowed them. But God removed the Shepherd of the flock from it for forty days, that the flock might show that its trust was fixed upon the calf. While God was feeding the flock with all delights, it chose for itself as its Shepherd the calf, which was not able even to eat. Moses who kept them in awe was removed from them, that the idolatry might cry aloud in their mouths, which the restraint of Moses had kept down in their hearts. For they cried : *Make us gods, to go before us.*[2]

19. But when Moses came down, he saw their heathenism revelling in the wide plain with drums and cymbals. Speedily, he put their madness to shame by means of the Levites and drawn swords. So likewise here, our Lord concealed His knowledge for

a little when the sinful woman approached Him, that the Pharisee might form into shape his thought, as his fathers had shaped the pernicious calf. But when the Pharisee's error came to a head within him, then the knowledge of our Lord was manifested against it and dispelled it ; *I entered into thy house ; thou gavest Me no water for My feet : But she has moistened them with her tears. Therefore her sins which are many are forgiven her.*[3] But the Pharisee when he heard our Lord naming the sins of the woman, *many sins*, was greatly put to shame because he had greatly erred. For he had supposed that our Lord did not even know that she was a sinner. Our Lord had before shown Himself as though not knowing her for a sinner. For He allowed him who had seen His signs, to show the doubt of his mind, that it might become manifest that his mind was bound in the ungodliness of his fathers. But the physician, who by his medicines brings out the hidden disease, is not the helper of the disease but its destroyer. For while the disease is hidden, it rules in the members, but when it is made manifest by medicines, it is rooted out. So then the Pharisee saw great things and doubted about small things. But when our Lord saw that his littleness made little of great things in his mind, He speedily showed him not only that she was a sinner, but even the multitude of her sins ; that he might be put to shame by little things,—he who had not believed in wonders.

20. God gave room to Israel to enlarge its heathenism in the wide desert ; whom God cut short with whetted sword, that their idolatry might not be spread abroad among the Gentiles. So our Lord allowed the Pharisee to imagine perverse things, that He might in turn duly reprove his pride. For concerning those things which the sinful woman was doing rightly, the Pharisee was thinking wrongly. But our Lord in His turn rebuked him, concerning the right things which he had wrongly withheld : *I*

---

[1] Ex. xxxii. 1.          [2] Ex. xxxii. 1.          [3] Luke vii. 44-47.

entered thy house ; thou gavest Me no water for My feet. Behold the withholding of that which was due ! But she has moistened them with her tears. Behold the payment of what was due ! Thou didst not anoint Me with oil. Behold the token of neglect ! But she has anointed My feet with sweet ointment. Behold the sign of zeal ! Thou didst not kiss Me. Behold the testimony of enmity ! But she has not ceased to kiss My feet. Behold the sign of love ! So then, by this enumeration our Lord showed that the Pharisee owed Him all those things and had withheld them ; but that the sinful woman had come in and rendered all those things which he had withheld. Because then she had paid the debts of him who wrongfully withheld them, the Just One forgave her, her own debt, even her sins.

21. Now the Pharisee, while he was doubting concerning our Lord, that He was not a prophet, pledged himself to the truth unawares, in saying—Had this man been a prophet, he would have known that this woman is a sinner. Therefore, if it should be found that our Lord knew that she was a sinner, He is, according to thy word, O Pharisee, a prophet. Our Lord, therefore, hastened to show both that she was a sinner, and that her sins were many ; that the testimony of his own mouth might confute him as a liar. For he was companion of those that said : Who is able to forgive sins, but God only ?[1] For from them our Lord received testimony, that, therefore, He Who is able to forgive sins, is God. Thenceforth, then, tne contention was this, that our Lord should show them whether He was able to forgive sins or no. So He speedily healed the members that were visible, that it might be made sure that He had forgiven the sins that were invisible. For our Lord cast before them the word which was expected to catch him that said it ; so that when they should rush forward to catch Him by it, according to their wish, they might be caught by Him according to His wish. Fear not, My son,

thy sins are forgiven thee.[2] While they were hastening to catch Him on the charge of blasphemy, they pledged themselves unawares to the truth. For Who is able to forgive sins but God only ? Accordingly, our Lord confuted them [as though saying] : "If I shall have shown that I am able to forgive sins, even though ye do not believe in Me that I am God ; yet abide ye by your word, which determined that whoso forgives sins is God." Therefore that our Lord might teach them that He forgives sins, He forgave that man his hidden sin, and caused him to carry his bed openly ; that by the carrying of the bed which carries [those that lie on it], they might believe in the slaying of the sin that slays.

This is a wonderful thing, that while our Lord there called Himself the Son of man, His adversaries, unawares, made Him to be God as forgiving sins. Accordingly, while they supposed that they had ensnared Him by their craftiness, He entangled them in their craftiness ; He made it a testimony to His truth. So their evil thoughts became unto them as bitter bonds ; and that they might not free themselves from their bonds, our Lord strengthened them by giving strength to him [to whom He said] ;—Arise, take up thy bed and go into thine house.[3] For the testimony could not again be undone, as though He were not God ; inasmuch as He forgave sins. Nor yet could it be falsely affirmed that He had not forgiven sins ; for lo ! He had healed [men's] limbs. For our Lord bound up His hidden testimonies in those which were manifest ; that their own testimony might choke the infidels. Accordingly our Lord made their thoughts to war against them, because they had warred with the Good One, who by His healing power warred against their diseases. For that which Simon the Pharisee imagined, and that which the scribes his companions imagined, they imagined in their hearts secretly ; but our Lord spread it forth openly.

Our Lord represented their hidden ima-

---

[1] Mark ii. 7.  [2] Matt. ix. 2.  [3] Matt. ix. 6.

ginations before them, that they might
learn that His knowledge reveals and shows
their secret things (;) so that though they
had not recognized Him by His open
signs, they might recognize Him when
He represented their secret imaginations ;
and that if only but by this,—that He
searched out their hearts,—their hearts
might perceive that He was God ;—that
at least when they saw that their imaginations could not be hidden from Him,
they might cease from imagining evil against
Him.   For they had imagined evil in their
heart ; but He exposed it openly, by this
[word] *Why are ye imagining evil in your
heart ?*  So that by this, that our Lord perceived their hidden imagination, they should
recognize His hidden Godhead.   For that
Godhead, by this very thing that they in
their error were reviling it, was by that reviling made known to them.   For they reviled our Lord in the body, and supposed
that He was not God, and cast Him down
below from on high ; but by the body He
was made known to them as being God, by
that body which was found passing to and
fro amongst them.   For they, by casting
Him down to the depth, attempted to show
this, that God Who is above, cannot in
bodily wise be born below.   But He by His
passage up to the height, taught them this ;
that for the body also that is sent down
below, it is not its nature to pass up to the
height rather than down to the depths ; so
that by the body which from below passed
on high upwards in the air, they might
learn of God that by His grace He descended down below from on high.

22. But why instead of a stern reproof
did our Lord speak a parable of persuasion
to that Pharisee ?  He spoke the parable to
him tenderly, that he, though froward,
might unawares be enticed to correct his
perversities.   For the waters that are con-
gealed by the force of a cold wind, the heat
of the sun gently dissolves.   So our Lord
did not at once oppose him harshly, that he
might not give occasion to the rebellious
to rebel again.   But by blandishment He

brought him under the yoke, that when he
had been yoked, He might work with him,
though rebellious, according to His will.
Now, because Simon was proudly minded,
our Lord began humbly with him, that He
might not be to him a teacher according to
his folly.   For if that Pharisee retained the
Pharisees' pride, how could our Lord cause
him to acquire humility, when the treasure
of humility was not under his hand ?  But
since our Lord was teaching humility to all
men, He showed that His treasury was free
from every form of pride.   But this was for
our sakes, that He might teach us, that whatever treasuries pride enters into, it is by
boastfulness that it gains access to them.
On this account *let not thy left hand know
what thy right hand doeth.*[1]   Our Lord then
did not employ harsh reproof, because His
coming was of grace :  He did not refrain
from reproof, because His later coming will
be of retribution.   For He put men to fear
in His coming of humility ; because *it is a
fearful thing to fall into His hands*[2] when He
shall come *in flaming fire.*[3]   But our Lord
bestowed the most part of His helps rather
by persuasion than by reproof.   For the
gentle shower softens the earth and penetrates all through it : but violent rain binds
and hardens the face of the earth, so that it
does not receive it.   For a harsh word ex-
cites wrath, and with it are bound up
wrongs.   And when a harsh word has
opened the door, wrath enters in, and at
the heels of wrath, along with it enter in
wrongs.

23. But because all helps attend on humble speech, He who came to render help
employed it.   Observe how mighty is the
power of a humble word ; for lo ! by it
vehement wrath is put down, and by it the
billows of a swelling mind are calmed.   But
hear whence this was.   That Pharisee
thought, *had this man been a prophet, he
would have known.*   Contempt as well as
blasphemy can be discerned here.   Hear
how our Lord in reply encountered this :

---

[1] Matt. ii. 3.        [2] Hebr. x. 31.        [3] 2 Thess. i. 7–8.

*Simon, I have somewhat to say unto thee.*
Love and reproof can be discerned here.
For this is a word of love such as friends use
with their friends. For when an adversary
reproaches his adversary, he speaks not to
him like this ; for the madness of anger does
not allow enemies to speak reasonably one
to another. But He Who prayed for them
that crucified Him, that He might show
that the fury of anger had no power over
Him, was about to put to the question those
that crucified Him, that He might show
that He was governed by reason and not
by anger.

24. Accordingly, our Lord placed a word
of conciliation at the beginning of His
speech, that by conciliation He might pacify
the Pharisee, into whose mind discord and
division had entered. He was the physician
who ranged His cures against the things
hurtful [to men]. Our Lord then shot forth
this word as an arrow, and set in the head
of it conciliation as the barb. And He anointed it with love, that soothes the members ; so that when it flew into him who
was full of discord, he was at once changed
from discord to harmony. For straightway
upon hearing that humble voice of our Lord,
saying,—*Simon, I have somewhat to say unto
thee*, that secret despiser returned his answer, *Say on, Lord.* For the sweet voice
entered his bitter mind, and begot of it
pleasant fruit. For he who before this voice
was one that secretly despised, after this
voice became one that openly honoured.
For humility, by its sweet utterance, subdues even its adversaries into rendering it
honour. For it is not over its friends that
humility tests its power, but over its enemies
it exhibits its victories.

25. Thus the heavenly King arrayed
Himself in armour of humility, and so conquered the bitter one, and drew from him
a good answer as a sure pledge [of victory].
This is the armour concerning which Paul
said, that by it *we humble the loftiness that
exalteth itself against the knowledge of God.*[1]

For Paul had received the proof of it in himself. For as he had been warring in pride,
but was conquered in humility, so is to be
conquered every *lofty thing which exalteth
itself* against this humility. For Saul was
journeying to subdue the disciples with hard
words, but the Master of the disciples subdued him with a humble word. For when
He to whom all things are possible manifested Himself to him, giving up all things
else, He spoke to him in humility alone,
that He might teach us that a soft tongue is
more effectual than all things else against
hard thoughts. For neither threats nor
words of terror were heard by Paul, but
weak words not able to avenge themselves :
*Saul, Saul, why persecutest thou Me ?*[2] But
the words which were thought not even
capable of avenging themselves, were found
to be taking vengeance by drawing him
away from the Jews and making him a
goodly vessel. He who was full of the bitter will of the Jews, was then filled with the
sweet preaching of the cross. When he was
filled with the bitterness of the crucifiers,
in his bitterness he made havoc of the
churches. But when he was filled with the
sweetness of the Crucified, he embittered
the synagogues of the crucifiers. Our Lord
then strove with humble voice with him,
who had been warring against His churches
with hard bonds. Thus Saul, who had been
binding the disciples with bitter chains, was
bound with pleasant persuasions ; that he
might not again cast the disciples into
bonds ; since he was bound by the Crucified, Who puts to silence evil voices, whom
all they that were set against Him could not
bind or injure. But when Paul ceased
from binding the disciples, he himself was
bound with chains by the persecutors. But
when he was bound with chains, he loosed
the bonds of idolatry by his bonds.

26. *Saul, Saul, why persecutest thou me ?*
He who had conquered His persecutors in
the world below, and ruled over the angels
in the world above, spoke from above with

---

[1] 2 Cor. x. 5.

[2] Acts ix. 4.

humble voice. And He Who while He was upon earth had denounced ten woes against His crucifiers, when He was in heaven, did not denounce even one woe against Saul, His persecutor. Now, our Lord denounced woe to His crucifiers, that He might teach His disciples not to be dismayed by His murderers. But our Lord spoke in humility from heaven, that in humility the heads of His church might speak, And if any one should say, "Wherein did our Lord speak humbly with Paul? for lo! the eyes of Paul were grievously smitten;" let him know that it was not from our merciful Lord that this chastisement proceeded, who spoke those words in humility; but from the vehement light that vehemently shone forth there. And this light did not strike Paul by way of retribution on account of his deeds, but on account of the vehemence of its rays it hurt him, as he also said: *When I arose, I could discern nothing for the glory of the light.*[1] But if that light was glorious, O Paul, how did the glorious light become a blinding light to thee thyself? The light was that which, according to its nature, illuminates above, but contrary to its nature, it shone forth below. When it illumined above, it was delightful; but when it shone forth below, it was blinding. For the light was both grievous and pleasant. It was grievous and violent towards the eyes of the flesh; and it was pleasant and delightful to those who are fire and spirit.[2]

27. *For I saw a light from heaven that excelled the sun, and its light shone upon me.*[3] So then mighty rays streamed forth without moderation, and were poured upon feeble eyes, which moderate rays refresh. For, lo! the sun also in measure assists the eyes, but beyond measure and out of measure it injures the eyes. And it is not by way of vengeance in wrath that it smites them. For lo! it is the friend of the eyes and beloved of the eyeballs. And this is a marvel; while with its gentle lustre it befriends and assists the eyes; yet by its vehement rays it

is hostile to and injures the eyeballs. But if the sun which is here below, and of kindred nature with the eyes that are here below, yet injures them, in vehemence and not in anger, in its proper force and not in wrath; how much more should the light that is from above, akin to the things that are above, by its vehemence injure a man here below who has suddenly gazed upon that which is not akin to his nature? For since Paul might have been injured by the vehemence of this sun to which he was accustomed, if he gazed upon it not according to custom, how much more should he be injured by the glory of that light to which his eyes never had been accustomed? For behold, Daniel also[4] was melted and poured out on every side before the glory of the angel, whose vehement brightness suddenly shone upon him! and it was not because of the angel's wrath that his human weakness was melted, just as it is not on account of the wrath or hostility of fire that wax is melted before it; but on account of the weakness of the wax it cannot keep firm and stand in presence of fire. When then the two approach one another, the power of the fire by its quality prevails; but the weakness of the wax on the other hand is brought lower even than its former weakness.

28. But the majesty of the angel was manifested in itself; the weakness of flesh in itself could not endure. For *my inward parts were turned into corruption.*[5] But yet men see men, their fellows, and faint before them: Yet it is not by their bright splendour that they are moved, but by their harsh will. For servants are terrified by the wrath of their masters, and those that are judged tremble through fear of their judges. But this did not befall Daniel on account of threatening or anger from the angel; but on account of his terrible nature and prevailing brightness. For it was not with threatening, the angel came to him. For if he had come with threatening, how could a mouth full of threatening become full of peace,

---

[1] Acts xxii. 11.  [2] Matt. iv. 11.  [3] Acts xxvi. 13.  [4] Dan. x. 5, 6.  [5] Dan. x. 8.

when it came, saying, *Peace be unto thee, thou man* of desire?[1] Thus that mouth that was a fountain of thunderings—for *the voice of his words was like the voice of many hosts,*[2] that voice became to him a fountain teeming with and containing peace. And when [the voice] reached the terrified ears which were athirst for the encouraging greeting of peace, there was opened and poured out [for Daniel] a draught of peace. And by the angel's later [word of] peace, those ears were encouraged, which had been terrified by his former voice first. For [he said], *Let my Lord speak because I have been strengthened.*[3] But because in that heart-moving vision the fiery angel was about to announce nothing concerning Him, [the Lord], on this account that majesty [of the angel] was forward to give the salutation of peace to the lowliness [of the prophet]; that by the gladdening salutation which that awful majesty gave, the dread should be removed which lay on the mind of the lowliness and that was terrified.

29. But what shall we say about the Lord of the Angel, Who said to Moses,—*No man shall see Me and live?*[4] Is it on account of the fury of His anger, that whoso shall see Him shall die? Or on account of the splendour of His Being? For that Being was not made and was not created: so that eyes which have been made and created cannot look upon it. For if it is on account of His fury that whoso shall look upon Him shall not live, lo! He would have granted to Moses to see Him because of His great love to him. Accordingly, the Self-Existent by His vision slays them that look upon Him; but He slays, not because of harsh fury but because of His potent splendour. Because of this He in His great love granted to Moses to see His glory; yet in the same great love He restrained him from seeing His glory. But it was not that the glory of His majesty would have been at all diminished, but that weak eyes could not suffice to bear the overpowering billows of His

glory. Therefore God, Who in His love desired that the vision of Moses should be directed upon the goodly brightness of His glory, in His love did not desire that the vision of Moses should be blinded amidst the potent rays of His glory. Therefore Moses saw and saw not. He saw, that he might be exalted; he saw not, that he might not be injured. For by that which he saw, his lowliness was exalted; and by that which he saw not, his weakness was not blinded. As also our eyes look upon the sun and look not upon it; and by what they see are assisted; and by what they see not, are uninjured. Thus the eye sees, that it may be benefited; but it ventures not [to look], that it may not be injured. So then through love God hindered Moses from seeing that glory that was too hard for his eyes: As also Moses through his love prevented the children of his people from seeing the brightness that was too strong for their eyes. For he learned from Him Who covered him, and spread His hand, and hid from him the splendour of the glory, that it might not injure him; so that he also should spread the veil and conceal from the feeble ones the overpowering splendour, that it might not hurt them. Now when Moses saw that the sons of perishable flesh could not gaze upon the borrowed glory that was on his face, his heart failed within him; for that he had sought to dare to gaze upon the glory of the Eternal Being; in whose floods, lo! those above and those below are plunged and spring forth; the depths whereof none can fathom; the shores whereof none can reach; whereof no end or limit can be found.

30. Now if any one should say, "Was it not then possible for God [to bring it to pass] that Moses should look upon that glory and not be injured; and that Paul likewise should look upon the light and take no hurt?" Let him that says this understand that though it is possible for the power and overruling force of God, that the eyes should change their nature; yet it is inconsistent with the wisdom and nature of God that the order of nature should be confused. For, lo! it is

---

[1] Dan. x. 19 (Peshitto).    [2] Dan. x. 6.
[3] Dan. x. 19.    [4] Exod. xxxiii. 20.

also easy for the arm of the artificer to destroy [his fabrics] ; but it is inconsistent with the good sense of the artificer to ruin goodly ornaments. And if any one wishes to say, concerning something which to himself seems meet ;—"It were meet for God to do this ; " let him know that it is meet for himself not to speak thus concerning God. For the chief of all things meet is this : that a man should not teach God what is meet. For it becomes not man to become God's instructor. For this is a great wickedness, that we should become teachers to Him, of Whom these created mouths of ours are unable to tell, in the formation of His handiwork. For it is an unpardonable iniquity, that the mouth in its boldness should teach what is proper to that God by Whose grace it learned to speak at all. If any one then shall say, "It had been meet for God to do this," I also, because I have a mouth and a tongue, may say, "It had been meet for God not to give to man freedom by which he thus reproaches Him Who is not to be reproached." But I do not dare to say that it was not meet for Him to give it ; lest I also make myself an instructor of Him Who is not to be instructed. For because He is just, He would have been reproached by Himself, had He not given freedom to men, as though through grudging He had withheld from lowly man the gift that makes great. Therefore He gave it betimes by His grace, that He might not be justly reproached by Himself ; even though through freedom, His own gift, lo! blasphemers wickedly reproach Him.

31. Now why were the eyes of Moses made to shine because of the glory which he saw, while on the contrary [the eyes of] Paul, instead of being made to shine, were made utterly blind? Yet we may be sure that the eyes of Moses were not stronger than those of Paul; for they were akin in one brotherhood of blood and flesh. But another power through grace sustained the eyes of Moses ; whereas no power was added in mercy to the eyes of Paul, beyond their natural power, which in wrath was

taken from them. But if we say that their natural power was taken away from them, and that [it was] on this account he was defeated and overcome by the overpowering light,—for had their natural power remained, they would have been able to endure that supernatural light. Yet let us be sure of this, that as often as anything transcendent is revealed, that surpasses and transcends our nature, our natural power is not able to stand before it. But if on the other hand another power beyond our natural one is added to us, then by that power received by us in excess of and beyond nature, we shall be able to stand before any strange thing which comes upon us supernaturally.

32. For, lo! the power of our ears and eyes is in us and is formed in us in its natural manner ; and yet our sight and hearing cannot stand before mighty thunderings and lightnings ; first, because they come with vehemence ; and secondly, because their potency suddenly surprises and astounds our feebleness. This is what happened to Paul. For the potency of the light suddenly surprised his feeble eyes and injured them. But the greatness of the voice brought low his strength and entered his ears and opened them. For they had been closed up by Jewish contentiousness as by wax. For the voice did not plough up the ears, as the light injured the eyeballs. Why? but because it was meet that he should hear, but not that he should see. Therefore the doors of hearing were opened by the voice as by a key : but the doors of sight were shut by the light that should open them. Why then was it meet that he should hear? Clearly because by that voice our Lord was able to reveal Himself as being persecuted by Saul. For He was not able to show Himself by sight as being persecuted ; for there was no way whereby this should be, that the son of David should be seen fleeing and Saul pursuing after Him.[1] For this happened in very deed with that first Saul and with the first David. The one was pursuing ; the other

---

[1] 1 Sam. xxiii. xxiv.

was being persecuted; they both of them saw and were seen, each by the other. But here the ear alone could hear of the persecution of the Son of David; the eye could not see that He was being persecuted. For it was in [the person of] others He was being persecuted, while He was Himself in heaven; —He Who beforetime had been persecuted in His own person while He was upon earth. Therefore the ears [of Saul] were opened and his eyes were closed. And He Who by sight could not represent Himself before Saul as persecuted, represented Himself by word before him as persecuted; when he cried and said;—*Saul, Saul, why persecutest thou Me?* Accordingly, his eyes were closed, because they could not see the persecution of Christ; but his ears were opened, because they could hear of His persecution. So then although the eyes of Moses were bodily eyes, as those of Paul, yet his inward eyes were Christian; for *Moses wrote of Me :*[1] but the outward eyes of Paul were open, while the inward [eyes] were shut. Then because the inward eyes of Moses shone clear, his outward eyes also were made to shine clearly. But the outward eyes of Paul were closed, that by the closing of those that were outward, there might come to pass the opening of those that were inward. For he who by the outward eyes was not able to see the Lord in His signs, he when those bodily eyes were closed, saw with those within. And because he had received the proof in his own person, he wrote to those who had their bodily eyes full of light ;— *May He illumine the eyes of your hearts.*[2] Therefore the signs manifested to the external eyes of the Jews, profited them not at all; but faith of the heart opened the eyes of the heart of the Gentiles. But because, had Moses come down in his accustomed aspect from the mountain, without that shining of countenance, and said, "I saw there the glory of God," the faithless fathers would not have believed him; so also, had Paul, without suffering blindness

of his eyes, said, "I heard the voice of Christ," the sons who crucified Christ would not have received it as true. Therefore He set on Moses as in love, an excelling sign of splendour, that the deceivers might believe that he had seen the Divine glory; but on Saul, as on a persecutor, He set the hateful sign of blindness, that the liars might believe that he had heard the words of Christ; that so thou might not again speak against Moses, and that these might not doubt concerning Paul. For God set signs on the bodies of the blind, and sent them to those who were in error, who used to make signs upon the borders of their garments. But they remembered not the signs on their garments, and in the signs of the body they greatly erred. The fathers who saw the glory of Moses, did not obey Moses; nor did the sons who saw the blindness of Paul believe Paul. But three times in the desert they threatened to stone Moses and his house with stones as dogs.[3] For *all the congregation bade stone them with stones.*[4] And thrice they scourged Paul with rods as a dog on his body. [?][5] Thrice was I beaten with rods.[6] These are the lions who through their love for their Lord were beaten as dogs; and were torn as flocks of sheep, those flocks that used to stone their guardian shepherds, in order that ravening wolves might rule over them.

33. But the crucifiers who corrupted the soldiers with a bribe, they perhaps said concerning Paul ;—" The disciples have bribed him with a bribe; therefore he associates with the disciples." For those who by the giving of a bribe strove that the resurrection of our Lord might not be preached, slandered Paul with the name of a bribe, that his revelation might not be believed. Therefore the voice astonished him, and the light blinded him, that his astonishment might pacify his violence, and his blindness might put to shame his slanderers. For the voice

---

[1] John v. 46.   [2] Eph. i. 18.

[3] Only one such threat is recorded (see margin); but cf. Exod. viii. 26, and xvii. 4.
[4] Num. xiv. 10.   [5] Rendering doubtful.
[6] 2 Cor. xi. 25.

astounded his hearing in this, that it said meekly to him ;—(*Saul, why persecutest thou Me ?*) : and the light blinded his sight, that when the slanderers should have said that he had received a bribe, and thereby was suborned to lie, his blindness which had been brought about by that light might confute them, showing that it was through it that he had been driven to speak what was true. So that those who supposed that his hands had received a bribe, and that because of it his lips lied, might know that his eyes had given up their light and because of this his lips proclaimed the truth. But again for another reason the meek voice accompanied the overpowering light ; namely, that as it were from meekness unto exaltation our Lord might produce help for the persecutor ; in like manner as also all His helps were produced, from lowliness unto greatness. For our Lord's meekness continued from the womb to the tomb. And observe that greatness comes close upon His lowliness, and exaltation on His meekness. For whereas His greatness was observed in divers things, His Divinity was revealed by glorious signs ; that it might be known that the One Who stood amongst them, was not one but two. For His nature is not humble nature alone, nor is it an exalted nature alone ; but there are two natures that are mingled, the one with the other ; the exalted and the humble. Therefore these two natures show forth their qualities ; so that by the quality of each of the two, mankind might distinguish between the two ; that it might not be supposed that He was merely one,—He Who was two by commingling : but that it might be known that He was two in respect of the blending, though He was one in respect of His Being. These things our Lord, through His humility and exaltation, taught to Paul also in the way to Damascus.

34. For our Lord appeared to Saul in meekness, since meekness was close to His greatness ; that because of His greatness it might be known Who He is Who spake meekly. For even as His disciples preached

on earth of our Lord in meekness and in exaltation,—in the meekness of His persecution, and in the exaltation of His signs,— so also our Lord preached of Himself in meekness and in exaltation in Paul's presence—in the exaltation of the potency of the light which flashed, and in the meekness of that meek voice which said ; *Saul, why persecutest thou Me?*—so that the preaching of Him which His disciples preached concerning Him in presence of many, should be like to that preaching which He preached concerning Himself. But even as, if He had not spoken meekly, it would not have been made known there that He was meek, so, had He not appeared there as an overpowering light, it would not have been made known there that He was exalted.

35. And if thou shouldst say ; " What necessity was there that He should speak humbly ? Could He not have convinced him also through the greatness of the light ? " Know, thou that questionest, that this rejoinder may be returned to thee ; that because it was necessary that He should speak humbly, He therefore spoke humbly. For by Him Who is wise in all things, there was done there nothing that was not meet to be done. For He Who has given knowledge to artificers to do each thing severally with the instrument meet for it, does He not Himself know that which He gives others the power of knowing ? Therefore whatsoever has been wrought or is being wrought by the Godhead, that very thing that is wrought by Him at that time, is for the furtherance of [God's] working at that time, even though to the blind the Divine orderings seem contrariwise. But that we may not restrain by constraint of words a wise enquirer, one that wishes to grow by true persuasion as the seed by the rain-drops ; know, O enquirer, that because Saul was a persecutor, but our Lord was endeavouring to make him persecuted instead of persecutor, therefore He of His wisdom made haste to cry—*Saul, why persecutest thou Me?*—in order that, when Saul who was being made a disciple, heard Him Who was mak-

ing him a disciple, saying, *Why persecutest thou Me?* he might know that the Master Whose servant he was becoming, was a persecuted Master, and so might quickly cast away the persecution of his former masters, and might clothe himself in the persecuted state of his persecuted Master. Now any master who wishes to teach a man anything, teaches him either by deeds or by words. But if he teach him neither by words nor by deeds, the man cannot be instructed in his craft. So that, even though our Lord did not teach Paul humility by deeds, yet by voice He taught him endurance of persecution which He could not teach him by deed. For before our Lord was crucified, He taught His disciples humble endurance of persecution by deed. But after He had finished His persecution by crucifixion, as He said, *Lo! all things are finished.*[1] He could not vainly return and begin again anything which once for all had been wisely finished. Or why again do ye seek for the crucifixion and shame of the Son of God?

36. For even though our Lord in His grace had beforetime brought the majesty of His Godhead into humility, yet afterwards in His justice He willed not again to bring back to humiliation the littleness of manhood which had been made great. But because it was necessary that the persecuting disciple should learn endurance of persecution, while yet it was impossible that the Master should again come down and be persecuted afresh; He taught him by voice that which could not be taught by deeds. *Saul, why persecutest thou Me?* The explanation of which utterance is this;—"Saul, why art thou not persecuted in Me?" But in order that Saul might not suppose that it was because of His weakness our Lord was persecuted, the strength of the overpowering light which shone upon him, convinced him. For if the eyes of Saul could not endure the shining of that light, how could the hands of Saul bind and fetter the disciples of the Lord of

that light? But his hands had fettered the disciples, that he might learn their power in their bonds; while his eyes could not endure the beams, that by their strength he might learn his own weakness. But had not the power of that light shone upon him, when the Lord said to him; *Saul, why persecutest thou Me?* Then because of the madness of the pride wherein Paul was set up at that time, he would perhaps have said this to Him, "I am persecuting Thee for this reason, because Thou hast said, *Why persecutest thou Me?* For who is there that would not persecute Thee, when Thou, with such strength, troublest Thy persecutor with these feeble cries." But the humility of our Lord was heard in the voice, and the power of the light shone forth in the beams. So Paul could not despise the humility of the voice, because of the glory of the light.

37. Thus were his ears brought into discipleship to the voice which he heard, because his eyes sufficed not to endure the beams which they saw. That marvel of the dawning of the light was shed forth upon his eyeballs and did them hurt; and the voice of the Lord of the light entered his ears, but did them no harm. But between the light and the Lord of the light, which ought to have been the stronger? For if the light which was created by Him was so overpowering, how much more overpowering He by Whom this very light was created! But if the Lord of the light was overpowering, as indeed He is overpowering, how did His voice enter the hearing and not harm it? even as that light which hurt the sight? But hear the wonder and the marvel which our Lord wrought by His grace. For our Lord willed not to humble that light which is His; but He being Lord of the light humbled Himself. But as the Lord of the light is greater than the light which is His, so great is the glory that the Lord of the light should humble Himself rather than humble the light.

38. As also in the night, while He was praying, it is written;—*There appeared to*

---

[1] John xix. 30.

*Him an angel strengthening Him.*[1] But here all mouths, celestial and terrestrial, are insufficient to give thanks to Him by Whose hand the angels were created ; that He was strengthened for the sake of sinners by that angel who was created by His hand. As then the angel from above stood in glory and in brightness, while the Lord of the angel, that He might *exalt* man who was degraded, stood in degradation and humility ; so also here that light flashed forth in manifestation ; but the Lord of the light, for the sake of helping one persecutor, spoke with humble voice and lowly words.

39. For this cause therefore that light which was overpowering, because it was not diminished, entered the eyeballs with overpowering manifestation and injured them. But the Lord of the light, because He had lowered Himself in order to help,— His lowly voice entered the ears that had need and helped them. But in order that the help of that voice which had become lowly, might not fail Him, therefore the strength of that light was not lowered, in order that because of that light, which was not lowered, the help of that voice which was lowered, might be believed. But this is a marvel, that until our Lord made Himself lowly in voice, Paul was not made lowly in deed ; for even as, before He came down and clothed Himself in a body, our Lord was in exaltation with His Father ; yet in His exaltation men did not learn humility ; but when He humbled Himself and came down from His exaltation, then by His humbleness humility was soon among men ; so again after His resurrection and ascension He was in glory at the right hand of God His Father, but by that His exaltation, Paul did not learn humility. Therefore He that was exalted and sat at the right hand of His Father, ceased from glorious and lofty speech, and He cried as one wronged and oppressed, with feeble and meek words, saying,—*Saul, Saul, why persecutest thou Me ?* Thus, humble

words prevailed over harsh bridles. For by humble words, as by bridles, the persecuted led the persecutor from the broad way of the persecutors into the narrow way of the persecuted. And since all the signs that were done in the Name of our Lord did not convince Paul, our Lord made haste to meet with humility him who was hastening on the way to Damascus in the vehemence of pride. Thus by His humble words, the harsh vehemence of pride was checked.

40. He then Who used humble words with Paul His persecutor, He also used humble sayings with the Pharisee. For so great is the power of humility that even God Who overcomes all did not overcome without it. Humility was able also in the wilderness to bear the burden of the stiff-necked people. For against the people who were more stubborn than all men, was set Moses who was more meek than all men. For God Who needs not anything, when He had set free the people, afterwards had need of the humility of Moses, that this humility might endure the wrath and murmuring of the People that provoked him. For humility alone could endure the gainsayings of that people, which the signs of Egypt and the prodigies (wrought) in the desert could not subdue. For when pride had wrought divisions amongst the people, humility by its prayer used to close up their divisions. If then the humility of the Stammerer endured six hundred thousand, how much more exceedingly did the humility of Him, Who gave speech to the Stammerer endure ? For the humility of Moses is a shadow of the humility of our Lord.

41. Our Lord then saw that Simon the Pharisee did not believe the signs and wonders which he had seen. He came to him to persuade him with humble words ; and humble utterances overcame him, whom mighty wonders had not overcome. What then are the wonders which that Pharisee had seen ? He had seen the dead raised to life, the lepers cleansed, the blind with eyes opened. These signs compelled that Pharisee to entertain our Lord as a prophet. But

---

[1] Luke xxii. 43.

he who entertained Him as a prophet, changed so as to despise Him for one who had not knowledge, saying (namely);—*Had this man been a prophet, He would have known that this woman*—who had approached Him—*is a sinner.* But we may despise the Pharisee and say, Had he been a man of discernment,[1] he would have learned from that sinful woman, who approached our Lord, not that He was a prophet, but the Lord of the Prophets. For the tears of the sinful woman testified, that it was not a prophet they were propitiating, but Him, Who, as God, was wroth with her sins. For, because the prophets sufficed not to raise sinners to life, the Lord of the prophets came down to heal those who were in evil case. But what physician is there who hinders the smitten, that they should not come to him, O blind Pharisee, as it befel that she came to our Physician! For why did the smitten woman approach Him,—she, whose wounds were healed by her tears? He Who had come down to be a fountain of healing amongst the diseased, was proclaiming this ;—*Let every one that is athirst, come and drink.*[2] But when the Pharisees, this man's companions, murmured at the healing of sinners, the Physician taught concerning His art, that the door is opened for the diseased and not for the whole, for *they that are whole need not a physician but they that are sick.*[3] Therefore the praise of the physician is the healing of the diseased ;—that the shame of the Pharisee who reproved the praise of our physician may be greater. But our Lord used to show signs in the streets ; and also when He entered into the house of the Pharisee, He showed signs which were greater than those He had shown outside. For in the street He made whole the bodies that were sick, but within He healed the souls that were diseased. Outside, He raised to life the mortality of Lazarus : but within, He raised to life the mortality of the sinful woman. He restored the living soul

to the corpse from which it had gone out ; And He expelled from the sinful woman the deadly sin which dwelt within her. But the blind (Pharisee) who was insufficient for great things, because of the great things which he saw not, belied those small things which he had seen. For he was a son of Israel who attributed weakness to his God, and not to himself. For (Israel said), *Though He smote the rock and the waters flowed, can He also give us bread ?*[4] But when our Lord saw his weakness, that it missed the great things and, because of them, the small things also, He hasted to put forward a simple word, as though for a babe that was being reared on milk, and was not capable of solid food.

42. For by that wherein thou knewest, O Pharisee, that our Lord was not a prophet, by that very thing it was proved that thou didst not know the prophets. For by this that thou saidst ;—*Had this man been a prophet, he would have known,* thou showest herein that (in thy esteem) whoever is a prophet knows all things. But lo ! some matters were hidden from the prophets ; how then dost thou attribute the revelation of all hidden things to the prophets ? But this unwise teacher who perverted the scriptures of the Prophets, did not even understand what he read in the scriptures. For it was not only that the greatness of the Lord was not discerned by that Pharisee, but he did not even discern the weakness of the prophets. For our Lord, as knowing all things, allowed that sinful woman to come in and receive His peace. But Elisha, as one ignorant, said to the Shunamite ;—Peace to thee *and peace be to the child.*[5] Accordingly he who supposed that our Lord was proved not to be a prophet, was himself proved not to know the Prophets. When the mind contains malice and cannot refrain, then that malice which is in it, is cunning in finding a pretext for opening a door ; but in case that pretext, in which the deceiver takes refuge is confuted, he knows that

---

[1] Parûshâ ; the resemblance of the word to Parishâ (= Pharisee) is here played on.
[2] John vii. 37.  [3] Matt. ix. 12.  [4] Ps. lxxviii. 20.  [5] 2 Kings iv. 26.

within this there is another concealed which he may employ.

Now observe this son of Israel, how he was like Israel in stubbornness. For heathenism was bound up in the mind of the People; therefore Moses was taken away from them, that the wickedness that was within them might become manifest. But that they might not be put to shame, and that it might not be known how they were seeking idols, they first sought for Moses, and then for idols. *As for this Moses, we know not what has become of him.*[1] And if God, Who cannot die, brought thee out of Egypt, why dost thou seek for a man, who at some time must die? Yet they did not desire Moses, that he should become a god to them; because Moses could hear and see and reprove; but they sought for a god who could neither hear nor see nor reprove. But whensoever Moses shall have died, what shall remain of him? For behold, thy God is a living God, and lo! He has revealed Himself to thee by living testimonies. For the bright cloud was at that time overshadowing them, and they had the pillar of light in the night-time. Water flowed for them from the rock, and they drank its streams. They were delighted every day by tasting that manna, the fame of which we have heard. How was Moses far from thee? Behold the signs of Moses surround thee. Or how does the person of Moses profit thee, when thou hast such a guide as this? If thy garments wear not old, and a temperate air refreshes thee, if the heat and the cold do not hurt thee, and thou hast rest from war, and art far removed from the fear of Egypt,—what thing then was lacking to Israel that he sought for Moses? Open heathenism was lacking to him. For it was not for Moses that he sought, but on the pretext of Moses' absence he followed after the calf. Thus briefly have we showed, that when the mind is full of anything, but an opposing reason meets it, then it forces it by violence to open for it a door to that which it desires.

---

[1] Ex. xxxii. 1.

43. Thou too, O Pharisee, athirst for blasphemy, what sawest thou in our Lord, to show that He was not a prophet? For lo! the things that belong to the Lord of the Prophets were seen in Him. For the gushing tears made haste to proclaim that they were shed as before God. The sorrowing kisses testified that they sought to win over the creditor to tear up the debt-bonds. The goodly ointment of the sinful woman proclaimed that it was a bribe of penitence. These medicines the sinful woman offered to her Physician, that by her tears He might wash away her stains, by her kisses He might heal her wounds, by her sweet ointment He might make her evil name sweet as the odour of her ointment. This is the Physician who heals men by the medicines which they bring to Him. These marvels were shown at that time; but to the Pharisee instead of these there appeared blasphemy. For what could be established in the weeping of the sinful woman, but that He can justify sinners? Else, judge thou in thy mind, O blind teacher, why was that mournful weeping in the joyful feast, so that, while they were making merry with food, she was in bitterness with her tears? Because she was a sinner, her deeds were unchaste, and these (deeds) she was wont to do. But if at that time, from the wantonness of sinners she was turned to chastity, then acknowledge, thou who saidst *He is not a prophet,* that He is One who makes those chaste that have been wanton. For by this, that thou knowest that she is a sinner, and by this, that thou seest her now penitent, search out where is the power that changed her. For he ought to have fallen down and worshipped Him Who, while silent, in His silence turned to chastity those sinners whom the Prophets by their vehement utterances could not turn to chastity. A wonderful and marvellous thing was seen in the house of the Pharisee; a sinful woman that sat and wept, and she who wept said not wherefore she wept; nor did He at Whose feet she sat say to her, Why weepest thou? The sinner did not need with her lips to

petition our Lord, because she believed that He knew, as God, the petitions that were hidden in her tears. Nor did our Lord ask her, What hast thou done? For He knew that by her pure kisses she was atoning for her transgressions. So then she, because she believed that He knew the things that were hidden, offered to Him her prayers in her heart; for knowing secret things He had no need of the outward lips. If then the sinner, because she knew that our Lord was God, sought not to persuade Him with her lips; and our Lord, because as God He discerned her thoughts, therefore questioned her not; dost not thou, O tyrant Pharisee, from the silence of both understand the position of both; that she was praying as to God in her heart, and that He as God was in silence searching out her thoughts? But the Pharisee could not see and understand these things, because he was a son of Israel, who though perceiving, saw not, and though he heard, understood not. Though then our Lord knew that that Pharisee thought evil thoughts concerning Him, He confuted him gently and not harshly. For sweetness came down from on high to break down the bitterness with which the Evil One had stamped us. Therefore our Lord taught that Pharisee of Himself and in Himself, as though saying, Even as I, though I knew the evil things in thy heart, yet gently persuaded thee, so though I knew the evil things of this woman, I mercifully received her.

But let us hear how long-suffering was drawn after the hasty thought, so as to draw it from haste to understanding. *A certain creditor had two debtors. One owed five hundred dinars, and the other fifty dinars.*—(Be not wearied, O hearer, at the length of the repetition of the parable, lest thou be contrary to Him Who in the parable was long-suffering for the sake of giving help.)—*At length, when neither of them had wherewithal to pay, he forgave them both. Which of them dost thou think would love him more? Simon said to Him, I suppose that he, to whom more was forgiven. Our*

*Lord said to him, Thou hast rightly judged.* Our Lord in His justice commended the perverse (Pharisee), because of the right judgment, which he had judged, though he in his wickedness had answered the good Lord concerning the mercy He had wrought. Now many things are laid up in this parable; for it is a treasury full of many helps. Why then did our Lord require that the Pharisee should pass judgment for Him between the two debtors? Was it not that the greatness, coming after the littleness, might show itself that nothing of the littleness was drawn after the greatness? For our Lord, since He knew the secret things, was long-suffering and questioned Simon, that those might be put to shame who, though not knowing, were hasty to blame, but not to enquire. For if, O man, before I heard thy judgment passed, I judged not of it, why didst thou, before thou heardest from Me, the case of the sinful woman, hastily blame? Now this was done for our instruction, that we might be swift to enquire, but slow to pass our sentence. For had that Pharisee been long-suffering, lo! that pardon which our Lord in the end gave to the sinful woman, would have taught him everything. Long-suffering is wont to acquire all things for those that acquire it.

44. But again; through the forgiveness of the two debtors, our Lord led into forgiveness him who was in need of forgiveness, yet in whose eyes the forgiveness of debts was hateful. For though the debts of the Pharisee himself needed forgiveness, yet the forgiveness of the debts of the sinful woman was hateful in his eyes. For had there been this forgiveness of debts in the mind of the Pharisee, it would not have been in his eyes disgraceful that that sinful woman should have come for forgiveness of her debts to God and not to the priests; for the priests could not forgive sins such as those. But this sinful woman from the glorious works which our Lord did, believed that He could also forgive sins. For she knew that whoso is able to restore the members of the body, is able also to cleanse

away the spots of the soul. But the Pharisee, though he was a teacher, did not know this. For the teachers of Israel were wont to be fools, put to shame by the despised and vile. For they were put to shame by that blind man to whom they said ;—*We know that this man is a sinner.*[1] But he said to them :—*How did He open my eyes ? lo ! God hears not sinners.*[1] These are the blind teachers who were made guides to others ; and their perverse path was made straight by a blind man.

45. But hear ye the marvel that our Lord wrought. Because that Pharisee supposed that our Lord did not know that the woman who touched Him was a sinner ; our Lord made the lips of the Pharisee like the strings of a harp ; and by his very lips He sang how she was trampling under foot his sins, though he knew it not. And he who as though he knew had blamed, was found to be a harp, whereto another could sing of that which he knew. For our Lord compared the sins of the sinful woman to five hundred dinars, and caused them to pass into the hearing of the Pharisee by the parable which he heard ; and again brought them forth from his mouth in the judgment he gave ; though Simon knew not, when he was judging, that those five hundred dinars denoted the sins of the sinful woman. And (the Pharisee) who thought concerning our Lord that He had not knowledge of her sins, was himself found not to have knowledge of them, when he heard of those debts in the parable, and gave judgment concerning them with his voice. But when it was explained to him at last by our Lord, then the Pharisee knew that alike his ears and also his lips were, as it were, instruments for our Lord, through which He might sing the glories of His knowledge.

For this Pharisee was the fellow of those scribes, whose sentence by their own mouths our Lord gave against them ;—*What then will the Lord of the vineyard do to those husbandmen ?*[2] They say unto Him, against

themselves :—*He will terribly destroy them, and will hire out the vineyard to husbandmen who will render unto Him the fruit in its season.* This is the Godhead to which all things are easy, which by the mouths, the very mouths that blasphemed it, pronounced the sentence of those very mouths against them.

46. Glory then be to Him the Invisible, who clothed Himself in invisibility, that sinners might be able to draw near to Him. For our Lord did not repel the sinful woman as the Pharisee expected ; inasmuch as He descended from the height which no man can reach unto, altogether in order that lowly publicans, like Zaccheus, might reach unto Him. And the Nature which none can handle, clothed Itself in a body, altogether in order that all lips[3] might kiss His feet as the sinful woman did. For the sacred soul was hidden within the veil of flesh, and so touched all unclean lips and sanctified them. Thus He Whom His appetite was supposed to invite to feasting, His feet invited to tears ; He was the good Physician, who came forth to go to the sinful woman who was seeking Him in her soul. She then anointed the feet of our Lord, who (anointed) not His head,—she who was trodden down in the dust by all. For those Pharisees who justified themselves and despised all (else), trod her down. But He the Merciful, Whose pure body sanctified her uncleanness, had pity on her.

47. But Mary anointed the head of our Lord's body,[4] as a token of the better part which she had chosen. And Christ prophesied concerning that which her soul had chosen. While Martha was cumbered with serving, Mary was hungering to be satisfied with spiritual things by Him Who also satisfies us with bodily things. So Mary refreshed Him with precious ointment, as He had refreshed her with His exalted teaching. Mary by the oil showed forth the mystery of His mortality, Who by His teaching mortified the concupiscence of her flesh.

---

[1] John ix. 24-31.  [2] Matt. xxi. 40-44.  [3] Is. vi. 7.  [4] Matt. xxvi. 7.

Thus the sinful woman by the flood of her tears, in full assurance was rewarded with remission of sins from beside His feet ; and she who had the issue of blood, stole healing from the hem of His garment. But Mary received blessing openly from His mouth, as a reward of the service of her hands upon His head. For she poured out on His head the precious ointment, and received from His mouth a wonderful promise. This is the ointment which was sown above and yielded fruit below. For she sowed it on His head and gathered its fruit from between His lips ;—*She shall have a name and this memorial in every place where My Gospel shall be preached.*[1] Accordingly, what she then received of Him, He is able to cause to pass unto all generations : and in no generation can any hinder it. For the ointment which she poured upon His head, gave its odour in presence of all the guests and refreshed Him ; so also the goodly name which He gave her, passes down through all generations and brings honour to her. Even as all who were at the feast were sensible of her ointment ; it was meet that all who come into the world should be sensible of her triumph. This is a loan whereof the increase is exacted in all generations.

48. Now Simeon the priest, when he took Him up in his arms to present Him before God,[2] understood as he saw [Him] that He was not presenting Him, but was being himself presented. For the Son was not presented by the servant to His Father, but the servant was presented by the Son to his Lord. For it is not possible that He, by Whom every offering is presented, should be presented by another. For the offering does not present him that offers it ; but by them that offer are offerings presented. So then He Who receives offerings gave Himself to be offered by another, that those who presented Him, while offering Him, might themselves be presented by Him. For as He gave His body to be eaten, that when

eaten It might quicken to life them that ate Him ; so He gave Himself to be offered, that by His Cross the hands of them that offered Him might be sanctified. So, then, though the arms of Simeon seemed to be presenting the Son, yet the words of Simeon testified that he was presented by the Son. Therefore we can have no dispute concerning this, because that which was said put an end to dispute ;—*Now lettest Thou Thy servant depart in peace.*[3] He then who is let depart to go in peace to God, is presented as an offering to God. And in order to make known by whom he was presented, he said,—*For lo ! mine eyes have seen Thy mercy.*[4] If there was no grace wrought on him, why then did he give thanks ? But rightly did he give thanks, that he was thought worthy to receive in his arms Him, Whom angels and prophets greatly desired to see. For lo ! *mine eyes have seen Thy mercy.* Let us understand then and see. Is *mercy* that which shows mercy to another, or is it that which receives mercy from another ? But if mercy is that which shows mercy to all, well did Simeon call our Lord by the name of the mercy that showed mercy to him,—Him Who freed him from the world which is full of snares, that he might go to Eden which is full of pleasures ; for he who was priest said and testified that he was offered as an offering, that from the midst of the perishing world he should go and be stored up in the treasure-house which is kept safe. For one for whom it may be that what he has found should be lost, to him it belongs to be diligent that it should be kept safe. But for our Lord it could not be that He should be lost ; but by Him the lost were found. So then, through the Son Who could not be lost, the servant who was very desirous not to be lost, was presented. *Lo ! mine eyes have seen Thy mercy.* It is evident Simeon received grace from that Child Whom he was carrying. For inwardly he received grace from that Infant, Whom openly he received in his

---

[1] Matt. xxvi. 13.  [2] Luke ii. 28.  [3] Luke ii. 29.  [4] Luke ii. 30.

arms. For through Him Who was glorious, even when He was carried, being small and feeble, he that carried Him was made great.

49. But inasmuch as Simeon endured to carry on his weak arms that Majesty which the creatures could not endure, it is evident that his weakness was made strong by the strength which he carried. For at that time Simeon also along with all creatures was secretly upheld by the almighty strength of the Son. Now this is a marvel, that outwardly it was he that was strengthened that carried Him Who strengthened him; but inwardly it was the strength that bore its bearer. For the Majesty straitened itself, that they who carried it might endure it; in order that as far as that Majesty stooped to our littleness, so far should our love be raised up from all desires to reach that Majesty.

50. So likewise the ship that carried our Lord; it was He that bare it, in that He stayed from it the wind that would have sunk it. Peace, for thou art shut up. While He was on the sea, His arm reached even to the fountain of the wind,[1] to shut it up. The ship bare His manhood, but the power of His Godhead bare the ship and all that was therein. But that He might show that even His manhood needed not the ship, instead of the planks which a shipwright puts together and fastens, He like the Architect of creation, made the waters solid and joined them together and laid them under His feet. So the Lord strengthened the hands of Simeon the Priest, that his arms might bear up in the Temple the strength that was bearing up all; as He strengthened the feet of Simeon the Apostle, that they might bear themselves up on the water. And so that name which bore the first-begotten in the Temple was afterwards borne up by the first-begotten in the sea; that He might show that as in the sea the drowning was borne up by Him, He did not need to be borne by Simeon on the dry ground. But our Lord bare Simeon up openly in the midst of the sea to teach that also on the dry land He supported him secretly.

51. Accordingly, the Son came to the servant; not that the Son might be presented by the servant, but that by the Son the servant might present to His Lord Priesthood and Prophecy, to be laid up with Him. For prophecy and priesthood, which were given through Moses, were handed down, both of them, and reached to Simeon. For he was a pure vessel, who sanctified himself that he might be like Moses, capable for both of them. There are small vessels which are capable for great gifts. There are gifts for which one is capable, by reason of their grace; yet many are not capable for them, by reason of their greatness. Thus, then, Simeon presented our Lord, and in Him offered both these things; so that that which was given to Moses in the wilderness, was received from Simeon in the Temple. But seeing that our Lord is the vessel wherein all fulness dwells, when Simeon was offering Him before God, he poured over Him (as a drink-offering) those two (gifts), priesthood from His hands and prophecy from His lips. Priesthood continued on the hands of Simeon, because of his purifications; and prophecy dwelt in operation upon his lips, because of revelations. When then these two powers saw Him who was Lord of both, they two united together and poured themselves into the vessel that was capable of both; that could contain priesthood and kingdom and prophecy. That Infant then, who was wrapped in swaddling clothes, because of His graciousness, clothed Himself in priesthood and prophecy because of His Majesty. For Simeon clothed Him in these, and gave Him to her who had wrapped Him in swaddling clothes. For when he gave Him to His mother, he gave along with Him the priesthood; and when he prophesied to her concerning Him, *This* (child) is *set for the fall and rising again,*[2] he gave prophecy also with Him.

---

[1] Mark iv. 39.

[2] Luke ii. 34.

52. Then Mary received her firstborn and went forth. He was outwardly wrapped in swaddling clothes, but secretly He was clothed with prophecy and priesthood. Whatsoever then was handed down from Moses, was received from Simeon, but continued and was possessed by the Lord of both. So then the steward first, and the treasurer lastly, handed over the keys of priesthood and prophecy to Him who has authority over the treasurer of them both. Therefore, His Father gave Him the spirit not by measure,[1] because all measures of the spirit are under his hand. And that our Lord might show that He received the keys from the former stewards, He said to Simeon : *To thee I will give the keys of the doors.*[2] But how should He have given them to another, had He not received them from another ? So, then, the keys which He had received from Simeon the priest, them He gave to another Simeon the Apostle ; that even though the People had not hearkened to the former Simeon, the Gentiles might hearken to the latter Simeon.

53. But because John also was the treasurer of baptism, the Lord of the stewardship came to him to receive from him the keys of the house of reconciliation. For John used to wash away in common water the blemishes of sins ; that bodies might become meet for the garment of the Spirit, given by our Lord. Therefore, because the Spirit was with the Son, He came to John to receive from him baptism, that He might mingle with the visible waters the invisible Spirit ; that they whose bodies should feel the moistening of the water, their souls should feel the gift of the Spirit ; that even as the bodies outwardly feel the pouring of the water upon them, so the souls inwardly may feel the pouring of the Spirit upon them. Accordingly, even as our Lord when He was baptised, was clothed in baptism and carried baptism with Him, so also when He was presented in the Temple, He put on prophecy and priesthood, and went forth

bearing the purity of the priesthood upon His pure members, and bearing the words of. prophecy in His wondrous ears. For when Simeon was sanctifying the body of the Child who sanctifies all, that body received the priesthood in its sanctification. And again, when Simeon was prophesying over Him, prophecy quickly entered the hearing of the Child. For if John leaped in the womb and perceived the voice of the Mother of our Lord,[3] how much more should our Lord have heard in the Temple ? For lo ! it was because of Him that John knew (so as) to hear in the womb.

54. Accordingly, each one of the gifts that was stored up for the Son, He gathered from their true tree. For He received baptism from the Jordan, even though John still after Him used to baptise. And He received priesthood from the Temple, even though Annas the High Priest exercised it. And again, He received prophecy which had been handed down amongst the righteous, even though by it Caiaphas in mockery platted a crown for our Lord, and He received the kingdom from the house of David, even though Herod held the place and exercised it.

55. This is He Who flew and came down from on high ; and when all those gifts which He had given to those of old time saw Him, they came flying from every quarter and rested on Him their Giver. For they gathered themselves together from every side, to come and be grafted into their natural tree. For they had been grafted into bitter trees, namely into wicked kings and priests. Therefore they hastened to come to their sweet parent-stock ; namely to the Godhead Who in sufficiency came down to the people of Israel, that the parts of Him might be gathered to Him. And when He received of them that which was His own, that which was not His own was rejected ; since for the sake of His own He had borne also with that which was not His own. For He bore with the idolatry of

---

[1] John iii. 34.  [2] Matt. xvi. 19.  [3] Luke i. 41.

Israel, for the sake of His **priesthood**; and He bore with its diviners, for the sake of His prophets; and He bore with its wicked dominion, for the sake of His holy crown.

56. But when our Lord took to Himself Priesthood from them, He sanctified by it all the Gentiles. And again, when He took to Himself prophecy, He revealed by it His counsels to all nations. And when he wove His crown, He bound the strong One who takes all men captive, and divides his spoils. These gifts were barren, with the fig-tree, which while it was barren of fruit made barren such glorious powers as these. Therefore as being without fruit, it was cut off, that these gifts might pass forth from it and bring forth fruit abundantly among all the Gentiles.

57. So He, Who came to make our bodies abodes for His indwelling, passed by all those dwelling-places. Let each one of us then be a dwelling-place for Him Who loves me. Let us come to Him and make our abode with Him. This is the Godhead Whom though all creation cannot contain, yet a lowly and humble soul suffices to receive Him.

## ON ADMONITION AND REPENTANCE.

1. Not of compulsion is the doctrine; of free-will is the word of life. Whoso is willing to hear the doctrine, let him cleanse the field of his will, that the good seed fall not among the thorns of vain enquirings. If thou wouldst heed the word of life, cut thyself off from evil things; the hearing of the word profits nothing to the man that is busied with sins. If thou willest to be good, love not dissolute customs. First of all, trust in God, and then hearken thou to His law.

2. Thou canst not hear His words, while thou dost not know thyself; and if thou keepest His judgments while thy understanding is aloof from Him, who will give thee thy reward? Who will keep for thee thy recompense? Thou wast baptised in His Name; confess His Name! In the

Persons and in the naming, Father and Son and Holy Spirit, three Names and Persons, these three shall be a wall to thee, against divisions and wranglings. Doubt not thou of the truth, lest thou perish through the truth. Thou wast baptised from the water; thou hast put on Christ in His naming; the seat of the Lord is on thy person and His stamp on thy forehead. See that thou become not another's, for other Lord hast thou none. One is He Who formed us in His mercy; one is He Who redeemed us on His cross. He it is Who guides our life; He it is Who has power over our feebleness; He it is Who brings to pass our Resurrection. He rewards us according to our works. Blessed is he that confesses Him, and hears and keeps His commandments! Thou, O man, art a son of God Who is high over all. See that thou vex not by thy works the Father Who is good and gracious.

3. If thou art wroth against thy neighbour, thou art wroth against God; and if thou bearest anger in thy heart, against thy Lord is thy boldness uplifted. If in envy thou rebukest, wicked is all thy reproof. But if charity dwell in thee, thou hast on earth no enemy. And if thou art a true son of peace, thou wilt stir up wrath in no man. If thou art just and upright, thou wilt not do wrong to thy fellow. And if thou lovest to be angry, be angry with the wicked and it will become thee; if to wage war thou seekest, lo! Satan is thy adversary; if thou desirest to revile, against the demons display thy curses.. If thou shouldst insult the King's image, thou shalt pay the penalty of murder; and if thou revilest a man, thou revilest the image of God. Do honour to thy neighbour, and lo! thou hast honoured God. But if thou wouldst dishonour Him, in wrath assail thy neighbour!

4. This is the first Commandment,—*Thou shall love the Lord thy God with all thy heart and thy soul, and with thy might* according as thou art able. The sign that thou lovest God, is this, that thou lovest thy fellow; and if thou hatest thy fellow, thy hatred is towards God. For it is blasphemy if thou

prayest before God while thou art **wroth.**
For thy heart also convicts thee, that in vain
thou multipliest words : thy conscience
rightly judges that in thy prayers thou pro-
fitest nought. Christ as He hung on the
height of the tree, interceded for His murderers ; and thou (who art) dust, son of the
clay, rage fills thee at its will. Thou keepest anger against thy brother ; and dost
thou yet dare to pray ? Even he that stands
on thy side, though he be not neighbour to
thy sins, the taint of iniquity reaches unto
him, and his petition is not heard. Leave
off rage and then pray ; and unless thou
wouldst further provoke, restrain anger and
so shalt thou supplicate. And if he (the
other) is not to encounter thee in fury, banish rage from that body, because it is holden
with lusts.

5. Thou hast a spiritual nature ; the soul
is the image of the Creator ; honour the image of God, by being in agreement with all
men. Remember death, and be not angry,
that thy peace be not of constraint. As
long as thy life remains to thee, cleanse thy
soul from wrath ; for if it should go to Sheol
with thee, thy road will be straight to Gehenna. Keep not anger in thy heart ; hold
not fury in thy soul ; thou hast not power
over thy soul, save to do that which is good.
Thou art bought with the blood of God;[1] thou
art redeemed by the passion of Christ ; for
thy sake He suffered death, that thou mightest die to thy sins. His face endured spitting, that thou mightest not shrink from
scorn. Vinegar and gall did He drink, that
thou mightest be set apart from wrath. He
received stripes on His body, that thou
mightest not fear suffering. If thou art in
truth His servant, fear thy holy Lord ; if thou
art His true disciple, walk in thy Master's
footsteps. Endure scorn from thy brother,
that thou mayest be the companion of Christ.
Display not anger against man, that thou be
not set apart from thy Redeemer.

6. Thou art a man, the dust of the earth,
clay, kinsman of the clod ; thou art the
son of the race of beasts. If thou knowest
not **thy honour ; separate** thy soul from animals, by works and not **by words. If thou**
lovest derision, thou art altogether as Satan ;
and if thou mockest at thy fellow, thou art
the mouth of the Devil ; if against defects
and flaws, in (injurious) names thou de-
lightest, Satan is not in creation but his
place thou hast seized by force. Get thee
far, O man, from this ; for it is altogether
hurtful ; and if thou desirest to live well, sit
not with the scorner, lest thou become the
partner of his sin and of his punishment.
Hate mockery which is altogether (the
cause of weeping), and mirth which is (the
cause of) cleansing. And if thou shouldst
hear a mocker by chance, when thou art not
desiring it, sign thyself with the cross of
light, and hasten from thence like an ante-
lope. Where Satan lodges, Christ will in no-
wise dwell ; a spacious dwelling for Satan is
the man that mocks at his neighbour ; a palace of the Enemy is the heart of the mocker.
Satan does not desire to add any other evil
to it. Mockery is sufficient for him to supply the place of all. Neither his belly nor
yet his purse can (the sinner) fill with that
sin of his. By his laughter is the wretch
despoiled, and he knows not nor does he
perceive it. For his wound, there is no cure ;
for his sickness, there is no healing ; his
pain, admits no remedy ; and his sore, endures no medicine. I desire not with such
a one to put forth my tongue to reprove
him : enough for him is his own shame ;
sufficient for him is his boldness. Blessed
is he that has not heard him ; and blessed
is he that has not known him. Be it far
from thee, O Church, that he should enter
thee, that evil leaven of Satan !

7. Narrow is the way of life, and broad the
way of torment ; prayer is able to bring a
man to the house of the kingdom. This is
the perfect work ; prayer that is pure from
iniquity. The righteousness of man is as
nothing accounted. The work of men,
what is it ? His labour is altogether vanity.[2]

---

[1] Acts xx. 28.

[2] Eccles. i. 3.

Of Thee, O Lord, of Thy grace it is that in our nature we should become good. Of Thee is righteousness, that we from men should become righteous. Of Thee is the mercy and favour, that we from the dust should become Thy image. Give power to our will, that we be not sunk in sin! Pour into our heart memory, that at every hour we may know Thy honour! Plant Thou truth in our minds, that we perish not among doubts! Occupy our understanding with Thy law, that it wander not in vain thoughts! Order the motions of our members, that they bring no hurt upon us! Draw thou near to God, that Satan may flee from thee. Cast out passions from thy heart, and lo! thou hast put to flight the enemy. Hate thou sins and wickedness, and Satan at once will have fled. Whatsoever sins thou servest, thou art worshipping secret idols. Whatsoever transgressions thou lovest, thou art serving demons in thy soul. Whensoever thou strivest with thy brother, Satan abides in peace. Whensoever thou enviest thy fellow, thou givest rest to Devils. Whensoever thou tellest the shortcoming of others who are not present, thy tongue has made a harp for the music of the devil. Whensoever hatred is in thy soul, great is the peace of the Deceiver. Whensoever thou lovest incantations, thy labour is altogether of the left hand.[1] If thou lovest unseemly discourse, thou preparest a feast for demons. For this is the worship of idols, the working of the lusts (of the flesh).

8. If so be thou givest a gift in pride, this is not of God. If thou art lifted up by reason of thy knowledge, thou hast denied the grace of God. If thou art poor and proud, lo! thy end is in thy torment. If thou art haughty and needy, lo! thy need is toward thy destruction. If thou art sick and criest out, lo! thy trouble is full of harm. If thou art in need of food, yet thy mind longs for riches; thy distress is with the poor, but thy torment with the rich. If thou shalt look unchastely, and shalt desire

thy neighbour's wife, lo! thy portion shall be with the adulterers, and thy hell with the fornicators. *Let thine own fountain be for thyself, and drink waters from thy well. Let thy fountains be for thyself alone, and let not another drink with thee.*[2] Require purity of thy body as thou requirest of thy yokefellow. Thou wouldst not have her commit lewdness, the wife of thy youth, with another man; commit not thou lewdness with another woman, the wife of a different husband. Let the defilement of her be hateful in thine eyes; keep aloof from it altogether. Chastity beseems the wife; purity is as her adornment; law becomes the husband; justice is the crown for his head. Desire not thou the bed of thy neighbour lest another desire thy bed. Preserve purity in thy marriage, that thy marriage may be holy. His conscience reproves the man, who corrupts the wife of his neighbour. He fears, and deceives through terror, whoso has engaged in fornication. Darkness is dearer to him than light, whose manner of life is not pure. Every hour he stands in dread, who commits adultery secretly. The adulterer is also a thief who breaks into houses in darkness. The very place reproves him, where he does the evil and wickedness. He enters the chamber and sins; in the darkness he does his will. The time will come when it shall be disclosed, when his secret deeds shall be manifested. With what eyes dost thou look towards God in prayer? What hands dost thou raise when thou askest pardon? Be ashamed and dismayed for thyself, that thou art void of understanding. If when thy neighbour see thee, thou art ashamed and dismayed, how much more shouldst thou be ashamed before God Who sees all? Thou art like the sow,[3] thy companion, that wallows altogether in mire. Even in seeing, thou mayest sin, if thy mind is not watchful; and in hearing thou mayest transgress, if thou dost not guard thy hearing. The fornicator's heart waxes wanton through speech that is full of uncleanness.

---

[1] *I.e.*, such as fits for a place on Christ's left hand, at the Judgment.

[2] Prov. v. 15–17.   [3] 2 Pet. ii. 22.

The passion hidden in the mind, sight and hearing awaken it.

9. He puts on garments of shame who desires to commit fornication, that from the lust of raiment, lewdness may enter and dwell in his heart. Make thou not snares of thy garments for that which is openly wanton. Speak not a word in craftiness, nor dig thy neighbour's well. Look not after the harlot ; be not snared by the beauty of her face. She is even as the dog that is mad, yea, much more bold than it. Modesty is removed from her face, she knows not what shame is. With spitting accept her person ; with reviling meet herself ; with a rod pursue her like a dog, for she is like one, and to be compared with such. Reject the sweetness of her words, lest thou fall into her net. She empties purses and wallets, and her gains are without number. Flee from her, for she is the daughter of vipers, that she tear not in pieces thy whole body.

10. Thou shalt not slander any man, lest they call thee Satan. If thou hatest the name, go not near to the act ; but if thou lovest the act, be not angry at the name. Count thyself rebuked first of all by the beasts and birds, how that every kind cleaves to its kind ; and so agree thou with thy yokefellow. Rejoice not in men's dishonour, that thou become not a Satan thyself. If evil should happen to him that hates thee, see thou rejoice not, lest thou sin. If thine adversary should fall, be thou in pain and mourning. Keep thy heart with all diligence,[1] that it sin not in secret ; for there is to be a laying bare of thoughts and of actions. Employ thy hands in labour, and let thy heart meditate in prayer. Love not vain discourse, for discourse that shall be profitable alike to the soul and the body lightens the burden of thy labour.

11. Does the poor man cry at thy door? Arise and open for him gladly : refresh him when he is wearied ; sustain his heart, for it is sad. Thou knowest by experience the affliction of poverty : receive not others in thy house, and drive not out the beggar. Have thou also a law, a comely law for thy household. Establish an order that is wise, that the abjects laugh not at thee. Be careful in all thy doings, that thou be not a sport for fools ; be upright and prudent, and both simple and wise.[2] Let thy body be quiet and cheerful, thy greeting seemly and simple ; thy discourse without fault, thy speech brief and savoury ; thy words few and sound, full of savour and understanding. Speak not overmuch, not even words that are wise ;[2] for all things that are overmany, though they be wise are wearisome. —To them of thy household be as a father. Amongst thy brethren esteem thyself least, and inferior amongst thy fellows, and of little account with all men. With thy friend keep a secret ; to those that love thee be true. See that there be no wrangling ; the secrets of thy friends reveal not, lest all that hear thee hate thee and esteem thee a mischief-maker. With those that hate thee wrangle not, neither face to face nor yet in thy heart. No enemy shalt thou have but Satan his very self. Give counsel to the wife thou hast wedded ; give heed to her doings ; as stronger thou art answerable that thou shouldst sustain her weakness. For weak is womankind, and very ready to fall. Be thou as a hawk, when kindled (to anger), but when wrath departs from thee, be gladsome and also firm, in the blending of diverse qualities. Keep silence among the aged ; to the elders give due honour. Honour the priests with diligence, as good stewards of the household. Give due honour to their degree, and search not out their doings. In his degree the priest is an angel, but in his doings a man. By mercy he is made a mediator, between God and mankind.

12. Search not out the faults of men ; reveal not the sin of thy fellow ; the shortcomings of thy neighbours, in speech of the mouth repeat not. Thou art not judge in

---

[1] Prov. iv. 23.

[2] Matt. x. 16.

creation, thou hast not dominion over the earth. If thou lovest righteousness, reprove thy soul and thyself. Be thou judge unto thine own sins, and chastener of thy own transgressions. Make thou not inquiry maliciously, into the misdeeds of men. For if thou doest this, injuries will not be lacking to thee. Trust not the hearing of the ear, for many are the deceivers. Vain reports believe thou not, for false rumours are not few.

13. Regard not spells and divinations, for that is communion with Satan. Love not idle prating, not even in behalf of righteousness. Discourse concerning thyself begin thou not, even in behalf of what is becoming. Flee and hide thyself from wrangling, as from a violent robber. See that thou be not a surety in a loan, lest thou sin. According as thou hast, assist him, (even) the man that is poorer than thou. Mock not the foolish man ; pray that thou be not even as he. Him that sins blame not, lest thou also be put to confusion. To him that repents of his sins be a helper and counsellor, and encourage him that is able to rise. Let him hold fast hope in God, and his sin shall be burned as stubble. Visit the sick and be not wearied, that thou mayest be beloved of men. Be familiar with the house of mourning, but a stranger to the house of feasting. Be not constant in drinking wine, lest thy shortcomings multiply. Cast a wall round thy lips, and set a guard upon thy mouth ; endure suffering with thy neighbour and share also in his tribulation. A good friend in tribulation is made known to him that loves him. In charity follow the deceased, with sorrow and with offerings, and pray that he may have rest in the hidden place whither he is going.

14. When thou standest in prayer, cry in thy soul : Have mercy on me, I am a sinner and weak ; be gracious, O God, to my weakness, and grant strength to me to pray a prayer that shall be pleasing to Thy Will. " Punish Thou not mine enemies, take not vengeance on them that hate me ; but grant them in Thy grace that they may become doers of Thy Will." At the time of prayer and petition, in contemplations such as these continue thou. Bow thy head before the Mighty One.

15. Do not thou resist evil, for he is evil from the Evil One, whoso resists evil.[1] Keep not back aught from any man, that if he perishes thou mayest not be blamed. Change not thy respect for a man's person, according to goods and possessions. Make all things as though they were not and God alone were in being. If thou shalt ask of thy neighbour and he shall not give thee according to thy wish, see that thou say not in anger a word that is full of bitterness. Oppose not thou [fit] seasons, for many are the changes. Put sorrow far from thy flesh,[2] and sadness from thy thoughts ; save only that for thy sins thou shouldst be constant in sadness. Cease not from labour, not even though thou be rich, for the slothful man gains manifold guilt by his idleness.

16. Be thou a lover of poverty, and be desirous of neediness. If thou hast them both for thy portion, thou art an inheritor on high. Despise not the voice of the poor and give him not cause to curse thee. For if he curse whose palate is bitter, the Lord will hear his petition. If his garments are foul, wash them in water, which freely is bought. Has a poor man entered into thy house? God has entered into thy house; God dwells within thy abode. He, whom thou hast refreshed from his troubles, from troubles will deliver thee. Hast thou washed the feet of the stranger? Thou hast washed away the filth of thy sins. Hast thou prepared a table before him? Behold God eating [at it], and Christ likewise drinking [at it], and the Holy Spirit resting [on it]. Is the poor satisfied at thy table and refreshed? Thou hast satisfied Christ thy Lord. He is ready to be thy rewarder; in presence of angels and men He will confess thou hast fed His hunger; He will give thanks unto thee that thou didst give Him drink, and quench His thirst.

---

[1] Matt. v. 39.          [2] Eccles. xi. 10.

17. O how gracious is the Lord ! O how measureless are His mercies ! Happy the race of mortals when God confesses it ! Woe to the soul which He denies ! Fire is stored up for its punishment. Be of good cheer, my son, in hope ; sow good [seed] [1] and faint not. The husbandman sows in hope, and the merchant journeys in hope, thou also lovest good [seed] ; in the hope look for the reward. Do not thou aught at all without the beginning of prayer. With the sign of the living cross, seal all thy doings, my son. Go not forth from the door of thy house till thou hast signed the cross. Whether in eating or in drinking, whether in sleeping or in waking, whether in thy house or on the road, or again in the season of leisure, neglect not this sign ; for there is no guardian like it. It shall be unto thee as a wall, in the forefront of all thy doings. And teach this to thy children, that heedfully they be conformed to it.

18. Yoke thyself under the law, that thou mayest be a freeman in very truth. Work not the desire of thy soul apart from the law of God. How many commandments must I write, and how many laws must I engrave ; which, if thou desirest thy freedom, thou canst learn all from thyself? And if thou lovest purity, thou wilt teach it to others also. Let nature be thy book, and all creation thy tables ; and learn from them the laws, and meditate things unwritten. The sun in his course teaches thee that thou rest from labour. The night in her silence cries to thee that a limit is set to thy works. The earth and the fruit of the tree cry that there is a season for all things. The seed thou sowest in the winter, in the summer thou gatherest its harvest. Thus in the world sow seeds of righteousness, and in the Resurrection gather them in. The bird in its daily gleaning reproves the covetous and his greed, and rebukes the extortion that grasps the store of others. Death, the limit of all things, is itself the reprover of all things.

19. Take thou refuge in God Who passes not away nor is changed. Restrain laughter by suffering, and mirthfulness by sorrow. Console suffering by hope, and sadness by expectation. Believe and trust, thou that art wise, for God is He Who guides thee ; and if His care leaves thee not, there is nothing that can harm thee. If one man by another man, the lowly by the great, can be saved, how much more shall the refuge of God preserve the man that believes? Fear not because of adversaries who with violence come upon thee. He will watchfully guard thy soul, and hurtful things become profitable. No one shall lead thee by compulsion, save only where there is freedom. No one falls into temptation, that passes the measure of his strength. There is no evil in chastisement, if so be that freedom is willing. The doings are not perverse of freedom, its will is perverted.

20. To men that are just and upright, temptations become helps. Job, a man of discernment, was victorious in temptations, Sickness came upon him, and he complained not ; disease afflicted him and he murmured not ; his body failed and his strength departed, but his will was not weakened. He proved perfect in all by sufferings, for as much as temptations crushed him not. Abraham was a stranger, from his place, his race [and his kindred]. But by this he was not harmed ; nay rather he triumphed greatly. So Joseph from the house of bondage was made to rule as king of Egypt. They of the company of Ananias and Daniel delivered others from bondage. See then, O thou that art wise, the power that freedom possesses ; that nothing can injure it unless the will is weakened. Israel with sumptuous living waxed fat, and kicked, [2] and forgot his covenant. He worshipped vain gods, and forgot the nature of his creation. The bondage that was in Egypt he forgat in the repose of the desert. As often as he was afflicted, he acknowledged the Lord alone ; but when he was dwelling in repose,

---

[1] Gal. vi. 9.

[2] Deut. xxxii. 15.

he forgot God his Redeemer. Seek thou not here repose, for this is a world of toil. And if thou canst wisely discern, change thou not time for time ; that which abides for that which abides not ; that which ceases not for that which ceases ; nor truth for lying ; nor body for shadow ; nor watching for slumber ; nor that which is in season for that which is out of season ; nor the Time for the times. Collect thy mind, let it not wander among varieties which profit not.

21. No one in creation is rich but he that fears God ; no one is truly poor but he that lacks the truth. How needy is he, and not rich, whose need witnesses against him, that even from the abject and the beggars he needs to receive a gift. He is truly a bondman, and many are his masters : he renders service to money, to riches, and possessions. His lords are void of mercy, for they grant him no repose. Flee, and live in poverty ; (as) a mother she pities her beloved. Seek thou refuge in indigence, who nourishes her children with choice things ; her yoke is light and pleasant, and sweet to the palate her memory. The sick in conscience alone abhors the draught of poverty ; the fainthearted dreads the yoke of indigence that is honourable. Who has granted to Thee, Son of man, in the world to find repose ? Who has granted to thee, thing of dust, to be rich amidst poverty ? Be not thou through desires needy and looking to others. Sufficient for thee is thy daily bread, that comes of the sweat of thy face. Let this be (the measure of) thy need, that which the day gives thee ; and if thou findest for thyself a feast, take of it that which thou needest. Thou shalt not take in a day (the provision) of days, for the belly keeps no treasure. Praise and give thanks when thou art satisfied, that therein thou provoke not the Giver to anger. In purity strengthen thyself, that thou mayest gain from it profit. In everything give thanks and praise unto God as the Redeemer, that He may grant thee by His grace, that we may hear and do His Will.

Thou to whom I have given the counsel of life, be not thou negligent in it. From that which is other men's (doctrine) have I written to thee ; see thou despise not their words. And if I depart before thee, in thy prayer make mention of me. In every season pray and beseech that our love may continue true. But as for us, on behalf of these things let us offer up praise and honour to Father, to Son, and to Holy Spirit, now and for ever. Amen.

## ON THE SINFUL WOMAN.

1. Hear and be comforted, beloved, how merciful is God. To the sinful woman He forgave her offences ; yea, He upheld her when she was afflicted. With clay He opened the eyes of the blind, so that the eyeballs beheld the light.[1] To the palsied He granted healing, who arose and walked and carried his bed.[2] And to us He has given the pearls ; His holy Body and Blood. He brought His medicines secretly ; and with them He heals openly. And He wandered round in the land of Judea, like a physician, bearing his medicines. Simon invited Him to the feast, to eat bread in his house.[3] The sinful woman rejoiced when she heard that He sat and was feasting in Simon's house ; her thoughts gathered together like the sea, and like the billows her love surged. She beheld the Sea of Grace, how it had forced itself into one place ; and she resolved to go and drown all her wickedness in its billows.

2. She bound her heart, because it had offended, with chains and tears of suffering ; and she began weeping (with herself) : "What avails me this fornication ? What avails this lewdness ? I have defiled the innocent ones without shame ; I have corrupted the orphan ; and without fear I have robbed the merchants of merchandise, and my rapacity was not satisfied. I have been as a bow in war, and have slain the good and the bad. I have been as a storm on the sea, and have sunk the ships of many. Why did I not win

---

[1] John ix. 6.  [2] Matt. ix. 2.  [3] Luke vii. 36.

me one man, who might have corrected my lewdness? For one man is of God, but many are of Satan."

3. These things she inwardly said; then began she to do outwardly. She washed and put away from her eyes the dye that blinded them that saw it. And tears gushed forth from her eyes over that deadly eye-paint.[1] She drew off and cast from her hands the enticing bracelets of her youth. She put off and cast away from her body the tunic of fine linen of whoredom, and resolved to go and attire herself in the tunic, the garment of reconciliation. She drew off and cast from her feet the adorned sandals of lewdness; and directed the steps of her going in the path of the heavenly Eagle. She took up her gold in her palm and held it up to the face of heaven, and began to cry secretly, to Him who hears openly: "This, O Lord, that I have gained from iniquity, with it will I purchase to myself redemption. This which was gathered from orphans, with it will I win the Lord of orphans."

4. These things she said secretly; then began to do openly. She took up the gold in her palm, and carried the alabaster box in her hands. Then hastily went she forth in sadness to the perfumer. The perfumer saw her and wondered, and fell into questioning with her; and thus he began to say to the harlot in the first words he spoke: "Was it not enough for thee, harlot, that thou hast corrupted all our town? What means this fashion that thou showest to-day to thy lovers—that thou hast put off thy wantonness and hast clothed thyself in modesty? Heretofore, when thou camest to me, thy aspect was different from to-day's. Thou wast clothed in goodly raiment, and didst bring little gold; and didst ask for precious ointment, to make thy lewdness pleasant. But lo! to-day thy vesture is mean, and thou hast brought much gold. Thy change I understand not; wherefore is this fashion of thine? Either

clothe thee in raiment according to thy ability, or buy ointment according to thy clothing. For this ointment becomes not or is suited to this attire. Can it be that a merchant has met thee, and brings great wealth; and thou hast seen that he loves it not, the fashion of thy lewdness? So thou hast put off thy lewdness and hast clothed thyself in meekness, that by various fashions thou mayest capture much wealth. But if he loves this fashion because he is a chaste man in truth, then woe to him! Into what has he fallen? Into a gulf that has swallowed up his merchandise. But I give thee advice, as a man that desires thy welfare, that thou send away thy many lovers who have helped thee nought from thy youth, and henceforth seek out one husband who may correct thy lewdness."

5. These things spake the perfumer, in wisdom, to the harlot. The sinful woman answered and said to him, to the perfumer after his discourse, "Hinder me not, O man, and stop me not by thy questioning. I have asked of thee ointment, not freely, but I will pay thee its value not grudgingly. Take thee the gold, as much as thou demandest, and give me the precious ointment; take thee that which endures not and give me that which endures; and I will go to Him who endures, and will buy that which endures. And as to that thou saidst, about a merchant; a Man has met me to-day Who bears riches in abundance. He has robbed me and I have robbed Him; He has robbed me of my transgressions and sins, and I have robbed Him of His wealth. And as to that thou saidst of a husband; I have won me a Husband in heaven, Whose dominion stands for ever, and His kingdom shall not be dissolved?" She took up the ointment and went forth.

6. In haste went she forth; as Satan saw her and was enraged; and was greatly grieved in his mind. At one time he rejoiced, and again at another he was grieved. That she carried the perfumed oil, he rejoiced in his inward mind; but that she was clad in mean raiment—at this doing of hers

---

[1] *Stibium.*

he was afraid. He clave then to her and followed her, as a robber follows a merchant. He listened to the murmurs of her lips, to hear the voice of her words. He closely watched her eyeballs (to mark) whither the glance of her eyes was directed; and as he went he moved by her feet (to mark) whither her goings were directed. Very full of craft is Satan, from our words to learn our aim. Therefore our Lord has taught us not to raise our voice when we pray, that the Devil may not hear our words and draw near and become our adversary. So then, when Satan saw that he could not change her mind, he clothed himself in the fashion of a man, and drew to himself a crowd of youths, like her lovers of former times; and then began he thus to address her: "By thy life, O woman, tell me, whither are thy footsteps directed? What means this haste? For thou hasteth more than other days. What means this thy meekness, for thy soul is meek like a handmaid's? Instead of garments of fine linen, lo! thou art clothed in sordid weeds; instead of bracelets of gold and silver, there are not even rings on thy fingers; instead of goodly sandals for thy feet, not even worn shoes are on thy feet. Disclose to me all thy doing, for I understand not thy change. Is it that some one of thy lovers has died, and thou goest to bury him? We will go with thee to the funeral, and with thee will (take part with thee) in sorrow."

7. The sinful woman answered and said to him, (even) to Satan, after his speech: "Well hast thou said that I go to inter the dead, one that has died to me. The sin of my thoughts has died, and I go to bury it." Satan answered and said to her, (even) to the sinful woman after her words: "Go to, O woman, I tell thee that I am the first of thy lovers. I am not such as thou, and I place my hands upon thee. I will give thee again more gold than before."

8. The sinful woman answered and said to him, even to Satan after his discourse: "I am wearied of thee, O man, and thou art no more my lover. I have won me a husband in heaven, Who is God, that is over all, and His dominion stands for ever, and His kingdom shall not be dissolved. For lo! in thy presence I say; I say it again and I lie not. I was a handmaid to Satan from my childhood unto this day. I was a bridge, and he trode upon me, and I destroyed thousands of men. The eyepaint blinded my eyes, and (I was) blind among many whom I blinded. I became sightless and knew not that there is One Who gives light to the sightless. Lo! I go to get light for mine eyes, and by that light to give light to many. I was fast bound, and knew not that there is One Who overthrows idols. Lo! I go to have my idols destroyed, and so to destroy the follies of many. I was wounded and knew not that there is One Who binds up wounds; and lo! I go to have my wounds bound." These things the harlot spake to Satan in her wisdom; and he groaned and was grieved and wept; and he cried aloud and thus he spake:—"I am conquered by thee, O woman, and what I shall do I know not."

9. As soon as Satan perceived that he could not change her mind, he began to weep for himself and thus it was that he spake: "Henceforth is my boasting perished, and the pride of all my days. How shall I lay for her a snare, for her who is ascending on high? how shall I shoot arrows at her, (even) at her whose wall is unshaken? Therefore I go into Jesus' presence; lo! she is about to enter His presence; and I shall say to Him thus: "This woman is an harlot." Perchance He may reject and not receive her. And I shall say to Him thus: "This woman who comes into Thy presence is a woman that is an harlot. She has led captive men by her whoredom; she is polluted from her youth. But Thou, O Lord, art righteous; all men throng to see Thee. And if mankind see Thee that Thou hast speech with the harlot, they all will flee from Thy presence, and no man will salute Thee."

10. These things Satan spake within him-

self, nor was he moved.[1] Then he changed the course of his thought, and thus it was that he spake. "How shall I enter into Jesus' presence, for to Him the secret things are manifest? He knows me, who I am, that no good office is my purpose. If haply He rebuke me I am undone, and all my wiles will be wasted. I will go to the house of Simon, for secret things are not manifest to him. And into his heart I will put it; perchance on that hook he may be caught. And thus will I say unto him: By thy life, O Simon, tell me; this man that sojourns in thy house is he a man that is righteous, or a friend of the doers of wickedness? I am a wealthy man, and a man that has possessions, and I wish like thee to invite him that he may come in and bless my possessions."

11. Simon answered and thus he said to the Evil One after his words: "From the day that (first) I saw Him I have seen no lewdness in Him, but rather quietness and peace, humility and seemliness. The sick He heals without reward, the diseased He freely cures. He approaches and stands by the grave, and calls, and the dead arise. Jairus[2] called Him to raise his daughter to life, trusting that He could raise her to life. And as He went with him in the way, He gave healing to the woman diseased, who laid hold of the hem of His garment and stole healing from Him, and her pain which was hard and bitter at once departed from her. He went forth to the desert and saw the hungry,[3] how they were fainting with famine. He made them sit down on the grass, and fed them in His mercy. In the ship He slept[4] as He willed, and the sea swelled against the disciples. He arose and rebuked the billows, and there was a great calm. The widow,[5] the desolate one who was following her only son, on the way to the grave He consoled her. He gave him to her and gladdened her heart.

To one man who was dumb and blind,[6] by His voice He brought healing. The lepers He cleansed by His word; to the limbs of the palsied[7] He restored strength. For the blind man,[8] afflicted and weary, He opened his eyes and he saw the light. And for two others who besought Him,[9] at once He opened their eyes. As for me, thus have I heard the fame of the man from afar; and I called Him to bless my possessions, and to bless all my flocks and herds."

12. Satan answered and said to him, to Simon after his words: "Praise not a man at his beginning, until thou learnest his end; hitherto this man is sober and his soul takes not pleasure in wine. If he shall go forth from thy house, and holds not converse with an harlot, then he is a righteous man and no friend of them that do wickedness." Such things did Satan speak in his craftiness to Simon. Then he approached and stood afar off, to see what should come to pass.

13. The sinful woman full of transgressions stood clinging by the door. She clasped her arms in prayer, and thus she spake beseeching :—"Blessed Son Who hast descended to earth for the sake of man's redemption, close not Thy door in my face; for Thou hast called me and lo! I come. I know that Thou hast not rejected me; open for me the door of Thy mercy, that I may come in, O my Lord, and find refuge in Thee, from the Evil One and his hosts! I was a sparrow, and the hawk pursued me, and I have fled and taken refuge in Thy nest. I was a heifer, and the yoke galled me, and I will turn back my wanderings to Thee. Lay upon me the shoulder of Thy yoke that I may take it on me, and work with Thy oxen." Thus did the harlot speak at the door with much weeping. The master of the house looked and saw her, and the colour of his visage was changed; and he began thus to address her, (even) the harlot, in the opening of his words :—"Depart thou

<hr>

[1] The text and rendering of these two places are doubtful.
[2] St. Mark v. 22.   [3] St. Matt. xiv. 15.
[4] St. Matt. xiv. 24.   [5] St. Luke vii. 11.

[6] St. Matt. xii. 22.   [7] St. Matt. ix. 2.
[8] St. John ix. 1.   [9] St. Matt. xx. 30.

hence, O harlot, for this man who abides in our house is a man that is righteous, and they that are of his companions are blameless. Is it not enough for thee, harlot, that thou hast corrupted the whole town? Thou hast corrupted the chaste without shame; thou hast robbed the orphans, and hast not blushed, and hast plundered the merchants' wares, and thy countenance is not abashed. From him thy heart [and soul] labour [to take]. But from him thy net takes no spoil.[1] For this man is righteous indeed, and they of his company are blameless."

14. The sinful woman answered and said to him, even to Simon when he had ceased: "Thou surely art the guardian of the door, O thou that knowest things that are secret! I will propose the matter in the feast, and thou shalt be free from blame. And if there be any that wills me to come in, he will bid me and I will come in." Simon ran and closed the door, and approached and stood afar off. And he tarried a long time and proposed not the matter in the feast. But He, Who knows what is secret, beckoned to Simon and said to him:—"Come hither, Simon, I bid thee; does any one stand at the door? Whosoever he be, open to him that he may come in; let him receive what he needs, and go. If he be hungry and hunger for bread, lo! in thy house is the table of life; and if he be thirsty, and thirst for water, lo! the blessed fountain is in thy dwelling. And if he be sick and ask for healing, lo! the great Physician is in thy house. Suffer sinners to look upon Me, for for their sakes have I abased Myself. I will not ascend to heaven, to the dwelling whence I came down, until I bear back the sheep that has wandered from its Father's house, and lift it up on My shoulders and bear it aloft to heaven." Simon answered and thus he said to Jesus, when He had done speaking:—"My Lord, this woman that stands in the doorway is a harlot: she is lewd and not free-born, polluted from her childhood. And Thou, my Lord, art a

righteous man, and all are eager to see Thee; and if men see Thee having speech with the harlot, all men will flee from beside Thee, and no man will salute Thee." Jesus answered, and thus He said to Simon when he was done speaking:—"Whosoever it be, open for him to come in, and thou shalt be free from blame; and though his offences be many, without rebuke I bid thee [receive him]."

\* \* \* \* \* \* \*

15. Simon approached and opened the door, and began thus to speak:—"Come, enter, fulfil that thou willest, to him who is even as thou." The sinful woman, full of transgressions, passed forward and stood by His feet, and clasped her arms in prayer, and with these words she spake:—"Mine eyes have become watercourses that cease not from [watering] the fields, and to-day they wash the feet of Him Who follows after sinners. This hair, abundant in locks from my childhood till this day, let it not grieve Thee that it should wipe this holy body. The mouth that has kissed the lewd, forbid it not to kiss the body that remits transgressions and sins." These things the harlot spake to Jesus, with much weeping. And Simon stood afar off to see what He would do to her. But He Who knows the things that are secret, beckoned to Simon and said to him:—"Lo! I will tell thee, O Simon, what thy meditation is, concerning the harlot. Within thy mind thou imaginest and within thy soul thou saidst, 'I have called this man righteous, but lo! the harlot kisses Him. I have called Him to bless my possessions, and lo! the harlot embraces Him.' O Simon, there were two debtors, whose creditor was one only; one owed him five-hundred [pence], and the other owed fifty. And when the creditor saw that neither of these two had aught, the creditor pardoned and forgave them both their debt. Which of them ought to render the greater thanks? He who was forgiven five hundred, or he who was forgiven fifty?" Simon answered, and thus he said to Jesus, when He had

---

[1] Text defective here.

done speaking :—"He who was forgiven five hundred ought to render the greater thanks." Jesus answered and thus He said : "Thou art he that owes five hundred, and this woman owes fifty. Lo! I came into thy house, O Simon ; and water for My feet thou broughtest not ; and this woman, of whom thou saidst that she was an harlot, one from her childhood defiled, has washed My feet with her tears, and with her hair she has wiped them. Ought I to send her away, O Simon, without receiving forgive-ness? Verily, verily, I say unto thee, I will write of her in the Gospel. Go, O woman, thy sins are forgiven thee and all thy transgression is covered ; henceforth and to the end of the world."

May our Lord account us worthy of hearing this word of His :—"Come, enter, ye blessed of My Father, inherit the kingdom made ready for all who shall do My will, and observe all My commandments." To Him be glory ; on us be mercy ; at all times. Amen ! Amen !

# APHRAHAT

## SELECT DEMONSTRATIONS.

# APHRAHAT

## LETTER OF AN INQUIRER.

1. Beloved, I send thee inquiries and questions, for I am compelled to seek further instruction of thee on many points. Do not thou refuse to hear me. My spirit urges me to warn thee about many topics[1] that thou mayest unfold for me the spiritual perceptions of thy mind, and mayest show me of all that thou hast apprehended from the holy books, that so my deficiency may be supplied by thee and my hunger satisfied by thy doctrine, and that thou mayest assuage my thirst from the fountain of thine instruction. Yet though many things are set in my thought to ask thee, they all are notwithstanding reserved with me, that when I come to thee, thou mayest instruct me on all subjects.

2. But before all things I desire that thou wouldst write and instruct me concerning this that straitens me, namely, concerning our faith; how it is, and what its foundation is, and on what structure it rises, on what it rests, and in what way is its fulfilment and consummation, and what are the works required for it. For I of myself firmly believe that God is one, Who made the heavens and the earth from the beginning; that He adorned the world by His handiwork; that He made man in His image; He it is that accepted the offering of Abel. He translated Enoch because of his excellence. He preserved Noah because of his righteousness. He chose Abraham because of his faith. He spake with Moses on account of his meekness. He it is that spake in all the prophets, and furthermore He sent His Christ

into the world. Since then, my brother, I thus believe in these things that so they are, I therefore, brother, request of thee that thou wouldest write and show me what are the works required for this our faith, that so thou mayest set me at rest..

## THE "DEMONSTRATIONS" OF APHRAHAT.

### *Demonstration I.*—OF FAITH.

§ 1. I have received thy letter, my beloved, and when I read it, it greatly gladdened me that thou hast turned thy thoughts to these investigations. For this thing that thou hast asked of me shall be freely granted,[2] for freely it was received. And whosoever has, and desires to withhold from him that seeks, whatsoever he withholds shall be taken away from him. Whoever of free grace receives, of free grace also does it behove him to give. And so, my beloved, as to that which thou hast asked of me, so far as my insignificance has apprehended, I will write to thee. And also whatsoever thou hast not sought of me, invoking God, I will explain to thee. Hear then, my beloved, and open the inward ears of thy heart unto me, and the spiritual perceptions of thy mind to that which I say unto thee.

§ 2. Faith is compounded of many things, and by many kinds is it brought to perfection. For it is like a building that is built up of many pieces of workmanship and so its edifice rises to the top. And know, my beloved, that in the foundations of the building stones are laid, and so resting upon stones the whole edifice rises until it is perfected. Thus also the true Stone, our Lord

---

[1] The beginning to this point is lost in the Syriac but has been preserved in the Armenian translation. We have borrowed it thence through the Latin translation of Graffin (*Patrologia Syriaca*, Tom. I.).

[2] S. Matt. x. 8.

345

Jesus Christ, is the foundation of all our faith. And on Him, on [this] Stone faith is based. And resting on faith all the structure rises until it is completed. For it is the foundation that is the beginning of all the building. For when any one is brought nigh unto faith, it is laid for him upon the Stone, that is our Lord Jesus Christ. And his building cannot be shaken by the waves, nor can it be injured by the winds. By the stormy blasts it does not fall, because its structure is reared upon the rock of the true Stone. And in this that I have called Christ the Stone, I have not spoken of my own thought, but the Prophets beforehand called Him the Stone. And this I shall make clear to thee.

§ 3. And now hear concerning faith that is based upon the Stone, and concerning the structure that is reared up upon the Stone. For first a man believes, and when he believes, he loves. When he loves, he hopes. When he hopes, he is justified. When he is justified, he is perfected. When he is perfected, he is consummated. And when his whole structure is raised up, consummated, and perfected, then he becomes a house and a temple for a dwelling-place of Christ, as Jeremiah the Prophet said :— *The temple of the Lord, the temple of the Lord, the temple of the Lord are ye, if ye amend your ways and your works.*[1] And again He said through the Prophet :—*I will dwell in them and walk in them.*[2] And also the Blessed Apostle thus said :—*Ye are the temple of God and the spirit of Christ dwelleth in you.*[3] And also our Lord again thus said to His disciples :—*Ye are in Me and I am in you.*[4]

§ 4. And when the house has become a dwelling-place, then the man begins to be anxious as to that which is required for Him Who dwells in the building. Just as if a king or an honourable man, to whom a royal name is given, should lodge in the house, there would be required for the King all the appurtenances of royalty and all the

service that is needed for the King's honour. For in a house that is void of all good things, the King will not lodge, nor will he dwell in the midst of it; but all that is choicest in the house is required for the King and that nothing in it be deficient. And if anything be deficient there in the house in which the King lodges, the keeper of the house is delivered over to death, because he did not make ready the service for the King. So also let the man, who becomes a house, yea a dwelling-place, for Christ, take heed to what is needed for the service of Christ, Who lodges in him, and with what things he may please Him. For first he builds his building on the Stone, which is Christ. On Him, on the Stone, is faith based, and on faith is reared up all the structure. For the habitation of the house is required pure fasting, and it is made firm by faith. There is also needed for it pure prayer, and through faith is it accepted. Necessary for it too is love, and with faith is it compounded. Furthermore alms are needed, and through faith are they given. He demands also meekness, and by faith is it adorned. He chooses too virginity, and by faith is it loved. He joins with himself holiness, and in faith is it planted. He cares also for wisdom, and through faith is it acquired. He desires also hospitality, and by faith does it abound. Requisite for Him also is simplicity, and with faith is it commingled. He demands patience also, and by faith is it perfected. He has respect also to long-suffering, and through faith is it acquired. He loves mourning also, and through faith is it manifested. He seeks also for purity, and by faith is it preserved. All these things does the faith demand that is based on the rock of the true Stone, that is Christ. These works are required for Christ the King, Who dwells in men that are built up in these works.

§ 5. And if perchance thou shouldest say : —If Christ is set for the foundation, how does Christ also dwell in the building when it is completed? For both these things did the blessed Apostle say. For he said :—*I*

---

[1] Jer. vii. 4 5.                [2] Levit. xxvi. 12.
[3] I. Cor. iii. 16, etc.         [4] John, xiv. 20.

as a wise architect have laid the foundation.[1] And there he defined the foundation and made it clear, for he said as follows :—*No man can lay other foundation than that which is laid, which is Jesus Christ.*[2] And that Christ furthermore dwells in that building is the word that was written above—that of Jeremiah who called men temples and said of God that He dwelt in them. And the Apostle said :—*The Spirit of Christ dwelleth in you.*[3] And our Lord said :—*I and My Father are one.*[4] And therefore that word is accomplished, that Christ dwells in men, namely, in those who believe on Him, and He is the foundation on which is reared up the whole building.

6. But I must proceed to my former statement that Christ is called the Stone in the Prophets. For in ancient times David said concerning Him :—*The stone which the builders rejected has become the head of the building.*[5] And how did the builders reject this Stone which is Christ? How else than that they so rejected Him before Pilate and said : —*This man shall not be King over us.*[6] And again in that parable that our Lord spake that a certain nobleman went to receive kingly power and to return and rule over them ; and they sent after Him envoys saying :—*This man shall not be King over us.*[7] By these things they rejected the Stone which is Christ. And how did it become the head of the building? How else than that it was set up over the building of the Gentiles and upon it is reared up all their building. And who are the builders? Who but the priests and Pharisees who did not build a sure building, but were overthrowing everything that he was building, as is written in Ezekiel the Prophet :—*He was building a wall of partition, but they were shaking it, that it might fall.*[9] And again it is written :—*I sought amongst them a man who was closing the fence and standing in the breach over the face of the land, that I might not destroy it and I did not find.*[1]

And furthermore Isaiah also prophesied beforehand with regard to this stone. For he said :—*Thus saith the Lord, Behold I lay in Zion a chosen stone in the precious corner, the head of the wall of the foundation.*[2] And he said again there :—*Every one that believeth on it shall not fear.*[3] And *whosoever falleth on that stone shall be broken, and every one on whom it shall fall, it will crush.*[4] For the people of the house of Israel fell upon Him, and He became their destruction for ever. And again *it shall fall on the image and crush it.*[5] And the Gentiles believed on it and do not fear.

7. And He shows thus with regard to that stone that it was laid as head of the wall and as foundation. But if that stone was laid as the foundation, how did it also become the head of the wall? How but that when our Lord came, He laid His faith in the earth like a foundation, and it rose above all the heavens like the head of the wall and all the building was finished with the stones, from the bottom to the top. And with regard to the faith about which I said that He laid His faith in the earth, this David proclaimed beforehand about Christ. For He said :—*Faith shall spring up from the earth.*[6] And that again, it is above, he said:— *Righteousness looked down from the heavens.*

8. And again Daniel also spoke concerning this stone which is Christ. For he said : —*The stone was cut out from the mountain, not by hands, and it smote the image, and the whole earth was filled with it.*[7] This he showed beforehand with regard to Christ that the whole earth shall be filled with Him. For lo ! by the faith of Christ are all the ends of the earth filled, as David said :—*The sound of the Gospel of Christ has gone forth into all the earth.*[8] And again when He sent forth His apostles He spake thus to them :—*Go forth, make disciples of all nations and they will believe on Me.*[9] And again the Prophet Zechariah also prophesied about that stone

---

[1] 1 Cor. iii. 10.  [2] 1 Cor. iii. 11.
[3] 1 Cor. iii. 16.  [4] John x. 30.
[5] Ps. cxviii. 22.  [6] Luke xix. 14.
[7] John xix. 15.  [8] Luke xix. 13, 14.
[9] Ez. xiii. 10.  [1] Ez. xxii. 30.

[2] Is. xxviii. 16.  [3] Is. xxviii. 16.
[4] Matt. xxi. 44.  [5] Dan. ii. 34.
[6] Ps. lxxxv. 12.  [7] Dan. ii. 34, 35.
[8] Ps. xix. 4.  [9] Matt. xxviii. 19.

which is Christ. For he said :—*I saw a chief stone of equality and of love.*[1] And why did he say "*chief*"? Surely because from the beginning[2] He was with His Father. And again that he spake of love, it was because when He came into the world, He said thus to His disciples :—*This is My commandment, that ye love one another.*[3] And again He said :—*I have called you My friends* (lovers).[4] And the blessed Apostle said thus :—*God loved as in the love of His Son.*[5] Of a truth Christ loved us and gave Himself for us.[6]

§ 9. And definitely did He show concerning this stone :—*Lo! on this stone will I open seven eyes.*[7] And what then are the seven eyes that were opened on the stone? Clearly the Spirit of God that abode on Christ with seven operations, as Isaiah the Prophet said :—*The Spirit of God shall rest and dwell upon Him,* (a spirit) *of wisdom and understanding, of counsel and of courage, of knowledge and of the fear of the Lord.*[8] These were the seven eyes that were opened upon the Stone, and *these are the seven eyes of the Lord which look upon all the earth.*[9]

§ 10. And also with reference to Christ was this (which follows) said. For he said that He was given as a light to all the Gentiles as the Prophet Isaiah said :—*I have given Thee as a light to all the Gentiles, that Thou shouldest be My redemption to the ends of the earth.*[1] And furthermore David also said ;—*Thy word is a lamp unto my feet and a light unto my paths.*[2] And also the word and discourse of the Lord is Christ, as is written in the beginning of the Gospel of our Saviour :—*In the beginning was the Word.*[3] And with regard to the light there again he bore witness :—*The light was shining in the darkness and the darkness comprehended it not.*[4] What then is this :—*The light was shining in the darkness and the darkness comprehended it*

not? Clearly Christ, Whose light shone in the midst of the people of the house of Israel, and the people of the house of Israel did not comprehend the light of Christ, in that they did not believe on Him, as it is written :—*He came unto His own, and His own received Him not.*[5] And also our Lord Jesus called them *darkness,* for He said to His disciples ;—*Whatsoever I say unto you in the darkness, that speak ye in the light,*[6] namely, *let your light shine among the Gentiles ;*[7] because they received the light of Christ, Who is the Light of the Gentiles. And He said again to His Apostles:—*Ye are the light of the world.*[8] And again He said unto them ;—*Let your light shine before men, that they may see your good works and glorify your Father which is in heaven.*[9] And again He showed with regard to Himself that He is the light, for He said to His disciples :—*Walk while the light is with you, ere the darkness overtake you.*[1] And again He said to them :—*Believe on the light that ye may be children of light.*[2] And again He said :—*I am the light of the world.*[3] And again He said :—*No man lighteth a lamp and putteth it under a bushel or under a bed, or putteth it in a hidden place, but putteth it upon the lampstand that every one may see the light of the lamp.*[4] And the shining lamp is Christ, as David said ;—*Thy word is a lamp unto my feet and a light to my paths.*[5]

§ 11. And furthermore the Prophet Hosea also said :—*Light you a lamp and seek ye the Lord.*[6] And our Lord Jesus Christ said :—*What woman is there who has ten drachmos and shall lose one of them, and will not light a lamp and sweep the house and seek her drachma that she lost?*[7] What then does this woman signify? Clearly the congregation of the house of Israel, to which the ten commandments were given. They lost the first commandment—that in which He warned

---

[1] Zach. iv. 2.
[2] The words for *chief* and for *beginning* are almost identical in the Syriac.
[3] John xv. 12.     [4] John xv. 15.
[5] Cf. Eph. ii. 4. 5.     [6] Cf. Eph. v. 2.
[7] Zech. iii. 9.     [8] Is. xi. 1, 2.
[9] Zech. iv. 10.     [1] Is. xlix. 6.
[2] Ps. cxix. 105.     [3] John i. 1.
[4] John i. 5.

[5] John i. 11.     [6] Matt. x. 27.
[7] Cf. Matt. v. 16.     [8] Matt. v. 14.
[9] Matt. v. 16.     [1] John xii. 35.
[2] John xii. 36.     [3] John viii. 12.
[4] Matt. v. 15 ; Mark iv. 21 ; Luke viii. 16.
[5] Ps. cxix. 105.     [6] Hos. x. 12.
[7] Luke xv. 8.

them saying :—*I am the Lord your God, Who brought you up from the land of Egypt.*[1] And when they had lost this first commandment, also the nine which are after it they could not keep, because on the first depend the nine. For it was an impossibility that while worshipping Baal, they should keep the nine commandments. For they lost the first commandment, like that woman who lost one drachma from the ten. So the Prophet cried unto them :—*Light you a lamp and seek ye the Lord.*[2] And furthermore the Prophet Isaiah also said :—*Seek ye the Lord, and when ye shall have found Him, call upon Him ; and when He is near let the sinner abandon his way and the wicked man his thought.*[3] For that lamp shone and they did not by it seek the Lord their God. And its light shone in the darkness and the darkness did not comprehend it. And the lamp was set up on the lamp-stand and those who were in the house did not see its light. And what then means this, that the lamp was set up on the lamp-stand? Clearly His being raised up upon the cross. And by this all the house was made dark over them. For when they crucified Him, the light was darkened from them, and shone amongst the Gentiles, because that from the time of the sixth hour (of the day) on which they crucified Him even unto the ninth hour there was darkness in all the land of Israel. And the sun set in midday and the land was darkened in the shining daytime, as is written in Zechariah the Prophet :—*It shall come to pass in that day, saith the Lord, I will cause the sun to set in midday, and will make dark the land in the shining daytime.*[5]

§ 12. Now I must proceed to my former subject of faith, that on it are reared up all the good works of the building. And again, in what I said with regard to the building, it was in no strange fashion that I spoke, but the blessed Apostle wrote in the first Epistle to the Corinthians, saying :—*I as a wise master-builder have laid the foundation, but* *every one buildeth on it.*[5] One builds silver and gold and goodly stones ; another builds reed and straw and stubble. In the last day that building shall be tried by fire ; for the gold and silver and goodly stones shall be preserved in the midst of the fire, because they are a firm building. But as for the straw and reed and stubble, the fire shall have power upon them and they shall be burned. And what is the gold and silver and goodly stones by which the building is raised up? Clearly the good deeds of faith, which shall be preserved in the midst of the fire ; because Christ dwells in that secure building, and He is its preserver from the fire. And let us consider and understand (this) from the example that God has given us also in the former dispensation, because the promises of that dispensation will abide sure for us. Let us then understand from (the case of) those three righteous men who were cast into the midst of the fire and were not burned, namely, Hananiah, Azariah and Misael, over whom the fire had no power, because they built a secure building and rejected the commandment of Nebuchadnezzar the king and did not worship the image that he made. And as for those who transgressed the commandment of God, the fire at once prevailed over them and burned them, and they were burned without mercy. For the Sodomites were burned like straw and reed and stubble. Furthermore, Nadab and Abihu were burned, who transgressed the commandment of God. Again, two hundred and fifty men were burned, who were offering incense. Again, two princes and a hundred who were with them were burned, because they approached the mountain on which Elijah was sitting, who ascended in a chariot of fire to heaven. The calumniators also were burned because they dug a pit for righteous men. Accordingly, beloved, the righteous shall be tried by the fire, like gold and silver and goodly stones, and the wicked shall be burned in the fire like straw and reed and stubble, and the fire shall have power upon them and they shall

---

[1] Ex. xx. 2.  [2] Hos. x. 12.
[3] Is. lv. 6, 7.
[4] Am. viii. 9. (Cf. the commentary ascribed to Ephrem in loco.) Cf. Zech. xiv. 6, 7.

[5] I Cor. iii 10, 12, sqq.

be burned ; even as the Prophet Isaiah said : —*By fire shall the Lord judge and by it shall He try all flesh.*[1] And again he said :—*Ye shall go out and see the carcases of the men who offended against Me, whose worm shall not die, nor shall their fire be quenched, and they shall be an astonishment to all flesh.*[2]

§ 13. And again the Apostle has commented for us upon this building and upon this foundation ; for he said thus ;—*No man can lay another foundation than that which is laid, which is Jesus Christ.*[3] Again the Apostle said about faith that it is conjoined with hope and love, for he said thus :—*These are three which shall abide, faith and hope and love.*[4] And he showed with regard to faith that first it is laid on a sure foundation.[5]

§ 14. For Abel, because of his faith his offering was accepted. And Enoch, because he was well-pleasing through his faith, was removed from death. Noah, because he believed, was preserved from the deluge. Abraham, through his faith, obtained blessing, and it was accounted to him for righteousness. Isaac, because he believed, was loved. Jacob, because of his faith, was preserved. Joseph, because of his faith, was tried in the waters of contention, and was delivered from his trial, and his Lord established a witness in him, as David said :—*Witness hath he established in Joseph.*" Moses also by his faith performed many wonderful works of power. By his faith he destroyed the Egyptians with ten plagues. Again, by faith he divided the sea, and caused his people to cross over and sank the Egyptians in the midst of it. By faith he cast the wood into the bitter waters and they became sweet. By faith he brought down manna and satisfied his people. By faith he spread out his hands and conquered Amalek, as is written :—*His hands continued*

*in faith till the setting of the sun.*[7] Also by faith he went up to Mount Sinai, when he twice fasted for the space of forty days. Again by faith he conquered Sihon and Og, the Kings of the Amorites.

§ 15. This is wonderful, my beloved, and a great prodigy that Moses did in the Red Sea, when the waters were divided by faith, and stood up on high like mountains or like mighty cliffs. They were checked and stood still at the commandment ; they were closed up as in vessels, and fast bound in the height as in the depth. Their fluidity did not overflow the boundary, but rather they changed the nature of their creation. Irrational creatures became obedient. The billows became rigid and were awaiting the vengeance, when the people should have passed over. Wonderful was it how the waves stood still and expected the commandment and the vengeance. The foundations (hidden) from the ages of the world were revealed, and that which from the beginning had been liquid suddenly became dry. *The gates lifted up their heads and the everlasting gates were lifted up.*[8] The pillar of fire entered and illuminated the entire camp. The people passed over by faith. And the judgment of righteousness was wrought upon Pharaoh and upon his host and upon his chariots.

§ 16. Thus also Joshua the son of Nun divided Jordan by his faith, and the children of Israel crossed over as in the days of Moses. But know, my beloved, that this passage of the Jordan was three times laid open by its being divided. First through Joshua the Son of Nun, and secondly through Elijah, and then through Elisha. For the word of the Book makes known that over against this passage of Jericho, there Elijah was taken up to heaven ; for when Elisha turned back from following him and divided the Jordan and passed over, the children of the Prophets of Jericho came out to meet Elisha and said :—*The spirit of Elijah rests upon Elisha.*[9] Furthermore when

---

[1] Is. lxvi. 16.					[2] Is. lxvi. 24.
[3] 1 Cor. iii. 11.					[4] 1 Cor. xiii. 13
[5] The allusion is to Heb. xi.
This sentence, connecting sections 13 (which relates to 1 Corinthians iii. and xiii.) and 14 (which echoes Hebrews xi.), seems to imply ( " *he showed* " ) that they are written by the same author,—in other words, to ascribe Hebrews to St. Paul.
[6] Ps. lxxxi. 6.

[7] Ex. xvii. 12. (Pesh.)		[8] Ps. xxiv. 7, 9		[9] 2 K. ii. 8-15.

the people crossed over in the days of Joshua the son of Nun (it was there), for thus it is written :— *The people passed over, over against Jericho.*[1] Also Joshua the son of Nun by faith cast down the walls of Jericho, and they fell without difficulty. Again by faith he destroyed thirty-one kings and made the children of Israel to inherit the land. Furthermore by his faith he spread out his hands towards heaven and stayed the sun in Gibeon and the moon in the valley of Ajalon.[2] And they were stayed and stood still from their courses. But enough ! All the righteous, our fathers, in all that they did were victorious through faith, as also the blessed Apostle testified with regard to all of them :—*By faith they prevailed.*[3] Again Solomon said:—*Many men are called merciful, but a faithful man who can find ?*[4] Also Job thus said :—*My integrity shall not pass from me, and in my righteousness will I persist.*[5]

§ 17. Also our Saviour used thus to say to every one who drew near to Him to be healed :—*According to thy faith be it unto thee.*[6] And when the blind man approached Him, He said to him :—*Dost thou believe that I am able to heal thee ?* That blind man said to Him :—*Yea, Lord, I believe.*[7] And his faith opened his eyes. And to him whose son was sick, He said :—*Believe and thy son shall live.* He said to Him :—*I believe, Lord ; help thou my feeble faith.*[8] And by his faith his son was healed. And also when the nobleman[9] came near to Him, by his faith was his boy healed, when he said to our Lord :—*Speak the word and my servant will be cured.*[1] And our Lord was astonished at his faith, and according to his faith it happened to him. And also when the chief of the Synagogue requested Him concerning his daughter, He said thus to him :—*Only firmly believe and thy daughter shall live.*[2] So he believed and his daughter lived and arose.

And when Lazarus died, our Lord said to Martha :—*If thou believest, thy brother shall rise.* Martha saith unto Him ;—*Yea, Lord, I believe.*[3] And He raised him after four days. And also Simon who was called Cephas because of his faith was called the firm rock.[4] And again when our Lord gave the Sacrament of Baptism to His apostles, He said thus to them :—*Whosoever believeth and is baptized shall live, and whosoever believeth not shall be condemned.*[5] Again He said to his Apostles :—*If ye believe and doubt not, there is nothing ye shall not be able to do.*[6] For when our Lord walked on the billows of the sea, Simon also by his faith walked with Him ; but when in respect of his faith he doubted, and began to sink, our Lord called him, *thou of little faith.*[7] And when the Apostles asked of our Lord, they begged nothing at His hands but this, saying to Him :—*Increase our faith.* He said to them :—*If there were in you faith, even a mountain would remove from before you.*[8] And He said to them :—*Doubt ye not, lest ye sink down in the midst of the world, even as Simon when he doubted began to sink in the midst of the sea.*[9] And again He said thus ;—*This shall be the sign for those that believe ; they shall speak with new tongues and shall cast out demons, and they shall lay their hands on the sick and they shall be made whole.*[1]

§ 18. Let us draw near then, my beloved, to faith, since its powers are so many. For faith raised up to the heavens (Enoch), and conquered the Deluge. It caused the barren to bring forth. It delivered from the sword. It raised up from the pit. It enriched the poor. It released the captives. It delivered the persecuted. It brought down the fire. It divided the sea. It cleft the rock, and gave to the thirsty water to drink. It satisfied the hungry. It raised the dead, and brought them up from Sheol. It stilled the billows. It healed the sick. It conquered

---

[1] Jos. iii. 17.  [2] Jos. x. 13.
[3] Heb. xi. 33.  [4] Prov. xx. 6.
[5] Job. xxvii. 5, 6.  [6] e. q. Matt. ix. 29.
[7] Matt. ix. 28.  [8] Mark ix. 22, 26.
[9] Lit. "king's servant," John iv. 46, which is here confused with Matt. viii. 8.
[1] Matt. viii. 8, 10.  [2] Mark v. 23-36.

[3] John xi. 23–27.  [4] Kipha-rock.
[5] Mark xvi. 16. Note that Aphrahat here cites the disputed conclusion of St. Mark's Gospel.
[6] Matt. xxi. 22.  [7] Matt. xiv. 31.
[8] Luke xvii. 5, and Matt. xvii. 19,; xxi. 21.
[9] (Apocryphal.)  [1] Mark xvi. 17, 18.

hosts. It overthrew walls. It stopped the mouths of lions, and quenched the flame of fire. It humiliated the proud, and brought the humble to honour. All these mighty works were wrought by faith.

§ 19. Now thus is faith; when a man believes in God the Lord of all, Who made the heavens and the earth and the seas and all that is in them; and He made Adam in His image; and He gave the Law to Moses; He sent of His Spirit upon the prophets; He sent moreover His Christ into the world. Furthermore that a man should believe in the resurrection of the dead; and should furthermore also believe in the sacrament of baptism. This is the faith of the Church of God. And (it is necessary)˙ that a man should separate himself from the observance of hours and Sabbaths and moons and seasons, and divinations and sorceries and Chaldæan arts and magic, from fornication and from festive music, from vain doctrines, which are instruments of the Evil One, from the blandishment of honeyed words, from blasphemy and from adultery. And that a man should not bear false witness, and that a man should not speak with double tongue. These then are the works of the faith which is based on the true Stone which is Christ, on Whom the whole building is reared up.

§ 20. Furthermore, my beloved, there is much besides in the Holy Books about faith. But these few things out of the much have I written to recall them to thy love that thou mayest know and make known and believe and also be believed. And when thou hast read and learned the works of faith, thou mayest be made like unto that tilled land upon which the good seed fell, and produced fruit a hundred-fold and sixty-fold and thirty-fold. And when thou comest to thy Lord, He may call thee a good servant and prudent and faithful, who on account of His faith, that abounded, is to enter into the Kingdom of his Lord.

*Demonstration V.*—OF WARS.

§ 1. This reflection has befallen me at this time concerning the shaking that is to take place at this time, and the host that has assembled itself for the sword. The times were disposed beforehand by God. The times of peace are fulfilled in the days of the good and just; and the times of many evils are fulfilled in the days of the evil and transgressors. For it is thus written:—*Good must happen, and blessed is he through whom it shall come to pass; and evil must happen, but woe to him through whom it shall come to pass.*[1] Good has come to the people of God, and blessedness awaits that man through whom the good came. And evil is stirred up as regards the host that is gathered together by means of the evil and arrogant one who glories; and woe also is there reserved for him through whom the evil is stirred up. But do not, my beloved, reproach the evil person who has inflicted evil upon many; because the times were beforehand disposed and the time of their accomplishment has arrived.

§ 2. Therefore because it is the time of the Evil One, hear in mystery that which I am writing for thee. For thus it is written:—*Whatsoever is exalted amongst men is despicable before God.*[2] And again it is written:—*Everyone who exalteth himself shall be abased, and everyone who humbleth himself shall be exalted.*[3] Also Jeremiah said:—*Let not the mighty glory in his might, nor the rich in his riches.*[4] And again the blessed Apostle said:—*Whosoever glorieth, let him glory in the Lord.*[5] And David said:—*I saw the wicked exalted and lifted up as the cedar of Lebanon; and when I passed by he was not, and I sought him and found him not.*[6]

§ 3. For every one that glories shall be humbled. Cain gloried over Abel his brother and slew him. And he was cursed and became a fugitive and a vagabond in the earth. Again the Sodomites gloried over Lot, and there fell upon them fire from heaven and burned them up and their city was overthrown upon them. And Esau

---

[1] Apocryphal; see Ps. Clem., Homil. xii. 29.
[2] Luke xvi. 15          [3] Luke xiv. 11.
[4] Jer. ix. 23.          [5] 2. Cor. x. 17.
[6] Ps. xxxvii. 35, 36.

gloried over Jacob and persecuted him, and Jacob received the birthright and blessings of Esau. And the children of Jacob gloried over Joseph, and (afterwards) fell down and worshipped him in Egypt. And Pharaoh gloried over Moses and over his people; and Pharaoh and his host were drowned in the sea. And Dathan and Abiram gloried over Moses, and they went down alive to Sheol. And Goliath threatened David, and he fell before him and was crushed. And again Saul persecuted David, and he fell by the sword of the Philistines. And Absalom exalted himself against him, and Joab slew him in the battle. Again Benhadad gloried over Ahab, and he was delivered into the hand of Israel. And Sennacherib blasphemed against Hezekiah and his God, and his host became dead carcases when one of the Watchers went forth and slew in the camp one hundred and eighty-five thousand at the prayer of Hezekiah and at the prayer of Prophet Isaiah, most glorious of the Prophets. Ahab exalted himself over Micah, and he went up and fell in Ramoth Gilead. Jezebel gloried over Elijah, and the dogs devoured her in the portion of Jezreel. Haman gloried over Mordecai, and his iniquity turned back upon his own head. The Babylonians gloried over Daniel and cast him into the den of lions, and Daniel came up victorious, and they were cast instead of him into the den. Again the Babylonians gloried and accused Hananiah and his companions, and they were cast into the furnace of fire; and they came up victorious and the flame devoured the accusers.

§ 4. Now Nebuchadnezzar said:—*I will ascend to heaven and exalt my throne above the stars of God and sit in the lofty mountains that are in the borders of the North.*[1] Isaiah said concerning him:—*Because thy heart has thus exalted thee, therefore thou shalt be brought down to Sheol, and all that look upon thee shall be astonished at thee.*[2] And Sennacherib also said thus:—*I will go up to the summit of the mountains and to the shoulders of Lebanon.*[3] *I*

*will dig and drink water and will dry up with my horses' hoofs all the deep rivers.* And because he thus exalted himself, Isaiah again said concerning him:—*Why does the axe boast itself against him that cutteth with it, or the saw exalt itself against him that saweth with it, or the rod lift itself up against him that wieldeth it?*[4] For thou, Sennacherib, art the axe in the hands of Him that cuts, and thou art the saw in the hands of Him that saws, and the rod in the hand of Him that wields thee for chastisement, and thou art the staff for smiting. Thou art sent against the fickle people, and again thou art ordained against the stubborn people, that thou mayest carry away the captivity and take the spoil; and thou hast made them as the mire of the streets for all men and for all the Gentiles. And when thou hast done all these things, why art thou exalted against Him Who holds thee, and why dost thou boast against Him Who saws with thee, and why hast thou reviled the holy city? and hast said to the children of Jerusalem:— *Can your God deliver you from my hand?*[5] And thou hast dared to say:—*Who is the Lord that He shall deliver you from my hands?* Because of this, hear the word of the Lord, saying:—*I will crush the Assyrian in My land, and on My mountains will I tread him down.*[6] And when he shall have been crushed and trodden down, *the Virgin, the daughter of Zion, will despise him, and the daughter of Jerusalem will shake her head and say:—Whom hast thou reviled and blasphemed, and against whom hast thou lifted up thy voice? Thou hast lifted up thine eyes towards heaven against the Holy One of Israel, and by the hands of thy messengers thou hast reviled the Lord. Now see that the hook has been forced into thy nostrils, and the bridle into thy lips, and thou hast turned back with thine heart crushed, who camest with thine heart uplifted.*[7] And his slaying was by the hands of his loved ones; and in the house of his confidence,[8] there was he over-

---

[1] Is. xiv. 13.    [2] Is. xiv. 15, 16.
[3] 2 Kings xix. 23, 24; Is. xxxvii. 24, 25.

[4] Is. x. 15.    [5] 2 Kings xviii. 35.
[6] Is. xiv. 25.
[7] 2. Kings, xix, 21-23, 28; Is. xxxvii. 22-24, 29.
[8] 2 Kings. xix. 37; Is. xxxvii. 38.

thrown, and fell before his god. And truly it was right, my beloved, that his body should thus become a sacrifice and offering before that god on whom he relied, and in his temple, as a memorial for his idol.

§ 5. Again the ram was lifted up and exalted, and pushed with its horns towards the west, and towards the north, and towards the south, and humbled many beasts. And they could not stand before him, until the he-goat came from the west and smote the ram and broke his horns and humbled the ram completely. But the ram was the King of Media and Persia, that is, Darius ; and the he-goat was Alexander, the son of Philip, the Macedonian. For Daniel saw the ram when he was *in the East before the gate of Shushan the fortress that is in the province of Elam, upon the river Ulai. And he was pushing towards the West and towards the North and towards the South. And none of the beasts could stand before him.*[1] And the he-goat of the goats came up from the region of the Greeks, and exalted himself against the ram. And he smote him and broke both his horns, the greater and the lesser. And why did he say that he broke both his horns ? Clearly because he humbled both the kingdoms which he ruled ; the lesser, that of the Medes, and the greater, that of the Persians. But when Alexander the Greek came, he slew Darius, King of Media and Persia. For thus the angel said to Daniel, when he was explaining the vision to him :—*The ram that thou sawest was the King of Media and Persia, and the he-goat the King of the Greeks.*[2] Now, from the time that the two horns of the ram were broken, until this time, there have been six hundred and forty-eight years.[3]

§ 6. Therefore, as for the ram, its horns are broken. And though its horns are broken, lo ! it exalts and uplifts itself against the fourth beast, that is *strong and*

*mighty and its teeth of iron and its hoofs of brass, and it shall devour and grind down, and trample with its feet whatsoever remaineth.*[4] O Ram, whose horns are broken, rest thou from the beast, and provoke it not lest it devour thee and grind thee to powder. The ram could not stand before the he-goat ; how shall it stand before that terrible beast, *whose mouth speaketh great things,*[5] and whatsoever it finds it couches over as a lion over his prey ? Whoever provokes the lion becomes its portion ; and whoever stirs up that beast, it shall devour him. And who is there that shall escape out from under the feet of that beast when it is trampling on him ? For the beast shall not be slain until the Ancient of Days shall sit upon the throne, and the Son of Man shall come near before Him, and authority shall be given to Him.[6] Then shall that beast be slain and its carcase shall perish. And the Kingdom of the Son of Man shall be established, an eternal Kingdom, and His authority from generation to generation.

§ 7. Be quiet, O thou that dost exalt thyself ; vaunt not thyself ! For if thy wealth has lifted up thy heart, it is not more abundant than that of Hezekiah, who went in and boasted of it before the Babylonians, (yet) it was all of it carried away and went to Babylon. And if thou gloriest in thy children, they shall be led away from thee to the Beast, as the children of King Hezekiah were led away, and became eunuchs in the palace of the King of Babylon.[7] And if thou dost glory in thy wisdom, thou dost not in it excel the Prince of Tyre, whom Ezekiel reproached, saying unto him :—*Art thou wiser than Daniel, or hast thou seen by thy wisdom the things that are hid ?*[8] And if thy mind is puffed up by thy years, that they are many ; they are not more in number than those of the Prince of Tyre who ruled the Kingdom during the days of twenty-two Kings of the house of Judah, that is, for four hundred and forty years.

---

[1] Dan. viii. 2, 4.　　　　　[2] Dan. viii. 20, 21.
[3] This *Demonstration* was therefore written in the year 648 according to the "era of the Greeks,"—*i.e.,* reckoning from B.C. 311-312. This year accordingly corresponds with the year 336-7 A.D. ; and the "ram."

[4] Dan. vii. 19.　　　　　[5] Dan. vii. 8.
[6] Dan. vii. 9, 13, 14, 22.　[7] 2 Kings. xx. 18 ; Is. xxxix 7.
[8] Ezek. xviii. 3.

And since the years of that King of Tyre were many, all the time he thus said in his heart, *I am God and sit in the seat of God in the heart of the seas.*[1] But Ezekiel said to him : *Thou art a man and thou art not God.* For while the Prince of Tyre was *walking without fault in the midst of the stones of fire*, there was mercy upon him. But when his heart was lifted up, *the cherub who overshadoweth, destroyed him.*[2]

§ 8. Now, what are the *stones of fire*, but the children of Zion and the children of Jerusalem? For in the ancient time, in the days of David and of Solomon his son, Hiram was a friend to those of the house of Israel. But when they were carried away captive from their place, he rejoiced over them and spurned them with his feet, and did not remember the friendship of the house of David. And as to that which I said that the children of Judah were called the *stones of fire*, it was not of my own thought that I said it, but Jeremiah the Prophet spake concerning them ; for when he was calling forth tears for them in the Lamentations, he said :—*The children of Zion were more excellent than precious stones.*[3] And again he said :—*How are the stones of the Sanctuary cast down at the head of all the streets ?*[4] And again He said by the Prophet :—*The stones were holy that were cast down in his land.*[5] And as to these very stones, the fire was burning in them, as Jeremiah said :—*The word of the Lord became in my heart like burning fire and it was hot in my bones.*[6] And again He said to Jeremiah :—*Lo ! I give My word in thy mouth as fire, and this people shall be as wood.*[7] And again He said :—*My words shall go forth as fire, and as iron that cutteth the stone.*[8] On this account the Prophets, amongst whom Hiram the Prince of Tyre was walking, were called *stones of fire*.

§ 9. And again (God) said to him :—*Thou wast with the Cherub who was anointed and overshadowing.*[9] For the king, who was anointed with the holy oil, was called a Cherub. And he was overshadowing all his people, as Jeremiah said :—*The anointed of the Lord is the breath of our nostrils, he of whom we said that in his shadow shall we live amongst the Gentiles.*[1] For they were sitting in the shadow of the king, while he was standing at their head. And when the crown of their head fell, they were without shade. And if any one should say that this word is spoken concerning Christ, let him receive that which I write for him without disputation, and thus he will be persuaded that it was said with reference to the king. For Jeremiah said in behalf of the people :— *Woe unto us, for the crown of our head has fallen !*[2] But Christ has not fallen, because He rose again the third day. For the king fell from the house of Judah, and never again was their kingdom set up. And as for that He said again :—*I will destroy the overshadowing Cherub.*[3] For the Cherub that He will destroy is Nebuchadnezzar, as it is written :—*He performed a work in Tyre, and there was given him by Tyre no hire for his host, and in return for the work of Tyre there was given him the land of Egypt.*[4] And why was hire not given by Tyre to Nebuchadnezzar? Clearly because its wealth went away in the sea, so that Nebuchadnezzar did not receive it. And at that time He destroyed *the overshadowing Cherub*, which is Nebuchadnezzar. For there are two Cherubs, one anointed and overshadowing, and one overshadowing but not anointed. For He said above :— *Thou wast with the Cherub anointed and overshadowing.*[5] And lower down He said :—*I will destroy thee the overshadowing Cherub ;*[6] and did not say "anointed." For Nebuchadnezzar was not anointed; but David and Solomon were, and the other kings who arose after them. And how was Nebuchadnezzar called *overshadowing ?* Clearly on

[1] Ezek. xxviii. 2.   [2] Ezek. xxviii. 14, 15.
[3] Lam. iv. 2.   [4] Lam. iv. 1.
[5] Zech. ix. 16.   [6] Jer. xx. 9.
[7] Jer. v. 14.   [8] Jer. xxiii. 29.

[9] Ezek. xxviii. 14.   [1] Lam. iv. 20.
[2] Lam. v. 16.   [3] Ezek. xxviii. 16.
[4] Ezek. xxix. 18, 19.   [5] Ezek. xxviii. 14.
[6] Ezek. xxviii. 16.

account of the vision of the tree, when he saw a tree in the midst of the earth, beneath which dwelt all the beasts of the wilderness and on its branches dwelt all the birds of heaven, and from it all flesh was fed. When Daniel interpreted his dream to him, Daniel said to him :—*Thou art the tree, that tree which thou sawest in the midst of the earth, and beneath thee dwell all the nations.*[1] On this account he was *the overshadowing Cherub ;* who destroyed the Prince of Tyre, because he rejoiced over the children of Israel, for that they were carried away captive from their land, and because his heart was exalted. This Tyre also lay waste seventy years like Jerusalem which sat in desolation seventy years. For Isaiah said concerning it :— *Tyre shall wander seventy years, as the days of one king, and shall commit fornication with all the kingdoms that are upon the face of the earth.*[2]

§ 10. O thou that art exalted and lifted up, let not the vaunting of thine heart mislead thee, nor say thou, I will go up against the rich land and against the powerful beast. For that beast will not be slain by the ram, seeing that its horns are broken. For the he-goat broke the horns of the ram.[3] Now the he-goat has become the mighty beast. For when the children of Japhet held the kingdom, then they slew Darius, the king of Persia. Now the fourth beast has swallowed up the third. And this third consists of the children of Japhet, and the fourth consists of the children of Shem, for they are the children of Esau. Because, when Daniel saw the vision of the four beasts, he saw first the children of Ham, the seed of Nimrod, which the Babylonians are ; and secondly, the Persians and Medes, who are the children of Japhet ; and thirdly, the Greeks, the brethren of the Medes ; and fourthly, the children of Shem, which the children of Esau are. For a confederacy was formed between the children of Japhet and the children of Shem. Then the government was taken away from the children of Japhet, the

younger, and was given to Shem, the elder ; and to this day it continues, and will continue for ever. But when the time of the consummation of the dominion of the children of Shem shall have come, the Ruler, who came forth from the children of Judah, shall receive the kingdom, when He shall come in His second Advent.

§ 11. For in the vision of Nebuchadnezzar, when he saw it, which Daniel made known and showed to Nebuchadnezzar, when he saw the image which stood over against him, *the head of the image was of gold, and its breast and arms of silver, and its belly and thighs of brass, and its legs and feet of iron and potter's clay.*[4] And Daniel said to Nebuchadnezzar :—*Thou art the head of gold.*[5] And why was he called the head of gold ? Was it not because the word of Jeremiah was fulfilled in him ? For Jeremiah said :—*Babylon is a golden cup in the hand of the Lord, that makes all the earth to drink of its wine.*[6] And also Babylon was called the head of all the kingdoms, as it is written :—*Babylon was the head of the kingdom of Nimrod.*[7]

§ 12. And he said that *the breast and the arms of the image were of silver.* This signified concerning a kingdom which was inferior to it ; namely, Darius the Mede. For (God) put the kingdom into the balance. For the kingdom of the house of Nimrod was weighed and was found wanting. And since it was wanting, Darius received it. Because of this he said that *his kingdom was inferior.*[8] And because it was inferior, the children of Media did not rule in all the earth. Now *the belly and thighs of the image were of brass,* and he said :—*The third kingdom shall rule in all the earth.*[9] It is the kingdom of the children of Javan, who are children of Japhet. For the children of Javan came in against the kingdom of their brethren. For Madai and Javan are sons of Japhet.[1] But Madai was foolish and incapable of gov-

---

[1] Dan. iv. 17, 19.  [2] Is. xxiii 15, 17.  [3] Dan. vii. 7.

[4] Dan. ii. 31–33.  [5] Ib. ii. 38.
[6] Jer. li. 7.  [7] Gen x. 10.
[8] Dan. ii. 39.  [9] Ibid.
[1] Gen. x. 2

erning the kingdom, until Javan, his brother, came, who was wise and cunning, to destroy the kingdom. For Alexander, son of Philip, ruled in all the earth.

§ 13. And *the legs and feet of the image were of iron.* This is the kingdom of the children of Shem, who are the children of Esau, which is strong as iron. And he said :—*As iron breaks and subdueth everything, so also the fourth kingdom shall break and bruise everything.*[1] And he explained with reference to the feet and toes, that part of them was of iron and part of them of potter's clay. For he said :—*Thus they shall be mingled with the seed of man, and they shall not cleave one to another, as iron cannot be mixed with clay.*[2] This referred to the fourth kingdom. Because in the kingdom of the children of Esau[3] there was not a king, the son of a king, established to govern the kingdom ; but when the children of Esau were gathered together into a powerful city, then they made a senate. And from thence they used to set up as chief of the city a wise man to govern the kingdom, lest when the Governor of their kingdom should weigh them, they might be found wanting, and the kingdom might be taken away from them as the kingdom of the children of arrogant Nimrod was taken away and given to the children of foolish Madai. And this king who was set up, the seed of that former king was destroying him ; and they did not cleave one to another. But as to the seed of man which is compared with the clay, the meaning is this ; that when the king was chosen for the kingdom, he mingled himself with the root of the kingdom of iron.

§ 14. And he showed that *in the days of those kings, who shall arise in the kingdom, the God of heaven will set up a kingdom which shall not be destroyed and shall not pass away for ever.*[4] This is the Kingdom of King Messiah, which is that which shall cause the fourth kingdom to pass away. And above he said :—*Thou sawest a stone which was cut out, but not by hands ; and it smote the image upon its feet of iron and potter's clay and broke them to pieces.*[5] Now he did not say that it smote upon the head of the image, nor on its breast and arms, nor yet on its belly and thighs, but on its feet ; because that, of the whole image, that stone when it comes will find the feet alone. And in the next verse he said :—*The iron and the brass and the silver and the gold were broken to pieces together.*[6] For after them, when King Messiah shall reign, then He will humble the fourth kingdom, and will break the whole image ; for by the whole image the world is meant. Its head is Nebuchadnezzar ; its breast and arms the King of Media and Persia ; its belly and thighs the King of the Greeks ; its legs and feet the kingdom of the children of Esau ; the stone, which smote the image and brake it, and with which the whole earth was filled, is the kingdom of King Messiah, Who will bring to nought the kingdom of this world, and He will rule for ever and ever.

§ 15. Again hear concerning the vision of the four beasts which Daniel saw coming up out of the sea and diverse one from another. This is the appearance of them :—*The first was like a lion, and it had the wings of an eagle. And I saw that its wings were plucked away, and it stood up like a man upon its feet, and the heart of a man was given to it.*[7] And the second beast was like a bear, and *it raised itself up upon one side and there were three ribs in its mouth between its teeth.* And the third beast was *like a leopard, and it had four wings and four heads.* And the fourth beast was *exceedingly terrible and strong and powerful, and it had great teeth. It devoured and brake to pieces, and whatsoever remained, it stamped with its feet.* Now the great sea that Daniel saw[8] is the world : and these four beasts are the four kingdoms signified above.

§ 16. Now as to the first beast, he said concerning it, that it was like a lion, and it had the wings of an eagle. For the first

---

[1] Dan. ii. 40.       [2] Dan. ii. 43.
[3] This passage describes the Roman Republic and Empire.       [4] Dan. ii. 44.
[5] Dan. ii. 34.       [6] Dan. ii. 35.
[7] Dan. vii. 4-7.       [8] Dan. vii. 2.

beast was the kingdom of Babylon, which was like a lion. For thus Jeremiah wrote saying :—*Israel is a wandering sheep. The lions caused them to wander. First the king of Assyria devoured him. And this last was stronger than he, Nebuchadnezzar king of Babylon.*[1] So Jeremiah called him a lion. And he said :—*He has the wings of an eagle.* For thus it is written that, when Nebuchadnezzar went out to the wilderness with the beasts, he grew hair like (the plumage) of an eagle. And he said :—*I saw that its wings were plucked away and it stood upright upon its feet as a man, and a man's heart was given to it.*[2] For first, in the vision of the image, he was compared to gold which is more precious than anything which is used in the world. So in the vision of the beasts he is compared to a lion which excels in its might all the beasts. And again he was compared to an eagle which surpasses every bird. Whatsoever was written about him was fulfilled in him. For the Lord said concerning him : —*I have placed a yoke of iron upon the neck of all the nations, and they shall serve the king of Babylon seventy years. And also the beasts of the desert and the birds of heaven have I given to him to serve him.* For since the king was like the head of gold, men served him as a king. And when he went out to the wilderness, the beasts served him as a lion. And when his hair was like (the plumage) of an eagle, the birds of heaven served him as an eagle. But when his heart was lifted up, and he knew not that the power was given to him from heaven, the yoke of iron was broken from the neck of men, and he went forth with the beasts, and instead of the heart of a king there was given him the heart of a lion. And when he was lifted up over the beasts, the heart of a lion was taken away from him, and there was given him the heart of a bird. And when wings grew upon him like those of an eagle, he exalted himself over the birds. And then his wings also were plucked away and there was given to him a humble heart. And

when he knew that the Most High has authority in the kingdom of man, to give it to whomsoever He will, then as a man he praised Him.

§ 17. And as for the second beast, he said concerning him that *it was like a bear and raised itself up upon one side.* Because when the kingdom of Media and Persia arose, it arose in the east. *And three ribs were in its mouth.* Because the ram was pushing towards the West and towards the North and towards the South, towards three winds of heaven. These three winds it held, and pushed against, like the three ribs that were in the mouth of the bear ; until the he-goat came forth from the west, and smote the ram and took out the ribs that were in his mouth.

§ 18. And concerning the third beast he said that it was like a leopard, and it had four birds' wings on its back and that beast had four heads. Now this third beast was Alexander the Macedonian. For he was strong as a leopard. And as for the four wings and the four heads that the beast had, that was because he gave the kingdom to his four friends to govern after him, when he had come and slain Darius and reigned in his stead.

§ 19. And of the fourth beast he said that it was exceedingly terrible and strong and mighty, devouring and crushing and trampling with its feet anything that remained. It is the kingdom of the children of Esau.[4] Because after that Alexander the Macedonian became king, the kingdom of the Greeks was founded, since Alexander also was one of them, even of the Greeks. But the vision of the third beast was fulfilled in him, since the third and the fourth were one. Now Alexander reigned for twelve years. And the kings of the Greeks arose after Alexander, being seventeen kings, and their years were two hundred and sixty-nine years from Seleucus Nicanor to Ptolemy. And the Cæsars were from Augustus to Philip Cæsar, seventeen kings. And their

---

[1] Jer. l. 17.
[3] Jer. xxviii. 14; xxv. 11.
[2] Dan. iv. 30.

[4] The Romans are here signified, according to Rabbinical doctrine, as descendants of Esau.

years are two hundred and ninety-three years ;[1] and eighteen years of Severus.

§ 20. For Daniel said :—*I was considering the ten horns that were upon the head of the beast. For the ten horns were ten kings*[2] who arose at that time until Antiochus. And he said :—*A little horn arose from between those ten and three fell before it.*[3] For when Antiochus arose in the kingdom, he humbled three kings, and he exalted himself against the saints of the Most High and against Jerusalem. And he defiled the sanctuary.[4] And he caused the sacrifice and the offerings to cease for a week and half a week, namely, for ten and a-half years. And he brought in fornicators into the house of the Lord, and he caused the observances of the Law to cease.[5] And he slew righteous men and gave them to the birds of heaven and to the beasts of the earth. For in his days was fulfilled the word that David spoke :[6]—*O God, the Gentiles have come into thine inheritance, and have defiled Thy holy temple. They have made Jerusalem desolate. They have given the dead bodies of Thy servants as food to the birds of heaven, and the flesh of Thy righteous ones to the beasts of the earth. They have poured out their blood like water round about Jerusalem, and there is none to bury them.* For this was accomplished at that time, when the venerable and aged Eleazar was slain, and the sons of the blessed Samuna, seven in number,[7] and when Judas (Maccabeus) and his brethren were struggling on behalf of their people, when they were dwelling in hiding-places.[8] At that time *the horn made war with the saints,*[9] and their power prevailed. And the wicked Antiochus *spake words against the Most High, and changed the times and the seasons.*[1] And he made to cease the covenant of Abraham, and abolished the Sabbath of rest.[2] For he commanded the Jews that they should not circumcise. Therefore, (the Prophet) said concerning him;—*He shall think to change the times and the seasons and the laws, and they were given into his hand for a time, times, and half a time.*[3] Now the time and half a time is the week and a half, which is ten years and a half. Again he said :—*The judgment was set and they took away his authority from him, to injure and destroy him until the end of the kingdom.*[4] For the judgment came upon Antiochus, a judgment from heaven ;[5] and he became sick with a grievous and evil sickness, and on account of the smell of him as he rotted, no man could approach him, for worms were crawling and falling from him and eating his flesh because he oppressed the *worm Jacob.*[6] And his flesh rotted in his lifetime, because he caused the dead bodies of the sons of Jerusalem to rot and they were not buried. And he became defiled in his own eyes, because he had defiled the sanctuary of God. And he prayed and was not heard,[7] because he did not hearken to the groanings of the righteous whom he slew. For he wrote a letter and sent it to the Jews and called them "my friends," but God had not mercy on him, but he died in his torment.

§ 21. He said again :—*The saints of the Most High shall receive the Kingdom.*[8] What shall we say concerning this? Have the children of Israel received the Kingdom of the Most High? God forbid. Or has that people come upon the clouds of heaven? This has passed away from them. For Jeremiah said concerning them :—*Call them rejected silver, for the Lord has rejected them.*[9] Again he said :—*He will not again regard them.*[1] And Isaiah said concerning them : —*Pass by ; pass by ; approach not the defiled.*[2] And concerning the saints of the Most High (Daniel) said thus :—*They shall inherit

[1] The "kingdom of the Greeks" is here reckoned from the "era of the Greeks," B.C. 311-12, in the reign of Seleucus Nicanor, to the end of the Ptolemies ; B.C. 43,—269 years, as above. From B.C. 43 to the death of the Emperor Philip, A.D. 249, makes up (approximately) the 293 years of the text. Philip was reputed to have been the first Christian Emperor, (Euseb. *H. E.*, VI. 34 ; Jerome, *Chronicon*).
[2] Dan. vii. 8, 24.   [3] Dan. vii. 8.
[4] 2 Macc. vi. 2-4.   [5] 2 Macc. v. 26.
[6] Ps. lxxix. 1-3.   [7] 2 Macc. vi. 18-31 ; vii.
[8] 2 Macc. v. 27.   [9] Dan. vii. 21.
[1] Dan. vii. 25.

[2] 2 Macc. vi. 10, 11.   [3] Dan. vii. 25.
[4] Dan. vii 26.   [5] 2 Macc. ix. 5-12.
[6] Is. xli. 14.   [7] 2 Macc. ix. 13, 18, 19, 28.
[8] Dan. vii. 27.   [9] Jer. vi. 30.
[1] Lam. iv. 16.   [2] Is. lii. 11.

the Kingdom for ever.[1] For these *rested a little from the burden of kings and princes*,[2] namely, from after the death of Antiochus till the sixty-two weeks were fulfilled. And the Son of Man came to free them and gather them together, but they did not receive Him. For He came to obtain fruit from them, and they did not give it to Him. For their vines were *of the vine of Sodom and of the stock of Gomorrha, a vineyard*[3] in which thorns grew, and which *bore wild grapes*.[4] Their vine was bitter, and their fruit sour. The thorns could not be softened, nor could the bitterness change to the nature of wine, nor could the sour fruit change to a sweet nature.

§ 22. For Isaiah first set men of Judah as judges over them,[5] and there was planted amongst them a new and beloved planting. But these are those judges *who shall sit on twelve thrones and judge their twelve tribes*.[6] And thus He said to the judges :[7]—*Judge between Me and My vineyard, what further*, O ye judges, *should I have done to My vineyard, that I did not do ? For lo! I planted it with vine scions*, and they became strange vines. *I surrounded it with a fence* of heavenly Watchers *and I built its tower*, the holy Temple. *And I dug out its winepress*, the baptism of the priests. And I brought down rain upon it, the words of My Prophets. And I pruned it and trimmed it, from the works of the Amorites. *I looked that it should produce grapes* of righteousness, *and it produced wild grapes* of iniquity and sin. *I looked for judgment and behold oppression, and for righteousness and there was a cry. Hear*, O ye judges, *what I will do to My vineyard. I will break open its fence, and it shall be for down-treading. And I will tear down its tower, and it shall be for pillage. And I will make it to become a desert because it produced wild grapes. And it shall not be dressed and it shall not be pruned. And thorns and weeds shall grow up in it.*

*And I will command the clouds that they send not down rain upon it.* For the heavenly Watchers departed from the fence of the vineyard ; and the mighty tower on which they relied was torn down. The winepress, the cleansing away of their offences, was overthrown. *When the vine was without blemish, it did not prove of service. Now that the fire has devoured it and that it is laid waste, how shall it prove of service ? The fire has devoured its two branches and its inward parts are wasted.*[8] For its two branches are the two kingdoms, and its inward part which is laid waste is Jerusalem. Many servants were sent to them by the Lord of the vineyard.[9] And they slew them and did not send the fruit to the Lord of the vineyard. After the servants the beloved Son was sent, to receive from them the fruit and to bring it back to Him that sent Him. And they seized Him and cast Him out of the vineyard ; and they cut spikes from the thorns of the vineyard and fixed them in His hands. And He was hungry and asked food of them ; and they took and gave Him gall from the fruit of the vineyard. He was thirsty and asked of them drink ; and they gave Him vinegar and He would not drink it. And they platted a crown of thorns that had sprung up in the vineyard, and placed it on the head of the Son of the Lord of the vineyard. For from the time that the vineyard was made, it displayed these fruits. Therefore its Lord uprooted it and cast it in the fire ; and planted good fruit-bearing vines in the vineyard, and such as gladden the husbandman. For Christ is the vineyard, and His Father is the husbandman ; and they who drink of His cup are the vines. Therefore vineyard was formed instead of vineyard. And furthermore at His coming He handed over the kingdom to the Romans, as the children of Esau are called. And these children of Esau will keep the kingdom for its giver.

§ 23. And the holy People inherited an eternal Kingdom ; the holy people who were

---

[1] Dan. vii. 27.  [2] Hos. viii. 10.
[3] Deut. xxxii. 32.  [4] Is. v. 2.
[5] Is. v. 1. sqq.  [6] Matt. xix. 28.
[7] Is. v. 1–6.

[8] Ezek. xv. 4, 5.  [9] Luke xx. 10 sqq.

chosen instead of the People. For *He provoked them to jealousy with a people that was not a people. And with a foolish people He angered them.*[1] And He set free the holy people. For lo! every covenant of God *is freed from the burden of kings and princes.*[2] For even if a man has served the heathen, as soon as ever he draws nigh unto the covenant of God, he is set free. But the Jews are toiling in bondage amongst the Gentiles. For thus he said about the Saints ;—*They shall inherit the Kingdom that is beneath the heaven.*[3] But if he had said it about them (the Jews), why are they toiling in service amongst the Gentiles? And if they say that it has not taken place as yet ; then (we ask) is the Kingdom that shall be given to the Son of man, to be heavenly or earthly? And lo! the children of the Kingdom are sealed, and they have received their emancipation from this world. For since it exists now, it will not be willing to be subjected to the power of the King, Who shall come and take to Himself His Kingdom. But it will guard His pledges with honour, that when He shall come to bring to nought the Kingdom, he may come upon them not in anger. For when He, *Whose is the Kingdom,*[4] shall come in His second coming, He will take to Himself whatever He has given. And He Himself will be King for ever and ever. And His Kingdom shall not pass away, because it is an eternal Kingdom.

§ 24. For first, He gave the Kingdom to the sons of Jacob, and subdued to them the children of Esau ; as Isaac said to Esau :—*Thou shalt serve Jacob thy brother.*[5] And when again they did not prosper in the Kingdom, He took it away from the children of Jacob and gave it to the children of Esau *until He should come Whose it is.*[6] And they will deliver up the deposit to its Giver, and will not deal fraudulently with it. And the Guardian of the Kingdom is subject to Him to Whom all things are subject. Therefore this Kingdom of the children of Esau

shall not be delivered up into the hand of the hosts that are gathered together, that desire to go up against it ; because the Kingdom is being kept safe for its Giver, and He Himself will preserve it. And as to this that I wrote to thee, beloved, that the Kingdom of the children of Esau is being kept safe for its Giver, doubt not about it, that that Kingdom will not be conquered. For a mighty champion Whose name is Jesus shall come with power, and bearing as His armour all the power of the Kingdom. And search out and see that also by the poll-tax[7] He was enrolled amongst them. And as He was enrolled by the poll-tax amongst them, He will also succour them. And His standard abounds in that place, and they are clothed in His armour, and shall not be found wanting in war. And if thou shouldest say unto me :—"In the years of the Kings that preceded these, why did they conquer and subdue the beast?" It was because the chiefs and kings who stood up at that time in the Kingdom of the children of Esau did not wish to lead with them to the war the Man who was enrolled with them in the poll-tax. Therefore the beast was subdued a little, but was not slain.

§ 25. But concerning these things that I have written for thee, my beloved, namely, concerning that which is written in Daniel, I have not brought them to an end, but (have stopped) short of the end. And if any man dispute about them, say thus to him, that these words are not concluded, because the words of God are infinite, nor will they be concluded. For the foolish man says, "Here unto (these) words reach." And again, it is not possible to add to them or to diminish from them.[8] For the riches of God cannot be computed or limited. For if thou take away water from the sea, the deficiency will be imperceptible. And if thou remove sand from the sea-shore, its measure will not be diminished. And if thou count the stars of heaven, thou wilt not arrive at the sum of them. And if thou kindle fire from

---

[1] Deut. xxxii. 21.  [2] Hos. viii. 10.
[3] Dan. vii. 27.  [4] Gen. xlix. 10.
[5] Gen. xxvii. 40.  [6] Gen. xlix. 10.

[7] Luke ii. 1, 2.  [8] Deut. iv. 2.

a burning, it will not a whit be lessened. And if thou receive of the Spirit of Christ, Christ will not a whit be diminished. And if Christ dwell in thee, yet He will not be completed in thee. And if the sun enter the windows of thy house, yet the sun in its entirety will not come to thee. And all these things that I have enumerated for thee were created by the word of God. Therefore know thou, that, as concerning the word of God no man has reached or will reach its end. Therefore, have thou no disputation about these things, but say :—"These things are so. That is enough." But hear these things from me, and also enquire about them of our brethren, children of our faith. But whosoever shall mock at the words of his brother, even if he say, "mine are wise," yet hearken not to his words. And concerning what I wrote to thee about these forces that are being stirred up to war, it is not as though anything has been revealed to me that I have made known these things to thee, but attend to the words at the head of the letter :—*Every one who exalteth himself shall be humbled.* For even if the forces shall go up and conquer, yet know that it is a chastisement of God ; and though they conquer, they shall be condemned in a righteous judgment. But yet be thou assured of this, that the beast shall be slain at its (appointed) time. But do thou, my brother, at this time be earnest in imploring mercy, that there may be peace upon the people of God.

### Demonstration VI.—Of Monks.

§ 1. Expedient is the word that I speak and worthy of acceptance :—*Let us now awake from our sleep*,[1] and lift up both our hearts and hands to God towards heaven ; lest suddenly the Lord of the house come, that *when He comes He may find us in watchfulness.*[2] Let us observe the appointed time of the glorious bridegroom,[3] that we may

enter with Him into His bride-chamber. Let us prepare oil for our lamps that we may go forth to meet Him with joy. Let us make ready provision for our abiding-place, for the way that is narrow and strait. And let us put away and cast from us all uncleanness, and put on wedding garments. Let us trade with the silver that we have received,[4] that we may be called diligent servants. Let us be constant in prayer, that we may pass by the place where fear dwells. Let us cleanse our heart from iniquity, that we may see the Lofty One in His honour. Let us be merciful, as it is written, that God may have mercy upon us.[5] Let there be peace amongst us, that we may be called the brethren of Christ. Let us hunger for righteousness, that we may be satisfied[6] from the table of His Kingdom. Let us be the salt of truth, that we may not become food for the serpent. Let us purge our seed from thorns, that we may produce fruit a hundred-fold. Let us found our building on the rock,[7] that it may not be shaken by the winds and waves. Let us be vessels unto honour[8] that we may be required by the Lord for His use. Let us sell all our possessions, and buy for ourselves the pearl,[9] that we may be rich. Let us lay up our treasures in heaven,[1] that when we come we may open them and have pleasure in them. Let us visit our Lord in the persons of the sick,[2] that He may invite us to stand at His right hand. Let us hate ourselves and love Christ, as He loved us and gave Himself up for our sakes.[3] Let us honour the spirit of Christ, that we may receive grace from Him. Let us be strangers to the world,[4] even as Christ was not of it. Let us be humble and mild, that we may inherit the land of life. Let us be unflagging in His service, that He may cause us to serve in the abode of the saints. Let us pray His prayer in purity, that it may have access to the Lord of

---

[1] Rom. xiii. 11.   [2] Luke xii. 37.   [3] Matt. xxv. 4, 10.

[4] Matt. xxv. 21.   [5] Matt. v. 7.
[6] Matt. v. 6.   [7] Matt. vii. 24.
[8] 2 Tim. ii. 21.   [9] Matt. xiii. 46.
[1] Matt. vi. 20.   [2] Matt. xxv. 33-35.
[3] John xii. 25 ; Eph. v. 2.   [4] John xvii. 14.

Majesty. Let us be partakers in His suffering, that so we may also rise up in His resurrection.[1] Let us bear His sign upon our bodies, that we may be delivered from the wrath to come. For fearful is the day in which He will come, and who is able to endure it?[2] Furious and hot is His wrath, and it will destroy all the wicked. Let us set upon our head the helmet of redemption,[3] that we may not be wounded and die in the battle. Let us gird our loins with truth, that we may not be found impotent in the contest. Let us arise and awaken Christ, that He may still the stormy blasts from us. Let us take as a shield against the Evil One, the preparation of the Gospel of our Redeemer. Let us receive power from our Lord to tread upon snakes and scorpions.[4] Let us lay aside from us wrath, with all fury and malice. Let no reviling proceed out of our mouth, with which we pray unto God. Let us not be cursers, that we may be delivered from the curse of the law. Let us be diligent workers, that we may obtain our reward with those of old. Let us take up the burden of the day, that we may seek a more abundant reward. Let us not be idle workers, for lo! our Lord has hired us for His vineyard.[5] Let us be planted as vines in the midst of His vineyard, for it is the true vineyard. Let us be fruitful vines, that we may not be uprooted out of His vineyard. Let us be a sweet odour, that our fragrance may breathe forth to all around. Let us be poor in the world, and let us enrich many by the doctrine of our Lord. Let us not call anyone our father in the earth,[6] that we may be the children of the Father which is in heaven. Though we have nothing, yet we possess all things.[7] Though no man know us, yet they that have knowledge of us are many. Let us rejoice in our hope at every time,[8] that He Who is our hope and our Redeemer may rejoice in us. Let us judge ourselves right-

eously and condemn ourselves, that we may not hang down our faces before the judges who shall sit upon thrones and judge the tribes.[9] Let us take to ourselves, as armour for the contest,[1] the preparation of the Gospel. Let us knock at the door of heaven,[2] that it may be opened before us, and we may enter in through it.

Let us diligently ask for mercy, that we may receive whatsoever is necessary for us. Let us seek His Kingdom and His righteousness,[3] that we may receive increase in the land. Let us think upon the things which are above,[4] on the heavenly things, and meditate on them, where Christ has been lifted up and exalted. But let us forsake the world which is not ours, that we may arrive at the place to which we have been invited. Let us raise up our eyes on high, that we may see the splendour which shall be revealed. Let us lift up our wings as eagles, that we may see the body there where it is. Let us prepare as offerings for the King desirable fruits, fasting and prayer. Let us guard His pledge in purity, that He may trust us over all His treasury. For whosoever deals falsely with His pledge, they suffer him not to enter into the treasure-house. Let us be careful of the body of Christ, that our bodies may rise at the sound of the trumpet. Let us hearken to the voice of the bridegroom, that we may go in with Him into the bride-chamber. Let us prepare the marriage-gift for His bridal day, and let us go forth to meet Him with joy. Let us put on holy raiment, that we may recline in the chief place of the elect. Whosoever puts not on wedding raiment,[5] they cast him out into outer darkness. Whosoever excuses himself from the wedding shall not taste the feast.[6] Whosoever loves fields and merchandise, shall be shut out of the city of Saints. Whosoever does not bear fruit in the vineyard, shall be uprooted and cast out to torment. Whosoever has re-

---

[1] 2 Tim. ii. 11, 12.
[2] Joel, ii. 11.
[3] Eph. vi. 14-17.
[4] Luke x. 19.
[5] Matt. xx. 1
[6] Matt. xxiii. 9.
[7] 2 Cor. vi. 9, 10.
[8] Rom. xii. 12.

[9] Matt. xix. 28.
[2] Matt. vii. 7.
[4] Col. iii. 1, 2.
[6] Luke xiv. 18

[1] Eph. vi. 16.
[3] Matt. vi. 33.
[5] Matt. xxii. 13.

ceived money from his Lord, let him return it to its Giver with its increase.[1] Whosoever desires to become a merchant, let him buy for himself the field and the treasure that is in it.[2] Whosoever receives the good seed, let him purge his land from thorns.[3] Whosoever desires to be a fisherman, let him cast forth his net at every time. Whosoever is training for the conflict, let him keep himself from the world. Whosoever wishes to gain the crown, let him run as a winner in the race. Whosoever wishes to go down into the course to contend, let him learn to (contend) against his adversary. Whosoever wishes to go down to the battle, let him take unto him armour wherewith to fight, and let him purify himself at every time. Whosoever adopts the likeness of angels, let him be a stranger to men, Whosoever takes upon him the yoke of the saints, let him remove from him getting and spending. Whosoever desires to gain himself, let him remove from him the gain of the world. Whosoever loves the abode that is in heaven, let him not toil at the building of clay that will fall. Whosoever is expectant of being caught up in the clouds, let him not make for himself adorned chariots. Whosoever is expectant of the marriage-feast of the Bridegroom, let him not love the feast of this present time. Whosoever wishes to have pleasure in the banquet reserved there, let him remove drunkenness from himself. Whosoever prepares himself for the supper, let him not excuse himself,[4] nor be a merchant. Whosoever he be on whom the good seed falls, let him not allow the Evil One to sow tares in him. Whosoever has begun to build a tower, let him count up all the cost thereof.[5] Whosoever builds ought to finish, that he be not a laughing-stock to them that pass by the way. Whosoever sets his building on the rock, let him make its foundations deep, that it may not be cast down by the billows. Whosoever wishes to fly from the darkness, let him walk while

he has light.[6] Whosoever fears to fly in winter,[7] let him prepare himself from the summer-time. Whosoever looks forward to enter into rest,[8] let him make ready his provision for the Sabbath. Whosoever begs forgiveness of his Lord, let him also forgive his debtor.[9] Whosoever does not demand back a hundred dinars, his Lord forgives him ten thousand talents. Whosoever casts down his Lord's money on the banker's table,[1] will not be called an unprofitable servant. Whosoever loves humility, shall be heir in the land of life. Whosoever wishes to make peace, shall be one of the sons of God.[2] Whosoever knows the will of his Lord, let him do that will, that he may not be beaten much.[3] Whosoever cleanses his heart from deceits, *His eyes shall behold the King in his beauty*.[4] Whosoever receives the Spirit of Christ, let him adorn his inner man. Whosoever is called the temple of God,[5] let him purify his body from all uncleanness. Whosoever grieves the Spirit of Christ,[6] shall not raise up his head from griefs. Whosoever receives the body of Christ, let him keep his body from all uncleanness. Whosoever casts off the *old man*,[7] let him not turn back to his former works. Whosoever puts on the *new man*, let him keep himself from all filthiness. Whosoever has put on armour from the water (of baptism), let him not put off his armour that he may not be condemned. Whosoever takes up the shield[8] against the Evil One, let him keep himself from the darts which he hurls at him. Whosoever shall *draw back*, his Lord *has no pleasure in him*.[9] Whosoever thinks upon the Law of his Lord, shall not be troubled with the thoughts of this world. Whosoever meditates on the Law of his Lord, is like a tree planted by the waters.[1] Whosoever again has trust in his Lord, is like a tree that is set out by the river. Whosoever puts his trust in man

---

[1] Matt. xxv. 16.
[2] Matt. xiii. 44.
[3] Matt. xiii. 7.
[4] Luke xiv. 18, 19.
[5] Luke xiv. 29.

[6] John xii. 35.
[8] Hebr. iv. 11.
[1] Matt. xxv. 27.
[3] Luke xii. 47.
[5] 1 Cor. iii. 16. 17.
[7] Eph. iv. 22.
[9] Hebr. x. 38.

[7] Matt. xxiv. 20.
[9] Matt. xviii. 24.
[2] Matt. v. 9.
[4] Is. xxxiii. 17.
[6] Eph. iv. 30.
[8] Eph. vi. 16.
[1] Ps. i. 2, 3.

shall receive the curses of Jeremiah.[1] Whosoever is invited to the Bridegroom, let him prepare himself. Whosoever has lighted his lamp, let him not suffer it to go out. Whosoever is expectant of the marriage-cry, let him take oil in his vessel.[2] Whosoever is keeper of the door, let him be on the watch for his Master. Whosoever loves virginity, let him become like Elijah. Whosoever takes up the yoke of the Saints, let him sit and be silent. Whosoever loves peace, let him look for his Master as the hope of life.

§ 2. For, my beloved, our adversary is skilful. He that contends against us is crafty. Against the brave and the renowned does he prepare himself, that they may be weakened. For the feeble are his own, nor does he fight with the captivity that are made captive to him. He that has wings flees from him and the darts that he hurls at him do not reach him. They that are spiritual see him when he assails, and his panoply has no power upon their bodies. All the children of light are without fear of him, because the darkness flies from before the light. The children of the Good fear not the Evil, for He hath given him to be trampled by their feet. When he makes himself like darkness unto them, they become light. And when he creeps upon them like a serpent, they become salt, whereof he cannot eat. If he makes himself like the asp unto them, then they become like babes. If he comes in upon them in the lust of food, they, like our Redeemer, conquer him by fasting. And if he wishes to contend with them by the lust of the eyes, they lift up their eyes to the height of heaven. If he wishes by enticements to overcome them, they do not afford him a hearing. If he wishes openly to strive with them, lo! they are clothed in panoply and stand up against him. If he wishes to come in against them by sleep, they are wakeful and vigilant and sing psalms and pray. If he allures them by possessions, they give them

to the poor. If he comes in as sweetness against them, they taste it not, knowing that he is bitter. If he inflames them with the desire of Eve, they dwell alone, and not with the daughters of Eve.

§3. For it was through Eve that he came in upon Adam,[3] and Adam was enticed because of his inexperience. And again he came in against Joseph through his master's wife,[4] but Joseph was acquainted with his craftiness and would not afford him a hearing. Through a woman he fought with Samson,[5] until he took away his Nazariteship. Reuben was the first-born of all his brethren, and through his father's wife,[6] (the adversary) cast a blemish upon him. Aaron was the great high-priest of the house of Israel, and through Miriam[7] his sister he envied Moses. Moses was sent to deliver the people from Egypt, and took with him the woman who advised him to shameful acts,[8] and the Lord met with Moses, and desired to slay him, till he sent back his wife to Midian. David was victorious in all his battles, yet through means of a daughter of Eve[9] there was found a blemish in him. Amnon was beautiful and fair in countenance, yet (the adversary) took him captive by desire for his sister,[1] and Absalom slew him on account of the humbling of Tamar. Solomon was greater than all the kings of the earth, yet in the days of his old age his wives led his heart astray.[2] Through Jezebel, daughter of Ethbaal, the wickedness of Ahab was increased,[3] and he became altogether a heathen. Furthermore, the adversary tempted Job through his children and his possessions,[4] and when he could not prevail over him, he went and brought against him his armour, and he came, bringing with him a daughter of Eve, who had caused Adam to sink, and through her mouth he said to Job, her righteous husband :—*Curse God.*[5] But Job rejected her counsel. King

---

[1] Jer. xvii. 5, 7, 8.    [2] Matt. xxv. 6.

[3] Gen. iii. 6.    [4] Gen. xxxix. 7, ff.
[5] Judg. xvi. 15, ff.    [6] Gen. xxxv. 22.
[7] Num. xii. 1, ff.    [8] Exod. iv. 24 26.
[9] 2 Sam. xi. 2, ff.    [1] 2 Sam. xiii. 1, ff.
[2] 1 Kin. xi. 1-4.    [3] 1 Kin. xvi. 31, xxi. 5, ff.
[4] Job. i. 13, ff.    [5] Job ii. 9.

Asa also conquered the Accursed-of-life, when he wished to come in against him, through his mother.[1] For Asa knew his craftiness and removed his mother from her high estate, and cut in pieces her idol and cast it down. John was greater than all the prophets, yet Herod slew him because of the dancing of a daughter of Eve.[2] Haman was wealthy and third in honour from the King, yet his wife counselled him to destroy the Jews.[3] Zimri was head of the tribe of Simeon, yet Cozbi, daughter of the chiefs of Midian, overthrew him, and because of one woman twenty-four thousand of Israel fell in one day.[4]

§ 4. Therefore, my brethren, if any man who is a monk or a saint, who loves the solitary life, yet desires that a woman, bound by monastic vow like himself, should dwell with him, it would be better for him in that case to take (to wife) a woman openly and not be made wanton by lust. So also again the woman, if she be not separated from the solitary, it is better for her to marry openly. Woman then ought to dwell with woman, and man to dwell with man. And also whatever man desires to continue in holiness, let not his spouse dwell with him, lest he turn back to his former condition, and so be esteemed an adulterer. Therefore this counsel is becoming and right and good, that I give to myself and you, my beloved solitaries, who do not take wives, and to the virgins who do not marry, and to those who have loved holiness. It is just and right and becoming, that even if a man should be distressed, he should continue alone. And thus it becomes him to dwell, as it is written in the Prophet Jeremiah :—*Blessed is the man who shall take up Thy yoke in his youth, and sit alone and be silent, because he has taken upon him Thy yoke.*[5] For thus, my beloved, it becomes him who takes up the yoke of Christ, to preserve his yoke in purity.

§ 5. For thus it is written, my beloved, concerning Moses, that from the time the Holy One was revealed to him, he also loved holiness. And from the time he was sanctified, his wife ministered not to him. But it is thus written :—*Joshua, the son of Nun, was the minister of Moses from his childhood.*[6] And of Joshua again it is thus written concerning him, that *he used not to depart from the tabernacle.*[7] And the temporal tabernacle was not ministered to by a woman, because the Law did not allow women to enter the temporal tabernacle, but even when they came to pray, they used to pray at the door of the temporal tabernacle, and then turn back. Moreover, he commanded the Priests, that at the time of their ministry they should continue in holiness, and should not know their wives. And also concerning Elijah it is thus written, that at one time he dwelt in Mount Carmel, and at another he dwelt at the brook Cherith, and was ministered to by his disciple; and because his heart was in heaven, the bird of heaven used to bring sustenance to him; and because he took upon him the likeness of the angels of heaven, those very angels brought him bread and water when he was fleeing from before Jezebel.[8] And because he set all his thought in heaven, he was caught up in the chariot of fire to heaven,[9] and there his dwelling-place was established for ever. Elisha also walked in the footsteps of his Master. He used to dwell in the upper chamber of the Shunamite, and was ministered to by his disciple. For thus the Shunamite said ;—*He is a holy Prophet of God and passes by us continually, for thus it becomes his holiness that we should make for him an upper chamber and do for him the service that is (necessary) in it.*[1] Now what was the service necessary in the upper chamber of Elisha? Clearly the bed and table and stool and lamp-stand only. But what shall we say of John? He also used to dwell amongst men, and preserved his virginity honourably, and received the Spirit of God. More-

---

[1] 1 Kings. xv. 13.
[2] Matt. xi. 11; xiv. 6, sq.
[3] Esth. vi. 13.
[4] Num. xxv. 6–15.
[5] Sam. iii. 27, 28.
[6] Ex. xxxiii. 11.   [7] Ib.   [8] 1 Kings xvii. 3–5; xix. 1–8.
[9] 2 Kings ii. 11.   [1] 2 Kings iv. 8–10.

over, the blessed Apostle said concerning himself and concerning Barnabas :—*Had we then not power to eat and to drink and to lead about wives with us? But it was not becoming or right.*[1]

§ 6. Therefore, brethren, because we know and have seen that from the beginning it was through woman that the adversary had access unto men, and to the end he will accomplish it by her—for she is the weapon of Satan, and through her he fights against the champions. Through her he makes music at every time, for she became as a harp for him from the first day. For because of her the curse of the Law was established, and because of her the promise unto death was made. For with pangs she bears children and delivers them to death. Because of her the earth was cursed, that it should bring forth thorns and tares. Accordingly, by the coming of the offspring of the Blessed Mary the thorns are uprooted, the sweat wiped away, the fig-tree cursed,[2] the dust made salt,[3] the curse nailed to the cross,[4] the edge of the sword removed from before the tree of life and it given as food to the faithful, and Paradise promised to the blessed and to virgins and to the saints. So the fruit of the tree of life is given as food to the faithful and to virgins, and to those that do the will of God has the door been opened and the way made plain. And the fountain flows and gives drink to the thirsty. The table is laid and the supper prepared. The fatted ox is slain and the cup of redemption mixed. The feast is prepared and the Bridegroom at hand, soon to take his place. The apostles have given the invitation and the called are very many. O ye chosen, prepare yourselves. The light has shone forth both bright and fair, and garments not made with hands are prepared. The marriage cry is at hand. The tombs will be opened and the treasures laid bare. The dead shall rise and the living shall fly to meet the King. The banquet is laid, and the cornet shall encourage and the trumpets shall hasten (them). The Watchers of heaven shall speed, and the throne shall be set for the Judge. He that laboured shall rejoice, and he that was unprofitable shall fear. He that did evil shall not draw nigh unto the Judge. Those on the right hand shall exult, and those on the left shall weep and wail. Those that are in the light shall be glorified, and those that are in the darkness shall groan that they may moisten their tongue. Grace has gone by, and justice reigns. There is no repentance in that place. Winter is at hand ; the summer has passed away. The Sabbath of rest has come ; toil has ceased. Night has passed away ; the light reigns. As to death, its sting is broken and it is swallowed up in life.[5] Those that return to Sheol shall weep and gnash their teeth, and those that go to the Kingdom shall rejoice and exult and dance and sing praises. For those that take not wives shall be ministered to by the Watchers of heaven. Those that preserve chastity shall rest in the sanctuary of the Most High. The Only Begotten Who is from the bosom of His Father shall cause all the solitaries to rejoice. There is there neither male nor female, neither bond nor free,[6] but they all are the children of the Most High. And all the pure virgins who are betrothed to Christ shall light their lamps[7] and with the Bridegroom shall they go into the marriage chamber. All those that are betrothed to Christ are far removed from the curse of the Law, and are redeemed from the condemnation of the daughters of Eve ; for they are not wedded to men so as to receive the curses and come into the pains. They take no thought of death, because they do not deliver children to him. And in place of a mortal husband, they are betrothed to Christ. And *because they do not bear children, there is given to them the name that is better than sons and daughters.*[8] And instead of the groans of the daughters of

---

[1] I Cor ix. 4, 5.  
[2] Matt. xxi. 19.  
[3] Matt. v. 13.  
[4] Col. ii. 14.  
[5] I Cor. xv. 54, 55.  
[6] Gal. iii. 28.  
[7] Matt. xxv. 10.  
[8] Is. lvi. 5.

Eve, they utter the songs of the Bridegroom. The wedding-feast of the daughters of Eve continues for but seven days ; but for these (virgins) is the Bridegroom who departs not for ever. The adornment of the daughters of Eve is wool that wears out and perishes, but the garments of these wear not out. Old age withers the beauty of the daughters of Eve, but the beauty of these shall be renewed in the time of the Resurrection.

§ 7. O ye virgins who have betrothed yourselves to Christ, when one of the monks shall say to one of you, "I will live with thee and minister thou to me," thus shalt thou say unto him :—"To a royal husband am I betrothed, and Him do I serve ; and if I leave His service and serve thee, my betrothed will be wroth with me, and will write me a letter of divorce, and will send me away from His house ; and while thou seekest to be honoured by me, and I to be honoured by thee, take heed lest hurt come upon me and thee. Take not fire into thy bosom,[1] lest it burn thy garments ; but be thou in honour alone, and I also alone will abide in my honour. And as concerning these things which the Bridegroom has prepared for the eternity of his marriage feast, do thou make thee a wedding-gift and prepare thyself to meet Him. And as for me, I will make me ready oil, that I may enter in with the wise virgins and may not be kept outside the door with the foolish virgins."

§ 8. Hearken then, my beloved, unto that which I write unto thee, namely, whatsoever things become solitaries, monks, virgins, saints. Before all things it beseems the man on whom the yoke is laid, that his faith should be firm ; as I wrote to thee in the first epistle ; that he should be zealous in fasting and prayer ; that he should be fervent in the love of Christ ; and should be humble and mild and wise. And let his speech be peaceful and pleasant, and his thought be sincere with all. Let him speak his words duly weighing them, and set a barrier to

his mouth from harmful words, and let him put far from him hasty laughter. Let him not love the adornment of garments, nor again does it become him to let his hair grow long and adorn it, or to anoint it with sweet-scented unguents. Let him not recline at feastings, nor does it become him to wear gorgeous apparel. Let him not dare to exceed at wine. Let him put far from him proud thoughts. It does not become him to look upon gorgeous apparel. or to wear fine raiment. Let him put away from him a crafty tongue ; let him drive from him envy and wrath, and cast away from him crafty lips. The words that are spoken about a man, when he about whom they are spoken is not near, let him not hear nor receive, that he sin not, until he search them out. Mockery is a hateful fault, and to bring it up upon the heart is not right. Let him not lend and take interest, and let him not love avarice. Let him suffer wrong and not do wrong. Furthermore, let him put away from him turmoil, and words of jesting let him not utter. Let him not scorn any man who is repenting of his sins, and let him not mock his brother who is fasting, and him that cannot fast let him not put to shame. Where he is received, let him reprove, and where they receive him not, let him understand his own honour. In an acceptable time let him speak his word ; otherwise, let him be silent. Let him not for his belly's sake make himself despised by his begging, and to such an one as fears God let him reveal his secret ; but let him keep himself from the evil (man). Let him not speak in complaisance with a wicked man, nor with his enemy. And so let him contend as to have no enemy at all. When men envy him in that which is good, let him add to his goodness, and let him not be harmed because of envy. When he has, and gives to the poor, let him rejoice ; and when he has not, let it not grieve him. With a wicked man let him have no converse and with a contemptuous man let him not speak, lest he give himself to contempt. With a blasphemer let him not dispute, lest

---

his Lord be blasphemed on his account. Let him depart from a slanderer, and let no man please another man with speciousness of words. These things beseem solitaries who take up the heavenly yoke, and become disciples of Christ. For thus it befits the disciples of Christ to be like unto Christ their Master.

§ 9. Let us take pattern, my beloved, from our Saviour, Who though He was rich, made Himself poor ;[1] and though He was lofty, humbled His Majesty ; and though His dwelling place was in heaven, He had no place to lay His head ;[2] and though He is to come upon the clouds,[3] yet rode on a colt and so entered Jerusalem;[4] and though He is God and Son of God, He took upon Him the likeness of a servant;[5] and though He was (for others) rest from all weariness, yet was Himself tired with the weariness of the journey ; though He was the fountain that quenches thirst, yet Himself thirsted and asked for water ;[6] though He was abundance and satisfied our hunger, yet He Himself hungered when He went forth to the wilderness to be tempted;[7] though He was a Watcher that slumbers not, He yet slumbered and slept in the ship in the midst of the sea ;[8] and though He was ministered to in the Tabernacle of His Father, yet let Himself be served by the hands of men ; though He was the healer of all sick men, yet nails were fastened into His hands ; though His mouth brought forth things that were good, yet they gave Him gall to eat ;[9] though He injured no man and harmed none, yet He was beaten with stripes and endured shame ; and though he was Saviour of all mortals, He delivered Himself to the death of the cross.

§ 10. All this humility did our Saviour show us in Himself. Let us then also humble ourselves, my beloved. When our Lord went outside of His nature,[1] He walked in our nature. Let us abide in our nature, that in the day of judgment He may cause us to partake of His nature. Our Lord took from us a pledge when He went, and He left us a pledge of His own when he ascended. He that was without need, because of our need devised this expedient. What was ours was His even from the beginning, but that which was His, who would have given us ? But true is that which our Lord promised us :—*Where I am there ye also shall be.*[2] For whatsoever He took of ours, is in honour with Him, and (as) a diadem is bound upon His Head. So also that, which of His we have received, we ought to honour. That which is ours is held in honour with Him who was not in our nature : let us honour that which is His in His own nature. If we honour Him, we shall go to Him, Who took upon Him of our nature and so ascended. But if we despise Him, He will take away from us that which He has given us. If we deal fraudulently with His pledge, He will there take away that which is His, and will deprive us of all that He has promised us. Let us magnify gloriously the King's Son Who is with us, because a hostage for Him has been taken from us. Whoso holds the King's Son in honour, shall obtain many gifts from the King. That of ours, that is with Him, has sat down in honour and a diadem is bound upon His head, and He has sat down with the King. And we who are poor, what shall we do to the King's Son Who is with us ? He needs nothing from us, but that we should adorn our temples for Him ; that when the time is accomplished and He goes to His Father, He may give thanks to Him because of us, because we have honoured Him. When He came to us, He had nothing of ours, and also we had nothing of His, though the two natures were His and His Father's. For when Gabriel made announcement to the Blessed Mary who bore Him, the word from on high set out and came, and *the word became flesh and dwelt in us.*[3] And when He

---

[1] 2 Cor. viii. 9.  [2] Matt. viii. 20.
[3] Matt. xxvi. 64.  [4] Matt. xxi. 2–7.
[5] Phil. ii. 6, 7, 8.  [6] John iv. 6, 7.
[7] Matt. iv. 2.  [8] Matt. viii. 24.
[9] Matt. xxvii. 26, 34.
[1] *l.c.* when He took a nature which was not originally His.

[2] John xiv. 3.  [3] John i. 14.

returned to Him that sent Him, He took away, when He went, that which He had not brought, as the Apostle said :—*He has taken us up and seated us with Himself in the heavens.*[1] And when He went to His Father, He sent to us His Spirit and said to us :— *I am with you till the world shall end.* For Christ *sitteth at the right hand of His Father,* and Christ *dwelleth among men.*[2] He is sufficient above and beneath, by the wisdom of His Father. And He dwells in many, though He is one, and all the faithful each by each He overshadows from Himself, and fails not, as it is written :—*I will divide Him among many.*[3] And though He is divided among many, yet He sits at the right hand of His Father. And He is in us and we are in Him, as He said :— *Ye are in Me and I am in you.*[4] And in another place He said :—*I and My Father are one.*[5]

§ 11. And if anyone, whose conscience lacks knowledge, should dispute about this and say :—"Since Christ is one and His Father is one, how does Christ dwell, and His Father dwell, in faithful men? And how do righteous men become temples for God that He should dwell in them? If then it is thus, that to each several faithful man there comes a several Christ, and God Who is in Christ,—if it is so, there are for them Gods many and Christs without number." But hear, my beloved, the defence that is suited to this argument. From that which is visible let him that has thus said receive instruction. For every man knows that the sun is fixed in the heavens, yet its rays are spread out in the earth, and (light) from it enters by many doors and windows of houses ; and wherever the sunshine falls, though it be but as (the measure of) the palm of the hand, it is called the sun. And though it fall in many places, it is thus called, but the real sun itself is in heaven. Therefore, if it is so, *have they* many suns ? Also the water of the sea is vast, and when thou takest one cup from it, that is called water. And though thou shouldest divide it into a thousand vessels, yet it is called water by its name. Also when thou kindlest fire from fire in many places, the place from whence thou takest it, when thou kindlest it, lacks not, and the fire is called by one name. And because thou dividest it into many places, it does not on that account become possessed of many names. And when thou takest dust from the earth, and castest it into many places, it is not a whit diminished, and also thou canst not call it by many names. Thus also God and His Christ, though they are One, yet dwell in men who are many. And they are in heaven in person, and are diminished in nothing when they dwell in many ; as the sun is not a whit diminished in heaven, when its power is poured out in the earth. How much greater then is the power of God, since by the power of God the very sun itself subsists.

§ 12. Again I will remind thee, my beloved, also of that which is written. For thus it is written, that when it was a grievous burden to Moses to lead the camp alone, the Lord said to him :—*Lo ! I will take away of the Spirit that is upon thee, and will put it upon seventy men, elders of Israel.*[6] But when He took away some of the Spirit of Moses, and the seventy men were filled with it, Moses nothing lacked, nor could it be known that anything was taken away from his Spirit. Moreover the blessed apostle also said :—*God divided of the Spirit of Christ and sent it into the Prophets.*[7] And Christ was in nothing injured, for *it was not by measure that His Father gave unto Him the Spirit.*[8] By this reflection thou canst comprehend that Christ dwells in faithful men ; yet Christ suffers no loss though He is divided among many. For the Prophets received of the Spirit of Christ, each one of them as he was able to bear. And of the Spirit of Christ again there is poured forth to-day upon all flesh,[9] and the sons and the

---

[1] Eph. ii. 6.                    [2] Matt. xxviii. 20.
[3] Is. liii. 12.                  [4] John xiv. 20.
[5] John x. 30.

[6] Num. xi. 17.
[7] Cf. 1 Cor. xii. 11, 28, and Rom. xii. 36.
[8] John iii. 34.                  [9] Joel ii. 28, 29.

daughters prophesy, the old men and the youths, the men-servants and the hand-maids. Something of Christ is in us, yet Christ is in heaven at the right hand of His Father. And Christ received the Spirit not by measure, but His Father loved Him and delivered all into His hands, and gave Him authority over all His treasure. For John said :—*Not by measure did the Father give the Spirit to His Son, but loved Him and gave all into His hands.*[1] And also our Lord said :—*All things have been delivered unto Me by My Father.*[2] Again he said :—*The Father will not judge any man, but all judgment will He give unto His Son.*[3] Again also the Apostle said :—*Everything shall be made subject unto Christ except His Father Who hath subjected all unto Him. And when everything is made subject unto Him by the Father, then He also shall be made subject to God His Father Who subjected all to Him, and God shall be all in all, and in every man.*[4]

§ 13. Our Lord testifies concerning John, that he is the greatest of the Prophets. Yet he received the Spirit by limit, because in that measure in which Elijah received the Spirit, (in the same) John obtained it. And as Elijah used to dwell in the wilderness, so also the Spirit of God led John into the wilderness, and he used to dwell in the mountains and caves. The birds sustained Elijah, and John used to eat locusts that fly. Elijah had his loins girded with a girdle of leather ; so John had his loins girded with a cincture of leather. Jezebel persecuted Elijah, and Herodias persecuted John. Elijah reproved Ahab, and John reproved Herod. Elijah divided the Jordan, and John opened up baptism. The spirit of Elijah rested twofold upon Elisha, so John laid his hand on our Redeemer, and He received the Spirit not by measure. Elijah opened the heavens and ascended ; and John saw the heavens opened, and the Spirit of God which descended and rested upon our Redeemer. Elisha received two-fold the Spirit of Elijah ; and our Redeemer received that of John and that of heaven. Elisha took the mantle of Elijah, and our Redeemer the imposition of the hand of the priests. Elisha made oil from water, and our Redeemer made wine from water. Elisha satisfied with a little bread a hundred men only ; and our Redeemer satisfied with a little bread five thousand men besides children and women. Elisha cleansed Naaman the leper, and our Redeemer cleansed the ten (lepers). Elisha cursed the children and they were devoured by bears, but our Redeemer blessed the children. The children reviled Elisha, but the children glorified our Redeemer with Hosannas. Elisha cursed Gehazi his servant, and our Redeemer cursed Judas His disciple and blessed all His (other) disciples. Elisha raised to life one dead man only, but our Redeemer raised up three to life. On the bones of Elisha one dead man revived, but when our Saviour descended to the abode of the dead, He quickened many and raised them up. And many are the signs that the Spirit of Christ wrought, which the Prophets received from Him.

§ 14. Therefore, my beloved, we also have received of the Spirit of Christ, and Christ *dwelleth in us*, as it is written that the Spirit said this through the mouth of the Prophet : —*I will dwell in them and will walk in them.*[5] Therefore let us prepare our temples for the Spirit of Christ, and let us not grieve it that it may not depart from us. Remember the warning that the Apostle gives us :—*Grieve not the Holy Spirit whereby ye have been sealed unto the day of redemption.* For from baptism do we receive the Spirit of Christ. For in that hour in which the priests invoke the Spirit, the heavens open and it descends and *moves upon the waters.*[6] And those that are baptized are clothed in it ; for the Spirit stays aloof from all that are born of the flesh, until they come to the new birth by water, and then they receive the Holy Spirit. For in the first birth they are born with an ani-

---

[1] John iii. 34, 35.  [2] Matt. xi. 27.
[3] John v. 22.  [4] 1 Cor. xv. 27, 28.
[5] Levit. xxi. 12.  [6] Gen. i. 2.

mal souls which is created within man and is not thereafter subject to death, as he said :—*Adam became a living soul.*[1] But in the second birth, that through baptism, they received the Holy Spirit from a particle of the Godhead, and it is not again subject to death. For when men die, the animal spirit is buried with the body, and sense is taken away from it, but the heavenly spirit that they receive goes according to its nature to Christ. And both these the Apostle has made known, for he said :—*The body is buried in animal wise, and rises again in spiritual wise.*[2] The Spirit goes back again to Christ according to its nature, for the Apostle said again :—*When we shall depart from the body we shall be with our Lord.*[3] For the Spirit of Christ, which the spiritual receive, goes to our Lord. And the animal spirit is buried in its nature, and sense is taken away from it. Whosoever guards the Spirit of Christ in purity, when it returns to Christ it thus addresses him :—" The body into which I went, and which put me on from the water of the baptism, has kept me in holiness." And the Holy Spirit will be earnest with Christ for the resurrection of that body which kept Him with purity, and the Spirit will request to be again conjoined to it that that body may rise up in glory. And whatever man there is that receives the Spirit from the water (of baptism) and grieves it, it departs from him until he dies, and returns according to its nature to Christ, and accuses that man of having grieved it. And when the time of the final consummation shall have come, and the time of the Resurrection shall have approached, the Holy Spirit, that was kept in purity, receives great power from its nature and comes before Christ and stands at the door of the tombs, where the men are buried that kept it in purity, and awaits the (resurrection) shout. And when the Watchers shall have opened the doors of heaven before the King,[4] then the cornet shall summon, and the trumpets

shall sound, and the Spirit that waits for the (resurrection) shout shall hear, and quickly shall open the tombs, and raise up the bodies and whatsoever was buried in them, and shall put on the glory that comes with it. And (the Spirit) shall be within for the resurrection of the body, and the glory shall be without for the adornment of the body. And the animal spirit shall be swallowed up in the heavenly Spirit, and the whole man shall become spiritual, since his body is possessed by it (the Spirit). And death shall be swallowed up in life,[5] and body shall be swallowed up in Spirit. And by the power of the Spirit, that man shall fly up to meet the King and He shall receive him with joy, and Christ shall give thanks for the body that has kept His Spirit in purity.

§ 15. This is the Spirit, my beloved, that the Prophets received, and thus also have we received. And it is not at every time found with those that receive it, but sometimes it returns to Him that sent it, and sometimes it goes to him that receives it. Hearken to that which our Lord said :—*Despise not one of these little ones that believe on Me, for their angels in heaven do always behold the face of My Father.*[6] This Spirit then goes frequently and stands before God and beholds His face, and whosoever injures the temple in which it dwells, it will accuse him before God.

§ 16. I will instruct thee of that which is written, that the Spirit is not at every time found with those that receive it. For thus it is written about Saul, that the Holy Spirit, which he received when he was anointed, *departed from him,*[7] because he grieved it, and God sent to him instead of it a vexing spirit. And whenever he was afflicted by the evil spirit, David used to play upon the harp, and the Holy Spirit, which David received when he was anointed, would come, and the evil spirit that was vexing Saul, would flee from before it. So the Holy

---

[1] Gen. ii. 7.  [2] 1 Cor. xv. 44.  [5] 2 Cor. v. 4.  [6] Matt. xviii. 10.
[3] 2 Cor. v. 8.  [4] 1 Thess. iv. 16.  [7] 1 Sam. xvi. 14, *ff.*

Spirit that David received was not found with him at every time. As long as he was playing the harp, then it used to come. For had it been with him always, it would not have allowed him to sin with the wife of Uriah. For when he was praying about his sins, and was confessing his offences before God, he said thus :—*Take not Thy holy spirit from me.*[1] Also concerning Elisha it is thus written, that, *while he played upon his harp, then the spirit came to him and he prophesied and said :—Thus saith the Lord, ye shall not see wind nor rain, yet this valley shall be made many pits.*[2] And also when the Shunamite came to him because of her son that was dead, he said thus to her :—*The Lord hid it from me and did cause me not to know it.*[3] Yet, when the King of Israel sent against him to slay him, the Spirit informed him before the messenger came upon him, and he said :—*Lo! this son of iniquity has sent to take away my head.*[4] And again he made known about the abundance that came about in Samaria the day after. And again the Spirit informed him when Gehazi stole the silver and concealed it.

§ 17. Therefore, my beloved, when the Holy Spirit departs from a man who has received it, until it returns and comes to him, then Satan draws near unto that man, to cause him to sin, and that the Holy Spirit may leave him altogether. For as long as the Spirit is with a man, Satan fears to come near him. And observe, my beloved, that our Lord also, Who was born from the Spirit, was not tempted by Satan until in baptism He received the Spirit from on high. And then the Spirit led him forth to be tempted by Satan. This, then, is the way with man ; that in the hour in which he perceives in himself that he is not fervent in the Spirit, and that his heart is inclining to the thought of this world, he may know that the Spirit is not with him, and may arise and pray and keep vigil that the Spirit of God may come to him, that he be not overcome by the adversary. A thief does not dig into a house, until he sees that its master is departing from it. Thus also Satan cannot draw near to that house which is our body, until the Spirit of Christ departs from it. And be sure, my beloved, that the thief does not certainly know whether the master of the house is within or not, but first *he applies his ear*, and looks. If he hears the voice of the master of the house within it saying :—"I have a journey to go," and when he has searched out and seen that the master of the house has set out to perform his business, then the thief comes and digs into the house and steals. But if he hears the voice of the master of the house admonishing and commanding his household to watch and guard his house, and saying to them, "I also am within the house," then the thief will fear and flee, that he may not be taken and captured. Thus also Satan, he has not the knowledge beforehand to know or see when the Spirit will depart, that so he may come to rob the man ; but he too listens and watches, and so assails. But if he hears a man in whom Christ dwells speaking shameful words, or enraged, or quarrelling, or contending, then Satan knows that Christ is not with him, and he comes and accomplishes his will in him. For Christ dwells in the peaceful and the meek, and lodges in those that fear His word, as He says through the prophet :—*On whom shall I look, and in whom shall I dwell, but in the peaceful and the meek who fear My word?*[5] And our Lord said :—*Whoever walks in My commandments and keeps My love, We will come to him and make Our abode with him.*[6] But if he hears from a man that he is on his guard and is praying and meditating in the Law of his Lord by day and by night, then he turns back from him, for he knows that Christ is with him. And if thou shouldest say, "How manifold is Satan! for lo! he fights with many ;" then hear and learn from that which I proved to thee above

---

[1] Ps. li. 13.  [2] 2 Kings iii. 15-17.  [3] 1 Kings iv. 27.  [4] 2 Kings vi. 32.  [5] Is. lxvi. 2.  [6] John xiv. 23.

concerning Christ, that no matter to what extent He is divided amongst many, yet He is not a whit diminished. For, as the house, through the window of which a little sunlight enters, is altogether illumined, so the man into whom a little of Satan enters, is altogether darkened. Hear that which the Apostle said :—*If Satan is transfigured to an angel of light, it is no wonder if his ministers also are transfigured to ministers of righteousness.*[1] And again our Lord said to His disciples :—*Lo, I have given you authority to tread upon the power of the adversary.*[2] And the Scriptures have made known that he has power and also ministers. Moreover Job said concerning him :— *God made him to wage his war.*[3] These ministers then that he has, he causes to run in the world, to wage war. But be sure that he will not fight openly ; because from the time of the coming of our Saviour, (God) has given authority over him. But he will surely plunder and steal.

§ 18. But I will explain to thee, my beloved, concerning that word which the Apostle said, by which can be weighed the doctrines that are instruments of the Evil One and doctrines of deceit. For the Apostle said :—*There is an animal body and there is a spiritual body, seeing that it is thus written :—The first Adam became a living soul and the second Adam a quickening spirit.*[4] So they[5] say that there will be two Adams. But he said :—*As we have put on the image of that Adam who was from the earth, so we shall put on the image of that Adam who is from heaven.*[6] For Adam who was from the earth was he that sinned, and the Adam who is from heaven is our Saviour, our Lord Jesus Christ. They then that receive the Spirit of Christ, come into the likeness of the heavenly Adam, Who is our Saviour, our Lord Jesus Christ. For the animal shall be swallowed up in the spiritual, as I wrote unto thee above. And the man that grieves the spirit of Christ, will be animal in his resurrection ;

because the heavenly spirit is not with him, that the animal might be swallowed up in it. But when he shall arise he shall continue in his natural state, naked of the Spirit. Because he stripped off from him the Spirit of Christ, he shall be given over to utter nakedness. And whosoever honours the Spirit, and it is guarded in him in purity, in that day the Holy Spirit shall protect him, and he shall become altogether spiritual, and shall not be found naked ; as the Apostle said :—*And when we shall have clothed ourselves, may we not be found naked.*[7] And again he said :—*We shall all sleep, but in the resurrection we shall not all be changed.*[8] And again he said :—*This which dies shall put on that which dies not, and this which is corruptible that which is incorruptible, and when this which dies shall have put on that which dies not, and this corruptible that which is incorruptible, then shall be accomplished that word which is written that death is swallowed up by victory.*[9] Again he said :— *Suddenly as the twinkling of an eye, the dead shall rise incorruptible and we shall be changed.*[1] And they who shall be changed shall put on the form of that heavenly Adam and shall become spiritual. And those who shall not be changed, shall continue animal in the created nature of Adam, namely, of dust ; and shall continue in their nature in the earth below. And then the heavenly shall be caught up to heaven and the Spirit that they have put on shall cause them to fly, and they shall inherit the kingdom that was prepared for them from the beginning. And they that are animal shall remain on the earth by the weight of their bodies, and shall turn back to Sheol, and there shall be weeping and gnashing of teeth.

§ 19. In writing this I have reminded myself, and also thee, my beloved ; therefore love virginity, the heavenly portion, the fellowship of the Watchers of heaven. For

---

[1] 2 Cor. xi. 14, 15.　　　[2] Luke x. 19.
[3] Job xl. 14.　　　[4] 1 Cor. xv. 44, 45.
[5] *Scil.*, heretics.　　　[6] 1 Cor. xv. 49.

[7] 2 Cor. v. 3.
[8] 1 Cor. xv. 51. This transposition of the negative is supported by many Greek and Latin authorities, but not by the Peshitto.
[9] 1 Cor. xv. 53, 54.　　　[1] 1 Cor. xv. 52.

there is nothing comparable with it. And in those that are thus, in them Christ dwells. *The time of summer is at hand, and the fig-tree has budded and its leaves have come out* [1]—the signs that our Redeemer gave have begun to be fulfilled. For he said :—*People shall rise against people and kingdom against kingdom. And there shall be famines and pestilences and terrors from heaven.* [2] And lo ! all these things are being accomplished in our days.

§ 20. Therefore read in this whatever I have written unto thee, thou and the brethren, the monks that love virginity. And be on thy guard against scorners. For whosoever scorns and mocks his brother, the word that is written in the Gospel fitly applies to him ; namely, when our Lord wished to take account with the avaricious and with the Pharisees. For it is written : —*Because they loved money, they mocked Him.* [3] So also now those that do not agree with these things mock in the same way. Read then and learn. Be zealous for reading and for doing. And let the Law of God be thy meditation at every time. And when thou hast read this epistle, on thy life (I adjure thee), my beloved, arise and pray, and remember my sinfulness in thy prayer.

### Demonstration VIII.—Of the Resurrection of the Dead.

§ 1. At all times controversies arise on this matter, *how the dead shall rise and with what body they shall come ?* [4] For lo ! the body wears out and is corrupted ; and the bones also, no doubt, as time lengthens out over them, waste away and are not to be recognised. And when thou enterest a tomb in which a hundred dead men are buried, thou findest not there an handful of dust. And thus say those that reflect on these things :—" We know of course that the dead shall rise ; but they will be clothed in a heavenly body and spiritual forms. And if it is not so, these hundred dead that were buried in one tomb, of whom after a long time elapses there remains nothing at all there, when the dead shall be quickened, and shall be clothed in a body and rise, unless they shall be clothed in a heavenly body, from whence shall their body come ? For lo ! there is nothing in the tomb."

§ 2. Whosoever reflects thus is foolish, and without knowledge. When the dead were brought in, they were something ; and when they were there for a long time, they became nothing. And, when the time shall have come that the dead shall rise, that nothing shall become something according to its former nature, and a change shall be added to its nature. O thou unwise who reflectest thus, hear that which the blessed Apostle said when he was instructing a foolish man like thee ; for he said :—*Thou fool, the seed which thou sowest unless it die is not quickened ; and that which thou sowest is not like that which grows up into its blade, but one bare grain of wheat or barley or some other seedling. And to each one of the seeds is given its own body. But God clothes thy seed with its body as He wills.* [5]

§ 3. Therefore, O fool, be instructed by this, that each of the seeds is clothed in its own body. Never dost thou sow wheat and yet reap barley, and never dost thou plant a vine and yet it produced figs ; but everything grows according to its nature. Thus also the body that was laid in the earth is that which shall rise again. And as to this, that the body is corrupted and wastes away, thou oughtest to be instructed by the parable of the seed ; that as the seed, when it is cast into the earth, decays and is corrupted, and from its decay it produces and buds and bears fruit. For the land that is ploughed, into which seed is not cast, produces not fruit, even if that land drinks in all the rain. So the grave in which the dead are not buried, from it men shall not issue forth in the quickening of the dead, though the full voice of the trumpet should

---

[1] Matt. xxiv. 32.　　[2] Luke xxi. 10, 11.
[3] Luke xvi. 14.　　[4] 1 Cor. xv. 35.

[5] 1 Cor. xv. 36–38.

sound within it. And if, as they say, the spirit of the just shall ascend into heaven and put on a heavenly body, they are in heaven. And He Who raises the dead dwells in heaven. Then when our Saviour shall come, whom shall He raise up from the earth? And why did He write for us :—*The hour shall come, and now is, that the dead also shall hear the voice of the Son of Man, and they shall live and come forth from their tombs?*[1] For the heavenly body will not come and enter into the tomb, and again go forth from it.

§ 4. For thus say those who are stubborn in folly :—Why did the Apostle say,—*Different is the body which is in heaven from that which is on earth?*[2] But he that hears this, let him hear also the other thing that the Apostle said :—*There is an animal body, and there is a spiritual body.*[3] And again he said :—*We shall all sleep, but we shall not all be changed.*[4] And again he said :—*This that shall die must clothe itself with that that shall not die, and this which is corruptible must clothe itself with that which is incorruptible.*[5] Again he said :—*We must all stand before the judgment-seat of Christ, that every man may be rewarded in his body for everything that before time was done by him, whether good or evil.*[6] Again he said :—*What shall those do that are baptized for the dead? For if the dead rise not, why are they baptized for them?*[7] Again he said :—*If there is no resurrection of the dead, then is Christ not risen, and if Christ is not risen then your faith is vain, and our preaching. And if so we are found false witnesses in that we testified of God, that He raised up Christ, Whom He raised not up.*[8] Therefore, if the dead rise not, there is no judgment. And if there is no judgment, then *let us eat and drink, for to-morrow we shall die. Be not deceived; evil communications corrupt good purposes.*[9] Now as to this that the Apostle said :—*The body that is in heaven is different from that*

*which is on the earth,* let this word be thus understood by thee. When the body of the just shall arise and be changed, it is called heavenly. And that which is not changed is called earthly, according to its earthly nature.

§ 5. But hear, my beloved, another word like this, which the Apostle has spoken. For he said:—*The spiritual man judgeth everything, and he is judged by no one.*[1] And again he said :—*They that are spiritual are spiritually minded, and they that are carnal are carnally minded.*[2] And again he said:—*When we were in the flesh, the weaknesses of sins were working in our members that we might become fruits for death.*[3] Again he said:—*If the Spirit of Christ is in you, ye are spiritual.*[4] All these things the Apostle said, while he was clothed in the flesh but was doing the works of the Spirit. Thus also in the Resurrection of the dead, the righteous shall be changed, and the earthly form shall be swallowed up in the heavenly, and it shall be called a heavenly body. And that which shall not be changed, shall be called earthly.

§ 6. Concerning then this Resurrection of the dead, my beloved, according to my power I will instruct thee. For from the beginning God created Adam; moulded him from the dust of the earth, and raised him up. For if, while Adam was not, He made him from nothing, how much easier now is it for Him to raise him up; for lo! as a seed he is sown in the earth. For if God should do those things that are easy for us, His works would not appear mighty to us. For lo! there are amongst men artificers who make wonderful things, and those who are not artificers of the works stand and wonder how they were done; and the work of their fellows is difficult in their eyes. How much more should not the works of God be as a marvel! But for God this was no great thing, that the dead should be quickened. Before seed was sown in the earth, the earth produced that which had not been cast

---

1 John v. 25, 28, 29.    2 1 Cor. xv. 40.
3 1 Cor. xv. 44.    4 *Ib.* xv. 51.
5 *Ib.* v. 53.    6 2 Cor. v. 10.
7 1 Cor. xv. 29.    8 *Ib.* v. 13-15.
9 *Ib.* v. 32, 33.

---

1 1 Cor. ii. 15.    2 Rom. viii. 5.
3 Rom. vii. 5.    4 Rom. viii. 9.

into it. Before it had conceived, it bore in its virginity. How then is this difficult, that the earth should cause to spring up again what had been cast into it, and after conception should bear? And lo! her travail-pains are near; as Isaiah said, *Who hath seen anything like this and who hath heard such things as these? that the earth should travail in one day, and a people should be born in one hour?* [1] For Adam unsown sprang up; unconceived he was born. But lo! now his offspring are sown, and wait for the rain, and shall spring up. And lo! the earth teems with many, and the time of her bringing forth is at hand.

§ 7. For all our fathers, in hope of the Resurrection and the quickening of the dead, were looking forward and hastening; as the blessed Apostle said, *If the righteous had been looking forward to that city from which Abraham went forth, they would have had an opportunity of again turning back and going to it; but they showed that they were looking forward to one better than it, namely that which is in heaven.* [2] They were looking forward to be released and to go speedily thither. And from that which I am writing unto thee, understand and observe that they were looking forward to the Resurrection. For Jacob our father, when he was dying, bound Joseph his son with an oath, and said to him, *Bury me in the tomb of my fathers, with Abraham and Sarah and Isaac and Rebecca.* [3] And why, my beloved, did Jacob not wish to be buried in Egypt, but with his fathers? He showed beforehand, that he was looking forward to the quickening of the dead; that, when the Resurrection shout should be raised and the sound of the trumpet (heard), he might rise up near to his fathers, and might not at the time of the Resurrection be mingled with the wicked who shall return to Sheol and to punishment.

§ 8. Thus also Joseph bound his brethren by an oath, [4] and said to them:—*When God shall remember you, take up my bones from hence with you.* And according to the word of Joseph his brethren did, and kept the oath a hundred and twenty-five years. At that time when the hosts of the Lord went out from the land of Egypt, then Moses took up the bones of Joseph when he went forth. [5] And the bones of the righteous man were more precious and better in his estimation than the gold and the silver that the children of Israel took from Egypt when they spoiled them. And the bones of Joseph were forty years in the wilderness; and at that time when Moses fell asleep, he gave them in inheritance to Joshua the son of Nun. The bones of Joseph his father were better in his estimation than all the spoil of that land which he subdued. And why did Moses give the bones of Joseph to Joshua? Clearly, because he was of the tribe of Ephraim the son of Joseph. And he buried them in the land of promise, that there might be in that land a treasure, (even that of the bones of Joseph (that were) buried therein. And also at the time that Jacob was dying, he blessed his tribes, and showed them what would happen to them *in the latter days,* and said to Reuben:—*Reuben, thou art my firstborn, my might and the beginning of my strength. Thou hast gone astray; as water, thou shalt not abide, because thou wentest up to thy father's bed. Truly thou defilest my couch and wentest up.* [6] From the time that Jacob fell asleep until the time that Moses fell asleep two hundred and thirty-three years elapsed. Then Moses wished by his priestly power to absolve Reuben from his transgression and sin, in that he had lain with Bilhah, his father's concubine; that when his brethren should rise, he might not be cut off from their number. So he said in the beginning of his blessing :—*Reuben shall live and not die, and shall be in the number.* [7]

§ 9. And also when the time came that Moses should sleep with his fathers, he was grieved and distressed, and he sought of his Lord and entreated that he might pass over

---

[1] Is. lxvi. 8.     [2] Heb. ix. 15, 16.     [5] Exod. xiii. 19.     [6] Gen. xlix. 3, 4.
[3] Gen. xlix. 29, 31.     [4] Gen. l. 24.     [7] Deut. xxxiii. 6.

to the land of promise. And why, my beloved, was the righteous Moses grieved because he did not enter into the land of promise ? Clearly, because he wished to go and be buried with his fathers, and not be buried in the land of his adversaries, in the land of Moab. For the Moabites hired Balaam the son of Beor to curse Israel. Therefore Moses wished not to be buried in that land, lest the Moabites should come and take vengeance on him by taking up and casting forth the bones of that righteous man. And the Lord performed an act of grace towards Moses. For He brought him forth to Mount Nebo, and showed him all the land, making it pass before him. And as Moses gazed upon all the land, and gazed upon the mountain of the Jebusites where the Tabernacle was to dwell, he was grieved and wept when he saw the tomb in Hebron where his fathers Abraham, Isaac and Jacob were buried, that he should not be buried with them, nor his bones cast upon their bones, that he might rise along with them in the Resurrection. But when he had seen all the land, his Lord encouraged him and said to him, "I myself will bury thee and hide thee, and none shall know thy tomb." *So Moses died according to the word of the mouth of the Lord, and He buried him in a valley in the land of Moab over against Beth-Peor, where Israel had sinned, and no man has known his sepulchre unto this day.*[1] Two goodly benefits did his Lord accomplish for Moses in not making known his tomb to the children of Israel. He rejoiced that his adversaries should not know it, and cast forth his bones from his tomb ; and in the second place, that the children of his people should not know it, and make his tomb a place of worship, for he was accounted as God in the eyes of the children of his people. And understand this, my beloved, from hence, that when he left them and went up to the mountain, they said:[2]—*As for this Moses who brought us up from the land of Egypt we know not what has become of him.* So they

made them a calf and worshipped it, and they remembered not God Who brought them up from Egypt by means of Moses *with a mighty hand and an uplifted arm.*[3] Because of this, God had respect unto Moses, and did not make known his tomb ; lest, if He should make known his tomb, the children of his people might go astray, and make them an image, and worship it and sacrifice to it, and so by their sins disquiet the bones of the righteous man.

§10. And Moses again proclaimed clearly the Resurrection of the dead, for he said as from the mouth of his God :—*It is I that cause to die and it is I that make alive.*[4] Again also Hannah said thus in her prayer :—*The Lord causeth to die and quickeneth ; He bringeth down to Sheol and bringeth up (therefrom).*[5] The Prophet Isaiah also said thus : —*Thy dead shall live, O Lord, and their bodies shall rise, and they that sleep in the dust shall awake and praise thee.*[6] David also proclaimed, saying :—*For lo ! for the dead Thou workest wonderful things, and the mighty ones shall rise and make confession unto Thee, and those that are in the tombs shall recount Thy grace.*[7] And how *in the tombs* shall they *recount the grace* of God ? Clearly, when they shall hear the sound of trumpet summoning them, and the cornet sounding forth from on high, and the earthquake that shall be, and the tombs that shall be opened, then the mighty ones shall arise in glory, and recount one to another in the tombs, saying, "Great is the grace that is performed towards us. For our hope was cut off ; yet (another) hope has arisen for us. We were imprisoned in darkness, and have come forth to the light. We were sown in corruption, and have risen in glory. We were buried naturally, and we have risen spiritually. Again we were sown in weakness, and have risen in power." This is the grace that they shall tell of in the tombs.

§ 11. And it was not only in words, my

---

[1] Deut. xxxiv. 5, 6.          [2] Ex. xxxii. 1.

[3] Deut. v. 15.
[5] 1 Sam. ii. 6.
[7] Ps. lxxxviii. 10, 11, 12.   (Pesh.)

[4] Deut. xxxii. 39.
[6] Is. xxvi. 19.

beloved, that God said:—"I quicken the dead," but also in deeds He showed it to us by many testimonies; that we might have no hesitation (concerning it). He showed it beforehand plainly; for through Elijah a wonder was manifested, (in proof) that the dead shall live and that they that sleep in the dust shall arise. For when the son of the widow died, Elijah raised him up and gave him to his mother. And Elisha again, his disciple, raised up the son of the Shunamite; that the testimony of two might be established and confirmed for us. And also again when the children of Israel cast a dead man on the bones of Elisha, that dead man revived and arose. And the witness of three is certain.

§ 12. And also through the Prophet Ezekiel, the Resurrection of the dead was manifestly shown, when God brought him forth to the valley and showed him many bones, and made him pass by them round about them, and said to him:—*Son of Man, will these bones live?* And Ezekiel said to Him:[1]—*Thou knowest, O Lord of lords.* And the Lord said to him:—*Prophesy, O Son of Man, over these bones; prophesy and say to the dry bones, Hear the word of the Lord of lords.* And when he had caused them to hear those words, there was a shaking and a noise, and the bones were gathered together, even those that were crushed into pieces and broken. And when the Prophet saw them, he was astonished, for they came together from all sides, and each bone received its fellow, and each joint approached its fellow-joint, and they ordered themselves, one on another. And their dryness was made moist, and the joints were united by the ligatures, and the blood grew warm in the arteries, and skin was stretched over the flesh, and hair grew up according to its nature. But they lay prostrate and there was no breath in them. Then again He commanded the Prophet, and said to him:—*Prophesy unto the spirit and say to it, Come, O spirit, from the four winds, and breathe upon these slain men that they may live.* And when he caused them to hear this second word, *the spirit entered into them, and they revived and stood up upon their feet, a very great host.*

§ 13. But why, my beloved, was it that those dead did not rise because of the one word (spoken) through Ezekiel, and why was not their resurrection, both of bones and spirit, accomplished (through that one word)? For lo! by one word the bones were fitted together, and by another the spirit came. It was in order that full perfection might be left for our Lord Jesus Christ, Who with one utterance and one word will raise up at the last day every body of man. For it was not the word that was insufficient, but its bearer was inferior. And with regard to this, understand and observe that when Elijah also, and Elisha his disciple, raised the dead, it was not with one word that they raised them up, but after they had prayed and made intercession and delayed no little time, then they arose.

§ 14. And our Lord Himself, in that His first Coming raised up three that were dead, that the testimony of three might be made sure. And He raised up each one of them with two words each. For when He raised up the widow's son, He called him twice, saying to him, *Young man, young man, arise.*[2] And he revived and arose. And again, He twice called the daughter of the chief of the synagogue, saying to her, *Damsel, damsel, arise.*[3] And her spirit returned and she arose. And after Lazarus died, when He came to the place of burial, He prayed earnestly and cried with a loud voice and said, *Lazarus, come forth.*[4] And he revived and came out of his tomb.

§ 15. And concerning all this that I have explained to thee, that those dead persons were raised with two words each, it was because for them two resurrections take place; that former one, and the second, that which is to come. For in that resurrection in which all men shall rise, none shall fall again; and by one word of God, sent forth

---

[1] Ez. xxxvii. 1–10.  [2] Luke vii. 14.  [3] Mark v. 47.  [4] John xi. 43.

through Christ, all *the dead shall rise in the twinkling of an eye, speedily.* For He Who brings it to pass is not feeble or insufficient. For with one word of summons He will cause all the ends (of the world) to hear, and all that are laid (in the grave) shall leap forth and rise up ; and no word shall return void to Him that sent it forth, but as it is written in the Prophet Isaiah,[1] who compares the word to rain and snow ; for he said :—*As the rain and the snow come down from heaven and return not thither, but fertilize the earth and cause it to bring forth and give seed to the sower and bread for food, so shall the word be that goes forth from My mouth, and it shall not return to Me void, but shall accomplish whatsoever I desire and shall accomplish that for which I shall have sent it.* For the rain and the snow do not return to heaven, but accomplish in the earth the will of Him that sends them. So the word that He shall send through His Christ, Who is Himself the Word and the Message, shall return to Him with great power. For when He shall come and bring it, He shall come down like rain and snow, and through Him all that is sown shall spring up and bear righteous fruit, and the word shall return to His sender ; but not in vain shall His going have been, but thus shall He say in the presence of His sender :—*Behold, I and the children that the Lord has given Me.*[2] And this is the voice through which the dead shall live. Concerning it our Redeemer testifies, saying :—*The hour shall come when even the dead shall hear the voice of the Son of Man and shall come forth from their tombs ;*[3] as it is written, *In the beginning was the voice, that is the Word.*[4] Again He said, *The Word became a body and dwelt amongst us.*[5] And this is that voice of God which shall sound from on high and raise up all the dead.

§ 16. Again, our Lord explained to the Sadducees with regard to the resurrection of the dead, when they brought forth to Him the parable of the woman who was married to seven husbands, and said to Him :—*Lo ! the woman was wife of them all ; in the Resurrection of the dead, to which of them shall she be wife ?*[6] Then our Lord said to them :—*Ye do greatly err, and ye know not the Scriptures nor the power of God. For they who are worthy of that world and of that Resurrection from the dead, they that are men do not take wives, nor are the women married to husbands, for they cannot die, for they are as the angels of God and children of the Resurrection. But concerning the Resurrection, that the dead shall rise, have ye not read in the Scripture that God said to Moses out of the bush, "I am the God of Abraham, of Isaac and of Jacob." And lo ! He is not God of the dead, for they all are alive unto Him.*[7]

§ 17. And there are those who even while they live are dead unto God. For He laid a commandment on Adam and said to him, *In the day that thou shalt eat of the tree, thou shalt surely die.*[8] And after he had transgressed the commandment, and had eaten, he lived nine hundred and thirty years ; but he was accounted dead unto God because of his sins. But that it may be made certain for thee that a sinner is called dead even when he lives, I will make it clear to thee. For thus it is written in Ezekiel the Prophet, *As I live, saith the Lord of lords, I desire not the death of the dead sinner.*[9]

§ 18. Moreover our Lord said to that man who said to Him :—*Let me go and bury my father, and I will come to Thee.*[1] And our Lord said to him, *Let the dead bury their dead, but go thou, preach the Kingdom of God.* But how is this word understood by thee, my beloved? Didst thou ever see the dead burying their dead? Or how shall a dead man arise to bury another dead man? But receive this explanation from me, that a sinner, while he is living, is dead unto God ; and a righteous man, though dead, is alive unto God. For such death is a sleep, as

---

[1] Is. lv. 10, 11.  [2] Is. viii. 18.  [3] John v. 25.
[4] John i. 1.  [5] John i. 14.

[6] Matt. xxii. 28.  [7] Matt. xxiii. 29–32.
[8] Gen. ii. 17.  [9] Ez. xviii. 23, 32 ; xxxiii. 11.
[1] Luke ix 59, 60.

David said, *I lay down and slept, and awoke.*[1] Again Isaiah said, *They that sleep in the dust shall awake.*[2] And our Lord said concerning the daughter of the chief of the synagogue, *The damsel is not dead, but sleeping a slumber.*[3] And concerning Lazarus, He said to His disciples :—*Our friend Lazarus has fallen asleep ; but I go to waken him.*[4] And the Apostle said :—*We shall all sleep, but we shall not all be changed.*[5] And again he said :—*Concerning those that sleep, be ye not grieved.*[6]

§ 19. But it is right for us to be afraid of the second death,[7] that which is full of weeping and gnashing of teeth, and of groanings and miseries, that which is situated in outer darkness. But blessed shall be the faithful and the righteous in that Resurrection, in which they expect to be awakened and to receive the good promises made them. But as for the wicked who are not faithful, in the Resurrection woe to them, because of that which is laid up for them ! It would be better for them according to the faith which they possess, were they not to arise. For the servant, for whom his Lord is preparing stripes and bonds, while he is sleeping desires not to awake, for he knows that when the dawn shall have come and he shall awake, his Lord will scourge and bind him. But the good servant, to whom his Lord has promised gifts, looks expectantly for the time when dawn shall come and he shall receive presents from his Lord. And even though he is soundly sleeping, in his dream he sees something like what his Lord is about to give him, whatsoever He has promised him, and he rejoices in his dream, and exults, and is gladdened. As for the wicked, his sleep is not pleasant to him, for he imagines that lo ! the dawn has come for him, and his heart is broken in his dream. But the righteous sleep, and their slumber is pleasant to them, in the day-time and the night-time, and they take no thought of all that long night, and like one

hour is it accounted in their eyes. Then in the watch of the dawn they awake with joy. But as for the wicked, their sleep lies heavy upon them, and they are like a man who is laid low by a great and deep fever, and tosses on his couch hither and thither, and he is terrified the whole night long, which lengthens itself out for him, and he fears the dawn when his Lord will condemn him.

§ 20. But our faith thus teaches, that when men fall asleep, they sleep this slumber without knowing good from evil. And the righteous look not forward to their promises, nor do the wicked look forward to their sentence of punishment, until the Judge come and separate those whose place is at His right hand from those whose place is at His left. And be thou instructed by that which is written, that when the Judge shall sit, and the books be opened before Him and the good and evil deeds recited, then they that have wrought good works shall receive good rewards from Him Who is good ; and they that have done evil deeds shall receive evil penalties from the just Judge. For towards the good, He changes not His nature ; and He proves Himself just because He justly condemns many. But towards the evil He changes His nature, in that world where grace is lost in justice ; and He proves Himself just to all. And grace will not be joined with justice towards them. Like as grace avails not (to remedy) detriment, so justice (avails not to assist) grace. For grace is far from the judge, but justice urges the judge. If grace be nigh to any one, let him turn himself towards it, and not deliver himself into the hands of justice, lest it condemn him, exacting for his shortcomings the penalty at his hands. And if grace be far from any one, justice will bring him to the trial, and by it he will be condemned, and go away to the torment.

§ 21. But hear, my beloved, this proof that retribution shall take place at the end. For when the Shepherd divides His flock and sets some on His right hand and some on His

---

[1] Ps. iii. 4.  [2] Is. xxvi. 19.
[3] Matt. ix. 26.  [4] John xi. 11.
[5] 1 Cor. xv. 51.  [6] 1 Thess. iv. 13.
[7] Rev. ii. 11; xx. 14; xxi. 18.

left,[1] until He shall have acknowledged the service of the good, then He will cause them to inherit the kingdom ; and until He shall have rebuked the evil and they are condemned, then He will send them to the torment. And as to them that sent messengers after the King, saying, *This man shall not be king over us,*[2] when He shall receive the kingdom and return, then His adversaries shall be slain before Him. And the labourers who hastened and were wearied in the vineyard, shall not receive the reward till the labour shall cease. And the traders who received the money, when the Lord of the money shall come, then shall He exact the usury. And the virgins who, while waiting for the bridegroom, slumbered and slept because He delayed to come, when they shall hear the cry, then they shall awake and trim their lamps ; and they that are wise shall enter in ; and the foolish shall be shut out. And they who were before us in entering the faith, without us *shall not be made perfect.*[3]

§ 22 From all these things, understand thou, my beloved, as it has been made certain for thee, that as yet no one has received his reward. For the righteous have not inherited the kingdom, nor have the wicked gone into torment. The Shepherd has not as yet divided His flock. And lo ! the workmen enter into the vineyard, and as yet have not received the reward. And lo ! the merchants are trading with the money. And as yet their Lord has not come to take the account. And the King has gone to receive the Kingdom, but as yet He has not returned the second time. And those virgins that are waiting the bridegroom are sleeping up to the present time, and are awaiting the cry when they will awake. And the former men who toiled in the faith until the last men shall come, shall not be made perfect.

§ 23. But they who are babes in understanding say :—" If no one has received his

reward, why did the Apostle say, *When we shall depart from the body, we shall be present with the Lord ?* "[4] But recollect, my beloved, that I instructed thee concerning this matter in the *Demonstration concerning Solitaries,*[5] that the spirit which the righteous receive, according to its heavenly nature, goes to our Lord until the time of the Resurrection, when it shall come to put on the body in which it dwelt. And at every time it has the memory of this in the presence of God, and looks eagerly for the Resurrection of that body in which it dwelt, as the Prophet Isaiah said about the Church of the Gentiles :—*They that make mention of thee shall be faithful and stand before the Lord, and thou shalt not give them rest.*[6] But as to the wicked, they have none to make mention of them before the Lord, because the Holy Spirit is far removed from them, because they are animal, and are buried after the manner of animals.

§ 24. And again, (the followers of) doctrines, which are instruments of the Evil One, are offended by the word which our Lord spake, *No one has ascended up to heaven but He Who came down from heaven, the Son of Man, Who was in heaven.*[7] And they say, "Lo ! our Lord testified that no earthly body has ascended to heaven." In their ignorance they cannot apprehend the force of this. For when our Lord instructed Nicodemus, he did not apprehend the force of the saying. Then our Lord said to him :—"*No one has ascended into heaven, so as to come down and* relate to you whatsoever is there. For *if I have spoken unto you of those things that are in the earth, and ye believe not, how shall ye believe if I shall speak unto you of those things which are in heaven?*[8] For lo ! no other witness besides Me has come down from thence, to bear witness concerning those things which are in heaven, so that ye should believe.

---

[1] Matt. xxv. 32, *ff*.  
[3] Hebr. xi. 40.  
[2] Luke xx. 9, *ff*.

[4] 2 Cor. v. 8.  
[5] See *Dem.* VI. 14.  
[6] Is. lxii. 6, 7. This quotation differs widely from the Peshitto, as well as from the Hebrew and the Septuagint.  
[7] John iii. 13.  
[8] John iii. 12.

For Elijah went up thither, but he came not down along with Me to bear witness, that the testimony of two might be sure."

§ 25. But as for thee, my beloved, have no doubt as to the Resurrection of the dead. For the living mouth (of God) testifies :— *I cause to die and I make alive.*[1] And both of them proceeded out of one mouth. And as we are sure that He causes to die, and we see it ; so also it is sure and worthy of belief, that He makes alive. And from all that I have explained to thee, receive and believe that in the day of the Resurrection thy body shall arise in its entirety, and thou shalt receive from our Lord the reward of thy faith, and in all that thou hast believed, thou shalt rejoice and be made glad.

### Demonstration X.—OF PASTORS.

§ 1. Pastors are set over the flock, and give the sheep the food of life. Whosoever is watchful, and toils in behalf of his sheep, is careful for his flock, and is the disciple of our Good Shepherd, who gave Himself in behalf of His sheep.[2] And whosoever brings not back his flock carefully, is likened to the hireling who has no care for the sheep. Be ye like, O Pastors, to those righteous Pastors of old. Jacob fed the sheep of Laban, and guarded them and toiled and was watchful, and so received the reward. For Jacob said to Laban :—*Lo ! twenty years am I with thee. Thy sheep and thy flocks I have not robbed and the males of thy sheep I have not eaten. That which was broken I did not bring unto thee, but thou required it at my hands ! In the daytime the heat devoured me and the cold by night.*[3] *My sleep departed from my eyes.* Observe, ye Pastors, that Pastor, how he cared for his flock. He used to watch in the night-time to guard it and was vigilant ; and he used to toil in the daytime to feed it. As Jacob was a pastor, so Joseph was a

pastor and his brethren were pastors. Moses was a pastor, and David also was a pastor. So Amos was a pastor. These all were pastors who fed the sheep and led them well.

§ 2. Now, why, my beloved, did these pastors first feed the sheep, and were then chosen to be pastors of men ? Clearly that they might learn how a pastor cares for his sheep, and is watchful and toils in behalf of his sheep. And when they had learned the manners of pastors, they were chosen for the pastoral office. Jacob fed the sheep of Laban and toiled and was vigilant and led them well ; and then he tended and guided well his sons, and taught them the pattern of pastoral work. And Joseph used to tend the sheep along with his brethren ; and in Egypt he became guide to a numerous people, and led them back, as a good pastor does his flock. Moses fed the sheep of Jethro his father-in-law, and he was chosen from (tending) the sheep to tend his people, and as a good pastor he guided them. Moses bore his staff upon his shoulder, and went in front of his people that he was leading, and tended them for forty years ; and he was vigilant and toiled on behalf of his sheep, a diligent and good pastor. When his Lord wished to destroy them because of their sins, in that they worshipped the calf, Moses prayed and besought of his Lord and said :—*Either pardon the people for their sins, or else blot me out from Thy book that Thou hast written.*[4] That is a most diligent pastor, who delivered over himself on behalf of his sheep. That is an excellent leader, who gave himself in behalf of his sheep. And that is a merciful father who cherished his children and reared them up. Moses the great and wise shepherd, who knew how to lead back the flock, taught Joshua the son of Nun, a man full of the spirit, who (afterwards) led the flock, even all the host of Israel. He destroyed kings and subdued the land, and gave them the land as a place of pasturage, and divided the resting-places and the sheepfolds to his

---

[1] Deut. xxxii. 39.      [2] John x. 11, sq.
[3] Gen. xxxi. 38, 40.

[4] Ex. xxxii. 31, 32.

sheep. Furthermore, David fed his father's sheep, and was taken from the sheep to tend his people. *So he tended them in the integrity of his heart and by the skill of his hands he guided them.*[1] And when David numbered the flock of his sheep, wrath came upon them, and they began to be destroyed. Then David delivered himself over on behalf of his sheep, when he prayed, saying :— *O Lord God, I have sinned in that I have numbered Israel. Let Thy hand be on me and on my father's house. These innocent sheep, in what have they sinned ?*[2] So also all the diligent pastors used thus to give themselves on behalf of their sheep.

§ 3. But those pastors who did not care for the sheep, those were hirelings who used to feed themselves alone. On this account the Prophet[3] addresses them, saying to them :—*O ye pastors who destroy and scatter the sheep of my pasture, hear the word of the Lord. Thus saith the Lord: Lo! I will visit My sheep as the pastor visits his flock in the day of the whirlwind, and I will require My sheep at your hands. O foolish pastors, with the wool of the sheep do ye clothe yourselves and the flesh of the fatlings do ye eat, and the sheep ye do not feed. That which was sick ye did not heal, and that which was broken ye did not bind up. The weak ye did not strengthen, and the lost and the scattered ye did not gather together. The strong ones and the fatlings ye did not guard, but with harshness ye subdued them. The good pastures ye yourselves graze upon, and what remains ye trample with your feet. The pleasant waters do ye drink, and whatever remains ye defile with your feet. And My sheep have eaten the trampled (herbage) which your feet have trampled, and they have drunk the waters which your feet have defiled.* These are the greedy and base pastors and hirelings, who did not feed the sheep, or guide them well, or deliver them from the wolves. But when the Great Pastor, the chief of pastors, shall come, He will call and visit His sheep and will take knowledge of His

flock. And He will bring forward those pastors, and will exact an account from them, and will condemn them for their deeds. And those who fed the sheep well, them the Chief of Pastors will cause to rejoice and to inherit life and rest. *O stupid and foolish pastor, to whose right hand and to whose right eye I committed my sheep. Because thou didst say concerning the sheep, let that which dieth, die, and let that which perisheth perish, and whatever is left, let them devour the flesh of one another; therefore, behold I will make blind thy right eye and I will wither up thy right arm. Thy eye which regarded a bribe shall be blinded, and thy hand which did not rule in righteousness shall waste away.*[4] *And as for you, my sheep, the sheep of my pasture, ye are men; but I am the Lord your God.*[5] *Behold henceforth I will feed you in a good and rich pasture.*[6]

§ 4. *The good shepherd giveth himself for the sake of his sheep.*[7] And again He said :— *I have other sheep and I must bring them also hither. And the whole flock shall be one, and one shepherd, and My Father because of this loveth Me ; that I give Myself for the sake of the sheep.*[8] And again He said ;—*I am the door of the sheep. Every one that entereth by Me shall live and shall go in and go out and find pasture.*[9] O ye pastors, be ye made like unto that diligent pastor, the chief of the whole flock, who cared so greatly for his flock. He brought nigh those that were afar off. He brought back the wanderers. He visited the sick. He strengthened the weak. He bound up the broken. He guarded the fatlings. He gave himself up for the sake of the sheep. He chose and instructed excellent leaders, and committed the sheep into their hands, and gave them authority over all his flock. For He said to Simon Cephas :—*Feed My sheep and My lambs and My ewes.*[1] So Simon fed His sheep ; and he fulfilled his time and handed over the flock to you, and departed. Do ye

---

[1] Ps. lxxviii. 72.  [2] 2 Sam. xxiv. 17.
[3] Ezek. xxxiv. 2-4, 9, 10-12, 18, 19.

[4] Zech. xi. 9, 17.  [5] Ezek. xxxiv. 31.
[6] Ezek. xxxiv. 14.  [7] John x. 11.
[8] John x. 16, 17.  [9] John x. 9.
[1] John xxi. 15-17.

also feed and guide them well. For the pastor who cares for his sheep engages in no other pursuit along with that. He does not make a vineyard, nor plant gardens, nor does he fall into the troubles of this world. Never have we seen a pastor who left his sheep in the wilderness and became a merchant, or one who left his flock to wander and became a husbandman. But if he deserts his flock and does these things he thereby hands over his flock to the wolves.

§ 5. And remember, my beloved, that I wrote to thee concerning our fathers of old that they first learned the ways of tending sheep and in that received trial of carefulness, and then were chosen for the office of guides, that they might learn and observe how much the pastor cares for his flock, and as they used to guide the sheep carefully, so also might be perfected in this office of guidance. Thus Joseph was chosen from the sheep, to guide the Egyptians in the time of affliction. And Moses was chosen from the sheep, to guide his people and tend them. And David was taken from following the sheep, to become king over Israel. And the Lord took Amos from following the sheep, and made him a prophet over his people. Elisha likewise was taken from behind the yoke, to become a prophet in Israel. Moses did not return to his sheep, nor did he leave his flock that was committed to him. David did not return to his father's sheep, but guided his people in the integrity of his heart.[1] Amos did not turn back to feed his sheep, or to gather (the fruit of) trees, but he guided them and performed his office of prophecy. Elisha did not turn back to his yoke, but served Elijah and filled his place. And he[2] who was for him as a shepherd, because he loved fields and merchandise and vineyards and oliveyards and tillage, did not wish to become his disciple; and (therefore) he did not commit the flock into his hand.

§ 6. I beseech you, ye pastors, that ye set not over the flock, leaders who are foolish and stupid, covetous also and lovers of possessions. Every one who feeds the flock shall eat of their milk.[3] And every one who guides the yoke shall be ministered to from his labour. The priests have a right to partake of the altar, and the Levites shall receive their tithes. Whoever eats of the milk, let his heart be upon the flock; and let him that is ministered to from the labour of his yoke, take heed to his tillage. And let the priests who partake of the altar serve the altar with honour. And as for the Levites who receive the tithes, they have no portion in Israel. O pastors, disciples of our great Pastor, be ye not like hirelings; because the hireling cares not for the sheep. Be ye like our Sweet Pastor, Whose life was not dearer to Him than His sheep. Rear up the youths and bring up the maidens; and love the lambs and let them be reared in your bosoms; that when ye shall come to the Chief Pastor, ye may offer to Him all your sheep in completeness, and so He may give you what He has promised: *Where I am, ye also shall be.*[4] These things, brief as they are, will be sufficient for the good pastors and leaders.

§ 7. Above, my beloved, I have written to remind thee of the character that becomes the whole flock. And in this discourse I have written to thee about the pastors, the guides of the flock. These reminders I have written to thee, beloved, as thou didst ask of me in thy dear letter.

§ 8. The Steward brought me into the King's treasury and showed me there many precious things; and when I saw them my mind was captivated with the great treasury. And as I looked upon it, it dazzled my eyes, and took captive my thoughts, and caused my reflections to wander in many ways. Whosoever receives thereof, is himself enriched, and enriches (others). It lies open and unguarded before all that seek it; and though many take from it there is no deficiency; and when they give of that which

---

[1] Ps. lxxviii. 72.    [2] *Sc.* Gehazi.    [3] 1 Cor. ix. 7. sq.    [4] John xii. 26.

VOL. XIII.—25

they have received, their own portion is greatly multiplied. They that receive freely let them give freely [1] as they have received. For (this treasure) cannot be sold for a price, because there is nothing equivalent to it. Moreover the treasure fails not ; and they that receive it are not satiated. They drink, and are still eager ; they eat, and are hungry. Whosoever is not thirsty, finds not ought to drink ; whoever is not hungry, finds nothing to eat. The hunger for it satisfies many, and from the thirst for it flow forth water-springs. For the man who draws nigh to the fear of God is like the man who in his thirst draws near to the water-spring and drinks and is satisfied, and the fountain is not a whit diminished. And the land that needs to drink in water, drinks of the fountain, but its waters fail not. And when the land drinks, it needs again to drink, and the spring is not lessened by its flowing. So is the knowledge of God. Though all men should receive of it, yet there would come no lack in it, nor can it be limited by the sons of flesh. He that takes from it, cannot take away all ; and when he gives, he lacks nothing. When thou takest fire with a candle from a flame, though thou kindle many candles at it, yet the flame does not diminish when thou takest from it, nor does the candle fail, when it kindles many. One man cannot receive all the King's treasure, nor when a thirsty man drinks of the fountain, do its waters fail. When a man stands on a lofty mountain, his eye does not (equally) comprehend the near and the distant ; nor, when he stands and counts the stars of heaven, can he set limits to the hosts of the heavens. So when he draws nigh unto the fear of God, he cannot attain to the whole of it ; and when he receives much that is precious, it does not seem to be diminished ; and when he gives of that which he has received, it is not exhausted, nor has it come to an end for him. And remember, my beloved, what I wrote to thee, in the first dis-

course, about faith, that whoever has freely received ought to give freely as he has received, as our Lord said :—*Freely ye have received, freely give.* [2] For whosoever keeps back part of anything he has received, [3] even that which he has obtained shall be taken away from him. Therefore, my beloved, as I have been able to obtain now from that treasure that fails not, I have sent unto thee from it. Yet though I have sent it to thee, it is all with me. For the treasure fails not, for it is the wisdom of God ; and the steward is our Lord Jesus Christ, as He testified when He said :—*All things have been committed to Me by My Father.* [4] And while He is the steward of the wisdom, again, as the Apostle said :—*Christ is the power of God and His wisdom.* [5] This wisdom is imparted to many, yet nothing is lacking, as I explained to thee above ; the Prophets received of the spirit of Christ, yet Christ was not a whit diminished.

§ 9. Ten treatises have I written unto thee, my beloved. Whatsoever thou hast asked of me, I have explained to thee without (receiving) ought from thee. And that which thou enquiredst not of me, I have given unto thee. I have asked thy name and written unto thee. I have asked of myself thy question, and I have answered thee as I was able, for thy persuasion. Whatsoever I have written unto thee, meditate in these things at every time ; and labour to read those books which are read in the church of God. These ten little books that I have written for thee, they borrow one from another, and depend one upon another. Separate them not one from another. From *Olaph* to *Yud* I have written for thee, each letter after its fellow. Read thou and learn thou and the brethren, the monks, and the faithful, they from whom mocking is far removed ; as I wrote unto thee above. And remember that which I pointed out to thee, that I have not brought these matters to an end, but short of the end. Nor are these

---

[1] Matt. x. 8.

[2] Matt. x. 8.
[4] Matt. xi. 27.

[3] Matt. xxv. 29.
[5] I Cor. i. 24.

things sufficient ; but hear thou these things from me without wrangling, and enquire concerning them with brethren who are apt for persuasion. Whatsoever thou hearest that assuredly edifies, receive ; and whatever builds up strange doctrines, overthrow and utterly demolish. For wrangling cannot edify. But I, my beloved, as a stonecutter have brought stones for the building, and let wise architects carve them out and lay them in the building ; and all the labourers that toil in the building shall receive reward from the Lord of the house.

*Demonstration XVII.*—OF CHRIST THE SON OF GOD.

§ 1. (This is) a reply against the Jews, who blaspheme the people gathered from among the Gentiles ; for they say thus, "Ye worship and serve a man who was begotten, a son of man who was crucified, and ye call a son of men, God. And though God has no son, ye say concerning this crucified Jesus, that He is the Son of God." And they bring forward as an argument, that God said :—"*I am God and there is none else beside Me.*"[1] And again he said :—"*Thou shalt not worship another God.*"[2] Therefore, (say they), ye are opposing God in that ye call a man, God.

§ 2. Concerning these things, my beloved, so far as I, in my insignificance, can comprehend, I will instruct thee about them, that while we grant to them that He is man, and (while) we at the same time honour Him and call Him God and Lord, yet it is not in any novel fashion, that we have so called Him, nor that we have applied to Him a novel name, which they themselves did not employ. Yet it is a sure thing with us, that Jesus our Lord is God, the Son of God, and the King, the King's Son, Light of light, Creator and Counsellor, and Guide, and the Way, and Redeemer, and Shepherd, Gatherer, and the Door, and the Pearl, and the Lamp ; and by many (such) names is

He surnamed. But we shall leave aside all (the rest) of them, and prove concerning Him, that He Who came from God is the Son of God, and (is) God.

§ 3. For the venerated name of Godhead has been applied also to righteous men, and they have been held worthy to be called by it. And the men with whom God was well pleased, them He called, My sons, and My friends. When He chose Moses His friend and His beloved and made him chief and teacher and priest unto his people he called him God. For He said to him :—*I have made thee a God unto Pharaoh.*[3] And He gave him His priest for a prophet, *And Aaron thy brother shall speak for thee unto Pharaoh, and thou shalt be unto him as a God, and he shall be unto thee an interpreter.*[4] Thus not alone to the evil Pharaoh did He make Moses God, but also unto Aaron, the holy priest, He made Moses God.

§ 4. Again, hear concerning the title Son of God, by which we have called Him. They say that "though God has no son, ye make that crucified Jesus, the firstborn son of God." Yet He called Israel "*My firstborn,*" when He sent to Pharaoh through Moses and said to him, *Israel is My firstborn ; I have said unto thee, let My Son go to serve Me, and if thou art not willing to let (him) go, lo ! I will slay thy son, thy firstborn.*[5] And also through the Prophet[6] He testified concerning this, and reproved them and said to the people, *Out of Egypt have I called My son. As I called them, so they went and worshipped Baal and offered incense to the graven images.* And Isaiah said[7] concerning them, *Children have I reared and brought up, and they have rebelled against Me.* And again it is written, *Ye are the children of the Lord your God.*[8] And about Solomon He said, *He shall be to Me a son, and I will be to him a Father.*[9] So also we call the Christ, the Son of God, for through Him we have gained the knowledge of God ; even as He called Israel

---

[1] Deut. xxxii. 39.    [2] Exod. xxxiv. 14.

[3] Ex. vi. 1          [4] Ex. vii. 1.
[5] Ex. iv. 22, 23.     [6] Hos. xi. 1, 2.
[7] Is. i. 2.          [8] Deut. xiv. 1.
[9] 2 Sam. viii. 14.

*My firstborn son,* and as He said concerning Solomon, *He shall be to Me a son.* And we call Him God, even as He surnamed Moses by His own Name. And also David said concerning them :—*Ye are Gods and children of the Highest, all of you.*[1] And when they amended not themselves, therefore He said concerning them :—*As men shall ye die, and as one of the princes shall ye fall.*[2]

§ 5. For the name of Divinity is given for the highest honour in the world, and with whomsoever God is well pleased, He applies it to him. But however, the names of God are many and are venerable, as He delivered His names to Moses, saying to him :—*I am the God of your fathers, the God of Abraham and the God of Isaac and the God of Jacob. This is My Name for ever, and this is My memorial unto generations.*[3] And He called His name *Ahiyah ashar Ahiyah, El Shaddai and Adonai Sabaoth.*[4] By these names is God called. The great and honourable name of *Godhead* He withheld not from His righteous ones ; even as, though He is the great King, without grudging He applied the great and honourable name of Kingship to men who are His creatures.

§ 6. For by the mouth of His prophet God called the heathen King Nebuchadnezzar, *King of Kings.* For Jeremiah said :—*Every people and kingdom that shall not put his neck into the yoke of Nebuchadnezzar, King of Kings, My servant, with famine and with sword and with pestilence will I visit that people.*[5] Though He is the great King, He grudges not the name of Kingship to men. And (so), though He is the great God, yet He grudged not the name of Godhead to the sons of flesh. And though all fatherhood is His, He has called men also fathers. For He said to the congregation :—*Instead of thy fathers, shall be thy children.*[6] And though authority is His, He has given men authority one over

another. And while worship is His unto honour, He has yet allowed it in the world, that one man should honour another. For even though a man should do worship[7] before the wicked and the heathen and *them that refuse grace,* yet is he not censured by God. And concerning worship He commanded His people, *Thou shalt not worship the sun or the moon or all the hosts of heaven; and also ye shall not desire to worship any creature that is upon the earth.*[8] Behold the grace and the love of our good Maker, that He did not grudge to men the name of Godhead and the name of worship, and the name of Kingship, and the name of authority ; because He is the Father of the created things that are over the face of the world, and He has honoured and exalted and glorified men above all creatures. For with His holy hands He fashioned them ; and of His Spirit He breathed into them, and a dwelling-place did He become unto them from of old.[9] In them doth He abide and amongst them doth He walk. For He said through the prophet, *I will dwell in them, and walk in them.*[1] Furthermore also the Prophet Jeremiah said :—*Ye are the temple of the Lord, if ye make fair your ways and your deeds.*[2] And of old David said: —*Thou, Lord, hast been a dwelling-place unto us for generations ; before the mountains were conceived and before the earth travailed, and before the world was framed ; from age to age Thou art God.*[3]

§ 7. How dost thou understand this ? For one prophet says :—*Lord, Thou hast been our dwelling-place.* And another said :—*I will dwell in them and walk in them.* First, He became to us a dwelling-place, and afterwards He dwelt and walked in us. For the wise both things are true and simple. For David says :—*Thou, Lord, hast been our dwelling-place for generations, before the mountains were conceived and before the earth travailed, and before the world was framed.* And thou knowest, my beloved, that all cre-

---

[1] Ps. lxxxii. 6.     [2] *Ib.* 7.     [3] Exod. iii. 6, 15.
[4] Gen. xvii. 1 ; Exod. iii. 14; Jer. xxxii. 18. The Hebrew has "*Jehovah Sabaoth.*"
[5] Jer. xxvii. 8. The Hebrew has "King of *Babylon,*" and so the Peshitto. But Nebuchadnezzar is addressed as "King of Kings," Daniel ii. 37.
[6] Ps. xlv. 17.

[7] *I.e.,* homage, outward reverence.
[8] Deut. iv. 17.
[9] Gen. ii. 7 ; Ps. xc. 1.
[1] Lev. xxvi. 12.     Jer. vii. 4, 5.
[3] Ps. xc. 1, 2.

ated things that are above and that are beneath were created first, and after them all, man. For when God determined to create the world with all its goodly things, first He conceived and fashioned man in His mind ; and after that Adam was conceived in His thought, then He conceived the created things ; as he said :—*Before the mountains were conceived and the earth travailed ;* because man is older and more ancient in conception than the creatures, but in birth the creatures are older and more ancient than Adam. Adam was conceived and dwelt in the thought of God ; and while in conception he (man) was held in His (God's) mind, He (God) by the word of His mouth created all the creatures. And when He had finished and adorned the world, when nothing was lacking in it, then He brought forth Adam from His thoughts, and fashioned man by His hands ; and Adam saw the world completed. And He (God) gave him authority over all that He had made, just as a man who has a son and desires to make for him a marriage feast, betroths to him a wife and builds for him a house, and prepares and adorns all that is needed for his son ; then he makes the marriage feast and gives his son authority over his house. So after the conception of Adam, He brought him forth and gave him authority over all his creation. Concerning this the Prophet said :—*Thou, Lord, hast been our habitation for generations, before the mountains were conceived, and before the earth travailed, and before the world was framed. From age unto age Thou art the Lord.* That no one should suppose that there is another God, either before or afterwards, he said :—*From age and unto age,* just as Isaiah said :—*I am the first and I am the last.*[1] And after that God brought forth Adam from within His thought, He fashioned him, and breathed into him of His Spirit, and gave him the knowledge of discernment, that he might discern good from evil, and might know that God made him. And inasmuch as man

knew his Maker, God was formed and conceived within his thought, and he became a temple for God his Maker, as it is written, *Ye are the temple of God.* And (so) He Himself said :—*I will dwell in them and walk in them.* But as for the sons of Adam, who do not recognise their Maker, He is not formed within them, and does not dwell in them, and is not conceived in their thought ; but they are accounted before Him as the beasts, and as the rest of the creatures.

§ 8. Now by these things the stubborn will be convinced, that it is nothing strange that we call Christ the Son of God. For behold, He (God) conceived all men and brought them forth from His thoughts. And they will be forced to own that the name of Godhead also belongs to Him (Christ), for He (God) associated the righteous also in the name of God. And as to this, that we worship Jesus through Whom we have known God, let them be ashamed, inasmuch as they fall down and worship and honour even the heathen of the unclean Gentiles, if they possess authority ; and (for this) there is no blame. And this honour of worship God has given to the sons of Adam, that by it they might honour one another—especially those who excel and are worthy of honour amongst them. For if they worship, and honour with the name of worship, the heathen—those who in their heathen wickedness deny even the name of God—and yet do not worship them as their maker, as though they worshipped them alone, and so do not sin ; how much more does it become us to worship and honour Jesus, Who converted our stubborn minds from all worship of vain error, and taught us to worship and serve and minister to the one God, our Father and our Maker. And (taught us) to know that the kings of the world call themselves Gods by the name of the great God, and are infidels and force men to infidelity, and men fall down and worship before them and serve and honour them, like carven images and idols, yet the law never censured these, and there is no sin. As Daniel also used to do worship to Nebuchadnezzar,

---

[1] Is. xliv. 6 ; xlviii. 12.

King of Babylon, the infidel and compeller to infidelity, and was not censured. Joseph also gave worship to Pharaoh, and it is not written that it was a sin for him. But as for us, we are certain that Jesus is God, the Son of God, and through Him we know His Father, and (have) all of us (turned away) from all other worship. Therefore it is impossible for us to repay Him Who bore these things for us. But by worship let us pay Him honour in return for His affliction that was on our behalf.

§ 9. Furthermore, we must prove that this Jesus was beforehand promised from ancient times in the Prophets, and was called the Son of God. David said :—*Thou art My Son ; to-day have I begotten Thee.*[1] Again he said :—*In the glories of holiness, from the womb, from of old, have I begotten thee, a child.*[2] And Isaiah said :—*Unto us a child is born, unto us a Son is given, and His government was upon His shoulder, and His Name shall be called Wonderful, and Counsellor, and mighty God of the ages, and Prince of peace. And to the increase of His government and to His peace there is no end.*[3] Therefore tell me, O wise doctor of Israel, who is He that was born and whose name was called *Child* and *Son* and *Wonderful* and *Counsellor*, the *mighty God of the ages*, and *Prince of peace, to the increase of* whose government and to whose *peace* (he said), *there is no end ?* For if we call Christ the Son of God, David taught us (this) ; and that we call Him God, this we learned from Isaiah. *And His government was laid upon His shoulder ;* for He bare His cross, and went out from Jerusalem. And that He *was born* as *a child,* Isaiah again said :—*Lo, the virgin shall conceive and bear ; and His name shall be called Immanuel, which is, our God with us.*[4]

§ 10. And if thou shouldest say that Christ has not yet come, I will grant this also to thy contentiousness. For it is written that when He shall come, *the Gentiles shall ex-*

*pect Him.*[5] Lo ! I, one of the Gentiles, have heard that Christ is to come. And when as yet He had not come, I beforehand have believed on Him ; and through Him I worship the God of Israel. When He comes, will He then blame me because before His coming I beforehand believed on Him ? But, thou fool, the prophets suffer thee not to say that Christ has not yet come ; for Daniel confutes thee,[6] saying :—*After sixty-two weeks shall Messiah come and shall be slain. And in His coming shall the Holy City be laid waste, and her end shall be with a flood. And until the accomplishment of the things that are determined, shall she continue in desolation.* Thou expectest and hopest that, at the coming of Christ, Israel shall be gathered together from all regions, and Jerusalem shall be built up and inhabited. But Daniel testifies that, when Christ comes and is slain, Jerusalem shall be destroyed, and shall continue in desolation until the accomplishment of the things which are determined, for ever. And concerning the suffering of Christ, David said :—*They pierced my hands and my feet, and all my bones cried out. They gazed and looked upon me, and divided my garments amongst them, and upon my vesture did they cast the lot.*[7] And Isaiah said :—*Lo ! My servant shall be known and shall be revealed and shall be lifted up, so that many shall be astonished at Him. As for this man, His visage shall be marred more than that of man, and His aspect more than that of the sons of men.*[8] And he said :—*He will purify many nations, and kings shall be amazed at Him.*[9] And he said in that passage :—*He came up as a little child before Him, and as a root from the dry ground.*[1] And in the end of the passage he said :—*He shall be slain for our sins ; He shall be humiliated for our iniquity ; the chastisement of our peace is upon Him, and by His bruises shall we be healed.*[2] By what wounds were men healed ? David was not slain ; for he

[5] Gen. xlix. 10. So in Peshitto; and similarly in Septuagint.
  [6] Dan. ix. 26, 27.
  [8] Is lii. 13, 14.
  [1] Is. liii. 2.
  [7] Ps. xxii. 17–19.
  [9] Is. lii. 15.
  [2] Is. liii. 5.

[1] Ps. ii. 7.
[3] Is. ix. 6, 7.
[2] Ps. cx. 3 (Pesh.).
[4] Is. vii. 14 ; Matt. i. 23.

died in a good old age, and was buried in Bethlehem. And if they should say that it is spoken of Saul, for Saul was killed in the mountains of Gilboa in the battle with the Philistines, and if they should say that they *pierced his hands and his feet*, when they fastened up his body on the wall of Beth-shan; yet it does not fitly apply to Saul. When the limbs of Saul were pierced, his bones were not conscious of suffering, because he was dead. It was after Saul died, that they hanged his body and those of his sons on the wall of Bethshan. But when David said, *They pierced my hands and my feet, and all my bones cried out*, he said in the next verse :—*O God, abide for my help, and deliver my soul from the sword.*[1] Now Christ was delivered from the sword, and ascended from out of Sheol, and revived and rose the third day, and so *God abode for His help*. But Saul called upon the Lord and He did not answer him; and he asked through the Prophets, but no answer was given to him. And he disguised himself and inquired by soothsayers, and learned from thence. He was worsted before the Philistines, and he slew himself with his own sword, when he saw that the battle had overcome him. Moreover in this passage David said :—*I will declare Thy name unto my brethren, and in the midst of the congregation will I glorify Thee.*[2] How can these things apply to Saul? And again David said :—*Thou didst not give Thy holy one to see corruption.*[3] But all these things fitly apply to Christ. When He came to them, they did not receive Him; but wickedly judged Him by false witness. And He was hung upon the tree by His hands, and they pierced His hands and His feet with the nails which they fastened in him; and all His bones cried out. And on that day a great prodigy happened, namely, that the light became dark in the middle of the day, as Zechariah prophesied, saying :— *The day shall be known unto the Lord. It*

*shall not be daytime, and it shall not be night; and at the evening time there shall be light.*[4] Now what is the day that was distinguished by the prodigy, that it was neither daytime nor night, and that at the evening time there was light? Evidently the day on which they crucified Him, for in the midst of that day there came darkness, and at the eveningtime there was light. And again he said :—*That day there shall be cold and frost.*[5]—As thou knowest, on that day on which they crucified Him, it was cold, and they had made them a fire to warm themselves when Simon came and stood with them. And again he said :—*The spear shall arise against the shepherd, and against the man, My friend;*[6] *and it shall smite the shepherd, and the sheep of his flock shall be scattered; and I will turn back My hand upon the pastor.*[7] And furthermore David said concerning His Passion :—*For My meat they gave gall, and for My thirst did they give Me vinegar to drink.*[8]—Again he said in that passage :—*They have persecuted Him Whom Thou hast smitten; and have added to the affliction of Him that was slain.* For they added many (afflictions) to Him, much that was not written concerning Him, cursings and revilings, such as the Scripture could not reveal, for their revilings were hateful. But, however, *the Lord was pleased to humiliate Him and afflict Him.*[9] *And He was slain for our iniquity,*[1] *and was humiliated for our sins*, and *was made sin* in His own person.[2]

§ 11. We worship those mercies, and bow the knee before the Majesty of His Father, Who converted our worship to Him. We call Him God, just as Moses (was called God); and Firstborn, and Son, just as Israel (was called); and Jesus (Joshua), just as Joshua

---

[1] Ps. xxii. 17, 18.    [2] Ps. xxii. 23.
[3] Ps. xvi. 10.

[4] Zech. xiv. 7.
[5] Zech. xiv. 6. So in Peshitto; also in Septuagint. Cp. margin of Revised Version.
[6] This is so read in one Syriac MS.; for " *the sheep, my friends*," which the other gives.
[7] Zech. xiii. 7; S. Matt. xxvi. 31; S. Mark. xiv. 27.
[8] Ps. lxix. 22, 27.    [9] Is. liii. 10.
[1] *Ib.* liii. 5.
[2] 2 Cor. v. 21.

the son of Nun was so called; and Priest, like Aaron, and King, like David; and great Prophet, like all the Prophets; and Shepherd, like the shepherds who tended and guided Israel. And so did He call children, as He said:—*Strange children shall hearken unto Me.*[1] And He has made us brothers unto Himself, He said:—I *will declare Thy name unto My brethren.*[2] And we have become friends unto Him, as He said to His disciples:—*I have called you friends,*[3] even as His Father called Abraham *My friend.*[4] And He said unto us:—*I am the good Shepherd, the Door, the Way, the Vine, the Sower, the Bridegroom, the Pearl, the Lamp, the Light, the King, God, Saviour, and Redeemer.* And by many names is He surnamed.

§ 12. This brief argument have I written unto thee, my beloved, that thou mayest make defence against the Jews, concerning this that they say, that God has no son, and concerning this that we call Him God, the Son of God, King, and Firstborn of all creatures.[5]

*Demonstration XXI.*—Of Persecution.

§ 1. I have heard a reproach, which has greatly vexed me. The unclean (the heathen) say, that this people, which is gathered together out of all nations, has no God. And thus say the impious:—"If they have a God, why does He not avenge His people?" And darkness more exceedingly has thickened upon me, because the Jews also reproach us, and magnify themselves over the children of our people. It happened one day, that a man, who is called wise amongst the Jews, questioned me, saying:—Jesus, Who is called your Teacher, wrote for you, that *If there shall be in you faith like one grain of mustard, ye shall say to this mountain, Remove, and it shall remove from before you; and (ye shall say) even, Be lifted up and fall into the sea, and it shall obey you.*[6] So apparently there is in all your people not one wise man, whose prayer is heard, and who asks of God that your persecutors should cease from you. For clearly it is written for you in that passage, *There is nothing which ye shall not be able to do.*

§ 2. And when I saw that he was blaspheming and speaking much against the Way (the Christian religion), my mind was disturbed, and I understood that he would not admit the interpretation of the words that he quoted to me. Then I also questioned him on sayings from the Law and from the Prophets, and said to him:—Do ye trust that even when ye are dispersed God is with you? And he professed to me, "God is with us, because that God said unto Israel:—*Even in the lands of their enemies, I yet did not forsake them, nor did I make void My covenant with them.*"[7] In answer I said to him:—"Right good is this that I have heard from thee, that God is with you. Against thy words will I also speak unto thee. For I said the Prophet said unto Israel, as from the mouth of God:—*If thou shalt pass through the sea, I will be with thee, and the rivers shall not overflow thee; and if thou shalt walk upon fire, thou shalt not be burned, and the flame shall not scorch thee; because the Lord thy God is with thee.*[8] Thus there is not one righteous and good and wise man out of all your people, who could pass through the sea and live and not be drowned; or (through) the river without its overflowing him; or who could walk over fire and see whether he would not be scorched and whether the flame would not burn him. And if thou shalt bring to me an explanation, I will not be persuaded by thee, just as thou also dost not accept from me the interpretation of the words as to which thou hast questioned me."

§ 3. Furthermore I questioned him about another saying that is written in Ezekiel; namely, that he said to Jerusalem:—*Sodom*

---

[1] Ps. xxiii. 45.
[2] Ps. xxii. 23.
[3] John xv. 15.
[4] Is. xli. 8.
[5] Col. i. 15.

[6] Matt. xvii. 19; xxi. 22.
[7] Lev. xxvi. 44.
[8] Is. xliii. 2, 3.

*and her daughters shall be built up as of old, and thou and thy daughters shall become as of old.*[1] So he explained this saying to me, and began to make a defence, and said to me, "As to this that God said to Jerusalem by the Prophet, *Sodom and her daughters shall be built up as of old, and thou and thy daughters shall become as of old;* this is the force of the passage, that Sodom and her daughters shall be in their place as of old, and shall be made subject to Israel; and Jerusalem and her daughters shall be in the splendour of royalty as of old." When I heard this defence from him, it was very contemptible in my eyes, and I said to him:—"Inasmuch as the words of the Prophet were said in wrath, is the whole passage wrathful, or is part of it wrathful and part of it gracious?" He answered:—"A wrathful passage is altogether wrath, and there is no peace in it." And I said to him:—"Since thou hast instructed me that there is no peace in that wrathful passage, hear without contention and blaspheme not, and I will instruct thee about this saying. For from the top to the bottom the whole passage is said in wrath. For he said to Jerusalem:—*As I live, saith the Lord God, Sodom and her daughters did not do at all as thou and thy daughters have done.*[2] And he said to her (Jerusalem):—*Be abashed and accept thy shame, that thou hast overcome thy sisters in thy sins, and they are justified rather than thou.*[3] Since he says that Sodom and her daughters were justified rather than Jerusalem and her daughters, and that Jerusalem overcame Sodom in her sins, it is right that when Israel shall be gathered together, its seat should be in Sodom and Gomorrha. For *their vine is of the vine of Sodom, and of the planting of Gomorrha. Their grapes are bitter and their clusters gall unto them.*[4] And Isaiah also calls them *rulers of Sodom, and people of Gomorrha.*[5] For if Israel is gathered together, in Sodom and Gomorrha ought they to dwell with the rulers of Sodom and with the people of Gomorrha; and on the vine of Sodom and planting of Gomorrha to eat bitter grapes and gather clusters of gall; and to eat the eggs of the basilisk and to clothe themselves with spiders' webs,[6] to be used with *wild grapes of the vineyard,*[7] and to be turned into *reprobate silver.*[8] And Sodom and her daughters, who were justified rather than Jerusalem, shall be built up as of old. And Jerusalem, that surpassed Sodom in her sins, shall continue in her sins, *and shall remain in desolation until the accomplishment of the things determined for ever.*[9]

§ 4. And Ezekiel said:—*This is the iniquity of Sodom and of her daughters, that they did not take by the hand the poor and needy; and when I saw these things in them, I overthrew them.*[1] And consider and see that, from the time that Sodom was overthrown until Jerusalem was built, there were eight hundred and ninety-six years. From the time that Abraham was informed by God through the Angel that *at this time next year I will return to thee, and Sarah thy wife shall have a son,*[2] from that time till Jacob entered Egypt was a hundred and ninety-one years: and the children of Jacob were in Egypt two hundred and twenty-five years. So all the years from the time that Isaac was conceived and Sodom overthrown were four hundred and sixteen years, and from the Exodus of Israel from Egypt till the great edifice of Jerusalem was built up by Solomon, and the temple was built, there were four hundred and eighty years. Therefore all the years from the conception of Isaac and the overthrow of Sodom till the great building of Jerusalem, were eight hundred and ninety-six years. And from the great building of Jerusalem until the destruction of Jerusalem there were four hundred and twenty-five years. The sum of all the years from the time of the overthrow of Sodom until Jerusalem was laid waste, was one thousand three hundred and twenty-one. These are all the years that

---

[1] Ezek. xvi. 55.    [2] Ezek. xvi. 48.
[3] Ezek. xvi. 52.    [4] Deut. xxxii. 32.
[5] Is. i. 10.

[6] Is. lix. 5.    [7] Is v. 2.
[8] Jer. vi. 30.    [9] Dan. ix. 27.
[1] Ezek. xvi. 49.    [2] Gen. xviii. 14.

Sodom and her daughters were laid waste before Jerusalem. And she that was more just than Jerusalem is not yet inhabited. Therefore the whole sum of the years from the overthrow of Sodom till the six hundred and fifty-fifth year of the Kingdom of Alexander, the son of Philip of Macedon,[1] is two thousand two hundred and seventy-six years. And from the time that Jerusalem was laid waste by the Babylonians until the present time is nine hundred and fifty-five years. And Jerusalem has been inhabited, after the Babylonians laid it waste, during those seventy weeks about which Daniel testified. Then it was laid waste in its last destruction by the Romans, and it shall not be inhabited again for ever, for *it abideth in desolation until the accomplishment of the things determined.*[2] So then, all the years of the former and latter desolation of Jerusalem have been four hundred and sixty-five years, and when thou dost deduct from them the seventy years of Babylon, they have been three hundred and ninety-five years.

§ 5. All this argument have I written to thee, because the Jews pride themselves, (saying), "It has been covenanted to us, that we shall be gathered." For if Sodom, whose iniquity was not so great as that of Jerusalem, is not as yet inhabited, and if we say thus, that it will not be restored for ever, how shall Jerusalem be restored, whose iniquity is greater than that of Sodom and her daughters? As for Sodom God has not had mercy on her for two thousand two hundred and seventy-six years; and shall we say that He will have mercy on Jerusalem? For up to the present there are but three hundred and ninety-five years from the day that she was laid waste, according to the calculation that has been written above. But as to this that he said, *Sodom and her daughters shall be possessed as of old,*[3] and with regard to Jerusalem he said, *Thou and thy daughters shall become as of old,* this is the force of the passage;

that they shall not be inhabited for ever; for the Lord also thus cursed the land against which He was wroth :—*It shall not be sown, nor shall it produce, nor shall any herb spring up in it, but it shall be like Sodom and Gomorrha, against which the Lord was wroth and towards which He was not appeased.*[4] Therefore be sure, my hearer, that Sodom and her daughters shall not be inhabited for ever; but they shall be as of old, namely, as in that time when they were not as yet inhabited, and as in the time when the Lord was wroth with them and was not appeased towards them. And Jerusalem and her daughters shall be as of old, (that is) as in the former time when the mountain of the Amorites lay in desolation, whereon Abraham built the altar, when he bound upon it Isaac his son ; and as it was desolate when David bought the threshing-floor from Araunah the Jebusite, and built there the altar. For consider and see that this mountain whereon Abraham offered his son is the mountain of Jebus, which is Jerusalem. And this place of the threshing-floor that David bought of Araunah is that whereon the Temple was built. Thus Jerusalem shall be in desolation as of old. And consider that when Ezekiel prophesied this passage, Jerusalem still was sitting in her greatness, and those who were in her were rebelling against the King of Babylon. And that which the Prophet spoke, he said in wrath and reproach against Jerusalem.

§ 6. Consider and observe, my hearer, that if God had given a hope to Sodom and to her fellows, He would not have overthrown them with fire and brimstone, the sign of the last day of the world, but would have delivered them over to one of the kingdoms to be chastised. As it is written that when Jeremiah caused the nations and kingdoms to drink the cup of wrath, he said concerning each one of the cities, that after they shall *drink the cup, I will turn back the*

---

[1] *I.e.*, A.D. 344, in which year this was written. Cp. *Dem.* XXII. 25.
[2] Dan. ix. 27.
[3] Ezek. xvi. 55.

[4] Deut. xxix. 23.

*captivity of Elam*, of Tyre, of Zidon, *of the children of Ammon, and of Moab*, and *of Edom*.[1] Concerning each one of these kingdoms he said :—*In the last days I will turn back her captivity*. Now we see that Tyre was inhabited, and was opulent after she had *wandered seventy years*,[2] and after she had received the reward of her harlotries and after she had *committed fornication with all kingdoms*. And *she took the harp, and played it sweetly, and multiplied her music*. And also the region of Elam is inhabited and opulent. And with regard to Babylon Jeremiah said :—*Babylon shall fall, and shall not rise*.[3] And lo! unto this day does it continue in desolation, and will do so for ever. And also about Jerusalem he said :— *The virgin of Israel shall fall, and shall not rise again. She is forsaken upon the ground and there is none to raise her up*.[4] For if the prophecy is true which Jeremiah spake about Babylon, also that about Jerusalem is true and worthy of faith. And Isaiah said unto Jerusalem :—*I will not again be wroth with thee, nor will I reprove thee*.[5] Of a truth He will not again be wroth with her, nor will He reprove her for ever; for that which is in desolation He will not reprove, nor will she provoke him to wrath.

§ 7. As to those that reproach us (saying) :—"Ye are persecuted and are not delivered," let them be ashamed themselves, that at every time they have been persecuted, even for many years before they were delivered. They were made to serve in Egypt two hundred and twenty-five years. And the Midianites[6] made Israel serve in the days of Barak and Deborah.[7] The Moabites ruled over them in the days of Ehud;[8] the Ammonites in the days of Jephthah;[9] the Philistines in the days of Samson,[1] and also in the days of Eli and of Samuel the Prophet;[2] the Edomites in the days of Ahab; the Assyrians in the days of Hezekiah.[2]

The king of Babylon uprooted them from their place and dispersed them;[4] and after he had tried and persecuted them much, they did not amend, as He said to them :— *In vain have I smitten your sons, for they did not accept chastisement*.[5] And again He said :—*I have cut off the Prophets, and slain them by the word of My mouth*.[6] And to Jerusalem He said :—*By afflictions and scourges be instructed, O Jerusalem, lest thy life depart from thee*.[7] But they forsook Him, and worshipped idols, as Jeremiah said concerning them :[8]—*Go to the distant isles, and send to Kedar, and consider well and see, whether there has been (anything) like this, whether the nations change their gods, those that are no gods. But My people has changed My honour for that which is not profitable. Be astonished, ye heavens, at this; and quake and fear greatly, saith the Lord: because My people have done two wickednesses; they have abandoned Me, the fountain of the water of life, and they have gone and dug for themselves cisterns, broken cisterns which cannot hold water.* For the broken cisterns are the fear of images and idols. And He calls the heavens to astonishment, because they worshipped the hosts of the heavens. And the heavens shall receive as a penalty, that *they shall be rolled up as a scroll, and all the host of them shall fall down*.[9]

§ 8. All this discourse that I have written unto thee, my beloved, from the beginning, was because the Jew reproached the children of our people; but now, as far as I can comprehend, I will instruct thee about the persecuted, that they have received a great reward, while the persecutors have come to scorn and contempt.

§ 9. Jacob was persecuted, and Esau was a persecutor. Jacob received the blessings and the birthright, while Esau was cast out from both. Joseph was persecuted, and his brothers were persecutors; Joseph was exalted and his persecutors bowed down

---

[1] Jer. xxv. 15-27 ; xlviii. 47 ; xlix. 6, 39.
[2] Is. xxiii. 15, 16, 17.          [3] Jer. li. 64.
[4] Amos v. 1, 2.                    [5] Is. liv. 9.
[6] Rather, the Canaanites.        [7] Judges iv. 2.
[8] Judges iii. 12.                  [9] Judges xi. 5.
[1] Judges xiii. 1-24.              [2] 1 Sam. iv. 1. sq.
[3] 1 Kings xx. 11.

[4] 2 Kings xviii. 9, 13 ; xxv. 1. sq.   [5] Jer. ii. 30.
[6] Hos. vi. 5.                           [7] Jer. vi. 7, 8.
[8] Jer. ii. 10-13.                       [9] Is. xxxiv. 4.

before him, and so his dreams and his visions were fulfilled. Joseph who was persecuted was a type of the persecuted Jesus. His father clothed Joseph in a tunic of divers colours ; and His Father clothed Jesus with a body (taken) from the Virgin. His father loved Joseph more than his brethren, and Jesus is the dear and beloved one of His Father. Joseph saw visions and dreamed dreams ; Jesus fulfilled the visions and the Prophets. Joseph was a shepherd with his brethren ; and Jesus is the Chief of Shepherds. When his father sent Joseph to visit his brethren, they saw him coming and plotted to kill him ; and when His Father sent Jesus to visit His brethren, they said :— *This is the heir ; come, let us kill him.*[1] His brethren cast Joseph into the pit ; and His brethren brought down Jesus into the abode of the dead. Joseph ascended from the pit ; and Jesus arose from the abode of the dead. Joseph, after he arose from the pit, had authority over his brethren ; and after Jesus arose from the abode of the dead, His Father gave Him a great and excellent name,[2] that His brethren should serve Him, and His enemies be put beneath His feet. After that Joseph was made known to his brethren, they were abashed and feared and were amazed at his greatness ; and when Jesus shall come at the last time, when He shall be revealed in His Majesty, His brethren will be abashed and fear and be dismayed before Him, because they crucified Him. Moreover, Joseph, by the counsel of Judah, was sold into Egypt ; and Jesus, by the hands of Judas Iscariot, was delivered over to the Jews. When they sold Joseph, he answered nothing to his brethren ; Jesus also spake not and gave no answer to the judges who judged Him. His master wrongfully delivered over Joseph to the prison ; and His countrymen wrongfully condemned Jesus. Joseph delivered over his two garments, one into the hand of his brethren, and the other into the hand of his master's wife ; and Jesus delivered over

His garments and divided them between the soldiers. Joseph, when thirty years old, stood before Pharaoh and became lord of Egypt ; and Jesus, when about thirty years old, came to the Jordan to be baptized, and received the spirit, and went forth to preach. Joseph nourished Egypt with bread ; and Jesus nourished the whole world with the bread of life. Joseph took to wife the daughter of the wicked and unclean priest ; and Jesus espoused to Himself the Church (taken) from the unclean Gentiles. Joseph died and was buried in Egypt ; and Jesus died and was buried in Jerusalem. Joseph's bones his brethren brought up from Egypt ; and Jesus His Father raised from the abode of the dead, and took up His Body with Him to heaven uncorrupted.

§ 10. Moses also was persecuted, as Jesus was persecuted. When Moses was born, they concealed him that he might not be slain by his persecutors. When Jesus was born they carried Him off in flight into Egypt that Herod, His persecutor, might not slay Him. In the days when Moses was born, children used to be drowned in the river ; and at the birth of Jesus the children of Bethlehem and in its borders were slain. To Moses God said :—" *The men are dead who were seeking thy life ;*[3] and to Joseph the angel said in Egypt :—*Arise, take up the child, and go into the land of Israel, for they are dead who were seeking the life of the child to take it away.*[4] Moses brought out his people from the service of Pharaoh ; and Jesus delivered all nations from the service of Satan. Moses grew up in Pharaoh's house ; and Jesus grew up in Egypt when Joseph brought Him there in flight. Miriam[5] stood on the edge of the river when Moses was floating in the water ; and Mary bare Jesus, after the Angel Gabriel had made the annunciation to her. When Moses sacrificed the lamb, the firstborn of Egypt were slain ; and when they crucified Jesus the true

---

[1] Matt xxi. 38.  [2] Phil. ii. 9.

[3] Ex. iv. 10.  [4] Matt. ii. 20.
[5] Miriam, Mariam, Maria, Mary, are all of them forms of the same name.

Lamb, the people who slew Him perished through His slaying. Moses brought down manna for his people; and Jesus gave His Body to the nations. Moses sweetened the bitter waters by the wood; and Jesus sweetened our bitterness by His cross, by the wood of the tree of His crucifixion. Moses brought down the Law to his people; and Jesus gave His covenants to the nations. Moses conquered Amalek by the spreading out of his hands; and Jesus conquered Satan by the sign of His cross. Moses brought out water from the rock for his people; and Jesus sent Simon Cephas (the rock) to carry His doctrine among the nations. Moses lifted up the veil from his face and spake with God; and Jesus lifted up the veil from the face of the nations, that they might hear and receive his doctrine. Moses laid his hand upon his messengers (apostles), and they received priesthood; and Jesus laid His hand upon His apostles, and they received the Holy Spirit. Moses ascended the mountain and died there; and Jesus ascended into heaven and took his seat at the right hand of His Father.

§ 11. Also Joshua the son of Nun was persecuted as Jesus our Redeemer was persecuted. Joshua the son of Nun was persecuted by the unclean nations; and Jesus our Redeemer was persecuted by the foolish people. Joshua the son of Nun took away the inheritance from his persecutors and gave it to his people; and Jesus our Redeemer took away the inheritance from His persecutors and gave it to strange nations. Joshua the son of Nun caused the sun to stand still in the heavens, and took vengeance on the nations his persecutors; and Jesus our Redeemer caused the sun to set in the midst of the day, that the persecuting people which crucified Him might be ashamed. Joshua the son of Nun divided the inheritance unto his people; and Jesus our Redeemer has promised to give to the nations the land of life. Joshua the son of Nun caused Rahab the harlot to live; and Jesus our Redeemer gathered together and gave life to the Church, though polluted by the harlotry (of idolatry). Joshua the son of Nun on the seventh day overthrew and cast down the walls of Jericho; and Jesus our Redeemer, on His seventh day, on the Sabbath of the rest of God, this world shall be dissolved and fall. Joshua the son of Nun stoned Achor, because he stole of the accursed thing; and Jesus our Redeemer separated Judas from the disciples, His friends, because he stole of the money of the poor. Joshua the son of Nun, when he was dying, laid down a testimony among his people; and Jesus our Redeemer, when He was taken up, laid down a testimony among His apostles.

§ 12. Also Jephthah was persecuted, as Jesus was persecuted. Jephthah, his brethren drove out from the house of his father; and Jesus, His brethren drove out and lifted up and crucified. Jephthah though persecuted arose as leader to his people; Jesus though persecuted arose and became King of the Nations. Jephthah vowed a vow and offered up his firstborn daughter as a sacrifice; and Jesus was lifted up as a sacrifice to his Father for all the Gentiles.

§ 13. Also David was persecuted, as Jesus was persecuted. David was anointed by Samuel to be king instead of Saul who had sinned; and Jesus was anointed by John to be High Priest instead of the priests, the ministers of the Law. David was persecuted after his anointing; and Jesus was persecuted after His anointing. David reigned first over one tribe only, and afterwards over all Israel; and Jesus reigned from the beginning over the few who believed on Him, and in the end He will reign over all the world. Samuel anointed David when he was thirty years old; and Jesus when about thirty years old received the imposition of the hand from John. David wedded two daughters of the king; and Jesus wedded two daughters of kings, the congregation of the People and the congregation of the Gentiles. David repaid good to Saul his enemy; and Jesus taught,

*Pray for your enemies.*[1] David was the heart of God ;[2] and Jesus was the Son of God. David received the kingdom of Saul his persecutor ; and Jesus received the kingdom of Israel His persecutor. David wept with dirges over Saul his enemy when he died ; and Jesus wept over Jerusalem, His persecutor, which was to be laid waste. David handed over the kingdom to Solomon, and was gathered to his people ; and Jesus handed over the keys to Simon, and ascended and returned to Him who sent Him. For David's sake, sins were forgiven to his posterity ; and for Jesus' sake sins are forgiven to the nations.[3]

§ 14. Elijah also was persecuted as Jesus was persecuted. Jezebel the murderess persecuted Elijah ; and the persecuting and murderous congregation persecuted Jesus. Elijah restrained the heavens from rain because of the sins of Israel ; and Jesus by His coming restrained the Spirit from the prophets, because of the sins of the people. Elijah destroyed the servants of Baal ; and Jesus trampled upon Satan and his hosts. Elijah raised to life the son of the widow ; and Jesus raised to life the son of the widow, as well as Lazarus and the daughter of the ruler of the Synagogue. Elijah sustained the widow with a little bread ; and Jesus satisfied thousands with a little bread. Elijah was taken up in a chariot to heaven ; and our Redeemer ascended and took His seat on the right hand of His Father. Elisha received the spirit of Elijah ; and Jesus breathed upon the faces of His Apostles.

§ 15. Also Elisha was persecuted as Jesus was persecuted. Elisha was persecuted by the son of Ahab, the son of the murderer ; and Jesus was persecuted by the murderous people. Elisha prophesied, and there came about abundance in Samaria ; and Jesus said :—*Whosoever eateth of My body and drinketh of My blood shall live for ever.* Elisha satisfied a hundred men with a little bread ; and Jesus satisfied four thousand men, besides women and children, with five loaves. Elisha made oil out of water ; and Jesus made wine out of water. Elisha delivered the widow from her creditor ; and Jesus delivered the indebted nations. Elisha made the iron to swim and the wood to sink ; and Jesus raised up that which was sunk in us, and sank that which was light. A dead man (laid) upon the bones of Elisha recovered life ; and all the nations, who were dead in their sins, were cast upon the bones of Jesus and recovered life.

§ 16. Hezekiah also was persecuted as Jesus was persecuted. Hezekiah was persecuted, and was reproached by Sennacherib his enemy ; Jesus also was reproached by the foolish people. Hezekiah prayed and overcame his adversary ; and by the crucifixion of Jesus was our Adversary overcome. Hezekiah was king of all Israel ; and Jesus is King of all the nations. Because Hezekiah was sick, the sun turned backwards ; and because Jesus suffered, the sun was darkened from its light. The enemies of Hezekiah became dead corpses ; and Jesus, His enemies shall be cast down beneath His feet. Hezekiah was of the family of the house of David ; and Jesus was, in the flesh, the son of David. Hezekiah said :— *Peace and truth shall be in my days ;*[4] and Jesus said to His disciples :—*My peace I leave with you.*[5] Hezekiah prayed, and was healed of his sickness ; Jesus prayed, and arose from the abode of the dead. Hezekiah after he arose from his sickness added to his years ; and Jesus after His Resurrection received great glory. Hezekiah, after the prolongation of his life, death was given dominion over him ; but Jesus, after that He rose, death shall not again have dominion over Him for ever.

§ 17. Josiah also was persecuted as Jesus was persecuted. Josiah was persecuted, and Pharaoh the Lame[6] slew Him ;[7] and Jesus was persecuted, and the people that were made lame by their sins slew Him.

---

[1] Luke vi. 28.                    [2] 1 Sam. xiii. 14.
[3] 1 Kings xi. 12, 36 ; xv. 4, etc.

[4] 2 Kings xx. 19.                    [5] Job xiv. 27.
[6] *I.e.*, Pharaoh *Nechoh*,—a Rabbinical interpretation of the surname.                    [7] 2 Kings xxiii. 29.

Josiah cleansed the land of Israel from uncleanness ; and Jesus cleansed and caused to pass away uncleanness from all the earth. Josiah hallowed and glorified the name of his God ; and Jesus said :—*I have glorified and will glorify* (*His Name*).[1] Josiah because of the iniquity of Israel *rent his clothes ;*[2] and Jesus because of the iniquity of the people *rent the vail of the Holy Temple.*[3] Josiah said :—*Great is the wrath that shall come upon this people ;* and Jesus said :—*There shall come wrath upon this people, and they shall fall by the edge of the sword.*[4] Josiah cast out uncleanness from the Holy Temple ; and Jesus cast out the unclean traders from His Father's house. For Josiah the daughters of Israel mourned and wailed, as Jeremiah said :—*O daughters of Israel, weep for Josiah ;*[5] and over Jesus did the daughters of Israel weep and mourn, as Zechariah said :—*The land shall mourn, families over families.*[6]

§ 18. Daniel also was persecuted as Jesus was persecuted. Daniel was persecuted by the Chaldeans, the congregation of heathen men ; Jesus also the Jews, the congregain of wicked men, persecuted. Daniel the Chaldeans accused ; and Jesus the Jews accused before the governor. Daniel they cast into the pit of lions, and he was delivered and came up out of its midst uninjured ; and Jesus they sent down into the pit of the abode of the dead, and He ascended, and death had not dominion over him. Concerning Daniel they expected that when he had fallen into the pit he would not come up again ; and concerning Jesus they said, *Since He has fallen, He shall not rise again.*[7] From (harming) Daniel the mouth of the ravenous and destructive lions was closed ; and from (harming) Jesus was closed the mouth of death, (though) ravenous and destructive of (living) forms. They sealed the pit of Daniel, and guarded it with diligence ; and the grave of Jesus did they guard with diligence, as they said, *Set guards to watch at the tomb.*[8] When Daniel came up, his accusers were ashamed ; and when Jesus rose, all they who had crucified Him were ashamed. The King who judged Daniel was greatly grieved[9] at the wickedness of his accusers the Chaldeans ; and Pilate who judged Jesus was greatly grieved because he knew that *for malice the Jews were accusing Him.*[1] At the prayer of Daniel, the captivity of his people went up from Babylon ; and Jesus by His prayer turned back the captivity of all the nations. Daniel interpreted the visions and dreams of Nebuchadnezzar ; and Jesus explained and interpreted the visions of the Law and the Prophets. When Daniel explained the vision of Belteshazzar, he received authority over the third part of the kingdom ; and when Jesus fulfilled the visions and the Prophets, His Father delivered unto Him all authority in heaven and in earth. Daniel saw wonders and uttered secrets ; and Jesus revealed secrets and fulfilled what is written. Daniel was led away among the hostages in behalf of his people ; and the body of Jesus was a hostage in behalf of all nations. For Daniel's sake the wrath of the King was appeased from the Chaldeans, so that they were not slain ; and for Jesus' sake the wrath of His Father was appeased from all nations, so that they were not slain and died not because of their sins. Daniel *besought of the king, and he gave* his brethren authority *over the affairs of the province of Babylon ;*[2] and Jesus besought of God, and He gave His brethren, His disciples, authority over Satan and his host.[3] Daniel said concerning Jerusalem, that until the things determined, she should remain in desolation ; and Jesus said concerning Jerusalem, *There shall not be left in her stone upon stone, because she knew not the day of her greatness.*[4] Daniel foresaw the weeks that should remain over for his people ; and Jesus came and fulfilled them.

§ 19. Hananiah also and his brethren

[1] John xii. 28.  [2] 2 Kings xxii. 11, 13.
[3] Matt. xxvii. 51.  [4] Luke xxi. 23, 24.
[5] 2 Chron. xxxv.25 ; Lam. iv. 20.
[6] Zech. xii. 12 ; Luke xxiii. 27, 28.
[7] Ps. xli. 9.

[8] Matt. xxvii. 64.  [9] Dan. vi 14.
[1] Matt. xxviii. 18, 24.  [2] Dan. ii. 49.
[3] Matt. x. 1 ; Luke x. 17, 18.  [4] Luke xix. 44.

were persecuted as Jesus was persecuted. Hananiah and his brethren were persecuted by Nebuchadnezzar ; and Jesus, the people of the Jews persecuted. Hananiah and his brethren were cast into the furnace of fire, and it was cold as dew upon the righteous. Jesus also descended to the place of darkness, and burst its gates and brought forth its prisoners. Hananiah and his brethren came up from the furnace of fire, and the flame burned their accusers ; and Jesus revived and came up from the midst of darkness, and His accusers and they that crucified Him shall be burned in flames at the end. When Hananiah and his brethren came up from the furnace, Nebuchadnezzar the King trembled and was amazed ; and when Jesus arose from the abode of the dead, the people that crucified Him were terrified and trembled. Hananiah and his brethren worshipped not the image of the King of Babylon ; and Jesus restrained the nations from the worship of dead images. Because of Hananiah and his brethren, the *nations and languages glorified God Who had delivered them* from the fire ; [1] and because of Jesus, the nations and all languages shall glorify (God) Who delivered His Son, so that He saw no corruption. On the garments of Hananiah and his brethren the fire had no power ; and on the bodies of the righteous, who have believed in Jesus, the fire shall have no power at the end. [2]

§ 20. Mordecai also was persecuted as Jesus was persecuted. Mordecai was persecuted by the wicked Haman ; and Jesus was persecuted by the rebellious People. Mordecai by his prayer delivered his people from the hands of Haman ; and Jesus by His prayer delivered His people from the hands of Satan. Mordecai was delivered from the hands of his persecutor ; and Jesus was rescued from the hands of His persecutors. Because Mordecai sat and clothed himself with sackcloth, he saved Esther and his people from the sword ; and because Jesus clothed Himself with a body and was

illuminated, He saved the Church and her children from death. Because of Mordecai, Esther was well pleasing to the king, and went in and sat instead of Vashti, who did not do his will ; and because of Jesus, the Church is well pleasing to God, and has gone in to the king, instead of the congregation which did not His Will. Mordecai admonished Esther that she should fast with her maidens, that she and her people might be delivered from the hands of Haman ; and Jesus admonished the Church and her children (to fast), that she and her children might be delivered from the wrath. Mordecai received the honour of Haman, his persecutor ; and Jesus received great glory from His Father, instead of His persecutors who were of the foolish People. Mordecai trod upon the neck of Haman, his persecutor ; and as for Jesus, His enemies shall be put under His feet. Before Mordecai, Haman proclaimed, *Thus shall it be done to the man, in honouring whom the king is pleased ;* [3] and as for Jesus, His preachers came out of the People that persecuted Him, and they said :—*This is Jesus the Son of God.* [4] The blood of Mordecai was required at the hand of Haman and his sons ; [5] and *the blood of Jesus*, His persecutors took *upon themselves and upon their children.* [6]

§ 21. These memorials that I have written unto thee, my beloved, concerning Jesus Who was persecuted, and the righteous who were persecuted, are in order that those who to-day are persecuted for the sake of the persecuted Jesus, may be comforted, for He wrote for us and comforted us Himself ; for He said :—*If they have persecuted Me, they will also persecute you. And because of this they will persecute you, that ye are not of the world, even as I was not of it.* [7] For He wrote before for us :—*Your fathers and your brothers and your family will deliver you up, and all men shall hate you for My name's sake.* [8] And again He taught us :—*When they shall bring you before rulers and before magistrates, and before*

---

[1] Dan. iii. 28, 29.　　[2] Ps. xvi. 10 ; Acts iii. 31 ; xiii. 37.

[3] Esth. vi. 11.　　　　　　　　[4] Matt. xxvii. 54.
[5] Esth. vii. 10 ; ix. 10.　　　[6] Matt. xxvii. 25.
[7] John xv. 20, 19 ; xvii. 14.　[8] Luke xxi. 16, 17.

*kings that hold the world, meditate not before the time what ye shall say, and how ye shall make defence; and I will give you a mouth and wisdom, that your enemies may not be able to overcome you, because it is not ye that speak, but the Holy Spirit of your Father; He shall speak in you.*[1] This is the spirit which spoke by the mouth of Jacob to Esau, his persecutor; and the spirit of wisdom which spoke before Pharaoh by the mouth of the persecuted Joseph; and the spirit which spoke by the mouth of Moses in all the prodigies which he did in the land of Egypt, and the spirit of knowledge which was given to Joshua, the son of Nun, when Moses laid his hand upon him, so that the nations which persecuted him came to a complete end before him; and the spirit that uttered psalms by the mouth of the persecuted David, by which he used to sing psalms and soothe Saul his persecutor from the evil spirit; and the spirit which clothed Elijah, and through him reproved Jezebel and Ahab his persecutor; and the spirit which spoke in Elisha, and prophesied and made known to the king his persecutor about all that was to happen thereafter; and the spirit which was fervent in the mouth of Micaiah when he reproved Ahab his persecutor saying:—*If thou shalt at all return back, the Lord hath not spoken by me;*[2] and the spirit which strengthened Jeremiah, so that he stood boldly, and by it reproved Zedekiah; and the spirit that preserved Daniel and his brethren in the land of Babylon; and the spirit that delivered Mordecai and Esther in the place of their captivity.

§ 22. Hear, my beloved, these names of martyrs, of confessors, and of the persecuted. Abel was murdered, and his blood cried out from the earth. Jacob was persecuted, and fled and became an exile. Joseph was persecuted, and sold and cast into the pit. Moses was persecuted, and fled to Midian. Joshua the son of Nun was persecuted, and made war. Jephthah and Samson and Gideon and Barak, these also were persecuted. These are they of whom the blessed Apostle said:—*Time fails me to narrate their victories.*[3] David also was persecuted at the hands of Saul, and he walked *in the mountains and in dens, and in caves.*[4] Samuel also was persecuted, and mourned over Saul. Furthermore Hezekiah was persecuted, and bound up in affliction. Elijah was persecuted, and walked in the desert. Elisha was persecuted and became an exile; and Micaiah was persecuted, and cast into prison. Jeremiah was persecuted, and they cast him into the pit of mire. Daniel was persecuted, and cast into the pit of lions. Hananiah also and his brethren were persecuted, and cast into the furnace of fire. Mordecai and Esther and the children of their people were persecuted, at the hands of Haman. Judas Maccabæus and his brethren were persecuted, and they also endured reproach. The seven brethren, sons of the blessed woman, endured torments by bitter scourgings,[5] and were confessors and true martyrs, and Eleazar, aged and advanced in years as he was, proved a noble example and made (his) confession and became a true martyr.[6]

§ 23. Great and excellent is the martyrdom of Jesus. He surpassed in affliction and in confession all who were before or after. And after Him was the faithful martyr Stephen whom the Jews stoned. Simon (Peter) also and Paul were perfect martyrs. And James and John walked in the footsteps of their Master Christ. Also (others) of the apostles thereafter in divers places confessed and proved true martyrs. And also concerning our brethren who are in the West, in the days of Diocletian there came great affliction and persecution to the whole Church of God, which was in all their region. The Churches were overthrown and uprooted, and many confessors and martyrs made confession. And (the Lord) turned in mercy to them after they were

---

[1] Matt. v. 19, 20; Luke xi. 11; xxi. 14, 15.
[2] 1 Kings xxii 28.
[3] Heb. xi. 32, sq.
[5] 2 Macc. vii. 1, sq.
[5] Heb. xi. 38.
[6] 2 Macc. vi. 18, sq.

persecuted. And also in our days these things happened to us also on account of our sins; but also that what is written might be fulfilled, even as our Redeemer said:—*These things are to be.*[1] The Apostle also said:—*Also over us is set this cloud of confession;*[2] which (is) our honour, wherein many confess and are slain.

## Demonstration XXII.—Of Death and the Latter Times.

§ 1. The upright and righteous and good and wise fear not nor tremble at death, because of the great hope that is before them. And they at every time are mindful of death, their exodus, and of the last day in which the children of Adam shall be judged. They know that by the sentence of judgment death has held sway, because Adam transgressed the commandment; as the Apostle said:—*Death ruled from Adam unto Moses even over those who sinned not, so that also upon all the children of Adam it passed,*[3] even as it passed upon Adam. And how did death rule from Adam unto Moses? Clearly, when God laid down the commandment for Adam, He warned him, and said: —*On the day that thou shalt eat of the tree of the knowledge of good and evil, thou shalt die the death.*[4] So when he transgressed the commandment and ate of the tree, death ruled over him and over all his progeny. Even over those who had not sinned, even over them did death rule through Adam's transgression of the commandment.

§ 2. And why did he say:—*From Adam unto Moses did Death rule?* And who is so ill-furnished with knowledge as to imagine that only from Adam to Moses has death had dominion? Yet let him understand from this that he said:—*Upon all men it passed.* Thus, upon all men it passed from Moses until the world shall end. Yet Moses preached that its kingdom is made void. For when Adam

transgressed the commandment whereby the sentence of death was passed upon his progeny, Death hoped that he would bind fast all the sons of man and would be king over them for ever. But when Moses came, he proclaimed the resurrection, and Death knew that his kingdom is to be made void. For Moses said:—*Reuben shall live and not die, and shall be in number.*[5] And when the Holy One called Moses from the bush he said thus to him:—*I am the God of Abraham, of Isaac, and of Jacob.*[6] When Death heard this utterance, he trembled and feared and was terrified and was perturbed, and knew that he had not become king for ever over the children of Adam. From the hour that he heard God saying to Moses:—*I am the God of Abraham, of Isaac, and of Jacob,* Death smote his hands together, for he learned that God is King of the dead and of the living, and that it is appointed to the children of Adam to come forth from his darkness, and arise with their bodies. And observe that our Redeemer Jesus also, when He repeated this utterance to the Sadducees, when they were disputing with Him about the Resurrection of the dead, thus said:— *God is not (God) of the dead, for all are alive unto Him.*[7]

§ 3. And that God might make known to Death that his authority is not for ever over all the progeny of the world, He translated Enoch to Himself, because he was well-pleasing, and made him deathless. And again He took up Elijah to heaven, and Death had no dominion over him. And Hannah said:—*The Lord maketh to die and causeth to live; He bringeth down to Sheol and raiseth up.*[8] Furthermore Moses said as from the mouth of God:—*I make to die and I cause to live.*[9] Again the Prophet Isaiah also said: —*Thy dead shall live, and their dead bodies shall rise again; and the sleepers of the dust shall be awakened, and shall glorify Thee.*[1] When Death heard all these things, amaze-

---

[1] Matt. xxiv. 6; Luke xxi. 9.　[2] Heb. xi. 1.
[3] Rom v. 14, 12.　[4] Gen. ii. 17,

[5] Deut. xxxiii. 6.　[6] Ex. iii. 6.
[7] Luke xx. 38.　[8] 1 Sam. ii. 6.
[9] Deut. xxxii. 39.　[1] Is. xxvi. 19.

ment seized him, and he sat him down in mourning.

§ 4. And when Jesus, the slayer of Death, came, and clothed Himself in a Body from the seed of Adam, and was crucified in His Body, and tasted death ; and when (Death) perceived thereby that He had come down unto him, he was shaken from his place and was agitated when he saw Jesus ; and he closed his gates and was not willing to receive Him. Then He burst his gates, and entered into him, and began to despoil all his possessions. But when the dead saw light in the darkness, they lifted up their heads from the bondage of death, and looked forth, and saw the splendour of the King Messiah. Then the powers of the darkness of Death sat in mourning, for he was degraded from his authority. Death tasted the medicine that was deadly to him, and his hands dropped down, and he learned that the dead shall live and escape from his sway. And when He had afflicted Death by the despoiling of his possessions, he wailed and cried aloud in bitterness and said, " Go forth from my realm and enter it not. Who then is this that comes in alive into my realm ? " And while Death was crying out in terror (for he saw that his darkness was beginning to be done away, and some of the righteous who were sleeping arose to ascend with Him), then He made known to him that when He shall come in the fulness of time, He will bring forth all the prisoners from his power, and they shall go forth to see the light. Then when Jesus had fulfilled His ministry amongst the dead, Death sent Him forth from his realm, and suffered Him not to remain there. And to devour Him like all the dead, he counted it not pleasure. He had no power over the Holy One, nor was He given over to corruption.

§ 5. And when he had eagerly sent Him forth and He had come forth from his realm, He left with him, as a poison, the promise of life ; that by little and little his power should be done away. Even as when a man has taken a poison in the food which is given for (the support of) life, when he perceives in himself that he has received poison in the food, then he casts up again from his belly the food in which poison was mingled ; but the drug leaves its power in his limbs, so that by little and little the structure of his body is dissolved and corrupted. So Jesus dead was the bringer to nought of Death ; for through Him life is made to reign, and through Him Death is abolished, to whom it is said :—*O Death, where is thy victory ?*[1]

§ 6. Therefore, ye children of Adam, all ye over whom Death has ruled, be mindful of Death and remember life ; and transgress not the commandment as your first father did. O Kings, crowned with the diadem, remember Death, which will take away the diadems that are set upon your heads, and he shall be king over you till the time, when ye shall rise again for the judgment. O ye haughty and uplifted and proud, remember Death, which shall destroy your haughtiness, and dissolve the limbs, and separate the joints, and the body and its forms shall be given over to corruption. The lofty ones shall be brought low by Death, and the fierce and stern ones shall be buried away in his darkness. He shall take away all the pride, and they shall corrupt away and become dust, until the judgment. O ye rich, remember Death ; for when the time shall come and ye shall draw nigh to him there, ye shall not use your wealth and possessions. He will not place dainty viands before you, nor will he prepare for you a rich banquet. There the body of the gluttons who used to live delicately shall be corrupted. They shall cease from their luxury and shall not remember it. There the worm shall consume their bodies, and they shall clothe themselves in darkness over their fair apparel. They remember not the ending of this world, that Death shall confound them when they descend to him. So they shall sit in oppression and in the shadow of death, and shall not remember this world, until the end shall be and they shall rise again for the judgment. O ye rapacious and extortioners

---

[1] 1 Cor. xv. 55.

and plunderers of your fellows, remember
Death, and multiply not your sins ; for in
that place sinners repent not ; and he who has
plundered his fellows' goods shall not possess his own, but shall go to the place where
man shall make no use of wealth.  And he
shall come to nought and pass away from
his honour, but his sins shall be laid up
against the day of judgment.

§ 7.  O ye that trust in this world, let this
world be despised in your eyes ; for ye are
sojourners and aliens in the midst of it, and
ye know not the day that ye shall be taken
out of it.  For suddenly shall Death come,
and separate and lead away the loved children from their parents, and the parents
from their darling children.    He leads
away for himself the precious only-begotten
children, and their parents shall be deprived
of them and shall come into contempt.  He
separates precious friends unto himself, and
their beloved weep for them lamentably.
He leads away and takes prisoners unto himself them that are desired for their beauty,
that he may put to shame their forms and
corrupt them.   And those that are glorious
in aspect he leads away to himself, and
they become dust until the judgment.   He
leads away betrothed maidens from their
spouses, and binds them captive in his
bridal-chamber, in his place of gloom.   He
leads away and separates betrothed husbands from the virgins who were designed
for them and betrothed in their name ; and
these shall sit in bitter mourning over them.
He leads away and separates unto himself
all the beautiful youths who supposed that
even unto old age they would not see death.
He leads away and gathers unto himself
the loved infants of days, with whom their
parents were not satiated.   He leads away
to himself the wealthy, the sons of luxury ;
And *they leave their possessions as the waves of
the sea.*[1]  He leads away to himself the skilful artificers, who were raising up the world
by their wonderful works.  He leads away
to himself the subtle and the wise, and they

become simple, not distinguishing good
from evil.  He leads away to himself the
richly endowed of this world, and their endowments are destroyed and shall not be
established for ever.   He leads away to
himself the mighty and the great ones, and
their might is brought low and weakened,
and comes to an end.  Them that were confident that their might would not be brought
lower, in the day of death, men that are
of lower degree than theirs gather together
their bodies.  They that trust that in their
death they shall be buried with honour,
it befalls them that the dogs devour them.
And they that trust that they shall be
buried in the place wherein they were born,
know not but that in the land of their captivity they shall even be gathered (to the
grave) with insult.   They that trusted in
their possessions, that they should give
them in inheritance to their children, from
them it is hidden that they shall be plundered by their enemies.   Death leads away
to himself the brave and the warriors, who
thought to lay waste the great world.  Death
leads away them that adorn themselves
with all pleasant things, and the burial of
an ass befalls them when they are buried.
Death rules over the unborn, and takes them
captive to himself before they are born.
Death leads away to himself them that are
honoured with pomps, and they come into
contempt when they descend to him, to the
realm of darkness, where there is no light.
He is not ashamed before Kings (that are)
crowned with the diadem.  He is not
abashed before the lofty and the fierce ones
who lay waste the lands.   Death respects
not the persons of the honourable, nor does
he receive a bribe from the rich.   Death despises not the poor, nor does his soul scorn
him that has nothing.   Death honours not
them that live in magnificence, nor with
him are the good distinguished from the bad.
He takes no account of the aged, rather than
of children in respect of honour.   The lords
of prudence he makes without understanding, and them that used to make haste
and vex themselves, in acquiring possessions

---

[1] Ecclus. xxix. 18.;

there with him, these are stripped of their gains. He leads away to himself slaves and their masters ; and there the masters are not honoured more than their servants. *Small and great are there, and they hear not the voice of the oppressor. The slave who is freed from his master* [1] there pays no regard to him who used to oppress him. Death binds and makes captive to himself the keepers of prisoners, and the prisoners who were shut up. By means of Death the prisoners are released, and fear not again because of their oppressors.

§ 8. They that live daintily fear death; but the afflicted look forward with hope that they shall be speedily taken away. All the rich tremble because of death ; but the poor desire it, that they may rest from their labour. Death terrifies the mighty when they remember him ; but the sick look forward with hope to him that through him they may forget their pains. Again the young children are afraid of death, for when it comes upon them they shall leave their pleasures ; but the old men advanced in years pray for it, they that are in need of daily bread.

§ 9. The sons of peace remember death ; and they forsake and remove from them wrath and enmity. As sojourners they dwell in this world, and prepare for themselves a provision for the journey before them. On that which is above they set their thoughts, on that which is above they meditate ; and those things which are beneath their eyes they despise. They send away their treasures to the place where there is no peril, the place where there is no moth, nor are there thieves. They abide in the world as aliens, sons of a far land ; and look forward to be sent out of this world and to come to the city, the place of the righteous. They afflict themselves in the place of their sojourning ; and they are not entangled or occupied in the house of their exile. Ever day by day their faces are set upwards, to go to the repose

of their fathers. As prisoners are they in this world, and as hostages of the King are they kept. To the end they have no rest in this world, nor is (their) hope in it, that it will continue for ever. They that acquire possessions, rejoice not in them, and they that beget children, death fills them with sorrow. They that build cities, shall not be left in them ; and those that hasten and toil for anything, are in no wise to be distinguished from fools. O man without sense, whosoever he be whose trust is in this world !

§ 10. Remember, my beloved, and compare and consider in thy mind, who is there of former generations who has been left in this world so as to continue for ever ? Death has led away the former generations, the great ones and the mighty and the subtle. Who is there that acquired great possessions, and at the time when he departed took them with him ? That which was gathered together from the earth returns back into its bosom ; and naked does a man depart from his possessions. The wise, when they acquire goods, send some of them before them, as Job said :—*My witnesses are in heaven ;* and again :—*My brethren and my lovers are with God.* [2] And our Lord commanded them that acquire possessions to *make for themselves friends* in heaven, and also to *lay up treasures* there. [3]

§ 11. Do thou also remember death, O wise scribe, that thy heart be not lifted up, so that thou shouldest forget the sentence of judgment. Death leaves not aside the wise, nor respects the persons of the subtle. Death leads away to himself the wise scribes, so that they forget that which they have learned, until the time comes in which all the righteous shall rise again.

§ 12. In that place they shall forget this world. There they have no want ; and they shall love one another with an abundant love. In their bodies there shall be no heaviness, and lightly shall they fly *as*

---

[1] Job iii. 18, 19.

[2] Job xvi. 19 ; *ib.* xvi. 20.
[3] Matt. vi. 20 ; Luke xvi. 9.

doves to their windows.[1] In their thoughts they shall not there remember wickedness at all, nor shall anything of uncleanness arise in their heart. In that place there shall be no natural desire, for there they shall be weaned from all appetites. There shall not arise in their heart anger or lasciviousness ; also they shall remove from them all things that gender sins. Fervent in their heart will be the love of each other ; and hatred will not be fixed within them at all. They shall have no need there to build houses, for they shall abide in light, in the mansions of the saints. They shall have no need of woven raiment, for they shall be clothed in eternal light. They shall have no need of food, for they shall recline at His table and be nurtured for ever. The air of that region is pleasant and glorious, and its light shines out, and is goodly and gladsome. Planted there are beautiful trees, whose fruits fail not, and whose leaves fall not. Their boughs are glorious, their perfume delightful, and of their taste no soul shall grow weary for ever. Spacious is the region, nor is it limited ; yet its inhabitants shall see its distance even as that which is near. There the inheritance shall not be divided, and no man shall say to his fellow :—"This is mine and that is thine." They shall not be bound there in the desire of covetousness, nor shall they go astray there concerning remembrance. There a man shall not love his neighbour with especial reverence, but abundantly shall they all love one another after one fashion. They shall not marry wives there, nor shall they beget children ; nor shall there the male be distinguished from the female ; but all shall be sons of their Father Who is in heaven ; as the Prophet said :—*Is there not one Father of us all ; is there not one God Who created us ?*[2]

§ 13. And as regards that which I said ; that there they shall not take wives, nor is male distinguished from female, our Lord and His Apostles have taught us. For our Lord said :—*They that are worthy of that*

*world, and of that resurrection from the abode of the dead, shall not take wives, nor shall (women) become wives to men ; for they cannot die ; but they are as the angels in heaven, and are the children of God.*[3] And the apostle said :— *There is neither male nor female, neither bond nor free ; but ye are all one in Jesus Christ.*[4] For, as for Eve, to spread abroad generation, God took her out from Adam, that she might become the mother of all living ; but yet in that world there is no female ; even as in heaven also there is no female, nor generation, nor use of concupiscence.' In that place there is no deficiency, but fulness and perfection. The aged shall not die and the young shall not grow old. And it is in expectation of growing old and dying that young men take wives and beget children, that when the fathers shall have died the children may rise up in their stead. Now all these things have their use only in this world, for in that place there is no want, nor any deficiency, nor concupiscence, nor generation, nor ending, nor failure, nor death, nor termination, nor old age. There is neither hatred, nor wrath, nor envy, nor weariness, nor toil, nor darkness, nor night, nor falsehood. There is not in that place any want at all ; but it is full of light, and life, and grace, and fulness, and satisfaction, and renewal, and love, and all the good promises that are written but not yet *sealed.* For there is there *that which eye hath not seen and ear hath not heard, and which hath not come up into the heart of man,*[5] that which is unspeakable and which a man cannot utter. And the Apostle said :—*That which God hath prepared for them that love Him.*[6] Though men shall say much, they shall not be able to express it. That which eye hath not seen, they are unable to relate ; and that which ear hath not heard, it is not right to speak of in such wise as to compare it with anything that the ear has heard and the eye has seen. And that which has not come up unto the heart, who is there dares to speak

---

[1] Is. lx. 8.  [2] Mal. ii. 10.

Luke xx. 35, 36.  [4] Gal. iii. 28.
[5] 1 Cor. ii. 9.  [6] *Ib.*

of it, as though it was like anything that has come up into the heart? But this is right for a speaker, to liken and call that place the abode of God, and the place of life, the perfect place, the place of light, the place of glory, the Sabbath of God, the day of rest, the repose of the righteous, the joy of the just, the abode and dwelling-place of the righteous and the holy, the place of our hope, the sure abode of our trust, the place of our treasure, the place that shall assuage our weariness and remove our afflictions, and soothe our sighs. To these things it is right for us to liken, and thus to call, that place.

§ 14. Again, Death leads away to himself kings, the founders of cities, who strengthen themselves in splendour. And he does not leave aside the Lords of the countries. Death leads away and takes captive to himself the avaricious who are not satisfied nor say "Enough"; and he is greedy for them with a greater greed than theirs. Death leads away to himself the despoilers who were not by their grace restrained from despoiling their fellows. Death leads away to himself the oppressors, and through death are they restrained from iniquity. Death leads away to himself the persecutors, and the persecuted have rest till they go to him. Death leads away to himself them that swallow up their fellows, and the down-trodden and oppressed have rest for a little until they themselves also are led away and go thither. Death leads away them that abound in meditations, and all they have thought upon is dissolved and brought to nought. Men meditate upon many matters, and death comes upon them suddenly, and they are led away; and thereafter they remember nothing that they have thought upon. There is one that makes plans for many years, and (the knowledge) is withheld from him that he shall not survive to-morrow. Some son of Adam is uplifted and vaunts himself over his fellow; and death comes upon him and brings to nought his vaunting. The rich man plans to add to his possessions, and

he knows not that he shall not continue to possess even that which he has acquired. Death leads away to himself all the children of men, and binds them fast in his abode until the judgment. Also over those that have not sinned is he king, because of the sentence of judgment that Adam received for his sins.

§ 15. And the Life-giver shall come, the Destroyer of Death, and shall bring to nought his power, from over the just and from over the wicked. And the dead shall arise with a mighty shout, and Death shall be emptied and stripped of all the captivity. And for judgment shall all the children of Adam be gathered together, and each shall go to the place prepared for him. The risen of the righteous shall go unto life, and the risen of the sinners shall be delivered unto death. The righteous who kept the commandment shall go, and shall not come nigh unto judgment in the day that they shall rise; as David asked, *And bring not thy servant into judgment;* [1] nor will their Lord terrify them in that day.

§ 16. Remember that the Apostle also said, *We shall judge angels.* [2] And our Lord said to His disciples, *Ye shall sit on twelve thrones, and judge twelve tribes of the house of Israel.* [3] And Ezekiel said concerning righteous men, [4] that they shall judge Ahola and Aholibah. Since, then, the righteous are to judge the wicked, He has made clear concerning them that they shall not come into judgment. And as to what the apostles say, that *We shall judge angels*, hear, and I will instruct thee. The angels who shall be judged by the apostles are the priests who have violated the law; as the Prophet said, *The lips of the priest shall guard knowledge, and the law shall they inquire of his mouth; because he is the angel of the Lord, the most mighty.* [5] The angels who are *the priests, of whose mouth the law is inquired*, when they transgress the law, shall be judged at the

---

[1] Ps. cxlii. 2.
[2] Cor. vi. 3.
[3] Matt. xix. 28 ; Luke xxii. 30.
[4] Ezek. xxiii. 24, 25
[5] Mal. ii. 7.

last by the apostles, and the priests who observe the law.

§ 17. *And the wicked shall not arise in the judgment, nor sinners in the congregation of the righteous.*[1] And even as the righteous who are perfected in good works shall not come into the judgment to be judged, so of the wicked also whose sins are many, and the measure of whose offences is overflowing, it shall not be required that they should draw nigh unto the judgment, but when they have risen again they shall turn back to Sheol, as David said, *The wicked shall turn back to Sheol, and all the nations that forget God.*[2] And Isaiah said, *All the nations are as a drop from the bucket, and as the turning of the balance. And the isles as a grain of sand shall be cast away, and all the nations are esteemed as nothingness by Him. For destruction and the sword are they esteemed by Him.*[3] Therefore learn and be persuaded, that all the nations that know not God their Maker, are esteemed by God as nothingness, and shall not come nigh to judgment, but as soon as they have risen shall turn back to Sheol.

§ 18. But all the rest of the world who are called sinners shall stand in the judgment and be rebuked. Those in whom there is a little shortcoming will the judge rebuke, and make known to them that they have offended. And He will give them the inheritance of life after the judgment. And understand that our Lord has made known to us in His Gospel, that every man according to his work shall receive his reward. He that received money, showed the increase on it. He whose pound or talent produced tenfold, received life, perfect, in nothing lacking. He whose pound or talent produced fivefold, received the half of ten. One was given a tenfold authority and one a fivefold. Now consider and see, that the increase of five is less than that of ten; and the labourers who demand the reward excel them that received it in silence. They who toiled all the day, with bold face receive the

reward and demand it, in confidence that He will add more to them. While they who worked one hour receive it in silence, and know that through grace they receive mercy and life. The sinners whose sins are many shall be condemned by the place of judgment, and shall go into torments. And from that time and onwards, judgment shall rule over them.

§ 19. Furthermore, hearken unto the Apostle who said, *Every man according to his work shall receive his reward.*[4] He that toiled little, shall receive according to his remissness; and he that made much speed, shall be rewarded according to his speed. And Job also said, *Far be it from God to do iniquity; and far be it from Him to do sin. For according to a man's works will He reward him, and a man shall receive according to his ways.*[5] And also the Apostle said, *Star excels star in brightness. So also is the resurrection of the dead.*[6] Therefore know that, even when men shall enter into life, yet reward shall excel reward, and glory shall excel glory, and recompense shall excel recompense. Degree is higher than degree; and light is more goodly than light in aspect. The sun excels the moon, and the moon is greater than the stars that are with her. And observe that the moon and the stars are also under the power of the sun, and their light is swallowed up in the splendour of the sun. And the sun has no power along with the moon and the stars, that he may not abolish the night which has been separated from the day. And when the sun was created, he was called a luminary. And observe that the sun and the moon and the stars are all called luminaries; but luminary excels luminary. The sun obscures the light of the moon, and the moon likewise darkens the light of the stars; and star excels star in its light.

§ 20. And understand (this) also, from that which is of this world, those who labour with toil, and from the hired men

---

[1] Ps. i. 5.  [2] Ps. ix. 17.  [3] Is. xl. 15, 17.

[4] I Cor. iii. 8.  [5] Job xxxiv. 10, 11.
[6] I Cor. xv. 41, 42.

who work with their fellows. There are some who hire their fellow-men by day-wages, and (these) receive the wage of their toil; and there are some who are hired for the month, and compute and receive the wage for the time, at the time agreed. And the day-wage is distinguished from the monthly wage; and yearly exceeds monthly wage.

§ 21. And also again, understand it from the authority that is in this world. There are some who please the king by their activity, and receive honour from those in authority. One receives a crown from the king, to become governor in one of the countries. And under the authority of another, the king places towns; and also he excels his inferiors in his attire. Some receive presents and gifts, and one honour is distinguished from another. There is one to whom the king gives the honour of being steward over all the treasury. Another, according to his lower condition, serves the king, and his authority is only to provide the daily food.

§ 22. Also in respect of penalty, I say that all men are not equal. He that has done great wickedness is greatly tormented. And he that has offended not so much is less tormented. Some *shall go into outer darkness, where there is weeping and gnashing of teeth.*[1] Others shall be cast into the fire, according as they deserve; for it is not written that they shall gnash their teeth, nor that there is darkness there. Some shall be cast into another place, a place where *their worm shall not die, and their fire shall not be quenched, and they shall become an astonishment to all flesh.*[2] In the faces of others the door shall be closed and the Judge will say to them:—*I know you not.*[3] And consider that, as the reward for good deeds is not equal for all men, so it is also for evil deeds. Not in one fashion shall men be judged, but every man according to his works shall receive his requital, because the Judge is clothed in righteousness and regards not the persons of men.

§ 23. And even as I have showed thee concerning the world, how one honour excels another, of those that kings and rulers of this world give to those beneath them; also concerning this I have showed thee, that even as kings have good gifts to give to those honoured by them, so also they have prisons and chains and fetters, which are various kinds of bonds. One man offends the king with a grievous offence, and without inquiry he is delivered over to death. Another offends, yet is not deserving of death; he is put in bonds until he is judged; and is chastised, and the king remits his offence. There is another whom the king has held in regard; and outside the prison house he is kept in freedom, without chains and without bonds. He that is put to death is distinguished from him that is bound; and the punishment of one exceeds that of another, according to the desert of his offence. But come thou to our Redeemer, Who said:—*Many are the mansions in My Father's house.*[4]

§ 24. My beloved, men who are inferior in understanding, dispute about this that I write to thee, and say:—"What is the place in which the righteous shall receive a good reward; and what is the place in which are torments, in which the wicked shall receive the punishments of their works?" O man that thinkest thus, I will ask thee, and tell thou me, why is death called death, and why is Sheol called Sheol? For it is written that when Korah and his companions made a schism against Moses, *the earth opened her mouth and swallowed them up, and they went down alive into Sheol.*[5] Therefore that was the mouth of Sheol that was opened in the wilderness. David also said, *The wicked shall turn back to Sheol.*[6] We say that to Sheol, in which Korah and his companions were swallowed up, thither shall the wicked be turned back. For God has power, if He chooses, to give inheritance of

---

[1] Matt. vii. 12.      [2] Is. lxvi. 24.
[3] Matt. xxv. 12.

[4] John xiv. 2.      [5] Num. xvi. 32, 33.      [6] Ps. ix. 17.

life in heaven, and if it please Him, in the earth. Jesus our Lord said, *Blessed are the poor in spirit, for theirs is the kingdom of heaven.*[1] And to one of those who were crucified with Him, who believed on him, He swore :—*Thou shalt be with Me to-day in the garden of Eden.*[2] And the Apostle said, *When the righteous shall rise again, they shall fly upwards to meet our Redeemer.*[3] But, however, we say thus : That which our Redeemer said to us is true :—*Heaven and earth shall pass away.*[4] And the Apostle said, *Hope which is seen is not hope.*[5] And the Prophet said, *The heavens shall pass away as smoke, and the earth as a garment shall wear away; and its inhabitants shall become like it.*[6] And Job said concerning those that sleep, *Till the heavens wear out, they shall not be aroused, nor shall they wake out of their sleep.*[7] From these things be thou persuaded that this earth, in which the children of Adam are sown, and the firmament that is over men, (even) that firmament which is set to divide the upper heavens from the earth and this life, shall pass away, and wear out, and be destroyed. And God will make a new thing for the children of Adam, and they shall inherit inheritances in the Kingdom of Heaven. If He shall give them inheritance in the earth, it shall be called the kingdom of heaven. And if in Heaven, it is easy for Him to do. For with the kings of the earth also, although each one of them abides in his own place, yet every place to which their authority extends, is called their kingdom. So the sun is a luminary set in the heaven, yet for every place to which its rays extend, its authority suffices, whether on sea or on land. And observe that the princes of the world also have banquetings and delights, and in every place or state into which they go, their banquetings are with them ; and in whatever place pleases them, they make a prison-house. For the sun in twelve hours

circles round, from the east unto the west ; and when he has accomplished his course, his light is hidden in the night-time, and the night is not disturbed by his power. And in the hours of the night the sun turns round in his rapid course, and turning round begins to run in his accustomed path. As for the sun that is with thee, thou wise man, from thy childhood till the completion of thy old age, thou knowest not where he runs in the night-time, so as to circle round to the place of its course. Is it necessary for thee to inquire into those things that are hidden from thee ?

§ 25. These memorials I have written for our brethren and beloved, the children of the Church of God, that when these come into their hands in various places, and when they read in them, they may also remember my insignificance in their prayers, and may know that I am a sinner also, and fall short ; but that this is my faith, that I have set forth from the beginning and written, in these chapters written (by me). *Faith* is the foundation, and upon faith (rest) the works that become it. And after Faith (I wrote) that there are two commandments of *Love*. And after Love, I have written of *Fasting*, in its demonstration also along with its works. And after Fasting, I wrote of *Prayer* in its fruit and in its works. And after Prayer, I have written about *War* and about whatever Daniel wrote concerning the kingdoms. And after War, I have written of the exhortation for *Monks*. And after the Monks, I have written about *Repentance*. And after Repentance, I have written about the *Resurrection of the dead*. And after the Resurrection of the dead, I have written about *Humility*. And after Humility, I have written of the *Pastors*, the teachers. And after the Pastors, I have written about the *Circumcision* in which the people of the Jews pride themselves. And after the Circumcision, I have written about the *Passover*, and about the fourteenth day. And after the Passover, I have written about the *Sabbath*, in which the Jews are puffed up. And after the Sabbath, I have written an

---

[1] Matt. v. 3.
[2] Luke xxiii. 43.
[3] 1 Thess. iv. 17.
[4] Matt. xxiv. 35.
[5] Rom. viii. 24.
[6] Is. li. 6.
[7] Job. xiv. 12.

*Exhortation,* on account of the dissension which happened in our days. And after the Exhortation, I have written about *Meats,* those that the Jews deem unclean. And after the Meats, I have written about the *Gentiles,* that they have entered in and become heirs instead of the original people. And after the Gentiles, I have written and proved that *God has a Son.* And after the *Son of God,* I have written against the Jews, who speak injuriously about *Virginity.* And after the apology about Virginity, I have written again *Against the Jews,* who say :—"It is appointed for us to be gathered together." And after that defence, I have written about *Almsgiving to the Poor.* And after the Poor, I have written a demonstration about *The Persecuted.* And after the Persecuted, I have written at the end about *Death and the Last Times.* These twenty-two discourses have I written according to the twenty-two letters of the alphabet. The first ten I wrote in the six hundred and forty-eighth year of the kingdom of Alexander the son of Philip the Macedonian, as is written in the end of them. And these twelve last I wrote in the six hundred and fifty-fifth year of the kingdom of the Greeks and of the Romans, which is the kingdom of Alexander, and in the thirty-fifth year of the Persian King.[1]

§ 26. These things I have written according to what I have attained to. But if any-one shall read these dicourses, and find words that do not agree with his thought, he ought not to scorn them; because whatsoever is written in these chapters was not written according to the thought of one man, nor for the persuasion of one reader; but according to the thought of all the Church, and for the persuasion of all faith. If he shall read and hear with persuasion, it is well ; and if not, it is meet for me to say that I wrote for those open to persuasion and not for mockers. And if again any reader should find words that are spoken by us in one fashion, and by another sage in another fashion, let him not be disturbed at this ; for every man speaks to his hearers according to what he can attain to. So I, who have written these things, even if some of the words do not agree with what other speakers have said, yet say this ; that those sages have spoken well, yet it seemed good to me to speak thus. And if any man shall speak and demonstrate to me about any matter, I will receive instruction from him without contention. Everyone who reads the sacred scriptures, both former and latter, in both covenants, and reads with persuasion, will learn and teach. But if he strives about anything that he does not understand, his mind does not receive teaching. But if he finds words that are too difficult for him, and he does not understand their force, let him say thus, "Whatsoever is written is written well, but I have not attained to the understanding of it." And if he shall ask about the matters that are too hard for him of wise and discerning men who inquire into doctrine, then, when ten wise men shall speak to him in ten different ways about one matter, let him accept that which pleases him ; and if any please not him, let him not scorn the sages ; for the word of God is like a pearl, that has a beautiful appearance on whatever side you turn it. And remember, O disciple, what David said, *From all my teachers have I learned.*[2] And the Apostle said :—*Thou readest every Scripture that is in the Spirit of God. And prove everything; hold fast that which is good; and flee from every evil thing.*[3] For if the days of a man should be many as all the days of the world from Adam to the end of the ages, and he should sit and meditate upon the Holy Scriptures, he would not comprehend all the force of the depth of the words. And man cannot rise up to the wisdom of God ; as I have written in the tenth discourse. But, however, the words of all speakers who do not take from the great treasure, are accursed and to be despised. For the image of the king (on his coin) is received wher-

---

[1] Sc., in the years 337 and 344, A.D.

[2] Ps. cxix. 99. [3] 1 Thess. v. 21, 22 ; 2 Tim. iii. 16.

ever it goes ; but (the coin) in which there is base metal, is rejected and is not received. And if any one should say, "These dis-courses were spoken by such an one ;" let him carefully learn that to be careful to inquire about the speaker is not commanded him.   I also according to my insignificance have written these things, a man sprung from Adam, and fashioned by the hands of God, a disciple of the Holy Scriptures.   For our Lord said :—*Every one that asketh re-ceiveth, and he that seeketh findeth, and for him that knocketh it shall be opened.*[1]   And the prophet said :—*I will pour out my spirit upon all flesh in the last days, and they shall prophesy.*[2]

Therefore whoever shall read anything that I have written above, let him read with persuasion, and pray for the author as a brother of the Body ; that through the peti-tion of all the Church of God ; his sins may be forgiven.   And let whoever reads un-derstand what is written :—*Let him that hears the word, communicate to him that causes him to hear, in all good things.*[3]   And again it is written, *The sower and the reaper shall rejoice together.*[4]   And *Every man according to his labours shall receive his reward.*[5]   And *There is nothing hidden that shall not be revealed to every man.*[6]

---

[1] Matt. vii. 8.                          [2] Joel ii. 28.

[3] Gal. vi. 6.                          [4] John iv. 36.
[5] 1 Cor. iii. 8.                          [6] Matt. x. 26.

# S. GREGORY THE GREAT

## INDEX OF TEXTS

# INDEX OF SUBJECTS

# EPHRAIM SYRUS AND APHRAHAT

## INDEX OF TEXTS

# INDEX OF SUBJECTS